LIBRARY

D1035931

My Life

F
1788
.22
c 3
A 5
2007

FIDEL CASTRO

My Life

Edited by IGNACIO RAMONET
Translated by ANDREW HURLEY

ALLEN LANE
an imprint of
PENGUIN BOOKS

To Alfredo Guevara

To my children, Tancrède and Axel

ALLEN LANE

Published by the Penguin Group
Penguin Books Ltd, 80 Strand, London WC2R ORL, England
Penguin Group (USA) Inc., 375 Hudson Street, New York, New York 10014, USA
Penguin Group (Canada), 90 Eglinton Avenue East, Suite 700, Toronto, Ontario, Canada M4P 2Y3
(a division of Pearson Penguin Canada Inc.)
Penguin Ireland, 25 St Stephen's Green, Dublin 2, Ireland
(a division of Penguin Books Ltd)
Penguin Group (Australia), 250 Camberwell Road, Camberwell, Victoria 3124, Australia
(a division of Pearson Australia Group Pty Ltd)
Penguin Books India Pvt Ltd, 11 Community Centre, Panchsheel Park, New Delhi – 110 017, India
Penguin Group (NZ), 67 Apollo Drive, Rosedale, North Shore 0632, New Zealand
(a division of Pearson New Zealand Ltd)
Penguin Books (South Africa) (Pty) Ltd, 24 Sturdee Avenue, Rosebank, Johannesburg 2196, South Africa

Penguin Books Ltd, Registered Offices: 80 Strand, London WC2R ORL, England

www.penguin.com

Fidel Castro: Biografía a dos voces first published in Spain by Random House Mondadori 2006
Revised edition published 2007
This translation first published by Allen Lane 2007
1

Copyright © Ignacio Ramonet and Random House Mondadori, 2006, 2007
Translation copyright © Andrew Hurley, 2007

The moral right of the author and translator has been asserted

All rights reserved
Without limiting the rights under copyright
reserved above, no part of this publication may be
reproduced, stored in or introduced into a retrieval system,
or transmitted, in any form or by any means (electronic, mechanical,
photocopying, recording or otherwise) without the prior
written permission of both the copyright owner and
the above publisher of this book

Set in PostScript Adobe Sabon
Typeset by Rowland Phototypesetting Ltd, Bury St Edmunds, Suffolk
Printed in Great Britain by Clays Ltd, St Ives plc

ISBN: 978-0-713-99920-4

www.greenpenguin.co.uk

Penguin Books is committed to a sustainable future
for our business, our readers and our planet.
The book in your hands is made from paper
certified by the Forest Stewardship Council.

Contents

Straits of Florida

HAVANA

Matanzas   Cárdenas

S. Cristóbal   Güineso

Pinar del Río   Gulf of
Batabanó   Colón

La Fe   Santa Clar

Cape
San Antonio   Isle of Pines
(now Isle
of Youth)   Bay of Pigs/
Playa Girón   Cienfuegos

Escambray Mountains ▲

C A R I B B E A N

Ar
Jara
(Queen's Gar

S E A

Cayman Islands

0   50   100   150 km

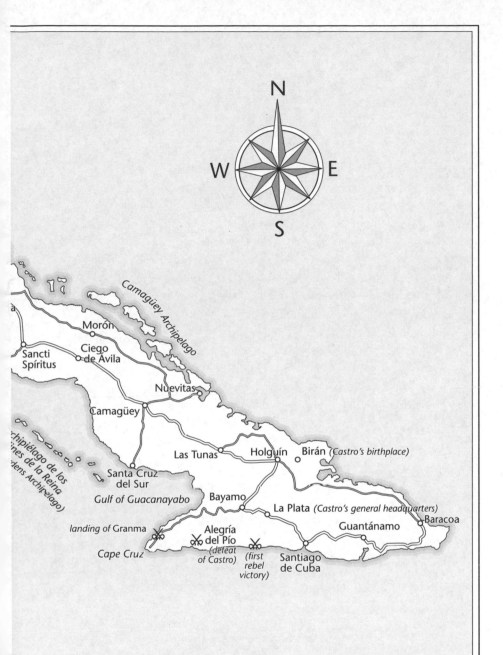

N

W E

S

Camagüey Archipelago

Morón

Ciego de Ávila

Sancti Spíritus

Nuevitas

Camagüey

Las Tunas   Holguín   Birán *(Castro's birthplace)*

Santa Cruz del Sur

Gulf of Guacanayabo   Bayamo

La Plata *(Castro's general headquarters)*

Guantánamo

Baracoa

landing of Granma

Cape Cruz

Alegría del Pío
(defeat of Castro)

(first rebel victory)

Santiago de Cuba

Archipiélago de los Jardines de la Reina (Gardens Archipelago)

CUBA

A Hundred Hours with Fidel

It was two o'clock in the morning, and we'd been talking for hours. We were in his personal office in the Palacio de la Revolución, a big, austere room with a high ceiling and a large expanse of windows framed with light-coloured curtains that opened out on to a broad balcony from which one could see one of Havana's main avenues. An immense bookshelf on one wall, and before it, a long, heavy desk covered with books and documents. Everything very neat. In among the books on the bookshelves and on small tables at each end of the couch were a bronze figure and bust of the 'Apostle of Liberty' José Martí,[1] a statue of Simón Bolívar, one of Antonio José de Sucre,[2] and a bust of Abraham Lincoln. In one corner, a wire sculpture of Don Quixote astride his skinny steed Rocinante. And on the walls, in addition to a large oil portrait of Camilo Cienfuegos, one of Castro's main lieutenants in the Sierra Maestra, three framed documents: a handwritten letter by Simón Bolívar, a signed photograph of Ernest Hemingway holding up a huge swordfish ('To Dr Fidel Castro – May you hook one like this in the well at Cojímar. In friendship, Ernest Hemingway'), and a photograph of his father, Angel Castro, on his arrival from distant Galicia in 1895.

Sitting before me – tall, robust, well built, his beard almost white, wearing his ever-present impeccable olive-green uniform with no ribbons or decorations and showing not the slightest trace of weariness despite the lateness of the hour – Fidel answered calmly, sometimes in a voice so low that it was just a whisper, almost inaudible. This was in late January 2003, and we were beginning the first series of long conversations that would bring me back to Cuba several times over the succeeding months, through to December 2005.

The idea for this conversation had come up a year earlier, in February 2002. I'd gone to Havana to give a lecture at the Havana Book Fair. Joseph Stiglitz, winner of the Nobel Prize for Economics in 2001, was also there. Fidel introduced me to him by saying, 'He's an economist and an American, but the most radical one I've ever seen. Beside him, I'm a moderate.' Fidel and I started talking about neoliberal globalization and the World Social Forum in Porto Alegre, which I was just returning from. Fidel wanted to know all about it – the subjects that had been debated there, the seminars, the participants, the forecasts ... He expressed his admiration for the alternative globalization movement: 'A new generation of rebels has emerged,' he said, 'many of them Americans, who are employing new methods of protest and making the lords of the world tremble. Ideas are more important than weapons. Except for violence, all arguments should be used to combat globalization.'

As always, ideas rushed like a bubbling stream from Fidel. Stiglitz and I listened in fascination. He had an all-encompassing vision of globalization, its consequences and ways of confronting them; his arguments, of a great modernity and cleverness, made patent those qualities that many biographers have noted in him: his sense of strategy, his ability to 'read' a concrete situation, and his quickness at analysis. To all that was added experience accumulated over so many years of governing, resistance and combat.

As I listened to him, it struck me as unfair that the newer generations knew so little about his life and career and that, as unconscious victims of constant anti-Castro propaganda, so many of those in Europe who were committed to the alternative globalization movement, especially the young people, considered him a relic of the Cold War, a leader left over from a stage of modern history that had now passed, a man who had little to contribute to the struggles of the twenty-first century.

Even today, and even in the inner circles of the Left, many people criticize, distrust, even outright oppose the Castro regime in Havana. And though throughout Latin America the Cuban Revolution continues to inspire enthusiasm among leftist social movements and many intellectuals, in Europe it is the subject of controversy. It is increasingly difficult, in fact, to find anyone – for or against the Cuban Revolution – who, asked to sum up Castro and his years in power, can give a serene, dispassionate opinion.

I had just published a short book of conversations with Subcomandante Marcos, the romantic, galactic leader of the Zapatistas in Mexico.[3] Fidel had read it and found it interesting. I suggested that he and I do something similar, but on a larger scale. He has never written his memoirs, and it's almost certain that for lack of time he never will. What I proposed would be, then, a kind of 'autobiography à deux', though in the form of a conversation; it would be Fidel Castro's political testament, an oral summing-up of Fidel Castro's life by Fidel himself at almost eighty and more than half a century after the attack on the Moncada barracks in Santiago de Cuba in 1953 – the moment when, to some degree, his public life began.

Few men have known the glory of entering the pages of both history and legend while they are still alive. Fidel is one of them. He is the last 'sacred giant' of international politics. He belongs to the generation of mythical insurgents – Nelson Mandela, Ho Chi Minh, Patrice Lumumba, Amílcar Cabral, Che Guevara, Carlos Marighela,[4] Camilo Torres,[5] Mehdi Ben Barka[6] – who, pursuing an ideal of justice, threw themselves into political action in the years following the Second World War. These were men who hoped to change a world of inequalities and discrimination, a world polarized by the Cold War between the Soviet Union and the United States. Like thousands of progressives and intellectuals around the world, among them the most brilliant of men and women, that generation honestly thought that Communism promised a bright and shining future, and that injustice, racism and poverty could be wiped off the face of the earth in a matter of just decades.

At that time – in Vietnam, Algeria, Guinea-Bissau, over half the planet – the oppressed peoples of the earth rose up. Most of humanity was still, back then, subject to the infamy of colonization. Almost all of Africa and much of Asia were still under the domination, under the *thumb*, of the old Western colonial powers. Meanwhile, the nations of Latin America, theoretically independent for 150 years, were being exploited by privileged minorities and often subjugated by cruel dictators (Batista in Cuba, Trujillo in the Dominican Republic, Duvalier in Haiti, Somoza in Nicaragua, Ydígoras in Guatemala,[7] Pérez Jiménez in Venezuela,[8] Stroessner in Paraguay . . .) who were installed as leaders and supported by Washington.

Fidel listened to my suggestion with a slight smile, as though the idea of it amused him. He looked at me with mischievous eyes, and with a touch of irony asked me, 'Do you really want to waste your time talking to me? Don't you have anything more important to do?' Of course I said I really did, and I didn't, respectively. Dozens of journalists from all over the world, among them the most famous and respected, had spent years waiting for a chance to talk to Fidel. For a professional journalist, could there be any interview more important than this one – with a man who was unquestionably one of the most significant figures of the last sixty years? Is Castro not the longest-serving head of state in the world today?[9] As a comparison, we should recall that the same day that Fidel, then thirty-two years old, entered Havana in victory after defeating Batista's army – 8 January 1959 – General

Charles de Gaulle was being installed as the first president of the Fifth Republic in France.

Fidel Castro has had to deal with no fewer than ten US presidents (Eisenhower, Kennedy, Johnson, Nixon, Ford, Carter, Reagan, Bush I, Clinton and Bush II). He has had personal and sometimes friendly relationships with some of the world's most important leaders since 1945 (Nehru, Nasser, Tito, Khrushchev, Olof Palme,[10] Willy Brandt, Ben Bella, Boumedienne,[11] Arafat, Indira Gandhi, Salvador Allende, Brezhnev, Gorbachev, Mitterrand, Jiang Zemin, John Paul II, King Juan Carlos of Spain, Nelson Mandela . . .), and he has known some of the major intellectuals, artists and personalities of our time (Jean-Paul Sartre, Simone de Beauvoir, Ernest Hemingway, Graham Greene, Arthur Miller, Pablo Neruda, Jorge Amado, Oswaldo Guayasamín, Henri Cartier-Bresson, Oscar Niemeyer, Julio Cortázar, José Saramago, Gabriel García Márquez, Claudio Abbado, Yves-Jacques Cousteau, Harry Belafonte, Angela Davis, Jesse Jackson, Danielle Mitterrand, Costa-Gavras, Gérard Depardieu, Danny Glover, Robert Redford, Jack Nicholson, Steven Spielberg, Eduardo Galeano,[12] Diego Maradona, Oliver Stone, Noam Chomsky and many, many others).

Under his leadership, his little country (100,000 square kilometres, less than 40,000 square miles, with a population of about 11 million people) has conducted a very powerful foreign policy, of far-reaching consequences – it has even stared down the United States, whose leaders have not been able to overthrow him or kill him, or even jostle the Revolution off its path.

In October 1962, a Third World War almost broke out because of the US government's opposition to the installation of Soviet nuclear missiles in Cuba – missiles whose function was, above all, to defend the nation and prevent a second invasion like the one that had been carried out in 1961 at Playa Girón (the Bay of Pigs) with the direct support of the US military, but an invasion this time carried out directly by the US, and aimed at overthrowing the Cuban government.

Since 1960, the United States has been waging economic warfare against Cuba, and has kept the country, unilaterally and despite ever-increasing opposition by the United Nations,[13] under a devastating trade embargo, strengthened in the nineties by the Helms-Burton Act and the Torricelli Amendment and strengthened once again by the Bush administration in May 2004.[14] This embargo has obstructed the country's normal development and helped aggravate its precarious financial and economic situation,[15] with tragic consequences for its inhabitants.

The United States has also pursued a permanent and ongoing ideological and media war against Havana, with powerful broadcasting stations – Radio Martí and TV Martí – installed in Florida and flooding the island with propaganda, as in the worst days of the Cold War. The US authorities, sometimes through fronts such as the National Endowment for Democracy (NED), an NGO created by Ronald Reagan in 1983, finance groups abroad that spread propaganda hostile to Cuba.[16]

For example, according to the Associated Press, in 2005 the NED distributed $2.4 million to organizations that militate in Europe for regime change in Cuba. And then there's the United States Agency for International Development (USAID), which depends directly on the government of the United States and since 1996 has delivered over $65 million to anti-Castro groups, based mainly in Florida. In May 2004, the Bush administration created a supplementary fund of $80 million earmarked to strengthen aid to those same groups.[17] Dozens of reporters around the world are paid to spread disinformation about Cuba.[18]

Some of this money is used to underwrite terrorist organizations hostile to the Cuban government – Alpha 66 and Omega 7 among them. These organizations have their headquarters in Florida, where they run training camps and from where they regularly send armed commandos into Cuba to carry out bombings and acts of sabotage, all this with the tacit complicity of the US authorities. In the past forty years there have been over 3,500 deaths in Cuba from terrorist attacks, with almost 2,000 other people injured for life – more than almost any other country – and the country has suffered accordingly.[19]

In 2005, with absolute contempt for Cuba's sovereignty – under the pretence that the island is, so to speak, a US 'internal affair' – Washington had no scruples in naming a 'Cuban Transition Coordinator', a man called Caleb McCarry, who had previously been posted to Afghanistan.

On 10 July 2006, a report to the president of the United States by the Commission for Assistance to a Free Cuba, which is co-chaired by Secretary of State Condoleezza Rice and Secretary of Commerce Carlos Gutierrez, demanded that everything possible be done so that 'the Castro regime's succession strategy may not succeed'.[20] This document states that the amount the United States has sent to aid its allies in Cuba – those people whom writer Ernest Hemingway, in a very different context, called the 'fifth column'[21] – totals some $68.2 million, and notes that that sum is sent directly to 'dissidents', who will be trained and receive equipment and materials.

This is an undeniable attempt by a great power to destabilize a small country.[22] The president of the Cuban parliament, Ricardo Alarcón, has said, 'so long as this policy exists, there will be Cubans conspiring with the Americans, accepting their money; . . . I know of no country that does not classify such activity as a crime'.[23] And he is perfectly correct in calling it a crime if we consider the following note to the Americans' 'plan': *For reasons of national security and effective implementation, some recommendations are contained in a separate classified annex.*

Despite the persistent attacks by the United States and the 600 assassination attempts against Fidel Castro, Cuba has never responded with violence. For forty-eight years, not a single act of violence encouraged or sponsored by Cuba has occurred in the United States. Quite the contrary – Castro made a statement after the attacks against New York and Washington on 11 September 2001 in which he said that the United States' 'attitude against us in no way lessens the profound grief we feel for the victims [of those attacks] . . . We have said on many occasions that whatever our relations with the administration in Washington may be, no one will ever set out from Cuba to commit a terrorist attack on the United States.' And then, for yet greater emphasis, Castro added, 'May they cut off my hand if they find a single word aimed at denigrating the American people. We would be little better than ignorant fanatics if we were to blame the American people for the differences between our two governments.'

As a reaction to the constant aggressions against Cuba directed from abroad, within the country the government has preached unity-to-the-death. It has maintained the principle of a single political party, and has often severely sanctioned any difference of opinion or disagreement, applying in its own way St Ignatius Loyola's old motto: 'In a besieged fortress, all dissidence is treason.' Thus, Amnesty International's 2006 report on human-rights violations criticized the Cuban authorities' attitude towards civil freedoms (freedom of association, freedom of opinion, freedom of movement) and reminded the world that 'nearly seventy prisoners of conscience [remain] in prison' in Cuba.[24] Whatever its justification may be, this is a situation that is indefensible. As is the death penalty, which has been abolished in almost every developed country in the world (with the notable exceptions of the United States and Japan). No person who believes in democracy can countenance the existence of prisoners of conscience and the continued use of the death penalty.[25]

These critical reports by Amnesty International do not, however, allege any cases of torture in Cuba, or 'disappearances', or the murder of journalists, or political assassinations, or protest marchers beaten by police. Nor has there ever been a popular uprising against the regime – not a single case in the Revolution's almost fifty years. The reports do show, however, that in some countries in the region that have stayed under the mass media's radar – Guatemala, Honduras, El Salvador, the Dominican Republic, even Mexico, not to mention Colombia, for example[26] – women, union members, government opponents, journalists, priests, judges, mayors and leaders of civilian society continue to be murdered with impunity, and without these violations of human rights' arousing any international media attention at all, much less outrage.

To all this one must add that those countries, and most of the poor nations of the world, are afflicted by terrible ills: the constant violation of millions of citizens' economic, social and cultural rights; scandalous infant mortality rates; short life expectancies; hunger; illiteracy; homelessness; unemployment; lack of health care; desperate poverty that leads to begging, children living in the streets, and shantytowns; drug addiction and drug trafficking; high crime rates; and all sorts of minor criminality . . . phenomena all but unknown in Cuba.

As is the official cult of personality. Although the face of Fidel is often in the press, on television and in the street, there is no official portrait, nor is there a statue or coin or avenue or building or monument dedicated to Fidel Castro or any other living leader of the Revolution.

Despite the unceasing harassment from abroad, this little country, clinging to its sovereignty, has achieved undeniably admirable results in the area of human development: the abolition of racism, the emancipation of women, the eradication of illiteracy, a drastic reduction in infant mortality rates,[27] a higher level of general knowledge . . . In questions of education, health, medical research and sports, Cuba has achieved results that many developed nations would envy.[28]

Cuba continues to be one of the most diplomatically active countries in the world. In the sixties and seventies, it supported armed opposition movements in several countries in Central America (El Salvador, Guatemala, Nicaragua) and South America (Colombia, Venezuela, Bolivia, Argentina). Its armed forces, sent halfway around the world, took part in military campaigns of great impact, particularly in the wars of Ethiopia and Angola. The Cuban armed forces' intervention in Angola, in fact, brought about the defeat of elite divisions from the Republic of South Africa and unquestionably hastened the fall of South Africa's racist apartheid regime and the release from prison of Nelson Mandela, who never misses an opportunity to remember his friendship with Fidel Castro and the debt he owes the Cuban Revolution.

In the eighties, Cuba took a leadership position in the Non-Aligned Movement and directed an intense international campaign to refuse repayment of the Latin American nations' foreign debt. In the wake of the débâcle in the Socialist camp in Eastern Europe and the Soviet Union's collapse in 1991, the Cuban Revolution went through some very hard years, a time called the 'special period', but it did manage to survive, to the great surprise of most of its adversaries.

For the first time in its history, Cuba has no dependence on an empire – neither Spain nor the United States nor the Soviet Union. Fully independent at last, the country has begun a kind of second political life – to the left of the international Left, associated with all the international progressive movements and forces, and part of the vast offensive against neoliberalism and globalization.

In this new geopolitical context, the Cuban Revolution is still, thanks to its successes and despite its not inconsiderable shortcomings (economic difficulties, colossal bureaucratic incompetence, widespread small-scale corruption, the harshness of daily life, food and other shortages, power cuts, a chronic lack of public – and, of course, private – transport, housing problems, rationing, restrictions on certain freedoms), an important reference for millions of the disinherited of the planet.

Although Cuba in no way intends to 'export' its socio-political model, in many places in the world women and men protest, struggle and sometimes die trying to attain social objectives such as those achieved by the Cuban Revolution. This is particularly true in Latin America, where solidarity with Cuba and the vindication of the figure of Fidel Castro have never been so strong.

From Hugo Chávez' electoral victory in Venezuela in December 1998 through to December 2006, candidates from the Left have been elected – democratically, at the polls – across the continent: Néstor Kirchner in Argentina, Lula da Silva in Brazil, Tabaré Vázquez in Uruguay, Martín Torrijos in Panama, René Préval in Haiti, Michelle Bachelet in Chile, Evo Morales in Bolivia, Daniel Ortega in Nicaragua and Rafael Correa in Ecuador. In other countries, only what is widely considered to be fraud has prevented the candidate of the Left from winning – as happened in July 2006 in Mexico with Andrés Manuel López Obrador, with a losing margin of 0.56 per cent of the votes cast![29]

This situation in Latin America is totally unprecedented. Not so long ago, under a number of pretexts, a military coup (the most recent of which occurred on 11 April 2002 in Venezuela, against President Hugo Chávez) or direct military intervention by the United States (the most recent of which occurred in December 1989 in Panama against President Manuel Noriega) would put a quick end to any attempt at economic and social reform, regardless of its support by the majority of the country's population. We must remember that democratically elected leaders such as Jacobo Arbenz in Guatemala, João Goulart in Brazil, Juan Bosch in the Dominican Republic and Salvador Allende in Chile, to cite just four of the most famous cases, were toppled (in 1954, 1964, 1965 and 1973, respectively) by military coups backed by the United States in order to prevent structural reforms in highly inegalitarian societies – reforms which would have affected the interests of the US and (in the days of the Cold War, which lasted from 1947 to 1989) brought about a shift of alliances that Washington had no intention of allowing.

In the geopolitical context of the time, the only Left-leaning experiment that managed to survive was Cuba's. But we have all seen at what cost. Pressures and aggressions have forced the country to harden itself in the extreme, and, in order to escape the political isolation and economic strangulation imposed by the United States, to privilege for more than twenty years a none-too-natural alliance with the distant Soviet Union, whose sudden disappearance in December 1991 caused Cuba grave difficulties. Thus, with the exception of Cuba's, all attempts to change the structures of property or to more fairly distribute the continent's wealth were brutally cut short . . . until just a few years ago.

Why is something the United States didn't allow for decades being accepted now? Why can a red (or at least pink) tide wash over so many Latin American states without being pushed back, as it always was before? What has changed? In the first place, one would have to note one extraordinarily persuasive reason: the failure, all across Latin America, of the some-times quite radical neoliberal experiments of the nineties. In many countries, these policies led to unacceptable and finally intolerable results: privatizations that entailed selling off the national patrimony at bargain-basement prices; massive corruption; brazen looting on a national scale; the massive impoverishment of the middle and working classes; and the destruction of entire industries. Finally, and perhaps foreseeably, the citizens rebelled. In Venezuela, in Bolivia, in Ecuador, in Peru and in Argentina, civil insurrections brought down presidents who were democratically elected but thought that once they won the elections they could do as they pleased throughout their terms of office – even, finally, betray their platforms and their people.

Thus, the popular uprising in Argentina in December 2001, which led to the downfall of President Fernando de la Rua, and especially the dramatic failure of the neoliberal policies imposed in the period from 1989 to 1999 by President Carlos Menem, are, in a way, the equivalent in South America of the fall of the Berlin Wall on 9 November 1989 in Europe: the final rejection of a dogmatic, arrogant and anti-popular model.

Another fundamental reason: since the Gulf War in 1991 and even more since 11 September 2001, the essential geopolitical concerns of the United States, which is the 'godfather' (in the Mafia sense) of this region it considers its 'backyard', have shifted towards the Near and Middle East, where there are both oil and the United States' main current enemies. This change of focus has allowed the emergence of a number of leftist experiments in Latin America, and has no doubt prevented their northern neighbour from quickly nipping them in the bud, as it would have done before. This has been an opportunity for Havana, which has seen the number of new, solid allies in the region grow as it has reached both political and economic agreements with its continental counterparts, and particularly with the Bolivarian Venezuela of Hugo Chávez. We should recall that at the Mercosur Summit in Córdoba, Argentina, in 2001, Fidel Castro signed an important trade agreement with the member-countries of that association, among them Brazil and Argentina. Not only was this an open challenge to the American embargo but also a show of support on the part of the Southern Cone nations for a small country which for almost fifty years has refused to relinquish its national sovereignty to the greatest superpower on the planet.

What will happen when the Cuban president dies – of natural causes? It is obvious that changes will take place, since no one in the power structure in Cuba (neither the state nor the Party nor the armed forces) has Castro's authority – an authority that invests him with his four-fold role as the Revolution's theorist, military leader,[30] founder and strategist, for over forty-eight years, of its policies. Some analysts predict that the current system will soon fall, or be toppled, as happened in Eastern Europe after the fall of the Berlin Wall. They are mistaken. They are victims of the same wishful thinking that afflicts American neoconservatives, who have convinced themselves that all authoritarian regimes, without exception, are simply hollow shells that will collapse at the first push. It is this wishful thinking, we should remember, that has led the United States into the morasses of Afghanistan and Iraq. It is very unlikely that in Cuba we will see a transition like those of Eastern Europe, where a system imposed from without, and hated by a large part of the population, simply crumbled into dust in a short period of time.

On 31 July 2006 we had some proof of this statement when, due to a complicated surgical procedure following what was described as an 'acute intestinal attack that triggered severe haemorrhaging', Fidel Castro, for the first time since 1959, and then only 'provisionally', turned over all his responsibilities and functions to a team of seven government officials presided over by Raúl Castro.[31] Many adversaries rushed to announce the imminent collapse of the regime and an insurrection by the country's populace. The Cuban-American National Foundation immediately called for a 'military or civilian uprising' to bring down the regime. And on 2 August George W. Bush also called for an insurrection, broadcasting this message to the people of the island: 'We support you in your efforts to establish ... a transition government committed to the path of democracy'[32] and threatening reprisals against supporters of the Revolution who opposed a 'free Cuba'. But the days passed and by late December, all observers noted that life continued normally throughout Cuba.

Though his opponents find it hard to believe, the fact is that the majority of Cubans (though admittedly not all) are loyal to the Revolution. It is a loyalty founded on patriotism – a patriotism which, unlike what happened in the Communist countries of Eastern Europe, has its roots in the country's historical resistance to the annexationist intentions of the United States.

Whether his detractors like it or not, Fidel Castro has a place in the pantheon of world figures who have struggled most fiercely for social justice and with greatest solidarity come to the aid of the oppressed. As Frei Betto, the Brazilian Catholic theologian and former adviser to President Lula, put it, 'Fidel Castro has freed his country not just from hunger, but also from illiteracy, begging, criminality, and subservience to the empire.'

For all these reasons – to which, in March and April 2003, was added my disagreement with the long prison terms to which some seventy non-violent dissidents were sentenced and the execution by firing squad of three boat hijackers – I thought it inconceivable that Fidel Castro, a leader of such high profile, criticized so fiercely by so much of the West's press, not present his personal version, give his own direct statement on the major struggles of his life.

Fidel Castro, so prolix in his speeches, has given very few long interviews, and in fifty years only four such conversations have been published: two with Gianni Miná, one with Frei Betto and one with Nicaraguan writer and former Sandinista minister Tomás Borge. After almost a year of waiting, I was told that he had agreed to my request, that he would have his fifth long conversation with me, and it has turned out to be the longest and most complete of them all.

I prepared myself extensively, as though I were about to run a marathon. I read or reread dozens of books, articles and reports and consulted various friends, many of whom knew better than I the complex history, the many twists and turns, of the Cuban Revolution and were able to suggest questions, subjects to pursue, critiques. To them I owe any interest readers may find in the questions I asked Fidel Castro for this book-interview.

The book-interview is a hybrid genre. It is at once old – given that one of its first examples, Goethe's *Conversations with Eckermann*, appeared in 1835[33] – and contemporary, because recent recording techniques have made this sort of work relatively common. It belongs simultaneously to the realm of 'journalism' and the realm of 'essay'. *Journalism* because the interview is one of the reporter's tools *par excellence*, although it's newer than one might think: the first modern interview, between Horace Greeley and Mormon leader Brigham Young, was published by the *New York Tribune* on 20 August 1859.[34] And *essay* because the breadth and length of a book free the interview from the usual qualities of superficiality, speed and improvisation imposed by the modern radio, television and internet media.

Time, for a book, is slower, and its status different – and this, by definition, allows the person interviewed to reread his or her (his, in this case) statements, make changes and corrections, introduce lost or forgotten details and add, if need be, useful information. Freed from the exigencies of 'live and direct', the interviewer can rearrange the questions, organize them so as to give the dialogue a better rhythm and coherence. In the present case, I have wanted this also to be a book of contemporary history, and that desire has led me to supplement the Cuban president's statements with numerous notes aimed at clarifying the context, providing information on the historical, cultural and political figures mentioned by Castro and me, and recall historical events; I have also included a chronology with useful parallels in time and geography.

Before we sat down to work in the silence and semi-obscurity of Fidel Castro's personal office – since part of the interviews were filmed for a documentary[35] – I wanted to get to know the public figure a little better, get a little closer to him, see him going about his daily work, handling the routine matters of state and of his life. Until that point, I had spoken with Fidel only in brief professional encounters, and on very specific subjects for stories I was doing on the island or when I was taking part in some conference or other event there, such as the Feria del Libro de La Habana, the Havana Book Fair. He agreed to that, and invited me to accompany him for several days on several trips, both inside Cuba (to Santiago, Holguín, through Havana) and abroad (to Ecuador).

During all that time – in his official vehicle, a heavy black armoured Mercedes from the eighties with a machine gun rolling around on the floor; in his presidential plane, an old Soviet Ilyusin Il-18 not manufactured since 1970; or walking, or having lunch or dinner – we talked about the topics of the day, his experiences in the past, his present-day concerns, every subject imaginable, and without a tape recorder. I would later reconstruct those conversations in my notebooks from memory, since we had agreed that he would be able to reread and alter his responses before publication.

What I discovered during this time was a private, almost shy Fidel, a polite, affable man who pays attention to each person he talks to and speaks without affectation, yet with the manners and gestures of a somewhat old-fashioned courtesy that has earned him the title of 'the last Spanish gentleman'. He is always attentive to others, aware of them as persons – especially those he works with, his staff, and his escorts – and he never raised his voice. I never heard him give an order. But still, wherever he is, he exercises absolute authority – it is the force of his overwhelming personality. Where he is, there is but one voice: his. He makes all the decisions, big and small. Although he consults the political authorities in charge of the Party and the government very respectfully, very 'professionally' during the decision-making process, it is Fidel who finally decides. There is no one within the circle of power that Fidel moves in, since the death of Che Guevara, who has an intellectual calibre comparable to his own. In that respect, he gives the impression of being a man alone, with no close friends, no intellectual peers.

He is a leader who lives, so far as I could see, modestly, austerely, in almost spartan conditions: there is no luxury; his furniture is sober; his food is frugal, healthy, macrobiotic. His are the habits of a soldier-monk. Most of his enemies admit that he is one of the very few heads of state who has not taken advantage of his position to enrich himself.

He sleeps about four hours a night, and sometimes one or two more during the day, when he has a chance. His workday, all seven days a week, usually ends at five or six in the morning, as the sun is rising. More than once he interrupted our conversation at two or three in the morning because, weary but smiling, he still had to attend an 'important meeting.' . . . One trip, one drive from here to there, one meeting, one visit, one public appearance follows upon another incessantly, and dizzyingly. His assistants – all young men in their thirties, and brilliant – are drained at the end of the workday. They are virtually asleep on their feet, exhausted, unable to keep up with that indefatigable eighty-year-old.

Fidel is always asking for notes, reports, cables, international and national news, statistics, summaries of TV or radio broadcasts, the results of national opinion polls. He is constantly making or receiving telephone calls via the mobile phone carried by his personal assistant, Carlitos Valenciaga . . . He is a man of infinite curiosity, and he never stops thinking, pondering, rallying his staff of advisers. Always alert, in action, at the head of a small General Staff – his group of assistants – ready to engage in the day's new battles. Ready to remake the Revolution, every day. There is nothing more alien to him than dogma, precept, rules, 'the system', revealed truth. He is the very definition of an anti-dogmatic leader. He is an innate and instinctive transgressor – subversive, anti-authoritarian – and, though it may be too obvious to say it, a rebel.

Seeing Fidel Castro in action is inspiring – it's watching politics on the move. Always full of ideas, thinking the unthinkable, imagining the unimaginable, with a creativity that one has to call genius. In that sense, one might say that he is a political *creator*, as others are creators in the field of painting or music. He is incapable of having an idea that's not a Big Idea, and his mental daring is spectacular.

Once a project has been discussed and approved, no obstacle can stop him. As de Gaulle used to say, 'City hall will go on.' That's the way Fidel thinks, too. All is *un fait accompli* – *dicho y hecho*, as the Spanish phrase would have it: 'Said, and done.' He believes passionately in what he is doing, and his enthusiasm moves others not just to believe, but to *do*. That must be the definition of charisma. 'It's ideas that transform the world, the way tools transform matter,' he often says.

Before his health crisis in late July 2006, Castro, despite his age, was a man of impressive physique – tall (1.85 metres, a little over six feet), athletic, robust. The *comandante* exerts a powerful attraction on the numerous visitors he receives, many from abroad, and he, like the great actors, knows how to use that undeniable seduction.

Brilliant and baroque, Fidel Castro has a visceral need to communicate with the public. He is aware that one of his main qualities is his ability to speak – to convince and persuade. He is better than anyone at capturing an audience's attention, holding them in his power, subjugating them, electrifying them, and eliciting storms of applause. There is no spectacle that can compare with Fidel Castro giving a speech. Standing, his body swaying, his hand often on the microphone, his voice thunders, his eyes fix on the crowd, he pauses ... then moves his arms like a bronco-rider, raises his index finger and points at the suddenly tame crowd. Because it is true, as Spanish essayist Gregorio Marañon says, that 'a great orator to the masses must master the gestures of a lion-tamer.'

The writer Gabriel García Márquez, who knows him well, describes the way Fidel addresses crowds: 'He always begins almost inaudibly, his path uncertain, but he takes advantage of any glimmer, any spark, to gain ground, little by little, until suddenly he casts off – and takes control of his audience. It is inspiration, an irresistible, blinding state of grace, which is only denied by those who have not had the glorious experience of living through it.'

His mastery of the art of oratory, so many times described, is prodigious. Nor am I talking about his public speeches, which everyone knows about, but rather a simple after-dinner conversation. A torrent of plain words of great impact. A verbal avalanche that he always accompanies with the dancerlike gestures of his expressive hands.

On 1 December 2006, in Havana, Rodrigo Borja, former president of Ecuador, told me that talking once with then-French president François Mitterrand, Borja had asked him, 'What political leader that you've known personally has made the greatest impression on you?' And Mitterrand had answered, 'I'm going to name three: de Gaulle, Gorbachev and Fidel Castro.' 'Why Castro?' Borja had asked puzzled. 'Because of his ability to anticipate the future, and his sense of history,' said Mitterrand.

And it's true: Fidel has a profound sense of himself in history, and an extreme sensitivity to everything touching upon national identity. He quotes José Martí, the hero of Cuban independence, whom he reads and rereads much more than any figure in the history of the socialist or labour movement. Martí, in fact, is his principal source of inspiration. But he is also fascinated by the sciences, and scientific research. He is impassioned by medical progress, the possibility of healing children – all the children. And the fact is, thousands of Cuban doctors are to be found in dozens of poor countries, healing the poorest and most needy.[36]

Moved by humanitarian compassion and internationalist solidarity, he has a dream, which he has talked about a thousand times, of bringing health and knowledge, medicines and education, to every corner of the planet. Is that an impossible dream? Not for nothing is his favourite literary hero Don Quixote. Most of the people who speak with Castro, and even some of his adversaries, admit that he is a person who acts out of ambitions that are noble, out of ideals of justice and equity. This quality, which makes one think of those words of Che Guevara: 'A great revolution can only be born out of a great feeling of love,' made a profound impression on American film-maker Oliver Stone. 'Castro,' he said, 'is one of the wisest men there are; he is a survivor and a Quixote. I admire his Revolution, his faith in himself and his honesty.'[37]

Castro likes precision, accuracy, exactitude, punctuality. Whatever the subject he may be talking about, he does mathematical calculations at amazing speed. No approximations for Fidel. He remembers the smallest detail. During our conversations, the excellent historian Pedro Alvarez Tabío was often at Castro's side, helping him, when necessary, with the exact detail, date, name, situation . . . Sometimes his insistence on accuracy has to do with his own past ('What time did I get to Siboney the night before the attack on Moncada?' 'At such-and-such an hour, *comandante*,' replies Pedro); sometimes it has to do with some marginal aspect of a distant event ('What was the name of that vice president of the Bolivian Communist Party who wouldn't help Che?' 'So-and-so,' answers Pedro). There is, then, this second memory alongside Fidel's own – which is formidable to begin with – and Pedro's, like Fidel's, is astounding.

Fidel's is a memory *so* rich, though, that it sometimes seems to prevent him from thinking synthetically. His thoughts branch, everything is connected to everything, and the branches form long chains of links. The pursuit of a subject leads him, through an association of ideas, through the recollection of such-and-such a situation or person, to call up a parallel subject, and another, and another, and another, until we are far from the central issue – so far that the interlocutor fears, for a moment, that he's lost the thread. But Fidel retraces his steps after a while and returns to the original topic.

At no time during the more than hundred hours of conversation did Fidel put any limitation on the questions or issues that we could discuss. He never asked, although it wouldn't have been strange to do so in such a wide-ranging project, for a list of questions or subjects to be talked about. He knew – we had discussed this earlier – that I wanted to go over all, without exception, of the long list of reproaches, criticisms and reservations inspired by the Cuban Revolution in both his adversaries and some of the Revolution's friends. As the intellectual he is, he is not afraid of debate. On the contrary, he needs it, requires it, encourages it. He is always ready to 'litigate', and with anybody. With tons of arguments. And with an impressive mastery of rhetoric. With great respect for his interlocutor, great tact. He is a fearsome arguer and polemicist – highly educated – who is put off only by bad faith and hatred.

If there are any questions or subjects missing in this book, that absence is attributable only to my own shortcomings as an interviewer, never to Castro's refusal to speak about this or that aspect of his long political life. Furthermore, one must recognize that some dialogues, due to the intellectual disparity between the person asking the questions and the person answering, become monologues. There was no intent, in these conversations, to polemicize or debate – the journalist takes no sides – but rather to elicit a 'personal interpretation' of the biographical and political career of this man who is now a part of history.

I have never liked those narcissistic interviewers who never stop attacking their interlocutor and are eager to demonstrate that they're cleverer, more intelligent and better prepared than the person they are interviewing. That type of journalist doesn't listen to the person being interviewed, often cuts them off, and eventually frustrates the reader. Nor do I like those who think of the interview as a police interrogation in which there's a cop on one side of the table and a suspect on the other, or as an inquisitorial relationship with a perpetrator of crimes standing before a harsh judge whose job it is to extract a confession. For this kind of interviewer, journalism is first and foremost a 'trial' – even, sometimes, a meting-out of justice – and stands above all other tribunals.

There is also the dishonest and cowardly notion of the interview as a genre that allows the person interviewed to be stabbed in the back by the interviewer, under the pretext that journalism is free and 'objective' (on behalf of a perverted notion of freedom of the press), and allows the interviewer to do what he or she likes with the interviewee's statements: keep certain passages and throw out others, take a statement out of context, omit details, cut out qualifications and leave statements 'bald', and never allow the person interviewed to reread his or her own words before publication.

One of the objectives of these conversations with Fidel Castro was to allow one of the most implacably attacked figures in the world of the last fifty years, and at the same time one of the most censored, to have his say, to make his argument to the world. Apparently some people believe that journalistic courage consists of bending to the 'censorship of the consensus'; that is, lazily repeating the 'facts' and interpretations sung in chorus by the mass media over the past five decades. As in Pavlovian training, in some countries the simple mention of the word 'Cuba' automatically triggers a litany of clichés, repeated *ad nauseam* by people acting under the Goebbelsian principle that sufficient repetition of any statement creates belief in that statement. No one takes the trouble to verify that single and unilateral version of the facts that some present as the result of 'revelations' or, more fashionably, 'investigation'.

Another of this book's objectives is to try to lift the veil from the 'Fidel Castro enigma'. How does a boy born in an isolated, rural, rustic place to wealthy, conservative and relatively uneducated parents, then educated by Franco-supporting Jesuits in Catholic schools for the children of the elite, a young man who rubbed elbows with the offspring of the *haute bourgeoisie* in the classrooms of law school, wind up turning into one of the great revolutionaries of the second half of the twentieth century?

And I also wanted to bring out from behind the armour-plating of his many public functions the private Fidel – my belief being that a person may manage to hide his true personality in an interview lasting ten minutes or an hour or two hours, but in an interview lasting as long as these conversations did, no one can do that. In a hundred or more hours, the person interviewed, willy-nilly, reveals his soul, drops the mask at some point, shows his true humanity (or lack thereof), his true self. The reader can see that here.

The long sessions of work with Fidel Castro in January, February and then May 2003 produced a first draft of this book. But months passed, and the text wasn't ready for the press. Meanwhile, in Cuba and around the world, life and events unfolded. The gap between the subjects we had talked about and the new problems that had appeared (the war in Iraq, the new situation in Latin America, the spread of corruption in Cuba, the broken knee suffered by Fidel Castro in Santa Clara) grew wider. In the autumn of 2004, then, I returned to Havana and met Fidel again, so that we might talk further about some of the subjects we had touched on earlier. Then, finally, in late 2005, long hours of supplementary conversations allowed us to bring the book up to date and complete it.

In response, or as a complement to a response, to certain questions, there were times when Castro, feeling it was pointless to repeat things he'd already said, suggested that I look at some of his recent speeches or statements. And he authorized me, with the assistance of Pedro Alvarez Tabío, to introduce passages from those statements into the text of our interview. He wanted to use his own words, and I thought it natural that he would want to see them reproduced here in this book that constitutes, without question, a 'look back' over his life and thought – those additions would give the book a new breadth and significance.

Finally, by common accord, we also decided to add notes that would give readers some new facts and show the evolution of some of the subjects we had taken up over the course of our conversations. I have introduced those 'updating' notes in cases where they seemed to me essential for the reader's understanding of events.

Let me say, too, that it never crossed my mind that we should speak about Castro's private life, his wife or his children.

Fidel Castro had promised me that he would reread all his answers, but obligations of state prevented that, so the first edition of this book came out in Spain in April 2006, in Cuba a month later, without his having personally reread it.

But the *comandante* likes to keep his promises, so he took upon himself the task of rereading and modifying his responses after the book had already been published – and he decided at that point, as is his habit, to devote himself entirely to the task at hand. So he added the detailed, meticulous reading to his many regular duties, reducing his short nights even further in order to bring added precision to this book, complete a phrase here and there, change oral expression into a more written style. He even consulted with some of the figures mentioned in our conversations in order to verify that what he had said about them was true. Several of these figures – Raúl Castro and Hugo Chávez, for example – reminded him of interesting sidelights or other details that he then also included in his replies.

All those who were in contact with Fidel Castro during those months of June and July 2006, and particularly his closest assistants, have stressed how caught up he became in this process of rereading, which once more demonstrates his almost maniacal obsession with perfection. Some have even suggested that this absorbing task, added to the efforts he made a few days earlier, around the time of the Mercosur Summit in Córdoba, Argentina, may have contributed to the extreme stress that led, apparently, on 26 July 2006, to that severe attack of diverticulitis and resulting haemorrhage that we all now know about.

In the first days of August, after complicated surgery, in his hospital bed, Castro picked up the book again and started rereading the last chapters. He himself told Argentine writer Miguel Bonasso, 'I kept correcting the book at the worst moments, from the very first. I wanted to finish it because I didn't know how much time I'd have.'

This version of the book has, then, been totally revised, amended and completed personally by Fidel Castro, who finished rereading it in its entirety in late November 2006.

What are the main differences between the first edition in Spanish and this one [in Spanish]?[38] One entire chapter has been added, Chapter 24, 'Fidel and France', which was not in the first edition because it was not ready in time. It is the last chapter Fidel reread, corrected and completed. The vast majority of the retouching done by Castro – one day historians may arrive at the exhaustive list[39] – has to do with the style of the answers and more specific or more accurate details and descriptions, especially in Chapter 8, 'In the Sierra Maestra', that greatly clarify the context yet in no way change the content.

On four occasions, however, Castro wanted to add important observations; I feel they have enriched the book enormously. In the first chapter, he considerably expanded his comments on his mother, Lina. Castro, a reserved, almost modest man, had never expressed himself publicly so fully on the subject of his mother. In Chapter 13, he added important letters between himself and Nikita Khrushchev during the 'Cuban missile crisis' in October of 1962. These letters are not completely unknown, but they are documents that only a very few specialists have ever seen. Chapter 25, 'Latin America', is where perhaps the greatest number of changes have been made. Specifically, the part of that chapter in which Castro talks about his actions during the coup against President Hugo Chávez of Venezuela on 11 April 2002 has been expanded. With these new details – which are *entirely* new and have never been seen before, especially the retranscription of telephone conversations with some of the high-ranking military officers loyal to President Chávez – this chapter is now an exceptional historical document.

Finally, in Chapter 26, which discusses the 1991 Gulf War, Fidel Castro makes public for the first time the two personal letters he sent to Saddam Hussein, urging the Iraqi leader to withdraw from Kuwait.

On one occasion, Castro 'censored' his first statement. This, too, was in relation to Saddam Hussein, and also in Chapter 26. In the first [Spanish] edition of the book, to the question 'What do you think about Saddam Hussein?' Castro had replied: 'How shall I put it? . . . A disaster. An erratic strategist. Cruel with his own people.' These words were deleted in the version sent to press by Castro. Why? This is my personal explanation: when Fidel Castro made that first statement to me, in May 2003, after the taking of Baghdad by the US army, Saddam Hussein was a free man, and one might even have conjectured that he had taken charge of a part of the armed resistance. Judging a man who fights with weapons in hand, Fidel didn't hide his attitude towards the Iraqi leader: 'An erratic strategist. Cruel with his own people.' Three and a half years later, with Saddam a prisoner of the Americans, condemned to death and about to be executed, Castro took back what he'd said. One does not judge a humiliated, humbled man so severely, no matter what he's done.

The fall of the Berlin Wall, the disappearance of the Soviet Union and the historic failure of authoritarian state Socialism seem not to have altered Fidel Castro's dream of establishing in his country a society of a new kind – less unequal, healthier, better educated, without privatizations or discriminations, and with a culture that embraces the entire world. And his close new alliance with Venezuela and President Hugo Chávez, Bolivia and Evo Morales, and other countries in Latin America has strengthened his convictions.

In the winter of his life and now, due to health concerns, a little distanced from power, he is still driven to defend the energy revolution, the environment, against neoliberal globalization and internal corruption. He is still down in the trenches, on the front line, leading the battle for the ideas he believes in – ideas which, apparently, nothing and no one will ever make him give up.

Ignacio Ramonet
Paris, 31 December 2005
Limeil-Brévannes, 31 December 2006

I

The Childhood of a Leader

Childhood in Birán – Don Angel – The batey *– Fidel's mother – Living in
the teacher's house – Colegio de La Salle – Echoes of the war in Spain –
The Jesuits of the Colegio de Dolores*

*Historical roots are important, and in that regard, I wanted to ask you:
You were born into a relatively well-to-do family, you studied at religious
schools for the wealthy, you later studied law. With that sort of upbringing,
you could have been a* conservative *leader, couldn't you?*
Perfectly well could have, because a man is not entirely the master of his
own destiny. A man is also the child of circumstances, of difficulties, of
struggle. Problems gradually sculpt him like a lathe sculpts a piece of metal.
A man is not born a revolutionary, I'd venture to say.

So how did the revolutionary in you come forth?
I made myself into a revolutionary. I've reflected from time to time about
the factors that had to do with that. Beginning with the fact of the place
where I was born, way out in the country, on a large estate.

Could you describe the place where you were born?
I was born on a farm. Towards the north-centre of the former province of
Oriente, not far from the Bay of Nipe, and near the sugar-cane *central*
Marcané.[1] The farm was called Birán. It wasn't a town, or even a village –
just a few isolated houses. My family's house was there, alongside the old
Camino Real, as the dirt and mud path was called that ran from the capital
of the municipality [sic] southward. The roads at that time were just big
mud-tracks. People travelled on horseback or in oxcarts. There were no

motorized vehicles yet, or even electric light. When I was little, we lit the house with wax candles and kerosene lamps.

Do you remember the house you were born in?
It was a house constructed in Spanish architecture, or rather Galician. I should point out that my father was a Spaniard, a Galician, from the village of Láncara, in the province of Lugo, the son of poor *campesinos*. And in Galicia, the custom was to shelter the animals underneath the house. My house was inspired by that architecture in Galicia, because it was built on wooden piles, like stilts. These piles were over six feet tall, which was the usual way of building houses in Galicia. I remember that when I was three or four years old, the cows slept underneath the house. They'd be brought in at nightfall, and they'd sleep under the house. And they'd be milked there, tied to some of the piles. Under the house there was also, just like in Galicia, a little pen with pigs and fowl – at various times there'd be chickens, ducks, guinea hens, turkeys and even a few geese.

I've been visiting Birán. And I've seen that house where you were born, which is, as you say, a very original sort of structure.
It was a wooden house. The piles were made of a very hard wood, *caguairán*, and then laid on top of those piles was the floor. The house, I imagine, was originally square. Later on, an addition was made to it: at one corner a kind of office was built. Then it was expanded to make a bathroom area, a pantry for foodstuffs, a dining room and a kitchen. Then on top of the original square area of the house there was a second floor, smaller, which we called the 'mirador'. And it was there that I was born, on 13 August 1926, at two o'clock in the morning, as the story goes.

   In those surroundings, from the time I was a very young boy I lived among the sights and the work of the country – the trees, the sugar cane, the birds, the insects . . .

What's remarkable about Birán is that one feels, almost palpably, the strong entrepreneurial character of your father, don Angel.
He was a man of great will, great determination. He taught himself to read and write, with great effort. Without question he was a very active man – he moved around a lot, he was a go-get-'em kind of person, and he had a natural talent for organization.

Under what circumstances did your father come to Cuba?

My father was the son of *campesinos*; they were extremely poor. When I visited Galicia in 1992, I went to Láncara, the town he'd lived in, and I saw the house he'd been born in. It's a tiny little house, about thirty feet long by about eighteen to twenty feet wide. Made of fieldstone, which is a material that's very abundant in that area [and that's] used traditionally by Galician *campesinos* to build their houses. In that little rustic house lived the whole family, and I suppose the animals did, too. The bedroom and kitchen were in one room. There was no land, not a square yard. Families farmed isolated plots scattered over the countryside.

When he was very young, sixteen or seventeen years old, my father was recruited in Spain for military duty, but he was over twenty when he came to Cuba for the second War of Independence, which began in 1895. No one knows exactly how he came, under what conditions. After I was old enough to do so, I never talked about those things with my father. He would – from time to time, at a dinner, with a group of friends, that sort of thing – he would tell stories. But my older sister, Angelita, and Ramón, the second oldest – they're both still alive – they might know something, because they talked to him more than I did. And then later, when I went to Havana to school and became involved in revolutionary activities, organized the attack on Moncada, was in jail, and later in the *Granma* expedition, my younger brothers and sisters, like Raúl, who's four years and some months younger than me, and then two girls, Emma and Juana, who stayed there at home, talked with my father quite a bit, and by then he probably talked more about those things, though I wasn't there to hear him.

Through them I've learned about some things, and the theory is that my father was one of those poor boys from Galicia that some rich man gave money to so he'd go into military service as a replacement for him. And it's apparently quite true that my father was one of those *campesinos*, one of the ones recruited that way. You know what those wars were like.

Recruitment was by lottery, and the wealthy could pay the poor to do their military service, or go to war, in their place.[2]

Well, it must have been as you say; there were many cases in which a rich man would be ordered to perform his military service or go off to war and he'd come up with a certain amount of money and give it to a man who didn't have any, who lived very badly, on a little piece of land or doing some sort of labour in the country.

My father was sent here as a Spanish soldier, and he was stationed in the great tract of cleared land between Júcaro and Morón. And among other things, it turned out that the huge clearing in the woods where the garrison had been constructed was used by [Cuban rebel] invaders from Oriente, under the command of Maceo and Máximo Gómez,[3] shortly after the death of Martí.

The enormous clearing where the garrison had been built had to be crossed at all costs – a difficult operation. It was on a fortified line that ran north–south, in the narrowest part of the centre of the island, quite a few kilometres long, it might be almost 100 kilometres, over sixty miles, from Morón in the north to Júcaro, a port city on the south coast. I know that my father was stationed along that line, but I don't think he was still there when Maceo came through. The Cubans travelled through there constantly, or farther to the north, they went into a place called Turiguanó, a kind of island joined to Morón by a very swampy area. There, on that road, was my father, stationed there. That's what I know; my brothers and sisters may know more.

You don't remember any conversations with your father about this?
I once heard him talk about some of this, when I was going off to the working-men's camps in Pinares de Mayarí, because I liked to be anywhere but at home. Home represented authority, and that got my dander up, and the rebel spirit in me began to emerge.

So as a youngster you were a rebel?
I had several reasons for being one. Faced with a certain Spanish authoritarianism, and even more so the particular Spaniard giving the orders . . . so it was authority, respect in general . . . I didn't like authority, because at that time there was also a lot of corporal punishment, a slap on the head or a belt taken to you – we always ran that risk, although we gradually learned to defend ourselves against it.

Your father was authoritarian?
He had a little temper. He couldn't have done what he did, build himself up – so young, first during the war, far from his family and his country, and later from nothing, without a cent, without family, the first in his family to read and write, by his own efforts and no one else's – [couldn't have built] a *latifundio*, [accumulated] wealth, without a strong character. Like most

Galician immigrants, he was modest and hard-working, with a spirit of humility. And yet [he had] great character and determination. But he was never unfair. He never said no to anyone who came to him for help. [He was] always ready to listen, ready to lend a hand when other people were in difficulty. He himself had been in need when he was a boy and growing up. I know he was orphaned at a very early age – eleven; he lost his mother. His father remarried and, well, his childhood was one of suffering and turbulence. But he had the noble virtues of the Galician emigrant: kindness, hospitality, generosity.

There are many stories of his generosity. Even kindness. A man with a good heart who always helped his friends, labourers, people who were having a hard time. Sometimes he'd complain, he'd grumble, but he never let anyone leave without an answer to his problem. When the *tiempo muerto* came,[4] when the harvest was over and there was very little work, then often a man would come and say, 'My children are hungry . . . we have nothing, I need work.' At that time there was a system called the *ajuste*:[5] 'You clear this land for so much.' This *ajuste* was another of the ways that were common in Cuba for landowners to lower their costs; it consisted of a contract with a family or a worker to clear a cane field, and you'd give him so much per *caballería* or per *roza*; they didn't use hectares, like now. I think a *caballería* was about eighteen *rozas*.[6] Every country in Central and South America used different measurements. Thank goodness the metric system came along, invented in the times of the French Revolution. So as I was saying, there would be a contract: 'All right, for twenty pesos, I'll *ajustar* this for you.'[7] My father would invent some new field that needed clearing or some sort of non-essential chores in order to make jobs for people, even though it wasn't financially profitable for him. I realized this as I got a little older, when I'd work in the office during my holiday time. There, I'd give out purchase orders to the workers so they could get goods from the stores even when they weren't hired to work. He was a kind and noble man.

After the War of Independence, in 1898, did your father decide to stay in Cuba?
No, he was repatriated to Spain after the war, in 1898, but apparently he liked Cuba, so, along with a lot of other Galician emigrants, he came back to Cuba the next year. It's documented that he landed in the port of Havana in December 1899. Without a penny and without any family at all, he went to work. He ended up, I have no idea how, in the eastern provinces. It was

the period when the great American plantations were spreading through the forests of hardwood, which would be cut down and used for fuel in the sugar *centrales* – that same wonderful hardwood that El Escorial palace was made from, and other famous buildings and ships, like that formidable *Santísima Trinidad*, the largest and most powerful warship of its time, which was built in the shipyards of Havana and then sank in a storm after being boarded by the English at the Battle of Trafalgar in 1805.

So anyway, the Americans would hire people to cut down the trees and plant sugar cane. The land is always fertile where there's been a forest; the first harvests are excellent.

And your father worked for the Americans?
My father began to work in Oriente province as a simple labourer for the famous United Fruit Company, which had plantations in the north-central part of the province. Then he organized a group of workers and hired himself out to the Yankee company with this group of men under him. I think my father at one time had – I heard this once – as many as 300 men, and that left him a profit. Some talent as an organizer, he had. But he didn't know how to read or write; he learned, gradually, but it wasn't easy. He began with a small business that cut down forests for planting sugar cane or producing firewood for the *centrales*. And that way he began to turn a profit as an organizer of that group of workers, who, I imagine, were immigrants, mostly Spaniards and men from the islands – Haiti and Jamaica.

How much land did your father finally end up owning?
He ended up buying about, approximately 900 hectares, a little over 2,000 acres, which belonged to him, and then later he leased several thousand hectares from two Cuban generals who had fought in the War of Independence – no one knows even today how they came by that land. Vast forests of pine, most of them virgin. The land stretched over mountains and into valleys, up on to a big plateau about 1,800 feet high, a great tableland that pine trees grew on, a natural forest. My father cut the pine forests of Mayarí. Seventeen trucks loaded with pinewood came down out of there every day. The income, also, from sugar cane and livestock was considerable, because he owned other land, mostly flatlands, but some pre-mountain land as well. Around 10,000 hectares, about 25,000 acres, in all.

An extraordinary amount of land.
If you add it up, my father, as owner of part of it and leaseholder of another part, controlled no less than 11,000 hectares of land.

A considerable amount.
Yes, it was considerable. I can tell you this story, because I, really, under those conditions, belonged to a family that was more than *relatively* well-to-do. It was, on that scale, quite well-to-do. I mean, I don't say it out of pride, but rather just because it's the case – [I want] to tell things accurately.

So you're the son of a millionaire.
Well, not of a millionaire. No one would ever have said that my father was a millionaire. In those days, being a millionaire was a colossal thing – a millionaire was somebody who really, really had a lot of money. A millionaire, for example – at that time, when a dollar was worth something and a worker would earn an average of a dollar a day – was a man who had a million times what a person earned in a day. My father's properties couldn't be assessed at that high a price. My father can't be said to have been a millionaire, although he was very well-to-do and had a solid financial position. Although in that poor, suffering society we children were treated like the children of rich people. I can assure you that a lot of people would come up to us and be nice out of pure self-interest, although we really never realized that.

In Birán, your father built not only a house but little by little, there alongside the Camino Real, other buildings as well – a bakery, an inn, a tavern, a school, houses for the Haitian workers . . . A real little town.
Well, where we lived there was no town, just some buildings. It was what you might call a *batey*.[8] When I was little, the dairy was underneath the house. Later, a dairy was built about forty yards from the house, and across the road [there was] a blacksmith shop where the tools, ploughs, all that would be repaired. And very close to that, a small slaughterhouse was built. And then about forty yards away, in another direction, was the bakery, and not far from that, a primary school, a little state school. Also, alongside the road, there was a store, with a storage shed for provisions [non-perishables] and whatnot, and on the other side of the road the post office and telegraph office. Not far away were some very poorly built barracks-like buildings, some huts with dirt floors and palm-leaf roofs, where, as you say, a few

dozen Haitian immigrants lived in poor conditions; they worked during the cultivation and harvesting of the sugar cane, which was the farm's major activity. Near the house there was a big orange grove where my father personally oversaw the pruning, with a big two-handed pair of shears; there were about twelve or fourteen hectares, thirty to thirty-five acres there, and all kinds of fruit trees, sometimes just one or two and sometimes in little groups; there were plantains, papaya, coconuts, soursops, sugar-apples,[9] a little of everything. And three big apiaries with forty-something beehives that yielded lots and lots of honey. I could still walk through that orange grove with my eyes closed today – I knew where every single kind of fruit tree was; I'd peel the oranges with my fingers, and I'd spend my whole summer and Christmas holidays out there. Nobody ate more oranges than I did.

And there was also a big arena for cockfights. Were there cockfights?
Yes. About 100 yards from our house, and along that road, was the cockfight enclosure that you're talking about. It was a place where every Sunday during the harvest season, and also Christmas Day and New Year, Easter Saturday and Easter Sunday, there would be cockfights. In the country, that was the sport.

A local entertainment.
Yes, because there was very little entertainment. People played dominoes. People also played cards; my father, when he was a young soldier, loved to play cards; he was apparently an excellent card player. And in my house there was also, from the time I was about three years old, one of those wind-up phonographs, an RCA Victor [i.e., Victrola], I think it was, to play music. Nobody even had radio. I think my father was the only one who did, and I was big by the time radio came – I mean, I must have been seven or eight years old. No! Older! I must have been ten or twelve, because that was 1936 or 1937 – the Spanish Civil War had already started by the time there was a radio and a small generator there, a little motor that ran for a couple of hours. It charged several 'accumulators', as they were called back then – batteries – and almost every day we had to give it a little rainwater.

And all that belonged to your father?
All except the little schoolhouse and the post office, which were public – all the rest belonged to my family. By the time I was born, in 1926, my father

had already accumulated a certain degree of wealth, and he was very well-to-do as a landowner. Don Angel, 'don Angel Castro', they called him, a person who was very highly respected, a man of great authority in that almost feudal area and time. That's why I tell you that I was the son, really, of a landowning family; my father had been buying land little by little for years.

Talk to me about your mother.
Her name was Lina. She was Cuban, from the western part of the island, from the province of Pinar del Río. Her family was originally from the Canary Islands. She, too, was of *campesino* origin, and her family was very poor. My maternal grandfather was a carter, he transported sugar cane in an oxcart. When they moved to the area of Birán, my mother, who was then thirteen or fourteen years old, came with her parents and her brothers and sisters from Camagüey, where they'd gone by train from Pinar del Río, seeking their fortune. Then they travelled a long, long way by oxcart, first to Guaro and finally to Birán.

My mother was practically illiterate, and, like my father, she learned to read and write practically on her own. With a great deal of effort and determination, too. I never heard her say that she'd gone to school. She was self-taught. An extraordinarily hard-working woman, and there was nothing that escaped her attention. She was a cook, a doctor, a caretaker of all of us – she provided every single thing we might need, and she was a shoulder to cry on for any problem we might have. She didn't spoil us, though; she was a stickler for order, savings, cleanliness. She was the 'overseer', you might say, for all the daily tasks and routines inside and outside the house; she was the family economist. Nobody ever knew where she got the time and energy to do everything she did; she never sat down, I never saw her rest one second the whole day.

She brought seven children into the world, all of us born in that house, although there was always a midwife to help at the delivery. There was never a doctor, never could have been – there was no such thing in that remote part of the country.

Nobody ever worked as hard to see that her children went to school; she wanted us to have what she'd never had a chance for. Without her, I assure you that I – who always loved to study – would be a functional illiterate. My mother, although she wasn't saying so every minute, adored her children. She was a strong-willed woman, brave and self-sacrificing. She was strong and unwavering in the face of the sufferings that some of us unwittingly caused her. She was never bitter about the agrarian reform and the redistribution of that land, which she truly loved.

She was very, very religious, in her faith and her beliefs, which I always respected. She was somehow comforted by the pains of being a mother, and she also accepted her role as the mother of the Revolution that she'd suffered so much over, even though, since she was just a poor, humble *campesina*, she'd never had the least possibility of knowing anything about the history of humanity and the deeper causes for the events she lived through in Cuba and the world.

She died on 6 August 1963, three and a half years after the triumph of the Revolution.

And your father, when did he die?
He died earlier. He was quite a bit older than my mother. He died on 21 October 1956. Two months after my thirtieth birthday, and two months before we started back from Mexico with the *Granma* expedition.

Did your father speak the Galician language?
Yes, but he never used it.

Did you ever hear him speak it?
I heard him say some phrases in Galician a few times. There were other Galicians in that area, and my father may have spoken Galician with them, it's possible. But there were also Spaniards from other provinces; there were Asturians, for example, who didn't speak Galician. Apparently the Galicians had adapted to Spanish, they could speak it, they could be understood better that way, of course, and besides, they weren't going to speak Galician to the Cubans, because nobody would understand them. To a worker, they had to speak Spanish – to everybody, even to their girlfriend or their wife they had to speak Spanish, because [those people] wouldn't know Galician, so that's why I almost never heard him speak Galician.

When the Civil War broke out in Spain, you were about ten years old, I believe.
I hadn't turned ten yet. I was born on 13 August 1926, and the war in Spain started on 18 July 1936. So I was nine years and eleven months old; I already knew, of course, how to read and write.

Do you remember, for example, whether your father was worried about that war, concerned about it, whether he talked about the Spanish Civil War?
In Birán there were two factions in the group of twelve or fourteen Spaniards who lived and worked there.

Spaniards who met with your father, who came to your house?
Who worked with him doing various things, or as labourers. There was an Asturian who was the bookkeeper, and who also had a good education. He'd say that he spoke seven languages, and I almost believe it, because he . . . when we got radio in my house and something would come over the radio in English or even German, he'd translate it. He knew Latin, he wrote in a beautiful Gothic hand. This little Asturian – I say *little* Asturian because he was really short – unquestionably knew more than anybody else there, he was more educated and had wider general knowledge. He knew about Greece, he would talk about Demosthenes; he was the first person I ever heard talk about Demosthenes, the great orator, and what Demosthenes was like, the fact that he would put a little stone in his mouth to cure his stuttering. It was that Asturian who talked to me about that and other things.

That group, and a few more, when the war broke out were on the rebel side – the people who were against the Republic were called the rebels.

The side of the Franquistas?
Right. And there was another group, which supported the Republicans. They were farm workers, and some of them didn't know how to read or write. Although a Cuban named Valero was one of that group, too – the man who was in charge of the telegraph office, the post office, he was a Republican, like a lot of the workers. One of the group of workers was a cook, because since his job on the farm had been taking care of the livestock he'd come down with I don't know what kind of rheumatism, and finally he could hardly walk, so they sent him to be the cook for the house. With all respect for his memory, by the way, and I really liked him a lot, he was *not* a very good cook, or at least there was a lot of complaining in my house about his cooking. His name was García; he was totally illiterate.

Illiterate?
Yes. In my childhood I can assure you that in Birán fewer than 20 per cent of the people who lived there knew how to read and write, and even those

did so with great difficulty. Very few made it to the sixth grade. There I had the experiences that enable me today to understand how much an illiterate person suffers. No one can imagine, because there's such a thing as self-esteem . . . What is an illiterate person? He's the guy on the last rung of the social ladder way down there, the man who has to ask a friend to write a letter to his girlfriend for him. In Birán, the people who didn't know how to read and write would ask the ones who did to write a letter to the woman they were courting, for example. But it wasn't that they dictated a letter – tell her so-and-so and so-and-so – that he dreamed about her last night and that he's not eating for thinking about her, that sort of thing, if that had been the sort of thing he wanted to tell her. No, he'd tell the one who knew how to read and write, 'No, no, you just write whatever you think I ought to write to her.' To win over the girlfriend! I'm not exaggerating. I lived during a time when things were like that.

Do you, personally, recall anything of the discussions or the arguments about the Spanish Civil War?

In 1936 I was sent as a live-in student, a boarder, to a school in Santiago de Cuba, and that summer, when the war started, I was at home on holiday in Birán; at that point I must have been, I don't know, not ten years old yet, I don't know whether I'd finished second grade . . .

So what happened? When I arrived in Birán from Santiago, on holiday from school, since I knew how to read and write, Manuel García, the cook who limped in one leg, a hard-working man who during this time I'm talking about lived in a little house near the post office – Manuel García runs up to ask me to read the newspaper to him. He was a fire-breathing Republican – just to show you the spirit of class, I often ask myself why he was such a fanatical Republican, and so anti-clerical, I must say for the sake of the truth – and so I would read the newspaper to him and give him news about the war in Spain. So that was how I learned about that war, before I'd even turned ten years old. I would read several newspapers to him. One that came to Birán was called, I think, *Información*, and others, such as *El Mundo*, *El País* and *El Diario de Cuba*, but the main newspaper that came there was the *Diario de la Marina*.

Which was a Havana newspaper.

No, no, not a Havana newspaper – it covered the entire republic. It had been a pro-Spanish newspaper since the War of Independence and it was the most right-wing of any newspaper that ever existed in the country down to the triumph of the Revolution. It had a rotogravure section, too, which came out on Sunday. It was very famous. It had pages and pages of advertisements, very thick, and it came to García's small wooden house and I'd go to his house to read it to him. I'd read it to him cover to cover. The 'rebels' were called just that – 'rebels', but it was almost like praise.

The ones who took Franco's side.
The 'Nationalists', which were also called that ['Nationalists']. The others were the 'reds', the 'little reds', pejoratively, but sometimes, very kindly, the paper would call them 'Republicans'. That was the main newspaper that came to Birán – the most weighty, you might say, as well as the thickest, with lots of news, good paper and advertisements, and I would read it to García for hours on end. Although from time to time some other newspaper or other would show up. The one with the most news about the war in Spain was the *Diario de la Marina*.

I remember that war, almost from the beginning. I remember the capture of Teruel by the Republican troops, for example.

And the Ebro front?
The Ebro front was later, almost at the end.

The battle of Madrid?
Yes, Madrid under siege. The trouncing the Republicans gave Mussolini's soldiers in Guadalajara when they advanced on Madrid, and, as I told you, when the Republicans advanced and took Teruel. And the counter-offensive by General Mola to retake the city, and other news that would come in from the people in Burgos, which was the Franquista capital. What was the name of that fortress where the Franquistas were besieged?

The Alcázar, in Toledo.
The Alcázar. I read all about the battle of the Alcázar in Toledo to García, and I'd practically be on his side! I'd even try to make him feel better. I'd say, 'But listen, listen, the battle of Teruel is going well' – I remember that – 'It's all right, look what they've accomplished; look, they're fighting here and here and here.' Every piece of news that was good for the Republicans that could be given, I'd give it to him. That was the situation that was there in Birán, exactly, just exactly the way I'm telling you.

Did your father favour one side or the other, or was he not interested?
No, my father was against the Republic.

Against the Republic?
Yes, yes, and some others were, too – the Asturian, the bookkeeper, in fact, and some others. I think almost the majority of the Spaniards who were in Birán took that position, against the Republic. But there was another group, one that García and some other Spaniards were in, and Valero, the Cuban telegrapher, where they were all Republicans to the death. And once in a while they'd all play dominoes against each other – one ideological side against the other.

A war of dominoes.
Those who were for and against the Republic would get together. They'd face off in spirited games of dominoes. A little like *Don Camilo*, that famous novel by Guareschi,[10] with the priest and the Communist. When I was on holiday, either during the summer or for Christmas, I'd be at home for two weeks, and during Holy Week [prior to Easter], too. I don't know who might have read the news to García when I was at school. He didn't have a radio – my father in that big house was the only one who had one.

Thanks to this Manuel García, then, you must have followed the Spanish war very closely.
Yes. Which is why I remember the Civil War so well, the run-up to the Second World War, when Republican ideas and Western 'democratic' ideas – I'd put quotation marks around 'democratic' – faced off against the genocidal, hegemonic and imperialist ideas of Nazi Germany. What happened in Spain and why the Spanish Republic fell, and what sort of 'non-intervention' was it that the so-called Western democracies had engaged in, in the face of Hitler and Mussolini's intervention since the very beginning of the war? What did all that mean? That was what helped lead to the Second World War.

The first battles were waged right there, in Spain, and there you could find the leftists and rightists, the so-called 'Nationalists', supported by Mussolini and Hitler, and the Spanish Republic, the Left mixed into the 'democratic system', although it was more advanced than could be conceived at that time, the most just, the most popular, because the Spanish Republic was already defending the idea of progress within a society that was almost feudal, a society that had never become industrialized at all, that lived off the income from its colonies for many years. They're a very combative people, the Spanish.

There, the two sides clashed and shot one another by firing squads – they even executed priests. There were priests who were with the Republic and priests – possibly a majority – who were with the rebels or Nationalists – the Franquistas. At that time, the Spanish teachers at my school, in Santiago, talked about the Spanish Civil War. From the political point of view they were Nationalists, we might say more accurately that they were Franquistas – all of them, without exception. They talked a lot about the horrors of the war – about the Nationalists, even priests, who were being shot by the firing squads. But they didn't talk about the Republicans who were being shot by firing squads. Because the Spanish Civil War was very, very bloody, and on both sides there was a policy of *mano dura* – an iron hand.

I remember that after the war was over, one of my teachers would tell me long stories about the number of Republican prisoners shot by firing squads in Spain when the Civil War ended. I was attending the Colegio de Belén, which was also run by the Jesuits, in Havana, and Padre Llorente – he had been a medic during the war – told me stories about how after the war tens of thousands of people – no one even knew how many – had been shot by firing squad, and he'd been assigned to be the medic in charge of examining them to find out whether they were alive or dead before they were buried. He would tell me details of what he'd seen. It had made such a terrible impression on him. There were some Catholics and Christians who were on the side of the Republic, quite a few.

I've talked about my memories of that episode. Of course, since then I've read quite a bit about the subject, but I'm telling you the things I knew then.

The Battle of the Ebro took place in about 1938, if I remember rightly. That was the last Republican offensive . . . Movies have been made of that, and books written. But from the time I was about ten years old, reading the newspapers, I saw for myself how that war unfolded.

Do you think that interest in the war in Spain, when you were such a young boy, had any influence on your development?
Oh, yes. The importance of the international scene. But all boys like war. Like everybody else, I also liked films, the Westerns, and what's more, I took them seriously.

Though they were very racist at that time, weren't they, very anti-Indian?
We took seriously all those tricks the cowboys did. As a boy I did, I mean. Later, grown up, almost an adult, I watched them as comedies – that round-house right the guy threw at the guy across the bar, that red bottle of whisky. I remember all those details. The revolvers that never ran out of bullets except when the plot needed them to run out. There were no machine guns back then, but lots and lots of shooting, and when somebody was being chased on horseback and ran out of bullets, they'd reach up and grab a tree limb.

All the boys would watch those movies. Boys are brought up watching violence from the moment they're born . . . So anyway, reading all that news about the war – how could I ever have imagined all the things that would happen in the world after that!

Afterwards came the Second World War.
I also remember the exact day when the world war broke out – 1 September 1939. I was a little older then, about thirteen, and I read about all of it: the taking of the Ruhr, the annexation of Austria, the occupation of the Sudetenland, the Molotov–Ribbentrop Pact, the invasion of Poland. I wasn't very aware of the significance of the events, but as things went on I learned about it all.

I can remember the basic battles and the things that happened from the beginning of the Second World War in 1939 to 1945, when the atomic bombs were dropped on Japan. I can talk about that subject a great deal, because my interest in it has always remained. But even before that, there had been the war in Ethiopia, when I was just starting school.

You remember the war in Ethiopia?
Yes, you could buy these little biscuits with trading cards about that war, 'the Italians in Abyssinia', as it was called.

It was called the 'Abyssinian War'.[11]
That's right, the 'Abyssinian War' it was called at the time. You could buy these little biscuits that had – so kids would buy them, you know – a collection of trading cards, except for ten or twelve that almost never appeared. Some of them, I think they never even printed, so that kids would drive their parents into bankruptcy buying biscuits.

I became almost an expert on that war in Abyssinia, collecting and playing with those cards. I was in [Colegio de] La Salle by this time, in Santiago de Cuba, and I learned to play with the trading cards that came with the biscuits; you'd lean them up against the wall like this, holding the top edge with your right thumb and then flip them, so they'd go flying off. The one that landed on top of the other would win, and you could keep it . . . I had put my little marks up on the wall and I'd test the wind, all sorts of things like that – I had a whole technique, and it seemed to really work. Goodness knows how many I finally had.

I still remember the images and the colours on the ones that actually did get printed . . . All the kids always trying to complete the set, but they never did.

There were always some cards missing?
Some of them would deliberately never be printed, to make kids buy them, you know. Capitalism . . . I don't recall a single complete collection.

One day this kid came along and told me he had a beautiful album on Napoleon Bonaparte. It wasn't those little trading cards printed on thin cardboard; the ones he had were on some other kind of paper, very elegant, they looked like photographs, and the collection was complete . . . I still have it somewhere. Eusebio Leal[12] came across it not long ago. The kid offered to trade it to me for all those hundreds of trading cards I had on the Abyssinian war. I took him up on it immediately – the album was a real jewel.

So you were very definitely interested in [the] war.[13]
Listen, the Bible talks quite a bit about dramatic events, dramatic wars. From the first grade, in Sacred History – that's what they called that subject in my school – you have the punishment of Babylon, the enslavement of the Israelites, as the Jews were called, the crossing of the Red Sea, Joshua and his trumpets bringing down the walls of Jericho, Samson and his herculean strength, able to pull down a temple with his own hands, the Tablets of the Law, the golden calf worshipped as an idol . . . I used that image in *History Will Absolve Me*, to express a Socialist philosophy. I said, 'We do not believe in golden calves.' That was when I defended myself after the assault on the Moncada barracks in Santiago de Cuba. That was in 1953, and here we are, talking about 1936. At that time I was, as I say, more or less ten years old.

But the war in Abyssinia came before the war in Spain – you were even younger then.
You're right, the Abyssinian War was a little earlier. I think I must have

been in the second grade at Colegio de La Salle. I must have been about nine. I'll tell you, [my interest in that war] helped me get a wonderful album on Napoleon that the city historian, who knows everything, and whom I'd probably told my story about that album, found – either that one or one exactly like it. The yellowish colour of the cards makes me think it was the same one that I'd played with for several years, looking at those images and imagining the famous battles. The battle of Arcole, for example, when at a crucial moment Napoleon picked up the flag and crossed the bridge and shouted, 'Follow your general!' That impresses any boy. And then Austerlitz and all the other battles. The main episodes of Napoleon's life were right there, in pictures. Naturally, it was great entertainment, and I was crazy about that leader, as I was crazy about Hannibal, crazy about Alexander the Great and other famous people that the elementary-school history books never cease writing about. Back then, I wished Hannibal had taken Rome – maybe because of his daring in crossing the Alps with his elephants, or maybe because he was the underdog. I also liked the Spartans and their defence of the Gates of Thermopylae with just 300 men. And I'll tell you, I console myself today by thinking that my Napoleon album was *much* better than any Wild West movie.

You liked military leaders, warriors.
All boys do. They start, as I say, in Sacred History. The Old Testament is full of wars and other exciting episodes: Noah's Ark, the flood, the forty days of rain . . . It even says, in Genesis, that after the flood, Noah planted a vineyard, planted grapes and made wine, and he drank a little more than he should have and one of his sons made fun of his father and Noah cursed him! He condemned him to be a slave and to be black![14] That's one of the things that are in the Bible that I think the Church itself ought to rectify some day, because it sounds as if being black is a curse from God . . . As it's a curse, a punishment, to be a woman, and to be the one that's responsible for original sin.

You're asking the Catholic Church to rectify that?
Well, actually, I'm not asking that the Church amend itself or change in matters of faith. But John Paul II himself, who was very brave, very deter- mined, said that the theory of evolution is not irreconcilable with the doctrine of creation.

I've spoken with cardinals and bishops from time to time about this subject. There are these two points. I believe that with the wisdom possessed by an institution that has endured for 2,000 years, they should contribute to the notion of women's equality, to women's not being blamed for all the suffering in the world, to getting rid of the idea that being black is a punishment from God, just because a son of Noah made a little fun of his father.

You, too, rebelled first against your father, didn't you?
Well, I didn't rebel against my father; that was hard, because he was a man with a good heart. I rebelled against authority.

You couldn't bear authority.
That has a history. It didn't just spring up full-blown when I was ten or twelve years old, because I'd started being a rebel several years before that, at like six or seven, say.

What other memories marked your early childhood in Birán?
I remember many things. And some of them must necessarily have had an influence on me. But, for example, death did not mark my childhood. Although I did lose an aunt, Antonia, who died in childbirth before I was three years old. I still remember that sadness in the family, that air of tragedy among the adults. She was one of my mother's sisters, [and she was] married to a Spaniard that worked with my father in Birán – he was the overseer of a sugar-cane area. Soto was his name. I remember walking along a little dirt path through the sugar cane, with the women crying, till we got to a small wooden house. I remember that, but it must not have made a very strong impression on me because I didn't know what it was all about, I wasn't aware of death.

I also remember the first time I saw a locomotive. Everything about a steam locomotive is impressive – its wheels, its noise, its power, its whistle. They would come to pick up sugar cane to be processed. And I thought they were fabulous monsters.

When I was in primary school, I must've been about seven or eight years old, I remember hearing people talk about the flight of Barberán and Collar.[15] There in Birán, people would say, 'Barberán and Collar flew over here' – they were two Spanish pilots that crossed the Atlantic and then were going on to Mexico. At the end of the flight, there was no news from Barberán and Collar. People are still arguing today about where they must've fallen, whether it was into the sea between Pinar del Río and Mexico or in the Yucatán or in some other place. But nothing more was ever heard from them, these two guys who had dared to cross the Atlantic in a little prop plane when aviation was still in its infancy. They perished in a little plane carrying I don't know how many tanks of petrol, because that was the only thing they could do back then. They took off – did a thing as daring as that, crossing the Atlantic – they took off from Spain and reached Cuba; then they took off again, headed for Mexico, but they never made it.

I saw hurricanes, cyclones, from the time I was a very little boy. Hurricane winds, waterspouts, storms with terrible winds. I even felt an earthquake once when I was probably four or five years old.[16] Our house started shaking; everything just shook. All those natural phenomena must have marked me in some way.

What else, as you see it, had an influence on the formation of your personality?

A privilege and a piece of luck. I was the son of a landowner, not the *grandson*. If I'd been the grandson of a rich family I'd have been born . . . I'd have had an aristocratic birth, and all my friends and all my culture would have been marked by a sense of superiority over other people. But in fact, where I was born everybody was poor – [my peers were] children of farm workers and extremely poor *campesinos*. My own family, on my mother's side, was poor, and some of my father's cousins, who came over from Galicia, were poor, and my father's family in Galicia was also very poor.

No doubt what has had the greatest influence is that where I was born, I lived with people of the most humble origins. I remember the illiterate unemployed men who would stand in line near the cane fields, with nobody to bring them a drop of water, or breakfast, or lunch, or give them shelter, or transport. And I can't forget those children going barefoot. All the children whom I played with in Birán, all those I grew up with, ran around with, all over the place, were very, very poor. Some of them, at lunchtime, I would bring them a big can full of the food that was left over from meals at my house. I would go with them down to the river, on horseback or on foot, with my dogs, all over the place, to throw rocks, to hunt birds – a terrible thing but it was common to use a slingshot. On the other hand, in Santiago and later in Havana, I went to schools for the privileged; there were definitely landowners' children *there*.

So you also lived with them.

They were the children of people with money. And of course, I was friends with them, we played together, we played sports together and all that. But I didn't exactly 'live' with them in wealthy neighbourhoods.

There [at school], we had other things in our heads, mainly sports or classes, outings and all that. I played a lot of sports, and climbed mountains, two spontaneous hobbies. The people that ran the Colegio de La Salle also had a farm in Santiago, on a peninsula where there's a refinery today – Renté [the farm] was called. There was a beach to swim at; they had put out some stakes like this, made of palm canes as they called them, because it was a bay, to make a closed bathing area in the water, because there was the danger of sharks, a real danger, although not as much as you might think. There were diving boards – the first, the second, and the third . . . I should've been a high diver, because I remember that when I got there, the first time I dived, I dived off the highest one, kind of challenging the rest of the boys, you know – Who wants to dive off the high dive? So I, *bam!*, I jumped – feet first, by the way; thank goodness I didn't go head first. The diving board was pretty high but I jumped off it without really thinking about it.

Did you know how to swim?

I had learned how to swim when I was I don't know how old in the pools and rivers back in Birán, and all that with the same people I was always going off adventuring with.

Your friends, the poor boys, the boys of humble origins?

Yes, all those people, my playmates and my friends. I didn't acquire bourgeois culture. My father was a very isolated landowner, actually. My parents didn't go out to visit people and only rarely had visitors. They didn't have the culture or the customs of a family from the wealthy class. They worked all the time. And our only contact was with the people who lived there, in Birán.

Among the boys you played with, were there any black boys?

In my house, I was never told, 'Don't play with this boy or that boy!' Never. And I would go over to the huts and poor houses, the barracks where the Haitians lived, and I finally got scolded for it at home. Not because of social considerations, though – it was out of health considerations, because I would go over there to eat roasted corn on the cob with them. My parents threatened to send me to Guanajay, which was a reformatory west of Havana.

For rebellious children?
My parents would say to me, 'We're going to send you to Guanajay if you keep eating that roasted corn over there with those Haitians!' They threatened to do that more than once – for other things, too. When I began to know about the world, to my mind the best school I ever went to was the childhood I lived out there in the country in the place I lived in. The country was freedom.

Later, because I was the son of a rich man, I was the victim of exploitation.

The victim of exploitation?
Exploitation.

In what sense?
It's simple, I'll tell you about it. My childhood circle was the Birán public school. I had an older sister and an older brother, Angelita and Ramón, who went to that school, and although I still wasn't old enough to be there, I was sent to the same school and they put me at a desk right at the front of the room. There were about twenty-five students, from very poor families in general. I still remember the dates. I don't know how I learned to write, probably by watching the other kids, sitting there in the front row, because they made me sit there.

Then, I remember, I think it was in 1930 . . .

You'd have been four years old.
Four years old. I learned to read and sort of scribble by watching the others, and the teacher with the chalk up at the blackboard – and [I'd play] pranks, too, just like the son of a landowner. The teacher would always come to our house, she ate with our family. And at school there'd be punishments, once in a while a smack with a ruler, I recall. Once in a while I had to get down on my knees, too, and they'd put some coins like this, in your outstretched hands, and you'd have to kneel there, holding your arms out – it wasn't as if they'd have us stay like that for three hours, but listen . . . And sometimes they'd put down grains of corn.

For you to kneel on?
Oh, yes. I well remember those schoolhouse tortures, although they didn't happen every day, or even all that often. They were really more just ways of scaring us.

Let's call a spade a spade: torture.
By that time I was already very rebellious, because, well, there are long stories about things. If you want, I'll tell you some of them later, I'll tell you things that helped me to become a rebel. I found myself needing to solve problems at a very early age, and that helped me acquire a certain awareness of injustice and of the things that happened in that world. But we're not talking about that, and you're not going to be very interested in it.

I am interested.
When the time comes, if you like, I'll tell you about some of them. But I'll add these factors about what in my view we've been talking about: what was it that made me a revolutionary? What factors influenced my life, despite my social origins as the son of a landowner, and despite the fact that kids are self-centred and that kids are vain, too, and become a little aware of their social position?

You were the only rich person in the little school in Birán?
I was the only one, aside from my brother and sister, who were a little older. There was nobody there who was even a little rich, or owned a store. Their parents were day labourers, sharecroppers, or maybe owned just a little piece of land. The children were all the children of very, very poor people.

Was that why your parents decided to send you to Santiago, so you could be among children from another social stratum?
No, I don't think that even crossed their minds. What did my parents do with me? At the age of six, they sent me to Santiago de Cuba, with the story, thought up by the teacher, that I was a 'very intelligent little boy'. They had already decided that the schoolteacher in Birán, whose name was Eufrasia Feliú, would take my sister, the oldest of us, Angelita, who was three years and four months older than me, to her house in Santiago. If I was six, she must've been nine or ten years old. So she was sent there, and my parents included me in the deal: it would be good for the *muchachito* to go to Santiago too, to improve his education in the teacher's house. That made

my head spin – I was curious what that would be like, so I went without a second thought.

What sort of impression did Santiago make on you, coming as you did from the country?
Santiago was a small city at that time, compared with what it is today, but it made a tremendous impression on me; I thought it was huge. It made a strong impression, very similar to the one later when I was sixteen and saw Havana for the first time, the capital of the Republic. Here in Havana I saw big houses, four- or five-storey buildings that looked huge to me. The city that I had been familiar with, Santiago, had little houses, one storey; buildings several storeys tall were the exception. So when I saw Havana it also made a tremendous impression on me. But I should add that in Santiago, when I was six years old, I saw the open sea for the first time. I was coming from the country, inland, the hills. And when, for the first time, at the outlet of the bay in Santiago, I saw the open sea, I was stunned.

What was the teacher's house like in Santiago?
It was a wooden house on the Intendente hill, in the *barrio* of El Tívoli, a relatively poor *barrio* . . . And it was a narrow, dark, damp house, very tiny, a little living room with a piano, two bedrooms, a bathroom, and the porch with a beautiful view of the Sierra Maestra and, very nearby, the Bay of Santiago.

The little house, with its wooden walls and its roof of faded and broken roof-tiles, faced a small plaza, just a dirt clearing, with no trees. Next door was a row of one-room houses. Then down in the next block there was a little store that sold coconut nougat sweets, made with brown sugar. In front of the house, across the small plaza, I recall there was a big house that belonged to Yidi, Yidi the Moor, they called him, who was very rich. And behind [the house] was an 'institute', as it was called, a secondary school. I was witness to some very important days there. I recall that the school was occupied by soldiers, because all the students there were against Machado.[17] I recall one thing I saw at the institute while it was occupied – the soldiers beating a civilian with their rifle butts; I guess he'd said something to them. I recall some of those scenes well, because we lived right there and we saw them.

There was an atmosphere of tension; the soldiers would stop people just going by. The town mechanic in Birán, Antonio he was called, was imprisoned by them at that time. I later learned that he was arrested because they claimed he was a Communist. I recall that his wife went to visit him in prison and took me with her, as young as I was. The jail was at the end of the Alameda in Santiago, a gloomy, sombre place, with filthy, grimy, mildewed walls. I shiver when I remember the jailers, the bars, the prisoners' looks . . .

In that little house I went to live in in Santiago, the roof would leak when it rained and everything would get wet. It rained more inside than outside. They would put pails and buckets down to catch the water. There was terrible damp in that house. It was there that my sister and I were taken. There in a little room with a rickety old bed, lived the lady's father, Néstor, and in the other room lived the teacher's other sister, Belén, who was a pianist. She was a pianist and a noble person, but she didn't have a single student.

Was there electricity?
Yes, there was electricity by then, but they didn't use it very much. The house was mostly lit with oil lamps, because I guess the oil cost less.

So how many people lived in that house?
First there were the three sisters, I think their parents were Haitians; I'm not sure whether [the sisters] had gone to school in France or in Haiti. They were mestizas. One became a schoolteacher, the other a piano teacher, and the third one was a doctor, and when I went there she had died not long before. The two sisters, as I said, lived with their father, Néstor, whose wife had died. Then there was my sister, me – that is, there were five of us counting the teacher, who kept teaching in Birán during the school year but came home during the holidays. There was also a *campesina, una guajirita,*[18] Esmérida, whom they brought in a little later as a maid. They never paid her a penny. So that made six of us. And later, my older brother Ramón came one day and I convinced him to stay, which meant that there were seven of us when the teacher was there. And all five or six or seven of us ate out of a *cantinita.*[19]

This is at what period?
It was the period of the Machado dictatorship, what was called the *machadato.* There was terrible hunger all over the country. Machado was toppled, basically, by hunger, because to top things off, besides the economic crisis

47

that took place in 1929, the United States imposed a commercial accord on us from the very earliest years of the dependent republic – an accord that forced us not to produce many things but rather to import them. Although the US bought sugar from us at the time, when the crisis came in 1929 the US also imposed tariffs on sugar. So that limited the amount of sugar that was exported, and the price was just rock-bottom. So the economy became even more depressed, and there was hunger throughout Cuba.

It was a time of economic crisis and also of political repression.
Machado had begun his term with a certain degree of support from the people because of the nationalistic measures he had taken, and he built public works, certain factories, but he was authoritarian, and very soon his regime turned bloody. There was, for example, opposition from students. In particular, from Julio Antonio Mella, the founder of the Fundación Estudiantil Universitaria [FEU] and the Communist Party, at the age, I think, of twenty or twenty-one.[20] Mella was an emblematic figure for students, workers and the people in general. He was later assassinated over in Mexico on Machado's orders.

Mella was an extraordinarily capable and precocious young man, one of the main figures to emerge after Martí. He would even talk about a 'workers' university', a brilliant idea. At that time, students would go to university and start to hear him talk about history and his heroes. Of course by this time the famous Bolshevik Revolution had already occurred, in 1917, and Mella, no doubt inspired by the radicalism of that revolution and the principles behind it, had founded the Communist Party. Inspired, too, by José Martí. Mella was very Martí-an and was very sympathetic to the Bolshevik Revolution. That must have had a great influence on the fact that he, along with a Marxist who'd been a friend of Martí's, Carlos Baliño, founded the first Communist Party in Cuba.

Machado was toppled in 1933, right?
Right. Machado was toppled in the struggle in 1933, in August, and later, in September, the 'Sergeants' Uprising' took place. I'd just turned seven. The Sergeants emerged with the aura of having rebelled against the officers who'd been Machado's accomplices. So at that point, everybody came out from underground, the various organizations, some of them were left-wing, others more or less inspired by right-wing ideas, some even by some of Mussolini's Fascist ideas, so there was a little bit of everything.

Within the university community, there were students – they'd formed a Directorate – who had fought against the dictatorship, had suffered casualties – even some very well-known professors [were part of that group]. And within one of the most combative of those groups there appeared a physiology professor named Ramón Grau San Martín,[21] who was nominated and finally elected president of Cuba. In his administration, which came into power after the 4th of September Movement, three weeks after the fall of Machado, Antonio Guiteras[22] was appointed secretary of state. Guiteras was a very courageous, very daring young man who had taken part in the struggle, captured an army barracks in San Luis, in Oriente province, been very determined in his employment of armed struggle against Machado.

Antonio Guiteras.
Guiteras enforced the laws, he expropriated the telephone company and other Yankee businesses, which was unheard-of in Cuba, and he passed laws authorizing syndicates, unions, limiting a day's work to eight hours – a whole series of progressive measures that characterized that administration.

One of those measures, which was well meaning but turned out not to be totally fair, was called the Nationalization of Labour Act, and it eventually led, though that was not its objective, to the cruel expulsion from the country of a large number of Haitians. The administration, whose strongest minister, toughest and most determined minister, was this man Guiteras, passed the Nationalization of Labour Act to protect Cuban workers from the exclusion they were subjected to by the many Spanish businessmen on the island, who gave first preference for jobs to family members brought in from Spain.

That administration, which was initially a pentarchy, a government of five leaders, before it turned over the presidency to Professor Grau San Martín, coincided with the three months during which this law and other related laws benefiting the Cuban people were passed, but by then the Yankees, through US ambassador Sumner Welles, had begun to influence Batista, despite the fact that the president of the United States at the time was no less than Franklin Delano Roosevelt, who was then promoting his 'good neighbour policy' for Latin America.

Despite the character and nature of the political system in [the United States] – which after Great Britain and France was a strong, and growing, imperial power, [even though it was] immersed in the worldwide economic crisis that hit the people of that country so hard – Roosevelt, in my opinion, was one of the finest statesmen our neighbour to the north has ever had. A man whom I, as a high school student, liked and looked up to. He was crippled. That warm voice he used in his speeches was attractive.

Roosevelt, who may have admired the spirit and combativeness of the Cuban people, and certainly wanted better relations with Latin America, not to mention that he could foresee the uncertain future of the world with Hitler coming to power, has the merit of having suspended the Platt Amendment[23] and giving his go-ahead to an agreement called the Hay–Quesada Treaty, in which the Americans gave Cuba back the Isle of Pines, the Isla de Pinos – today, the Isla de Juventud – which had been occupied and its future left undefined.[24]

Was it occupied militarily by the United States?
The Americans had occupied Isla de Pinos since 1898.

It was not administered by the government of the Republic?
No. It had been an American possession since the years of the Platt Amendment. So *it* was recovered, but Guantánamo still belongs to the Americans. The Platt Amendment gave the United States, by constitutional law, the ability to intervene in all of Cuba's internal affairs.

That amendment was signed in 1902.
It was imposed in 1901 and not abolished until 1934; I don't remember the exact date.

That government with Guiteras lasted only about three months. Then, in 1934, Fulgencio Batista simply swept them from power. Antonio Guiteras was assassinated in 1935, when he tried to go to Mexico to make preparations for [an anti-Batista] struggle, as Mella had done before and as we did afterwards.

During the period of the revolutionary government of 1933 there was some fighting, a few skirmishes and fights, one of them in Havana at the Hotel Nacional, where a group of army officers who supported the deposed Machado regime had taken refuge, among them some who were well trained, expert marksmen. Finally, little by little, they were cleared out by soldiers under the Sergeants, but they fought hard.

There were also the ABCs, a group of men who had been against Machado, and whose ideas, actually, were pretty fascistic; they started an uprising, they took over police stations, engaged in some combat here and there, and the last fire fight took place in the former fortress at Atarés. All that against the progressive administration and against Guiteras' laws.

Batista managed to take over the entire leadership of the army. It became *his* army. Later, due to pressures from the United States ambassador, he removed the government and appointed another president. Batista was promoted to colonel, other sergeants were promoted by Batista to the rank of lieutenant-colonel; there were no generals. Some of the former lower-ranking officers and all the sergeants were promoted by Batista to lieutenant, captain, *comandante*, lieutenant-colonel . . . I think the only [full] colonel was the head of the army, Fulgencio Batista.

This took place in 1934. Batista ruled for seven years, until a Constituent Assembly in 1940. During all that time, I was in Santiago, at the teacher's house at first, then at the Colegio de La Salle, and later at the Colegio de Dolores, with the Jesuits. It was in 1942 that I went off to Havana to the Colegio de Belén, which was also a Jesuit school, as I told you, and famous for being the best school in the country. And I graduated from Belén in 1945.

That's what I can tell you about the first years of my life.

2

The Forging of a Rebel

The first rebellions – The 'house of hunger' – The political atmosphere –
The dictatorships of Machado and Batista – In trouble – Havana – The
Colegio de Belén

Your formative years coincide, then, with two tragic periods: the first
dictatorship of Fulgencio Batista and the Second World War.
All of that unquestionably had an influence on my education and upbringing,
but especially on the evolution and development of political and revolutionary forces [throughout the world]. Because also towards the end of the
thirties, the famous 'popular fronts' had emerged. But I don't want to talk
about that right now.

What was your education like in the teacher's house?
They didn't teach me a thing, I was never given a single lesson. They never
sent me to any school. I was just there. There wasn't even a radio in that
house. The only thing I ever heard was the piano: *do, re, mi, fa, sol, la, ti,*
bang, bang, bang. Can you imagine, a couple of hours every day listening
to that piano? It's amazing I didn't turn out to be a musician.

The teacher's sister, the pianist, was supposed to give me my first-grade
classes, elementary school; I never had *one*. Boy, if I start that story I'll never
finish it. If you want, I'll tell it to you later, and I'll tell you how I learned to
add, multiply, subtract and divide, all by myself, from the back cover of a
writing tablet, one of those school notebooks, with a red cover, and on the
back cover there were addition, subtraction, multiplication and division
tables. I'd sit down all by myself and study, and I memorized them, and
that's how I learned arithmetic; but that was all I learned. Because they
didn't even *teach* me that. The lessons consisted of me sitting down by myself

to study the tables on the back cover of an exercise book. The fact is that I spent over two years there wasting my time.

So young, you must have missed your family.
They just sent me off to a place where I learned almost nothing and went through all sorts of hardships. And I was hungry, to boot, without knowing that it was hunger, because I just thought it was appetite.

Incredible.
Some very serious things happened. That was where I first rebelled, very early, maybe at the age of eight. By that time I was not living where I studied, because that story has two stages . . .

With that experience, didn't you lose affection for your parents?
No, I loved them, at least respected them, both my father and my mother. I felt more for my mother, it's only logical, she's the one you're closest to.

Despite the fact that they had sent you off to a boarding school with that teacher in Santiago?
A boarding school? That wasn't being sent away to *school*! What happened was that I was sent into *exile*, starved, confusing hunger with appetite!

Who did you blame for that?
I couldn't really blame my parents, or anybody. Honestly, at first, I didn't know what in the world was happening. I couldn't really understand it, or judge the situation. [All I knew was that] I was happy in Birán and all of a sudden they sent me off to a place where I was far from my family, from my home, from the countryside that I loved so much. And subjected to unfair treatment by people who were not my relatives.

Did you have any playmates?
Yes, fortunately, a boy named Gabrielito, Gabrielito Palau. His parents owned some business or other, they were in a little better financial position and had a better house, which was also near the plaza. There, and on the side streets near the plaza, he and I and some other boys would play. He was there for a long time, until after the triumph of the Revolution, working in television. And he's still working today, I think, in television. It's been a while since I've heard anything about him.

But the rest of the time, it was hard to live there. And I soon tired of that life, that house, that family, those rules. It was the instinctive reaction of a small mistreated animal.

What rules?
That family had a French upbringing. They spoke French perfectly, and they had a very good formal education. And all those rules, all those rules of etiquette, they taught them to me from the very beginning. You had to speak very politely, you couldn't raise your voice, you couldn't say a single improper word. Once in a while they would also spank you, to keep you in line. And if I didn't behave, they threatened to send me off to school to live, to the Colegio de La Salle, where I attended first grade in the final stage of that odyssey. Among other things, they'd caused me to waste about two years. At that age today, kids in Cuba are entering the *third* grade.

You were an abused child, in a word.
Well, it was terrible. During the first few months, I even had to make my own shoes. You can imagine the scolding I got one day because I broke a needle – a needle for cloth[, not leather] . . . My shoes came unsewn along the seam on each side. They'd fallen apart. So I tried to repair them, and it wasn't the first time. I used regular sewing thread, of course, much too fine, but that's all there was. I got into trouble for that. I'd never gone barefoot, so I [thought I] had to mend them. I don't remember now how the dispute turned out. It was fixed somehow.

Of course I don't want to exaggerate – it wasn't like a concentration camp. And there were mitigating circumstances: the teacher's family was poor. They lived on her salary; that was all they had. And the government back then often didn't pay teachers their salary. Sometimes they'd have to wait three months or more to be paid. That created uncertainty, of course, and self-centredness. Every centavo, the way it was spent, became a question of life and death for that family.

And you say you were hungry there?
I was hungry there. In Birán, my parents were always making me eat, and in Santiago I liked the food a lot. Suddenly I discovered that rice was very tasty, and sometimes they'd serve the rice with a piece of sweet potato, or some *picadillo*[1] – I don't remember that there was ever any bread – but the problem was that the same little bit of food, for six or seven people, was

supposed to last through lunch and dinner – the food that was sent in at lunch. The food came from the house of one of the teacher's cousins, whom they called Cosita, 'Little Bit' or 'Little Thing'. She was a very fat lady, I don't know why they called her Cosita; apparently she was the one who ate all the food. The cooking would be done at her house, and another cousin, Marcial – who could ever forget that name! – would bring over the *cantinita*, which would have a little rice, some beans, sweet potato, plantains, a little *picadillo*, as I said, on rare occasions, and that would be divided up. I remember using the edge of my fork to pick up the last grain of rice on my plate.

If it was so dreadful, how is it possible that your older brother, Ramón, was also sent off to that house?

Because one day Ramón showed up in Santiago, I don't remember why, and he brought one of those little leather pouches that you keep coins in, and it had quite a few pesetas [twenty-centavo pieces], several reales [ten-centavo pieces], some five-centavo coins, and even a one-centavo piece. At that time, a popsicle[2] cost one centavo, a coconut-and-brown-sugar sweet, one centavo. I envied the other boys – kids are pretty self-centred – because the neighbour kids, although they were poor, had one or two or three centavos. But since the people that were bringing me up brought us up in the French manner – all of a sudden I'd been plunged into that French upbringing that the teacher and her sister had had, and they'd explain that asking for something was very bad manners. The kids knew I was supposed to follow that rule of theirs, that I wasn't allowed to ask for things, so when any of them got their hands on a popsicle or a coconut sweet, if I asked them for a bite of it, they'd run and tell the teacher or her sister on me.

I remember one day I asked the teacher's sister for a centavo – she was a very, very nice person, but very poor. I'll never forget her getting so upset, so irritated with me, and exclaiming, 'I've already given you eighty-two centavos!' It was true, and she wouldn't give me any more – I never again dared asked her for another penny.

When Ramón came for a visit several months later, with all that capital in his little pouch, a pouch just full of coins, I thought it was a huge fortune – I could see it transformed into popsicles and coconut sweets! – I talked him into staying, told him what fun we'd have. And by doing that, actually, I made the poverty all the worse, because now there was another mouth to feed out of the same *cantinita*.

Later, I became more aware of the situation [in the house, i.e., the poverty]. It was a year or so later, because one day my parents discovered what was going on.

Your parents hadn't realized what you and your brother and sister were going through?
One day my father came; I'd just had the measles or some disease like that – my hair was long, because they didn't even cut our hair, I was thin as a rake, as you can imagine, and my father didn't realize a thing! They told him it was because of the measles I'd just been through.

Another day, my mother came – by now the teacher, her sister and her father had moved to another house, because things had got a little better, there were three of us now as pupils, so they were getting 120 pesos every month – and my mother discovered that all three of us were skinny and half starving to death. That day she took us out of there and carried us to the best café in town – I think we devoured every bit of ice cream in the place. La Nuviola, the café was called. It was also mango season; she bought a sack of mangoes, the little ones, 'Toledo mangoes' they're called, delicious, and that sack didn't last ten minutes, or the ice cream either, we ate every bit of it. And the next day she took us home to Birán.

Recently, talking to my older sister, Angelita, I was still criticizing her [Angelita]. She knew how to read and write – why didn't she write home and tell them about what I couldn't yet understand? I'd come from the country, from the fields of Birán. Birán was like a paradise of abundance, and [my parents] had to scold us to make us eat: 'Eat this soup, eat that meat, eat this, eat that.' After we'd spent all day long eating this and that, things from the store or the pantry at home, that night at the table they'd have to force us to eat. My sister should have told our parents what was happening, so I was giving her a brotherly scolding for not doing it. But she told me why she hadn't. 'It's that I wasn't allowed to send the letters I wrote; they intercepted them,' she told me.

By that time, with three students at forty pesos each, that must have been a profitable business.
Yes, by that time – I don't remember the exact date – their situation had improved considerably. Three of us from Birán – forty plus forty plus forty: 120. That was much more than $3,000 today in any Third World country. Plus you have to add the fact that the Haitian consul arrived on the scene

– he'd married the piano teacher ... So there was quite a considerable improvement.

The teacher, naturally, saved up money and even went on a trip to the United States, to Niagara Falls. She brought back some little flags as souvenirs. What misery! You have no idea the hours I spent listening to her talk about Niagara Falls. I must have hated those stories, because it was Niagara this and Niagara that, the same stories over and over – just the opposite of that poem by Heredia, 'Ode to Niagara'.[3] I had it up to *here* with Niagara Falls when that lady came back – who aside from that trip had gone out and bought furniture, which we paid for with our hunger.

I'm telling you this in all honesty and clarity ... So then and there, we had ourselves a rebellion.

You rebelled against the teacher?
When I went back to Birán, the first time, when my mother rescued us, was when I became aware of the crime, because everybody could see that all three of us had been practically starved, and we went back home – which we had truly, desperately longed to return to – as sworn enemies of that teacher, who would come to our house to have lunch, and she'd always pick the best pieces of chicken out of the rice ... Then when my mother took us back home to Birán, it was during term time, so the teacher was there giving her lessons. And Ramón and I organized our first action against her.

Rebellion.
No, it wasn't exactly a rebellion. Our first act of vengeance, you might say revenge, and it was with a slingshot, though [all we did was make a lot of] noise, because the roof of the schoolhouse was zinc, those wavy sheets of galvanized zinc. It was getting dark. We'd made slingshots out of a forked branch of a guava tree and some strips of rubber. There was a bakery nearby, and we took all the firewood for the oven and made ourselves a parapet, a fort, and we organized a bombardment that lasted like half an hour ... or maybe not that long, maybe a lot less time, but I thought it was wonderful! The rocks landing on that zinc roof ... By the time two or three were hitting the roof, there'd be two or three more in the air – we considered ourselves experts at that. You couldn't even hear the yells and screams that we imagined the teacher was making for the noise of the rocks hitting that roof. And the teacher was living there ... Oh, we were vengeful little devils!

What we could hardly imagine was that later, our parents would make peace with the teacher and I'd be sent to her house in Santiago again. But that time, my luck ran out: Ramón stayed in Birán. Asthma saved him.

No! You're kidding!
Yes, but this time there was no starvation – [the starvation before] had caused too much of a scandal. But it was still a waste of time. I wasted months of my time there, because I was still not doing a thing, just hanging around the house and studying the multiplication tables on my own, every single day. Come January they sent me to the first grade, at Colegio de La Salle, as a day student. For the first time in my life I began to go to real lessons.

By this time, the transition after Machado's fall, Batista's action, had taken place, and I remember just about this time the big strike in March of 1935. Behind the house was the secondary school, the '*instituto de segunda enseñanza*', where they held the classes for high school. It was occupied by the army – that was where we saw so many abuses. Twenty-one years later, the *compañeros* in the 26th of July Movement[4] attacked it, on 30 November 1956, when we landed near Las Coloradas, from Mexico.

That same school?
Yes, the same building, although it was no longer a school by then, because they made an army barracks or police station or something out of it when Batista returned to power. In 1956, there was a police station there. In my days as an elementary school student, it was still an *instituto de segunda enseñanza*, but right after that, it was turned into a barracks for the army or the police, when I was living in the teacher's house. Soldiers also hung out there, roaming around; they'd 'captured' the school. I know that on 30 November 1956 the people in the 26th of July Movement, who were under the leadership of Frank País[5] there in Oriente province, attacked it. They wanted the action to coincide with our landing; they calculated the days, and on 30 November they attacked. But that turned out to be two days before the landing. We'd been delayed forty-eight hours by sea conditions and the boat and other reasons, and they attacked on the 30th, the date, according to their calculations, that the *Granma* was supposed to arrive. I didn't want the actions to be simultaneous, I wanted to land first.

What other memories do you have of those years?
Well, about that time, quite a while before I entered the school, a romance occurred between the teacher's sister [the piano teacher] and the Haitian

consul. They were very nice people, mestizos[6] who spoke perfect French. So into that house comes a new figure: the Haitian consul, Louis Hibert his name was. There was a change in the status quo. The family moved into a house – next door – which was better, so now our roof didn't leak, and there was more space. And there was a little less hunger, too, because the income had increased, as I said. The teacher may have started getting her salary. Anyway, the sister married the Haitian consul, who earned a salary, the food was a little better, although, well . . .

They were the ones who took me to the cathedral in Santiago to baptize me, because I was called 'the Jew' – that's what they called people that weren't baptized. Although I think, of course, that the nickname 'Jew' had to do with religious prejudice, anti-Semitism. People called me 'Jew' and I didn't know why. So you see the prejudices of the time.

You hadn't been baptized?

No, I was baptized after I'd turned eight. What happened was that while we waited for the millionaire – a friend of my father's who was going to be my godfather – and the priest and I to manage to get together on the same day so I could be baptized, years had passed. My brother and sister were already godchildren, *ahijados*, as they were called, of one aunt or another; but me, at that age, like eight years old, they decided to baptize. What happened was that they were waiting for the millionaire who was going to be my godfather, whose name was Fidel Pino Santos. That's where my name comes from, so I can't be too proud of it. I was born on 13 August, and St Fidel's Day is 24 April[7] – St Fidel of Sigmaringen. Later I've tried to find out who he was . . .[8] 13 August is St Hipólito Casiano,[9] but I was given the name Fidel after the man who was going to be my godfather, a wealthy – *very* wealthy – man who came to our house from time to time in Birán, in the country.

So your real godfather was the Haitian consul?

Yes. The Haitian consul married the piano teacher, my teacher's sister. And the two of them were my godfather and godmother at my baptism. I remember that my godfather, that Haitian consul, took me one day to visit a very large passenger ship, the *La Salle* – it had two smokestacks, it was a transatlantic ship that was full of Haitians, like sardines in a tin, who'd been expelled from the country because of that Labour Nationalization Act I was telling you about earlier. So I've seen Haitians from the thatch houses where

I ate roasted corn on the cob sent to that luxury liner they were expelled from Cuba on, to face who knows what terrible hardships in their own country – which was and is even poorer than Cuba. They were sent from one terrible life of misery and poverty to another even worse one.

They were deported from Cuba?
That's right. During the years of the sugar boom they'd come by the tens of thousands to help with the planting, cultivating and harvesting of the sugar cane. They worked in the cane fields as practically slaves, with great sacrifice, very low wages. I believe the slaves in the nineteenth century actually had better conditions than those Haitians. The slaves were the property of a slave owner who took care of them the way you take care of an animal. The slave owners cared for the animal's health, fed the animal, but the capitalist doesn't watch over the health of the supposedly free worker, the former slave, or feed him.

When the so-called Revolution of 1933 came along, which really was a struggle against those abuses, it gave in to the call for a nationalization of labour and the demand that preference in hiring be given to Cubans, and that led to this event I was telling you about. But that law, which was based on good intentions, led to cruel measures; it was mainly used to throw out thousands and thousands of Haitians who'd come to Cuba and lived on the island for over twenty years. Their population grew, there were too many Haitians, so they shipped them off to Haiti in that cruel, merciless way, in that boat full of deportees. Truly inhuman ... And I was taken to witness that; I had no idea, of course, how valuable that experience would be to me later, how much it would help me understand the world.

How many years did you spend in the teacher's house?
I spent three Three Kings' Days[10] there. That's the only way I have of calculating that's more or less accurate. And while we're on the subject of the Three Kings, I'll tell you a story – I said before that it's surprising I'm not a musician ... well, I think I *could* have been a musician, because my godmother was a pianist, so she played the piano all day long – it's a pity it never occurred to her to give me lessons, to put my time to good use – and the other thing is that every year, the Three Kings brought me a little musical instrument, every single time. The first one was a little cornet made out of cardboard, with a metal mouthpiece; the second one was another cornet, a little trumpet that was half cardboard and the other half aluminium; and

the third one, *another* cornet, all aluminium, with three keys . . . Three Three Kings' Days, which is not to say three years, but if I was sent there in September to go to school, then the first Three Kings' Day was in January, and then there was the second one and the third one, but in all, it wouldn't have been more than two years and eight months, say. You also have to subtract the time we were in Birán, when we bombed the roof of the school the teacher was also living in.

When I was little I'd write long, long letters to the Three Kings that brought me those cornets, and I'd put out lots of grass under the bed, glasses of water for the camels, and so on, and ask for everything a kid could think of: a train, even a film projector . . . And what I always got was a little cornet; that was it.

In the new house, there was a vine on the porch with big wide leaves that gave a little shade, and I would sit under it in a chair or on the floor, which had red tiles, and study and go over those times tables, over and over again . . . I mean, I gave myself my own lessons. Since then, I've always taught myself things, been self-taught in so many ways.

In that new house I slept in a little passageway that opened out on to the street behind the house, on a couch, nothing else, one of those couches made out of . . . wicker? This was a time when there were bombs going off all the time in Santiago. Almost every night there'd be one or several explosions. I remember one night when there were over twenty or thirty bombs; every few minutes, *bam!* I had the impression that a bomb might go off at any moment right there, right next to me. I didn't know why there were bombs going off, or why people were setting them off. In that little back street, huddled up in the hallway, where I lived, I'd have to go to sleep to the noise of those bombs.

Who was setting off the bombs?
The anti-Machado or anti-Batista revolutionaries, I imagine.

Against Machado?
Yes, against Machado, and later against Batista, because Batista's coup came on 4 September 1933. Those bombs must have been in the last months of the struggle against Machado, and immediately afterwards came some three months of a government that called itself revolutionary.

The 'Sergeants' Uprising,' as I told you, was a relatively revolutionary action, but before that, civilians had been fighting, until August 1933, against the government of Machado, who'd reelected himself, so to speak, for a second term, in the midst of a great crisis. It was the time of the terrible crisis [the Depression] that began in 1929, and as I told you, there was terrible hunger in the country. People fought against Machado, but then came a kind of truce when Machado fell. In September, Fulgencio Batista, who was a sergeant in the army, a stenographer for military tribunals, led a coup d'état, which was organized by another sergeant, but Batista became the leader, he took command. The sergeants joined up with the students and other revolutionary forces.

At that point, fighting broke out with the ABCs, the people from the fascistic ABC group. Maybe it was the ABCs that were setting off the bombs during that period, the last three months of 1933. I'm not sure whether that stage lasted until late December or early January, but then came the struggle against Batista.

I can't tell you who it was that set off as many as thirty bombs in one night, because the memories are all jumbled together in the haze of time and all I have are the memories of a child, basically. In 1933, when there came that famous Nationalization Act and the expulsion of the Haitians, I was living in the teacher's second house. I'm absolutely sure of that, so from that I can deduce that I must have gone to Santiago for the first time in late 1932, more or less. I can't be sure of the exact dates, I can only deduce an approximation from all the impressions I remember and the known events that were occurring in Cuba.

You would have been between six and seven years old . . .
No, about six. No more than six, no doubt about it, no more than six, because I spent less than a year in the teacher's first house.

I'm beginning to remember now that after that period in that [first] house I went to the other one, and bombs would still go off for a long time [after we moved]. That has to have been in late 1933. Machado fell in August of that year, and then came Batista's movement, an alliance that lasted about three months, a revolutionary government that was toppled sometime around the end of that year. There were groups – the ABC, for example – of fascistic tendencies, who fought against the revolutionary government and later allied themselves with Batista. So I wonder – who was setting off the bombs at that time?

In 1932.
No, in 1932 we know who it was. The question is: who was setting them off after that? Most likely is that this time it was the enemies of the Revolution. In late 1933 there was an uprising by those ABC people who'd turned against the government of physiology professor Grau San Martín, and Guiteras, his left wing [of the alliance]; perhaps the only ones who were strong enough to set off that many bombs were the ABC people.

In Santiago there was no university; the students had neither the organization nor the resources to set off as many as thirty bombs, as I recall; there may have been fewer, but to me it seemed as if there were a lot. Which is why I'm deducing that the bombs I heard on that wicker couch were after August, not before, maybe late 1933, or even perhaps later, after the first rebellion in Birán had already happened, or the revenge I told you about. I'd already been sent back to Santiago and enrolled in the Colegio de La Salle, where I was a day student, I'd go back and forth. I was in the first grade as a day student as a result of that miserable time, that agony.

You walked back and forth by yourself?
Yes, back and forth, and I had lunch at home. Lunch had improved, because by that time they'd adopted the French habit of eating vegetables; they served vegetables and a few other things, it wasn't the *cantinita* any more. Food at that time was cheap, almost nobody had any money, and very few people had jobs. My family, as I said, sent 120 pesos a month, which at that time was a fortune.

I had to go back and forth to eat lunch and go back to school in the afternoon. I was sick of all that, I tell you. I was studying on my own. A third Three Kings' Day had come and gone. It must have been in February 1935, I'd have to look to see whether there are any papers around [that say for sure]. Whatever the case, they threatened to send me away to school to live if I didn't behave like an angel. And that was exactly what I wanted to do.

In order to escape from that house.
I'd developed an awareness of what was going on there because of the first time, and I was bored with all those French rules, that French way of living. One day I broke all the French rules, all the manners. They made me eat vegetables – beets, carrots, *chayote*. I wasn't used to that. *Chayote* seemed so tasteless to me, and beets were disgustingly sweet. Some [vegetables]

I wouldn't eat again until years and years afterwards. It was the French custom, and the discipline was feudal. One day I rebelled – 'I won't do it,' whatever it was, 'I refuse'; 'I won't do this other thing, I refuse.' My rebellion wasn't actually against the French manners and ways of doing things, it was against the abuses I'd been the victim of.

You rebelled.
What else could I do? It was instinctive. Really, it was the first conscious rebellion of my life . . . And it turned out the way I'd wanted it to. They sent me straight to the Colegio de La Salle as a boarding student – first grade, the second semester of first grade. Then I was happy, because I was with all the other boys. We'd play, and on Thursday and Sunday they'd take us to a place down by the ocean where there was a big area where there were all sorts of places for sports and adventures. I was finally a happy boy.

And do you harbour any resentment against that family?
Really, I don't blame them for what happened. They lived in that society; I can't say they were a bunch of perverts or child abusers or anything. That society was full of injustices, great hardships, many inequalities, much need, a great deal of sacrifice on the part of the people who lived in it; it fostered terrible selfishness, self-interest, it caused people to look out for number one, you know, to try to make a profit off just about anything. It didn't encourage feelings of kindness and generosity. They had to live, and they discovered that there was a way to do that: by exploitation. In the last analysis, they were exploiting the rich man's son. They had nothing. I was a victim of exploitation, because of what the money my family sent represented for that poor family. I suffered the consequences.

When you later read Dickens' Oliver Twist *and* David Copperfield, *for example, you must have had the impression that you'd lived that experience.*
You're not going to believe me when I tell you that I didn't read some of those books until years after I'd graduated, because in the schools I went to they didn't teach French literature, English literature, American literature. They would barely mention a play by Shakespeare, for example. All the books were Spanish. That famous *Uncle Tom*[11] I didn't read until I was practically out of school. We were privileged boys going to schools for the wealthy, the upper class, yet we had big gaps in art, painting, music. The most they did for me, in like third grade, was put me in a chorus, but I was

kicked out of it when they discovered – I can't imagine how – that I couldn't carry a tune in a bucket.

Remember that from the middle of the fifth grade in elementary school to graduation, almost all my teachers were Spaniards, and nationalists. Their ideology was right-wing, Franquista, reactionary, yet they were the best in terms of discipline, character, austerity.

And [they were] religious, too.
They were people I came to know very well, especially the Jesuits, whom I studied with for over seven years – people of character, educated people. Even though you had to pay to study there, the schools weren't expensive, there was no spirit of mercantilism. The priests didn't collect a salary. They lived a very austere life. They were rigorous, self-sacrificing, hard-working. They helped me, I must say, because they stimulated my love of nature, my love of the outdoors. I loved to climb mountains. When I saw a mountain, I saw it as a challenge. I would be seized with the idea of climbing that mountain, getting to the top. Sometimes the bus would have to wait four hours because I was climbing a mountain. I'd go by myself or with one or two of the others; sometimes it would take longer than we'd calculated to get back, and nobody ever punished me for it at all. Those teachers, if they observed some characteristic – a spirit of sacrifice, effort, risk – that the student showed, they would encourage it, stimulate it. They were concerned with the student's character.

You studied under the Jesuits for many years, didn't you?
Yes. But not in the first few grades; that was with the La Salle brothers, in Colegio de La Salle, from first through to fifth, because I'd skipped from third to fifth. I was there for almost four years. I enjoyed living at the school. They'd take us to the country and the ocean, as I said, on Thursdays and Sundays. We'd go to a small peninsula on the Bay of Santiago. They had a beach for swimming and sports facilities. There were baseball fields, a place to swim, fish – [we'd] hike, play sports. I was happy there, twice a week. Later, in the Colegio de Dolores, in Santiago de Cuba, the Jesuits didn't have a country place like that, although it was a better school, and I was older.

Among your schoolmates, all boys from well-to-do families, were there any black students?
At La Salle they admitted black boys, but very few. In my class, the only

one was Alejandro Larriñaga, a livewire, smart. I'll never forget him. In the other two, the Colegio de Dolores and Belén, with the Jesuits, there was not a single black, or even a mulatto, or a mestizo either. The rich people's children went to those schools. We were all supposedly white.

Did you not think it odd that there were no blacks?

I asked some questions, not because I actually had much awareness or education in the subject, but since it was a little strange to me, I asked. In La Salle there *was* one – I mentioned him. But in the Jesuit schools, in the more distinguished schools, where the *haute bourgeoisie* sent their boys, there were no blacks or mestizos. The ones in charge would give explanations, you know, but it was very hard to justify.

They chose?

They were schools for the rich, and they just didn't admit any. Even had there been any who could pay, they wouldn't have admitted them. They didn't, of course, make a student applying for admission take a blood test, the way the Nazis might have. But unquestionably, if you weren't obviously white, you wouldn't be admitted to the school.

Even if you could afford it?

That's right. They didn't admit them. Despite how rebellious the Jesuits are – despite the fact that they've rebelled against political authorities and hierarchies.

And recently in Latin America there have been very outspoken Jesuits, very defiant of authority.

Recently, some of the most rebellious personalities, such as the priests at the University of El Salvador and other [priests], have been Jesuits, very courageous men who've even given their lives. Apparently they got that from the origins of their order. St Ignatius was a soldier.[12] I remember the hymn, the anthem: 'Fundador sois Ignacio y general de la compañía real, que Jesús . . .'[13] It was an anthem of war [against the devil and his minions], and St Ignatius was a general of the order. That's why I may criticize, but I'm also capable of recognizing that they were far superior in their education to the priests at La Salle. They had made a vow in perpetuity, and they had to study a very great deal, study for several years longer. In Cuba, there have been eminent figures who've been Jesuits; eminent astronomers [sic] who forecast hurricanes, such as Padre Viñes; others have been excellent teachers of Spanish and literature, such as Father Rubinos.

The Jesuits also have a clear idea of organization, right?, a concept of discipline – a military concept, in fact.
They know how to form boys' characters. If you do risky, difficult things, engage in that sort of activities, they see that as proof of an enterprising, determined character – a 'get-up-and-go' sort of character. They don't discourage it. Plus, in the schools I went to, they were Spaniards, so they combined the traditions of the Jesuits – that military spirit, their military organization – with the Spanish character and personality. The Spanish Jesuits know how to inculcate a great sense of personal dignity in a boy, the sense of personal honour – they appreciate character, honesty, straightforwardness, uprightness, a person's courage, his ability to make sacrifices. Those are values that they know how to instill, to bring out.

It's a good school, then, definitely, for a revolutionary?
It was useful to me, despite the fact that it discriminated against blacks and was a school for young men of the *haute bourgeoisie*. Once I read a literary work called *La forja de un rebelde*,[14] 'The Forging of a Rebel', which tells how a rebel, and I'm not talking about a revolutionary, is partly forged by life and his own experiences. I say 'partly' because a person's character, temperament, also has an influence. And I think that my temperament, which is partly inborn, was also forged with the Jesuits.

St Ignatius himself is a good example. A man who set out to conquer minds with a military strategy.
He was a soldier, and he organized a military order. I don't remember much more, but the anthem or hymn I learned, and that they still have, is an anthem of war. But that itself didn't hold a lot of interest for me. I liked the kind of healthy, austere life I lived in those schools.

Anyway, you preferred sports.
When I was in high school, I was, above all, a sportsman and a mountain climber. My main activities were sports and exploring. I loved them! I hadn't climbed Pico Turquino, and I really wanted to. Once I was about to do it, with one of the priests at the Colegio de Belén, Padre Amando Llorente – who hadn't graduated, he was at the practice stage – the brother of another

Llorente, Segundo Llorente, who was a missionary in Alaska with the Eskimos and wrote magnificent, interesting reports on 'the land of eternal ice'. One summer we were in the port of Santiago about to leave for the place where Pico Turquino was. I was even carrying – I'd brought it along from the house of my own accord – a Browning shotgun. By that time, when I was graduating from high school and about to enter university, my father, who was proud of his son's great achievement, didn't keep very good tabs on me. But anyway, a leak in the schooner, which was impossible to repair overnight, ruined our plans. Padre Amando Llorente – Jesuit, young, a Spaniard from the region of León – was a friend of mine, because he was a great believer in sports and exploration.

During the first expedition to the Yumurí Valley I had been made one of the leaders of the explorers because it would be the leader who'd stay up all night, on guard, you see, like a sentinel. The explorers had their uniform, they lived out in the countryside, in tents. I added some activities on my own initiative, like mountain-climbing . . . And finally, since I was pretty outstanding, they made me the overall leader of the school explorers. It was my first position in the ranks of the school authority. But I also took part in all the sports, and I was finally chosen, my last year – the school had over 1,000 students – the best at sports in the school. I was outstanding at basketball, football, baseball, almost all the sports.

Of course, I devoted a lot of my time to sports; I'd go to class, but I never paid any attention, and then I'd go study. I did what I recommend to students every day that they *not* do. So I turned into even more of a self-taught man, you might say, an autodidact in mathematics, algebra, physics, geometry – I'd study those theorems and whatnot on my own. And then, also, I was lucky enough to get good grades on my final exams, sometimes higher than my grades in the first exams. During the course, the Jesuits wouldn't say anything, and then when the time was approaching for final exams – *bam!* – notification would go out to a tutor I had, who was a friend of my father's, the same one that was going to be my godfather – a very wealthy man, he had a loan company, he was in the Congress of the Republic, he had a house in Havana, since he was a representative [to the House of Delegates], and his son, with the same machinery and the same money, was a senator – and he was a kind of tutor of mine – they would call him, at his home, and tell him that I was going to fail every subject. All three years I was there, they always predicted the same thing at the end of the semester.

Because you didn't seem interested in your studies.
I'll tell you – I never paid any attention in any lesson. Maybe agriculture, I don't know why, maybe a teacher that awakened my interest in the subject. I would study from the books; I would even stay up late at night to study, till the wee hours of the morning, because I was in charge of turning out the lights in the study hall at the end of the day. When everybody else would go off to sleep, instead of turning out the lights and leaving I'd stay there reading until two or three o'clock in the morning, and then go off to bed. So mathematics and everything else, I learned on my own.

Was your brother Raúl also with you?
There's a story there. He was back in Birán; he was five years younger than I was, he was the youngest; when I was at home we'd always pick on him. He was sent off to school with us to La Salle when he was about four and a half. He'd come with our mother to visit us and [this one time] he wanted to stay. He cried, kicked, threw such a tantrum that she had to let him. [We lived] in a room with four boys – there was Ramón, Raúl, me and Cristobita, who was the son of the manager of a saw mill for a foreign company, the Bahamas Cuban Company, which exploited part of the pine forests around Mayarí with my father. Raúl tended to misbehave a little at that time, I would sometimes have to scold him, but Ramón always came to his defence.

He was the oldest.
Ramón was the oldest. So Raúl was there with us, boarding, at La Salle.

And you more or less brought Raúl up?
When I went home for holidays, all I heard was criticism from our parents, sso I told them, 'Let me take charge of this, I'll take care of him,' and so I started watching over him. He kind of ran wild there.

Later, I gave him some books to read, and he became interested in them. I awakened his interest in studying, and then I got the idea that he had wasted so much time, he [might be able to catch up and] go on to the university. And there was a way to do that, which was to enter what was called the Administration major; it was a branch of the university that was part of Social Sciences and Law. It wasn't very hard; if you majored in that you could later study letters, diplomatic law, even become a lawyer. So that idea came to me and I convinced my parents and he came to Havana.

But by then, I was spending my time indoctrinating everybody. There's a story to that, but I've got ahead of myself.

You told me that your first act of rebellion took place in the teacher's house. When did the others take place?

There were two more, and almost a fourth one. That is, from the teacher's house, I was sent to the Colegio de La Salle. As a boarder. And there I did first, second and third grades. Then I skipped the fourth grade and went into the fifth, and one day in Santiago there was a big fight between the vice-principal, who was the brother in charge of the students, and me. So that was my second 'uprising'. Unfair things happened, and they took me out of that school and sent me to another one. My parents wanted to keep me from going to school, as a punishment, because of the principal of that school.

I'll explain. There were two different principals there – the first one was Brother Fernando, a good man, and the other was Neón Marí. Because Brother Bernardo, an inspector [vice-principal] who was in charge of the boarding students, was always going around hitting the students, I stood up to him, and I got punished for it. It was the third time this vice-principal had hit me . . . The last two hadn't been so bad, but the first one was terrible. It was because of a fight I had with another boy in a boat we boarders were taken to sea in, on Thursdays and Sundays. We'd crossed the bay [coming back], and we were walking along the avenue, up a street that was pretty steep, because the school was in a high part of the city, past the Parque Céspedes – so anyway, the street we were going up was in a red-light district, a place where there was a lot of prostitution. And so the women started pestering the brothers, one or two of them that were wearing cassocks – 'Hey, padre, come on, come over here,' and things like that. The boys, with all that carrying-on, well, naturally, they all laughed.

The fight had started while we were coming back [in the boat] from the beach, and we hadn't finished it . . . It was a miracle we didn't fall on top of the motor, because the motor didn't even have a cover. The boat was called *El Cateto*, the hick or hayseed. But the others separated us, and the fight was suspended, so to speak, till we got back to school. He was a good kid. Years later I had news of him; he was working in one of the Revolution's activities. I'm not going to say what his name was, but he was the vice-principal's favourite, the apple of his eye – one of those things that happens; I mean that tendency to show special attention to one of the students. I'm not implying anything out of the ordinary in the student. Those brothers, many of them excellent teachers and individuals, were, however, members of a less disciplined, less strict order than the Jesuits. We may not have liked that situation [the favouritism shown certain boys] very much, we resented it.

But at any rate, I can't recall now what it was that started the fight on the boat. But the fight between us had to be put off. And when we got back to the school, I went over to him and said, 'Stand up'; he stood up, and I hit him with a roundhouse right. We traded a few punches, and then the others stepped in to separate us again. The consequences were not long in coming. I was in the fifth grade, and for the first time, Brother Bernardo, the school vice-principal, hit me.

But otherwise, I was happy in that school, because I had the freedom of sport, the ocean, fishing . . .

But what exactly happened?

Well, in simple terms, I had a fight with a boy that was the vice-principal's favourite, that vice-principal's favourite, as I just told you.

At La Salle there was a big tank, a cistern, under the upper part of a long central courtyard; under that part of the courtyard was the water, you see. The courtyard had two levels.[15] On three sides of that top part of the courtyard there was just a single storey, and on that level of the building were the dining hall, then immediately the sacristy, then the chapel was in the corner and occupied part of the central side; on the other side [of the courtyard], a study hall, and to the right along the passageway, to your left, there were several classrooms. All that part, which was built of wood, surrounded the upper courtyard.

That day, almost at dark, there was a religious ceremony in the chapel. After the fistfight with that boy, I, very prudently or cautiously – because I think I must have foreseen that something was going to happen – sneaked into the sacristy, from which point you could see the activity down at the altar in the chapel. While I was up there, then, the big thick door to the sacristy from the courtyard opened, and a finger goes like this, the vice-principal was standing there and wanted to see me – instinct always knows things, doesn't it? He had no respect even for the liturgy. He had me follow him, he made me walk along the passageway, turn to the right at the next corner, then down the hall a little way further, and he stopped in front of the classrooms and he says to me, 'What happened with what's-his-name?' And I say, 'Well, what happened is this . . .' I was standing there in front of him, and he didn't even let me finish, with his right hand he slapped me as hard as he could. I was totally unprepared.

He just slapped you.

Then, just as hard, another one, with his left hand. They were the hands of a relatively strong man, raised against a boy in the first semester of the fifth grade. I was dazed ... my ears rang. It was night by now. It was terrible ... Shameful, and abusive.

The boy I'd had the fight with was no forty-pound weakling, you understand. He was a big sturdy teenage boy that could give as well as he could take. The vice-principal, this brother, was twice as strong as I was, and he was a young man.

Weeks later, it happened a second time – he smacked me good, twice, because I was talking in the queue as we were going upstairs to the dormitory. He smacked me on the side of the head twice, not very hard. But inside, it hurt much worse.

Because of the humiliation.

The method of physical aggression, of violence, seemed inconceivable to me. The third time – it was the last dressing-down I got – I was leaving the dining hall after breakfast. They would give you a few minutes to drink a little milk and eat one or two small bread rolls. There was butter in green glass containers – we'd eat two or three rolls really quickly and butter two or three more to take with us. The appetite at that age is something ...

We were in a queue, there was a little courtyard, the cover of the big water tank that I mentioned, and we were scuffling to see who'd be the first to touch a column where the queue ended, because the one who touched it first got to bat. We'd have eight or ten minutes out there to play ball with this rubber ball we had.

So we were scuffling, tugging and pushing to get to the column, and all of a sudden I felt somebody hit me two or three times on the side of my head. It was the vice-principal again ... But that was the last time, because I just blew up. I was so furious that I took those buttered rolls and threw them right in the vice-principal's face, as hard as I could, and then I ran at him and jumped on him like a little tiger – biting him, kicking him, hitting him with my fists, in front of the whole school. That was my second rebellion. I was a student and he was a figure of authority who abused and humiliated a student.

Every so often the boys, when they were mad, would say, 'I'm gonna smash your head with an inkwell!' Or 'I'm going to do –' whatever . . . I never said I was going to smash anybody's head with an inkwell, but the third time [he hit me], I decided I wasn't going to take it any more. That vice-principal had a hard time getting me off him.

So I see the principal, Neón Marí, who was nearby, in the study hall at the end of the passageway – I went up to him and I said to him, 'Listen, this just happened . . .' But he cut me off: 'No, all he did was give you a little shove.' But if he hadn't seen the vice-principal hit me, he'd certainly seen the kicking and hitting and biting that I was doing. That was all the justice I ever got from the head of the school. But the arbitrary vice-principal had taken a heavy moral blow to his abusive authority. All the students said I was right. I doubted he'd ever try to hit me again, or any other student, either. The inkwell had done its job, for sure. No one knew what was going to happen [i.e., the boys were waiting for the vice-principal to have his revenge].

We were in the first quarter of the fifth grade, and we would get one of three grades for conduct each week: white, for the ones who behaved well; red, which wasn't given very often at all, for the ones who behaved badly; and green, which was really rare, for the ones who behaved *really* badly.

And you got green.
No. The day came, and I waited and waited. White: students X, Y, Z and so on. Red: students X, Y, Z and so on. Green: nobody . . . I didn't get white or red or green, none of them – no rating at all. For the moment, he ignored me, and I ignored him. I never behaved any better, out of pride, dignity. It was several weeks till Christmas. And we never exchanged a word, that whole time.

When Christmas came, my parents came to get me, my mother and father, and the principal told them – you're going to laugh – told my mother and father that their three children were *los tres bandidos más grandes que habían pasado por la escuela* – 'the three biggest rascals that had ever gone through that school'.

Imagine, Raúl, a rascal – he must have been in the first grade, must have been six years old. Ramón, who was a saint, I swear to you. And my misbehaviour – I told you what my great sin was. So at that, my parents took us home to Birán.

Did your parents believe him?

That's the worst part of it – they did! Especially my father, because I found out that he started telling all his friends when they came to the house. The Asturian was in the office, and when we got to Birán, he says to me, 'Time to settle accounts.' Settle accounts – punishment, for sure. Of course we kids, I mean, we were always going to get into some kind of trouble – for example, we got our hands on the answer book, the answers to the maths problems, that the teachers used. I'm not sure how we came to have that book. It was Ramón who got it. I never asked him. But the point is, we were punished for hours and hours every day, on account of Neón Marí's intrigues. I heard people say that when friends of the family came to Birán, people who owned land or businesses here and there, my father would tell them about the 'tragedy' and what the principal of La Salle had told him. So it was decreed that we were not to be sent off to any other school

Ramón, who loved to ride tractors and farm pickups and things, was happy about that. Raúl was too little to have an opinion. I was the one hurt by it, I was the injured party, I was the one humiliated. I could see how unfair all the things were that had been attributed to me, how unfairly I'd been slapped and hit. And now I was punished [yet again] by not being allowed to go back to school.

So I had to rebel again. I told them they had to take me to school. I demanded that they send me to school. I put up a fight. This time it was in my own house. 'I won't accept you not letting me study,' I declared. That rebellion was a pretty good one, because of some other things I said – I don't mean I was going to do all the things I said I'd do, but I did say them.

Who did you say them to, your father?

I told my mother, who then passed them on. Because Three Kings' Day came and went, and it was the seventh of January, and we were always taken back to school on the day after Three Kings' Day. But nothing happened, nothing was said about going back to school, no packing, no nothing – I had no place to go, I was just punished. So I got tough.

At eleven years old?

Well, yes, I must have been eleven, because I was in the fifth grade, and that's when I said a terrible thing.

What did you say?

I said that if they didn't send me to school I was going to burn the house down.

Your own house?

Yes, it was made of wood.

But you didn't really intend to do that, did you?

I'm sure I wouldn't have. But I said I would, and I must have said it very seriously, because I was determined to put up a fight against that injustice that was being done against me at school and at home. I think I made my point – they saw my point.

Your mother took you seriously?

My mother was always the peacemaker. My father, very understanding – he may have liked how firm I was in defending my right to go to school. Whatever the case, my parents decided to send me off to school again. It was the dry season, so I was sent in this station wagon that took passengers, a *pisicorre* we call them, off to Santiago, down these dusty dirt roads. That was in about 1938, close to the congressional elections. They sent me off to the house of a businessman there, a man named Mazorra, who was the owner of a store called La Muñeca. A Galician, married to a woman from Santiago, Carmen Vega, a tall, muscular mulatto woman, twice as tall as her husband was, although she didn't boss him around or anything . . . That little Galician fellow didn't take any nonsense, and if he had to pick up a house-slipper and swat you with it, he'd do it, and cause a commotion, too. He was not one to be bossed around. He owned a clothing store, as I said. Doña Carmen was his second wife. She had a son by an earlier marriage, and at that time this son was totally dedicated to the electoral campaign for a paediatrician running for representative who'd offered the son a job, and then there was another son that she'd had with Mazorra, Martincito, who was studying to be a civilian pilot, in the United States.

One day during this time there was an unfortunate accident. The training plane had something wrong with it, the son jumped out with a parachute, they sent for the father immediately, you can imagine that story . . . There was also a daughter, Riset, who was in the third year of high school – she had three little white ribbons on her blue skirt, and she was also from that marriage, don Martín and doña Carmen, a dark-skinned, very pretty girl. I had a crush on her. At that age, kids fall in love with a girl even if she's older than they are – the teacher, some girl down the street, almost every girl alive. Well, but I won't say anything else about that . . . We were talking about politics, right? Which is where the last rebellion of my childhood took place.

Against the businessman?
Mazorra was the owner and head of the family in the house we lived in, on the second floor. It was a long house, and not very wide. I slept in a tiny room at the end of the hall. It was while I was there that I listened to the second fight between Joe Louis and Max Schmeling on the radio – a terrific fight, although it didn't last long, right? – first round, or second, and KO.

Joe Louis won, right?
Yes, Joe Louis.[16] Later, there was a lot of publicity about this Max Schmeling because he was one of the German paratroopers who attacked the island of Crete, in the Second World War, on the eve of the invasion of the USSR. He was a paratrooper and a symbol of 'German racial superiority', but he'd been humbled pretty seriously by that defeat at the hands of no less than Joe Louis, a black man. Enough said.

You were telling me about the fourth rebellion.
The fourth one, because I was sick of that house. But let me tell you some of the things I did, the tricks I played.

Tell me about them.
Shall I?

Absolutely.
Well, that'll be the last one for tonight. It was like this: Mazorra, this businessman, was climbing the social ladder. With his wife, who was this mulatto woman – tall, strong – he'd already made it into the middle class, and they were building a house in Vista Alegre, the upper-class neighbour-hood [in Santiago].

I'd been sent off to the Colegio de Dolores, run by the Jesuits, where the sons of the aristocrats, the Santiago *haute bourgeoisie*, went. Doña Carmen was happy to have her boarder going there, because that way she could rub elbows with all the rich people who also sent their sons there. She and the

Spaniard, as I said, were building their house in Vista Alegre. They even took me to see where it was. I still remember this. Anyway, this family of high social rank had to have their boarder in that school, and he had to be the best student there. And certain things happened to this boarder . . .

What happened to him?

My sister Angelita was studying to be admitted to high school. Emiliana Danger, a black woman, excellent teacher, was my sister's seventh-grade teacher, preparing her for high school. So during that holiday period I didn't go home to Birán, or they didn't send me home – I went from the fifth to the sixth grade. But I couldn't enter the institute, the high school, when I finished sixth grade, because I wasn't old enough; I think you had to be thirteen, something like that. So anyway, Miss Danger took an interest because I was a good student, I was attentive, I answered all the questions and knew the book – *that* thick – by heart, the book that you had to learn in order to get into high school. She was very enthusiastic. She was the first person I ever met who could make *me* enthusiastic about something. She was determined that I was going to study so I could do the sixth and seventh grades and the first year of high school all at the same time, so that when I finished the sixth grade and reached the age, whatever it was, I could take the exam for the seventh grade and the first year of high school.

So I was all excited, all full of enthusiasm, when I had the misfortune, right at the beginning of that semester, to be diagnosed with what they said was appendicitis. At that time, they took out everybody's appendix, so me, of course, because of a little stomach ache, an insignificant pain, they took mine out, too. They did like in the United States, they operated on people even if they didn't really need to be operated on. So I had to go have my appendix out. We were members of the Colonia Española, a very good cooperative [health care, hospital] institution, because there were thousands of Spaniards, and for a peso, or a peso and a half, you received hospital services. So even middle-class families had access to inexpensive and relatively good hospital care.

I must say that the Spanish co-ops, the health facilities, were the closest thing you'll ever see to a socialist cooperative, because they had a number of doctors, nurses, clinics, wings and everything, and they collected enough money to give good medical service. A family like mine, for a peso and a half or two pesos per person, was 'insured', so to speak, against medical emergencies; we had access to medical services. If you needed an operation, they'd do it and also give you your medications. So anyway, they operated on me with local anaesthesia – back then it was [either] spinal anaesthesia, general, or local . . . I still don't know why the devil they operated on me with local anaesthesia . . . I'll never forget that operation. It hurt quite a bit, but the worst of it was that seven days later . . . you know that back then, they didn't let you move for a week.

I didn't know that.
Now they get you up and make you walk around right away, to avoid blood clots and embolisms and other problems, but medicine back then was antiquated . . . Seven days later they got me up, took out my stitches, and in forty-eight or seventy-two hours the incision turned out to be infected. Fortunately, it was superficial, it wasn't internal, because back then there was no penicillin or anything of the sort. They opened the incision again, completely, and I had to stay in the hospital for three months. I had to forget about Miss Danger's plan, and I started the sixth grade at Colegio de Dolores, where I entered halfway through the fifth grade. I spent my first quarter of the sixth grade in the hospital . . .

Unable to go to school.
Unable to go to school. Now – what had I done in the fifth grade? I couldn't get very good grades – the change of school, teachers, classes, textbooks . . . But my guardian, the businessman's wife, the lady there where I was staying, doña Carmen, demanded that I get the best grades in school. So I was forced to do something.

I thought about it, and I said to myself, Well, the system is that you take your report card home, they sign it – there, in the house where I was staying – and you take the report card back to school . . . There were several grades: Excellent, Outstanding, Very Good, Good, Fail. There were five possibilities, and with [this family's] social pretensions, they wanted me to get all Excellents. I had to get Excellent in every subject. Or otherwise, they'd take away the money I got every week, five centavos to buy an Argentine comic book I liked, *El Gorrión*.[17]

You liked comic books?
I liked them a lot. Back then I also read *De tal palo, tal astilla*,[18] a series, and I also liked cartoons at the cinema. Every Thursday, five centavos, and twenty centavos on Sunday: ten for the movies, five for an ice cream, and

five for a little pork sandwich, which was cheap, right? Total: twenty-five. And they would warn me: if I didn't get Excellent in every subject, they'd take away my twenty-five centavos.

So I made a plan. I have no trouble telling this story, and I'm even glad I did it. I said to myself: What would happen if I lost my report card? I'll take the old one to them and they can sign it, but I'll keep it, and at school I'll tell them I lost the report card. Sure enough, they gave me a new one, so then I had two, one with my real grades – they weren't failing, but they weren't what doña Carmen expected – and the other one with the grades that I'd put in myself.

You forged them?
Yes, the grades. Since I had two report cards, I'd put my grades down on one of them, which *Doña* Carmen would sign, the lady I was living with, and on the other one were my real grades, which *I* signed. The problem came at the end of the semester, when the lady I was living with thought I was the most brilliant student that had ever gone to that school, so she has herself a long black dress made, because all the rich people's kids went there, the children of her future neighbours in Vista Alegre, and I was going to carry off all the honours . . .

All the prizes?
A brilliant student!

You gave yourself the highest grades?
All tens. Not a single nine, nothing lower than a ten, because I had to be sure I got the highest [marks]. When the end of the school year came, I didn't have any plan yet for how I was going to get away with all that, because that was when they gave out the prizes for the most outstanding student in this subject and that subject, the Excellents, in this very solemn ceremony.

I think I had some sort of prize in something, geography I think, because I liked it.

So this afternoon they started giving out the awards. Excellent: Enrique Peral, I remember was his name. Language, first prize: So-and-so; second . . . I started acting as though I was so surprised – me, who had to have excellent grades, wasn't being called up for a single prize – and I had no reasonable explanation available – I put on this astonished expression: you mean I didn't win first place? So the ceremony was over and I hadn't won first place, or second place, or any place at all – I was nowhere to be seen. Or maybe one prize, as I said. And so when the time came to say something, I had the answer: 'Oh, I remember now what happened. Since I didn't come in till the middle of the year, I don't have the points from the first quarter. That's why I didn't win anything.' So that was some consolation; doña Carmen accepted that explanation, and everybody was happy. I'll never forget that I had to invent that whole story, had to think fast, you know.

The sixth grade was when the appendicitis came, and the operation, and the three lost months, the return to the Spaniard's house for the same story all over again, and by then I was sick of having to have the highest grades all the time, all that vanity and keeping up appearances. I decided I was leaving that house. Really, I didn't even study, because when you try to study under those conditions, when they make you study for hours every afternoon you start daydreaming, your mind starts wandering. So I do the same thing again, and they threaten to send me off to a boarding school . . . It was the same prescription as in my godmother's house when they had to send me off as a boarder to the Colegio de La Salle. I rebelled, I broke every rule you can think of, I refused to obey any of them, and they had to send me packing. But then I had a good experience as a boarder, so I started to get good grades, and by the seventh grade I was an excellent student.

By the rules, without having to falsify your grades.
Yes, a good student by the rules, and without studying too hard, with just a little attention, and not having to stop playing sports. By this time I was studying English, and I think the war was getting closer – this was in 1939 – which is when, as I mentioned, I sent a letter to Roosevelt. We were studying English out of a textbook by a teacher in Santiago de Cuba, and this textbook told about the Blake family. We were studying things about the house, the dining room, the names for food, coins, that sort of thing . . . I even told Roosevelt that I'd like to have 'ten dollars'. *A ten dollars green bill.*[19] I think I even talked about minerals, the pine forests in Mayarí, iron for his warships, all that sort of thing. And I got a reply – you know how it is, they're very organized, they have teams of people working for the president. So one day I get out of class and I find myself the centre of this huge ruckus at school: Roosevelt had sent a letter to Fidel! There was a copy of it on exhibition on the bulletin board. After the triumph of the Revolution, the Americans found my letter and published it, thanks to which I have a

copy of it, because I didn't keep one. And there are people who've told me that if Roosevelt had only sent me $10 I wouldn't have given the United States so many headaches!

Ten dollars would have won him a good friend.
Well, now I've told you things. We haven't set any time limit, and I have to talk about this just as it happened.

You've told me about your four childhood rebellions. What lesson can be learned from your behaviour then?
Well, naturally, that I wasn't born a revolutionary but that I did, as I've told you, rebel from time to time. I think that very early on, in school, at home, I started to see and live through things that were unfair, unjust. I'd been born on a large tract of land in the country, and I knew how that was. I have an indelible memory of what capitalism was in the country. The images of so many poor, hard-working, humble people there in Birán will never be erased from my mind – hungry, barefoot, people living there and nearby, especially the men and women who worked for the large American sugar companies, where the situation was much worse, in the *tiempo muerto*, and they would come to my father and ask for his help. As I said, my father was not a selfish landowner, or miserly in any way.

I was also the victim of certain things. Little by little I began to acquire notions of justice and dignity, certain central values. So my character was moulded by the hard tests I had to pass, difficulties I had to overcome, conflicts I had to face, decisions I had to make, rebellions . . . I started to question that whole society, on my own – perfectly normal, a habit of thinking with a certain logic, analysing things. With no one to help me, really. Very early on, all those experiences led me to see abuses, injustice, or the simple humiliation of another person, as inconceivable wrongs. I began to acquire awareness. I never resigned myself to abuses. I acquired a profound sense of justice, ethics, a sense of equality. All that, in addition to a temperament that was unquestionably rebellious, must have exerted a strong influence on my political and revolutionary vocation.

In your childhood, you most definitely developed into the role of rebel.
It may have been the particular circumstances of my life that made me react that way. I faced certain problems even as a young child, and little by little I developed – that may, indeed, explain my role as a rebel. You hear people

talk about 'rebels without a cause', but it seems to me, as I think back over it, that I was a rebel with many causes, and I'm grateful to life that I've been able, throughout all these years, to continue to be one. I am one even today, and maybe for even better reasons – because I have more ideas, more experience, because I've learned a great deal from my own struggles, because I have a better understanding of this world we were born into, this world we live in – globalized, and at a decisive moment in its history.

3

Entering Politics

The university – Eduardo Chibás – Cayo Confites –
'El Bogotazo' – Thinking about Moncada

*I imagine that afterwards, during the time you were at university, you must
have had some disappointments, some disillusionments that contributed to
your understanding of other people.*

Yes. The first person to betray us was, in fact, the son of that telegraph
operator in Birán – Valero, the Spanish Republican I mentioned when we
were talking about the Spanish Civil War. The telegraph operator's son was
one of the first people to betray us when the struggle against Batista started.
He was a *compañero*. He lived here in Havana. For my part, I came here,
went to the university, began my work, and he was a friend, a supporter –
he sympathized with us, [he was] in the Party. I trusted him. That's the
mistake. You shouldn't trust someone just because he's a friend.

How did he betray you?

We were using a mimeograph machine to print up a clandestine newspaper,
a flyer, a manifesto, trying to create a clandestine revolutionary publication
and also a radio station, using short-wave radio ... Because our launch
platform, so to speak, was the existence of a people's party, the Orthodox
People's Party of Cuba, which had quite a large following. It had been
founded by a very popular political leader named Eduardo Chibás.[1] And
many young people were followers. They were workers, labourers, they had
no class awareness, but they all harboured a terrible hatred for Batista, for
corruption, for theft, for the coup of 10 March 1952, several weeks before
the elections, when Batista already knew he'd lost.

This son of Valero's informed Batista's police of – I believe I'm correct –

the location of the mimeograph machine we were using to print up our little newspaper, *El Acusador* ('The Accuser'). That's where I published our first manifesto, which I wrote a year after Chibás' death, on 16 August 1952, four months after Batista's military coup.

You were influenced politically by Chibás?
Chibás was the leader of a popular party, a people's party, as I said, which was fiercely opposed to theft, speculation, corruption. He was constantly denouncing those wrongs, and others. He often denounced Batista.

His prestige stemmed from a weekly radio programme. It was broadcast on Sunday, from 8 to 8.30 p.m., for years. He won great respect. It was, in our country, the first instance of the political impact of radio. Chibás was born out of that medium and he became very popular because of his strong political personality, speaking to the people for half an hour every Sunday. He had a huge audience.

Chibás denounced corruption.
Mainly. He wanted to sweep the thieves out of government. And once in a while, he would denounce an 'octopus' – the electricity company, the telephone company – when there was some rate increase. He was an advanced thinker in civic terms, but revolutionary social change was not his main objective. A new political period was beginning . . .

I came in contact with Chibás' followers during my first year at the University of Havana, [when I was] studying law. He was known for his principled, upright opposition to Batista and his constant denunciations of corruption.

From the students who had fought against Machado in the thirties had emerged the Partido Revolucionario Cubano (Auténtico) – the (Authentic) Cuban Revolutionary Party. It evoked the memory of the Revolutionary Party that had been created by Martí, but it added 'authentic' to its name because there had been another Cuban Revolutionary Party. Chibás belonged to this Authentic Party, which was founded in 1934 by Grau San Martín and which won the elections in 1944. Then just two and a half years later, in 1947, Chibás, who was now a senator, in turn founded the Partido del Pueblo Cubano, the Cuban People's Party, or Orthodox Party, and he started denouncing all the immoralities of the administration backed by the party he'd belonged to for years[2] but which in a very short time started showing its moral and political weaknesses. There was just nothing left of that revolutionary spirit that had existed in 1933. Do you know how political parties are founded?

No.

Sometimes, in the case, for instance, of a revolutionary workers' party, all it took was ten or twelve people. How many people did Lenin, for example, have when he founded the Party in Minsk, the capital of Belorussia? About ten, if I remember correctly. That's in the history of the Bolshevik Party. If you look, it was just three or four of us who created the embryo of the movement that attacked the Moncada barracks. From the beginning – it's strange – we had a small corps of leaders and a small executive committee of just three people. Chibás' party, on the other hand, was formed on the basis of a strong tendency within the so-called Cuban Revolutionary Party, which was then in power, and with the support of a great many personalities, well-known leaders who weren't happy with [that party's] demagogic, tolerant and corrupt policies adopted years earlier, in 1933, by the man who was president of the Revolutionary administration of the time. So you see two such different ways of creating a political organization. Radical revolutionary parties are often born in the underground, clandestinely – they're created and led by a very few people. They are more solid, as a general rule, and tend to last longer.

Didn't Chibás commit suicide?
Chibás committed suicide; that's another story.

I'd like for you to tell me why Chibás committed suicide. I mean, how is it that a man who wants to change the destiny of his country comes to commit suicide. Isn't there a contradiction there?
He fell into a terrible depression. Why? Chibás had denounced the minister of education, who was a person with some degree of political acumen, political experience, and who in his time had fought against Machado and Batista, as both student and professor – he'd been on the Left. Actually, the people with the most political savvy were those who had been Marxists or pro-Marxists, because a lot of politicians didn't even know what a society was.

Anyway, this man who was the minister of education in a corrupt and almost completely discredited administration was accused by Chibás of owning farms in Guatemala. So this man defied Chibás, quite spectacularly, to prove it. And Chibás couldn't. Apparently, some source he'd trusted had given him that information without providing the necessary proof. Chibás came under terrible pressure – he was accused of lying and of slander. So he fell into a terrible depression and shot himself in the stomach after his Sunday radio programme – no one was able to stop him. He died a few days later.

Weeks later, I said, 'You don't have to go all the way to Guatemala,' and I showed, with irrefutable documentation, the dozens of properties that leading figures in the administration – including the president of the Republic – had bought in Cuba with dirty money, plus other scandalous immoralities. Those articles were published by the daily *Alerta* – a newspaper with a great deal of influence, above all its special Monday edition, which set records for circulation – in the days preceding Batista's coup. Which is why the people in that administration later blamed me for having undermined the constitutional government with those shocking denunciations.

The man who inherited Chibás' radio programme after his death was José Pardo Llada, who never attacked Batista, which Chibás of course had done systematically. Chibás would talk about Batista and his people and often remind everybody of his bloody past, calling them the 'Palmacristi and Escape-Act colonels' – Palmacristi was an oil, castor oil I believe, and it was one of the methods [they used] for torturing people, as Mussolini's Fascists had done, and the 'Escape Act' was a law that allowed authorities to kill prisoners if they tried to escape, so of course these officers used that as a pretext to kill their enemies.

Chibás' dramatic death gave great impetus to the party he'd founded, but the fact that now there were no more denunciations made it easier for Batista, whom Chibás had constantly denounced, to carry out his coup. Chibás was a popular figure who'd have been able to offer some resistance to the usurper's coup.

Did you have a radio broadcast?
Weeks before the coup, I requested the radio slot that Chibás had had, in order to denounce Batista. There were strong indications of his intention to mount a military coup. As I explained, I had access to *Alerta*, the highest-circulation newspaper. Its editor was a brilliant newspaperman, and at the time a valuable ally of Chibás' and a candidate for senator in Chibás' party. But the old relationship he'd maintained with Batista led me to think – although he was always very deferential to me – that he wouldn't get involved in a matter as delicate as that. I had a fifteen-minute radio programme every day on Radio Alvarez, but it was local – it reached Havana

and part of what today is the province of Havana, but that was it. The leadership of the Orthodox Party, whom I informed of Batista's conspiratorial activities, promised to look into it. All they did was talk to some of their members, teachers in a school where they gave classes to high-ranking active-duty army officers, and the answer was that 'everything was quiet'. They didn't give me the Sunday radio slot, and the denunciation was never made. Unfortunately, several weeks later, events proved me right, and in a very dramatic way.

Chibás' radio slot was inherited by José Pardo Llada, as I said, who had known a little about Marxism in his youth. He became very popular through a twice-a-day radio news broadcast that gave the news and then ended with a brief editorial. He habitually defended all the strikes and all the labour causes. He got 71,000 preferential votes in the 1950 elections – incredible! So you see the growing effects of the mass media.

Chibás had become a national leader on the basis of that half-hour, from eight to eight-thirty every Sunday night for years and years, and Pardo Llada became a popular phenomenon, too, with his news programme twice a day. And on top of that, everyone, even the unions and other organizations, went to him, to make denunciations and spread news. I don't want to talk about him, but Pardo Llada was no Chibás – he didn't do what Chibás did: systematically denounce Batista and keep him on the defensive. Had Chibás not died, there'd have been no coup. But I was prevented from making my own denunciations from that prestigious and influential bully-pulpit by jealousies, rivalries, mediocrities and naivetés. A subjective factor came into play in events.

Chibás committed suicide in August 1951. You were twenty-five, and you'd graduated from law school, right?
That's right. Chibás' death was in 1951, almost ten months before the presidential election of 1952. He had been an important figure since the time of the struggle against Machado. He was the son of a wealthy family, from Oriente, the area of Guantánamo. Curiously enough, he'd gone to the same schools as I had – he'd studied under the Jesuits, at the Colegio de Dolores in Santiago, and here in Havana, at Belén. He was an anti-Machadista and a senator when the Partido Auténtico came into power, in 1944. I was in my last year of high school that year, when the presidential elections were won by a physiology professor who was in power for three months in 1933, and later pushed out by Batista.

Grau San Martín?

Yes, Grau was elected president in 1944, at the end of the Second World War, when the world was saturated with propaganda in favour of democracy, sovereignty and all those other things that went with all the political preaching throughout the war years.

Then Batista himself, under a certain amount of pressure, folded – he'd been elected president after the constitution was approved, in 1940. At that time he was pretty progressive in some respects, because of the influence of the Communists, who at that time were allied with him in a popular front.

Munich[3] was the place where the attempt took place by France and England – the two great colonial powers, the biggest in the world – to push Hitler into attacking the USSR. I don't think, however, that those imperialist plans should ever have justified the pact between Hitler and Stalin. It was hard, very hard. All the Communist parties, which were characterized by their discipline, were forced to defend the Molotov–Ribbentrop Pact and to bleed themselves to death politically. These were very difficult and costly steps, but they came one after another, and the most disciplined Communists in the world, those most loyal to the great October Revolution – and I say this with the greatest respect for their self-sacrifice and firmness – were the Communist parties of Latin America, and among them, the Cuban Communist Party, for which I always had and still do have the highest regard.

Even before the Molotov–Ribbentrop Pact, the need to unite against the Fascists led in Cuba to the alliance between the Cuban Communists and Batista, when Batista had already launched a bloody repression of that famous strike in April of 1934 – a strike that came after Batista's cunning coup against the provisional government of 1933, which was unquestionably revolutionary in nature, and the result in large part of the heroic struggle of the labour movement and the Cuban Communist Party, led at the time by Martínez Villena,[4] formerly by Mella and Baliño. Before that anti-Fascist alliance, Batista had murdered I don't know how many people, had stolen I don't know how much money. He'd always been, since his betrayal in late 1933, a pawn of Yankee imperialism.

So there were Communists in the Batista government.

That's right. The order came down from the International, where there was not a true collective leadership. [The Communists in his government] were, however, as I've said, wonderful people. Some of them, like Carlos Rafael

Rodríguez[5] – a supremely honest man whom I remember with great affection; he was with me in the Sierra Maestra when Batista launched his last offensive – were ministers and held other posts, as disciplined members of a party that was compelled almost without appeal to follow the International's order.

In June 1944 the Second World War wasn't over yet, although the red flag, dyed with the blood of millions of Soviet soldiers who died defending Socialism, flew over the Reichstag in Berlin. Japan was still resisting, and the Alliance still held. Two atomic bombs were used over defenceless Japanese civilian cities as a way of terrorizing the world. Almost immediately after that came the worldwide wave of repression of Communism. In the United States, you had the rise of McCarthyism, a period during which brave progressive men and women, such as the Rosenbergs, were executed, others imprisoned, and many harassed and persecuted. In Cuba itself, under the administration of that physiology teacher, honoured Communist labour leaders were brutally murdered. The historical lesson is that a revolutionary party can carry out tactical movements, but it mustn't commit strategic errors.

Our own Revolution has benefited from the saving kindnesses of inter-nationalism, and suffered the hateful, almost fatal harm done by chauvinism in the world. Chauvinism is the bane of sincere internationalism, and without internationalism there is no salvation for humanity.

When did you graduate from university?
I graduated from law school in September 1950. I was twenty-four years old. In 1952, in the June elections – frustrated by Batista's coup on 10 March of that same year – I ran for a seat in congress as representative of the province of Havana, but on my own, in virtue of the fights that I, as a student, had fought.

And not as a candidate of the Orthodox Party?
From the early years of my career, I had been associated with people at university who sympathized with the Orthodox Party that Chibás had founded. Since its beginnings, I had been a strong sympathizer of that movement, too. Later I began to see certain things that didn't sit well with me; I began to acquire a more radical political awareness, and I was learning more and more about Marx and Lenin. I was also reading Engels and other authors and works on economics and philosophy, but mainly political works – the political ideas, the political theories of Marx.

What works by Marx were you familiar with?

What I liked most by Marx, apart from the *Communist Manifesto*, were *The Civil Wars* [*sic*] *in France, The Eighteenth Brumaire,*[6] the *Critique of the Gotha Programme* and other works of a political nature. I was impressed by his austerity, his self-sacrifice, and the rigour and seriousness of his research. Of Lenin's works, [I read] *The State and the Revolution* and *Imperialism: A Superior Phase of Capitalism.* Not to mention his critical reflections on so many subjects. I was very impressed by Engels' work on the history of the working class in England. I also remember very well another of his books that I thought was very interesting, *The Dialectic of Nature,* where he talked about the fact that one day the sun would go out, that the fuel that feeds the fire of that star that gives us light would be exhausted, and the sun's light would cease to exist. And Engels wrote that despite the fact that he couldn't possibly have read Stephen Hawking's *A Brief History of Time*[7] or know anything about Einstein's theory of relativity.

When the coup took place, on 10 March 1952, I recall that many people sat down to read Lenin's article 'What Is To Be Done?', trying to find a kind of prescription for what to do under those circumstances. One day it occurred to me to read Curzio Malaparte's *Coup D'État: The Technique of Revolution,*[8] but that wasn't before Moncada – I read it later, in prison, out of sheer curiosity, since it seemed to me absurd that a coup d'état, or the seizure of power, the result of so many factors and circumstances, might be a simple question of *technique.* Malaparte produced a fantasy, a novel: if you can control communications, the railways and other strategic points, then you control the state. That's not what happened in Venezuela, the coup against Chávez on 11 April 2002, which brought together the traitorous military commanders educated in the doctrines of imperialism, all that clique of yellow unionists, the big factory owners, the owners of the television stations and the principal opinion media, the old corrupt parties, the thieves and robbers of every kind, and a force with fascistic ideas and extremely powerful resources, determined to destroy the Bolivarian process. That is the real technique of a counter-revolutionary coup d'état, rehearsed and proven time and time again by the forces of imperialism to eliminate any attempt to change society in Latin America.

Back then, when the coup took place here in Cuba . . .

On 10 March 1952.

That's right, 1952, when with a small group of excellent *compañeros,* among whom were Abel,[9] Montané[10] and others, I organized and trained most of the 1,200 men – very good, clean young men whom I talked to personally, explaining to them the objectives and rules that would govern our organization. They came, almost without exception, from the Orthodox Youth.

For the assault on Moncada?

That movement began not with the intention of carrying out a revolution all by ourselves, but rather on the basis of another premise: everyone would fight to return to the situation prior to 10 March, and with that, to the constitutional and political situation destroyed by the coup. I believed everyone would come together to wipe out Batista's tyranny. It was clear to me that Batista had to be overthrown by arms and that constitutional government had to be restored. To me, it was simple: join hands to fight the traitorous coup of the tenth of March. Until that day, I, who had a pretty well-formed idea of what should be done in Cuba, was using legal means, although they led, on the basis of my ideas, to the idea of the revolutionary seizure of power. The coup destroyed all that. In the new situation, it was in the interest of all the island's political forces, I thought, to return to the starting point.

You had begun to take an interest in politics at university, while you were studying law?

When I got to the university I was a political illiterate. The university, as I've said, was dominated by a group closely tied to the government of Grau San Martín. From the moment I entered, that first year, I could see an atmosphere of force, of fear, of weapons. There was a university policy totally controlled by groups linked to the power establishment of the moment. It was a bulwark in the hands of a corrupt government. The main leaders at the university also had positions, posts, privileges and every governmental resource. And during the same period, Chibás' rebellion against the Auténticos took place, which would result in the founding of the Cuban People's Party, the Orthodox Party. When I got to the university, that incipient movement already existed.

When did you arrive at the university?

I entered the university on 4 September 1945. As the son of a landowner, as I explained, I was able to finish the sixth grade and then, having passed the exams for the seventh grade, I was able to enter a preparatory institute, a pre-university school. Later I was able to come to Havana, where the university was, because my father had money – so I graduated from high school and entered the university. Was I better than any of those hundreds of poor kids in Birán, almost none of whom ever reached the sixth grade and none of whom graduated from high school, none of whom entered university?

What person who hadn't been able to go to high school would be able to go to university? The children of *campesinos*, or labourers, kids who lived on a sugar-cane plantation or in one of the many towns that weren't Santiago de Cuba, or Holguín, maybe Manzanillo and two or three others in the former Oriente province, could never dream of even graduating from high school, much less graduating from university. Because back then, after high school, [if you wanted to go to university] you had to come to Havana. And the University of Havana was not a university for the poor – it was a university for the middle class, a university for the country's wealthy. Although those youngsters [who attended] often rose above the self-centred ideas of their class, and many were idealists capable of struggle [for social causes]; thus they fought throughout the history of Cuba.

At the university, which I arrived at with only a spirit of rebelliousness and some elementary ideas about justice, I became a revolutionary, I became a Marxist-Leninist, and I acquired sentiments and values which I still hold today and for which I have struggled throughout my life.

In that university atmosphere, then, you began your political education.
That's right. I began to react against so many things like those we were seeing. What I had was a rebellious spirit, hungry for ideas and knowledge, filled with curiosity and energy. Because from all the experiences I'd lived through, I sensed from a very young age that there were a great many things to do [in my life].

In a relatively short time, on my own and with very little knowledge of economics or other essential subjects, I started becoming what today I would call a 'utopian Communist' – on the basis of life, experience, those first understandings I acquired of the traditional political economy that occurs in a capitalist society. I got a little of that subject, but very badly taught and very elementary, in my last year of high school.

And if I tell you that I became a revolutionary at that university, it's because I came in contact with certain books. But before I'd read any of those books I was already questioning the political economy of capitalism, because even then, at such an early stage of my education, it seemed to me irrational. In the first year of my studies, there was a very demanding professor of political economy, Portela his name was – there was no textbook from a publisher, just a stack of 900 mimeographed pages! [Portela] was very famous, and very tough. He was a terror. I was lucky, though, because he gave an oral examination; I answered without any problem at all and got a surprisingly high grade.

And this was a class that explained the laws of capitalism but hardly talked at all about the various other economic theories. As I studied the political economy of capitalism, I began to have serious doubts, began to increasingly question the system, because I'd lived on a large estate, a *latifundio*, and I remembered things and had dreamed about solutions, like so many other utopians in the world.

What sort of student were you?
I was a dreadful, terrible example as a student, because I never went to classes. In high school, as I told you, I never attended a lesson. Since I had to be in the classroom – I was a boarding student, after all – I'd just let my imagination fly [during the lesson period] and study at the end of the term, just before the exams. At the university I never went to class, either. What I'd do was talk to other students in the park, in the Patio de los Laureles; I'd just talk out there – there were small benches – with the guys, and especially with the girls, because they paid a little more attention to me, they were better educated.[11] There were always several students sitting around listening while I explained my theories. What I wouldn't give today to remember the arguments I used to try to persuade them, and what I was trying to persuade them of!

From my third year on, I couldn't be an official student leader because I had to opt for what they called *matrícula libre* – 'open enrolment', you might call it, I suppose – due to reasons I may explain at another time. Still I had a lot of influence there – I stood out, you might say, among the students.

From that time on, I studied *por la libre*, as they called it, which meant that you're not enrolled in any particular course, you can enrol in all the subjects you want, and I signed up for fifty.

Fifty?
Fifty, *por la libre*. It was only in the last stage of my time there that I dedicated myself to really studying, and I had three majors: law, diplomatic law and social sciences. Anybody who was going for three degrees had access

to a scholarship. By then my political ideas were very well defined, but I wanted to go deeper, increase my knowledge of economics, and I was thinking about a fellowship that would allow me to study in Europe, or even in the United States. When I decided to really buckle down and study, I'd study fifteen or sixteen hours a day. I'd have breakfast, lunch and dinner with a book in front of me, never taking my eyes off what I was reading.

Your father was rather right-wing, all your education had taken place in conservative religious schools – when was it during your time at university that you found yourself on the Left?
I've told the story of when I arrived at the university. The number of people on the Left, by the way, was minimal – just a tiny number. In my years as a student at what, twenty years earlier, was the prestigious university where Mella was the presiding spirit, and just twelve years before *that*, the university where, under the inspiration of Rubén Martínez Villena's Communist Party, students had joined the revolutionary strike and the street protests that accelerated the fall of Machado, of the 15,000 students enrolled in 1945, after the war, with McCarthyism and anti-Communism all the rage, there were no more than fifty active, known anti-imperialists. Back then, there were only a very, very few students from the working classes, or the countryside. Other political and ethical subjects occupied the young people's attention, but not exactly the subject of radically changing society. The leftists saw me as a queer duck – they'd say, 'Son of landowners and a graduate of the Colegio de Belén, this guy must be the most reactionary person in the world.'

During the first few days, as I had in high school, I devoted a lot of time to sports, but after the first few weeks of that first year I started to also take an interest in politics, and I took my first steps in that direction, until within two or three months I'd completely forgotten about basketball, baseball, football and all the rest. I dedicated my life entirely to politics. I was a candidate for representative of my class. And I was elected: 181 votes in favour, 33 against.

So I dedicated more and more of my time to that. As the election for the president of the FEU (*Federación Estudiantil Universitaria*, University Student Federation) drew near, I started to strongly oppose the government's candidate. That translated into countless dangers for me, because it ran counter to the interests of the mafia that, as I told you, dominated the university.

What sort of dangers?

The physical threats and pressures were enormous. When the FEU elections were almost upon us – I was in the second year of law school – this mafia, irritated by my insubordination, decided after several incidents to use stronger methods of intimidation: they forbade me to enter the university. I couldn't enter any university facilities.

So what did you do?

Well, I cried. That's right. I went off to a beach to meditate, and at the ripe old age of twenty, I lay face down on the sand and cried – tears welled up in my eyes. The problem was extremely complex. I was up against all the powers and all the impunities. They were armed, and they had no scruples about killing; they had the support of all the police agencies and Grau's corrupt administration. The only thing that had contained them [so far] had been a moral force, the growing mass of students who supported me. No one had faced them openly in their feudal empire at the university, and they weren't going to tolerate any more defiance, any more challenges to their authority. They also had the university police on their side. I ran the real risk of being killed in what would be alleged to be inter-group rivalry. I cried, but I decided to go back – to go back ready to fight, although I was aware that it might mean my death.

A friend of mine got me a gun, a Browning fifteen-shot pistol, similar to the one I use today. I was determined to go down fighting, and not to accept the dishonour of not being at the university. And so began my first, very idiosyncratic armed struggle against the government and the powers of the state. But that struggle wasn't characterized by the use of weapons; instead, it translated into a series of incredible risks and acts of defiance. There were very few times I could carry a gun like that day. I ran the risk of being arrested by the police and sent for an emergency trial – they were fast, and there was no bail. With that procedure, the enemy could easily take me out of circulation. So that became perhaps one of the hardest and most dangerous stages of my life. I went back [to the university] that day with five young men who spontaneously, out of sheer admiration for my solitary struggle, volunteered to go with me – all armed just like me. That action paralysed those who'd forbidden me to enter the university, but I couldn't get away with it for ever. I soon found myself obliged to be alone most of the time, and most of the time unarmed, until finally, on 26 July 1953 . . . For seven years, in all my activity in the struggle, I remained unarmed, the only exceptions being when I joined the expedition against Trujillo and when I took part in the popular uprising in Bogotá. On not a few occasions I'd be accompanied by a group of people without weapons – that was my only possible protection. Constantly denouncing the government, with contempt for the risks and dangers, is like a whip in the hands of a lion tamer. I was taught that dignity, morality and truth are unconquerable weapons. But since the day I disembarked from the *Granma*, 2 December 1956, I've never been unarmed again.

But did you know how to use a weapon? What experience did you have with weapons?
I was a good shot. My experience stemmed from having been born in the country and having many times used the rifles in my house, without anybody's permission – a Winchester, a Browning shotgun for bird-hunting, the revolvers, every gun you can think of.

You would shoot?
Back in Birán I'd made up this story that the buzzards ate the chickens. I mean, *I* didn't invent it, people said that buzzards ate eggs and chicks. There was a pole near the house, a sort of radio antenna I believe it was, and buzzards would often perch on it. Once in a while, I'd decide that I was going to protect the henhouse, because people said the buzzards were dangerous to the chicks, which wasn't true. They were really scavengers, the clean-up men, you know? – they ate carrion, when a large animal died.

They're scavengers; they don't attack live animals.
From the time I was little, I would always wander around Birán with a gun. In my house we had one of those semi-automatic rifles that have four rounds in the chamber [*sic*, for magazine]. If you put a round in the chamber, you could shoot five times in two seconds. We also had like three rifles, a little old and rusty, but they could use modern bullets – they were called Mausers. There were also two .44 calibre Winchester rifles, like the ones that Buffalo Bill used, with several rounds in the chamber.

Did you ever actually use the Browning [pistol] you took to the university?
At that point, no. The great battle for the national FEU was resolved, miraculously enough, without casualties, but the risks I ran, as I said, were considerable. That was the way the university I entered in 1945 was. With

its ups and downs, very difficult conditions for me, many vicissitudes, many anecdotes. But that would be a long story. I've said enough about that.

Although I could add that some young people, students who in good faith allied themselves with the previous university leadership and were my adversaries in those episodes, years later joined the Revolution – there were even some who gave their lives. I hold no grudge against them whatsoever, and I am grateful for their subsequent acts of solidarity. Today that type of conflict doesn't happen in our university, where a population of over half a million young people takes classes and where a solid socialist and anti-imperialist awareness maintains its spirit of combativeness in defence of the Revolution and of the *patria*. What a tremendous gift that is!

And in the midst of all that comes the Cayo Confites expedition against Trujillo, the dictator of the Dominican Republic.[12]

Yes, in July 1947, at the age of twenty-one, I joined the Cayo Confites expedition to fight against the dictatorship of Trujillo, since in my first year I'd been designated chairman of the FEU's Committee for Dominican Democracy. I'd also been named chairman of the Committee for Puerto Rican Independence. I'd taken those responsibilities very seriously. We're talking about 1947, and from that time on I harboured the idea of an irregular war. I was convinced, on the basis of the experience of Cuba, the wars of independence, and other analyses that you could fight against a conventional modern army by using the methods of irregular warfare, guerrilla warfare. My idea was a guerrilla struggle in the mountains of the Dominican Republic, instead of launching a badly trained, inexperienced force against Trujillo's regular army.

Seeing the chaos and disorder that prevailed in the Cayo Confites expedition, I made plans to go off to the mountains with my company as soon as we arrived in the Dominican Republic, since in the crossing I'd wound up as the leader of a company. Cayo Confites was in 1947, and the assault on Moncada was in 1953, just six years later. I'd already had the idea for that sort of struggle, and it materialized in the Sierra Maestra. I believed in irregular warfare out of instinct – I'd been born in the country, I knew the mountains, and I realized that [the Cayo Confites] expedition was a disaster. It confirmed my conviction that you couldn't fight head-on against an army in Cuba or the Dominican Republic, because the army had a naval element, an air element, it had everything. It was stupid not to acknowledge that.

You were in Bogotá on 9 April 1948, the day Jorge Eliécer Gaitán, a very popular political leader, was killed. You lived through an insurrection there that has since been called the 'Bogotazo' – the Bogotá uprising, you might say.[13] What was that experience like?

That was an experience of great political importance. Gaitán represented hope and development for Colombia. His death detonated an explosion – the uprising of the people, a people seeking justice . . . The crowd seizing weapons, the police joining the fray, the destruction, the thousands of deaths . . . I joined the people; I grabbed a rifle in a police station that collapsed when it was rushed by a crowd. I witnessed the spectacle of a totally spontaneous popular revolution. I've talked about that experience in detail, it's out there somewhere in a book by the Colombian historian Alape.[14]

But I can tell you that that experience led me to identify myself even more with the cause of the people. My still incipient Marxist ideas had nothing to do with our conduct – it was a spontaneous reaction on our part, as young people with Martí-an, anti-imperialist, anti-colonialist and pro-democratic ideas.

During this time, on the eve of Gaitán's assassination, I'd been in Panama meeting with students who'd just been subjected to a cunning aggression by the Yankee forces who were occupying the Canal Zone – they'd been machine-gunned as they were protesting, demanding the return of the Canal. Several were killed and wounded. I recall one of the streets we marched down, lined with bars, a gigantic brothel, kilometres and kilometres long. There were some kids in the hospital, one of them paralysed by a wound to his spinal column – I visited him, filled with admiration for those courageous young people.

Before that, I'd passed through Venezuela – Rómulo Betancourt was the president at the time, the leader of the Democratic Action Party. He wasn't the man he would later become. The revolution in Venezuela[15] had awakened a great deal of sympathy in Cuba. Carlos Andrés Pérez was at that time a young fellow who worked for the governing party's official newspaper. Rómulo Gallegos,[16] a humble, honest man and a prestigious political and literary figure, was the newly elected president of Venezuela. Until just a short time before, I'd been enrolled in the expeditionary force against Trujillo, which had considerable support from progressive and revolutionary movements in Central America and the Caribbean, among them, of course, Acción Democrática, Democratic Action [Betancourt's party]. Chávez hadn't been born yet.

In Colombia, Gaitán had united the liberals; he had enormous influence within the universities. We made contact with the students, and we even met him, Gaitán, we met him, and he decided to support the congress of Latin American students that we wanted to organize. He wanted to inaugurate it. Our effort coincided, though purely by accident, with the creation in Bogotá of the OAS (Organization of American States).

I recall that when we were in Bogotá trying to create a federation of Latin American students, we came out, among other things, for the Argentines in their struggle for the Malvinas[17] and also for the independence of Puerto Rico, the overthrow of Trujillo, the return of the Panama Canal, and the sovereignty of the European colonies throughout the hemisphere. That was our programme – which was anti-imperialist and anti-dictatorial.

When Batista's coup took place, on 10 March 1952, do you think that with the struggles at the university, the experience of Cayo Confites, your experience in the 'Bogotazo', plus your activities in the inner workings of the Orthodox Party, you may have already had the beginnings of a theory of society, a theory of the seizure of power?

At the time, I'd read many of the books published on the Wars of Independence in Cuba. When I entered the university I came into closer contact with ideas about political economy and very soon, with the texts that were assigned in those classes, I became aware of the absurdities of capitalist society.

Later on, I encountered the Marxist material, as I told you. I was already involved in political issues, but in my first year at the university I hadn't gone very deeply into the subject that was called 'political economy' – so I never even took the examination in it. It was taught, as I've mentioned, by a certain professor, very hard, very strict, Professor Portela. The text was almost 1,000 pages of material printed on long and sometimes illegible mimeograph pages. I've mentioned that already. When I decided to go deeply into it, I started to come across theories of the law of value and added-value and the various interpretations of its causes. It was the political economy that was imparted to the children of the bourgeoisie. That's where I began to question the system.

On my own I came to the conclusion that the capitalist economy was absurd. What I'd already become, before I'd come into contact with Marxist or Leninist material, was a utopian Communist. A utopian Communist is someone whose ideas don't have any basis in science or history, but who sees that things are very bad, who sees poverty, injustice, inequality, an insuperable contradiction between society and true development. And I also had an ethics; I told you that our ethics came fundamentally through Martí.

I was helped a very great deal by life, the way I lived, and the way I saw the way I lived. When people talked about the 'crisis of overproduction' and the 'crisis of unemployment' and other problems, I gradually came to the conclusion that the system didn't work. The courses in History of Social Doctrines and Labour Legislation, which had texts written or compiled by people who'd been educated in theories of the Left,[18] helped me to think more deeply about these things.

One of the first of Marx's texts I read, as I said, was *The Communist Manifesto*. It made an enormous impact on me. I started to see and understand certain things, because I'd been born on a *latifundio*, which was, in addition, surrounded by other huge *latifundios*, and I knew what life was like there for those people. I'd had the experience, at first hand, of what imperialism was, domination, one government subservient to another government that was corrupt and repressive. The Orthodox Party denounced those abuses, that corruption. But I was already to the left of that party.

From that time on, I avidly read Marxist literature, to which I was more and more attracted. Within me, certain sentiments of justice and certain ethical values were already deeply rooted. I had an abhorrence of inequalities, of abuses. I felt that I had been conquered, so to speak, by that literature. It was like a political revelation of the conclusions that I'd reached on my own. I once said somewhere that if Ulysses was captivated by the songs of the sirens, I was captivated by the irrefutable truths of the Marxist denunciations. I'd already developed utopian ideas; now I felt I was on firmer ground.

Marxism taught me what society was. I was like a blindfolded man in a forest, who doesn't even know where north or south is. If you don't eventually come to truly understand the history of the class struggle, or at least have a clear idea that society is divided between the rich and the poor, and that some people subjugate and exploit other people, you're lost in a forest, not knowing anything.

In the circles you moved in, that way of thinking must not have been too common . . .
Well, to many people, the society as it was seemed the most natural thing in the world, like the family you're born into or the town you live in. It was

familiar – old habits. If all your life you've heard, 'So-and-so owns a horse; So-and-so owns a *bohío*;[19] and So-and-so owns this immense tract of land and everything on it,' then none of that ever seems so strange to you. The concept of property was universal, applicable to everything, even to your children. This is So-and-so's child, and this is So-and-so's wife – I mean, everything belongs to somebody. That concept of property applies to every-thing – a horse, a lorry, a farm, a factory, a school – except assets that are public.

A citizen is born into a capitalist society and is immediately immersed in the concept of property. For him, everything is property, and a pair of shoes, his child, his wife, is as sacred to him as that factory where there's a Mr So-and-so who's the owner and another man who's the manager and does you the favour of giving you a little job and pats people who are ignorant, who can't even read and write, on the back. Because capitalists are great users of psychology, which socialists often don't use. The socialist adminis-trator, the socialist manager thinks that working well, doing a good job, is the duty of the worker, while the capitalist knows that the worker produces added-value. Sometimes the capitalist doesn't really know, consciously, what added-value is. It's all so natural for him – he gets organized, gets a little money together, sets up a business, gets rich – even very, very rich.

Back then, I mean, people lived in such conditions of inferiority and subservience that they even looked upon one of those politicians, knowing that he was the richest and most corrupt guy in the world, with admiration!

It was when I started to formulate theories – as my studies in economics began – that I learned that there was a man named Karl Marx, and that there was a thing called Socialism, that there were people called Marxists, and Communists, and utopians. That was when I discovered that I was one of those utopians, you see?

Do you think that it was during those years that the stage of your political education ended, and that you now possessed the knowledge, the elements that would push you to begin a political life?
I'd come a long way in comparison with the day I entered the university a few years earlier, but there were still a lot of things to learn – and there still are.

What were the three essential things I learned from those great revolution-ary thinkers? From Martí, inspiration, his example and many other things; but in essence, ethics – above all, ethics. When he spoke that phrase I'll never be able to forget – 'All the glory in the world fits into a grain of corn' – it seemed extraordinarily beautiful to me, in the face of all the vanity and ambition that one saw everywhere, and against which we revolutionaries must be on constant guard. I seized upon that ethics. Ethics, as a mode of behaviour, is essential, a fabulous treasure.

From Marx, I received the concept of what human society is; otherwise, someone who hasn't read about it, or to whom it hasn't been explained, it's as though they were set down in the middle of a forest, at night, without knowing which way north is, or south, east or west. Marx told us what a society is and the history of its evolution. Without Marx, you can't formulate any argument that leads to a reasonable interpretation of historical events – what the tendencies are, the probable evolution of a humanity that has not yet completed its social evolution.

You and I and many other people in the world are worried about doctrines and theories such as neoliberal globalization, today so fashionable, which would terrify a man who lived during the period of colonialism; they would terrify Martí, when Cuba was a colony of Spain; they would terrify humanity just thirty years ago. Many important things, about which one now has awareness. So human history . . .

And your own personal history, no?
Well, I told you that there was also considerable influence from the fact of having been born in the countryside, and of being the son of a large land-owner rather than the *grandson* of a landowner. I lived through all that, so I was already familiar with it when I read Marx, because I'd seen with my own eyes what life was like on those *latifundios*. My father's *latifundio* was possibly the most humane of them all, and not just because he was my father. He was there, he would talk to people, he would see them suffer when they came to ask him for something, ask him some favour – and he could make a decision.

There in Birán, on the other *latifundios*, which belonged to American companies, the stockholders were in New York, and the people who were here[, in Cuba, and actually on the property,] were the administrators and overseers, who didn't have the option of helping anybody. They had a budget and they had to stay within it. Che Guevara looked for and studied the documents, on the way the plantations belonging to those big transnational companies were run – I know you're interested in Che – he studied the way it was: 'There was not a centavo to help anyone.' My father – I told you how much land he owned – was there; he would go out and see the people every day, they'd come up to him, he didn't have a bodyguard or anybody to go places with him; he would go out alone, by himself, he'd ride for kilo-metres and kilometres, and people would have access to him. They didn't have access to the president of a company like the United Fruit Company and others in New York, which is why the conditions were more humane there [on my father's farm]. I saw all that [in Birán], and it helped a great deal – it was the raw material for my philosophy of aiding those who have nothing.

I told you that I sometimes went hungry; I told you a lot of things, the things I went through. It was very easy for me, then, to understand that we lived in a society of inequalities and injustices.

When did you decide to move from theory into practice?
Remember that I was already about halfway an internationalist; I'd been in Bogotá in 1948, I'd joined the students there. We already had a programme. Remember that that programme, that platform if you will, contained, among other things, the fight for the Malvinas, the return of the Panama Canal. I'd been in the Cayo Confites expedition and on other assignments. And most important of all: by 10 March 1952, the day of Batista's coup d'état, I'd already been a convinced Marxist-Leninist for several years. I say that because of the values I'd acquired, because of what I'd learned in all those years at the university. Without those lessons, I wouldn't have been able to play any role at all.

If Christopher Columbus hadn't had a compass, he wouldn't have got anywhere. But the compass existed. I had a compass; it was what I'd found in Marx and in Lenin. And the ethics – I repeat – that I had found in Martí. Other factors may have had an influence, too – I enjoyed sports very much and climbed mountains. Circumstances have their influence on a person; life helped me.

When Batista's coup took place in 1952, I'd already formulated a plan for the future. I decided to launch a revolutionary programme and organize a popular uprising. From that moment on, I had a clear idea of the struggle ahead and of the fundamental revolutionary ideas behind it, the ideas that are in *History Will Absolve Me*.[20] I already had the idea that a revolutionary takeover of power was necessary. It all stemmed from what was going to happen after the 1 June elections that year. Nothing was going to change. The frustration and disillusionment were going to be repeated all over again. And it was not possible to go back again, back over those long-travelled roads that led nowhere.

4
The Assault on the Moncada Barracks

Preparation – The men – The weapons –
The strategy – The farm in Siboney – The attack – The retreat

When did you decide to attack the Moncada barracks?

I suspected – there were signs – that Batista was planning a coup. I reported my suspicions to the leaders of the Orthodox Party and they asked people they trusted to look into it. They did, and they came back and told the directorate, which I was not a member of, that there was no danger, everything was quiet. I told you this.

When did we decide to attack Moncada? When we became convinced that nobody was going to do anything, that there was not going to be any fight against Batista, and that many of the existing groups – in which there were lots and lots of people who were members of several [groups] at the same time – were not prepared, not organized, to carry out the armed struggle that I was hoping for.

A professor at the university, Rafael García Bárcena, for example, came to talk to me, because he wanted to seize the Columbia military base in Havana, which was one of the regime's major bulwarks. He says to me, 'I've got people inside [the garrison] that will support us.'

'You want to take over Columbia,' I said to him, 'and they're going to pave the way for you? Don't talk to anybody else, then – we've got enough men and we can keep [the action] totally secret.' But he did just the opposite! He talked to over twenty organizations, and within a few days all of Havana, including the army, knew what this professor was planning – a good, decent man, who gave some of those classes that more or less high-ranking military personnel take as part of their education. Bárcena was one of their professors. As you might expect, everybody was sent to prison, including the professor.

But even before that perfectly predictable outcome, which came a few weeks after my conversation with Bárcena, when we discovered that the takeover of Columbia was now common knowledge, we decided to act right away with our own forces, which were superior in number, discipline and training to all the other juntas. It pains me to say that, but it's true. Among those organizations, one of the most serious and combative was the University Student Federation, the FEU. But the FEU's most brilliant pages, under the leadership of José Antonio Echeverría,[1] who'd just entered the university, and of the Revolutionary Directorate, which he'd created in 1956, were yet to be written.

We analysed the situation and formulated a plan. We'd chosen Santiago de Cuba as the place to begin the struggle. I never talked to Bárcena again. One day, when I was driving back from Santiago, I was listening to the radio and heard the news that he and several groups of civilians had been arrested on street corners near the Columbia military camp.

How did you put together the group of militants who were going to attack Moncada?

I'd done quite a bit of proselytising and speech-making – because I already had a clear idea of how to make a revolution – and I had the habit of studying each and every combatant who volunteered, determining his motivations and ensuring that he understood the rules of organization and conduct, explaining our goals and principles, explaining what I could and should explain. Without that approach, you couldn't have conceived the plan for Moncada. On what basis? What forces were you going to have? Who were your combatants, what were their motivations, their backgrounds, and how many of them were there? If you can't count on the working class, the *campesinos*, the under-class, the poor and humble, in a country terribly exploited and suffering, then none of it makes any sense. There was no class consciousness [in Cuba at the time], except for those who were members of the Popular Socialist Party, who were pretty well educated politically; there was, though, what I sometimes called a class instinct. There was Mella, a young, brilliant university leader who, along with a fighter from the War of Independence, had founded the Communist Party of Cuba in 1925. I've mentioned him more than once. But in 1952 that party was politically isolated – imagine, this was the heyday of McCarthyism and [Cuba was] under the influence of a ferocious imperialist campaign, with all the resources imaginable at its disposal, to be used against anything that smelled the slightest bit like Communism. There was an enormous lack of political culture.

Did it take you long to gather all those men together?
It went relatively quickly. I was amazed at how fast, using the right arguments and a number of examples, you could persuade somebody that that society [we lived in] was absurd and that it had to be changed. Initially, I began the job with a handful of teams. There were a lot of people who were against theft, misappropriation of funds, unemployment, abuse, injustice, but they thought it was all attributable to bad politicians. They couldn't see that it was the system that created all of that.

We know that capitalism's influences, invisible to the majority of people, act on the individual without the individual's awareness. Many people were of the opinion that if you brought an archangel down from heaven, the most expert of them all, and gave him the job of governing the Republic, that would bring about administrative honesty – you could create more schools, no one would steal the money to be used for public health and other pressing needs any more. They couldn't see that unemployment, poverty, the lack of land – all those calamities couldn't be fixed even by an archangel, because those enormous tracts of land, the *latifundios*, that system of production would not allow anything, anything at all, to be done. I was totally convinced that the system had to be done away with.

The kids I recruited were Orthodoxists, very anti-Batista, very good, honest kids, but they lacked any political education. They had class instinct, I would say, but not class consciousness.

As I explained at the beginning, we began to recruit and train men not in order to make a revolution, but rather to engage – this seemed perfectly elementary – in a struggle, along with others, to reestablish the constitutional status quo of 1952, when [the constitutional system] was short-circuited, two months and twenty days before the elections, by Fulgencio Batista, a man who had great influence in his old and unpurified military and who conceived the coup when he became convinced that he had no chance whatever of winning the elections.

We organized as a fighting force – not, I repeat, in order to make a revolution but rather to join all the other anti-Batista forces, because after the coup on 10 March 1952, it was elementary that all those forces had to be united. The party that had won the 1948 elections, the Authentic Party, was in power and it was pretty corrupt, but Batista was much worse. There was a constitution, there was a whole electoral process under way, and eighty days before the June elections, on 10 March 1952, Batista launched his coup.

The elections were going to be held on 1 June. He was his party's candidate, but the polls said he had no chance whatsoever of being elected; clearly the party that Chibás had founded, the Orthodox Party, was going to win by a wide majority. So Batista launched his military coup. [And almost immediately,] everybody began to organize and make plans to bring down that illegal, despotic government.

How many men did your group have?

We didn't have a centavo, we didn't have anything. What I did have was a relationship with a party, the Orthodox Party, which had a lot of young people in it, all very anti-Batista – they were like the antithesis of Batista. In that respect, there was no other organization comparable to it in the country. The ethical and political stature of the youth wing of the party was very high. I couldn't say that they had, as I said to you earlier, a high level of political awareness, revolutionary awareness, class consciousness, because when all was said and done, the leadership of that party, like always, except in Havana, where there was a large group of intellectuals and professionals, had gradually fallen into the hands of landowners and other wealthy men.

But the majority of the party were good men, honest, hard-working people, even some from the middle class – [they weren't] even particularly anti-imperialistic, because the subject of imperialism was simply not discussed. It was discussed only within the circles of the Communist Party – that was how low the revolutionary spirit of the Cuban people had fallen after the Second World War; it had been crushed under the overwhelming weight of the Yankees' ideological and advertising machinery.

How many men did you train for the assault?

We trained 1,200 young men. That exact figure, 1,200, shows that when we reached that number we stopped recruiting future combatants. We'd created a small army. I spoke with each one of them; I strove very assiduously to do that – hours and hours every day. My argumentation with them was essentially political – we had to get organized and be prepared. Our intentions were clear, [but] we never mentioned concrete plans. Discipline was essential.

Within a few months we had recruited the 1,200 men I mentioned. I put 50,000 kilometres, over 30,000 miles, on that car! Whose engine blew, by the way, a few days before Moncada – a beige Chevrolet, licence plate 50315. I still remember it. So then I exchanged it for another car, which we rented a few days before 26 July.

We infiltrated other organizations. There was one that belonged to the party of the corrupt [Orthodox Party] administration that had been over-thrown on 10 March – it was conspiring against Batista, too. It had a large stockpile of weapons, a little of everything – what it didn't have was men. Former military leaders under that administration were organizing the troops they did have, and looking for more. Using Abel's personality, dyna-mism and mental agility, we convinced them that they could count on three groups of 120 young men each, all well trained, whom they inspected in groups of forty at various places around Havana. They were impressed. That was all they wanted. Although it was a lot. But we were overambitious. They got suspicious and broke off contact. All the young men and leaders were new. They must have smelled our strategy. [If they realized that it was me, Fidel Castro, that was behind the infiltration, they'd have dropped us like a hot potato, because] you couldn't even mention my name to them. I'd written several articles denouncing that administration's [i.e., the Orthodox Party administration, which this group had supported] terribly serious, immoral acts, and *Alerta*, the country's highest-circulation newspaper, pub-lished them, one after another, with all relevant proof, in its special Monday edition. That took place several months after the death of Chibás and just a few weeks before the coup, so they blamed me for undermining the govern-ment and making the coup possible.

We recruited and trained 1,200 men, as I was saying, in less than a year – quite a number. They were almost all members of the Orthodox Youth, and we came to have tremendous discipline and unity of vision. They trusted in our efforts, they believed in our arguments, and they nourished our hopes.

So all of them were very young, then.
Yes, all of them, all of them. They were young guys – twenty, twenty-two, twenty-three, twenty-four years old. Over thirty, [there were] maybe two: Dr Mario Muñoz, the detachment doctor, and Gildo Fleitas, who worked in the office at the Belén school, so I'd known him since then. It had been seven years since I graduated from high school there in 1945. The others came from cells we organized in various cities, with outstanding young men of unquestionable honour and humanity. There were a lot of young men like that, all over the country. The city we got the most from was Artemisa,

which at that time belonged to the province of Pinar del Río – Artemisa provided between twenty and thirty future combatants, an excellent group. There were also others from all around Havana and several cities in the former province of Havana, which included the territory of what are today two provinces.

At that time there were many organizations of various kinds, and many young men who were in one, and another, and another at the same time.

I'd recruited some people that I already knew, but I didn't know most of them, because I wasn't around the official leaders of the Orthodox Party very much . . . I mean, I was close to some of them: Max Lesnik, whom our nation knows and respects because he's doing courageous work today in Florida, fighting some of our unscrupulous adversaries there; then there was Ribadulla and even a leader of the Orthodox Youth, a guy named Orlando Castro, who'd run for the House of Deputies before the coup and later went to Venezuela and became a millionaire over there. At first, many of them were there just hanging out, you might say, and talking political talk.

I used the headquarters of the Orthodox Party in Havana, at 109 Calle Prado, because a lot of people went there every day to talk and get the news. That was very useful for my purposes – camouflage and disinformation. There were no leaders there, just the office staff. I'd meet in a little room with small groups of five, six or seven young men. I explained that [recruitment] work to you. What we were doing was persuading, indoctrinating and taking the first steps toward organizing. You had to study them, and you couldn't reveal your plans. The Orthodox Party was a party of the middle class, poor people, workers, *campesinos*, clerks, professionals, students . . . There were also some unemployed people in it. Some of [the men I interviewed] worked in stores; others, in factories, such as Pedro Marrero, or were self-employed, such as Fernando Chenard, a photographer. And there were others, such as the Gómez brothers, who were cooks at the Belén school, that I'd known there, as I had Gildo Fleitas – wonderful people.

I recall that in the days following the coup on 10 March 1952, among the first people who joined were Jesús Montané and Abel Santamaría. I organized a small circle of Marxist studies in Guanabo, where someone lent me a house, and the material I used was Mehring's biography of Marx;[2] I liked that book, which has a beautiful story. Abel and Montané sat in on the course. I discovered one thing: the easiest thing in the world, under those circumstances, was converting somebody to Marxism. I'm not bad at speech-making, preaching the word.

It must be due to your Christian education.
Maybe. By this time I had got past my period as a utopian Communist, when I hadn't yet read Marx or other socialist authors. As I told you, during that [first] phase of my political education, the place I was born and the particular experiences I had lived through were very useful to me.

That society was chaotic, it lacked all semblance of rationality.

And during this time were you a lawyer [i.e., were you in practice]?
I was the first professional revolutionary in the Movement – under the circumstances, I was supported by the militants. They worked, I was the professional revolutionary, because as a lawyer, I defended very poor people – I didn't charge anything and I didn't have any other job. Besides, I was devoting my full time to the Revolution.

Montané had an account in the bank, not very big, maybe 2,000 or 3,000 pesos, and a relatively well-paying job, and Abel, for his part, was earning a good salary for the time. He had an apartment in a building in El Vedado; his sister, Haydée,[3] lived there with him. I met the three of them after Batista's coup.

My money went for petrol for the car, the rent on my house, and basic living expenses. I should add that the car, licence plate 50315, wasn't entirely mine – I'd bought it on instalments. I had to make a monthly payment or it would be repossessed by the credit company right off the street. More than once Abel and Montané had to rescue it when they got paid.

Some historians have noted that many of those who took part in the assault on the Moncada barracks were the sons of Spaniards, and especially Galicians. Can you confirm that?
Yes, I was struck by that. One day I just happened to be looking at the list of the main organizers and leaders of the Moncada attack and I was struck by the fact that many of us were the sons of Spaniards. I mean, there was already the famous case of José Martí, the hero of our independence, who was the son of Spanish parents on both sides. And I should say that in Cuba's struggles for independence down through history, many Spaniards and Galicians have taken part. I think there were a little over 100 Galicians, some of them very noteworthy, who made common cause with the Cubans.

In our 26th of July Movement, the second in command, Abel Santamaría – a brave, extraordinary *compañero* – was the son of a Galician too. So the two main leaders were sons of Galicians. But there was also Raúl, who played a very noteworthy role and who, of course, is also the son of a Galician.

Other historic leaders of the 26th of July Movement, such as Frank País and his brother Josué, were also the sons of Galicians – Galicians from Galicia, and I stress that because in Cuba, practically all Spaniards were called Galicians, a little pejoratively. In our revolutionary process, in the struggle in the Sierra Maestra, several sons or grandsons of Galicians, such as Camilo Cienfuegos, distinguished themselves as military leaders, and we hadn't met one another in a social club,[4] but rather on the street, in the struggle.

And were all of you sympathetic to Marxism?

By then, all the principal leaders thought that way: Abel, Montané, and I. Raúl was not a leader yet, because he was very young. He was attending the university; he hadn't been there long. There was a fourth leader, Martínez Ararás,[5] who was very capable and active as an organizer, but what he liked was action; he didn't bother much about theory. He was given the mission to take the barracks at Bayamo; he was the commander of the detachment sent to attack the troops posted in that city.

If we hadn't studied Marxism – this story is longer, but I'll only say this about it – if we hadn't read Marx's books on political theory, and if we hadn't been inspired by Martí, Marx and Lenin, we couldn't possibly have conceived the idea of a revolution in Cuba, because with a group of men, none of whom has gone through a military academy, you can't wage a war against a well-organized, well-armed, well-trained army and win a victory starting practically from scratch. Those ideas were the essential building blocks of the Revolution.

At the time, your brother Raúl was a member of the Young Socialists, which was part of the Communist Party, correct?

Well, Raúl was already very left-wing, but really, I was the person who introduced him to Marxist-Leninist ideas. He came with me to Havana, lived with me in a tiny penthouse there, right across the street from a barracks, in fact, where today stands the famous Hotel Cohíba.[6]

The Hotel Meliá Cohíba?

That's right, the Meliá Cohíba, built by Cuba with its own money, and which the Meliá chain operates under a management contract. There was a barracks complex on that site; its buildings weren't very tall – there weren't any tall buildings near the ocean. What Raúl did, in keeping with what he interpreted Marxist doctrine to be, was join the youth branch of the Communist Party.

He joined on his own?
Yes, he always had his own mind.

You were never in the Communist Party?
No. And that was well calculated and thought out. But that's another story. That moment may come, and I'll tell you about it.

Where did you and the others train to prepare for the assault?
At the university was where we trained our men. We even organized and trained some commando groups. We were helped out by a man who was quite expert, a guy who hung out in revolutionary circles – he was so strange that he aroused more suspicion than enthusiasm among us. But he didn't know anything about our plans, and he never saw a weapon. What we were doing looked more like some kind of sporting activity.

At the University of Havana?
Yes, the University of Havana. Pedrito Miret[7] was also there – he was an instructor.

Did you do target practice at the University of Havana?
No, no, we did that somewhere else. At the University of Havana, it was assembling and disassembling rifles and firing practice, with blanks, with Pedro Miret. Pedrito set up his training centre in the Hall of Martyrs. The university was quite autonomous, and students had no problem mobilizing. For a while, throughout one whole early stage, University Hill had a certain degree of immunity, so that was where everybody went to protest. Batista and his army must have laughed at those 'practices' of ours.

Miret was an engineering student. I had a lot of friends at the university, and I met Miret. I started organizing our people into cells of six, eight, ten or twelve men, and training them; each one had its leader. I did the political work and the organizational work. I never showed my face around the training sites at the university. I was practically underground, so far as Batista and the other organizations were concerned.

Did Miret have any particular military experience?
No, none. Nobody had studied in military schools. Honestly, none of those who took part in that struggle. I mean, well, except for one soldier we'd recruited – who was attached, by the way, to the Havana barracks ... Do you know where we trained to learn to shoot rifles?

Somewhere on the outskirts of Havana?
No, at firing ranges in Havana. We disguised some of our *compañeros* as good upstanding members of the bourgeoisie – businessmen, whatever, depending on what you looked like, your style, your abilities. We'd register them first, for example, in hunting clubs, and they'd invite us to their clubs to practise clay-pigeon shooting. Actually, we were able perfectly legally to train 1,200 men, although only some of them were trained in live fire. Batista's forces of repression didn't pay us much attention, because they knew we didn't have a cent, we didn't have a thing. Naturally, I made myself pretty scarce at all those places.

   The ones that had millions were the former government. They also had weapons; they'd brought them in from abroad – they had all the contacts and all the resources for that.

You'd had some military training during the 'Bogotazo'.
Well, yes, when I was in the 'Bogotazo', but especially at home in Birán – from the time I was ten or eleven years old, I was always fooling around with some gun or other, and I was a good shot.

You had also trained quite a bit in Cayo Confites, hadn't you?
Yes, I even had training in shooting mortars and other weapons. It's true that I had been in what was almost a war. Remember, there were a lot of my enemies in that expedition, but despite that I signed up – only because I was president of the Committee for Dominican Democracy. We talked a little bit about that before. There's a story there, how that expedition was organized and armed, who organized it, and at what point all that was done. It was in 1947. The Second World War was over; Trujillo had been in power for years, and Cuban students had a great deal of antipathy towards him.

Did you really get any military experience out of that adventure?
There were absolutely no tactics or strategy involved over there.

Not to mention that it didn't work.
That's a long story. How did they recruit more than 1,000 men? They picked them up on the street.

They were a bit lumpen, no?
Well, but lumpen [who are] well prepared, well trained can be good. I don't want to use that word pejoratively.[8] But they lacked any ideological preparation, any political education. What I learned most from the Cayo Confites expedition was how *not* to organize something like that, how to choose your people.

It helped you avoid errors later, down the line.
Since back then I'd been thinking about an irregular war, as I told you, because [in Cayo Confites] there'd been an army that wasn't an army. They even had fighter jets, and they thought, well, we'll disembark on the coasts of Santo Domingo [the capital of the country], which would have meant they were going to hit that army of thousands of men, organized, trained and well armed by the United States of America, head-on – this was an army that also had warships and military aircraft. That expedition was pure chaos. Commands were given out on the basis of politics; each 'personality' got a command. Among them there was one tremendous crook, Rolando Masferrer, who at one time had been on the Left, he had been a Communist, he'd taken part in the Spanish Civil War, and he'd had a certain amount of intellectual education, but later he was one of Batista's worst thugs, a man who organized paramilitary groups and committed numerous crimes. It would take [the Dominican] army a matter of hours to totally wipe out that expedition – it barely had time to disembark.

Let's talk about the assault on Moncada. Do you think that attack was, without question, a failure?
The Moncada barracks could have been taken, and if we'd taken Moncada we'd have toppled Batista, without question. We'd have seized several thousand weapons. Total surprise, added to our cunning and complete deception of the enemy. We were all dressed as sergeants, mimicking the antecedent, the 'Sergeants' Uprising', which had been led by Batista himself, in 1933. He wasn't the principal organizer, but since he had a little more education, and he was clever, and he was the stenographer for the army general staff, he was made leader of the sergeants too. In Santiago de Cuba, it would have

taken them hours to recover from the chaos and confusion that would have been created in their ranks, and that would have given us time for the subsequent steps.

You think the plan of attack was a good one?

If I were to organize a plan for taking the Moncada barracks again, I would do it exactly the same way; I wouldn't change a thing. What failed there was that we lacked sufficient combat experience. Later, we picked it up . . .

Luck, chance, also had a decisive influence, in that the plan, which was really quite good in terms of concept, organization, secrecy and other factors, failed because of a detail that could have easily been overcome. If I were to be asked today, 'What could have been done better?', I would talk about an alternative formula,* because if we'd triumphed at Moncada, we'd have triumphed too early. Although it wasn't calculated that way, the support of the USSR was essential after the triumph of 1959. We wouldn't have had that support in 1953. In 1953, the spirit and policy of Stalin prevailed in the USSR. Although Stalin had died a few months earlier, in March 1953, it was still the 'Stalin era' in July. And Khrushchev was not Stalin.

At that time, I hadn't read anything about the daring operations that had been carried out in the Second World War. I had, however, read quite a bit about the military feats in our own history. I can tell you the factors that had an influence on our guerrilla tactics and the procedures we used in our struggle. You're going to be amazed at some things. But I hadn't read, for example, the history of Mussolini's rescue by Skorzeny when the Fascist political regime collapsed in Italy.[9] It goes without saying that I read every book that came into my hands about the Second World War written by the Soviets and the Germans, especially after the triumph of the Revolution.

There are basic principles as to what one should or can do when certain situations occur. Had we satisfactorily overcome what was probably just a small obstacle, the Moncada barracks would without a doubt have fallen.

Did you attack only Moncada or were there other objectives at the same time?

We attacked two barracks complexes. Besides Moncada, there was the Bayamo barracks, as a check to the counter-attack. We planned to blow up or

---

* [Here, Castro apparently contradicts himself, but what he seems to be saying is that he would reformulate the question: it isn't that he would change the plan of attack, but that his plans for what to do after a victory would be more thoroughly thought out. – Trans.]

at least put out of commission the Central Highway bridge over the River Cauto, a few kilometres north of Bayamo, because the first reinforcements would probably come [via that route] from the regiment at Holguín, and then from the rest of the country. By air, they didn't have enough forces, and the other way was the railway, which was much easier to defend against. You derail the train or pull up rails – it's much easier than neutralizing a strong, solid bridge made of steel and concrete. We sent forty men to take the Bayamo barracks; the intention was to defend ourselves against a foreseeable attack by the enemy coming along the Central Highway at a point more than 200 kilometres from Santiago.

The counter-attack would come by land. To avoid being bombarded by air, we planned to get out of the barracks complex right away and cache the weapons at various points around Santiago, so as to distribute them later to the people, on the basis of their tradition of fighting for independence. On 10 March, when that city's regiment didn't immediately join the coup – some of the officers were against it, although when those particular officers were removed the regiment did join the coup – the city of Santiago mobilized to support [the regiment]. The city totally rejected, totally hated that coup.

You made very meticulous plans for this assault. On the day before the attack, everyone that was going to take part in it began gathering, in small groups and very discreetly, at a place outside Santiago, the Siboney farm. We all arrived from Havana the day before, hours before the attack. Then we left for Moncada from the farm.

When you arrived at the farm, most of the men hadn't been told what the objective was, isn't that right? Well, once they arrived at the farm from Havana, each group with its leader . . . I left last, at 2.40 a.m. on Saturday the 25th, so I didn't sleep a wink for forty-eight hours before the attack. I got to the farm on the night of the 25th. Abel Santamaría was there waiting for me, and the others in guest houses that had been rented in the city, and everybody with their cars so as to be able to move out when the word was given . . . Nobody knew about the farm; the only people who knew about it were Abel, Renato Guitart,[10] and I. Oh, and Elpidio Sosa and Melba[11] – and Haydée, later on.

The farm had been rented in April 1953, three months before the attack. All the details were handled by Renato, a young fellow from Santiago, who was the only person who knew the objective. A very clever guy – very good, very brave and determined. He had an excellent knowledge of the city of Santiago and its environs. He was the main keeper of a very important secret, and the only person who knew what the target of the armed attack was to be.

Of those who came from Oriente, Abel was the first one [to join us? to learn of the attack?]; then came Elpidio Sosa. The combatants were all mentally prepared; they would be notified and everything would be by surprise. We had mobilized them several times to one place or another, simulating a possible action, and then we'd sent everybody back home. This time, though, was the real thing; we knew them all much better now. Each nucleus had its own leader. We rented the cars that would transport them from Havana, almost 1,000 kilometres, over 600 miles.

In Santiago?
No, in Havana, for us to travel almost 1,000 kilometres to Santiago – we travelled from Havana. We attacked on the morning of 26 July, and I had left Havana on the morning of the 25th, at the time I told you. I went by way of Santa Clara. I bought some glasses, eyeglasses there. Yes, because I had a little myopia – myopia decreases with age.

You'd forgotten your glasses?
No, no, I hadn't forgotten them; it would be hard to forget your glasses, but I don't remember what happened – whether there was some problem with them, or whether I wanted another pair or what. The question is that there, at an optician's in Santa Clara, I needed to have some made, so I did. Then I continued on, made a stop in Bayamo, I stopped to see the people that were going to attack the barracks in that historic city, stopped in Palma Soriano to make contact with Aguilerita, another very committed Oriental, and I arrived at the Siboney farm, on the outskirts of Santiago, at nightfall on the 25th. Just a few hours before the attack. Almost all the others had come from Havana in cars, down the Central Highway. Several cars flew a little flag of the Batista-ites, the fighters of the 4th of September. Not me – I was better known, and anybody who saw me with a 4th of September flag would have said, 'What in the world is going on?'

So anyway, we had chosen the Siboney farm because it was the most strategic place. It seemed to be the most out-of-the-way of the various places where you might bring a big group together. Along the highway that runs in front of the farm you could see from Santiago all the way to the ocean, right to the point, in fact, where the Americans disembarked in 1898, in the Spanish-American War. That's Siboney, and from there the highway today runs along the coast to near Guantánamo. That spot was perfect for our plan. There were trees, among them some mango trees with very dense foliage. We set up a fake chicken farm there, with incubators and everything. We hid some of the guns in a well near the house. But most of the weapons arrived at almost the same time we did. I told you that there was just one fellow from Santiago, Renato Guitart; everybody came from Oriente so as not to arouse suspicion.

But the driver of your car was from Santiago, wasn't he?
No, the driver drove down from Havana.

When you came from Havana?
Right, when I came from Havana. The driver was Mitchell, Teodulio Mitchell. So anyway, we arrived at the farm around nightfall. As we were arriving in the city, it was beginning to get dark. I immediately made contact with Abel Santamaría; each group was in one of the various guest houses where they'd gone as they arrived.

It was carnival time; we chose the day [for our raid] because of that, too, because a lot of people came to Santiago and there was a lot of noise and music and carrying-on. That carnival atmosphere, which was famous, was good for us, but unexpectedly it worked against us, because it led to certain measures at the barracks complex, which were the main cause of later difficulties. From the farm, we'd drive to the barracks – it was all prepared, the cars were well hidden there at the farm.

How did you hide the cars?
The cars were driven into these shed-like structures; there weren't many cars, anyway. There were sixteen cars, and we had planted some plants so nobody could see how many cars there were. All anybody who passed by there would have seen would have been the henhouses and incubators.

Where did you hide the weapons?
In a well near the house – it looked as if it had been sealed up, with a little tree on top. We kept most of our weapons there. A lot came in at the last moment. There were weapons bought on Friday in Havana that had arrived only several hours before. We had planned every detail.

For the attack that was to take place on Sunday the 26th?

A considerable number of weapons that were used in the actions on Sunday at 5.15 in the morning had been bought on the afternoon of Friday the 24th. We bought some in Santiago, too, in normal businesses, in a gun shop where they were just ordinarily for sale, so when they came in, there was no reason to put them in the well. Those that arrived on Saturday had been taken into the bedrooms and put in other places in the house.

They were essentially light arms?

I'll tell you. The best weapon we had was a shotgun, for hunting, a Belgian shotgun. I was familiar with it because my father had one in our house in Birán, as I told you. There was a light American semi-automatic M-1 rifle and a bolt-action Springfield, also American-made; a .45-calibre Thompson submachine gun, with the magazine underneath – it could use a box or a drum magazine. And the M-1, too – semi-automatic, light, American. The M-1 was the rifle everybody liked – it was light, small, efficient, semi-automatic. But the most effective weapons for the type of action we were carrying out were .12-gauge Belgian hunting shotguns, with nine-shot cartridges; you could fire up to five cartridges in a matter of seconds. I was carrying one of those. For combat at close range, they were much more effective than a machine gun, because in one shot they shoot nine projectiles, any one of which can be fatal. We had several dozen of those. Not sawn-off.

Didn't you have some with the barrel sawn off?

In the history of political movements, often, and in Cuba itself, a sawn-off shotgun was used in actions of this kind. But we didn't need a sawn-off shotgun. Some of them were single-shot, for hunting large game, apparently, but we had very few of those.

We also had .22 rifles. The .22 was a good weapon under certain specific conditions. But there are other conditions in which the .22 has no advantage, such as in the face of a .30–06 at a distance greater than 150 yards.

They aren't so effective.

If the target is really far off they aren't effective. Shotguns aren't very good, either, in that case.

They don't have enough range?

For combat at a little longer distance you can use a .22 rifle, but to attack the barracks, the ideal weapon was a shotgun. And the .45-calibre submachine gun, an automatic weapon, but we only had one of those, or maybe two. The semi-automatic .22 has a good range, and it could use metal bullets. You'd buy what could more or less be effective for you, and you had to be happy with whatever you found.

How did you get the weapons?
The semi-automatic .12-gauge shotguns, we bought in gun shops. Everything was quiet in Cuba after Batista's coup; the coup leaders felt so safe and secure that you could buy weapons in any gun shop. I saw to organizing the purchase of almost all the weapons, one by one, and of raising money. We had to disguise people as bourgeois types and as sport hunters, we had to use a certain degree of cunning with sellers, [had to] seem to be carrying out completely commercial operations. We even bought some guns, as I told you, in a gun shop in Santiago de Cuba.

What weapon did you yourself carry?
As I told you, I carried a Belgian .12-gauge shotgun. It's a weapon that can be loaded with several shells. It worked pretty well. The only M-1 we had belonged to Pedrito Miret. We had one or two Thompson submachine guns, a Springfield, and two Winchesters that had a cover that opened to the side and used the same calibre bullets as the Springfield, .30–06. The Winchesters came from my house in Birán. In my parents' house there were shotguns, four or five of them, which they always had in the house. I knew they were there in Birán, so at the end, since there was a tremendous shortage of weapons, I had to get them wherever I could . . .

Raúl learned how to take apart the Winchesters under Pedro Lago, who worked on the farm as a night watchman. He got two of them off the gun rack in the house and left for Marcané – from there, he moved on to Holguín, from where he sent one of the two guns in a package by mail to Havana. He got on the Santiago–Havana bus with the other one. He put the gun up front, in the front seats, and he sat in the back, so that if the bus was searched he could decide what to do.

Your brother Raúl says that you also had a Browning submachine gun, a .45-calibre.
There were one or two Thompsons of that calibre. I think I recall that there was just one, which came from the university. There was no Browning

.45-calibre submachine gun. The automatic weapon I remember of that manufacturer's used a cartridge clip, it was a .30–06. The soldiers in the army had that gun. We didn't have a single one.

To sum up, we had one M-1, one Thompson, one Springfield, [and] two Winchesters. The rest were .22 rifles, semi-automatic or repeaters, and .12-gauge shotguns. I can also remember several pistols that some of us carried individually. The most fearsome weapon, as I say, was the .12-gauge semi-automatic shotgun with four shells of nine shot each in the chamber and one in the barrel [sic].[12] In a matter of seconds you can get off forty-five potentially fatal projectiles. You can put anybody out of combat with it, in an almost hand-to-hand confrontation, which was the kind of combat we expected, because we were going to be inside the barracks complex with the soldiers very close. A deadly weapon.

Listen, with what we carried we could have taken Moncada; there was no problem – we could have done it with even fewer people than we had. That was clear from the calculations we'd done. There was a regiment of soldiers and a squad from the Rural Guard: 1,500 men, approximately, whose command posts and dormitories would be taken in a surprise attack at dawn.

The little semi-automatic .22 rifle is a medium-distance weapon of war, good for what we wanted it for, which was to take over the barracks and capture all its weapons. The real weapons of war were in the hands of the army, the soldiers there. Our mission was to seize their weapons – otherwise, what was the point of attacking the barracks? Once the Moncada barracks complex was captured, we'd have been in possession of several thousand weapons, since in addition to the soldiers' own weapons we'd be able to take over the weapons belonging to the reserves and the navy and the police, which were much weaker forces and would almost certainly never have tried to resist once the regiment was taken out of action.

What arms did the soldiers at Moncada have?
A little of everything. They had various kinds: five-shot Springfields, semi-automatic Garands and M-1s, Thompson submachine guns, automatic rifles and .30–06s and .50-calibre tripod machine guns, mortars and so on.

How many combatants took part in the attack?
A hundred and sixty men. Forty that we used in Bayamo to take the barracks there and prevent the counter-attack from the Central Highway, and 120

for the assault on Moncada. I was to go in with ninety of them, inside the barracks.

All armed?
Yes, of course, all of them, all of them.

And in uniforms?
Everybody wearing a uniform of Batista's army and the rank of sergeant.

How did you get the uniforms?
We made them in Havana, at Melba Hernández' house – she's still alive – and Yeyé's [Haydée Santamaría]. Everybody helped out. We also, as I told you, had a man inside the barracks, one of our own who'd infiltrated the main barracks in Havana, and this guy bought most of the uniforms – I'll never know how he managed! He was good, that guy. When you start looking for people for a certain job, you find them. He helped us tremendously in getting caps, visors and a number of army uniforms that were already made.

And how were you going to recognize each other in the midst of all those soldiers stationed in the barracks themselves?
You know how we recognized each other? Besides the kind of guns, which were unmistakable? The shoes! Our shoes weren't military-issue. We all wore low-cut street shoes – but the rest, the fatigue caps and everything, standard-issue. You can imagine what a job it was to make all those uniforms, caps and all. Melba Hernández' family helped us a lot, and Yeyé, who was just a young thing. They weren't related, they were just friends. Yeyé came from the centre of the island, the province of Las Villas, and she was with her brother in Havana because he was a bookkeeper for one of those agencies there, a car dealer. His salary was at least 300 pesos, three-something. Montané had a similar job.

And at that little farm, there was space for 120 men to sleep?
No, no, we all met there, but there was no time to sleep.

Where did they sleep?
As they arrived, they went to guest houses in the city that had been rented beforehand. All those details had been organized by Abel. There were several

guest houses, and each man went to the one his group was assigned to. The timing, to coincide with the carnival, which attracted a lot of visitors, made our movements easier.

They arrived, mobilized at night. They started arriving [at Siboney] between ten and eleven at night. Because the attack was going to be at five the next morning, and there was no reason to have them there [any longer than overnight]. They received their instructions at the farm.

When you arrived at the Siboney farm, it was the moment of truth for your comrades. Were they aware of the objective?
They were mentally prepared – as I told you, we'd mobilized them several times, for firing practice with the .22s or other objectives.

But did they know they were going to attack the Moncada barracks?
No. They learned at the farm what the objective was to be, because they were trained in the idea that they wouldn't know, but that they'd be mobilized. Several times they'd been mobilized for other things.

So, well, then a problem arose. There was a cell of five university students who were real fire-eaters – we called them that because they were the super-tough guys, they thought they were the bravest of us all, etc., but when they found out that we were going to take the Moncada barracks they backed out. Inviting them along had been almost a courtesy. Because Pedrito Miret had trained several hundred students, and some of them got wind of our activity. They didn't belong to the main organization at the university, but rather to a sort of free-lance combatant group – but very gung-ho, you know, they were ready to have the world for breakfast. To avoid complications with them, we'd promised to include them in any serious action.

So they joined and came to Santiago. It was a kind of alliance, or micro-alliance, we had with this little group. They were active enemies of Batista and had shown that they wanted to go into action. Which was why the guys in this little group were mobilized – these 'tough guys', or apparently tough guys, because the students in general were very brave.

And at the farm, when they found out that the objective was the assault on the barracks, they didn't go?
No. When they saw all the preparations and everything, saw troops arriving – because all this time our troops were coming in, group after group, in all that period, well trained for combat . . . When they learned just before

dawn what the plan was, and we handed out uniforms, weapons and every-thing, they got cold feet . . . That group of tough, go-get-'em, gung-ho kids backed out.

So I said to them, 'All right, stay behind and leave after we do, at the end of the caravan, and follow us – we aren't going to force you to fight.'

What was the plan of attack?
My group's mission was to take the garrison headquarters, and it would have been easy. Wherever we sent people, they took everything by surprise, total surprise. The day we'd chosen, the 26th of July, was a very important day, because the *fiestas* in Santiago are on 25 July – the day of carnival.

I had 120 men, and I divided them into three groups – one went ahead to take a civilian hospital that bordered the rear of the barracks. That was the safest objective, and that's where I sent the second-in-command of the organization, Abel, an excellent kid, very intelligent, agile, daring. The girls, Haydée and Melba, were with him, and our medic, Dr Mario Muñoz, whose mission was to tend our wounded, who'd be sent there to them. At the back there was a wall that was excellent because it overlooked the rear part of the barracks dormitories.

The second group was to take the Audiencia building, the Palacio de Justicia, several storeys tall, with a kid who had been made leader. Raúl, my brother, also went with them – we'd recruited him and he came along as a rank-and-file combatant.

Me, with the third group, ninety men – my mission was to take the guard post and the General Staff offices with eight or nine men while the rest took the barracks. When I stopped, the other cars were to stop in front of the barracks. The soldiers were going to be asleep and they'd be pushed out of the barracks dormitories into the rear courtyard – overlooking the courtyard, from above, was the building where Abel and the men who'd taken the Audiencia would be. The soldiers were going to be in their underwear, because they wouldn't have had time to get dressed or pick up their weapons. There was no help for that, and all of us were dressed as sergeants, which was our insignia.

In theory, there doesn't seem to have been much danger.
Abel at the back [was] apparently in the least danger. Those who were to take the Audiencia shouldn't have much problem, either. I – knowing, of course, that Abel would be the one to take my place if I were killed – sent

him to that [relatively safe] position. I sent Raúl, who had only recently been recruited, with the group that was going to carry out a relatively more dangerous, important mission, though also, in my judgement, not particularly complicated. I had on my conscience all the weight of responsibility to my parents for including Raúl, at his age, in that rash and daring action. As was my duty and real necessity, I assigned myself the most complicated mission, behind the group made up of Jesús Montané, Ramirito Valdés, Guitart and several kids from Artemisa that was to take the entrance and lower the chain that blocked vehicle access. I had excellent combatants with me for this.

What time did you and your men set out from the farm?
About 4.45.

And what time did the attack begin?
At exactly 5.15 we attacked, because at that hour the soldiers had to be asleep, and it needed to be before they woke up. We attacked at 5.15. We needed a certain amount of light and at the same time, to [attack] when all the soldiers were still asleep.

Was it light yet?
Santiago is in the eastern part of the island, and in summer the sun comes up about twenty minutes earlier than in Havana. There was enough light to attack. All of that was calculated. Had it not been, we couldn't have attempted such an action. The job was not easy with men who, though trained in small groups, had never worked together – you had to sort out all the pieces, put the jigsaw puzzle together, and give each man his mission.

The attack began at 5.15. How was it carried out?
For this operation, which was intended to take two objectives, I had 120 men, as I said, minus those students who backed out, and about sixteen cars. There were at least eight of us in each car. With one that we left for the guys who backed out and another one that broke down, that meant two cars fewer. But we went on. The first car, carrying the men who were to be on the roof of the hospital, behind Moncada, started out, then the men that were going to occupy the roof of the Audiencia – they had further to go than we did. My group had ten or twelve cars, and it was to go to the main entrance of Moncada. I was in the second, about 100 yards behind, down

the highway from Siboney to Santiago. The sun was beginning to come up, and we were planning this total surprise, before reveille sounded. It was July, and the sun comes up earlier there in Oriente. So we were to arrive practically at daybreak. As you entered the city you had to cross a narrow little bridge, single file, one after another, each car, and that slowed us down a little.

Approximately 100 yards ahead, the first car was going down Avenida Garzón; it turned right down a side street towards the entrance to the barracks. I followed it, and the others followed behind.

Riding in that first car were Ramirito Valdés' men – Jesús Montané, Renato Guitart and a couple more. Montané had volunteered for the mission of taking the entrance. I was about eighty yards behind them at that point, about the right distance to continue on at a certain speed while they were overpowering the sentinels at the entrance and taking down the chains that prevented cars from driving into the interior of the installation. [There was a large interior courtyard.]

The first car stopped when it reached its objective and the men jumped out to neutralize the guards and take their weapons. It was at that point that I saw, about twenty yards or so in front of my car and to the left, a foot patrol of two soldiers with Thompson machine guns coming down the pavement. They realized that something was going on at the guard post, which was about sixty yards from them, I'd say, and they were in a position – or so it looked to me – to fire on Ramirito, Montané and the rest, who'd managed to disarm the guards already.

In a fraction of a second, two ideas went through my mind: neutralize that patrol that threatened our *compañeros*, and get [the two soldiers'] weapons. When I saw that the soldiers were aiming towards the entrance, which meant they'd turned their backs to me, I slowed the car and drove up closer, to capture them. So I was driving, holding the shotgun with my right hand and a pistol in my left, and I draw up alongside them, with my door half open. I was intending to do two things at once: keep them from firing on Ramirito and Montané's men and get the two Thompsons they were carrying.

There was another way of going about it, which I later saw perfectly clearly, when I'd gained a little more knowledge and experience. What I should have done was forget about them and just keep going. If those two soldiers had seen one car and another and another and another coming in, speeding towards them, they would never have fired. But that's not what I did

– what I did was try to come up from behind them and capture them by surprise. When I was probably about six feet away, they must have heard some noise, because they swung around, saw my car, and probably instinctively pointed their weapons at us. So I drove the car into them and jumped out.

The men with me jumped out too. The personnel in the cars that were coming up behind did the same thing. They thought they were inside the barracks facilities. Their mission was to take the dormitories and push the soldiers into the rear courtyard – barefoot, in their underwear, unarmed and half asleep, they'd be our prisoners.

What was it that didn't work, then?

The presence of that patrol, which had been assigned, I imagine, because of the carnival festivities, marching back and forth between the entrance to the barracks facilities and Avenida Garzón, was something we hadn't known anything about, and because they were so close to the guard post, they threw the plan off in a serious way. In our attempt to neutralize and disarm the patrol – in driving the car into them – all our men jumped out of their cars, with their weapons. One of the men who was with me, as he got out of the passenger side of the front seat, fired his weapon – the first shot heard in that most unusual combat. And at that, a lot more started firing. The firing kept spreading, and as it did the alarms started going off – the noise was deafening, unbelievable. All the men who'd been in the cars behind me got out, according to plan, and rushed into a long, relatively large building [constructed] in the same architecture as the other military facilities in the headquarters there. It was the military hospital, and they rushed into it thinking it was the objective they were supposed to occupy.

A building that was not one of your objectives?

The problem was that the combat that was supposed to take place *inside* the barracks complex was taking place *outside*. And in the confusion, some of the men captured the wrong building. By the time we got out of the cars, the foot patrol had disappeared. I immediately ran into the hospital to pull out the personnel who'd taken it by mistake. I got them all out – they were still on the ground floor. I managed to do that pretty quickly. I could almost get the caravan reorganized with six or seven cars, because despite everything, the guard post at the entrance had been taken.

Ramirito and Montané's group had already taken the sentry post at the gate, let down the chain, and entered one of the barracks inside the complex.

Then they headed towards the weapons depository. When they got there, they found that the army band was sleeping there. Apparently the weapons had been moved to the main barracks. The situation was pretty much the same in the other barracks, which hadn't been able to react to our surprise attack.

For their part, Abel's group occupied the building they were supposed to, and the group that Raúl was in took the Palacio de Justicia.

But by this time everybody was shooting.
Well, in those first moments the soldiers were still getting dressed – putting on their shoes, running around and getting organized, taking down their weapons – and it was only the guard posts that were firing, although it was mostly for the sake of the noise. The Rural Guard slept in one of the barracks, too, alongside the army regiment. They didn't sleep with their rifles by their beds, of course, and didn't have any commanders in the first few moments – some of the regimental officers were sleeping in their own homes. None of the officers or enlisted men in Moncada knew what was happening.

The combat took place outside the barracks, so the huge, decisive advantage of surprise had been lost.

I went, as I said, into the hospital building, and I managed to pull out and reorganize a small number of *compañeros* in several cars, intending to drive to the General Staff offices, when suddenly a car came up from behind and flew past us, drove to the entrance to the barracks complex, then backed up just as fast as it had come in and backed right into my car. Just like that! One guy, on his own initiative, in the midst of the increasing gunfire, pulled up, then backed up and ran into my car. So I got out again.

Under those adverse and unexpected circumstances, the men showed remarkable tenacity and courage. Heroic individual initiatives took place, but there was no longer any way to overcome the situation we'd created. The combat [was] under way, and this inevitable disorganization in our ranks . . .

We'd lost contact with the group in the car that had taken the sentry post. Abel's and Raúl's men, with whom we had no communication, could only go by the sound of the gunfire, which was now decreasing on our side, while the enemy, who'd recovered from the surprise and got itself organized, was defending its positions. *Compañero* Gildo Fleitas – I've already told you about him – was standing very calmly at the corner of a building near where we'd run into the foot patrol and observing the situation, which was desperate. I spoke to him for a few seconds. It was the last time I ever saw him. From the very first moments I realized there was no possible way of achieving our initial objective. You can take a barracks complex with a handful of men if the soldiers are asleep, but a barracks with more than 1,000 troops, awake and heavily armed – there was no way to take it. More than the shooting, I remember the deafening, bitter sounds of the alarm sirens that thwarted our plan.

It had become a mission impossible.
The complex could have been taken with the plan we'd formulated. Were I to make a plan again for a mission like that, I'd do exactly the same thing. The only difference, based on our experience, would be not to have paid the slightest attention to that foot patrol. Those things go through your head in a fraction of a second. Protecting our *compañeros* in danger was my main motivation.*

When did you decide to order the retreat?
The gunfire was still going strong. I explained to you, in considerable detail, what happened. But recalling it, in all honesty and with absolute objectivity, I believe that no more than thirty minutes had passed, maybe much less, when I resigned myself to the fact that the objective was now impossible. I knew the details better than anyone, and I knew on what basis that decision [to retreat] had to be made. I'd conceived and elaborated the plan in every detail.

There came a moment when I began to give orders to pull back. What did I do? I was in the middle of the street, not far from the guard post. I had my .22-calibre rifle, and on the roof of one of the main buildings in the complex there was a .50-calibre machine gun that could take out the entire street, because it was aimed directly at that point. A man was fidgeting with it, he was apparently by himself, he looked like some kind of monkey, jumping

* [(in 1st ed.:) If my car had gone on without stopping, and then another and another and another, those guards would have frozen in their tracks – they'd never have fired. The way to keep them from firing on Ramirito and Montané and their men was for them to see one car after another drive through there, to be surprised that we were attacking. We'd have taken the barracks complex in a walk. If you get out of the car dressed as a sergeant, with a gun in your hand and you yell, 'On the ground, everybody!', 'Everybody down!', you take the headquarters. Abel and the others would already have achieved their objectives, and would be standing over the rear courtyard of the complex. That was the plan.]

around trying to ready the gun and fire. I had to do something about him while the men got into the cars and retreated. Every time he tried to use the machine gun, I'd shoot at him. I was pretty keyed up, as you can imagine . . .

Now there was no one [from our group] to be seen, not a single combatant on foot. I got in the last car and while I was sitting there, in the back seat on the right, all of a sudden one of our men appeared – he just shows up, and he's about to be left behind. The car was full, but I got out and gave him my place. And I ordered the car to leave.

And I stood there, in the middle of the street, all by myself, totally alone. Unbelievable things happen in circumstances like that. There I was, all by myself in the street in front of the entrance to the barracks complex. It goes without saying that at that point I cared absolutely nothing about dying . . . And all of a sudden, I was rescued by another car. I don't know how, or why, but a car was coming towards me, and it pulled up beside me and picked me up. It was one of the kids from Artemisa, driving a car with several *compañeros* in it, and he drove up to me and rescued me. I was never able later – there was just no time – to ask him about all the details. I've always wished I could talk to that man to find out how and why he jumped back into the hell of that firefight. But as in so many other things, you think you've got 100 years to do it . . . And the man unfortunately died more than ten years ago.

He was with your group?

Yes, one of ours. Santana was his name. Apparently he realized that I'd been left behind so he came back to find me. He was one of the ones who'd got out, and apparently at some point he realized I hadn't so he turned back to look for me. There must be something written, some *testimonio*[13] or other about that episode.

I was absolutely alone out there . . . I had my .22 and that was it, and I didn't know what kind of gunfight might break out, or what the end of it all might have been . . . Of course I might have tried to retreat down some alley or something.

Did you fire during all this?

Yes, several times, at that man that was trying to fire his .50-calibre machine gun at us from the roof – but he never got a shot off.

You kept him from firing?
Yes. He'd move around and try to use the machine gun, I'd fire, and he'd duck. Then a few seconds later he'd be trying to make the machine gun work and I'd fire again. Several times he tried to use it, but I don't know, he apparently had second thoughts and never did, because it happened just the way I'm telling you. And while I was busy keeping the guy with the machine gun busy, our cars were retreating, with the personnel who'd accompanied me on the mission to penetrate the barracks complex and take it.

Under these circumstances, people act almost on their own initiative. This Santana who came back to pick me up did that, I believe, on his own initiative. There was nobody to give him that order. He drove in, drove over to me, and picked me up. The car was full, but I said, 'Let's go to El Caney.' There were several cars waiting out in the avenue, waiting for those of us who had trained them. But one or two of them in the lead didn't know where El Caney was, so instead of going straight down Avenida Garzón through Vista Alegre, they turned right, towards Siboney. There were three or four cars; the one that had picked me up was the second or third one in the little caravan.

I knew El Caney well – it was a place where there had been an important battle at the end of the second War of Independence in 1898. There was a relatively small barracks there. My idea was to drive there and surprise them and take it, in order to give support to the men at Bayamo. I didn't know what was happening in Bayamo. I assumed that they'd taken the barracks. And that was the main concern at that point. But our men had taken a hard blow already, and it's difficult to get them into action again.

What did the other groups do?
Of the group that was with me, when we retreated we didn't see any of them anywhere. We later learned that some of them, such as Pedro Miret, had taken cover somewhere, but we weren't sure – there was no contact with them.

The group that had taken the Palacio de Justicia realized what had happened and the leader came down with his little patrol, including Raúl. At the exit there was a sergeant with several men, and he ordered them to surrender. The leader of the group [of our men] turned over his weapons, so Raúl, who was just a private, you might say, and the others also turned over theirs, but just then Raúl saved them, and saved himself. He acted quickly, very very quickly – the sergeant was holding a pistol on them, and Raúl saw that his hand was shaking, so Raúl grabs the pistol and takes the squad that was taking them prisoner, prisoner! If he hadn't, the same thing that happened to all the others would have happened to them: torture and execution . . . When they got out of there, they looked for an escape – somewhere to go, somewhere to change clothes, get moving, and then they dispersed.

Had you foreseen this at all?
No, we hadn't foreseen this.

You hadn't made plans for a possible retreat?
No, how the devil were we going to foresee such a thing? How can you foresee a retreat in an operation like that?

But if something went wrong, there was no provision for a retreat?
No, no. In an operation conceived in that way, the way I explained it to you, how are you going to retreat if you're inside the barracks complex and you've lost control of the men stationed there? They had posts at all the possible entrances and exits – how are you going to retreat?

We had, though, managed to do the essential thing, which was to achieve total surprise up until unexpectedly and coincidentally running into that foot patrol, and you've got to regret not knowing what might have happened. But I have not the slightest doubt that the soldiers in there would have been taken prisoner, and in a question of minutes, just like that, as I said. There'd have been tremendous confusion in their ranks, and our uniforms would have contributed to that confusion.

Did Abel's men, seeing all this, try to get out?
No, they stayed there, waiting, because the people in the hospital tried to protect them. Everybody in the hospital supported them – they disguised them and tried to protect them when it became clear that the mission had failed and they no doubt thought we were all dead. My mind was calm about them, because Abel knew the plan perfectly. My instantaneous concern when the car came to rescue me was how to support the men that attacked the Bayamo barracks.

You'd have to talk to Melba, who still remembers, and all this has been written about – it's only once in a very rare while that I talk about this. What's the name of that historian who wrote about the early years? He's got the story, because he questioned everybody. What was his name? The one who wrote that history, the Frenchman?

Robert Merle. A wonderful book.[14] But I'm interested in your version, your personal version.
Yes, I never had the chance to tell Merle what I'm telling you.

How many casualties did your men suffer?
There were five killed in the combat and another fifty-six who were murdered [later]. The five killed in combat were Gildo Fleitas, Flores Betancourt, Carmelo Noa, Renato Guitart and Pedro Marrero. Almost all of them were in the first car, those who took up positions in the first building inside the complex after they'd taken the sentry post. Several of them, though, did manage to survive. Wait . . . Gildo wasn't in that group, because Gildo was with me as we tried to get a group of cars together again to penetrate the barracks complex.

You must have been terribly crestfallen by that situation.
At that moment I was terribly bitter about what had happened. But I was ready to go on with the struggle. I said, 'Those men in Bayamo are going to be hung out to dry.' Assuming, you see, that they'd taken the barracks.[15] So, as I said, my idea was to go to the barracks in El Caney and attack it, to support the men in Bayamo, to create a combat situation in the area of Santiago de Cuba. Yes, my idea was to take the avenue that went straight to the highway to El Caney, and there were about twenty of us. But the car in front, as I said, made a mistake and turned right, and the next one turned off after it. So there was no way to cut off that car and carry out the operation in El Caney before they learned what had happened at Moncada. I wasn't driving, you see, I'd been picked up by another car.

Did you still have your uniforms on?
Yes, we did.

And you had your weapons?
We had our weapons, all of them, up to the very last minute, even for several days afterwards.

Did you go back to the farm, then?
Yes, we went back to Siboney to regroup after the attack. Several cars had gone there, so I found a little of everything there – men who wanted to keep going and others who were taking off their uniforms. Some of them were

stashing weapons, [there were] men wounded, people who couldn't walk
. . . A very sad sight.

I got there and what I did was convince a group . . . and I and nineteen other
men took off into the mountains. I couldn't give any support to the men at
Bayamo. I wasn't going to give myself up, I wasn't going to surrender or
anything of the sort – there was no sense [in doing that], not because I was
going to be killed but because the idea of surrendering was just inconceivable
to us.

5

The Backdrop of the Revolution

*Bolívar – Slavery and independence – Autonomists and pro-Americans –
The two Wars of Independence – Carlos Manuel de Céspedes –
Máximo Gómez – Antonio Maceo – José Martí*

**Comandante, *the year 2003 was not just the 150th anniversary of the birth
of José Martí but also the fiftieth anniversary of the assault on the Moncada
barracks. Might one say that 26 July 1953 marked the beginning of the
Cuban Revolution?***

That wouldn't be completely fair, because the Cuban Revolution began with
the first War of Independence in 1868, which started in Oriente province
on 10 October of that year. The war was led by a very well-trained and
well-educated Cuban, Carlos Manuel de Céspedes.[1] In that area, slavery was
not so widespread. Slavery was, however, deeply entrenched in the western
part of the country, which had the great coffee plantations and later the
sugar-cane plantations. These properties experienced a real boom on account
of the slave rebellion on the French plantations.

The slave rebellion in Haiti,[2] in 1791?

That's right, in Haiti. Many of those French landowners came to Cuba, to
Oriente province, nearest Haiti – [the two islands] are separated by just the
Windward Passage, as it's called.

There had always been some traffic, even in the times of the indigenous
peoples, between Cuba and the region that's now Haiti, on the western side of
the island that the Spaniards named Hispaniola. Those tribes, in part Caribs,
were more combative [than other indigenous groups], and they offered quite
a bit of resistance to the Spaniards, and some crossed over to the eastern
side of Cuba [in retreat from the Spaniards' incursions into their lands].

So when the conquest and colonization of Cuba began, there were some native people here who had come over from Hispaniola, and these people put up a certain degree of resistance in that area, in the east. One of them was named Hatuey. Hatuey is one of Cuba's important historical figures, the first person who made any attempt to resist [the Spanish invasion], because the indigenous tribes that were native to our country were very peaceable. The *conquistadores* came in with horses, swords, crossbows, harquebuses and so on, and the native peoples were not able to resist them, but some of them actually tried.

The difference in technological progress was just too great.
The Spaniards arrived with 800 years of warfare behind them, and they flooded these islands with warriors – *conquistadores*, conquerors. They were a people who had fought for their own independence, against the Arab occupation.

And at one point, you were saying, the slaves rebelled in Haiti.
In 1791, when the slave rebellion led by Toussaint L'Ouverture took place in Haiti, there were about 400,000 slaves there.[3] A few hundred – maybe 2,000 or 3,000, but all it took was a few hundred – French planters and slave owners fled here to Cuba. Some of them brought some of their slaves with them, and they settled in the easternmost part of Cuba.

In the rest of the island there was no slavery?
I told you that where slavery was most widespread was the *western* part of the country. In the former province of Oriente, there was some slavery, but on a smaller scale, because most of the agriculture in that area was dedicated to raising cattle and smaller-scale crops. It was the [eastern] part of Cuba that had the largest number of individual landowners; after it came Camagüey, with large tracts of land, which was mostly cattle-raising country, and which also had very few slaves.

But from the centre of the island westward, many, many coffee and sugar-cane plantations were based on slave labour, and in Matanzas and Havana provinces there were hundreds of small sugar-cane *centrales*, whose machinery was often driven by animal power. Cuba became the world's largest producer and exporter of coffee [after the slave rebellion in Haiti], since it moved into the coffee markets that had formerly been dominated by that country.

In the 1840s, two great hurricanes wiped out the coffee plantations, but sugar cane is more resistant to hurricanes and drought – it's a safer crop. A hurricane can reduce the [sugar cane] harvest by 20 or 25 per cent, but the entire plantation isn't lost. It was a better crop, but it also needed many, many slaves.

At the time, twenty or thirty years before the first War of Independence began, in 1868, there were approximately 300,000 slaves in Cuba.

Of a total population of how many inhabitants?
I couldn't say exactly, but I calculate between one and one and a half million people, maybe, including the slaves. The rest of the population were descendants of Spaniards in the first period of colonization, the 'criollos', as they're called, who were the owners of the land and the plantations, and the mestizos born to Spanish fathers and Indian mothers, and later a mixture of Spanish, Indian and black blood. Those Peninsular Spaniards controlled the island's administration, trade, internal order and defence.

The greatest number of slaves was on the sugar-cane plantations, owned by the criollos. That fact had tremendous influence, because after the wars of independence in Spanish America, the only colonies Spain had left in the hemisphere were Cuba and Puerto Rico. Although there was an independence movement in Santo Domingo in 1821, which went so far as to proclaim its brotherhood with the Colombia of Simón Bolívar, Spain reoccupied Hispaniola for a time in the nineteenth century. But [on Hispaniola, in what is now the Dominican Republic, then called Santo Domingo], the wars were fought more against neighbouring Haiti [than against Spain, for independence]. Between 1850 and 1860, more or less, before our first War of Independence, a certain number of Dominicans came to Cuba. Some of them had served in the Spanish army, so they came to Cuba as Spanish citizens, although they had been born in Santo Domingo. They had military experience, and afterwards – they were *campesinos*, farmers – they joined the Cuban patriots.

How did that first War of Independence begin?
The 1868 war was started by a group of landowners. They had some education, and a certain amount of culture. Many of them were lawyers. They were liberal in their thought, they favoured independence, and they tended to be small-scale slave owners – some of them owned sugar-cane plantations. Big plantations of coffee, with large numbers of slaves, were only in the region of Guantánamo, [in the east,] near Haiti.

The leader of the *independentista* revolution, a very distinguished, cultured man, was Carlos Manuel de Céspedes, as I said, and he owned one of the small sugar-cane *centrales*. The conspiracy started in Camagüey province and spread to include practically all the landowners of the eastern part of the island. Of course those conspiracies are always discovered in one way or another, and the authorities even sent out an arrest order, but the leaders of the revolution had friends in the post offices. Carlos Manuel de Céspedes learned that he was about to be arrested and he moved the date of the uprising forward – he launched it on 10 October 1868, on his sugar-cane *central*. He freed his small group of slaves. There weren't many, but he set them free without one moment's hesitation, thereby decreeing the revolutionary abolition of slavery in Cuba.

Was it common in those days to free slaves?
No, not at all, so that was a grand gesture, you might say, an unprecedented gesture, the opposite of what happened in South America. Because in South America, when the War of Independence began in 1810 – triggered by France's occupation of Spain and the establishment of a new monarchy when Napoleon made his brother, Joseph Bonaparte, king – the Spanish colonies rose up not against Spain but against the Napoleonic monarchy imposed on Spain, which is how the patriotic juntas came to be created in South America and other parts of the hemisphere that were Spanish colonies.

The first of the juntas was created in Venezuela, in April 1810, and it was called the 'Conservative Junta of the Rights of Fernando VII' – that is, the king dethroned by Napoleon. There had been a precursor of independence in Venezuela – Francisco de Miranda,[4] a famous figure. Miranda had even taken part in the American Revolution, the United States' own War of Independence, because Spain under Charles III sent soldiers born in South America, and also in Cuba – blacks, mestizos and criollo Spaniards alike – to fight for the colonies' independence. This was in 1776, before the French Revolution, which began thirteen years later, in 1789. Lafayette, a future participant in the French Revolution, also took part in that war, alongside many Spanish volunteers.[5] The rivalry between France and England, of course, was bitter, and Spain was on France's side. So there were Cubans, people born in Cuba, who fought for the independence of the United States.

There are strange links one finds in history . . . Miranda, a Spanish officer, born in Venezuela, decided to desert from the colonial army while he was posted in Cuba, so it was in Havana that he began the long anti-imperialist struggle that led him to conceive the project for what would be Colombia – that is, the liberation and unification of all our peoples into one great independent political bloc. He emigrated to France, became a distinguished military commander under the leaders of the French Revolution, and fought against those who tried to invade revolutionary France – and he distinguished himself immensely. But at a certain point he fell out of favour, as often happened [in revolutionary France], and he was almost guillotined at one point. But then the authorities realized their error. What saved him was the immense service he'd given France. He had been all over Europe, he'd become famous, and he was the precursor of South American independence. He even disembarked in Venezuela to start the fight; that was August 1806.

Did this occur before Simón Bolívar began the fight for the independence of Spanish South America?

Oh, long before. When these events I'm telling you about took place – the events that led to the installation of a Napoleonic monarchy in Spain – the juntas were created out of a sense of loyalty to Spain [under the thumb of Napoleon], although there were people in the juntas who were strong supporters of independence. One of those was, in fact, Simón Bolívar. They created the Caracas junta, the first in Spanish America to declare independence – and there was Bolívar, a very young officer at the time.

Bolívar had gone to Italy with his tutor and mentor Simón Rodríguez, and on 15 August 1805, on Monte Sacro, he made his famous vow to fight for the independence of Venezuela. It's hard to imagine that incredible premonition.

Did they free the slaves?

No, they – the criollos, I mean – didn't initially free the slaves. There was just not enough awareness of the problem at that time. José Tomás Boves,[6] a clever Asturian, took advantage of that contradiction. Boves went to the *llaneros*,[7] who were Indians and mestizos, fearsome horsemen, in those broad plains full of almost-wild horses, and there he carried out, in his own way, a sort of agrarian reform: since the land belonged to the criollo rebels, he expropriated it and distributed the land, distributed the haciendas, and turned the *llaneros* into what we might call the lords and masters of all of that, and at the head of a force of these pro-Spanish troops he advanced across the plains, in the most devastating way, mercilessly burning and killing. It was a fierce class war between Venezuelan and Venezuelan, promoted by the Spanish colonialists. That was the so-called Poor Men's Rebellion of 1814.

Arturo Uslar Pietri,[8] a very famous Venezuelan author who's quite brilliant as a writer although not so much as a politician, performed a great service to posterity by writing a novel about that episode; it's called *Las lanzas coloradas*. 'The Red Lances'. Its descriptions are so vivid that you can practically hear the thunder of horses galloping across the plains. It was that army of poor *llaneros*, slaves and semi-slaves with their unstoppable cavalry that defeated the *independentista* Venezuelans and finally reached Caracas. And at that point there begins an episode unparalleled in this continent's wars of independence: the retreat of the population of Caracas to the east. This action is known in Venezuelan history as the 'eastward emigration', and it was led personally by Bolívar. It cost the lives of countless women, children, young people and elderly. What an incredible price the Venezuelan people paid for their independence, and with what dignity and integrity they bore up under [the struggle]!

This took place after the creation of the Second Republic, which had been born out of that memorable series of battles known as the 'Admirable Campaign'. Bolívar marched from the Magdalena River, in New Granada, now Colombia, in late 1812, and in August 1813 he entered Caracas, where he was proclaimed the 'Liberator'.

But before that, at the time the First Republic was proclaimed, in 1810, Bolívar was not yet a political and military leader; it was Miranda who was called to serve, and who was supported by those involved in the revolution. And Miranda, in the face of imminent defeat, made peace. He was on the point of taking an English ship at La Guaira when Bolívar and a group of officers unhappy with the peace Miranda was making with Spain arrested him. Miranda had acquired many French customs – certain habits, bathing, the life lived by distinguished people, the nobles, that sort of thing – and instead of being aboard the English ship, he had stayed on shore that night, where he could rest more comfortably. That gave [Bolívar and the others] time to arrest him.

But Spain had retaken power, thanks to the llaneros' *offensive.*
No, no. The *llaneros* acted afterwards, when independence was reestablished and the Second Republic was created in 1813. What I just told you about happened before, when Miranda signed a treaty of peace with Spain. Bolívar and his friends had to escape, and they managed to capture a ship. Miranda

was turned over to the Spanish commander, Domingo Monteverde. Bolívar sailed [north-]west, towards the island of Bonaire, which was a Dutch possession, disembarked in the neighbourhood of the Magdalena River, in Venezuela, and upriver, with a handful of men, he began an overwhelming offensive – an action that history has called the 'Admirable Campaign'.

Some of the patriotic [i.e., pro-independence] troops were still within the territory of New Granada. Bolívar arrived, called them together, and started the war again. They recaptured Caracas and reestablished the patriotic administration. But the slaves were still not freed. At that point – 26 March 1812, a Maundy Thursday – an earthquake struck, and Bolívar made that famous declaration, 'If Nature opposes our designs, then we shall fight against her and make her obey.' Terrible earthquake, wonderful turn of phrase!

It was after the second defeat of the Republic that he retreated from Venezuela and went off to Jamaica. He somehow miraculously survived a plot to assassinate him. And it was there that he wrote his famous *Letter from Jamaica*, and there, too, in 1816, that he came in contact with President Pétion of Haiti.[9] Pétion began to exert an influence on Bolívar with regard to the freeing of the slaves; he helped him with arms, and Bolívar made a vow that was now absolutely consonant with his revolutionary thinking: he promised to abolish slavery. He had learned the great lesson of what had happened with the First and Second Republics. So then the struggle for the Third began. His expedition left Haiti and disembarked on Venezuelan soil, and there, on 6 July 1816, he delivered the 'Ocumare Manifesto'. One of its first paragraphs states: 'That unfortunate portion of our brothers who have groaned under the hardships of slavery is now free. Nature, justice and policy call for the emancipation of the slaves; from this time forward, in Venezuela there shall be one single class of men, and all shall be citizens.'

From the island of Margarita the Liberator came down to the Orinoco to what today is Ciudad Bolívar, and there, in Angostura, he formulated the ideas for the Constitution of 1819 and decreed the abolition of slavery. José Antonio Páez, a patriotic *llanero*, brought many of those Indian and mestizo *llaneros* with him when he joined the struggle, and from those events on, victory was assured. That just gives you an eloquent example of the relationship between independence and the abolition of slavery.

In Cuba, was Céspedes the first to free the slaves?
Yes – when Carlos Manuel de Céspedes began that first War of Independence. The decree was applied throughout Oriente and Camagüey. Many of

the freed slaves then joined the patriots. That war lasted ten years. And it was there that the brilliant Dominican-born leader Máximo Gómez[10] emerged. And another leader, brilliant as well, a black man.

Antonio Maceo?
That's right, Maceo, the most brilliant of our soldiers, a black man, born in 1845 in Santiago de Cuba. He was twenty-three when the war started.

Apparently, some of the criollos who rebelled against Spain in 1868 did so in the hope of joining the United States. Is that true?
The idea of independence had to face many different currents of thought throughout the eighteenth and nineteenth centuries, among them reformist currents, autonomist currents and annexationist currents.

Spanish colonialism was different from the British version. The Spaniards are not the British – their colonialism was not the same; they were a different type of colonialist, [there was] even a different treatment of the slaves. One positive thing about the Spaniards: they allowed African slaves to have their [religious] rites, they authorized them. In some sense, it was a way of keeping them quieter, because in this climate, in this territory, with the exploitation and mistreatment to which the slaves were subjected, there were many rebellions; many slaves escaped and then were ruthlessly hunted down – but they were allowed to keep their customs and their religious traditions.

Think how different it was in the United States. In the United States the slaves were not allowed to worship in their own ways; as a result, practically all there is is Christianity, including Catholicism. There are other religions, of course – Islam, Judaism, Buddhism – but there are hardly any forms of worship of African origin. Here, on the other hand, Catholicism was almost universal; there was hardly any presence of other Christian religions, but there did exist, among that mass of slaves, certain African-inspired forms of worship. And by virtue of religious syncretism, some of the figures of the Catholic church were used with different names and introduced into the rites and rituals of the Africans,[11] through the gods that they had, gods [the African slaves] believed in. That was an important difference.

That may be why some criollos wanted to join the United States.
There was a certain degree of annexationist sentiment among some of those patriots, even some who revolted, because it had not been very long at all since the War of Secession in the United States, which lasted from 1861 to

1865, in which the North had won the war and Abraham Lincoln had emerged as an extremely prestigious figure.

But since the early nineteenth century there had been some degree of annexationist sentiment among many slave-owning criollo landowners in Cuba, especially in the western region of the island – a desire to become a part of the United States. The English had prohibited slave trafficking, and the Cuban criollos were afraid that the British would decree – and impose on the whole Caribbean – the abolition of slavery. What England had already abolished was the *trafficking* of slaves – that is, the transport of slaves from Africa. So an annexationist sentiment emerged, and it was encouraged in the United States by the Southerners, who were opposed to the Northerners and competed for votes in the Senate. If the Southerners created a new slave state in the South, the Northerners created another one [that was slave-free], until the moment came when the Northerners, who for logical economic reasons and out of more liberal ideas opposed the system of slavery, won the majority. That's the moment at which the War of Secession broke out and slavery was abolished. That was in 1861.

The image of Abraham Lincoln, the Northern leader, was very much esteemed already, but until then, in the western part of Cuba, the slave owners – the immense majority of them, not all of them, there are always exceptions – wanted to join the South. An annexationist sentiment emerged, but as I said, this sentiment prevailed in the western part of Cuba but extended only slightly into the eastern region, where the [Cuban] War of Independence originated.

Did they really plan to secede from Spain and join the United States?
Carlos Manuel de Céspedes didn't, nor did the immense majority of those who rebelled, but in the region of Camagüey [in the east-centre of the island] there was some influence from people who had annexationist ideas, fundamentally, I think, due to hatred of Spain. At that point, there was some influence from the fact that after a bloody civil war, slavery had just been abolished in the United States and a figure as prominent and attractive as Abraham Lincoln, later assassinated, had emerged. When our first War of Independence began, in 1868, that annexationist sentiment had not been totally eradicated in some of those people, who viewed Céspedes as something of a *caudillo*.[12]

He was, on the other hand, an extraordinary man – patriotic, daring, generous. He launched the struggle [for independence] before he could be arrested, he freed the slaves, he accepted the position of general-in-chief, and he adopted a flag very different from that of the United States. Those people were very formalistic – in the middle of the war they got together a group of men to draft a constitution, had long involved discussions, much debate, even on the matter of the flag. Due to obvious rivalries and reservations on the part of some of the framers about Céspedes's flag, the flag that the struggle had begun with was rejected.

Finally, the one adopted was the one brought in by General Narciso López[13] in 1850, which was very similar to the flag of Texas, with a star inside a triangle. For a long time, Narciso López was seen in Cuba as a hero. He had been one of the Spanish military leaders who fought in the Battle of Carabobo, in 1821, the battle that sealed Venezuela's independence, which came three years later.

Did he fight alongside Bolívar?
No, Narciso López, a distinguished officer in the Spanish army, fought with the Spanish, *against* Bolívar. He returned to Spain, then came to Cuba, [changed sides,] joined the patriots, then had to flee, so he fled to the United States. It's very strange that he should emerge as a liberator of Cuba, at the head of a force that came down from the United States, which always wanted to devour our island. Narciso López organized an expedition that was financed by Southern slave-holders – that's where the idea of a flag inspired by the Texas flag came from. In the midst of great historical confusion, his flag was the first to be raised in a war against Spanish oppression, and it remained as the symbol of a war of independence, when actually it was a war of annexation.

Historians later discovered all this, but for a long time, even after the supposedly sovereign Republic of Cuba had been instituted, that war was considered to be a patriotic war. As is obvious, imperialism and its allies had no interest in clarifying that episode.

In the Constituent Assembly of 1868–9, when the Parliament was created – it was an *itinerant* Parliament, in the midst of an irregular war, you can imagine what a complicated situation that must have been – that flag, not the flag of Carlos Manuel de Céspedes, was adopted.

Still, that flag of doubtful origin did become the flag of Cuba that is flown today.
Yes, because it is a symbol of glory. Adopted in that Constituent Assembly,

it is the flag of the heroic struggles of our people, and [it has been] the glorious flag of all Cubans for more than 135 years of unceasing battle for independence yesterday and Socialism today. It has been washed clean of its alien origins a thousand times over by the purest and most patriotic blood that has ever been spilled, and thanks to which Cuba exists today, in confrontation with the most powerful empire that has existed in all the history of humanity. It became the national flag and it has flown over all our struggles, down to this day.

If I understand correctly, many Cuban criollos were not seeking to make Cuba independent, but rather to break Cuba's ties to Spain in order to become a state of the United States, and in particular one of the Southern states, which were slave states, and anti-abolitionist.

In Cuba, what there was was a slave society, in which the great majority of the rich were slave owners and annexationists, who feared the abolition of slavery. It was different in the eastern area, with the exception of Guantánamo, where there was slavery, and deeply entrenched. So in the first few years of the war, Maceo, that black leader who was beginning to distinguish himself, was sent off by Máximo Gómez to invade Guantánamo, where he fought bloody battles against the Spanish forces on the coffee plantations in order to free the slaves. Many French names are still to be found in Santiago de Cuba and all that region, because slaves were given the name of the plantation owners [who had originally come over from St Domingue/Haiti]. That's the reason for the many, many French surnames.

That first war, in 1868, was lost by the patriots.

That's right, and unquestionably due to a lack of unity in the last stage of the war.

But although the war was lost, you say that it marked the beginning of the Cuban Revolution.

That's where we say the Revolution began. For us, the great struggle began at that point, and it went on for ten years! It's incredible how much resistance was put up against the Spaniards, who were both powerful and very stubborn, plus against a number of Cubans who were opposed to independence – they tended to be the plantation owners, so even though the slaves had been freed in the United States in 1862, slavery wasn't abolished here until 1886. Still, all the freed slaves in the eastern half of the island – wherever the patriotic troops reached, from Oriente province almost to Matanzas – joined the War of Independence. They were led, generally speaking, by people who of course had more education and wider culture. There were many brilliant black officers among the leaders. I mentioned Maceo, who was born in Santiago de Cuba, a patriotic man of humble origins who possessed a remarkable gift for command, great intelligence, and a good level of culture, despite his very modest background.

That war, too, had its internationalist aspects. Often coming from great distances, many foreigners joined the ranks of patriotic Cubans. I might, for example, mention the case of Henry Reeve, whom the *mambises*[14] called 'El Inglesito', the little Englishman, although he was American – born in Brooklyn, New York. As a young man he'd fought with the forces of Abraham Lincoln against the Southern secessionists, and after the Civil War he came as a volunteer to Cuba to fight against the slave holders and colonialists. Here, he attained the rank of brigadier general. He fought under one of our greatest heroes, General Ignacio Agramonte, and after Agramonte's death his commanding officer was Máximo Gómez, who had great regard for his bravery and his qualities as both leader and combatant. After seven years of heroic action in that war, he fell in combat against the Spaniards in 1876, at just twenty-six years of age.

What happened after that war?
After the Ten Years' War, there was a hiatus. The country was exhausted. Then came what was called the 'Guerra Chiquita', the Little War – some disembarkations and other actions. But there weren't enough forces, Cuba hadn't recovered from that destructive ten-year-long struggle, so it wasn't until 1895, seventeen years later, that the second war began.

And its principal protagonist was José Martí.
Yes, Martí, who was born 150 years ago, in January 1853 ... When the first War of Independence broke out, the war of 1868, Martí was fifteen years old. He was the son of a Spanish officer, a Spanish army captain.

Who'd taken part in the war ... ?
No, he hadn't. He'd been in Cuba, he belonged to the Havana garrison, but at the time of his son's birth there was no war going on. Martí was born in 1853, so when the war started, he was fifteen years old.

He had a remarkable, a singular talent, and as a very young man, in his adolescence, he was imprisoned; he was shackled and made to work in the quarries. He had a good tutor who was characterized by his *independentista* ideas. A miracle of a man, with extraordinary talent. He was held prisoner in the quarries, and later he wrote wonderful things: *El presidio político en Cuba*, 'The Political Prison in Cuba', for example. In Spain he wrote *La República española ante la Revolución cubana*, 'The Spanish Republic's Response to the Cuban Revolution', because a movement had emerged that established a republic in Spain, the republic of 1874, and that republic was waging a bloody war against Cuba, which wanted to be independent. He discussed all the contradictions: *El presidio político en Cuba* and *La República española* later . . . what extraordinary documents! And at sixteen and twenty years old – it's incredible!

What did Martí do afterwards? Did he stay in Spain for a while?
Afterwards? Well, he went to school there. He was not strong physically – his physical constitution was not good – he was in exile, he'd been out of the country since he was very young. Later, he went to Mexico and Guatemala. He returned to Cuba after the 'peace of Zanjón', which ended the Ten Years' War, and after a second exile in Spain, on his way back to Latin America he passed through France and England. He spent some time in Venezuela, too. In 1880 he arrived in the United States.

You clearly feel great admiration for José Martí.
The merit of Martí, the greatest merit is the following: The war that was fought between 1868 and 1878 came to an end; by that last year Martí had become a young intellectual and a patriot – a poet, a writer, a man of *independentista* ideas – and at the age of twenty-five this young man took the first steps on the road that would bring him to the command of the veterans of that hard and glorious Ten Years' War – veterans that he himself had reunited for just that purpose. There's nothing in the world harder than bringing military veterans together, especially if the man who wants to do that is an intellectual who's been away in Spain and never been to war. And Martí managed to bring them back together! What talent and abilities! What thought, what resolve, what moral strength! He formulated a doctrine, he propounded a philosophy of independence and an exceptional humanistic philosophy. Martí spoke about hatred more than once: 'We harbour no hatred for the Spaniard . . .' He was very understanding in that regard.

That was his principal merit?

His greatest merit, from my point of view, is that he managed to bring together extremely famous generals and lead them, politically. He had great, great character, he was a superb debater, and at a certain point he even broke with some of them. But he united the Cubans abroad, organized them into a revolutionary party, gave rousing speeches, raised money – he did concrete things [i.e., as opposed to theorizing about independence], and of a wide variety. He developed an idea of a united Latin America – he was a great admirer of Bolívar, a great admirer of Juárez,[15] all the men who fought for the independence of the nations of Latin America. He wrote that the day he arrived in Venezuela, 'before he'd washed off the dust of the road, the first thing he did was visit the statue of Bolívar, there in Caracas – a beautiful act. It's a pity his thinking is not better known throughout 'Our Americas'.

Of course later, Martí became better and better known in Cuba. He had managed to bring together all those famous generals who'd done great deeds of war, make them adherents to his cause and his party. He organized the war, and when it was about to begin, his armaments were seized, up there in the United States.

And despite everything he went on with his plans to begin the war?

That's exactly right. His arms had been seized, but despite everything he gave the order and came, he didn't postpone the decision to begin the struggle – the order had already been given. And he had no money left; he raised a little, he went to Santo Domingo, met with Máximo Gómez, the most outstanding military strategist [in the Caribbean]. Maceo was in Central America. The main leaders were in various places, some of them even in the United States. Martí organized their disembarkations here. The war began in the area of Matanzas, an area of sugar-cane plantations and many slaves, and also in the area of Oriente province, where the tradition of insurrection was still alive. Martí went to Santo Domingo, drew up a manifesto, what's called the 'Montecristi Manifesto', in which he set out the major programme of the *independentista* revolution. With tremendous effort, from a German ship that happened to be sailing through that area, the *Norstrand*, he managed to board and then came ashore on a small boat on a stormy night. He landed at a place called Playitas, with six or seven men.

Those who came over from Central America, such as Maceo, had also been through a very hard time, as hard as ours after the *Granma* landing in

1956. But they were combatants from before. And some had belonged to groups who had put down the native peoples in the area and kept them down, [so they'd] been very well indoctrinated by the Spaniards; they were fearsome ... Maceo found himself isolated after his landing near Baracoa, but he managed to reach the area near Santiago, and by the time Martí and Máximo Gómez landed ten days later, Maceo already had thousands of men on horseback.

That war, its tactics, its guerrilla techniques – did all that serve as a model for you in the Sierra Maestra after 1956?
In the 1895–8 war, the Cubans faced over 300,000 Spanish combatants. It was a terrible war, the Vietnam of the nineteenth century. And the Cuban combatants, the *mambises*, were forced to wage an 'irregular' war. In the view of the time, the strategy was to invade [and cripple] the rich areas of the western part of the island. The *mambises* burned everything in their path.

In that we were different, because we introduced an innovation that better suited our particular conditions: we didn't destroy the sugar industry. If you destroy that industry, you have no way of collecting taxes, or buying supplies and equipment and sometimes even bullets, weapons, [so] you have no way of ambushing troops that are moving in to protect the industry. We had another idea. The tactic of the combatants in 1895 was the torch – they burned everything, sugar cane and sugar factory. They burned all the *centrales* from one end of the island to the other, because the money to finance the Spanish side of the war came from the sugar industry. This colony, you see, Cuba, was the world's main exporter of sugar, and therefore supplied Spain with endless resources. We exported sugar to the United States, Europe, anywhere, and the idea of those combatants was to destroy that source of funds.

What we did was *not* burn the sugar-cane *centrales* and [then] collect the taxes when we could. In the end, we collected so much money from taxes that when the war ended we had around $8 million in cash. Some proprietors wound up paying later, but they paid. Plus, the sugar *centrales* were the only source of employment, of subsistence, for the mass of labourers and *campesinos* who supported us.

In the 1895 war, were there rivalries between Martí and the other leaders, Maceo or Máximo Gómez?
Martí described that whole long process of preparations for the war, and

the war's beginnings. He kept a campaign diary and set down every detail. It was wonderful, what he wrote. And I have to add this: when Maceo believed that the little money they sent him for a landing in Cuba was not enough, Martí found himself in the position of having to assign another leader the task of organizing the expedition with the resources available. So Maceo – even though he was the most distinguished, the most experienced, the most prestigious commander – came [to Cuba] that way, under another officer, Flor Crombet, who'd been made temporary commander by Martí. Maceo landed, as I told you, in the area of Baracoa, under very, very difficult conditions, and he soon took command of thousands of men. On the ground, it was he who controlled the situation.

It was hard to persuade him that Martí had done the right thing, made the right decision, in face of such a desperate shortage of resources. Máximo Gómez and Martí arrived at the camp. Maceo greeted them, but almost as guests. There was a moment, and Martí wrote about this in his diary, when Maceo became bitter. The first day they arrived, they slept outside the camp, then later they came in and discussed things, and apparently the discussions – arguments, really – were heated. Martí says that Maceo complained of the way he'd been treated. He was still aggrieved. But he finally accepted the decision. He was an honest, noble, disciplined man, and he continued to behave that way through the entire war.

Did Martí take part in the struggle? As an intellectual, did he have any experience of military combat?
Well, due to the reasons I've explained to you, he'd had no possibility of gaining that experience. Within a few days of leaving Maceo's camp – this would be May, 19 May 1895 – an unexpected battle took place: a Spanish column was on the move and there was an encounter not far from where Martí was – Martí was ready to fight. Máximo Gómez, an experienced fighter, gave Martí an order, 'No, you stay here,' and he left him with a young orderly. It was like telling a man of such great professional pride, 'Look, you don't know anything about these things, just stay here.' Much the same happened to me in Bogotá in 1948. [Although I have to say,] I'd been in more combat actions, seen more danger, than the officers who ordered me to stay back.

In 1948, when Gaitán was killed.[16]
Yes, they told me more or less the same thing – 'No, you stay here.' It was

Cuban soldiers visiting Venezuela and staying in the consulate, where a fire-fight had just broken out at the entrance. But that's another story.

The people received Martí with great love and sympathy, they hailed him as their president: ¡*Viva el presidente!* ¡*Viva Martí!* He talked to the people, they got to know him, he had organized that whole [uprising], and they called him president – there was no other one.

And Máximo Gómez didn't like [the fact that Martí was called 'president']?
No, it wasn't that. The general-in-chief, a Dominican, Máximo Gómez, was an honourable, exceptional man, a man of great rigour, discipline, but he had a terrible temper. And he would say, referring to Martí – Martí wrote this in his diary – 'I won't have him called president' – as though fearing it would go to his head – 'I won't have it. As long as I live, Martí will never be president.' I'm not quoting exactly, but it's the essence, it's the way I remember it. But [Gómez] also said that because he didn't have a very high opinion of the position of president in a Republic at Arms, because in the middle of a war he thought such a position was impracticable – there was no way for there to be a seat of government. But he did see Martí as a man who had a special purity about him.

Then, when that day in May 1895 came, and suddenly this combat broke out, he told Martí to stay there with an orderly, a man named Angel de la Guardia. But Martí didn't stay, he motioned to the aide and he said, 'Young man, to the charge!' and he spurred his horse towards the powerful Spanish forces dug in in a cattle ranch. He died almost instantly.

It's de la Guardia who tells this story, in a valuable memoir published after the war. The details of the events leading up to his death are known to us from what Martí himself wrote and the details that were given by the orderly, de la Guardia, who saw him die. Before he went into combat, Martí was writing in his diary, drafting a letter to Manuel Mercado, a Mexican who was his great friend for many years.[17] In this letter, which was never finished, Martí confesses: 'Every day now I am in danger of giving my life for my country and my duty – since I understand it and have the spirit to carry it out – in order to prevent, by the timely independence of Cuba, the United States from extending its hold across the Antilles and falling with all the greater force on the lands of our America. All that I have done up to now, and all I will do, is for that.' And then he adds: 'It has had to be done in silence, and indirectly, for there are things that must be concealed in order to be attained: proclaiming them for what they are would give rise to obstacles too formidable to be overcome.' That's verbatim. He says this in his last, unfinished, letter.

That was the last thing that Martí wrote.
It's wonderful, what he says: to prevent, with the independence of Cuba and Puerto Rico, the United States from falling with all the greater force on the lands of America. 'All that I have done up to now, and all I will do . . .,' he says, and then he adds, 'It must be done in silence,' and he explains why. That is the incredible legacy left by this man to us Cuban revolutionaries.

Those are phrases that seem to have left their mark on you. Have you adopted them as your own, as your political programme?[18]
I have, yes. It was from those words that I began to acquire political awareness, right after I finished high school, because all the time before that I'd gone to religious schools my parents sent me to – La Salle, which was of French origins, first, until halfway through the fifth grade; Dolores, which was Jesuit, until my second year of high school; and Belén, in Havana, which was also run by Spanish Jesuits, just at the end of that terrible Spanish Civil War, in which both sides sent the other to the firing squads.

By the time I finished high school, I had read certain things; I was drawn to the Cuban patriots on account of their struggles – they teach you a little of that [in school]. But since this republic, everyone said, had been made independent by the Americans, there was no way for me to know what the role of the patriots in our War of Independence had been.

I did go, in Santiago de Cuba, to see El Morro;[19] I stood before that fortress and that bay to the south of which the famous naval battle between the Spanish and US fleets took place.[20] There was no way I could know what it had been like, or the reasons for the battle itself. I saw enormous shells in several places, which were reminders of the bombardments – I didn't learn about all that till later. At the time, there was no way for me to understand what sort of war it had been. At that time, a child in the fourth, fifth or sixth grade who didn't have a tutor, a mentor, someone to explain it to him, couldn't possibly have known anything about that.

But during your adolescence, then, you began to read Martí and to understand his political importance.
The first thing I read in my adolescent years was on the Wars of Independence, and certain texts by Martí. I became drawn to Martí when I began

to read his works. Just as Bolívar, in 1823, had an intuition about imperial-ism[, as you can see from his own words] – 'The United States seem destined by providence to plague the Americas in the name of liberty' – so Martí, too, had a foreboding. Martí was the first person to talk about imperialism, that nascent imperialism [of the US's]. He knew about expansionism, the Mexican-American War, and all the other wars, and he was strongly opposed to the United States' foreign policy. He was a precursor. Before Lenin, Martí organized a party to engage in revolution – the Cuban Revolutionary Party. It wasn't a Socialist party, because this was a slave-holding society in which a handful of free men and patriots were fighting for independence. Still, his thinking was very advanced, anti-slavery, *independentista* and profoundly humanist.

Had Martí read Karl Marx?

He had apparently read a little Marx, because in his works he talks about him. He has two or three magnificent phrases, when he mentions Marx, and one of them, I remember now, is, 'Given that he took the side of the poor, he deserves honour.'[21] And like that one, there are other phrases that praise Marx.[22]

Do you think that Marx's theses may in some way have influenced Martí's thought?

The point of departure of Marx's theory is the evolution of the forces of production in the most advanced capitalist countries. Marx believed that the emergence of the working class would bury the capitalist system. He wrote this at the exact time that the United States was invading Mexico and annexing Texas, which was the year 1845. And Marx wrote, I'm told, that he saw that annexation as positive, because it would contribute to the swift development of the forces of production, the working class, [it would] add to the contradictions and the crisis that would lead eventually to Socialism. That was his theory. People were not talking about the problem of colonies yet. Lenin was the first to address the problem of colonies, of colonialism, from a Socialist perspective.

What influence did Marx have on Martí? I'm not certain whether even the experts in Martí's thought know what [Martí] knew about Marx, but he did know that Marx was a fighter on the side of the poor. Remember that Marx was fighting for the organization of workers, founding the Communist International. And Martí certainly knew that, even though those debates centred almost exclusively on Europe, and Martí of course was fighting for the independence of a colonized, slave-holding country [in another hemisphere altogether].

One of the things that made the greatest impact on Martí was the dreadful, unjust shooting of the eight Cuban medical students in 1871. At that time – when they were shot, on 27 November – he was just eighteen years old. He wrote a wonderful poem, beside those other writings I mentioned: *A mis hermanos muertos el 27 de noviembre*, 'To My Brothers Killed on 27 November'. And he also learned about the shooting of the martyred workers in Chicago, that 1 May 1886,[23] who were later honoured by the creation of International Workers' Day on that same date every year. Martí fought, he began his war in 1895 and died in May of that year.

He died in action, fighting?

He died in action – Martí, who was an intellectual, but an intellectual of profound convictions.

He had dreams ... What admiration he felt for the Cubans fighting for their independence! He commemorated 27 November and 10 October, the date the first War of Independence was launched. He was the writer, almost biographer, the apologist of all those great patriots. With a very special style. His own speeches are not easy to understand – [they're] a river of ideas that rush from his mouth. I've sometimes expressed it in the following way: 'A cataract of ideas in a little *arroyo* of words.' Into those words he put a whole universe, one phrase after another; that was the style of his speeches. And he made famous speeches, especially the ones he gave on all the most important anniversaries and commemorative occasions.

As in all Western humanist thought, Martí's philosophy contains a certain amount of Christian ethics. He was a man of great ethical conviction ... The highest Christian ethics had exerted great influence on him, as had the heroic tradition of this hemisphere's wars of independence, the struggles in Europe, the French Revolution. He was a journalist, writer, poet, statesman, visionary.

He organized the [Cuban Revolutionary] Party – as I said, before Lenin organized his own – to guide the struggle for independence, and he had to fight against annexationist currents, which were still there, and also against autonomist currents, which didn't dare speak the word 'independence', and he had fierce arguments with the spokesmen for those currents. [He was] a man of peace, of sincere sentiments of peace, although he also believed in war, but he called people to a 'necessary and rapid war'; he wanted to organize it so that there would be the fewest victims possible. Of course he was anti-slavery and anti-racist in the extreme; he wrote wonderful things about that.

He believed in, and wanted, a republic 'for all and for the good of all': Cubans, Spaniards, all different ethnicities. And his manifesto is tremendous, the promise of a future, that manifesto signed by him and the man who was to be the military leader [of the struggle], Máximo Gómez, over there in Santo Domingo. It expresses his thoughts about what the republic should be, the most advanced republic that could be conceived under those circumstances. But it can't be said that he was a Marxist, though there is no doubt that he 'sympathized' with the workers and was therefore an admirer of Marx's objectives. He, too, then, 'deserved honour for putting himself on the side of the poor'.

He knew about everything, even about economics, and in admirable depth. There are texts by him, prophetic articles he wrote when the United States for the first time proposed a form of FTAA, a Free Trade Area of the Americas,[24] an economic community with Latin America. I don't know whether you're familiar with those texts, you who've written so much on neoliberal globalization and the FTAA. Martí fought against a form of FTAA, the equivalent for the time, and explained with infinite wisdom why an economic community of that sort was not in the interests of the countries of Latin America, why that alliance, that association, with a country that was much more developed, was not in their interest.

Martí rejected a free-exchange economic zone out of hand.

Martí wrote tremendous articles that could be republished today to combat the Yankee plans for annexation – just to show you the profound roots of certain ideas today. So you see with that, how universal his thought was.

In addition, he didn't think just about the independence of Cuba, but also about the independence of Puerto Rico, didn't he?

Yes, the independence of both of them. His objective was to secure the independence of both islands.

Incredible obstacles arose, obstacles he'd never imagined, as he was about to give the order to begin the war, when the date was set and the weapons were purchased – with great sacrifice, I might add, with money he collected among the workers in Tampa. Martí was a leader of the Cuban workers of the period, and an idol of the cigar makers in Tampa, who were the main contributors to the funds for independence.

Those cigar makers were Cuban émigrés who were working in Florida.
Cubans working there in one job or another, yes. They were very solid in their support – the emigrants, I mean, and especially those in Tampa, people who'd moved from here and were experts at rolling cigars, Cuban cigars. It was easy: Cuban tobacco was sent from here and they rolled it in Florida. He gave many of his speeches there; the base of his party was working-class, fundamentally those people. Although there was no way to talk about a Socialist republic, his programme was the most humane and most advanced of his time. If you follow the thread of that thought, you end up with a Socialist programme. It's what the New Testament says, too, and Christian teaching. With the teachings of Christ you can formulate a radical Socialist programme, whether you're a believer or not.

In particular the Sermon on the Mount.[25]
According to the Bible, the sermons and parables and thoughts of Christ were taken up by fishermen, who didn't know how to read or write. I sometimes say that Christ turned water into wine and multiplied the loaves and fishes,[26] and that's the same thing we want to do here – multiply the loaves and the fishes. Epulion, the rich man, paid the man who worked four hours the same as the man who worked eight,[27] and that's a *Communist* distribution, not even a Socialist one. And Christ even used violence at a certain moment, when he threw the moneylenders out of the temple.[28] Of course later there emerged certain currents which didn't have much Christianity about them, because they allied themselves with the rich . . .

At bottom, you are a great Christian.
Not long ago I was telling Chávez, the president of Venezuela – because Hugo Chávez is a Christian and talks about it a lot – 'If people call me Christian, not from the standpoint of religion but from the standpoint of social vision, I declare that I am a Christian.' On the basis of my convictions and the objectives I pursue.

It was the first doctrine that emerged at that time, in those days, which were barbaric times, and from it there emerged a group of very humane precepts. You don't have to be Christian, in the religious sense, to understand the ethical values and the sense of social justice that that philosophy gave the world.

Of course, I am a Socialist, a Marxist, and a Leninist – I have never stopped being those things, and never will.

And a Martí-an, too, of course . . .
Yes, of course; I was first a Martí-an and then became a Martí-an, Marxist and Leninist.

Do you inscribe yourself within the prolongation of Martí's thought?
My first political philosophy was Martí-an, but when the attack on the Moncada barracks took place, in 1953, I'd read quite a bit about Socialism, my Martí-an thinking was well developed, and I also had acquired radical Socialist ideas, a philosophy that I've adhered to firmly throughout my life. So when you say that the Revolution began on 26 July 1953, we say that it began on 10 October 1868, and continues down through history.

I've explained the role of Martí and why we became Martí-ans . . . Forgive me for going on so, but since we were on the subject I had to say some things.

6

'History Will Absolve Me'

The capture – Lieutenant Sarría – 'Ideas can't be killed' –
The trial – The allocution – Prison

From Siboney, then, you went off into the mountains.
I'd decided to continue the war. I managed to bring almost twenty men
[from our group back] together, although the weapons we had, which
were fine for attacking and occupying a military installation in virtually
hand-to-hand combat, weren't particularly good for another kind of war. I
went off into the mountains to continue the struggle. That's what I told our
compañeros – to the mountains.

The initial idea was to cross over to the other side of the cordillera, around
Realengo 18, the historic site of *campesino* struggles, and to continue the
fight we'd begun at Moncada in that area. We were at sea level, so we had
to climb to the top of the mountain range, over 3,000 feet, which was the
average height in that area. The soldiers [of the Batista forces], of course,
who were travelling in vehicles along highways and mountain roads, got
there before we did and secured the high points.

Of the nineteen men in our group, some were injured, others exhausted,
and they were in no condition to undertake forced marches, either during
the day or at night, in order to get out of that region saturated with soldiers
– [we had] no guides, no information, no water, no food or other minimum
supplies. The Batista forces would systematically torture prisoners in the
most horrific ways, and then they'd murder almost every one. That happened
dozens of times. All through Oriente province and the rest of the country,
people were outraged. The archbishop of Santiago, Monsignor Pérez
Serantes, and a number of other figures started to act, to try to save the
survivors of the assault.

In our attempt to break through the cordon on that route, we saw soldiers several times. Their rifles and .30–06 machine guns and other weapons had much greater range than the .22s and 12-gauge shotguns we had. By that time, I'd exchanged mine for a .22 with a longer range and greater accuracy.

The terrain was mountainous and rocky. Our little platoon was hit by new injuries from accidental gunshots. There was no medic. I decided to send a *compañero* to evacuate the wounded and the most physically exhausted to Santiago, and to request aid from the population to assist them. So I evacuated twelve men.

Under pressure from the population, the tortures and mass murders had been scaled down. Batista and his regime were beginning to show signs of nervousness. I still had eight men, five with some degree of responsibility in the organization, so they'd go on with us, we needed to keep them, although some were in pretty bad physical shape, and three of the eight were officers of greater responsibility: Oscar Alcalde,[1] head of the Directorate; José Suárez,[2] head of the Artemisa detachment; and me.

Despite these colossal obstacles, I never abandoned the idea of continuing our struggle. Since it looked doubtful, under those conditions, that we'd be able to cross the cordillera, I decided to change course. What we'd do was slip through the coastal plain over to the bay at Santiago de Cuba; I planned to go to a point known as La Chivera, cross the bay in a boat over to the other side, and advance from there to the Sierra Maestra, which was very close.

But there was no way to carry out that manoeuvre in the physical condition the lower-ranking members of our group were in. Fortunately, we three higher-echelon members would be able to attempt the crossing. We all sat down to analyse the situation. Alcalde, Suárez and I were in shape to move on foot. The other five would take advantage of the guarantees demanded, and in part obtained, by the Catholic Church and other institutions that the physical well-being and life of prisoners would be respected. Since there were a number of survivors being cared for already, the five would meet with them and take them news and instructions.

Once we'd made that decision, we decided to wait until that night to advance to the house of a *campesino* with a good reputation who had a farm that bordered the Santiago-to-Siboney highway. He would see to contacting the archbishop and making the arrangements [for the five *compañeros* to turn themselves in].

That night we advanced several kilometres to the house, to accompany our five *compañeros*. On the way, we hid their weapons. The other three of us continued our march [to the house] carrying our weapons.

We agreed on the details with the *campesino* and started back. We'd wait for night in a woody area not far from the highway. We were sure we'd be able to get through the woods early and get out into the heavy undergrowth of the scrubland and coastal vegetation and reach the bay quickly, before the enemy got wind of our new movement.

In that situation, my old mountain-climbing days were about to stand me in very good stead.

A few kilometres from the other shore of the bay we were planning to row to, to the north-west, there's a little village called El Cobre, and you could see several mountains rising up around it, very high and covered with forest. That was especially to the south-west of the village. And I'd climbed those mountains when I was at the Colegio de Dolores. Now we were planning to go down to the bay, get across to that shore, and march along the middle of that imposing range.

Who could have imagined at that point in our campaign that three and a half years later I'd be advancing eastward from Alegría de Pío trying to get to those same mountains?

But crossing the bay was no more than a dream. We made a stupid mistake. After walking two or three kilometres, retracing our path uphill, trying to find a place to stop and sleep and wait until the next night, instead of doing what we'd been doing every day except that one, which was sleeping in the woods, we found a *varaentierra* – a *varaentierra* is a little tiny house, a shed, really, where the *campesinos* keep their palm fronds and whatnot – and the three of us, who'd been cold, hungry and miserable for days and days, and who the next night would have to start a long march to the Bay of Santiago, allowed ourselves to give in to the temptation of sleeping in that little hut, close to where we'd hidden the weapons of those five *compañeros* we'd left at the *campesino*'s house, without taking into account the enemy's proximity. So we slept – without the cold and fog and wetness of the open woods.

I remember that before I was fully awake – we'd slept for four or five hours – I heard something that sounded like hoofbeats outside, and then a few seconds later, somebody smashes the door with a rifle-butt – *bam!* – the door flies open, and us in there asleep, we wake up with rifle barrels poking us in the chest. So they caught us. In that sad, ignominious way, we were surprised and captured. Within seconds, they had our hands tied behind our backs.

And you had no weapons with you?

We had ours, three of them, but mine was a .22 rifle with a big long barrel. Later, in Alegría del Pío, when we landed on the *Granma* in 1956, I found myself in almost the same situation, but this time I took certain precautions: I slept with the barrel of the rifle under my chin, because I kept falling asleep – I couldn't help it, after a terrible aerial attack in which five or six fighter planes with eight .50-calibre machine guns each fired on us for several minutes, forcing us to bury ourselves under the dry leaves of the sugar cane. That time, too, it was three of us, after another reversal . . . But that's another story.

For the moment I'll just say this: we were captured by that patrol. Why? People say that the *campesino* with whom we'd left our five *compañeros* for safekeeping started calling the archbishop or who knows who on the telephone. You can assume several things: one, that he was an informer, or two, that something happened, or three, that the archbishop's phone was tapped. And that was also probably the way the enemy authorities learned that I'd gone [to the *campesino*'s house] and then kept going.

So early that morning there were several patrols out searching, combing the woods, and one of them happened to come upon exactly the place where we were sleeping. And they captured us.

Those dozen or so soldiers were furious. The veins and arteries in their necks, I'll never forget, were all swollen and throbbing. They wanted to kill us on the spot! So a big argument broke out between us and the soldiers. We were tied up, and they sat us down on the ground with our arms tied behind us. They didn't recognize me. We were so scruffy looking that they didn't realize who we were. They asked me my name, and I gave them some name or other. I remembered a joke that had some guy's name in it – I think I told him 'Francisco González Calderín', I just blurted it out. If I'd spoken my own name there, nobody would've been able to hold those soldiers back. I acted on instinct.

The argument, as I said, started from almost the very beginning. They were screaming at us – 'Listen good, you blankety-blank, we're the heirs of the Liberation Army' and things like that. That's the way those miserable, murderous soldiers thought – somebody had put that in their heads. So we'd tell them, 'We're the only ones who are the heirs of the Liberation Army.'

You said that to them?

Yes, oh yes. 'We're the ones who are the heirs of the Liberation Army. You guys are the heirs of the Spanish army.' Oh, it was quite a scene, so the lieutenant said, 'Don't shoot,' trying to restrain them. He was a tall black man, thirty or forty years old. Pedro Sarría, his name was. Apparently he was studying law in his spare time. Anyway, he was trying to restrain these soldiers – they were big, heavyset guys, very well fed I would say – they trampled all the underbrush under their feet as they walked through those woods! They're standing there, with their rifles pointed at us like this, about to do what they did with prisoners [i.e., kill them], but never imagining that one of us was me. The lieutenant, sort of murmuring, kept saying, 'Don't shoot, don't shoot. Ideas can't be killed, ideas can't be killed.' So several minutes pass that way, a long time, and then something else bad happened.

Those enraged soldiers started to search inside and out around the shack, and they found the other five men's weapons that I told you about. Boy! That was a very, very difficult moment, very critical, when they found those five weapons, and their adrenalin started flowing again. They were running back and forth, and the lieutenant by now was *really* having a hard time reining them in. But he kept saying, 'Calm down! Take it easy!' He kept ordering them not to shoot, which is what they'd have dearly loved to do, and finally he managed to calm them down – don't ask me how, but he just kept saying, 'Don't shoot. You can't kill ideas.'

Nice phrase.
'You can't kill ideas,' he kept murmuring, almost as though he were talking to himself. I think, as a matter of fact, that I could hear him better than the soldiers could. So we were still alive. And they got us up and marched us out to the highway.

The lieutenant not knowing that you were Fidel Castro.
He still didn't know – I'll explain how it was. They got us up and they marched us out. Suddenly we heard shots coming from over the same way they were taking us. Apparently that was when the *campesino* [we'd left the men with] made contact with an army patrol and the patrol took our five men prisoner. And immediately through my mind passes the thought that it's all a trick, somebody firing so they could shoot us.[3]

I remember that those soldiers were furious, absolutely enraged. All this lasted several minutes – I don't know, eight, ten, fifteen minutes. When they heard the firing, [the soldiers] got all excited, they trampled the underbrush all over the place, and then they ordered us to hit the ground. They were yelling at us: 'Hit the ground!' but I said, 'I'm not going to do it, I'm not going to get down. If you want to kill me, kill me while I'm standing.' I just flatly disobeyed their order, I just stood there. So then Lieutenant Sarría, who was marching along very close to me, goes like this and says, 'You're very brave, *muchachos*,' he says. 'You're very brave boys.'

When I saw how that man was behaving I told him, 'Lieutenant, I want to tell you something – I'm Fidel Castro.' He said, 'Don't tell anyone, don't tell.' So from that point on, he knew my identity. You know what he did? We came to the house of a *campesino*, very close to the highway, and there was a truck parked there. They put me up in it with the other soldiers and the other prisoners. The driver was sitting here behind the steering wheel, me in the middle, and the lieutenant on the right. Then here came a car with Comandante Pérez Chaumont,[4] a murderer, a real thug, the commander of the soldiers who had been killing people all through that area, and he ordered Sarría to turn me over to him.

This Pérez Chaumont was his superior; [Sarría] was just a lieutenant.
[Pérez Chaumont] was the commander, but the lieutenant told him he wouldn't turn me over. 'This man is my prisoner,' and so on. He refused; he said he was responsible for me, and that he was taking me to Vivac. And that *comandante*, there was no way he could convince [Sarría], and the lieutenant took me to Vivac. If he'd taken me to the Moncada barracks, they'd have chopped me up and fried me – there wouldn't have been a piece of me left. Imagine, if I'd shown up there! Batista had told everyone in Cuba that we had slit the throats of the sick soldiers who were in the infirmary. Heaven only knows how much bloodshed that lie caused.

Sarría made the decision not to go down Avenida Garzón, which ran by the barracks complex, but to go around instead, to Vivac, which was an installation under the control of the police. Vivac was a civilian prison in the centre of the city, and a prisoner there would be under the jurisdiction of the courts. There was no way to take any of the eight of us to Moncada. All eight of us would almost certainly have been murdered. The barracks was full of bloodthirsty animals. Chaumont was one of the worst murderers in Moncada.

Everything had been planned. My death had even been announced in the newspapers.

Wasn't that after the Granma *landing?*
Yes, then too. But this time – it was on 29 July 1953 – the news was

published in the newspaper. I was still up in the mountains. I hadn't even been captured yet. It was published in *Alaja* and also in other newspapers. I died several times during those days.

I can't imagine it went easy for Lieutenant Sarría.
There were those who didn't want to forgive him for what he'd done. When Colonel Chaviano, who was the regiment commander – a captain promoted by Batista to colonel on 10 March – came on the scene, he went to Vivac to interrogate me personally. Which was where that photo of me was taken – me standing there in the jail with a photograph of Martí in the background. There were several photos taken in that office . . . I immediately assumed the responsibility . . . 'I'm the one responsible,' I told them.

They kept claiming that the operation had been financed with money from former president Carlos Prío Socarrás, who'd been overthrown by Batista on 10 March, but I told them we had no ties to Prío or anybody else, that that was totally false. I explained it to them. I had nothing to hide, and I took full responsibility: [I told them] we bought the weapons in gun shops, no one provided us with them, nobody else had any responsibility. Then they let some reporters in. One belonged to a well-known newspaper, and I was able to talk to him. The next day they confiscated all the newspapers that had been printed, picked them up, because in their euphoria they'd let them publish the news: 'Captured!' So now it wasn't so easy to kill me.

Before the interrogation I was held with a group of the surviving *compañeros*, but afterwards they separated me and put me in an isolation cell.

Did you later meet this Lieutenant Sarría?
Yes, of course, the war went on and he was still in the army, although the regime wasn't very pleased with him – they even jailed him when we were up in the Sierra Maestra fighting – because he'd been the one who'd captured me and kept them from murdering me. Of course I was the only one who knew about his famous phrases, which only years later I told about. After all, it was his patrol. I can imagine how they must have hated him . . .

When the war was over, in 1959, we promoted him to captain and made him aide to the first president of the Republic. Unfortunately, he didn't live many years longer; he had a malignancy, he went blind, and that wonderful man died. It's one of the stories that you tell and people can't believe.

Obviously you owe him your life.

Three times over!

He didn't say who you were, didn't turn you over to his superior.

When I saw that man acting in such a gentlemanly way, I stood up before
him like this and I said, 'I'm so-and-so.' And he says, 'Don't say anything to
anybody, don't tell.' I learned some of the other things later – how he refused
to turn me over to Pérez Chaumont[, for instance]. Look at the decisive way
he sat me next to the driver, with me in the middle and him [Sarría] on the
right. How do you explain that? He was a man who was going to school,
a brave and decent man. That's the reason I wasn't killed from the first
moment.

And he saved my life a third time when he refused to drive me to the
Moncada barracks, and took me to Vivac instead.[5]

So I was held there in the provincial prison in Boniato, and then, when
the trial started, on Monday 21 September 1953, I assumed my own defence.
And as [the defence] lawyer I started interrogating all those thugs and
henchmen, all the witnesses, and that was a sight to see . . . They couldn't
take it, they pulled me out of the trial because they couldn't prevent my
denunciations. They tried me later by myself, with another man who'd been
wounded, in a little room in the hospital.

You defended yourself? You didn't have a lawyer?

Of course, and I denounced it all.

And you ended with your famous allocution, 'History Will Absolve Me'.[6]

I thought that at any moment they might do something terrible, and in the
jail at Boniato where I was being held, when they forbade me to talk to
the *compañeros* who were in the same wing and walked right in front of
my cell, I went on a hunger strike. And I made my point. Then later they
isolated me again. I spent seventy-five days in an isolation cell; no one was
allowed to speak to me. But I found ways to maintain the minimum essential
communication.

They even changed the guards at one point, because I was able to befriend
several of them, so they found some more thugs, especially hateful towards
me, but of these new ones, too, one of them became a friend. Three [*sic*]
years later, he was in the infantry in the battle of Maffo in late 1958, and
our forces surrounded him. His well fortified battalion had put up a very

strong resistance. He'd made friends with me in the jail at Boniato; he was one of those *guajiritos* in the group of tough-as-nails soldiers that were sent in to guard us.

When they'd come in to bring me food while I was on hunger strike, I'd yell at them, 'I don't want that food; tell Chaviano' – who was the commander of the post – 'to shove it up his anus'. Of course I used a less technical word, which I won't repeat here. It may seem crazy on my part, but you have to understand the state of our emotions, since we knew everything they'd done, the horrendous tortures and terrible crimes they'd committed against our *compañeros* . . .

We'd been dead men for some time now, so doing what I did didn't cost a thing. I shot back at them with a hunger strike. And what happened was that it got their attention, and then they let me talk to Haydée, Melba and some others. Through them I learned a lot of things that had happened that I hadn't known anything about, things that were essential to my trial. Of course before that, I'd been passing little pieces of paper out – I'd toss them out sometimes, because there was a soldier that was always posted there outside, but we [the imprisoned group] managed to communicate with each other. Finally they agreed [to let me talk to the others], so I was able to eat. But those murderous jailers kept their word for just twenty-four hours and then they isolated me again. But I'd won a battle, so I didn't go back on my hunger strike. That may, in fact, have been what they wanted me to do, for whatever reason.

During the days when I was defying them, one of the higher-ranking officers came in to talk to me. You know what he said to me? He said, 'You're a decent man, you're an educated man; it's incredible, don't say those words.' All those words I was screaming at the jailers three times a day had them really concerned. You could hear me all over the prison, the soldiers, the prisoners, the civilian workers there, everybody. They were demoralized.

I had some printed material, although it wasn't allowed. I was very grateful for the knowledge I'd acquired as a student of social science and political science, some of which I was able to refresh [there in my cell]. I also had some material by Martí.

If Moncada had fallen, what were you planning to do?
If Moncada had fallen, 3,000 weapons would have fallen into our hands. Remember, we were all sergeants. A proclamation by the 'sergeants in revolt'

would have sown chaos among the ranks of the enemy. Some of the ones we'd have taken prisoner, with their names and personal information, would have sent messages to the commanders of units all across the province, telling them about a 'Sergeants' Uprising' – which, as I've said, had a clear and unique historical antecedent in the Republic of Cuba. We'd have invested three or four hours on disinformation, throwing everyone off.

Immediately afterwards we'd have started reporting who had really taken Moncada. That is, we'd have told people who we were. Meanwhile, all the weapons would have been distributed throughout the city so as to protect them from an air attack on the barracks complex, which was surely coming – you can be sure they wouldn't have cared whether their own soldiers were in there with us or not.

Our plan was to immediately get the weapons out of Moncada and distribute them to various buildings in the city, because the only immediate counter-attack possible was by air. The railway didn't worry us, because it was easy to cut; we were, however, concerned about the Central Highway, which is how they could have sent in reinforcements for a counter-attack, from the regiment in Holguín and other garrisons throughout that area. Which is why we attacked Bayamo. Bayamo was vital, because of the bridge over the Cauto River on the Central Highway. The town would have revolted, there was absolutely no doubt about that, because anybody who rebelled against Batista would have won the immediate support of the people.

So right at the beginning we'd have been 'sergeants', and from inside Moncada, in the first few minutes, no one would really have known what was happening. We were going to send messages to all the [regular army] units in the province.

With their own communications equipment.
Yes, with their own communications. Using the name 'sergeants of the so-and-so regiment' we'd have sent communiqués to all the other barracks and garrisons, in order to create confusion and paralysis while we got the weapons out of there.

It would look at first like a sergeants' movement, which would have created real chaos within the armed forces.

Then within two, three, four hours, we'd have started identifying ourselves and the first thing would have been to rebroadcast the speech by the leader of the Orthodox Party when he so dramatically shot himself.

Eduardo Chibás.
We were going to broadcast his last words from the radio station in Santiago.

You planned to occupy the radio station?
Of course, that was elementary. Once Moncada was taken.

Not simultaneously?
No, *hombre*, no – there was no need! What we had to take first was the barracks complex, so later we could take any other objective.

At first, we'd do the less public work, [a communiqué] from the communications room there in the barracks, which we'd have occupied, creating the maximum amount of confusion among the soldiers of the army.

After that first action, everyone would think that the army was fighting among itself, and that was what would do the damage and create confusion in the ranks while we organized and laid the ground for our next steps.

Then later, we'd occupy the radio station. All the material was ready: the laws that appeared later in *History Will Absolve Me*,[7] the exhortation to the people and the call to a general strike, because the time was ripe for that, don't doubt it for a second.

That was what we did on 1 January 1959, when, with the enemy defeated, [our] leaders launched the coup in Havana.

When you launched the attack on the Moncada barracks, were you thinking about the kind of government you were going to install if you won? Were you thinking about the USSR, for example?
We didn't think about the USSR or anything of the sort; that came later. We believed that there was such a thing as sovereignty on this planet, that it was a real, respected right after the two Wars of Independence in our nation, which had cost over 50,000 lives of a much smaller Cuban population. We believed that, and we believed that our right to wage a revolution would be respected – a revolution that was not yet Socialist but was the prelude to a Socialist revolution. To see that, you have to read the defence, the speech I made in court later known as 'History Will Absolve Me'; there you'll find all the basic elements of a future Socialist revolution, which didn't have to come immediately – it could be carried out gradually, progressively, but it would be solid and uncontainable. Although we wouldn't hesitate to radicalize it if necessary.

The attack on Moncada translated into the torture and death of many of your comrades and prison for others, and for you. Why didn't you draw from that failure, for example, the conclusion that the road to revolution by arms was, once and for all, impossible?

On the contrary. When we attacked Moncada, we had the idea of going off into the mountains with all the weapons seized in the barracks complex if the regime didn't collapse. And I'm sure it would have collapsed.

During that period there was no other guerrilla war in Latin America, was there?

In 1948, when I was an eyewitness to that uprising in Bogotá, there were some irregular groups at work in Colombia, but not under the later concept of guerrilla warfare that was applied in Cuba. In Latin America, many movements had existed and many armed actions had taken place. There was the Mexican revolution, which was a great inspiration for us; there had also been the heroic Sandino movement.

Sandino in Nicaragua, in the thirties.[8]

The 'general of free men' . . . Those are [our] historical antecedents.

During this period, were you familiar with Sandino's work?

Oh, yes, very much so. I knew Sandino's actions practically by heart. What he had was a little army; the books called it 'the mad little army'. And another thing, I'd also read a lot about what Maceo, Gómez and the other daring commanders in our wars of independence had done here in Cuba.

You knew a great deal about the wars in Cuba.

Yes. [Those wars] helped us in formulating a different strategy, because both Maceo and Máximo Gómez had cavalry, a very mobile army, and they had virtual freedom of movement. Almost all the battles were 'encounters' [battles that occurred when the opposing forces just came upon each other]. Our main combats, however, in the circumstances of *our* war, were planned, with cover, trenches prepared, all sorts of other essential measures taken. Never, at any time in the War of Independence, had a trench been dug – maybe over there in Pinar del Río somewhere, once. Almost all their battles were encounters, while we were forced to foresee ours, and plan them in advance.

What we thought at first to be the right way to fight a war in a forested mountain region at 4,000 feet above sea level, we later did on the plains, on the highways, in a coffee plantation, in a mangrove swamp, in a cane field. So it was all a matter of learning. Batista's forces, for example, in all the actions, always had aeroplanes over us, not to mention other advantages. Those were hard lessons we learned, because the difference [in strength and tactics] was enormous, and that enormous difference, in my opinion, was what taught us to formulate tactics, ideas, to compensate for the difference.

We were almost wiped out in the beginning, through a betrayal, but there came a moment when there was no longer any way to betray us in any fatal way, or hunt us down, or eliminate us. Our troops in the Sierra never walked into an ambush, ever. What usually happened was that *we* were hunting *them*; a heavily armed column would come along, for example – 300 men, an army – and we'd have just seventy or eighty men to strike and halt the enemy forces.

Were you familiar with the theses put forward by Giap,[9] Ho Chi Minh, Mao on revolutionary warfare?

I'll tell you, we knew that the Vietnamese were extraordinary soldiers; they defeated the French in Dien Bien Phu in 1954, but that was another kind of war, using masses of men, artillery and all that; they had a real army. We started from scratch, and we didn't have an army.

When Mao set out on the Long March in China, in 1935 [*sic*], he performed a military feat that very few of us in Cuba knew anything about. Since then, I've read a lot about it. A Long March wouldn't have been of any use to us here, although its tactics and political and military principles are of great value in any war. Mao was able to show that anything is possible, because they marched for 12,000 kilometres, almost 7,500 miles, fighting.

Our problem was that our struggle was carried out under very different conditions.

7
Che Guevara

Mexico – Meeting Che – Seeing eye to eye politically – Personality
and determination – Preparations for a guerrilla war – Training

After two years in prison on the Isle of Pines, you went into exile in Mexico,
and when you arrived there you met Ernesto 'Che' Guevara for the first
time. Would you tell me under what circumstances you met him?

It gives me great pleasure to talk about Che, really.[1] Many people know
about Che's motorcycle tour when he was in Argentina studying; his trips
through the interior of that country,[2] then to several Latin American countries – Bolivia, Chile, Peru and other places.[3] We mustn't forget that in 1952,
after the military coup in 1951, Bolivia experienced a powerful labour
and *campesino* movement that gave battle there and had a great deal of
influence.[4]

Most people know about his trip with his friend Alberto Granado, just
before Che graduated from medical school, when they visited several hospitals, and also know that they wound up in a leper colony out there in the
Amazon region working as doctors.[5] They know he travelled all over Latin
America; he went to the copper mines in Chuquicamata, in Chile, where the
work is exhausting; he crossed the Atacama desert; he visited the ruins at
Machu Picchu in Peru; he took a boat across Lake Titicaca – and in all these
places, coming to know the indigenous peoples and taking a great interest
in them. From there, as people also know, he moved on to Guatemala,
during the Arbenz regime.[6]

At that time, President Jacobo Arbenz was putting very progressive reforms
into place in Guatemala.

That's right. An important process of agrarian reform was taking place there, in which large banana plantations run by a big American transnational corporation were distributed among the *campesinos*. With the support of the United States the military carried out a coup, so the agrarian reform was immediately thwarted. Back then, talking about agrarian reform laws was 'Communist', it meant being automatically identified as a Communist.

But in Guatemala they had actually implemented one [i.e., an agrarian reform], and like everywhere else, the powerful immediately began to oppose it. As did the neighbours to the north, and their specialized institutions immediately began to organize counter-revolutionary actions to overthrow the elected president, Jacobo Arbenz. They were going to do this with a military expedition attacking from the border and with the complicity of military groups from the former army.

When our movement attacked the Moncada barracks on 26 July 1953, a number of our *compañeros* managed to escape from the country. Antonio 'Ñico' López[7] and some others went to Guatemala. Che was already there, so he lived through the bitter experience of Jacobo Arbenz's overthrow; he met our *compañeros* and went with them to Mexico.

Did your brother Raúl meet him before you did?
Yes, because one of the first to go off to Mexico was Raúl. People were beginning to accuse him of things, even of setting off bombs, so I told him, 'You've got to get out [of the country].' While we were in prison we'd conceived the idea of going to Mexico and organizing an armed return. It was a sort of tradition in Cuba. So Raúl went to Mexico, and there, through our *compañeros* who were already there, he met Che. Of course, Che wasn't Che yet; he was Ernesto Guevara, but since the Argentines are always saying '*¡che, hombre!*', '*che*' this and '*che*' that,[8] the Cubans started calling him 'el Che', and it stuck . . .

It took me a little longer to leave because I wasn't in any imminent danger, but I couldn't keep agitating in Cuba, so the moment came for me, too, when it was time to leave for Mexico. Among other things, I had to prepare for a quick return. In the weeks after we got out of prison, we had engaged in an intense campaign to take our ideas to the people, and to begin to create [social] awareness. We had structured our own revolutionary organization – the 26th of July Movement – and we'd shown that it was impossible to carry out the struggle by peaceful, legal means.

Did Che sympathize with your group's ideas?
He was already a Marxist. Although he wasn't a member of any party at
that time, he was, at that point, a Marxist by conviction. And there in Mexico
he was with Ñico López, who was one of the leaders of our movement, a
good *compañero*, modest – he'd been a member of the Orthodox Party, but
he was very radical, very courageous, and I'd talked to him a lot about
Marxism; he was already convinced. He'd taken part in the attack on the
Bayamo barracks complex. The fact that [Che's and my] ideas coincided
was one of the things that most helped along my bonding with Che.

I've explained at great length what our political philosophy was when we
attacked Moncada. I was a utopian Marxist. That explains to a degree my
bonding with Che. That congruence of so many ideas was perhaps one of
the things that aided that bonding.

Did you realize when you met him for the first time that Che was different?
He had a gift for people. He was one of those people that everyone immediately cares about – it was his naturalness, his simplicity, his sense of comrade-
ship and all his virtues. He was a doctor; he was working at a Social Security
Institute centre doing some sort of research, cardiac something or other, or
allergies, because he himself was allergic.

He had asthma, I believe.
Our little group there in Mexico liked him immediately. Raúl had already
struck up a friendship with him. When I arrived was when I met him. He
was twenty-seven.

He himself said[9] that our meeting took place one night in July 1955 in
Mexico City, on Calle Emparan, if I'm not mistaken, in the home of a Cuban
friend, María Antonia González. There was nothing surprising about our
immediate sympathy with one another: he'd been travelling around Latin
America, he'd visited Guatemala, he'd witnessed the American intervention
there, and he knew we'd attacked a military stronghold, he knew about our
struggle in Cuba, he knew how we thought. I arrived, we talked to each
other, and right there, he joined us.

He knew that in our movement there were even some petit-bourgeois
members and a bit of everything. But he saw that we were going to fight a
revolution of national liberation, an anti-imperialist revolution; he didn't
yet see a Socialist revolution, but that was no obstacle – he joined right up,
he immediately signed on.

He enlisted for the adventure.

He said just one thing to me: 'The only thing I ask is that when the Revolution triumphs in Cuba, you not forbid me, for reasons of state, from going to Argentina to make a revolution there.'

In his own country?

Yes, in his country. That's what he told me. By that time we were carrying out an incipient but strong policy of internationalism. What was our action in Bogotá, the fight against Trujillo, our defence of the independence of Puerto Rico, the return of the Panama Canal to Panama, Argentina's right to the Malvinas, and the independence of the European colonies in the Caribbean [if not internationalism]? We were not just some simple appendixes. Che had absolute trust in us. So 'Agreed,' I said to him, and there was no need for another word on the subject.

Did he start doing military training with you and your group?

He attended a tactics course with us that was given by a Spanish general, Alberto Bayo,[10] who'd been born in Cuba, in Camagüey province, in 1892, before independence in 1898. In the twenties he'd fought in Morocco, in the army air division, and later, as a Republican officer, fought in the Spanish Civil War and [then, when Franco triumphed, he'd] gone into exile in Mexico. Che attended all those classes in tactics. Bayo said he was his best student. They both played chess, so every night, there in the camp where they were before the arrests, they'd play chess every night.

Bayo never went beyond teaching what a guerrilla fighter should do to break through a perimeter when he's surrounded, on the basis of his experience of the times Abd el-Krim's Moroccans, in the war in the Rif, broke through the Spanish lines that encircled them.[11] He didn't formulate a strategy, however; it never occurred to him that guerrilla fighters might become an army, and that that army might defeat the other army – which was our essential idea.

That was what you and your group wanted to do?

When I say 'army', I'm talking about developing a [military] force that can defeat another army. That was our essential idea when we left for Mexico. The deeds of our small force in the initial months of the struggle in the Sierra Maestra strengthened that idea.

Your idea was to transform a guerrilla force into an army and wage a new form of warfare.

There are two kinds of war: an irregular war and a regular, conventional war. We created a formula for confronting that army of Batista's, which had planes, tanks, cannons, communications, everything ... We had neither money nor weapons. We had to find a way to overthrow the tyranny and make a revolution in Cuba. And success crowned our venture. I'm not going to tell you that it worked purely on its merits – luck played an important part. You can make mistakes, commit errors or do things as perfectly as possible, and there are still things you can't foresee. You can live or die, perish or survive because of one small detail, or because you did or didn't receive certain information on time. Remember the pain and grief with which I talked about the series of chance factors that thwarted our plans to take the Moncada barracks after so much organizational effort. And we've also talked about the stupid surprise that caught us off guard after we disembarked from the *Granma*. How many valuable lives could have been saved in either or both of those cases?

In Mexico, with Bayo, we trained many *compañeros*. I had to do the organizational work and find and acquire weapons, and I was training the men on the firing ranges. I had to 'move it' all the time; it was hard for me to attend Bayo's training sessions.

But Che attended the classes regularly, faithfully?

Yes, the theory courses and also the firing practices, and he was a very good shot. There in Mexico we practised our marksmanship at a range near Mexico City. It belonged to an old confederate of Pancho Villa's, and he'd leased it to us. When we disembarked, we had fifty-five rifles with telescopic sights. Our practice with those rifles consisted of shooting sheep that were turned loose 200 yards out on the firing range – without support for the rifle, free-handed. We could break a plate at 600 yards. Our men were very good shots. They'd send a man out 200 yards, and put a bottle down on the ground beside him – we'd aim with the telescopic sight; the sight gives you tremendous accuracy – and we'd fire hundreds of rounds. One of our volunteers was called the Korean.[12] We'd put a bottle down a foot from him; I made that shot many times, and a bullet never landed between the bottle and the man's foot – with the rifle on a support, of course. You can't do that just holding the rifle, without a support, because the slightest variation will hit him. Those practices gave us complete confidence in what we could do with one of those weapons.

[(in 1st ed.:) What we knew best was shooting, which is very different from knowing what's best to do and best not to. Later I formulated a tactic, as I said.]

Che had no military experience when he arrived there?
No, none. He had none.

But he learned?
He studied and practised, but he was with us as the group's medic, and he turned out to be an outstanding doctor; he saw to the health and well-being of our *compañeros*. Let me tell you one quality that sums him up, one that I most appreciated, among the many I observed in him . . . Che suffered from asthma. Near Mexico City, there's a volcano, Popocatépetl, and every weekend Che would try to climb Popocatépetl. He'd get his equipment in order – the mountain is tall, over 5,000 metres, almost 18,000 feet, with snow year-round – and he'd start the ascent. He'd make a tremendous effort, but he'd never make it to the top. The asthma prevented him. The next week he'd try again to climb Popo, as he called it, but he wouldn't make it. He never made it to the top, he never reached the peak of Popocatépetl. But he kept trying to climb the mountain, and he'd have spent his entire life trying to climb Popocatépetl. He made a heroic effort, although he never managed to reach that summit. So there you see his strength of character. That gives you some idea of his spiritual strength, his constancy.

His willpower.
When we were still a very small group, whenever a volunteer was needed for some job, the first to volunteer would always be 'el Che'.
   And another characteristic of his was that foresight, that almost prophetic clairvoyance that he showed when he asked me not to prevent him from going to Argentina to fight for the revolution there.

When he said he wanted to go to Argentina?
That's right . . . And later, during our own war, I had to make an effort to save him, because if I'd let him do everything he wanted to do, he'd never have survived. From the very first, he distinguished himself . . . Every time we needed a volunteer for a difficult mission, or to lay some surprise, recover some weapons that needed to be saved so the enemy wouldn't get their hands on them, the first to volunteer would be 'el Che'.

He'd volunteer to go on the most dangerous missions?
He'd be the first for *any* difficult mission; he was characterized by an extra-ordinary bravery, an absolute contempt for danger, but also, he'd sometimes propose that we do very difficult, very risky things . . . I'd tell him, 'No.'

Because he was running too many risks?
Listen, you send a man out for a first ambush, a second, a third, and a fourth, and fifth, and sixth – it's like flipping a coin: in a combat at the platoon or squad level, he dies like people that play Russian roulette.

It wasn't a problem that he wasn't Cuban?
Yes, it was, at times. In Mexico we had put him in command of a camp and there were those who started complaining that he was Argentine and this and that, and there was a big dust-up with me. I'm not going to mention names because they later came round. Yes, there in that camp in Mexico. Here, in our war, he was the medic, but because of his bravery, his qualities, we gave him the command of a column, and he distinguished himself in so many ways, through so many fine qualities.

Human, political, military?
Human and political. As a man, as an extraordinary human being. He was also a person of great culture, a person of great intelligence. And with military qualities as well. Che was a doctor who became a soldier without ceasing for a single minute to be a doctor. There were many combats we were in together. Sometimes I'd call the men of two columns together and we'd carry out a pretty complex operation, with ambushes and foreseeable movements of enemy troops.

We revolutionaries learned the art of war up there [in the Sierra] by fighting. We discovered that the enemy within its own positions is strong, but the enemy in motion is weak. A column of 300 men has the strength of the one or two platoons who lead it; the others don't fire in combat, or they just shoot in the air to make noise – they can't see the troops that are firing on their advance positions. That was one of the elementary principles we used: attack the enemy when he's weakest and most vulnerable. If we attacked positions, we'd always have casualties, we'd waste ammunition, we wouldn't always take the objective; the enemy was dug in, so he could fight with more information and more safely. Little by little, our tactics evolved; I'm not going to talk about that, but we gradually learned to fight against a strong adversary, and Column 1 was our elementary school.

At one point in Mexico, when you were training, you and your group were taken prisoner. Do you recall that?

Yes. There's a story behind that. We were captured. I was taken prisoner almost by chance. A little piece of paper here and another one there that the Mexican police discovered in the pockets of some [of our men] whom they'd arrested – some address, some telephone. None of them gave even the minutest information.

We were lucky; we started being followed by the Federales and not the Secret Police. The Federales were commanded by an army officer. They initially thought we were smugglers or something, because we made ourselves look suspicious because of certain measures we took against being kidnapped and killed by Batista's agents [in Mexico]. Our movements looked strange to them [the Federales]. It was a miracle we weren't killed in the incident that happened later.

Batista had influence among the Secret Police, he'd bought them off, so they supported him, and he had plans to kidnap us in Mexico. We were forced to take [counter-]measures, so one afternoon, just at nightfall, when we were moving from one house to another and were exposed, you see, several Federales, who were doing something else, saw us moving and decided to arrest us. They were pretty sharp, I must say. I was on foot – because we'd also observed some strange movements by some cars – and I had Ramirito thirty or forty yards behind me, walking along the left-hand side of the street. I was on the same side of the street, approaching the next corner. It was an area where there weren't many houses. On that corner a house was under construction. All of a sudden, a car came from behind us down that same street, screeched to a halt close to the corner, and out of it jumped a group of men. I hid behind a column in the construction site and tried to draw my Spanish automatic pistol, which had a twenty-five-round clip. At that exact moment, someone put the barrel of a gun to the back of my head. It was one of the Federales. They'd also captured Ramirito. And that was the beginning of a long odyssey for us in Mexico.

What had happened? I thought Ramirito and Universo [Sánchez] were behind me, backing me up, but they'd been captured, and just when I went to defend myself from the men getting out of the car, I was immobilized from behind. If I'd managed to fire, I can imagine how long I'd have lasted.

It was just when I was pulling out my gun that they jumped me and arrested me. They thought they'd arrested smugglers or something. There was almost no drug problem in those days; the authorities' attention was centred more on contraband. And they took us to police headquarters.

We were immediately relieved when they started talking to us. These were firm, tough men, with a get-the-job-done attitude. They were very capable when it came to capturing people and investigation, because they'd pick up some little piece of paper and they'd follow the trail. Boy, did I suffer there under arrest when I remembered that Cándido González – one of the *compañeros* that was always with me – had put a piece of paper in my pocket with the telephone number of a house we had where we'd stored a big lot of our best weapons, and that only he and I knew about! I hadn't remembered that piece of paper. Thank goodness the police, who'd followed all the trails, hadn't thought of investigating that telephone number more closely, because that would have been the end. But they still confiscated quite a few weapons by following other clues. You could see, though, that as they got to know us they began to have more respect for us.

Che wasn't with you at that point, when you were arrested?
No. Che was arrested while he was at the camp we trained at, Rancho Santa Rosa, in Chalco. They were looking for the place, they had some idea where it was and they were determined to find it. One day, the leader said to me, 'We know where that training camp is.' It was a trick. They looked for it for quite a while, and I don't know how they got some real clue, but they connected whatever it was with a story from somebody out at Chalco about strange movements by some Cubans out there, and finally they told me the exact location of the ranch. I knew there was a group of about twenty *compañeros* out there, and that they had weapons. Given the accuracy of his information, I told the head of the Federales, 'I want to ask you one thing; let me go out there with you, to avoid a confrontation,' and the commander agreed. So I went out there, I asked the Federales to let me go in alone; I climbed over a gate and jumped in. The *compañeros* were all so happy [to see me], they thought I'd been released . . . I told them, 'No, no, take it easy, don't move!' And I explained what was happening.

That's where they arrested Che. Some of them were out in the field behind the house, or doing other things, and they got away. Bayo was one of them. He wasn't caught, he wasn't there. Let me tell you something: several weeks earlier he'd gone on a fast for twenty days, just to prove his willpower. He was a true Spartan. During the Spanish Civil War, he'd captained an expedition to the Baleares. But he couldn't liberate [the islands] from the Franquistas.

After every adventure of war and its inevitable failure, he'd write a book, so now he wrote one while we were prisoners: 'My Frustrated Expedition to Cuba' it was called. To his dying day he never changed; he was always the same Bayo, that Spaniard who'd been born in Cuba and brought up in the Canary Islands.

He wasn't arrested?

No. Bayo wasn't taken prisoner; he wasn't there just then, but they did capture several dozen weapons, which were the ones we had there then, along with the ones that the *compañeros* trained with, but fortunately they weren't the most sophisticated or accurate ones. They didn't have telescopic sights. There was a goat's milk and cheese production operation there, run by some friendly neighbours; that was what the cover was.

But anyway, the police, who over the course of many days had been investigating very thoroughly, as I said, had found several clues, several leads, and finally they found the place. That was where Che was taken prisoner.

Were you and he together in jail?

Yes, we were in prison together for almost two months. When did he create a problem for us? When they interrogated him and asked him, 'Are you a Communist?' 'Yes, I'm a Communist,' he answered. And the newspapers over there in Mexico started reporting that we were a Communist organization, that we were conspiring to 'liquidate democracy' on the continent [South America] and I don't know what else . . . They took Che before the prosecutor, the prosecutor interrogated him, and Che even started arguing about the cult of personality, doing a critique of Stalin. Imagine Che involved in a theoretical discussion with the police, the district attorney and the immigration authorities over Stalin's errors! This took place in July 1956, and in February of that same year Khrushchev's critique of Stalin had taken place.[13] Che, of course, stuck to the official versions put out by the Soviet Party Congress. Che said to them, 'Yes, all right, they committed those mistakes, in this and that and the other,' and defended his theory of Communism and his Communist ideas. Imagine! He was an Argentine; at the time, that was riskier. I sincerely believe that in situations such as that, when the whole project was in danger, the best thing to do would have been disinform the enemy. But Che, who was so strongly influenced by the epic of Communist literature, couldn't be reproached for that tactical mess, which didn't keep him from going to Cuba with us.

Practically the last ones [to be released] were Che and me. I even think they took me out a few days before him. Lázaro Cárdenas,[14] actually, intervened on behalf of the Cuban prisoners, and the concern he showed contributed a great deal to our liberation. His name was venerated by the people, and his moral authority was capable of opening the doors of our prison.

It's been said that Che even had some Trotskyite sympathies. Did you see that in him at that point?

No, no. Let me tell you, really, what Che was like. Che already had, as I've said, a political education. He had come naturally to read a number of books on the theories of Marx, Engels and Lenin ... He was a Marxist. I never heard him talk about Trotsky. He defended Marx, he defended Lenin, and he attacked Stalin – or rather, he criticized the cult of personality, Stalin's errors ... But I never heard him speak, really, about Trotsky. He was a Leninist and, to a degree, he even recognized some merits in Stalin – you know, industrialization, some of those things.

I, deep inside, was more critical of Stalin [than Che was], because of some of his mistakes. He was to blame, in my view, for the invasion of the USSR in 1941 by Hitler's powerful war machine, without the Soviet forces ever hearing a call to arms. Stalin also committed serious errors – everyone knows about his abuse of force, the repression, and his personal characteristics, the cult of personality. But yet he also showed tremendous merit in industrializing the country, in moving the military industry to Siberia – those were decisive factors in the world's fight against Nazism.

So, when I analyse it, I weigh his merits and also his great errors, and one of those was when he purged the Red Army due to Nazi misinformation – that weakened the USSR militarily on the very eve of the Fascist attack.

He disarmed himself.

He disarmed himself, he weakened himself, and he signed that terrible German–Soviet pact, the Molotov–Ribbentrop Pact, and other things. I've talked about that before, I'm not going to add anything else.

8

In the Sierra Maestra

The Granma – *Alegría de Pío – First victories – Che in combat –*
Raúl and Camilo – War strategies – The defeat of Batista –
The triumph of the Revolution

You and your men landed on 2 December 1956, and a short time later, in
Alegría de Pío, you suffered a devastating attack.
It was on the 5th. We had done all our practice sailing runs with an empty
boat. We didn't know much about sailing, and when we loaded eighty-two
men, plus weapons, munitions, food and extra fuel into the *Granma*, it
slowed the boat down tremendously, so it took seven days for the trip
instead of five, and there were only a few inches of fuel left in the tanks. It
took us two days longer than we'd planned. And we were attacked three
days after we landed.

In Alegría de Pío, while we were marching towards the mountains, which
were still far off, the day of 5 December was dawning. We marched past a
little patch of heavy woods and undergrowth no more than a hectare in size,
a couple of acres maybe, and we walked 100 or 200 yards further, towards
the big patch of wooded land between the line of the coast on the south and
the strip of flat, fertile land planted in pasture and sugar cane to the north.
We came to the edge of those woods, explored it a bit, and then we spread
out, hundreds of yards from one another. It was a good spot, which overlooked a long stretch of the road we'd been walking, but the ground was
rocky, and covered with sharp stones. Once again, in the late afternoon,
we'd have had to walk another whole night to get through the [Batista
army's] perimeter. Some of the *compañeros* were totally exhausted. I decided
to camp on a little hill with smooth, soft soil a few yards from a field of new
sugar cane that you could chew and suck on. The men spread out with their

platoons to rest and wait for night to come on. The [army] post was just 100 yards from our camp. Overconfidence.

Late that afternoon, enemy spotter planes, small one-engine planes, started to explore. About four o'clock, fighter jets began flying low over the woods. And then about five, the first shots came, and seconds later, heavy infantry fire against us – we'd been too distracted by the noise of the fighter jets, and they caught us off guard.

We all dispersed, like crazy. I stayed more or less where I was, with two *compañeros*, in the cane field where some of our men had taken shelter – some of them had run right through it. Each man or small group had its own battle to fight. The three of us who were hunkered down in the sugar cane waited for night to fall – it wouldn't be long – and then we headed for those big woods. There we slept the best we could. Total forces: three men; total weapons: my rifle with ninety rounds and Universo's with thirty. That was what was left of my command.

The area was full of soldiers. We needed to march towards the east and bring as many of our dispersed *compañeros* back together again as we could. I wanted to head east along the edge of the woods; Faustino [Pérez], who like me was a member of the movement's leadership cadre, wanted to march through a broad swathe of sugar cane that couldn't have been more than about a metre tall, three feet tall. I did the wrong thing – I got furious with Faustino's stubbornness, and I said, 'You wanna go that way? Okay, that way it is!!' It's not hard to imagine what a terrible state of mind I was in after seeing all the work we'd been doing for two years go up in smoke in a question of minutes. Taking that route was a mistake. We'd walked several kilometres in broad daylight when I spotted a civilian plane, about medium-sized, that was circling about 3,000 feet above us. I realized the danger that implied, so we speeded up. In front of us there was a field of sugar cane that had been knocked down and three stands of marabu,[1] a thorny plant that grows spontaneously on abandoned land – these were growing in a kind of line about sixty yards to the east of us. Just a few yards from the spot where we were was the beginning of another old field of sugar cane. I said we had to get out of the scrubland immediately – it was just about ten yards in diameter – so we threw ourselves under the leaves and straw of the sugar cane that was just a few yards away. Almost simultaneously, the fighter jets, coming in from the east, started machine-gunning the scrub, passing over again and again for what seemed an eternity to us. The earth would shake under the firepower of the eight .50-calibre machine guns that each jet carried. A few yards away from the marabu, after each strafing I'd call out to Universo and Faustino, for whom, in spite of his hard-headedness, I had tremendous respect, and always will have – he was a true revolutionary. None of us was dead or injured. A few minutes without any strafing gave us the chance to crawl forward thirty or forty yards to a taller, thicker stand of sugar cane. There was no way to get any further away. The machine-gunning had stopped. The spotter planes took turns circling over the area, at very low altitude. We buried ourselves under the leaves and straw of the sugar cane and lay absolutely still.

At that point, I lived through one of the most dramatic moments of my life. Lying there in that cane field just yards from where we'd been strafed within an inch of our lives I got sleepy – very, very sleepy – and I said to myself, 'I know they're going to come in and go over this place on foot. They'll come to see what effect that tremendous attack had.'

They could not know who the men were out there in that field. But whoever they were, they attacked them with everything they had. All that happened a little after midday – I don't know the exact time. But I do know that we were underneath those leaves and straw, because they kept circling and circling overhead in those little spotter planes all the time, watching the area. Under the sugar cane, lying there like that, the exhaustion from all the tension you've lived through for days and days just comes over you.

Was that one of the most dramatic situations you've lived through?
Absolutely, one of the most dramatic, that one, that afternoon, at that hour. There was never any situation more dramatic. I've already told you about Sarría when I was captured after the assault on Moncada.

Yes, but this one was even more dramatic, wasn't it?
I remember when I could barely keep my eyes open. My rifle had two triggers: one trigger lightened the touch on the other, and the other one, practically all you had to do was touch it, so your shot would be very accurate.[2] The gun had a ten-power telescopic sight.

Under those circumstances, what did I do? When I realized there was no way I could stay awake, that I was sure to fall asleep, I lay down on my side and put the rifle butt between my legs and the end of the barrel under my chin. I didn't want to be captured alive if the enemy should come upon me while I was asleep. Having a pistol in that situation is better; you can take it out more easily and shoot at the enemy or shoot yourself, but with a rifle like the one I had, if they surprised you while you were sleeping you couldn't do anything. We were under the dry leaves, and the little prop plane up in the air above us . . . Since I couldn't move, I fell asleep and slept very deeply. I slept for about three hours; I was exhausted. As the afternoon went on, it got cooler.

Despite that tragic landing and the casualties, you weren't discouraged?
No. We started reorganizing with two rifles. Raúl, on the other hand, met us two weeks later with five guns. With the two we had, that meant we had seven. And that's when I said, for the first time, 'Now we can win this war.' I remember a phrase by Carlos Manuel de Céspedes, who, replying to the pessimists when he was in a similar situation and had only twelve men, said, 'We still have twelve men! That's enough to win Cuba's independence.' Raúl and I always had the same idea: get to the Sierra and continue the war.

So there was a moment when we kept fighting with just seven rifles, but at that point, aided by the *campesinos* who had picked up some guns from several of our murdered *compañeros* or some of our men who'd hidden weapons somewhere to be picked up later, we managed to put together an arsenal of seventeen guns, and with them we won our first victory.

What was the first victory?
The first combat was against a mixed patrol of army and navy troops. It took place forty-six days after we disembarked, on 17 January 1957 – we'd landed on 2 December 1956. That was our first victorious encounter, the first small but symbolic victory. Five days later, a platoon of paratroopers marching at the head of a column of 300 men fell into an ambush we'd planned down to the last detail – our fire inflicted about five casualties, and we occupied a Garand semi-automatic rifle with all its rounds. It would take a long time to tell everything that happened in those first two victorious combats: La Plata and Los Llanos del Infierno in Palma Mocha. We wound up with thirty men under arms, up from the nineteen that had been in the first combat.

Later, we had tremendous problems because of a very sensitive, vile betrayal – the man who betrayed us was the only guide we had. So we were then down to twenty men, and then twelve. After the disembarkation, and since that terrible reversal at Alegría de Pío, we'd been on our way to a quick recovery, and then came that betrayal.

What was the hardest part of that first period?
What was the hardest part? The learning curve. If we'd landed with eighty-two men in the right place, the place we'd planned to land at, the war might have lasted just seven months. Why? Because of experience. With those men and the experience we had, fifty-five weapons with telescopic sights, excellent marksmen, the war wouldn't have lasted seven months. On the *Granma*, I calibrated those fifty-five rifles for accuracy at 600 metres, over 650 yards. We had three makes of rifles, and each of them had a different variation, depending on the steel and the bullet, and on the *Granma*, at a distance of ten yards and with a geometric formula, I calibrated all the weapons. I spent over two days calibrating those rifles.

Che suffered from asthma, which must have made it very difficult for him to fight in a guerrilla war. When it came time to choose the men who would sail with you on the Granma, *you discarded others but not him. Did the asthma present any problems later on?*
Che came [to Cuba] on the *Granma*, of course . . . And of course everything was prepared as per our plan . . . Everyone had to be ready to leave [i.e., board ship] at any moment . . . No one knew when we'd be leaving. That night of 24 November 1956, when we mobilized towards a house on the bank of the Tuxpan River, Che took off without his asthma inhaler . . . But still, of course, he came with us on the *Granma* . . .

Without his asthma medication?
That's right. And several months later, up in the Sierra, after we met in February 1957 with Herbert Matthews, the reporter from the *New York Times*,[3] when we'd once again reached the figure of twenty combatants – we were more and more familiar with the terrain, more experienced at surviving, at handling ourselves under those difficult conditions, under constant, implacable pursuit from an enemy whose pride we'd wounded yet who still had absolute contempt for our modest forces – at that point a complicated situation arose with respect to Che's asthma.

We were attacked by a heavy column [of enemy troops]. Our march was dangerously slowed down due to a severe attack of asthma that suddenly came over Che. At that point, he could hardly walk. We had to climb a very steep mountainside; we were making our way up the incline towards a wooded area when a column of about 300 soldiers that was swinging around our left flank, higher than we were, on the firm ground of an elevation planted with pasture, spotted us, and they started firing at us with mortar shells, plus some rifle fire. Despite the shooting, we continued up the hill, practically dragging Che, trying to reach the wooded area before the enemy column. It was late by now, and night was beginning to fall. We reached the woods just minutes before a huge downpour – both sides, not more than 600 to 700 metres apart, were being deluged with rain. The rain forced us to keep going, to the other side of the peak on that cleared mountain top where – it was totally night by now – we found two *campesino* families, their houses separated by a few hundred yards. We were cold and soaked to the skin. Che couldn't even move.

He had an asthma attack?
Yes, a really severe attack. And that put us in a pretty complicated situation. There was no medication [for it]. He could have received it quickly from Manzanillo, at the point where we'd met with Matthews. Che hadn't said a word at the time. So now he was immobilized, with the army right on our heels. We didn't expect them to move at night through those woods, with the darkness and mud and whatnot. They'd no doubt move at sunrise, and they'd come right to us.

I introduced myself to the two *campesinos*, and drawing upon all my reserves of calm and sang-froid, I told them I was a colonel in the Batista army. There was nothing strange about that, if you consider the nearby explosions of the mortar shells and the intense rifle fire they'd heard until just a short while earlier. Sometimes that little ruse was necessary, because early on, the *campesinos* got very nervous when a rebel group visited them for the first time, because of the reprisals the army would take against them later. But my false identity had one flaw: I was too decent. I said to myself: 'I have to study these two, because I've got to find a way to get one of them to go for the medication.' I talked for hours with these two *campesinos*. I'm not going to mention the name of one of them, who was very definitely on Batista's side, but he said, 'Listen, send *mi general* greetings from me, and tell him such-and-such.' Oh, how he buttered me up! The other one was not so hearty – he was holding back. So I said to Isaac, which was his name, 'So, what do you think of this man?' – referring to Batista. And he said, 'Well, I was in the Orthodox Party.' The Orthodox Party was totally anti-Batista. 'But then,' Isaac went on, 'you've got to consider the work he's done . . .' All I could think about were the houses burned, and the horrors, and killing people . . . So I realized which side that one was really on. He was no sympathizer of Batista's; he held no brief for the man. So I said to him, 'Listen, I'm no colonel. I'm Fidel Castro.' He was so happy to hear that – his eyes went wide like this – he was so happy!

I told him, 'We're in a tough situation here – we've got a *compañero* in this situation, somebody's got to go to Manzanillo to get his medication. And we've got to find a place to hide him where he won't be discovered.' We gave [Isaac] some money for him to leave at first light and go to Manzanillo to get the medication. And he went.[4]

We found a spot that was well hidden and we left Che there with his weapon and another *compañero*. The rest of the group – there were eighteen of us at that point – went up a road that the army would have to go up, a wide, muddy road that led to Minas del Frío.

Back then we marched fast. Guillermo García[5] wore a sergeant's uniform and a helmet he'd taken in one of our first combats. We were psychologically hungry, so we were always sending ahead to plan something. So we'd arrived up in the Maestra[6] and suddenly confusion hit over the advance of some enemy troops close to our group, which was fragmented at the time, off doing various sorts of assignments. Conclusion: of the eighteen men in our group, six go one way – they were *campesinos* who'd joined up with us – so there were just twelve of us left, all from the *Granma*.

That same day, the commander of Batista's army – think of the coincidence! – gave a speech and he said, 'We're going to put that jug in the fire till the bottom breaks. There's just twelve of them left, and there's no alternative but to surrender or escape – if they can.' At that point Che was not with us, because he was back where we'd left him.

That *campesino*, by the way, José Isaac, accomplished his mission.

He brought back the medication?
He brought back the medication. When we split up, I gave Che an assignment – receiving the reinforcements of men and weapons that Frank País was sending up to us from Santiago de Cuba. Meanwhile, I was leading a small detachment eastward through the Sierra Maestra on a scouting mission. There was one problem with the recruits – we saw this months later: they weren't as experienced [as we were], so an ambush, for example, or some other action could go wrong. But they were all the more determined, because they wanted to do in one or two or three months what they'd heard that other men had done in a year. In situations like that, a recruit is terrific, under a good leader.

When the reinforcements arrived, several weeks later, there was a problem, because Che was an Argentine, and the new troops were a little chauvinistic.

Che was still considered an Argentine?
He wasn't a *comandante* yet. He was the medic for our troops, who was distinguishing himself . . .

How did he serve as the doctor for the guerrilla forces?
Che stayed behind with the wounded and he attended them with great skill. He was like that. As a doctor, he would remain behind with the sick, because out there in nature, in the rough, wooded terrain, with the combatants pursued from all different directions, what you might call our main force had to move after the encounter, leave a visible track so the medic with the men he was taking care of could safely stay behind. There was one point when he was the only medic, until others joined our struggle.

After the first combat we set up an ambush for those paratroopers; by now we had almost thirty men, as I said. There were no casualties in the first combat, none in the second. As a doctor, Che had nothing to do.

But the toughest combat was when we attacked the barracks in Uvero, right on the open coast.[7] [It was] an extremely risky action for us all, but while we were up in the mountains watching the movements of enemy troops in order to strike, we received news that a landing of armed Cubans had taken place in the northern [*sic*, for 'southern'] part of [Oriente, now Santiago] province. They belonged to another organization, which hadn't coordinated with anybody. We remembered how hard it was, how much we'd suffered in those first days after we'd landed, and as an act of solidarity with the men who had landed, we decided to carry out an action that was extremely daring from a military point of view, which was simply to attack a unit that was well dug in along the coast of the ocean, south of the Sierra, not far from our zone of movement.

It was daring, but we did it, as I said, to help a group that had no relationship to us but who were our compatriots; we knew what might happen to them and by this time we had a great deal of confidence in our own abilities. To provide them with support, we departed from our own doctrine. We carried out a daring attack in which a third of those who took part were either killed or wounded. And the action took place in broad daylight. Fortunately, we'd immediately destroyed the enemy's communications, so there were no gunships or planes that came to their aid.

I was carrying the rifle with the telescopic sight I showed you,[8] and at that stage, I would shoot first – that was the way to signal the beginning of the operation. To give you an idea of the amount of firing that went on in that wooden barracks, there were seven parrots and five of them were shot dead. At the beginning of the action, we had two platoons of reserves; they fired on the objective with me from a little heights nearby. We needed to see how the soldiers in the garrison reacted. There were some tree trunks stacked up behind the installation, because it was a forested area and timber was sent out from there to Santiago de Cuba. So [some of the soldiers] also got behind all that timber and fired on us, up towards the heights where we were dug in. The soldiers also had several tree-trunk bunkers that were hard to neutralize; they fired on the rebel forces from all of those.

In the encounter, several platoon and squad leaders distinguished themselves, such as Guillermo, who was in command of a squad from the group that attacked from the west and took the bunker over there – he along with Furri[9] and other brave men in the Santiago platoon.

At the first shots fired by us, Juan Almeida[10] was sent with his platoon over towards the main installation. When he got close, he opened fire and practically on foot they attacked a fortified point to his left. He was hit three times.

Ramiro Valdés, the second-in-command of Raúl's platoon, and very near Raúl [during this action], says that beside him, Julito Díaz had just been killed with a bullet to the eye.

The enemy, despite the tremendous surprise and the number of their casualties, had regrouped very quickly, really, and they were fighting furiously.

In the midst of that complicated situation, I sent Raúl, who'd been with me since the beginning of the attack, over to the main objective, in support of the men who were over there fighting so hard. That was the last reserves [we had]. Celia[11] was with me, and four or five other *compañeros* from the General Staff that had also been there since the beginning of the operation, over two hours before. Before that, I'd ordered Che to advance along the left flank; he had a submachine gun. He was with us in the command group – we saw that he was impatient, ready to reinforce the attackers over in that direction, so I sent him with two or three men to back up the combatants at that point, in the area where the enemy might be able to receive some support, although we knew where their troops were and how long it would take them to get there.

Curiously, the main platoon and squad leaders were all in that heavy fighting. Three of them – Raúl, Almeida and Ramiro – were in on the Moncada assault and had come over with the *Granma*, and two others, Guillermo García, the first *campesino* who joined us after Alegría de Pío, and Abelardo Colomé, whom we called 'Furri', was from Santiago and had been sent to us by Frank País.

We were lucky in that the planes never showed up, as I said, because fighting with the planes up above us would have been very serious business, or with gunships shooting high-calibre shells at our unprotected positions on the heights that overlooked the enemy's barracks. Had that happened, we'd have had to order a retreat, no doubt about it; we'd have had to retreat within an hour of beginning the action. [The enemy] had automatic and semi-automatic weapons and they defended themselves fiercely, fiercely. It was a company of special operations soldiers.

Che carried out the mission I'd sent him on. The battle at Uvero lasted about three hours. The enemy had eleven dead and nineteen wounded, among them the lieutenant commanding the barracks. We lost seven combatants and had eight wounded, several of them seriously. Once we'd achieved our victory, we provided aid to those who needed it. Che and the garrison doctor treated the enemy wounded, which there were more of than our own, and then they treated ours. Che treated all of them. You can't imagine that man's sensitivity!

We seized forty-five rifles – twenty-four Garand semi-automatics, twenty Springfields and a Browning submachine gun – and about 6,000 rounds of .30–06 ammunition, plus some other equipment – pistols, uniforms, boots, packs, cartridge belts, helmets and bayonets. We took a number of prisoners with us, while we had to leave two of our own wounded men there – we had to leave them because they couldn't move on their own.

You abandoned your wounded?
Let me explain. We held on to those prisoners in order to ensure that our two men who were wounded and had to remain behind at the garrison weren't murdered. Not that we would have taken reprisals, but it was a way of putting pressure on the enemy. If you have fifteen or sixteen prisoners, you have insurance, so to speak. The wounded from both sides, both theirs and ours, who couldn't move on their own, remained there. We took the prisoners that we could.

Che treated the wounded. He knew that one of our men was fatally wounded and didn't have long to live – a wonderful young man. What did [Che] do? He gave that dying boy a kiss when he left him . . . That really hit me when he told me that, painfully, remembering the moment when he realized there was no way to save him, so he leaned over and gave him a kiss on the forehead – [Che] knew he was inevitably going to die. The other man survived.[12] Of course we took the rest of our wounded with us, as we always did, among them Almeida. Also, in the last truck, Che left with us. I sent our men on ahead, and then we pulled out of the area as fast as we could, trying to get up to a higher altitude, in the woods, because at any moment the enemy's reinforcements might arrive, including planes . . . And sure enough, one of the garrison's soldiers had escaped – he hadn't been captured – and he ran off and told them, and that was when they learned of the attack.

We sent Che with a small group of men, so they wouldn't leave much of a trail, with our walking wounded, off to a place out in the country where they could be treated. [Che] had several armed men with him. So with his small group he stayed with the wounded and treated them. There were several columns of enemy soldiers approaching, and you knew there'd be a response to that daring and almost foolhardy attack . . .

We blazed a wide trail, advancing between enemy columns towards the north-west. That was where they had to follow us at some point, and that march wasn't easy. Che and his men stayed far back. It wasn't until a month or so later that Che rejoined our group, along with some *campesinos* who had joined him. Then, the first *comandante* we appointed was Che. There were two who had distinguished themselves a great deal: Che and Camilo.

Camilo Cienfuegos.

That's right, Camilo. He wasn't as intellectual as Che but he was very, very brave, an eminent leader, very daring, very humane. They respected each other, and loved each other very much. Camilo had distinguished himself, he'd been commander of the advance party, in Column 1, during the hardest days of those first few months. Now we assigned him to Che's column. Some time later, he made incursions into the lowlands and finally set up a front in that area – it was hard to do, we had no experience [in that terrain]. Camilo distinguished himself a great deal.

It was at that point, then, that you organized the various guerrilla fronts, with Che, Camilo and your brother Raúl?

Some of the troops with whom I'd returned from that combat, and several good officers with their enlisted men, among them Camilo and others, I sent with Che to form the second column, east of Turquino Peak [near the south coast] and not far from the first column. This was the First Front, with the original column and the new column under Che.

At that time, the original guerrilla column acted according to the tactic of attack and fall back and stay in motion, without a permanent territorial base. I always had command of Column 1, throughout the entire war. Out of that Column 1 came all the rest; Che's was the first, then Raúl's. Raúl crossed over from the Sierra Maestra into the mountainous region of the northeastern part of the island with fifty men; it was the first time we'd crossed the plains in that direction and they did it perfectly, they created the Second Eastern Front. In that big, distant region, Raúl was given the authority to create columns and appoint *comandantes*. So immediately, he created Juan Almeida's column, the third one, and [those two columns were then] the Third Front.

So Camilo's and Che's new columns, Raúl's, Juan Almeida's and several others in the east, the northwestern part of Oriente province, and the centre of the island, before or after the last enemy offensive – all of them stemmed from Column 1.

At that moment, you had no doubts, did you, that Che Guevara was an exceptional leader?
He was exemplary. He had great moral authority over his troops, great leadership. I believe he was a model for the revolutionary man.

People say he was perhaps a bit rash, a man who took unwarranted risks.
He was very daring. Sometimes he felt the best method was to use a group of soldiers loaded down with anti-personnel mines and other weapons. Camilo, on the other hand, preferred lighter troops. Che had a tendency to overload them. And sometimes he could have avoided a confrontation, a skirmish, a battle, but didn't. That was another difference between him and Camilo. Che was intrepid, but he also sometimes took too many risks . . . Which is why I'd sometimes say to him, 'You're responsible for these troops you're taking out there.'

So he was too daring sometimes.
Che wouldn't have come out of that war alive if some control hadn't been put on his daring and his tendency towards foolhardiness. I mean, when the

enemy's final offensive came, neither Camilo nor Che nor any of those leaders was in the front line. I sent Che to the recruits' school, where there were about a thousand recruits. Ramiro Valdés and Guillermo García stayed back at the place where their column fought Batista during the last offensive. Later, we brought them here too, to reinforce Column 1, but Che was assigned to the school, and also given the responsibility of defending the most westerly sector of the First Front, to confront the enemy if needs be.

And you did this so they wouldn't face too many risks?
That's right, because they were leaders. So I'd be able to use them later in strategic operations. Raúl's column on the Second Front was strategic, as was Almeida's on the Santiago Front, Che's in Las Villas, and Camilo's, which initially was sent to Pinar del Río.

In our defence against [Batista's] offensive we lost several brave, combative commanders who'd been extremely distinguished leaders. I had almost no leaders left in Column 1, but the ones I just named were very self-assured and reliable men, and all of them employed the same lessons no matter where they went, the same policy with the populace, with the enemy, and they were familiar with the experience we'd gained in the hard, critical months that had gone before – in a war to which every one of them was constantly bringing new contributions.

After Batista's last offensive, we sent Che to Las Villas with a column of 140 men and the best weapons. He had one of the bazookas we'd seized, good armaments, good soldiers. And [we sent] Camilo too. So we'd chosen two excellent leaders, although Camilo was carrying less weight. Che carried more, he insisted on carrying some anti-tank mines. He planned to use vehicles at some point, and he did that, I authorized him to do that, but when they started to pull out of the area they were hit by a hurricane – terrible wind, rain that brought floods and caused rivers to overflow their banks. Plus, both columns had to go through the plains around Camagüey, travel more than 400 kilometres, 250 miles through territory where Batista could call in the planes. It was a place where the 26th of July Movement was weak. They almost starved, as you can see from Camilo's and Che's writings.

It was a tremendous achievement those men, in a time of motorized infantry and aviation, were able to pull off – slogging through all that mud and marshland. And even under those adverse conditions they successfully fought several combats. It was a great achievement, and they wrote about it. Camilo wrote a detailed, moving report, and Che wrote about it in his campaign diary. Later he turned that into a book he titled *Passages from the Revolutionary War*, because he was in the habit of writing down everything that happened, and he had a real talent for storytelling – [he was] very brief, succinct. A later diary he wrote in Bolivia is a wonder of summation and brevity.

Let me pause for a moment to ask you about something else: when did you all decide to let your beards grow out as a symbol of the Revolution?

The story of our beards is very simple: it arose out of the difficult conditions we were living and fighting under as guerrillas. We didn't have any razor blades, or straight razors. When we found ourselves in the middle of the wilderness, up in the Sierra, everybody just let their beards and hair grow, and that turned into a kind of badge of identity. For the *campesinos* and everybody else, for the press, for the reporters we were '*los barbudos*' – the bearded ones. It had its positive side: in order for a spy to infiltrate us, he had to start preparing months ahead of time – he'd have had to have a six-months' growth of beard, you see. So the beards served as a badge of identification, and as protection, until it finally became a symbol of the guerrilla fighter. Later, with the triumph of the Revolution, we kept our beards to preserve the symbolism.

Besides that, a beard has a practical advantage: you don't have to shave every day. If you multiply the fifteen minutes you spend shaving every day by the number of days in a year, you'll see that you devote almost 5,500 minutes to shaving. An eight-hour day of work consists of 480 minutes, so if you don't shave you gain about ten days that you can devote to work, to reading, to sport, to whatever you like.

Not to mention the money you save in razor blades, soap, after-shave lotion, hot water . . . So letting your beard grow has a practical advantage and is also more economical. The only disadvantage is that grey hairs show up first in your beard. Which is why some of the men who had let their beards grow, cut them the minute the grey hairs started to show, because you could hide your age better without a beard.

In April 1958 there was a general strike against Batista, but you, who were up in the Sierra at the time, didn't support it. Why not?

That 9 April 1958 the general strike was declared, and it failed. At that point, we weren't in favour of the strike. The leadership cadre of the 26th of July Movement criticized us for that, and even said that we were not 'aware', not 'evolved', that we didn't have the degree of maturity that the Revolution has today. Yet I did sign the call for the strike because I could see that our *compañeros* in the Movement's leadership cadre were totally committed to it. So we supported it – concretely, by carrying out military actions in our territory against the enemy forces.

There were divisions, and there was a little exclusion. For example, although in the unions the Communists' influence was strong, there was prejudice [in the unions] against the Communists, which didn't happen with us up in the mountains. Some groups within the 26th of July Movement itself saw us as agitators; we were gaining prestige, we were making life difficult for Batista, and they thought the struggle would culminate in a military coup triggered by the 26th of July Movement and driven by the struggle carried out by the clandestine combatants and the guerrilla forces. We didn't see ourselves that way; we saw ourselves as the embryo of a small army – though experienced and daring – that with the total support of the people, right up to a general revolutionary strike, would defeat the enemy army.

Which is what happened in the end.
Which is exactly what happened, but the failure of that strike in April 1958 was a hard blow, because the failure caused such loss of morale among our people and at the same time encouraged the enemy forces, and [that encouragement] led to their last offensive against us.

Ten thousand men, consisting of fourteen battalions and I don't know how many additional independent infantry, artillery and tank units, supported by aviation and naval units, attacked Column 1's front lines, which was where the General Staff and Radio Rebelde were. They thought such an attack couldn't be resisted . . . That was the first time we'd defended our positions in close-range battle, and when they began the attack if we had 200 men it was a lot. I decided to move in troops from other fronts. I sent for Camilo, who was operating on the plains, and I sent orders to Almeida to send us support, some of his men, who'd opened another front in the eastern part of the Sierra Maestra, near Santiago. The only troops I didn't send for were Raúl's, because they were too far away. We fought for seventy straight days!

Once that last offensive was defeated, our forces, equipped with weapons seized from the enemy, grew from 300 to 900 armed men, and with them we invaded practically the whole country. When the counter-strike was over we organized, or rather reorganized, the columns. First we heavily re-equipped and reinforced two columns: Che's, with 140 men, and

Camilo's, with ninety. With those two, we advanced to the middle of the island. The number seems small, and it was, but those men's power of attack was fearsome. Camilo's was supposed to continue on to Pinar del Río but we stopped it in Santa Clara.

Why?

Why did we stop and not send Camilo on to Pinar del Río? Simply because we remembered the story of the invasion in the 1895 War of Independence, and that story carried a lot of weight. When Camilo came to the centre [of the island] it made no strategic sense to take the invasion there. And furthermore, certain circumstances having to do with the situation in Las Villas made it advisable that Camilo reinforce the joint military and political action that Che was going to be carrying out in that area. We realized that we were living in different times, and that the circumstances were very different, and that it didn't make any sense to take the invasion to Pinar del Río. At one point I said to Camilo, 'Stop in the centre, and join Che.'

After the failure of Batista's last offensive, did you decide to go on the counter-offensive?

The rebel columns were advancing in every direction through the country, without anyone or anything able to stop them. In a very short time, we had overcome and surrounded Batista's best troops. In Oriente province we had at least 17,000 enemy soldiers surrounded; if you add the operations forces and the garrisons for whom there was no escape, you see that no one could leave Oriente province, where the war had been going on since our disembarkation from the *Granma*.

Two frigates, of the three the enemy had, were trapped in the bay at Santiago de Cuba, they couldn't escape; eight machine guns we'd seized from the enemy totally covered the bay exit from the heights around the narrow channel.

When the war was over I visited the two frigates and realized that they'd run aground under the machine-gun fire; there were no commanding officers, no nothing, and the cannons wouldn't work from the deck because the frigates were manufactured for combat at sea from several kilometres' distance, not for meeting the fire from eight machine guns from 300 yards away. The metal and glass on their bridges were vulnerable to our machine guns – the calibre of the shells would have pierced them. They were completely defenceless.

On that occasion, you proposed an 'exit with dignity' to your military adversaries. What was that proposal?

The head of the enemy's operational forces, General Eulogio Cantillo, called for a meeting, and on 28 December 1958, I and a few other *compañeros* met with him in a dilapidated old sugar-cane *central*, the 'Oriente', near Palma Soriano. General Cantillo was no thug, and he was not known to be one of Batista's bloodthirsty, corrupt officers – he had a reputation for decency. He'd been to the [army] academy, one of the few [academy graduates] that Batista left in the army on 10 March 1952. [Cantillo] had even sent me a message when Batista launched the 10,000 men against us. I answered it, because he'd said that he was sorry about what was happening, that we were brave people and it grieved him that the country should lose people like us. I thanked him and told him that if he managed to defeat us, he shouldn't lament our fate, because if they managed to defeat the tenacious resistance they were going to meet, we would be writing a page of history that would one day be read and admired even by the children of the soldiers sent to fight us. Our reply was proud, perhaps arrogant, but gentlemanly.

Once in a while I'd exchange some communication with him – once, for example, when we had to release hundreds of enemy prisoners. We'd often exchange messages with commanders of nearby units or [those who were] in a difficult situation, to try to persuade them to put down their weapons; it was a style, a method of fighting. In complete confidence and trust, Cantillo arrived and talked to me. He came alone, in a helicopter. So you see how trusting he was. I remember what he told me: he acknowledged that he had 'lost the war' and he asked me for a formula to end it. I told him, 'Well, we can save a lot of officers and enlisted men who haven't committed any crimes. I suggest that you have the garrison in Santiago de Cuba revolt, in order to give shape to a civilian-military movement in cooperation with the Rebel Army.' Cantillo was the commander, too, of all the troops in the eastern region of the country. He agreed, he accepted my proposal, and we settled on a date. I told him, 'When this happens, within twenty-four hours Batista will no longer be in power.'

Still, he wanted to go to Havana; he claimed he had a brother, who was also a high-ranking officer in the army, the commander of the regiment in Matanzas. I asked him, 'What do you want to go to Havana for? Why run that risk?'

With me at that meeting was a former army officer, Comandante José Quevedo, commander of the battalion that had been surrounded and forced to surrender in El Jigüe after fighting so hard against us for ten days, from the 11th to the 21st July 1958. That battalion's prisoners had immediately been handed over to the International Red Cross. Later, [Quevedo] joined our forces. He had a very good reputation, and he reached the rank of general in the Revolutionary Armed Forces because of his performance and his services over so many years.

He had joined the rebel army?
He had been surrounded and I met him there, in El Jigüe, because the troops that had him surrounded and were fighting his battalion were under my direct command during the last enemy offensive. Several battalions had surrounded us, and we'd surrounded that other battalion. Our circle was tight, while theirs was strategic. We broke the balance when we defeated Quevedo's battalion. We took a lot of prisoners; [the battalion we'd defeated] had a lot of casualties, and we captured a large number of weapons. The balance tilted, you see, but we didn't immediately announce the victory, so the enemy wouldn't know how it had turned out.

We announced it forty-eight hours later; by that time, we'd armed some new troops and moved our forces into place against the other battalions, which we were beginning to surround, without wasting a minute.

Were you getting ready to attack Santiago de Cuba?
That happened five months after the defeat of the enemy offensive in August. We'd halted the attack on Santiago in late December, due to the meeting with Cantillo and his [surrender] agreement; we planned to carry out the attack with 1,200 men, approximately. They had 5,000. Still, we'd never had such a favourable balance of forces, and we were going to use the same tactics as in the Sierra Maestra: surround them and fight against reinforcements inside the city. That operation, according to my calculations, would last five days. From across the bay we'd smuggled in 100 weapons for the combatants in Santiago, because on the fifth day the city would rise up. Four battalions surrounded, four battles against the reinforcements, and then the uprising [– that was the plan].

That combat was going to last a maximum of six days – we'd delayed it; it was going to start around 30 December, more or less. After our meeting with Cantillo, we waited for him to keep our agreement. Camilo had an enemy battalion surrounded in Yaguajay and Che was beginning to penetrate the capital of Las Villas.

You were waiting for the agreement with the commander of the enemy forces in order to end the war?

That's right, and this General Cantillo finally went to Havana. I had imposed three conditions. And he agreed to them. I said to him, 'Well, go, if you've made up your mind to go, but first: we don't want a coup in the capital.' Our first condition was no coup in Havana. Second: 'We don't want anybody helping Batista escape.' Third: 'No contact with the US embassy.' Those were our three basic, very specific conditions, and the general agreed to them, and he left for Havana.

The time we'd agreed on came and went, and no news came of him. He'd left the commander of the garrison in Santiago in contact with me. So to make a long story short, Cantillo did exactly the opposite of what he'd agreed not to do: he had dinner with Batista the night of 31 December 1968, and went with him to the airport when Batista fled the country with a group of generals; second, he encouraged a coup in Havana; and third, he'd immediately got in touch, of course, with the American embassy . . . A cowardly betrayal! An act of treason!

What did you do then?

What did we do on 1 January 1959? Five years, five months and five days after the attack on Moncada on 26 July 1953? Exact numbers. That's the time that had passed since the attack on Moncada, including almost two years in prison, another almost two years outside Cuba preparing for an armed return, and another two years and one month at war.

On 1 January, when we heard on the radio that Batista had escaped and that there were signs of an impending coup in the capital, we ran to where Radio Rebelde was at the time, in Palma Soriano, and we sent instructions to our troops: 'Don't stop for a moment, accept no cease-fire.' To all the columns: 'Continue advancing and fighting.' And to the workers and the general population, we broadcast a call for a revolutionary general strike.

And unanimously, the workers voted to strike and even the people in the radio and television stations began airing our short-wave radio broadcasts from Radio Rebelde, which had a power of one kilowatt. They could do that by linking up one to another across the entire country, all the radio stations and television, which was in its infancy, so to speak. So by those means we could send instructions to all the troops. So I gave the entire country instructions and we were able to [leverage] the sympathies of the entire population.

Most of the labour unions were in the hands of a yellow pro-Batista and pro-Yankee group, but the workers went over the heads of their leaders and support for the strike became unanimous.

I drove in a Jeep to Santiago, skirting the cordillera so I could enter the city from the north. And on the way I met up with some uniformed men who were joining the cause. Since I'd given my word, I got in touch with the commander of the Santiago garrison. We'd exchanged some letters, and there were some questions remaining, because there was something I said that he had misinterpreted: 'If you don't meet our deadline of the 30th, we will attack and there will be no cease-fire until the garrison surrenders.' He had sent back a one-sentence reply: 'Soldiers do not surrender without a fight, or turn over their weapons without honour.' I wrote back to say that I hadn't ordered them to surrender, but simply warned him that once we started our attack there would be no cease-fire until the garrison had surrendered.

He wrote back saying, 'Trust the general,' referring obviously to General Cantillo, and he offered me a helicopter to fly me over Santiago de Cuba. I protested against the murder of two young men which had taken place the night before and told him I didn't need any helicopter. He [said he] was sorry for the murders. Now I was en route from Palma Soriano to the town of El Caney, north of the city, the same place where I tried to take the army barracks after Moncada, on 26 July 1953. That same day, 1 January, in less than eight hours, following orders broadcast by Radio Rebelde, our forces had brought an end to all resistance. Meanwhile, not knowing what had happened, due to a lack of communications, I was meeting with the officer cadre in the military barracks in Santiago and the operations units based in that city. And they were doing it [i.e., meeting me] very enthusiastically. I met about 300 officers. Three hundred officers of the troops who were defending Santiago de Cuba!

And I spoke to them; I explained the agreement we'd made with General Eulogio Cantillo, which he hadn't kept. I explained his betrayal, and they supported us, they came over to our side. I even appointed the commander of the Santiago garrison commander of the rest of the army.

Raúl says that when I told him I'd appointed Colonel Rego Rubido commander of the garrison and the army, he accepted out of discipline, but he didn't understand, so all he could say was, 'He must know what he's doing.' So Rego Rubido was commander of the army for a while, and he kept his word.

Meantime, Camilo and Che were entering Havana, I believe.

No, Che was attacking the city of Santa Clara. He'd already taken the main police station; an armoured train pulled in, very well protected, and Che's forces pulled up some track behind it; when the train started backing up, it derailed and they managed to seize all the guns and weapons on board and take the soldiers on board prisoner.

General Cantillo hadn't kept his word, so on that 1st of January I sent Camilo and Che the orders: 'Advance on Havana.' I told Camilo, 'You go to Columbia [military base],' and Che, 'You head for La Cabaña [another barracks, and also a prison].' They were still finishing the takeover of their objectives, but of course when the tyranny fell and the general strike started, all it took was one day for the rest of the army to surrender and for [Camilo and Che] to get organized and leave. I think they left that night, as fast as they could, or the next morning. At that moment I told them, 'Advance at full speed along the Central Highway.' The morale of Batista's people was very low . . . Che and Camilo organized two columns and advanced towards the capital. It took them a few hours to get there, but they finally arrived at their objectives. No one put up the slightest resistance, they didn't have to fire a single shot, and our people in Havana had almost everything under their control: total demoralization on the part of our adversaries, the entire country paralysed, an uprising in the cities, the people imposing their will all across the country.

Columbia and La Cabaña were the two large military barracks or encampments in Havana?

That's right. You see, the largest and most important fortress in Havana was Columbia, which is where Camilo went. The army's General Staff was headquartered there. The other large fortress, La Cabaña, was where Che went. The timing was perfect. They were military commanders and they had two powerful units – nothing could stop their advance. Camilo, at Columbia, set about reorganizing the forces, because there were even some American advisers there.

What Che started to do immediately, of course, once the fortress was secured and the war was over, was organize classes for all those *campesinos*, set up schools, and educate his people. He wanted his first action as military commander to be putting in place his literacy programme and teaching all the combatants.[13]

At the Columbia complex, Camilo encountered some former army officers who'd been held prisoner on Isla de Pinos – the Isla de Juventud today – for conspiring against Batista. They got out of prison on 2 January when the government fell. Some were officers of considerable prestige – the colonel who'd commanded the group wanted to organize that old army and maintain the morale of the men who were there. They'd arrived at Columbia before Camilo – the prison was just a few minutes from Havana by air. He took his group to the General Staff headquarters and they asked to speak to me – I was in Santiago. I told them, 'Tell Colonel Barquín' – this was the colonel I'm talking about; he was highly respected; he'd studied in the United States – 'that the only person I speak to in Columbia is Camilo. And in La Cabaña, Che.' They were trying to make deals and arrangements and so on, although we never gave them the slightest chance.

We didn't waste a minute, or a second. We had the backing of the entire country, which had taken over the streets and the entire nation.

What finally happened to General Cantillo?
Cantillo was arrested and sentenced to a number of years in prison, and then we released him.

When did you enter Havana?
I left Santiago for Bayamo on the 2nd. The operations troops headquartered in Bayamo who'd been fighting very hard against us had joined the 300 officers at El Caney, and they joined us as soon as I met them in a stadium in Bayamo. Actually, they greeted me very, very enthusiastically – it was hard to understand. I was advancing with 1,000 rebel soldiers towards Havana, where the situation with respect to the old army was unclear. I tried to keep those 2,000 men in the army, which was really hard.

I invited those 2,000 men, with their weapons – they had Sherman tanks, which we didn't know how to use, and artillery and so on – and since the situation in Havana was still uncertain, while Che and Camilo were arriving I made the decision [to enlist the 2,000 soldiers from the old army]. I came to Havana with 1,000 rebel combatants and 2,000 enlisted men belonging to the old army's best operations troops – the ones who until just a few days earlier had been engaged in fierce, bitter fighting with us in Guisa, Baire, Jiguaní, Maffo, and before that in the Sierra Maestra during the last offensive, and who'd lost maybe half of their troops in those battles – where, by the way, we always gave medical care to the enemy's wounded and freed the prisoners. Now, they were ready to fight alongside us. They were with me, driving the tanks and other heavy armaments – none of our people knew how to do that at the time – and they were delighted. I mean, they were witnesses to a mass welcome, a sea of people greeting us as we entered the city.

It took me eight days to reach Havana, because at every provincial capital I had to stop and make a speech and so on – there were crowds waiting for us everywhere along the line. A tank was the only thing that could get through – you couldn't get through in a truck or you'd be crushed. There was no resistance in Havana, which was the only place in the first seventy-two hours that might have been dicey. The strike was still going on; the people were excited about the strike even though there was no need for one now, but by that time, everybody was celebrating. *Todo el mundo estaba de fiesta.*

I arrived in Havana on 8 January 1959, after speaking to the crowds and rallying them all along the route. I went to Cienfuegos, where I'd been in jail during my student days and where the heroic rebellion of the sailors and revolutionaries had taken place. And Camilo and Che, in their solid positions, were waiting. In Havana, the 26th of July Movement had taken over all the police stations the very first day.

They'd been under your people's control since 1 January?
That's right, our people's. Even before Camilo and Che arrived, actually, the people from Action and Sabotage in the 26th of July Movement had taken over all the police stations. Many had died doing that. They were very brave, but they hadn't had the battle experience that we'd acquired up in the mountains. There were a lot of combatants from the lowland plains who'd preferred the risks of the city to climbing up and down mountains. Many of the ones who were excellent at fighting in cities were terrible guerrillas, because when you're fighting a guerrilla war, what's hard is climbing mountains, scrambling up and down hillsides, enduring all that hard physical effort, all the sacrifices . . . That's the way guerrilla warfare is, and that's the way men are.

And so the war ended.
Our army grew very quickly at the end, because in December 1958 I had, according to my calculations, just 3,000 armed men, but when we seized all those weapons on 1 January 1959, our army grew within just a few weeks to 40,000 men. But the war was won, in less than two years, by 3,000 men. One mustn't forget the time [it took].

9
Lessons from a Guerrilla War

Violence and revolution – Ethics with the campesinos *–*
Treatment of prisoners – Wartime justice in the Sierra

Do you think you and your people won the war because of your military tactics or because of your political strategy?
Both. Even before I went to prison, I had the plan for the war in the Sierra Maestra, the whole plan. We developed a warfare of movement, as I said – attack and fall back. Surprise. Attack, and attack again. And a great deal of psychological warfare. Burning the sugar cane to harass Batista,[1] force him to move and disperse troops, deprive him of resources and the support of the large landowners, sabotaging transportation routes and communications. But for us, guerrilla warfare was the detonator of another process whose objective was the revolutionary takeover of power. And with a culminating point: a revolutionary general strike and a general uprising of the populace.

You put your money on irregular warfare. Why was that?
I always trusted in the possibilities of an irregular war. Throughout history, in all wars since the times of Alexander and Hannibal, victory was always within the grasp of those who used the wiles of secrecy in their movements and surprise in their deployment of men and arms, terrain and tactics. How often those strategists used the sun or the wind against their enemies! The commander who knew best how to use his own resources, and in some cases even nature – that was the commander who won.

We put our imagination to work, and we found that we had to develop ideas able to overcome the immense obstacle of defeating a government that was backed by an army of 80,000 heavily armed men. We had very few resources, and we had to optimize our use of them, as well as the deployment of weapons and men. That was our fundamental problem.

But we soon developed the art of confusing the enemy forces, to force them to do what we wanted them to do. I would say that we developed the art of provoking the enemy forces, and of forcing them to stay on the move, based on a principle that we came to understand, which, as I told you, is that the adversary is strong when he's in his own positions, inside his own defences, but that he's weak when he's on the move, when he's pulled out of position. We developed the art of forcing the enemy to set out on marches, so we could attack him when and where he was most vulnerable.

You have to understand that in a forest, or in the mountains, for example, a column of 400 men has to move in single file. There are places where the terrain doesn't allow a force to advance unless it's one by one, and a battalion's combat ability in Indian file is minimal – it can't fan out. We'd take out the men in front, attack the centre, and then ambush the rear when it started retreating, on the terrain we'd chosen. Always by surprise, and in the place selected by us. Over time, we became pretty effective with that tactic.

You and your men developed the art of the ambush.
Well, ambushes are as old as warfare. We diversified the types of ambushes; we always made the first attack against the vanguard, which often caused the entire enemy column to withdraw, if its vanguard was wiped out. Then we'd also attack their flank, and last, when they were retreating, we'd mount a second ambush – when demoralized troops were trying to get back to their starting point and their rear guard turned into their vanguard.

You attack at night on a certain road, two, three times, and the enemy stops going out at night. You attack during the day, on foot, if they're on foot. If he mounts his troops on trucks, you attack when they're going up a hill or marching very slowly up a steep unpaved mountain road; you attack with automatic weapons if you can and you have them, or with whatever you've got. And if they armour their vehicles, you use landmines. If you're not able to surprise them any more, you have to invent other tactics.

You have always to be one step ahead of them. Surprise, that's the trick. Attack them in ways and in places they aren't expecting. When you do, the unit under fire always sends for reinforcements. If they don't get them, they surrender, [especially once] they came to realize that the revolutionary forces respected the lives and physical well-being of our prisoners.

But for you and your men, the military aspect was secondary to the political, I imagine. [Are you saying that] military strategy was the more important?
If the political front that we had proposed, the union of all anti-Batista forces, had happened from the beginning, the Batista regime would have collapsed of its own accord, maybe without another drop of blood being spilled. That was what we had hoped, that was what our tactics were aimed at. We're talking about tactics and how you win a war. Our tactics proved, in both political and military terms, to be the best in the concrete case of Cuba. That's why I have always said that you have to have a policy towards the populace and a policy towards your adversary. If you don't, you don't win. You can't kill innocent people, and you have to fight against the enemy's forces in combat. There's no other way to justify the use of violence. That is my conception of war.

You waged an informal war, but did you decide to obey the laws of war?
Yes, because that's a psychological factor of great importance. When an enemy comes to respect and even admire their adversary, you've won a psychological victory. They admire you because you've managed to defeat them, because you've hit them hard yet at the same time respected them, because you haven't humiliated them, you haven't insulted them, and especially because you haven't murdered them. And the moment came when we clearly had the upper hand in that respect. Our enemy respected us. Because they knew how wars were usually waged and how merciless the victors usually were with the conquered army.

You and your men, then, had made respect for prisoners a principle?
And there was no torture. Because what we were clear about, in the struggle against that regime, was that it tortured people and murdered people. I once said to those who accused us of violating human rights, 'I defy you to find a single case of extra-judicial execution; I defy you to find a single case of torture.'

Since the very beginning of the Revolution?
Since the triumph of the Revolution, and even before; since we began the struggle at Moncada, or later, when we landed in 1956. I remember that once, in the struggle against the *bandidos*, in the sixties, one of our commanders started to use certain methods of intimidation – he threw prisoners into the pool, put some on board helicopters – not really intending to throw

them out, but certainly to intimidate them. I got wind of that and I went to Escambray immediately, where this had taken place. He got a severe, severe dressing-down. He never [used physical torture], but it was a kind of psychological torture – whatever the case, it was unacceptable.

In addition, a police or intelligence agency that tortures doesn't really make headway, it doesn't develop the methods that ours developed – especially methods of infiltration, to seek out the truth. When someone was arrested, they would say they didn't remember where they were on such a day, but our intelligence organs knew, because it was all in a report. If you're asked, 'What did you do on Sunday, May something-or-other last year?', you may not remember, and the same thing would happen to them: who did they meet with? Who gave them their weapons? People were arrested only when there was irrefutable proof. Infiltration functioned very well, but physical violence never did – we simply never used it.

Were you and your followers the first guerrilla fighters to come up with that idea of not stealing from the campesinos, *not raping women, not torturing prisoners?*
No, no, I wouldn't say that at all, because I don't think that the Vietnamese patriots who began their struggle before we did, in 1946, or the Algerians, who also came before us, in 1954, raped women or stole from the countrypeople. I don't believe they did. There have been many struggles in which those principles have been respected. I have absolutely no evidence to the contrary.

The men and women who resisted the German soldiers, behind the Soviet–German front, didn't torture anyone, I believe, or rape women, because the ones who rape, steal, kill and burn, everywhere, are the forces of the reactionary regimes against which revolutionaries fight. Although no one knows what happened on those battlegrounds in the Second World War. I imagine there were cases of them shooting one another by firing squad, because there's no question that the Nazi troops didn't let any Bolsheviks escape with their lives, and I really don't know how the people in the Soviet resistance might have treated the Nazis who fell prisoner. I don't think they could do what we did. If they turned one of those Fascists loose, the next day he'd be killing Soviet men, women and children again. In cases like that, I'd have said they were perfectly justified in putting them out of action.

In Mexico, in 1910, there was a very fierce revolution that lasted for many years, and in Spain, too, in 1936, there was a bloody war . . .

And atrocities were committed on both sides.
In Spain there were even battles at the rear. That's what inspired Hemingway's novel *For Whom the Bell Tolls*.[2] The history of what happened at the rear during the Spanish Civil War was useful to us – knowing how the Republican guerrilla fighters behind the Franco forces managed to get their hands on the army's weapons. That book helped me conceive our own irregular war.

Hemingway's novel?
That's right, because while I was up in the Sierra, I remembered that book a lot . . . One day when we're talking about that I'll tell you.

Why don't you tell me now?
Well, if you want . . . You see, I read *For Whom the Bell Tolls* for the first time when I was a student. And over the years I must have read that novel at least three times. And I was also familiar with the movie that was made later. I was interested in that book because as I was saying, it deals, among other things, with a struggle in the rear of a conventional army. And it talks about life in the rear; it tells us about the existence of a guerrilla force, and how that guerrilla force may act in a territory that's supposedly controlled by the enemy. I'm referring to the very precise descriptions of war written by Hemingway in that novel.

We intuited what an irregular struggle might be like, from the political and military point of view. But *For Whom the Bell Tolls* allowed us to actually *see* that experience. Because in all his books, Hemingway describes things in a very realistic way, with great clarity. Everything is realistic and everything is convincing. It's hard to forget what you've read, because it's as though you'd lived through it, because he has the virtue of immersing the reader in the events of that cruel war, the Spanish Civil War. Later, we came to know that life as a guerrilla first-hand, up in the Sierra Maestra. So that book became a familiar part of my life. And we always went back to it, consulted it, to find inspiration, even when we were already guerrillas. And we tried to impose ethics on our struggle within the specific conditions of our country.

And I'll say it again: it cannot be said that we were the only guerrilla force with ethics.

But you and your followers made that ethics a fundamental principle.
Here, without that philosophy, combatants might have shot prisoners left

and right – heaven only knows what might've been done. There was a great deal of hatred for the injustice and the crimes [of that tyrannical government].

Did you and your followers use terrorism, for example, against Batista's forces? Or assassinations?
Neither terrorism nor assassinations. You know, we were against Batista but we never tried to assassinate him, and we could have done it. He was vulnerable – it was much harder to fight against his army in the mountains [than to kill him], much harder to try to take a fortress that was defended by a regiment. How many men were there in the Moncada barracks that 26 July 1953? Almost 1,000 men, maybe more.

Preparing an attack against Batista and killing him was ten or twenty times easier, but we never did that. Has tyrannicide ever served to make a revolution? Nothing changes in the objective conditions that engender a tyranny.

The men who attacked the Moncada fortress could have assassinated Batista on his farm, or on the road, the way Trujillo and other tyrants were killed, but we had a very clear idea: assassination does not solve the problem. They'll put someone else in the place of the man you killed, and the man you killed becomes a martyr to his people. The inadvisability of assassination is an old idea, arrived at and incorporated into revolutionary doctrine a long time ago.

There was also a great deal of discussion in the international Communist movement, whether it was right to get money by robbing banks. In the history of the Soviet Union, there are some who say that Stalin may have carried out some of those bank robberies. That – both the theory of assassination and the theory of bank robberies to get money – was really in contradiction with the most elementary common sense. Robbing banks was very much looked down on in Cuba, which is a country with a strongly entrenched bourgeoisie among whom banks were very highly respected. It wasn't a question of ethics, it was just a practical matter: whether you were going to help the Revolution or help the enemy.

What about the theory of an assassination attempt, or even just an attack, that may produce innocent victims?
Speaking just about war, we never faced that problem, because our war lasted [only] twenty-five months, and I cannot remember a single case of a

civilian death in any battle fought by Column 1. You'd have to ask the other commanders if they recall any cases in their operations.

For us it was a philosophy, a principle, that innocent people must not be sacrificed. It was always a principle – practically dogma. There was one case here in which some of the clandestine fighters in the Movement set off a bomb, which in fact *was* in the tradition of revolutionary struggles in Cuba. But we didn't want to do that, we disagreed with that method. We were truly concerned about the civilians in the battles where there might be some risk.

I mean, you saw Moncada, we showed you the floor plan, everything, and there was not a single civilian at risk there. The only civilians who were at risk were us revolutionaries, who were armed.

Apparently you'd given orders that deaths be kept to a minimum, even among Batista's forces. Is that true?
We weren't so concerned about the enemy soldiers who died in combat. We *were* concerned about those who surrendered or fell prisoner. If you aren't, you can't win. There are principles that are elementary in war and in politics. It wasn't because we were bleeding hearts. Ethics is not simply a moral issue – if ethics is sincere, it produces results.

In many places in the world today, violent groups seek to attain their political objectives by terror, blindly killing people. Do you disapprove of those methods?
I say to you that no war is ever won through terrorism. It's that simple. Because [if you employ terrorism,] you earn the opposition, hatred and rejection of those whom you need in order to win the war.

That's why we had the support of over 90 per cent of the population. Do you think that if we'd been sacrificing innocent people in Cuba we'd have achieved that level of support? Do you think that if we'd set off bombs, killed soldiers taken prisoner, killed civilians, we'd have obtained the arms that we obtained? We saved so many lives!

I told you earlier what happened in that battle at Uvero, when we attacked a garrison on the edge of the ocean – an extremely dangerous action. One of the toughest battles we fought, in which a third of the participants died or were wounded. We gave medical attention to a good many of the enemy's soldiers that we took prisoner, and we left them there so [their own] army could pick them up. We only took a few uninjured prisoners with us. They weren't immediately released.

211

From the very first battle, our medical supplies were used for *all* the wounded, without distinction – both ours and the army's. We had just nineteen men in that first combat, against a mixed garrison of sailors and soldiers; it was our first victory. I've spoken about that already. When it was over, there were several enemy troops dead, and of the rest, I think only one wasn't wounded. We didn't have a single casualty. It was two forty in the morning when we began that battle, which lasted almost an hour, because they resisted, they thought we'd kill them if they surrendered. Then, when it was all over, we gave them medication, we treated the wounded, and we left them the medical supplies they needed. One of our men stayed and took care of them, while we took the weapons and left the area before daybreak.

We shared our medical supplies, which were extremely limited, with our enemy's wounded. Sometimes we wouldn't have a single man injured. If there were wounded and injured on both sides, we treated both sides. If we'd had to choose between the life of one of our *compañeros* and the life of one of the enemy, of course we would save our *compañero*'s life, but if we didn't have a single man wounded, we'd leave the scarce medical supplies we had for the enemy, from the first battle to the last.

We'd give [our critics] everything we own, although this country doesn't have much, if they can find a single case of a soldier taken prisoner and executed, or a prisoner beaten, during the entire war of liberation.

Those ideas – because we were fighting against an extremely repressive regime which did precisely that, torture, murder – have been upheld for over forty-nine years, since the day we landed in the *Granma* on 2 December 1956. Figure out how many years it will be in December 2005.

Forty-nine years.
For forty-nine years, since we disembarked from the *Granma*, those guidelines have been in place: no assassination, no civilian victims, no use of the methods of terror. Why should we have done those things? It never occurred to us.

Don't forget what I've been telling you: we'd already done some reading in Marxism-Leninism, and I've told you what we thought. That influenced our strategies. Assassination is unnecessary, if you clearly understand that it makes no sense. I explained my reasons relating to the forms of expropriation of funds in the specific case of Cuba – that is, they're linked to a sense of the practical more than to an ethical principle. Neither the theorists of our wars of independence nor any Marxist-Leninist that I know of advocated assassinations or terrorist-style acts, acts in which innocent people might be killed. *That's* not contemplated in any revolutionary doctrine.

The errors committed when one is in power are another thing; that's another thing. I'm telling you our history. I do think we've written a new page [in history], especially with regard to maintaining a constant mode of behaviour throughout all these years, and despite our having lived through very hard, very tough, very serious episodes.

There were cases of [Batista] battalions who were surrounded and eventually surrendered. We [always] made a concession to the prisoners [in those cases]: the soldiers were allowed to go absolutely free. Those who were known to have committed crimes, if there were any, we offered not to apply the maximum sentence [i.e., death]. In our agreements with a battalion, or whatever unit, we allowed the officers to keep their personal sidearms. We had an invariable policy of respect for the adversary's integrity. If you kill them after they've surrendered, [the next ones] will fight you to the death, and besides, it costs you bullets, and lives. In a word, you don't win the war. The adversary will always have more weapons, resources and trained men.

There were cases of enlisted men who surrendered as many as three times, and three times we would release them. Besides, they'd left us their weapons. Their superiors would send them off to another area, or another province, but then our struggle would be taken there too . . . The enemy soldiers were our arms suppliers, and the *campesinos* were our main support and main suppliers of food. Batista's soldiers would go around stealing, burning houses and killing people. The *campesinos* could see that we, on the other hand, respected them – we paid them for the food and other things we got from them, even more than it was worth, sometimes. If we wanted to buy a chicken, or a hog, and there was nobody around, we'd leave a note telling them where to find the money when they got back. There was not a debt left by us in any little store anywhere. That was our policy with the populace. Otherwise, we wouldn't have won over anybody, and would never have won the war. The *campesinos* – don't think for a moment that they went to schools in revolutionary instruction. None of us knew the Sierra. But honestly – how else could we ever have won the war?

Only with that policy?
Without it, we'd never have won the war, and without certain operational concepts.

And yet up in the Sierra, you and your men had to institute what you called 'revolutionary justice', which led you to apply the death penalty.

Only in cases of betrayal. And the number of cases of persons sentenced to death was minimal. I remember that a rash of banditry broke out in a group that was collaborating with the Rebel Army, when there were only a few of us, not even 200 men – fewer, about 150. Although it was a movement that could defend itself and keep from being destroyed – but that was based on our treatment of the population, which was, as I said, all you could ask. We paid the *campesinos* with what very little we had for every single thing we got from them, even if they didn't want to accept it, and we paid them, I assure you, at a higher-than-market price. We showed, as I said, respect for their families, their children, their women, respect for their crops and their livestock – our respect was common knowledge. While Batista's army ran around burning, killing, stealing . . .

For us, then, an outbreak of banditry was fatal, and we had to execute those who engaged in it – it's that simple. Trials were held for several of the men who had been robbing houses or robbing stores. And that time, with a war being fought, the death penalty was applied. It was unavoidable and it was effective, because from then on, there was never another member of the Rebel Army who robbed a store. A tradition had been created. And an ethics was born out of it: total respect for the populace.

10

Revolution: First Steps, First Problems

Transition – Sectarianism – Public trials of torturers –
The Revolution and homosexuals – The Revolution and blacks –
The Revolution and women – The Revolution and machismo –
The Revolution and the Catholic Church

In January 1959 you and your followers didn't institute a policy of revolutionary change overnight; you began a sort of transition phase, isn't that right?
We had already put in place a government. I had said that I had no desire to be president – I wanted to show that I hadn't been in the struggle out of personal interest. We looked for a candidate, and we chose a magistrate who'd been against Batista, who'd actually acquitted revolutionaries who came before him in an important trial.

Manuel Urrutia?
That's right, Urrutia. He was highly respected. It's a shame he didn't have a bit less ambition and a bit more humility and common sense.

You didn't want to be president at that moment?
No, I had no interest in being president. What I wanted to pursue was the Revolution, the army, the development of our heroic Rebel Army. I mean, an election might come along at some point and I might run, but I wasn't really thinking about that at the time. I was interested in the laws that the Revolution would put in place, and in the application of the Moncada programme.

In other words, you waged that entire war with no personal desire to become president immediately afterwards?

I can assure you that that was the case, yes. Other factors may have come into play besides disinterestedness; there may have been a bit of pride, something of that sort, but the fact is, I wasn't interested. Remember, I'd been as good as dead for a long time. I was fighting to bring about a revolution, and titles weren't important to me. The satisfaction of the struggle, pride in the struggle and its eventual success, victory, is a prize much greater than any government position, and when I said I wasn't interested in being president, I did so after great deliberation. Our movement supported Urrutia for president, and we respected its decision. He and the 26th of July Movement, together, made the appointments to the cabinet, and there were those in the leadership cadre of the 26th of July Movement who were from the upper-middle class, even pretty right-wing, who'd joined us along the way, and others from the Left.

Some of them have written their memoirs, and many of them remained with the Revolution afterwards. They've had very interesting things to say, and they've been honest about what they thought, their discussions [perhaps 'arguments'] with Che and Camilo.

Did Che mistrust some of those leaders?

Che was very suspicious and very mistrustful of some of them, because he'd seen some problems during the strike in April 1958 and he thought that some of the members of the 26th of July Movement whom he'd talked to in Villa Clara during the war were incorrigibly bourgeois. Che was very much in favour of agrarian reform, and some of the others kept talking about a very moderate reform, with indemnifications and compensations and that sort of thing.

Che, nevertheless, was in favour of unifying all the revolutionary forces. On the other side there was a lot of anti-Communism; it was strong and influential, and Che rejected it. Here in Cuba, during the McCarthy era, things were pretty venomous; there was prejudice everywhere, in all the media. And to add to the anti-Communism of quite a few people, with their bourgeois and petit-bourgeois background, there was also sectarianism among many Communists.

Of the ultra-left-wing sort?

No, the Communists, the people in the PSP [Popular Socialist Party].[1]

BETTMANN/CORBIS

José Martí, poet and hero
of Cuban independence.

HULTON-DEUTSCH COLLECTION/CORBIS

Cuban combatants during the War of Independence against Spain, January 1896.

Angel Castro, Fidel Castro's father. 'He was a man of great will, great determination.'

Lina Ruz, Fidel Castro's mother. 'She was Cuban, from the western part of the island, from the province of Pinar del Río. Her family was originally from the Canary Islands.'

Fidel Castro (*right*) with his siblings Angelita and Ramón.

FOTOS: ARCHIVO FIDEL CASTRO

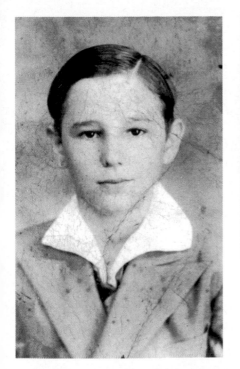

(*above*) In Colegio Dolores, school year 1940–41, Fidel Castro is second from right, looking at the camera. (*left*) Studio photograph from the same period.

Fidel Castro, university student leader, during a public speech.

AFP PHOTO/PRENSA LATINA

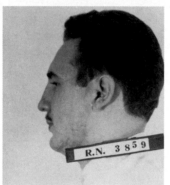

R.N. 3859

R.N. 3859

Fidel Castro arrested by the police and interrogated after the assault on the Moncada barracks in August 1953.

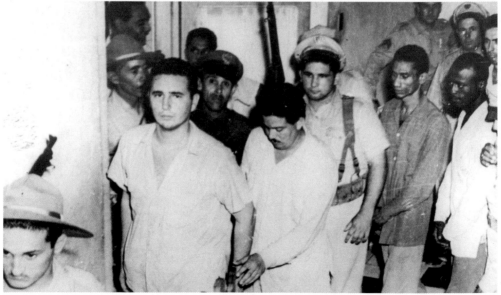

AGENCIA EFE

RENE BURRI / MAGNUM PHOTOS

With Raúl Castro and Juan Almeida, leaving prison on the Isle of Pines, 1955.

GREY VILLET//TIME LIFE PICTURES/GETTY IMAGES

Fulgencio Batista, president of Cuba, in 1957.

BETTMANN/CORBIS

Fidel Castro and some of the main leaders of the Revolution in June 1957. Among those around Castro here are Raúl Castro, Ernesto 'Che' Guevara, Juan Almeida, George Sotus and Guillermo García.

GILBERTO ANTE/ROGER VIOLLET/GETTY IMAGES

Sierra Maestra, 1957. Fidel Castro and Celia Sánchez surrounded by combatants.

CORBIS

Sierra Maestra. Fidel Castro with two of his men.

Vigente el plazo de 48 horas para que se rindan los rebeldes

Dirigentes oposicionistas visitaron al Primer Ministro para gestionar el cese del fuego. Han presentado también un plan de arreglo pacífico

SE DESCONOCE SI CASTRO ESTA EN CUBA

Díaz Tamayo cree que los rebeldes no están aún resueltos a rendirse y que disponen de víveres; considera que se encuentran muy fraccionados

News stories in the Cuban press after the arrival of the *Granma*. (*above*) '[Authorities give] rebels 48 hours to surrender. | Opposition leaders visited the Prime Minister to arrange for cease-fire. Also presented a plan for peace. | NOT KNOWN IF CASTRO IS IN CUBA. | Díaz Tamayo thinks the rebels are not yet resolved to turn themselves in, and have food supplies; believes they are very fragmented.' (*right*) 'No one who attempts a surprise attack on Cuba can possibly succeed, declares Batista.'

4 January 1959. Public speech in Camagüey. The Revolution has triumphed. Here, Castro is surrounded by some of the members of the 26th of July Revolutionary Movement.

BETTMANN/CORBIS

Fidel Castro speaks in an unidentified town during the 'March to Havana'.

BETTMANN/CORBIS

In La Plata, Sierra Maestra, smoking, surrounded by *campesinos* and combatants.

Two examples of the Cuban press's reaction to the attack on Playa Girón, Bahía de los Cochinos (the 'Bay of Pigs') and the US administration's activities: (*above*) 'Yankee invasion imminent: Roa to the UN to denounce the attack | Fatherland or Death! We shall conquer!' (*below*) 'Cynical official Yankee declaration | Kennedy confesses to being responsible for the invasion | "United States sent us to kill this nation" | Calviño, typical imperialist figure.'

NEAL BOENZI/NEW YORK TIMES CO./GETTY IMAGES

With Soviet president Nikita Khrushchev at the Theresa Hotel, Harlem, New York City, September 1960.

Front page of *Hoy* (Havana, 19 April 1961) during the October Crisis ('Cuban Missile Crisis'): 'Khrushchev's message causes great repercussions | Soviet Union asks UN to declare the United States Cuba's aggressor | Khrushchev's letter to Kennedy | Formidable demonstration in Mexico City in support of Cuba.'

AFP

Havana, during a mass meeting, with Che Guevara.

STEPHEN FERRY / GETTY IMAGES

With Che Guevara during a meeting.

LEE LOCKWOOD/TIME LIFE PICTURES/GETTY IMAGES

Raúl Castro and Che Guevara, relaxed, celebrating the 26th of July.

BETTMANN/CORBIS

22 August 1960. With Che Guevara in San Julián during a military parade.

ALFRED EISENSTAEDT/TIME LIFE PICTURES/GETTY IMAGES

At the UN with Antonio Núñez and Raúl Roa.

RALPH CRANE/TIME LIFE PICTURES/GETTY IMAGES

Fidel Castro during his speech to the UN General Assembly.

Because also, in a way, within the leadership sectarian methods and habits had evolved.

That party always maintained good relations with me, and later with the 26th of July Movement. It was in their bookstore on Calle Carlos III that I bought most of the classics of Marxist literature I read when I was a student.

When our movement, which had been born after the coup, was organized and launched its attack against the Moncada barracks complex in an attempt to bring down that spurious regime that was detested by the immense majority of the population, it did so in absolute secrecy, as an action of that sort can only be carried out. I've talked about this. In the subsequent repression, several Communist leaders, among them Lázaro Peña, were arrested by the repressive forces, which were looking for Blas Roca. Blas Roca, who happened to be in Santiago, had left the day before 26 July. In the same cell block where I was isolated in a cell with iron bars, I saw Lázaro Peña walking down the hallway with that noble, dignified expression on his face – he'd been unjustly accused of being an accomplice in the assault. Some leftists, outside the country, were talking about a *putsch*. I can't blame them, because no one can know the private thoughts of those who carry out such actions, nobody is in a position to know that a new tactic had emerged, of the thousand and one kinds of fighting that can be used to change a society. When those of us in our group were out on the street again – we'd been released due to public pressure – we renewed our contacts with our former Communist *compañeros* in the struggle for university autonomy. Flavio Bravo, former member of the directorate of the PSP youth, was my contact. In fact, the 26th of July Movement and the PSP were allies, and they had known about our plan to flee to Mexico, so the upper ranks of the Party directorate knew our plans and in principle were in agreement with them; certainly they wanted to maintain contact and continue to cooperate in the fight against tyranny.

The year 1956 passed. In Mexico we had serious problems, and many of us were even arrested. The situation in Cuba was still not critical. In the classic theses of the Communist movement, revolutionary action should always be preceded by great economic and financial crises. The conditions in that second half of 1956 didn't seem to be terribly favourable for a revolution to break out. Flavio Bravo visited us in Mexico. He brought us the opinion of his party's leadership and asked us to postpone our action. Flavio was like a brother. We may have given too much importance to our

217

own vow that in 1956 we would either be free or be martyrs. But no one renounces what he believes in, and I believed in what we were doing.

We left [Mexico], we disembarked [in Cuba], and three days later we had that terrible setback in Alegría de Pío. I've already told you that story. A fierce wave of persecution was unleashed against the dispersed expeditionaries: many were murdered. The Communists denounced and condemned the murders. The tyranny, emboldened, sated its hatred by murdering a great many revolutionaries in December, among them several Communist union leaders.

All seemed lost. Theories emerged as to the objective and subjective factors that had come into play, the causes of the difficulties – a leftist magazine not connected with the 26th of July Movement published all this – as told by one of the *compañeros* who'd come over on the *Granma* and was currently in prison. During those extremely difficult days, up in the Sierra Maestra several of us survivors continued to believe that even under these circumstances we had to fight for a victory. Certainly in the case of our country, subjective conditions played a considerable role.

There came a moment when the survivors of the *Granma*, with the support of the *campesinos* and the young reinforcements from Manzanillo, Bayamo, Santiago and other places, sent in by Frank País and Celia Sánchez Manduley, managed to reconstruct our detachment, which, now experienced and battle-hardened, though still small, barely 250 men, was able to extend its operations, with four columns, almost to Santiago de Cuba, and to invade the large strategic eastern region of the island.

The historical leader of the Popular Socialist Party, Blas Roca, was a man from a very humble background. He'd been born in Manzanillo and was self-taught, but he was a tireless advocate of spreading Marxist-Leninist ideas and developing the Communist Party in Cuba. Blas Roca had had to live outside Cuba for some time, for obvious reasons. During that time, Aníbal Escalante, as secretary of the Party, assumed the main leadership position. By the time of the triumph of the Revolution, he had great authority, and he acted as the virtual president of the Party. He was capable, intelligent and a good organizer, but he had the deeply rooted sectarian habit of filtering and controlling everything in favour of his Party. Those were the old tactics, the old obsessions, of a stage in the history of Communism – a ghetto mentality born of the discrimination, exclusion and anti-Communist feelings that people were subjected to for so long.

During the early days of the Revolution, once the war was over, they even did this with the 26th of July Movement, despite our excellent relations. These were misguided, mistaken methods, though used by unquestionably honourable, self-sacrificing people who were true revolutionaries and true anti-imperialists.

Aníbal Escalante introduced that method into the organization, and with it he created a serious problem of sectarianism that was doing great harm to the unit – this, when we'd already created the ORI[2] and had a national directorate. So I publicly denounced this – it was the only way to change the situation that had been created. What was sad about it was that Aníbal, within the leadership cadre of his party, backed the armed struggle against Batista.

Despite those unfortunate errors, unity was maintained. As far as I was concerned, I was able to overlook that political disloyalty. There was no vanity in me whatsoever – what should and always did prevail was modesty and unity in the conduct of those who aspire to change society and the world. I employed calm and equanimity in seeking unity in very difficult circumstances.

Aníbal was never a traitor, nor do I bear him any grudge, any ill will whatever. His brother César, who was the ideological secretary of the ORI, and who died prematurely just a few years after the triumph of the Revolution, was one of the most honest, disinterested and loyal Communists I've ever known in my life. His long, painful illness was very sad to us. I listened to his hopes for every new medication we found for him. Today, he might have been saved.

But going back to the initial thread of our conversation, I can say that the little island that was so alone during the arm-wrestling between the dominant empire and the Soviet government – the latter of which fell apart and the former of which became the single superpower – was able to resist, showing that nothing is impossible.

In real life, the grand political and historical events of the world and the battle between the followers of the Communards of Paris are mixed with the miseries of abject rulers of the empire that stole from us not just our wealth and the sweat of our people's brow, but also our independence and the most beautiful aspects of a country's history and tradition. Our people have performed the great deed you mentioned, and it is to be hoped that it will continue to write beautiful pages in history in its struggle for a better world.

When the war ended, you and your followers had promised to bring to trial and eventually put to death members of Batista's repressive forces, and you created the 'revolutionary tribunals' that carried out a purge that many observers characterized as excessive.

They were tried, and quite a few were given the death penalty.

Do you think that was a mistake?

Think what was a mistake?

Those public trials that were held in the weeks following the triumph of the Revolution, and those executions.

I think the error may have been in the manner, shall we say, that those trials were conducted, using public places and allowing the proceedings to be attended by a great number of our countrymen who were justly outraged by the thousands of crimes that had been committed. That might be in conflict, and in fact was in conflict, with our own ideas of justice. And it was very much exploited by the United States. We lost no time in rectifying what was unquestionably a mistake. But those guilty of genocide were tried and punished according to laws that had been passed long before by the Revolution, during the war. We don't regret having done it, although I do feel pity when I remember how bitter it must have been for [the accused] to experience the hatred that the people quite rightly felt for them because of their repugnant crimes.

I'd been in Venezuela during the 'Bogotazo', which we talked about, and I saw what an entire nation in rebellion is like. Here, when Machado fell, in 1933, Machado's people were dragged through the streets; there were lynchings, houses were invaded and attacked, people sought vengeance, revenge . . . So throughout the entire war, thinking about the mass violence that can accompany the victory of the people, we warned our country about that. We had a one-kilowatt short-wave station on top of a mountain at the end of the war – which had a higher [listener] rating, at certain hours, than all the other stations in Cuba combined, by the way – and we would tell people that our Movement did not want to see people dragged through the streets, or personal vengeance, because justice would be done. We were still very much influenced by the Nuremberg trials, which had taken place just some twelve years earlier, at the end of the Second World War.

No one says that this may have been the only revolution in which the main war criminals were tried and brought to justice, the only revolution that didn't rob or steal, didn't drag people through the streets, didn't take revenge, didn't take justice into its own hands. No one was ever lynched here. Not that some people wouldn't have liked to. Because the crimes committed by Batista's thugs and henchmen, those people who thought they could get away with anything, had been horrible. And if there were no lynchings, no bloodbaths it was because of our insistence and our promise: 'War criminals will be brought to justice and punished, as examples.'

We were applying the Moncada programme. Everybody was familiar with it. The punishment of the war criminals, though, was used [by our adversaries] to defame the Revolution, even though our conduct was exemplary. We committed the error I explained to you: too many people taking part in it . . .

There was a public trial in a sports coliseum.
Yes, but there's another issue, and it has to do with human nature. Thugs who commit monstrous crimes anywhere, almost everybody thinks they ought to be severely punished, but when the time comes and the [criminal] is sentenced and is about to be executed, there are people who react with sadness and even with pity.

With a sense of pity.
There is no link between people's awareness that the punishment is deserved, their conviction that the crimes committed were monstrous, and their emotional rejection of the death penalty. There were the Nuremberg trials, as I said, for the Nazi war criminals in which the tribunals condemned some of the accused to death, some to life sentences and other harsh sentences. I believe Rudolph Hess, who had parachuted into England, was in prison for I don't know how many years; others died, and those Nazis were the Olympic champions of barbarity.

Something happened to us: when it was a question of life or death for us – a serious case of treason or espionage – a court martial could apply the death penalty. But in two years of war, there were very few cases. You know what happened? Our men were repulsed by that job; we had to choose carefully the personnel to carry out their unpleasant duty in the very few cases when it was necessary to apply the death penalty.

Had you had to apply the death penalty earlier, in the Sierra?
Yes. Because there were people who put our entire force in danger. There

were traitors who brought the [Batista] army three times to where we were. One of the first ones who had joined the Rebel Army was captured by Batista's men and turned into a traitor.[3] There were scouts, the soldiers that went in and out carrying messages between the Sierra and down below, that would be captured. There were even some good men who fell into our ambush; they came as prisoners of the enemy with the mission, which they pretended they were going to carry out, of killing us, when their real intention was to inform us of what had happened. They survived the ambush by a miracle.

Batista's troops used pretty well-worn methods sometimes: if they saw that a man might be willing to betray us, they'd tell him they'd let him live and they'd offer him all sorts of things if he'd tell them where we were so we could all be wiped out, or if he'd come back to the camp and kill me.

But yes, we had to try people and execute them. There was no alternative, and there was no vacillation [on our part in doing so].

And what happened later, with the trials in Havana, was a mistake, but a mistake that was not motivated by hatred or cruelty. You try a man who's killed dozens of *campesinos*, but you try him in a courtroom where there are thousands of people, where repudiation of the murderer was universal.[4]

In a stadium, right?
It wasn't a Roman circus, you understand, it wasn't a baseball stadium, and that was used [against us] by the empire's publicity machine. We created tribunals that carried out traditional trials and punished those who'd committed war crimes. That case was the exception. But [I admit it:] you see a man who's being tried before thousands of people, and even if he's the worst sort of murderer, you tend to take pity on him.

It looked like an object lesson, a warning to others.
It was, but we rectified that.

One of the criticisms directed against the Revolution during those first years was that people say there was very aggressive behaviour, repressive behaviour, against homosexuals, that there were internment camps that homosexuals were sent to, locked up in and repressed. What can you tell me about that subject?
In a word, you're talking about the alleged persecution of homosexuals.

I should explain where that came from, why that criticism arose. I can guarantee you that there was no persecution of homosexuals, or internment camps for homosexuals.

But there are many reports, eyewitness testimony to them.[5]
What sort of problem occurred? In those first few years, we found that we had to mobilize almost the entire country, due to the risks that faced us, the risk of an imminent aggression by the United States, things that actually happened: the 'dirty war', the Playa Girón [Bay of Pigs] invasion, the October crisis [Cuban Missile Crisis] . . . During that whole stage, there were many prisoners.

Obligatory military service was instituted. Then we found we had three problems: the need for a certain level of education for service in the armed forces because of the sophisticated technology [used], because you can't serve with a second-, third-, or sixth-grade education – you had to have at least seven, eight, nine years of education, and later even more. We had to take some men out of the universities, and even use some who'd already graduated. To work in a ground-to-air missile battery, we needed college graduates.

In science, I imagine.
Quite right, as I'm sure you're aware. There were hundreds of thousands of men, and all of this had a kind of domino effect, not just on educational programmes, but also on important areas of the economy. There were people who weren't very well educated, and the country needed them because of the tremendous drain on centres of production. That was one problem we had to deal with.

Second, there were certain religious groups who, out of principle or religious doctrine, refused to be subordinated to a flag or to serve in the armed forces. Sometimes people would take that as a pretext for criticism or hostility.

Third, there was the homosexual situation. Homosexuals were not called up into military service. You're faced with the problem of a strong resistance against homosexuals, and when the Revolution triumphed, during this period that we're talking about, machismo was an element that was very much present in our society, and there was still widespread rejection of the idea of homosexuals serving in military units.

Those three factors led us not to call them up for military service, but that became a sore spot, because they were not called upon to make the hard sacrifice [for the country] and some people used that argument to criticize homosexuals even more harshly.

With those three categories of people who for one reason or another were excluded [from duty], the Unidades Militares de Ayuda a la Producción (UMAPs, or Military Units to Aid Production) were created, where people in those three categories were sent. That's what happened.

They weren't internment camps?
Those units were created all across the country, and they did certain kinds of work, mainly helping out in agriculture. That is, it was not just the category of homosexuals that was affected, although certainly part of them, those who were called up for compulsory military service, because it was an obligation that everyone in the country was taking part in.

That's how the problem came about, and it is true that they weren't internment camps, or punishment units – on the contrary, we tried to raise the morale of the people who were sent to the camps, present them with an opportunity to work, to help the country in those difficult times. There were also a lot of people who for religious reasons had the chance to help the country in another way; they gave their services not in combat units, but rather in labour units, and with respect to their material welfare, they even received the same benefits as hundreds of thousands of recruits who'd been drafted into the armed forces.

Of course later, in a visit I made to Camagüey, touring one of the agricultural installations, I became aware of the distortion the original plan had been subjected to, because I can't deny that there were prejudices against the homosexuals. I personally asked for a review of that issue. Those units lasted only about three years.

Later still, after the initial flaws had been corrected, there emerged our prestigious Youth Labour Army, which was founded over thirty years ago. Its members go through military training first, and then the rest of their time, they engage in production, for the country. They've worked in building housing, schools, repairing and constructing railways, and doing other jobs related to the economy and the infrastructure. Their work has also been decisive in agricultural production in those areas where there's a shortage of labour. Their meritorious role during difficult moments in the special period has earned them the people's gratitude and recognition.

Do you think those prejudices were an aspect of machismo?

It was a culture ... the same thing happened with other sectors [(in 1st ed.:) with women]. I can most assuredly tell you that the Revolution never encouraged those prejudices. On the contrary, we encouraged a struggle against various kinds of prejudice. With respect to women, there were prejudices, very strong ones, and with respect to homosexuals, too. At this point I'm not going to defend myself against all that – the part of the responsibility that I bear, I accept. *I* certainly had other ideas with respect to that problem. I had opinions, and for my part I instinctively opposed, and had always opposed, any abuse, any discrimination, because that society which had been based on injustice was saturated with prejudice. Homosexuals were most certainly the victims of discrimination. In other places much more than here, but they certainly were, in Cuba, victims of discrimination. Today a much more civilized, more educated population is gradually overcoming those prejudices.

I should tell you, too, that there were – and still are – very distinguished, outstanding personalities in culture, literature, very prestigious figures in many areas of knowledge, who were and are homosexual and who have enjoyed, and still enjoy, despite the prejudices, a great deal of privilege and respect in this country. So one shouldn't think about widespread sentiments. In the more educated, more sophisticated circles of our society there was less prejudice against homosexuals. [(in 1st ed.:) In the sectors of society with very little culture or education – a country at that time with 30 per cent illiteracy – there was strong prejudice against homosexuals, and among semi-illiterates, too, and even in many people who may have been professionals. That was a fact of our society.] So discrimination and machismo are today, and will increasingly be, inversely proportional to our compatriots' level of culture and knowledge [i.e., education].

And do you think that prejudice against homosexuals has been fought effectively?

I'd like to think that discrimination against homosexuals is a problem that is being overcome, and I do see it that way. I trust in that [progress] as I trust in the fact that our nation will soon be one of the most cultured, educated, sensitive and fair nations in the world. Old prejudices and narrow-mindedness will increasingly be things of the past.

At first, there were also conflicts between the Revolution and some churches, prejudices fed by anti-Socialists on the one hand and anti-religious persons on the other. The Party took the drastic step of not allowing believers into the Party. I consider myself largely responsible for that, because we saw it as leading to the risk of a conflict of loyalties. There were a lot of Catholics, for example.

Within the nucleus of the Party?
No, Catholics who were revolutionaries.

But who couldn't become members of the Party . . .
The principle was established that religious believers would not be allowed to enter the Party's ranks. Believers might be treated with every consideration and respect with regard to their political position, but they couldn't become a member of the Party. And don't think it didn't take work, years, to come to the decision that we had to open the Party's doors to religious believers.

You came around to that idea [of openness]?
Although I was of a different mind when the decision was made to exclude [religious believers] when the Party was created, I was almost one of the first to defend the idea of admitting believers. Over thirty years ago, I'd come in contact with Liberation Theology. I had my first encounter with representatives of that current of thought in 1971, in Chile. I met with a lot of priests and pastors of several denominations, and I met in the Cuban embassy with all of them. Then, after hours of meetings, I suggested the idea, which I'd been thinking about for some time, of a union between believers and non-believers, that is, between Marxists and believers, in support of the Revolution.

As the Sandinistas would say: 'Christianity and revolution – there's no contradiction.'
We said that much earlier, because the Sandinista revolution triumphed in 1979 and I defended that idea wherever I went: in Chile, when I visited Salvador Allende in 1971, and even in Jamaica when I visited Michael Manley in 1977. That was the policy that we had been applying. Almost all the churches [connected with Liberation Theology] were very receptive. I would declare [i.e., in speeches] that the revolutionary change needed in our hemisphere required Marxists and Christians to unite. I upheld those ideas, and I uphold them more and more today.

At one point, I said, 'We are suggesting the union of Marxists and Christians, but in the Party we don't apply those ideas, we still have the old ideas.'

Even fighting against prejudices and certain kinds of beliefs that arose wasn't easy, and we had to fight hard.

Did you have to fight, too, in the heart of the Revolution against discrimination against the black population?
There was no subjective discrimination. Because every revolutionary knows that among the cruellest sufferings that affect human society is racial discrimination.

Slavery, imposed through bloodshed and fire on men and women torn from Africa, reigned for hundreds of years in many countries in this hemisphere, including Cuba. In this nation slavery was abolished 120 years ago, in 1886, although it was just in name, formally. Men and women subjected to that abominable system continued to live for almost another three-quarters of a century as *apparently* free labourers in rundown barracks and shacks in the country and in the city, too, places in which large families would have a single room to live in, without schools or teachers, doing the lowest-paid labour – until the Revolution came.

You can't imagine, I had to speak three times, when I spoke against racial discrimination on a radio programme. At one point, our adversaries were spreading the rumour that we were going to take children away from their parents and send the children to Russia, can you imagine?, and that rumour spread, and was believed, because of the Goebbelian principle that a lie repeated often enough becomes the truth – but it wasn't just treacherous Goebbels who talked about that; it was that psychologist, too, Gustavo Lebón,[6] I think he was a French psychologist, who talked about the noxious influence of repeated lies, though Lebón's idea was in a slightly different sense.

Mass psychology.
I remember I had read Lebón's book on the importance of discipline in a military unit, and the importance of standing at attention and receiving an order, because people went to their deaths on the basis of an order given to them. What was the name of that book? I think it was *Psicología de las multitudes.*

More or less, yes. In French, La Psychologie des foules, *which is something like* The Psychology of the Masses.
And what's the author's name?

Gustave Le Bon.
Gustavo Lebón in my French! Although I read it a long time ago, I think I remember those basic ideas. I was attending the university at the time.

It's a classic.
So as I was saying, when I spoke on the radio for the first time, about racial discrimination, I had to speak two more times. Of course from the first moment we'd started applying the laws of the Revolution, and there was a prohibition against clubs, schools and all other institutions that didn't allow blacks, or even mulattoes, although we applied that prohibition with all possible care.

There were also hotels that didn't allow blacks.
Yes, yes, all sorts of places. Beaches, which were mainly private, and off-limits to blacks – often even to poor whites. Schools, too. The one I went to here [in Havana], the Colegio de Belén, as I told you, had 1,000 students, and it didn't admit blacks, or mulattoes either.

There was a little school attached to Belén, and there were some there. I spoke, when Pope John Paul II came, in January 1998, about those Catholic schools that didn't admit blacks, and I explained certain aspects of racial discrimination to him.

After the triumph of the Revolution, we were pretty ignorant about the phenomenon of racial discrimination, because we thought all we had to do was establish equality under the law, and that it would be applied, without discussion. But in a TV programme I talked about the subject: the disgusting 'balls'[7] that were thrown – 'balls' is a word we use in Cuba to mean rumours – like that one I told you about the kids being taken away from their parents and sent off to Russia. And some of those lies, repeated often enough, had their effect. I don't know whether Lebón ever talked about the fact that sometimes the more exaggerated and absurd the rumour is, the more risk there is that people will believe it.

After that came the October crisis,[8] in 1962; flights were suspended to the US, because before that, planes flew non-stop. We never put any restrictions on those people's ability to leave the country, and more than once we opened the way. We said, 'Come in privately owned boats and get your family members more safely.'

In addition to those lies [there were some relating to] racial discrimination. After my appearances on television [to denounce racial discrimination and to open schools and clubs to black students and members], people started saying that we were going to force people to marry people from other ethnic groups – whites marry blacks and vice versa, all that sort of thing. And not a few people were scared to death by that lie that stirred up prejudices, stirred up atavistic fears, fired up some people's superiority complexes.

How could Hitler make people believe they were superior to others and lead them into such crimes against other human beings when he himself had nothing of that Aryan look, that Aryan ideal he talked about? – nor did Himmler, or Goebbels . . . Imagine if cloning had existed back then! Imagine Fascism [i.e., Nazism] and cloning, racism and cloning!

That new eugenics may be one of the great threats in the future.
Scientific research has tried to show what the differences are between the various ethnic groups, and it hasn't come up with anything, except little things that have nothing whatsoever to do with talent. Science has come to the aid of those who fight against racism. Yet while science has incontestably shown the true intellectual equality of all human beings, discrimination still exists.

For us revolutionaries, fighting racial discrimination has been a sacred principle. But as I was telling you, when we were speaking about this subject for the first time, states of opinion and serious uneasiness were created in some of the population. I spoke again, three times I spoke, about the fight against discrimination – [I explained] that it didn't mean anybody was going to be forced to marry anybody; it was just that we were going to put an end to [racial] discrimination – the injustices, the inequalities in the workplace, in recreational activities, in education.

At the time, we were naïve enough to believe that decreeing total and absolute equality under the law would put an end to discrimination. Because there are two types of discrimination – one is subjective and the other is objective.

And are you satisfied today with the situation of the black population in Cuba? Or do you think that situation might still be improved?
No – it would be the height of vanity, chauvinism and smugness if we said we're satisfied. Even in societies such as Cuba's, which has grown up from a radical social revolution in which the people have achieved full and complete legal equality and a level of revolutionary education that has done away with most of the subjective component of discrimination, [racial

discrimination] still exists today in another form. I call it objective discrimination, a phenomenon associated with poverty and a historical monopoly on knowledge.

The Revolution, over and above the rights and guarantees achieved for all its citizens of whatever ethnic background or origin, has not had the same success in its fight to eradicate the differences in social and financial status for the black population of the country. Blacks don't live in the best houses; you find that they still have the hardest, most physically wearing and often worst-paid jobs and that they receive much less help from their family members no longer in Cuba, in dollars, than their white compatriots.

But I *am* satisfied with what we're doing in terms of discovering the root causes, which, if you don't make a determined effort to do something about them, tend to prolong people's marginalization down through subsequent generations. Where are its origins? Which group is it that fills the prisons, and why?

The social causes.

Why does marginalization exist? Slavery had been abolished long before the triumph of the Revolution in 1959. Seventy-three years had passed since the abolition of slavery in Cuba in 1886, 120 years ago now.

We have discovered that there is an inverse relation between knowledge, culture and crime; for example, the greater the knowledge, culture and access to university education, the less crime. In a country with 800,000 professionals and intellectuals, as we track down data, as we do research in prisons and a dozen places, we are gradually discovering the laws of that relationship.

The less culture, the more marginalization, crime and discrimination, right?

Yes, that's right. That's very important to us – encouraging access for the poorest among us, those who were the children of those who had never gone to college, to the best schools, the schools you're admitted to on the basis of your record and examinations.

You'd be amazed if you saw how many young people between twenty and thirty years old – and we're doing further research on this – are in prison, where, despite the enormous number of professionals and intellectuals in this country, only 2 per cent of those in prison are the children of professionals and intellectuals. When you go to our prisons, you discover that many [inmates] come from the marginalized *barrios*, they're the children of people whose families live in one room, in those forgotten *barrios*.

And the Revolution hasn't been able to put an end to that apparently inevitable destiny?
At first, we put an end to some of the marginalized *barrios*. But a culture of marginality already existed. Even though you built new houses, the phenomena that occurred in that place tended to continue to occur, unless a new culture arises on the basis of education. Professionals saw to their own – they taught them, sat down and did homework with them, so they could get into the best schools.

How many professionals have been educated and created by the Revolution? I'll tell you – millions. I think that at the present time the Revolution has at least three professionals or intellectuals – doctors, engineers and so on – at the university level for every citizen that had a sixth-grade education in 1959. Because today, there are many, many teachers, and almost all of them are university graduates. Among the nurses, both male and female, there are also many, many with university degrees.

The culture of marginality and all its consequences tend to propagate themselves. What do positive actions count for?

In some countries, that has increased a great deal, that positive discrimination.
Yes, but for us, it wasn't a question of laws or anything of the sort. We saw it as a question of justice and political ideas, political will, and here in Cuba, in fact, discrimination disappeared subjectively.

Sometimes a TV show on the efficiency of some [city's] police force would show a number of black and mestizo kids who'd broken the law . . . Because, in addition, there are two kinds of robbery: the ordinary kind, which is very irritating, and the white-collar kind, committed by administrators here or there . . . [The white-collar] criminal steals from society, but nobody's any the wiser – people are much more aware of the guy who breaks into your house, tears it apart, steals something, a piece of jewellery, some appliance, breaks things – and those are the crimes committed by the poor.

There came a time when I talked to the people who put on those TV shows that dealt with actions taken by crime-fighting agencies, because [the producers and directors] really did want to give people confidence in the police, and I told them, 'I wouldn't want to see another programme done in that particular way.' Each one in his office wanting to show the efficiency of [the police], and the ones who appeared in the pictures as criminals were mostly black and mestizo kids, along with a few whites. But usually the minorities. What good does that do, associating the crime that's most irritating to society with a particular ethnic group?

But we've come a long way – through ideological education, through the behaviour of the black population, through their loyalty to the Revolution. The poorest classes of society were among those most supportive of the Revolution.

Were they still discriminated against in other ways?
Well, many took advantage of new possibilities, but they weren't in the same situation as the others in terms of admission to universities, or the best schools, which you get into on the basis of your scholastic record, and also sitting an examination. The story of the people who helped with entrance examinations is incredible.

People might criticize us for taking so long to discover this, but we did discover it. One day I had to make a very critical speech about it, because all these problems needed dealing with, and as I told you, I'd had my experiences.

What remains is very much under the surface now, really, some subjective discrimination among people with some education, some culture, people who have lived for many years within the Revolution and have seen the enormous achievements [by blacks and mestizos]. But that discrimination is still reflected in this society, I must tell you.

Among the higher ranks of the government one still sees very few blacks.
That's right. You see blacks in some management positions, because we're still reaping the harvest of the fact that a lower proportion of blacks and mestizos were able to enter the universities. Universal military service lasted three years. And we took measures to encourage people to go to school, to study. When the time came that everyone had graduated from high school, then depending on their conduct they might go into military service for two years instead of three. We then reduced it further and gave many kids in military service who'd graduated from high school the chance to study one year at boarding school, taking an intensive course that would prepare them to enter university. A good number got in that way, the poorest got in that way, those who possibly wouldn't have been able to get into schools for students chosen by sitting an examination, for those who came from the higher social and cultural strata.

These were young men of the Revolution, their families were Revolution families, the ones I'm talking about – there were just differences of culture and knowledge. That was one of the measures we took.

Really, I'm very happy with the 106 Battle of Ideas programmes that are functioning today, many aimed at education, and the first thing I ask about is ethnic composition, an expression that had been erased from all the forms, because it seemed discriminatory.[9]

So you and your people now pay particular attention to ethnic composition?
Yes. In all the new schools, in teachers, professors, social workers, and cultural and artistic programmes. We are educating art instructors: there are fifteen teacher-training schools, one in each province, and plans are for 30,000 arts teachers, selected on the basis of their talent, to share their knowledge in educational centres and in communities over the next ten years, because there's a tremendous demand. The ethnic mix is different in each province. There are provinces where the black population is as high as 70 per cent.

In the provinces in the eastern part of the island, I imagine.
That's right. And in others, it's the other way round. In Holguín province, for example, the white population is the large majority. They're the descendants of farmers from the Canary Islands and other provinces in Spain. In areas where there were plantations worked by slaves, such as Guantánamo, or due to other historical factors, the percentage of whites, blacks and mestizos will vary.

In art schools – plastic arts, I mean, painting and sculpture – [the students] have to study music, dance and the dramatic arts, and they have to specialize in one of those disciplines and have basic knowledge in the others, because they might teach in a school and have to give lessons in the other disciplines, too.

There's an explosion of vocations, and we are educating some 16,000 young people, taking into account the ethnic composition, plus talent. It makes us very happy to see – in all these careers with such great social importance, careers that give young people the right to study in the university almost as a career – the ethnic mix. I'll tell you, I still look [at the ethnic composition,] and I ask, 'Tell me, how many admissions [are there] of such and such a type?' Just as you're asking. There are more in some institutions than in others.

Do you also look to see what the percentage is of women?
Fighting discrimination against women was tough; we even had to pass a law regulating morality, in a sense, the Family Law, stipulating a man's obligation to share household chores, cooking, childcare, with his wife ... We've made great progress in that area.

The immense majority of young people entering the universities was female. Because at the age of secondary school and pre-university, females are more studious and get better grades, in a word. And since they were admitted on the basis of their scholastic record ...

We send our doctors to many countries around the world. There are some countries where the local culture makes it hard for you to send a woman to provide medical services, but you'd call for young people to study medicine, males and females, and two out of three who applied would be women.

Sometimes, for a field of study, you'd say, 'Well, we have an urgent need for such-and-such,' and in those cases males would even be exempted from military service [to encourage them to attend school], but of every three admissions on the basis of transcripts, two would be women. We had to impose quotas – let's say 45 per cent men and 55 per cent women, because the vast majority of those who met the criteria [for admission] would be women. That process, for those reasons, translates into a tremendous growth in the number of women in the technical labour force, so that today, 65 per cent of the country's technical force is female.

A really spectacular advance.
Since women also have childbirth as a natural function, we give them, if they have children, a year off to raise their baby – not to encourage them to have more children, but because the best thing that can happen to a child when he comes into the world is to have his mother's influence, and his mother's milk.

There are other levels of so-called 'non-formal approaches' to the teaching of children. You have to educate the parents. It's much better when it's the mother [who spends those early months with a child]. The break-up of the nuclear family is closely associated with kids' dropping out of school and with their winding up in prison. But when one of the two parents is a professional, even when there's been a divorce – since generally speaking the children stay with the mother, if she's a professional – the negative effect is reduced considerably.

The [negative] effect in terms of marginalization, delinquency?

In 71 per cent of the cases of juvenile delinquents, 19 per cent lived with neither the mother nor the father. So when either the mother *or* father is present – it's usually the mother, that's the general rule – if they are well educated, you don't see the adverse effect that often comes with divorce, the break-up of the nuclear family; if both of them – or one of them, especially the mother – take care of the children, watch over them, etc., then there's hardly any difference. We look forward to the day when women will attain the highest professional and technical level possible for the welfare of the family and of society. Once women were terribly discriminated against, with access to only the most humiliating work; today, they are, by their own will and hard work, a decisive and prestigious segment of a society in which, as I've said, they constitute 65 per cent of the technical and scientific labour force.

Women have made their own way – they're a force to be reckoned with. What we may need to have in the future is a Federation of Cuban Men!

To defend themselves!

Exactly! Because you already see women rising, rising, and they're not at the top yet – but forty-six years since the triumph of the Revolution have not passed in vain.

Many women took part in the struggle to bring down Batista. You yourself have mentioned Haydée Santamaría and Melba Hernández, who were in the assault on Moncada, and we might mention other famous revolutionary women such as Celia Sánchez and Vilma Espín. So I'd like to ask you: were there women fighting up in the Sierra?

Oh, yes. I organized a unit of women in the Sierra, the 'Marianas'.[10] We showed that women could be as good at soldiering as men. I had to fight hard against machismo up there, because we had a group of the lightest weapons reserved for the women, and some men said, 'How can we give a woman an M-1?' – this was after Batista's last offensive – 'Why don't I get one?' I had a phrase I used with some of the men – I'll tell you what it was. I'd say, 'Listen, you know why [we're using women]? I'll tell you – because they're better soldiers than you are.'

I trained the first units of women combatants myself, and their performance was excellent, better than the average man's, and I'm not kidding. And they went into combat, they weren't there in offices or any of that. This is not a justification, it's a fact.

And do you think that Cuba is no longer a machista country?
Today we might say that we are the least machista country not in the world, I wouldn't say that, but at least in this hemisphere. We have created a culture of equality and respect, which you're aware is not something that you find in all of our societies.

I really haven't made a comparison, because our machismo was inherited, and we know very well how all that was inherited and cultivated in capitalist societies. That [machismo] was an inheritance, and we were quite ignorant. My own feelings were different – I've just mentioned that platoon of women in the Sierra. I had other opinions, I had a feeling of solidarity, because I saw and suffered over the way women were discriminated against in that exploitative society.

But, well, we're willing to listen to any statement that's related to this. I wouldn't say that machismo is totally a thing of the past, but there's an enormous difference from what was happening in those first few years that you're referring to, and I've told you in all honesty what that was like, and we take responsibility – it's a shame we didn't have enough culture, or that the circumstances weren't right, to prevent forms of discrimination that are unjust and that wound people. In just a few words, that's what I can say to that question.

Another accusation that was made against you in the early years of the Revolution is that there was religious persecution. You nationalized the Catholic schools, expelled some of the clergy and arrested priests. Do you think there were excesses there, too?
We nationalized all education, not just the Catholic schools. This is a radical, profound revolution, those are the words I use for it, and I can justify and show why – but there was not a single priest executed. And that is part of a policy and an idea – [it stems from] not just ethical principles, but also political principles. It was in the interests of imperialism, or the imperialist government of the United States, to portray the Cuban Revolution as an anti-religious revolution, based on the conflicts that occurred in the first few years and forced us to take certain measures. That's how the conspiracy got started, and, really, we couldn't just sit back and watch it happen. Very serious things happened.

What sort of things?
Well, for instance, Operation Peter Pan, the kidnapping, practically, of

14,000 of this country's children, after our adversaries invented the appalling lie that the Revolution was going to take children away from their parents, take away the parents' custody. Under that pretext, or due to that unfounded and absurd fear, 14,000 of this country's children were clandestinely sent to the United States, and several Catholic priests who were opposed to the Revolution took part in that kidnapping , as did Catholic priests in Miami.[11]

Fourteen thousand children were taken to the United States?
Yes, taken away because [our adversaries] invented a lie that claimed that a decree was about to be handed down that would take away parents' custody. When you're dealing with things involving such deep emotions, people go crazy, they're easily taken in because of the kind of lie it is, the circumstances of the moment, and the way the lie is spread. In this case, given an emotion such as the emotion of parenthood, that mad idea hit a nerve, it hit people's instinct – they couldn't process it. Which is why [our enemies] were able to scare even so many middle-class parents, and that made the exodus, the clandestine shipment of the children, much easier, and many families were separated for ever.

Later, reading those books by Sholokhov, the 'Don' books, several of them, I discovered on my own, I didn't know this, that as early as in the Sholokhov novels[12] those lies about custody appeared – they were very, very old tricks . . . Imagine, I had to say, 'And who's supposed to take care of all those kids if we take away the parents' custody?' It's been forty-six years and we *still* don't have enough facilities for the mothers who want to send their kids to childcare centres . . .

They said something even more terrible: they said we were going to turn the children into tinned meat.

My God!
That we were going to send them off to the Soviet Union, and in the Soviet Union they were going to be turned into tinned meat and sent back here in tins.

That's monstrous!
It's pure fantasy, although that didn't keep it from being believed – it was believed because those lies were associated with the most powerful human instinct, the instinct of a mother or a father, especially a mother's.

And they took the children away?
Oh yes, they took 14,000 of them.

But they were taken away gradually, clandestinely?
Not exactly, because those who wanted to leave could do so – even doctors, who were in such short supply in Cuba. They took half of our country's doctors. There wasn't a lot of paperwork, and the children were taken more, I'd say, fraudulently – they'd be sent away alone or with some friend, to get around the rules and with no assurance whatsoever as to what would become of them. They may have had to meet certain requirements as to passport and that sort of thing. Of course, no poor people, no marginalized people sent their children – they had faith in the Revolution, and they were the great majority. It was the higher-income sectors, and not a few wealthy families, but the children were not to blame in the slightest.

There were people who wanted to leave, and no one was stopping them, but what they did was unjustified. Many parents stayed behind, waiting, many of them thinking that the Revolution wouldn't last very long, and at that point they could send for their children. But whatever the case, 14,000 children were sent away. Many of them are adults now, and they criticize their parents. Up there in Miami there was no place to house them – they were even put in places that had been built as reformatories, wherever they could – a mass of parentless Cuban children scattered all over the United States.

And the Church bore some responsibility for this gigantic kidnapping?
That may be one of the saddest things about it. Some priests and members [of the clergy] at a higher level were involved in the operation, in both Cuba and Miami – it's something we haven't wanted to look into too closely. There was no law against citizens going to the United States. We threw up no obstacles – the most elementary identity requirements, that's all. There was no justification, at any rate, for sending the children [up there], with papers or without. The counter-revolution, backed by the government of the United States, fabricated that false decree, published it, and took away 14,000 children on the basis of fear and terror.

And you and your people didn't see what was happening?
We, as I say, never put any restrictions on people leaving, and they came and went – the American government threw the doors wide open to lure technical personnel, teachers, doctors, skilled labourers, and also then have

a pool from which to recruit invaders and soldiers who could attack this country. These were extremely serious events! What lie *didn't* they tell?

Very serious things happened along that line. We aren't going to blame Rome for what happened, or blame the Catholic Church, because there were many Catholics who were revolutionaries. But for counter-revolutionary activities, some were indeed sent to prison.

Priests?
Yes, though they weren't in prison long. In the Playa Girón expedition there were three priests among the mercenaries, but they were . . . What do you call those priests that preach to the army?

Chaplains?
That's right. We had a chaplain in the Sierra Maestra, too, a Catholic priest who joined the rebels. He was even promoted to the rank of *comandante*, and wore an olive-green uniform – Padre Sardiñas, very well known and much beloved. Not that our *compañeros* were practising Catholics, particularly, the kind who go to church, but here almost everyone used to be baptized, and if you weren't, as I told you, people called you 'Jew'.

I was telling you that it was not simply a question of principles, but also elementary political common sense: a priest shot by firing squad here – he'd have been an instant saint and martyr, a gift to the empire and an offence to many honest believers in Cuba and around the world.

Did the Cuban Revolution handle priests with kid gloves, then?
Some occurrences were very serious, but there was never a priest executed. And this is the only radical revolution that hasn't executed priests, shot them before a firing squad . . . In Mexico, you know about the *cristeros*,[13] and in many other revolutions the same thing happened. If you look at the history of France, where you, I believe, acquired much of your philosophy, though you weren't born in France . . .

The French Revolution was very anti-clerical.
Remember the three Estates. In the Revolution of 1789, the Estates killed one another, because the lower clergy was on the side of the Revolution and the ecclesiastical authorities were on the side of feudal power, although some of the authorities did pass over to the side of the Revolution. I don't know of a single revolution in which something of that nature hasn't happened.

Look, in the October Revolution, I doubt that anyone today would deny that in 1917 there was a revolution in the country that later came to be known as the Soviet Union – and there, too, events of that kind took place.

Then there was the Mexican revolution in 1910, an important social revolution, a true social revolution – not Socialist, but still a profound social revolution. And there one side murdered the other – including priests.

Then there was the Spanish Civil War. Spaniards are very religious people, and most of the Spaniards were on the side of the Republic, and there were priests on both sides shot by firing squads. That is, I don't remember a single revolution in which, with respect to the religious sphere, one side didn't employ firing squads against the other.

We are the exception to that. And that shows that we have been guided by certain political and ethical principles and ideas – both things. That's very important.

If people don't know that, if it's not reported, if the truth is hidden by those media that publish so much criticism of the Cuban Revolution, I'm not particularly concerned. You've ask me a question and I've explained. How many lies and slanders have been spread about the Cuban Revolution relating to torture and other things like that?

11

The Conspiracies Begin

The Revolution's first laws – Che in the administration – The agrarian reform – Che Guevara and voluntary labour – First acts of sabotage – Rupture with the US – Terrorism – Attempts on Fidel Castro's life

When the war ended, on 2 January 1959, you were just barely thirty-two years old and had no experience in government. How did you and your advisers set the Revolution in motion? I imagine there was a certain degree of disorder.

What did we do first? We kept our promise to bring the criminals to trial – something that had never happened, really, in this hemisphere. We kept our promise to confiscate all the goods and property stolen and misappropriated during the Batista years. We didn't go further back into the past because during the months of our struggle we had to achieve and maintain a degree of unity, and if we'd included goods and property stolen by prior govern-ments, I'll tell you, there wouldn't have been any property left in Cuba! There was a kind of *de facto* amnesty, on behalf of unity. Everyone complied with the decision made by the 26th of July Movement and the Rebel Army for the sake of unity among all those who to a greater or lesser extent had fought against the tyranny. We defended that idea.

What did you do next?

Another thing we did: we reinstated all the workers who'd been fired during the Batista period, in all the factories. Our accounts weren't particularly 'economics-based', and they didn't jibe very well with the ideas put forth by the Chicago Boys, or what today we call the 'pro-Yankee neoliberals'.

We also drastically reduced rents, which later became a new rent-reform that turned renters into buyers of real estate. Of course, we compensated the proprietors who had only a few housing units. All that brings us to May 1959.

That was when we created the agrarian reform laws, the first of which was passed on 17 May of that year.

We had to act in the face of idiocies, stupidities. Every few minutes there was a problem, because, for example, Urrutia said, with no warning, that all the casinos had to be closed – there was still gambling and all that sort of thing – and the reaction to that was pretty strong on the part of the people who worked in the casinos and in tourism and so on.

The casino workers protested. Didn't they march in the streets?
Every other day there was some dust-up because we were doing all these things.

Like creating 10,000 classrooms in education. There was no money; Batista had taken almost all the money with him. The Popular Socialist Party put in place certain anarchic measures, due to two things: rivalries between political organizations and the old pre-revolutionary habit of encouraging land distribution. I drew the line at that, I took a position and said that was not going to be done. We even issued an administrative order: 'The law will recognize no right to land taken by persons through their own means.' [On account of this kind of measure] there was going to be total chaos within a Revolution that had the support of more than 90 per cent of the population, according to the surveys. Because there were rivalries – and also disagreements, all that sort of thing.

That was during the first few months, and in May, on 17 May, we proclaimed the Agrarian Reform Act, and we announced it symbolically, up in the Sierra Maestra, at the La Plata headquarters.

It hadn't been a year since I entered that little village, Santo Domingo, where Sánchez Mosquera's first battalion burst in,[1] and the last reserve left to our command headquarters, which was the fundamental objective of the colossal force sent in by Batista in his last big offensive, was my rifle.

In the plane on the way to Oriente province, I introduced some additional elements into the law – elements I later discussed at command headquarters with the other ministers who were empowered to pass it, in accordance with the provisional constitution. These were things such as the idea of cooperatives, which was already in 'History Will Absolve Me'. Later we worked hard to establish agricultural cooperatives. We also favoured state agricultural corporations, because those enormous tracts of land[, the *lati-*

fundios that had been in the hands of wealthy Cuban landowners or large, usually US, corporations,] some being used to a certain degree for agriculture, or for livestock – how could we divide all that land up and distribute it as hundreds of *minifundios*, tiny tracts?

We established cooperatives in sugar-cane areas, and as a matter of fact in a relatively short time they became pretty successful. There was widespread ignorance about economics, and what prevailed were the old slogans and bywords of unions and *campesino* organizations, all very justifiable, but all within the framework of a capitalist society that had to be transformed. I recall, in the first weeks of 1960, the theatre at the CTC [Central de Trabajadores de Cuba, the Cuban Workers Central], which seated over 3,000 people, being full of representatives from the sugar-cane workers all clamouring for four shifts instead of three on the sugar-cane *centrales*. Leaders of the 26th of July Movement and the PSP competed furiously in support of that popular idea. How could you explain to that mass of people that that idea was financially ruinous, that what was needed was to create new jobs, not share out the ones that already existed? Socialism had not yet been proclaimed, nor could it be, yet. Companies and corporations were privately held, and many of the largest ones were Yankee. But our ideas *were* Socialist, and pretty radical. From the outset, we were going to be led into bankruptcy. I had to appeal to every recourse of my imagination to persuade them without giving our position away [i.e., that we were going to proclaim Socialism]. I think I convinced them. Today, no one would argue that I was wrong in doing so. I had the privilege always to be able to call on that great trust, which I have never betrayed. I couldn't say, 'Listen, what you're going to do is ruin businesses and industries,' but I did persuade them with arguments: 'It's not in our interest for this, that and the other reason.' We had to do some heavy arguing, even among the militants in the 26th of July Movement. There was also competition, rivalry, among the leadership, and you had to keep your eye on all that . . . In those first few months we signed all those laws.

What post did you hold at that time, or what were your responsibilities?
I had two positions, but at that time I was basically seeing to my duties as commander of a victorious army and people, which had suddenly had to assume power over the national territory. I'd turned down the position of head of state beforehand, and I was trying to cooperate loyally with the supreme political authority that we had designated. But actually what I was

doing was righting the wrongs done by our inexpert and unfortunately incapable president. The ministers were tired of Urrutia. He'd also somehow decided to take up the cause of anti-Communism, and to cap it all off, the presidency had gone to his head. Urrutia would send Machadito [José Ramón Machado Ventura], a doctor and former guerrilla fighter, today member of the Party Politburo, who at the time was Urrutia's aide, to accompany his wife on shopping trips to the most expensive shops in Havana. The man had decided this was some kind of banana republic . . .

Then there were the conspiracies that started springing up around the same time . . . There was one led by Huber Matos[2] in Camagüey – he was right-wing and had had certain relationships. There were all sorts of problems like that. During the days [when we were implementing] the agrarian reform, Che wasn't a minister, he was recovering his health in a place he'd been assigned near the ocean. There, Carlos Rafael Rodríguez, some other compañeros and I would visit him and more than once we met with him to discuss the bill for the Agrarian Reform Act. He still, of course, had the responsibility of commanding the forces stationed at La Cabaña.

Che was a military commander, because we had to stay alert. The minute some threat of invasion was announced, Raúl would take off to Oriente, Che to Pinar del Río, Almeida to the centre of the island, and me to Havana – we had divided the commands.

The same thing happened during [the invasion of Playa] Girón: Che to Pinar del Río, Almeida to the centre of the island, me to Havana, and Raúl to Oriente. I mean, during Playa Girón, or the October crisis, each of us had our [assigned] place, and each of us went there, no matter what we were doing.

Once victory was won, did Che Guevara insist that he wanted to leave, to go and lead the revolution in Argentina?
That commitment did exist, and I always told him, 'Don't worry, that commitment will be honoured.' But Che was very enthusiastic about the Revolution in Cuba. He even went, as I told you, to a beach near Cojímar, for his asthma. We'd all meet in a house there, in Tarará – it was Núñez Jiménez,[3] Carlos Rafael Rodríguez, some other compañeros and me – to discuss the Agrarian Reform Act, which [I felt] couldn't wait. Really, they all favoured a more moderate reform. Che was aware that there was going to be a big fight with the large Yankee corporations; he was no doubt remembering the [similar] experience in Guatemala, and he felt we should

be cautious; he expressed that opinion in a very intelligent and honest way. I should say, in all honesty, that Che was surprised that I wanted such a radical reform, much more radical than he wanted.

There were *latifundios* here of 200,000 hectares, almost a half-million acres, owned by foreign interests. Some American companies owned huge sugar-cane *centrales* and immense tracts of land. They owned land in lots of countries, of course, but here, historically, those corporations were very powerful and very influential. There was no alternative but to nationalize them, sooner or later. The process was speeded up, actually, not because we decided to speed it up or create conflicts with the United States. The problem was that the first Agrarian Reform Act, whether more radical or less, was absolutely unacceptable to a country [the US] whose corporations owned the best sugar-cane land in Cuba.

The law allowed a maximum of 100 *caballerías*,[4] and there were *latifundios* of 10,000 *caballerías* and more. If they were productive, and were actually in production, then we allowed up to 100 *caballerías*, but if not, the maximum was thirty. Those were the rules. That is, no company could have more than 100 *caballerías*. And then only if the land was in production; that is, no one could have more than 1,340 hectares, a little over 3,300 acres, and if the land wasn't in production, no one could have more than thirty *caballerías*, which is 402 hectares, or about 1,000 acres.*

In 'History Will Absolve Me', I talk about cooperatives, reforestation, industrialization, and I mention the 'golden calves'; I use symbolic language. At the time, no one believed in any programme put forth by any Cuban revolutionary, because lots of them had put forth programmes and none of them had followed through on them. Our problem, actually, was that we *over*-followed through on them.

There were hundreds of thousands of people in rural areas with no land, tens of thousands of *campesinos* who paid rent; others were what you might call squatters – they had no right to the land they worked and could be thrown off it at any time; they lived, especially, on state land up in the mountains. Others were sharecroppers; these were the worst off, because

---

* [(in 1st ed.:) At any rate, the others had wanted to allow 200 *caballerías*, but I said, 'Maximum 100.' Afterwards, I looked more closely, and I think we made a mistake there – we committed the sin of idealism. It cannot be denied that we committed errors of idealism. I was a part of that and I take responsibility for errors of idealism, because I believe we were taking a very big leap when in agriculture, instead of developing cooperativism, we developed state enterprises.]

they planted and grew the crops and the landowners kept a third or more of the harvest. All these lands were now distributed, parcelled out, there was no land left to distribute – what had to be done was legalize the parcels and grant [the *campesinos*] ownership of the land that they already occupied, and that's what we did.

Still, we didn't want to dismantle the sugar industry. The last land we nationalized was the large sugar-cane plantations, which were the largest of all the *latifundios*. Finally, we left the big agricultural corporations as collective state enterprises; today, they're cooperatives. As a matter of fact, during the 'special period',[5] when there were such terrible shortages of fuel, we decided the right thing to do was give the agricultural workers a little piece of land for family gardens; it helped the food supply. We didn't do what the Soviet Union had done at a certain difficult moment – carry out forced collectivization, which was extremely costly and bloody.

And also didn't work very well; in the Soviet Union, poor nutrition, food shortages of all kinds, lasted for many, many years.

We have never forced two pieces of land together. From the first day, the Cuban Revolution declared that the will of the *campesinos* would be respected and that no *campesino* would ever be pressured to join his land to someone else's in order to create bigger agricultural units, which may be more efficient per man and per hectare, although not always, but like everything imposed by force [not military or police force in this context, but 'by law'], always traumatic.

The cooperatives that emerged during the special period were born out of the state corporations that we already had, many of which were efficient and had tremendous technical futures, so long as they weren't over-bureaucratized or didn't fall victim to an obsession with gigantism. All of that occurred during our long, hard apprenticeship as revolutionary producers, and we still haven't resolved all the challenges that came up along the way as a result of situations in which the empire's despicable economic blockade clashed with our idealistic dreams, and [as a result] also of the hybrid formulas of capitalism and Socialism that caused confusion and chaos, in the attempt to change the exploitation of man by man as part of the search for a fairer society.

The most efficient and economical centres of agricultural production were born out of voluntary, conscious alliances of small independent farmers, who built houses, schools, health services, distribution centres, cooperatives for electrical power, water and so on, all of which brought an end to the isolation and sacrifice of many families. And today still other forms of production are being created or perfected – in my opinion, all perfectly possible, and in not a few cases successfully tested, so we know they can exist side by side with those we already have.

In the Soviet Union it was all or nothing. Zero collectivization during the years of the NEP,[6] and then total collectivization in a very short time, which caused terrible violence, conflicts and damage.

With respect to agrarian reform, I was very radical, what can I tell you? But I mean, if you're not radical you don't do anything – you organize a party, you hold twenty elections, and nothing happens. But me, I thought we had to strike a blow, and that blow was the Agrarian Reform Act.

And did Che follow you?
He was delighted. [For him,] there was absolutely no problem. He was reserved, a little, because he still had some of that caution from being a foreigner, despite his merits . . .

Because he was a foreigner?
He'd proposed initiatives for industries and things of that sort up in the Sierra. Then after the triumph of the Revolution the INRA (Instituto Nacional de Reforma Agraria, or the National Institute for Agrarian Reform) became a very powerful institution that took over the distribution of all the land. There was a certain amount of disorder in the INRA. There was one *compañero*, for example, who was the head of an agricultural development zone out there near Moa, and without consulting with anybody he nationalized Nicaro, a large nickel corporation owned by the United States government that was being built there – it was almost completed. Without a word to God or the devil, because there was a good dose of anarchy in those days – don't think it was easy. That was quite a brouhaha.

So I decided to go [out there] and discuss that [with him], but the company had already been nationalized – it was not a good idea to back off, so then we entered discussions and negotiations. There were things like that. Another case was the Ministry of Labour, which was very radicalized – it made important decisions as it saw fit. You mustn't think there was much discipline in those early years.

So by now the INRA was nationalizing not just land; it controlled industries, and it created a Department of Industries and Industrialization. I called

Che in to put him in charge of the Department of Industries. He was still a political and military figure, and in any situation, any threat of invasion, he was there as the military commander of a region – plus the fact that he was a political leader, a member of the Dirección Nacional de las Organizaciones Revolucionarias Integradas [the National Directorate of Integrated Revolutionary Organizations].

The ORI.

That's right. Three organizations were integrated in 1961: the 26th of July Movement, the Popular Socialist Party and the Revolutionary Directorate. The members of the National Directorate of the ORI met every week in Cojímar to discuss the basic problems. Che was on the Directorate, as was Raúl.

In the Department of Industrialization there in the INRA, we began to create what would become the Ministry of Industry. Then came a stage during which the Banco Nacional had no money; the resources we had were very limited, because the reserves had been stolen by Batista and we needed a president of the Banco Nacional. What was needed at that moment was a revolutionary. And because of our trust in Che's talent, discipline, abilities and integrity, he was made director of the Banco Nacional.

A lot of jokes were made about that. Our enemies always made jokes – although we did, too – but this joke, which was politically motivated, went like this: One day I said, 'We need an economist,' but somebody got confused and thought I'd said we need a Communist, so they brought in Che . . . But Che was the man who had to be there, you mustn't doubt that for a moment, because Che was a revolutionary, he was a Communist, and he was an excellent economist.

Excellent economist?

Yes, because being an excellent economist depends on what the person who stands at the head of the country's economy, in this case the person who stands at the head of the Banco Nacional de Cuba, wants to do with that economy and that bank. So, in his double character of Communist and economist, Che was excellent. Not because he had a degree in it, but because he had read a great deal and observed a great deal. Wherever Che was given responsibilities, he discharged them extremely well. I've mentioned his determination, his will. Anything you gave him to do, he was capable of doing.

Later, the bank's books were straightened out, but it didn't have much money and it was much more important to see to [the] industrialization [programme]. By that time, there were quite a few sugar *centrales*, industries and factories under the control of the state, because our adversaries began to take measures and we'd take countermeasures, and by the time we realized what was happening, the main industries had all been nationalized. We met every measure taken against the Revolution by stepping in [nationalizing]. A large number of industries – nickel, sugar cane and sugar – came into the hands of the Revolution, and to direct that new ministry we appointed Che. What a job he did – excellent! What discipline, what devotion, how studious he was, how self-sacrificing, how exemplary, how austere! Any job you gave him, he'd throw himself into, body and soul.

He was a political leader and a military leader, but his concrete job at that time was overseeing the Ministry of Industry. How he studied! That was the point at which he gave special attention to management methods.

Did he have disagreements with Carlos Rafael Rodríguez, who favoured applying the methods used in the Soviet Union?
Well, that was where certain problems arose between Che and others. [It was] an argument that seemed pretty Byzantine to me – I wasn't all that aware of exactly what was going on – because Che defended the method of budget financing while other *compañeros* tended to defend the method of financial self-management.[7]

Che's concern wasn't just how to guide the economy; he was not opposed to certain material incentives, but he always warned against the dangers entailed by the abuse of material incentives as the fundamental engine of production and the weight of those incentives in workers' minds.

So there were those friendly controversies and arguments, which never turned out to be very profound. Most of the revolutionary combatants' minds were on other things. I said, 'All right, each of you defend your position, discuss the merits of the *ideas*.' And I, as a utopian Communist, confess that on that subject I liked Che's ideas about the way to build the economy best,[8] which were very much like our guerrilla way of life in the mountains. I liked Che's moral appeal best, frankly.

Che gave great weight to the Communist conscience, Communist awareness, the value of example.

Che was one of those who argued in favour of voluntary labour, right?
Che was the creator of voluntary labour in Cuba. Every Sunday he'd go off
to do volunteer labour – one day in agriculture, another day to test some
machine or other, another day in construction. He'd do a little bit of
everything.

He maintained close contact with the labour centres; he would talk to the
workers, he'd go down to the docks sometimes, to the mines, sometimes
he'd go to the cane fields to cut sugar cane. If they were combining and he
had to climb up on a combine, he'd climb up on the sugar-cane combine. If
construction work had to be done, you'd see him there with a wheelbarrow;
if sacks had to be carried, he'd be there carrying sacks. He left us the legacy
of that *practice*, that *action*, which, through his example, won the sympathy
and solidarity of millions of our compatriots.

A true example! All those attitudes are so admirable. I appreciated those
characteristics of Che's.

Did he get along well with Raúl?
Raúl and Che were very close, although they sometimes argued. Che never
had arguments with me about political issues; nor, that I know of, did he
ever have disagreements [of that sort?] with Raúl. In some things, such as
the distribution of land by the *campesinos* themselves, I suspect both Che
and Raúl backed that, because they both had a great distrust of one faction
within the 26th of July Movement that was influenced by anti-Communist
currents – I don't know whether I'm slandering somebody here – I suspect
that, but I have no real proof. This happened in the first few months of the
Revolution, and the fact is, they both completely came into line with my
thinking that the agrarian reform couldn't be done that way [(in 1st ed.:),
with no rhyme or reason, chaotically].

We passed a very radical agrarian reform, and then we took it even further.
I fully assume the responsibility for this radicalism in the agricultural laws
and other areas of the Revolution. I may have shared certain elements of
idealism with Che, and Che with me, but I'm not in the least sorry about
that. Because through my long life as a revolutionary, the more I've learned
of the vices of capitalism, the more I'm persuaded of the importance of
example, ideas and awareness, and the more I'm persuaded that those are
fundamental elements that the Revolution managed to preserve.

In the first few months, when merchandise, which everyone thought was
eternal, ran out, when all the currency that [Batista] hadn't stolen had run

out, the oligarchs and the bourgeoisie were still running the economy, and they'd export products, under-invoice them, and leave part of the money abroad – if they sold the merchandise at $200 it would show up on the invoice as $150; they'd skim a little off the top. Our inexperience cost us dearly. There were [also] errors on our part that made it easy for the United States to freeze several million dollars belonging to the Cuban government that we hadn't taken out of American banks.

Earlier, you told me that immediately after the triumph of the Revolution, 'the conspiracies began'? What exactly were you referring to?
Sabotage, the infiltration of men and the draining off of military equipment in order to sabotage us and encourage uprisings and terrorist activities. Our country has been the object of the most prolonged economic war in history, and of a fierce and unceasing campaign of terrorism which has lasted more than forty-five years. They sent in planes to spray the cane fields with incendiary materials ... They hijacked our airliners and flew them to the United States, and many of those planes were destroyed, others confiscated. The owners of newspapers, as they do today in Venezuela against Chávez, encouraged attacks against the Revolution. The *Diario de la Marina*, one of the most important newspapers in Cuba, and other periodicals published statements by people who'd left for Miami.

It was all part of a war: pirate attacks on our coasts, on our fishing boats, on transport on its way to Cuba. They killed diplomats, they killed our *compañeros*, even in the United Nations ... They brought in dynamite from the United States – even white phosphorus! – they'd put it in a package of cigarettes, throw it in a theatre, in a store, causing fires and deaths. These were serious problems ... Since the first years after the triumph of the Revolution, throughout the length and breadth of the country, there were also armed groups who murdered *campesinos*, workers, teachers and people working in our literacy programmes; they burned houses and destroyed agricultural and industrial centres. Our ports, merchant ships and fishing boats have been subject to constant attacks. On 4 March 1960, at a dock in Havana, they blew up a French ship, the *La Coubre*, and more than 100 people were killed, among them six French sailors, and hundreds of Cubans were wounded. In March 1961 they set off explosions in a refinery; on 13 April of that same year they sabotaged and burned down the El Encanto department store in Havana ... The most disgusting thing was the hijacking and downing of a Cuban Airlines flight in October 1976, a plane full of passengers, killing seventy-three people, whose irrecoverable remains lie at the bottom of the sea, thousands of feet deep.

All that was organized by the United States?
Well, in the first few days and months those terrorist activities were organized by Batista elements, really – former police officers and Batista people mixed in with some counter-revolutionaries. But even then the US administration, using those elements, was working intensely against Cuba. In the months prior to the invasion of Girón, the CIA was frantically creating anti-Cuba and counter-revolutionary organizations – over time it created more than 300 of them. And today we know that in March 1960 President Eisenhower signed an order authorizing a 'powerful propaganda offensive' against the Revolution, and a clandestine plan of action to topple the Cuban government.[9]

From November 1961, after Playa Girón, to January 1963, that is, in fourteen months, there were a total of 5,780 terrorist actions against Cuba, and of those, 717 were serious attacks against our industrial facilities. As a result of this activity, 234 people in Cuba died. That terrorism, in total, produced more than 3,500 victims, more than 2,000 people mutilated. Cuba has had to face more terrorism than practically any other country on earth.

They also engaged in biological warfare against Cuba, sending in unknown viruses, I believe.
In 1971, under Nixon, the swine fever virus was introduced into Cuba in a container, according to a CIA source. And we had to sacrifice more than half a million hogs. That virus, which originated in Africa, was totally unknown on the island until then. And they introduced it twice.

And there were worse things than that: the type II dengue virus, which often produces potentially fatal haemorrhagic fevers in the human being. That was in 1981, and more than 350,000 people were infected; 158 people died, 101 of them children . . . The virus serotype was completely unknown at the time anywhere in the world; it had been created in a laboratory. In 1984 a leader of the Omega 7 terrorist organization, based in Florida, admitted that they had introduced that deadly virus into Cuba with the intention of causing the greatest number of victims possible . . .

And that's not to mention the attacks against me personally.

Attempts on your life?
There were dozens of plans, some of which came very close to succeeding.

In all, of plans that there are records of, there were over 600.[10] Different sorts of plans, ranging from sketches to plans in advanced stages; that is, plans were discovered at various stages of preparation. They were promoted in three ways: first, directly organized by the CIA; second, by creating supposedly independent groups and giving them all the necessary resources to act without direct intervention from American institutions; and third, by incitement, which can be very strong, it can create a hunter psychology in potential assassins, plant the idea that there's someone who should be hunted down – a licence to hunt somebody down ... then of course fund-raising, lots of resources for supposedly political groups, such as the famous Foundation and dozens of mafia groups headquartered in Miami and other parts of the world. Although the Foundation was used directly, at one point, to provide funds to and direct the terrorists.

The Cuban-American National Foundation?

That's right. Its line was political and lobbying work until the point at which, after the collapse of the Socialist camp and the USSR, it created an action group.[11] The guy who headed the Foundation, Jorge Mas Canosa, was the son of one of Batista's army officers. The ones who had the most influence in it were, first, the supporters of Batista and members of his regime, who took huge amounts of money with them when they left Cuba, and who were the leaders of the group. Later on, they would give financial support to all those groups, give them money; what they didn't have was an institutional group of their own for armed actions until, at the beginning of the 'special period', in 1992, they created one, but they worked with all those terrorists that the CIA had trained, and paid for all their assassination plans and their terrorist plans.

So the last method is incitement. They've managed to plant the idea in lots of people's minds that you have to do this big thing, which means assassinate that devil. They're 'assassination attempts by inducement', as I call them. Taking them all together, all the different kinds, there were, as I say, over 600, and some came pretty close to succeeding.

Chance sometimes intervened against them. There was an agent who had a cyanide pill and was about to put it into a chocolate milkshake in this place I often went to, a coffee shop in the Hotel Havana Libre. Fortunately, the ampoule [sic] froze, and just as he was about to throw it in, he realized that it was stuck to the ice in the freezer he'd put it in.

In Cuba at the time there was a mafia that ran gambling and contraband

and so on, gangsters whose business was hurt by the Revolution and who were later used by the US government in assassination plans and in plans for counter-revolution. In some hotels, they had people they'd put there, friends and so on. Although the vast majority were good people, exemplary, you could always find some that were willing to do things for money, which was a method they used all the time. That was confirmed by the United States Senate itself.[12]

In another assassination attempt, they planned to use a chemical agent that produced effects similar to LSD to contaminate the air in a TV studio where I went to make speeches on the radio. Another time they sprayed lethal poison on a package of cigarettes that I was supposed to smoke. At one point, when I visited Chile in 1971, they had me in the sights of a television camera with a gun inside it, just yards away. Of course, the ones who pulled the trigger would have died right there and then, and when their life was at stake, they didn't shoot.

The last spectacular assassination plan was [to be carried out] at that meeting in Panama – that was the plan Luis Posada Carriles was involved in, the man who blew up the Cuban plane in 1976, and who'd organized the group that was to carry out the execution.

At the Latin American Summit meeting?
That's right, in 2000. He was captured. And now the problem is that Washington refuses to extradite Posada Carriles;[13] they refuse to do it.

And all those plans and attempts were paid for by the United States.

In your view, what responsibility does Posada Carriles have in all these attacks against Cuba?
Posada Carriles and his accomplice Orlando Bosch are the most bloodthirsty exponents of imperialist terrorism against our nation. They have carried out dozens of horrific actions in numerous countries within the hemisphere, including even the territory of the United States. Thousands of Cubans and some citizens of other countries have lost their lives or been mutilated as a consequence of those cowardly and abominable acts by governments of the United States.

The same American institutions and services that trained these Cuban-born terrorists also trained, as we know, the men who organized the brutal attack on the Twin Towers in New York on 11 September 2001, in which several thousand Americans lost their lives.

Posada Carriles not only took part, along with Orlando Bosch – then head of the CORU [Coordinación de las Organizaciones Revolucionarias Unidas,[14] or Coordination of United Revolutionary Organizations], which was created by the CIA – in the destruction of the Cuban Airlines plane with seventy-three passengers on board, but also after that, and for many years, organized dozens of plans to assassinate the highest authorities of the Cuban Revolution, and he also planted a number of bombs in tourist hotels on the island, while Orlando Bosch, apparently a fugitive from American law enforcement, took part, along with Augusto Pinochet's forces of repression, in the kidnapping and assassination of important Chilean figures such as Carlos Prats and Orlando Letelier, as well as the disappearance of many of those who were fighting against Fascism in Chile, and even the kidnapping and murder of Cuban diplomats. Even from his prison cell in Venezuela, where he was jailed for eleven years, Orlando Bosch ordered his henchmen to carry out terrorist attacks.

These sinister figures always acted under the orders of American administrations and their special services, and [the terrorists] have been illegally exonerated [by the Americans] of all charges and possible punishment, as in the case of the pardon given Bosch by President George Bush, senior. In the case of Posada Carriles, his presence and movement on American soil have been tolerated for weeks by the current president of the United States, George W. Bush – which is a flagrant violation of the country's own laws by those whose highest responsibility it is to protect the American public from terrorist attacks.

All of Posada Carriles' terrorist acts, including the bombings of tourist hotels in Havana and the assassination plans, have been financed by the United States through the unfortunately famous Cuban-American National Foundation since its creation by Reagan and Bush in 1981. All of the money came from the United States. No one has ever acted with more deceit and hypocrisy.

Was the United States always behind these assassination attempts?
From the first moment [to this day], the American administration has been working to create an unfavourable image of the Cuban Revolution. They have carried out huge publicity campaigns against us, huge attempts to isolate Cuba. The objective has been to halt the influence of revolutionary ideas. They broke off diplomatic relations in 1960 and took measures to impose an economic blockade.

They had done the same thing with the Mexican revolution in the days of Lázaro Cárdenas, when he nationalized the oil industry in 1938; they said terrible things about that revolution. They did it again in 1954 against the Jacobo Arbenz revolution in Guatemala because he implemented an agrarian reform. They also launched a huge campaign against Salvador Allende and his reforms in Chile, and against the Sandinista revolution in Nicaragua. They've done it with all the revolutions, and today they're doing it with Hugo Chávez' Bolivarian revolution in Venezuela.

But against Cuba, Washington was able to tap anti-revolutionary Cubans for help.

That's right. Listen, I'm going to tell you something: what we've seen and what we've learned is that many of those who went to Miami, many of those who were involved in terrorist activities, were not actually planning to take part in bringing down the Revolution. They all lived under the conviction that it would be the United States and its powerful armed forces that would bring down the Revolution. Many of the rich and privileged who left Cuba and abandoned their homes and abandoned everything – it's not that we expelled them or took their homes away; they said, 'This will last four or five months; how long can a revolution last in this country?' and they left. But the counter-revolutionaries also had the conviction – and this has happened in other processes, too – that their despicable cause would win out in the end for one reason or another; and in this very special case, because the fight was with the United States, [what they were concerned with was] racking up points in one sense or another, being in some prison – although that wasn't so important – or in some counter-revolutionary guerrilla war in which they weren't looking to fight. They had no offensive spirit whatsoever; it was just to be sure their pro-Yankee behaviour got on the record.

They expected the United States to step in to bring the Revolution down.

12

The Bay of Pigs/Playa Girón

The attack – Mercenaries – US intervention – The military victory –
Treatment of the defeated combatants – The prisoner exchange –
The dirty war – The role of President Kennedy

This action took place on 17 April 1961, at Playa Girón, or what is known
in English as the Bay of Pigs.
Yes, that day an expedition of about 1,500 CIA-trained mercenaries, divided
into seven battalions of 200 men each and brought ashore on five landing
craft, landed on Playa Girón, Girón Beach, in the Bahía de Cochinos, the
Bay of Pigs. Before the landing, around dawn, a battalion of paratroopers
had been dropped in to take control of the two highways that run through
Zapata Swamp to the beach. A few miles out from the coast, on American
warships – among them an aircraft carrier, the USS *Essex* – Marines were
standing ready to disembark with naval and air support as soon as the
'provisional government' called on them. They were to have been airlifted
in as soon as the beachhead was established.

The mercenaries had a squadron of B-26 bombers piloted by not only
American crews but also officers from the former Batista air force; the
planes bore the insignia of the Cuban armed forces. They launched a surprise
attack on 15 April, hitting the bases used by our modest air force. This
attack was the announcement that the aggression was imminent. The next
day, at the burial of the victims, I proclaimed the Socialist nature of our
Revolution.

They chose an isolated location, Playa Girón, which is separated by a
large swamp from the rest of the area. It was [a place] very hard for us to
counter-attack because we'd have had to travel by the only two highways
that entered the area around the bay, through six or seven miles of otherwise

impenetrable swampland. That would have turned both those highways into a sort of gates of Thermopylae.[1]

But within about sixty hours – between dawn of the 17th and 6 p.m. on the 19th – we defeated them, after a terrible battle in which we lost more than 150 men and had hundreds of wounded. The battle was fought within sight of the American ships offshore. We took about 1,200 mercenaries prisoner, almost all the enemy forces who had been in the battle, the exceptions being, of course, the dead.

Those prisoners, you returned them not long afterwards, right?
That's right. After they'd been in prison for a short time, we demanded that the United States pay compensation in medical supplies and food for children. If it had happened in the US they'd have sentenced them all to life in prison, if they hadn't executed no telling how many first for treason, and the rest of them would still be in jail, for life. If we'd recruited over 1,000 Americans to invade the United States, anybody would have understood that sentence . . . Yet in December 2001, forty years later, five of our *compañeros* who were [in the United States] gathering information on terrorist acts against Cuba were given very lengthy prison terms – three were given life sentences, and one of those three was given *two* life sentences. Those are the five *compañeros* whom we call 'Heroes of the Republic of Cuba'.[2] What would they have done to over 1,000 Americans recruited by the government of Cuba to invade the United States? How many decades would they have spent in prison up there? While here, we tried to find a formula for the Playa Girón mercenary army, and we suggested compensation . . .

You traded [the prisoners] for medical supplies, I believe.
That's right, and for resources for producing foodstuffs. There was even some discussion of agricultural equipment, tractors, that sort of thing . . . What we wanted was to find a solution acceptable to our own people and then send [the invaders] home. What were we going to do with 1,200 'heroes' in jail? We preferred that the 1,200 so-called 'heroes' be sent back home up there.

I talked a great deal to all of them, because I took part in the capture of some of them, and I can tell you – this may be the only such case in history – after that terrible combat there was not a single case of prisoner abuse – no hitting them with rifle butts, nothing of the sort. Not a single case.

The prisoners were not mistreated?

Not a single case of abuse, and you can take it from somebody who got to Girón with the first [Cuban] combatants to arrive there.

[Our] final attack was at night. We didn't want them to be rescued by the Marines. The American fleet was a few miles offshore – aircraft carriers with dozens of the most advanced warplanes, landing equipment and Marines ready to go into action.

I'm not going into the whole history of that battle, but I *will* tell you that in those last minutes before we went out on to the beach, when I heard the enemy had an anti-tank barrier of 105-mm recoilless cannons, I put a commander in each of the three nearest tanks, [Soviet-made] T-34s, and asked them to head full speed at the barrier. It was almost night by now, and I sent them off at intervals of five minutes.

I was even caught in a bombardment by our own people, because, I mean, when a plane reported that they were landing more troops, I said, 'No, they're *reboarding*,' and I gave the artillery instructions to shoot a few salvos on land and a few into the water, and there were I don't know how many cannons, plus a complete 122-mm howitzer battery firing.

Of course none of the three [tank] commanders hesitated one second, but I couldn't control myself. I was expecting a formation of [our] heavy tanks with 122-mm cannons. I asked about them and [was told] they'd been delayed, it would be a while before they arrived. So I got up in one of the tanks that were sitting there, which turned out to be an SAU-100, a self-propelled 100-mm cannon that in the dark could hardly be distinguished from a tank, and I did the same thing – I drove right into the anti-tank barrier. I didn't know that the armoured vehicle [I'd got into], which had been fighting all afternoon, had no more than three or maybe five shells.

There's a famous photograph of you at Playa Girón, jumping off a tank.

Yes, I was in several tanks at various points during those actions, not just one. But that's another story . . .

I was explaining that from the first minutes, quite coincidentally, I was with the small vanguard that was advancing from the north along two different highways, one on the east and one on the west, and we entered Girón behind the tanks that had just been sent in minutes earlier, in total darkness. On each side of the highway I was on there were thick woods, and the ground was rocky down by the ocean. The anti-tank barrier disappeared and nobody fired.

I took part in the capture of nobody knows how many prisoners. I saved the life of one of them that same night. He kept saying, 'Kill me!' and he even had a beard. He had a bleeding ulcer. I told him, 'We don't kill prisoners.' We sent him to the hospital in a Jeep, at full speed. They saved his life.

None of the Playa Girón prisoners were mistreated?
Not one was even hit with a rifle butt, because that has always been our principle, as I said, and everybody knew it. The most admirable thing about it is that in all the combat fronts there were thousands of men that fought hard and saw over 150 of their beloved *compañeros* killed or wounded, and those men who fought so fiercely, I tell you, with such tremendous determination, were incapable of hitting even one of the prisoners with a rifle butt – a rifle butt, much less anything worse. And the enemy were paid mercenaries in the service of a foreign power – our men had no sympathy for them, as you can understand. I wonder whether there's any other case like it in the world.

That can also help to show why a conscience is more important than any discipline. There can be no discipline without conscience.

I mean, what happened in Vietnam? How many people did the American forces and their allies kill in Vietnam? Civilians, people captured, not just those who died in combat . . .

It has been calculated that 2 million Vietnamese lost their lives in the Vietnam War.
Many more – and you have to ask how many of those were in combat and how many were murdered. You know that happens in all wars of that kind. The French fought a war in Algeria, and how many Algerians were tortured and murdered? That's happened in a lot of places. In the war in Kosovo, in 1999, I don't know whether the NATO soldiers killed any, I don't know how much discipline those men had – what killed people there were the smart bombs and the Stealth bombers. [It was] a technological war, with B-52s that can fly all the way from the United States and so many other forms of death and destruction. Men hardly take part in battles any more, and battles are where the situation can arise in which a soldier kills prisoners.

The United States can't swear, in any of its modern wars, that its soldiers haven't committed atrocities. The Korean War was extremely cruel, and the United States had allies there in Vietnam. I don't know how the other allies might be, I have no way of knowing, but a lot of prisoners were killed there, and the puppet regime in Vietnam killed lots of people.

Now, find an example of a battle in which prisoners weren't mistreated. Later we took part in other battles – we were in Angola for fifteen years, from 1975 to 1990; we were at the decisive battle of Cuito Cuanavale.[3] You can go ask the South African army whether any of its men who were taken prisoner by us there were mistreated by Cuban troops, or beaten or struck in any way. They felt safe in our hands. There isn't a single case, I'll tell you. And we have shown our solidarity with many countries by going into combat for them . . .

We fought in Ethiopia, pushing back the aggression launched by Siad Barre[4] against the revolution there.[5] I'll tell you, our soldiers have never executed a prisoner, and have never mistreated one.

If in our war against Batista, which lasted twenty-five months, as I've told you, we had executed prisoners, we would never have won that war.

So Cuba returned the Playa Girón prisoners safe and sound.
Yes. And I've already mentioned the episodes after the battles, when people were full of adrenalin, enraged by the deaths, the men wounded, the tension of the battles, and this was during the first years of the Revolution, and many of our combatants were from the militias, volunteers who were there, labourers, *campesinos* and students, and there was not as much as a blow with a rifle butt. The men we returned to the United States are there, the ones who are still alive, in Miami – you can ask them, to see whether there's a single one of them who'll say he was so much as struck. There isn't a single case.

There was, though, an accident. I'll tell you about it. They were transporting the captured men to Havana, in a hurry. At the time the prisoners were transported in lorries, in eighteen-wheelers, etc. There were a lot of them, and we didn't have the organization we have now, but we wanted to move them to Havana quickly. One of the lorries was closed – it was an oversight on the part of one of the officers in charge of the transfer; someone didn't take the proper precautions, and there were cases of asphyxiation in that vehicle that was transporting prisoners.

Were there deaths?
Yes. It was completely accidental. What interest could we have [in killing them]? Our people didn't want a single one of them to die. I mean, the more prisoners we had, the bigger the victory – and there were a lot of mercenaries

taken prisoner that day. Because victory isn't measured just by the number of enemy casualties; we had many more casualties than they did.

The mercenaries were well trained, they had good weapons, but we were on the attack – attack, attack, attack, day and night, and we defeated them. Witnesses to what I'm telling you: thousands of soldiers and hundreds of officers in the US army.

They were attacking us with B-26 bombers they'd camouflaged with Cuban insignias, bombing the vehicles transporting our infantry. That's the way they tricked our troops – terrible things happened. But despite that, there wasn't a single prisoner mistreated.

We sentenced them to pay compensation of $100,000 per prisoner, or alternatively a prison sentence. What we wanted was payment of compensation, not because of any need for money but rather as a recognition by the United States government of the Revolution's victory – it was almost a kind of moral punishment.

There had to be some sanction.

Well, I mean, the men were prisoners and we negotiated. What's incredible is that the lawyer who negotiated with me, the CIA tried to use him to bring me a wetsuit, for diving, that was impregnated with enough mould spores and bacteria to kill me. The lawyer who was negotiating the liberation of the Playa Girón prisoners!

They had no scruples.

I can't say that he was actually in on the plan. But what we do know, what is definitely known, is that they tried to use him as the instrument. Donovan, the lawyer's name was, James Donovan. There's no indication that he took part consciously in the plan; he seems to have been used. Of course I'd never wear a wetsuit in this hot climate. Plus, you put one of those suits on and you have to carry more weight – it's useless in these waters. Anyway, among the dozens of plans to assassinate me, there's that one, because, as I said, a congressional committee investigated it and published [a report on] it.

The Church Commission? [6]

That's right. The US has investigated all of it; this is not some story I've made up. But imagine – what ethics! That's the man who was negotiating the release of those prisoners, many of whom could have been sentenced to death for treason. And we were freeing them!

Who were the men who landed in Playa Girón?
Who were those mercenaries? Some of them were war criminals who had
fled to the United States, because the officers and principal commanders
were almost all former officers in Batista's army, and among the invaders
there were many who were the sons of large landowners and wealthy
families. There you clearly see the class nature of the invasion.

Finally, how much compensation did Cuba receive in exchange for the
return of the prisoners?
I think in cash, $2 million, after the discussions with Donovan, and we
invested the money in incubators, bought from Canada, for our research in
poultry genetics. And another $50 million was the estimate, according to
Donovan, for the medical supplies and food for children. They charged a
lot for the medicines, you mustn't think they were much cheaper then than
they are now. But the amount of money wasn't the issue – we wanted to be
paid compensation.

And we were. So we were the ones who found the solution for all those
mercenaries who were in prison. The US government didn't have the
imagination for it. We even developed a certain degree of closeness to them,
because, really, in the end they told the whole truth, and told it publicly.
And the sanction had nothing to do with hate, or revenge. The victory was
the most important thing for us. Why would we want to hold 1,200 prisoners
here that the people in Miami would have turned into martyrs?

Weren't you afraid that when they got back to Miami they'd sign up for
more violent actions against Cuba?
Well, yes, really, some of the ones we sent back did return to Cuba, and
even set off bombs and carried out other hostile actions. Could we be blamed
for that? No. A shipload of 'heroes' is terrible, because every one of them
turns into a leader, every one of them is a 'hero'. So we sent them a thousand
and something tin-pot heroes.

And how many of the others have we sent back, the so-called 'dissidents'?
And who set them free? The government of Cuba. A witness to that is
Cardinal John O'Connor,[7] who was archbishop of New York. We sent him
off with thousands of people imprisoned for violent, serious crimes, many
of them terrorist actions, because there were thousands of counter-
revolutionary actions organized by the [various] US administrations against
Cuba during the first years of the Revolution.

After they'd served out just some of their sentences, we set them free. We'd tell the cardinal, 'Try to get a visa for them, because you know what they want is to go to the United States.' All those so-called 'dissidents' got privileges in the United States, jobs – even those who hadn't contributed very much at all to the attempts to destroy the Revolution . . .

That cardinal of New York, John O'Connor, I liked him. The Revolution set many thousands of counter-revolutionaries free, and some of them did in fact go back to their old ways – they formed groups, they trained, they spread lies and made up all sorts of stories. Which is why we have to act cautiously in these matters, because sometimes we're generous, we commute a sentence, we set a counter-revolutionary free, he goes off to the United States and starts organizing activities against Cuba, starts training – he can infiltrate our coastlines and that winds up costing the life of one of our compatriots.

Are you referring to the activities of Alpha 66 and Omega 7?[8]
Among others. I've told you that during the first few years, there were thousands of men involved in armed counter-revolutionary groups. The dirty war spread to all the provinces in the country, even the province of Havana. All it took was a swamp, a cane field – there was a dirty war all over the country. You might say that Cuba is the only revolutionary country in our times that has defeated the imperialist instrument of a dirty war, which is so costly and so debilitating to a Third World country.

When you talk about a 'dirty war', are you referring to actions such as assassinations in public places, for example?
No, no, I'm talking about armed irregular groups carrying out a kind of war against us, because the Americans are smart. While our Soviet friends were very slow and very academic, the Americans, the American military is more flexible. They saw immediately what formula we'd used to bring down Batista, to defeat that army, which was a combination of armed struggle and popular support.

And they thought they could use guerrilla tactics and strategy against you?
They tried. It was the first time they'd used that tactic. They had no respect for our patent on it! They tried it out on their own, and they did manage to organize groups. The 'fight against *bandidos*' cost us more lives than the war against Batista had. All of that was before Playa Girón. They went up into the

Sierra in Escambray, in the central region of the island, but we sent 40,000 troops up there, all volunteers, most of them from Havana – all volunteers.

When armed forces units were used in the dirty war, the recruits who took part were always volunteers, and it was because of this idea: in an internal struggle or an internationalist mission, all the combatants have to be volunteers.

Let me interrupt just for a moment. How do you explain the fact that the Sandinistas in Nicaragua, in the eighties, knowing Cuba's experience in that dirty war, didn't manage to eliminate the Contras, who were also financed, armed and trained by the United States?

I think a mistake was made there, but you can't blame them. In Nicaragua, an army was created to defend the country from outside aggression, aggression by the imperialist forces, but imperialism launched an internal war, and an internal war can't be fought, as I say, with regular soldiers, soldiers who have been drafted, as it were. Given the law of compulsory military service, you take a boy, you train him, you send him off to fight and he dies, and then the family thinks that the state, or the Revolution, or its laws, have sent their son to his death.

The highest price of a dirty war may have been paid by the Sandinistas because they instituted compulsory military service, which is something we never did to fight our dirty war. But there comes a moment when they let themselves be persuaded by academic theories, and that makes people depart from what the Revolution does best, that ability to create political and military tactics and formulas that lead to victory. If you allow yourself to be persuaded by the dogmas in books, you're lost.

Really, I always had an anti-academic mentality. Imagine, us carrying out a war under the defence principles and defence methods of 1959, 1960, 1961 and 1962, when today there are smart bombs, Stealth fighters invisible to radar, intelligent weaponry of all kinds, when you can destroy a tank from three or four miles away with missiles that can come within inches of their target, radar that can pick out your tanks and destroy them – you have to know how to use the weapons you have, and you have to stay completely away from all the books and all the formulas of academia.

And was that the way you won the dirty war in Escambray?

We surrounded Escambray, we divided it into four parts, we put a squad in every house in every zone to clean it out, and we cleaned it out quadrant by quadrant. Often perimeters have only relative value. A perimeter at night often lets you know the place where the enemy passed by, because they reach the line, they come up to it, throw a grenade, shoot and the men on the left and right of the point being attacked can't do much, so as not to wound their own men with friendly fire.

All it takes is 10 per cent of the civilian population, the *campesinos*, to provide a base for an irregular war, and up there in Escambray, due to certain circumstances, because of certain groups operating up in that area during the fight against Batista, the Revolution didn't have so much support, maybe 80 per cent. An irregular war can be waged with the support of 10 or even 5 per cent of the population.

The difference between our irregular war and the one *they* waged is that we were always in action, watching the enemy so as to strike at a fixed point or while they were in motion, either way, and they didn't have that spirit – the members of the groups that were waging the armed war against us that came to be called, after the war in Nicaragua, the 'dirty war'. They were experts at *avoiding* combat, *avoiding* pursuit – in that, they had some special talents for escape that we never developed, because our line, even though there weren't many of us, was to strike and strike again. The enemy, in contrast, dug out an underground shelter with lights and everything, little holes to breathe through, sucking in air like the crew of a submarine. If a battalion of the Revolutionary Army combed the area – a tough method, one man every ten yards searching everything – it would pass right over them and never discover a single *bandido*. They became real experts at avoiding combat, avoiding pursuit, but on the other hand, they never developed any spirit of offence at all. They became real experts at hiding, camouflaging, avoiding combat, avoiding pursuit – but they never developed the spirit of offence.

Later, in the eighties and nineties, the empire changed its tactics: they would send in mercenaries, lots of young kids trained in slaughter, in genocide, kids from El Salvador and other countries, and pay them $5,000 to set off bombs in Cuban hotels. They weren't Posada Carriles and other terrorists from the United States. Listen, we have a Salvadoran [Julio Cruz León] who came as a paid bomber – they paid him $5,000 – and he set off five bombs in one day. I mean, in a lot of countries for the right amount of money you can recruit thousands of mercenaries – sometimes for even as little as $2,000. [Our enemies] would pay for their return tickets and give them their money once they had set off their bomb and gone back.

Which is why that Salvadoran tried to set an Olympic record – he tried to make all five bombs go off at once. Meanwhile, in Miami, the Cuban-American National Foundation and all that mafia said the people who'd done it were members of our own Military Intelligence and State Security services, discontents, setting off bombs here in the hotels, and that that was the right thing to do – legitimate action, you know. They published lots of articles about that in the press.

There were also, later, other kinds of attacks.
Well, I've talked about the thousands of terrorist actions, the assassination attempts, the torching of the El Encanto department store, blowing up *La Coubre*, the passenger plane they blew up in mid-flight; I mentioned the attacks with viruses – swine fever, haemorrhagic dengue – that made thousands of people sick and killed over 100 children.

In the eighties there were also biological attacks on our agriculture. For example, a parasite called blue mould attacked our tobacco crops; later, an unknown mould destroyed our best strain of sugar cane, the Barbados 4362, and 90 per cent of the crop was lost. Such a thing had never happened before. The same thing happened with coffee; other crops were infested with a parasite, the melon thrips, or *Thrips palmi* Karny, which then attacked our potato crops. And there were other very destructive infestations like that, which caused many problems for our agriculture. It's very hard to prove, but everything indicates that these disasters were not just coincidental; there was really malicious intent. And those attacks are also complicated to fight, you have to go to science; a military solution in these cases is basically worthless.

Militarily speaking, did Cuba have enough men under arms to confront all these aggressions and all these threats?
Well, to defend the country, at one point, in the sixties, we needed hundreds of thousands of men, given that our adversary was no less than the United States.

It was a time when conventional wars were still fought as a confrontation between one man and another, or one group of men and another, between combatants, or brigades, battalions, armies. At that time, you had to expect a naval landing. The main way to occupy a country that's an island was a naval disembarkation – you had to take aerial landings into account, but that wasn't the fundamental method. The main [defensive] measure for us to take, then, was to defend the landing points. We watched the technological development of troop transports and all the possible places, especially in defence of the most strategic areas, from several points of view. With so many potential places for naval landings – and possible aerial landings, too – we were forced to prepare and mobilize the entire country.

By then, fortunately, the campaign against illiteracy had been started and was showing results, there were follow-up plans, and there were schools everywhere.

Which allowed you to have better-educated troops to handle modern military equipment.

That's right. At one point, for example, after the crisis in October 1962, we had to assimilate all the weapons of the 42,000 Soviets, among them surface-to-air missiles that require at least a high-school education plus special studies. Even the education of professionals in the universities was affected. We couldn't get as many students into medical schools as we wanted, the number of high-school graduates was insufficient, and many of those who graduated from high school went right on to become teachers pressed into service, some of them, or combatants handling modern technology – radar, communications. Practically all the equipment required well-qualified personnel.

So at one point a large number of soldiers who went into the army for three-year enlistments were high-school graduates or people with two years of university studies. We made some exceptions for careers where there was a super-high demand for personnel – medicine, for example, because out of the 6,000 doctors we had had before 1959, 3,000 of them had been lured away by the United States in the first few years.

It took us at least twenty years to be able to admit even 6,000 students to study medicine and get to the number of 70,000 we have now, almost all with one or two specialties. From the one school of medicine that existed at the time, we've increased to twenty-one, almost all in the ten years prior to the special period. The twenty-second is mainly for foreign students.

Both the landing at Playa Girón and the dirty war were authorized by President John Kennedy, who would later be a central figure, with you and Khrushchev, in the grave crisis that occurred in October 1962, which you've just mentioned. Yet when you talk about Kennedy, it doesn't sound as

though you bear any animosity towards him, and even that you almost
liked him. How do you explain that?
Well, with respect to Playa Girón, which was in April 1961, Kennedy really
inherited the plan from Eisenhower and his vice president Richard Nixon.
The invasion was a *fait accompli*; plans existed for destroying the Revolution,
despite the fact that at that point the Revolution wasn't even officially
Socialist.

The most important steps we had taken so far were agrarian reform and
nationalization of large industrial and commercial corporations and banks,
along with certain other measures of great social impact, such as the literacy
campaign, the reduction in rates for electricity and telephones, the urban
reform, the rent-control act, the confiscation of property of those who had
stolen from the government and the people. We'd done some very important
things, but we hadn't proclaimed ourselves as being Socialists, or openly
proclaimed Marxist-Leninist doctrines. Girón accelerated the revolutionary
process.

I should even say that our agrarian reform was, at the time, less radical
than the reform General MacArthur had instituted in Japan. Because when
the United States occupied Japan in 1945, MacArthur did away with large
land holdings and parcelled out the land and distributed it among the
peasantry and the poor. But in Japan the large tracts of land hadn't belonged
to big American companies, while in Cuba they had. So that's why we
weren't allowed to have an agrarian reform, just as it wasn't allowed in
Guatemala when Arbenz tried to implement one in 1954.

So then Kennedy, with reservations, scruples and some hesitation, put
Eisenhower and Nixon's plan into effect – he believed the plan developed
by the CIA and the Pentagon would have the support of the [Cuban] people,
that the people would rush into the streets to welcome the invaders and that
the militias wouldn't fight, that they'd rise against the country's government.
They may have believed their own lies and propaganda, and they most
certainly underestimated the Cuban people and our Cuban revolutionaries.[9]

Kennedy wavered, but in the end, given the difficulties that the Playa
Girón invasion was facing, he decided to give air support, but by the time
they were ready to do that, there were no mercenaries to support. In less
than seventy-two hours the overwhelming counter-attack by the Rebel Army
and the Revolutionary Militias had totally wiped out that expedition. A
hard defeat for the empire. And a great humiliation.

How did Kennedy react to that humiliation?
Well, on the one hand he imposed an economic blockade and backed pirate attacks and the dirty war. But he also reacted more intelligently, by developing a political programme aimed at social reform and economic aid for Latin American.

Kennedy proposed, after the defeat at Girón, an 'Alliance for Progress', plus the Peace Corps, a very astute strategy for putting the brakes on revolution. He proposed a plan to inject $20 billion into the region over a period of ten years, and this money was to go towards a programme of agrarian reform – agrarian reform! The administration that had never wanted to hear the phrase 'agrarian reform', that had considered it a 'Communist' idea, was now suggesting that there was a need for agrarian reform in Latin America. And they also proposed many other initiatives: housing construction, fiscal reforms, educational programmes, health programmes – almost exactly the same things *we* were doing.

In face of the Cuban Revolution, Kennedy was forced to launch initiatives of that kind. He realized that social and economic factors in the region could well lead to a radical revolution across the continent. There could be a second Cuban Revolution, but on a continent-wide scale, and perhaps even more radical.

In the end, many Latin American rulers stole all the money they could and the Alliance for Progress didn't solve a thing. Still, it was an intelligent reaction on Kennedy's part – he was a man of unquestionable intelligence.

13
The 'Cuban Missile Crisis' of October 1962

The world on the brink of nuclear war – The Soviets' 'betrayal' –
Failed negotiations – Letters between Castro and Khrushchev –
Khrushchev, Gorbachev, Putin – The Kennedy assassination

With Kennedy, you – and the rest of the world – lived through one of the
most dangerous international crises in world history: the so-called 'Cuban
Missile Crisis' of October 1962, what in Cuba is called the 'October Crisis'.
How do you see that situation now, forty-three years later?
It was a very tense moment, and there are many lessons to be learned
from that crisis. The world was on the verge of a thermonuclear war as
a consequence of the United States' aggressive, brutal policy against Cuba
– a plan, approved about ten months after the disastrous defeat they
suffered in Girón and about eight months before the crisis broke out, to
invade the island with the direct use of that country's naval, air and land
forces.

The Soviets managed to obtain absolutely trustworthy information
about that plan, and they notified Cuba of the existence of the danger,
although they weren't totally explicit – the truth is, they protected their
source. They said they'd come to that conviction after the meeting between
Khrushchev and Kennedy in Vienna. The details of the plan were learned
some twenty years later, when the documents related to the subject were
declassified and published by the US government.

The Soviets sent Sharaf Rashidov, Party secretary in Uzbekistan, and
Marshal Sergei Biryuzov, commander of the Strategic Rocket Forces in the
USSR, to talk to us. At the first meeting, Raúl and I were present.

After offering the information I mentioned, they asked what I thought
should be done to avoid the attack. I answered calmly: 'Make a public

statement warning the United States, just as they do in similar circumstances, that an attack on Cuba will be considered an attack on the Soviet Union.'

I then made my argument for that approach. They sat and thought about it for a while and then added that in order for it not to be just a simple statement, certain concrete measures had to be adopted. That was when they said they thought it was a good idea to install a minimal number of medium-range missiles in Cuba.

In my view, there was a clear desire [on their part] to obtain an improvement in the balance of power between the USSR and the United States. I confess I was none too happy about the presence of those weapons in Cuba, given our interest in avoiding the image of Cuba as a Soviet base, especially [as we might be seen in that way by] Latin America. So I replied, 'Let's take a break; I want to consult with the National Directorate of the Revolution about this delicate and extremely important matter.'

And we had that meeting around noon. At that meeting, I recall, besides Raúl there were Blas Roca, Che, Dorticós and Carlos Rafael. I told them what we'd been discussing and [explained that it appeared to me that] besides [the Soviets'] sincere desire to prevent an attack against Cuba, a subject to which Khrushchev was very committed, they were hoping to improve the balance of strategic forces, given what the presence of their missiles in Cuba would mean – it would be the equivalent of the window [recently] achieved by the United States through the presence of similar missiles in Turkey and Italy, which neighboured the Soviet Union.

I added that it would be inconsistent of us to expect the maximum support from the USSR and the rest of the Socialist camp should we be attacked by the United States and yet refuse to face the political risks and the possible damage to our reputation when they needed us. That ethical and revolutionary point of view was accepted unanimously.

When we got back to the place where the USSR's representatives were waiting for us, I told them that if this was a measure meant to protect Cuba from a direct attack and simultaneously strengthen the Soviet Union and the Socialist camp, then we agreed to the installation of as many medium-range rockets as might be necessary.

The rest of the time was spent on the relevant complementary measures. Forty-two medium-range rockets would be sent in. The naval, air and land forces in Cuba would be reinforced with missile-equipped patrol boats, a regiment of MiG-21 fighter planes, four brigades of motorized infantry well equipped with armoured personnel carriers and tanks, and a regiment of tactical nuclear arms that would be armed with nuclear warheads when the crisis broke out and whose commander would be empowered to use them without higher orders. Years later, McNamara would be horrified when he learned this. Batteries of surface-to-air missiles with a range of thirty kilometres would be deployed to protect the strategic nuclear arms.

This conversation took place five months before the crisis. There was not a second to lose. The effort was astounding.

Without that background, you can't have an idea of what happened in October 1962. Among other things, we discussed the preparation of all the relevant documents. The Soviets [said that they] would send them, and a short time later they did.

I studied them in great detail and realized that the draft of the accord or military agreement on the emplacement of the missiles had gaps from the political point of view and so couldn't be presented as a public document on such a delicate subject.

I rewrote it completely – wrote it out in longhand – and sent it with Raúl to Moscow. There, he discussed it with Minister of Defence Malinovski and with Khrushchev. It was accepted without changing a full stop or a comma.

The preparations began. I must in fairness tell you that the armed forces [of Cuba] and the Soviets acted with great efficiency to install the equipment in such a short time. First of all, we exerted great efforts in exploring, with the Soviets, sites on which to install the units and the armaments, including the medium-range missiles and all the elements to defend and protect them. Doing all that while still maintaining the strictest possible rules of compartmentalization, camouflage and discretion is perhaps the hardest thing you can imagine. Our armed forces and security agencies, backed by the Party and the mass organizations, acted with an efficiency that I don't think the world has ever seen. But despite these efforts, rumours circulated everywhere. Those who were disaffected with the Revolution would send messages any way they could to the United States, informing their family members and [government] functionaries of the movements they were observing. The press wasn't long in echoing the rumours. Kennedy was asked about it by the opposition and by the press.

A strange, byzantine discussion began between the Soviets and the government of the United States about the offensive versus defensive nature of the arms being sent to Cuba. Khrushchev assured Kennedy that the arms were defensive. In this case [i.e., the case of Cuba], Kennedy interpreted that to mean that there were no medium-range weapons. I think he believed, in his own way, Khrushchev's categorical assurance – Khrushchev, in fact, continued to insist that the weapons were defensive, not on any technical basis but rather because of the defensive purposes for which they'd been installed in Cuba. [But the] USSR had no need to go into those explanations. What Cuba and the USSR were doing was perfectly legal and in strict conformity with international law. From the first moment, Cuba's possession of armaments required for its defence should have been declared.

We didn't like the course the public debate was taking. I sent Che, who [at the time] was minister of industry and a member of the National Directorate of the ORI, to explain my view of the situation to Khrushchev, including the need to immediately publish the military agreement the USSR and Cuba had signed. But I couldn't manage to persuade him. Khrushchev's response was that he'd later send in the Baltic Fleet, so as to discourage too strong a response by the United States.

For us, for the Cuban leaders, the USSR was a powerful, experienced government. We had no other argument to use to persuade them that their strategy for managing the situation should be changed, so we had no alternative but to trust them.

How did the crisis begin?

The Americans detected the missile installations on 14–15 October. A U-2 spy plane flying at high altitude took photos of some launch ramps. The fact is, we know today that it was a member of the Soviet information services, Colonel Oleg Penkovsky, who gave the Americans the exact coordinates of the missiles that the U-2 then detected. Kennedy was informed on 16 October. Six days later, the crisis began.

What's hard to believe about Khrushchev's attitude is that while surface-to-air missile batteries were located all over the island, there'd been no attempt to prevent the adversary from spotting the Soviet–Cuban defence positions [with] spy planes overflying the island.

This was no longer a question that had to do with tactics or strategy. It was a decision that had to do with the willingness, or lack thereof, to maintain a firm stance in the situation that had emerged. From our point of view, which we stated then and that I still state today, allowing spy planes [to overfly Cuba] gave the adversary, for free, an extraordinary advantage. It gave them an entire week to organize their plan of response, both politically and militarily.

When the crisis broke out, Khrushchev didn't have a clear idea of what he should do. [His] first statement was a forceful, energetic condemnation of the position that Kennedy had taken.

What did Kennedy do at that point?*

On 19 October, Kennedy consulted with the US Joint Chiefs of Staff, who advised Kennedy to authorize a massive aerial attack on the missile installations. On 20 October, on the advice this time of Robert McNamara, his Secretary of State, Kennedy decided to impose a naval blockade on the island with 183 warships, among which were eight aircraft carriers, and 40,000 Marines on transport ships.

In Florida, 579 combat planes and five army divisions were assembled and put on alert, among which were two elite air divisions, the 82nd and 101st Airborne. But the American people, and people around the world, still didn't know what was happening.

When did Kennedy make the public announcement?

He spoke on television on 22 October, at 7 p.m. His speech was carried by every network, with a great sense of drama, and at that point the world became aware that there was this crisis and that we were on the brink of a nuclear war. He announced that the Soviet Union had to withdraw its missiles or it risked a nuclear war. And he also announced a naval blockade of Cuba, in order to prevent the arrival of more missiles. By this time, the Soviets had arrested Colonel Penkovsky and they knew that the Americans had all the information. And they also knew that Kennedy knew that Khrushchev had lied in his letter.

When was it that you were informed of what the Americans knew?

Really, I figured it out when, on the 22nd, there was a spectacular

---

* [(in 1st ed.:) Kennedy got in touch with Khrushchev, who at that point made an error, an ethical and political error. In a letter, Khrushchev lied to Kennedy; he told him that they were 'defensive' weapons, not strategic. Clearly they were weapons that could be used for defence, but they were offensive, too. There were some thirty-six [sic] medium-range strategic missiles here, and other weapons systems. And the Soviet general who commanded that operation had the authority, the power, under certain circumstances, to use those tactical weapons, as well as anti-aircraft weapons. I mean, he had a certain amount of authority to use them without even consulting with Moscow.

That letter of Khrushchev's was taken to Kennedy by Gromyko, Andre Gromyko, who was the Soviet minister of foreign affairs. That was on 18 October. At that point, the problem had not yet been made public. But then . . .]

announcement that Kennedy would be speaking that night at seven,[1] and I also saw a number of other indications. There was nothing it could be but a reaction to the presence of the missiles. I'd already asked the Soviet military command in Cuba to speed up as much as possible the construction of the missile-launching ramps. We had to be ready to fight. They worked day and night. On 16 October practically no launch ramp was ready; by the 18th there were eight, on the 20th there were thirteen, and on the 21st there were twenty. Things went very, very fast.

What did the Cubans do, faced with such grave danger?
As I told you, even before Kennedy spoke, we'd anticipated the reason for his appearance, so we decided to sound the combat alarm and mobilize down to the last man. Somewhere around 300,000 combatants were called to arms, all in a heightened spirit of defence. On 23 October I went on television to denounce the United States' policy, warn of the risk of invasion, mobilize the nation in its entirety, and declare our willingness to fight, whatever the dangers.

Did the US naval blockade ever become really effective?
Yes, of course. The blockade became effective on 24 October at two in the afternoon. And at that moment there were twenty-three Soviet naval vessels en route to Cuba. [(in 1st ed.:) . . . At any moment there could have been an incident, an American ship could have fired on a Soviet ship and nuclear war break out . . . There was tremendous tension, tremendous.]

In that situation, what did the UN do?
Well, there was that famous debate, which I would categorize as embarrassing, between the American ambassador, Adlai Stevenson, and the Soviet ambassador, Valerian Zorin. Stevenson [(in 1st ed.:) – as Colin Powell did on 4 February 2003, with false evidence in that case, to justify waging war on Iraq –] made a spectacular presentation to the United Nations Security Council in which he showed large aerial photographs of the strategic missile bases. The Soviet ambassador denied the evidence, denied that the proof was authentic. He rejected the debate. It was all *ad hoc*, all improvised – the man wasn't prepared to debate. He didn't attack, didn't denounce, didn't explain the powerful reasons that Cuba – a small country under constant threats both explicit and implicit from the superpower, under assault – had for requesting aid, and the USSR, faithful to its principles and its

internationalist duties, for providing it, and he got himself all tangled up in a mediocre argument that stemmed, ultimately, from the vacillations and public mishandling of the issue by Khrushchev in the months leading up to the crisis. He made the mistake of rejecting the real debate, which should have been over the sovereignty of Cuba, its right to defend itself, to protect itself. That was on 25 October 1962.

Meanwhile, I believe the Americans were still flying reconnaissance flights over Cuba, weren't they?
Yes, they were. They kept overflying the island, and they were allowed to do so with impunity, despite the anti-aircraft batteries that had been installed precisely to prevent that, prevent the open, brazen spying on our territory, observing every detail of our defences.

So they continued to send the U-2 spy planes, and they also started making low-altitude flights. We decided to fire on the American planes that had started making those low-level flights. You can't detect flights at more or less treetop level – it makes it easy for there to be a surprise attack. We pointed this out to the Soviet military officers in charge there, we told them that the low-level flights shouldn't be permitted. We had previously informed them that we were going to shoot them down. And we opened fire with anti-aircraft artillery.

On 27 October, in Oriente province, a battery of SAM missiles operated by the Soviets fired on and brought down a U-2 spy plane. It was at that point that the moment of maximum tension occurred. The American officer Rudolph Anderson, the pilot of the U-2, was killed. That was the sign that combat had practically begun. At any time, another incident could have occurred, and could have led to all-out war. And let me repeat that in Cuba, the people were very calm.

Did you think at any point that war was inevitable?
Well, it was a very tense moment. And we ourselves thought that conflict was inevitable. And we were determined to take that risk. It never occurred to us to give in to the adversary's threats.

But the Soviets did give in.
At that moment of maximum tension, the Soviets sent a proposal to the United States. And Khrushchev didn't consult with us about it. They proposed to withdraw the missiles if the Americans would withdraw their

Jupiter missiles from Turkey. Kennedy agreed to the compromise on 28 October. And the Soviets began to withdraw the SS-4s. That seemed to us absolutely the wrong decision. It occasioned great indignation.

Did you have the impression that the agreement had been reached behind your back?
We learned from news reports that the Soviets were making the proposal to withdraw the missiles. And it had never been discussed with us in any way! We weren't opposed to a solution, because it was important to avoid a nuclear conflict. But Khrushchev should have told the Americans, 'The Cubans must be included in the discussions.' At that moment they lost their nerve, and they weren't firm in their determination. Out of principle, they should have consulted with us.

Had they done that, the conditions [of the subsequent agreement] would most certainly have been better. There would have been no Guantánamo Naval Base; there'd have been no more high-altitude spy-plane reconnaissance . . . All of that offended us a great deal; we took it as an affront. And we protested. And even after the agreement, we kept firing on the low-level flights. So they had to suspend them. Our relations with the Soviets deteriorated. For years, all this had an influence on Cuban–Soviet relations.

I haven't wanted to tell you in great detail all the steps we took during that crisis, but it can't really be understood in all its political, moral and military aspects without the letters exchanged between Khrushchev and me during those days.[2]

I'll start by reading you the letter I sent to Khrushchev on 26 October 1962:

Dear *Compañero* Khrushchev,

After analysis of the situation and the reports in our possession, I consider aggression to be almost imminent – within the next twenty-four to seventy-two hours.

There are two possible variants: the first and most probable is an air attack against certain objectives with the limited aim of destroying them; the second, which is less probable though entirely possible, is invasion. In my view, this variant would demand a large force and is also the most repugnant form of aggression, which may deter them.

You may be sure that we will offer firm and determined resistance to an attack, whichever the case. The morale of the Cuban people is extremely high, and we will face the aggressor heroically.

I wish in these moments to give you, very briefly, a personal opinion.

Should the second variant take place and the imperialists invade Cuba with the intention of occupying [the country], the dangers of this aggressive policy for humanity are so great that after such an event the Soviet Union must never allow circumstances in which the imperialists might carry out a nuclear first strike against it.

I say this because I believe that the imperialists' aggressiveness has become extremely dangerous, and if they do indeed perform an act so brutal and in such brazen violation of universal law and morality as invading Cuba, that would be the moment to eliminate that danger for ever, in an act of the most legitimate self-defence. However hard and terrible the solution might be, there is no other.

This opinion is influenced by my having observed the evolution of this aggressive policy, the way the imperialists, in defiance of world opinion and [considering themselves] above principle and law, have blockaded the seas, violated our air space, and are now preparing for invasion, while they thwart every possibility of negotiation, despite knowing of the gravity of the situation.

You have been and are a tireless defender of peace; I understand how bitter these hours must be for you, when the results of your superhuman efforts are so seriously threatened. Until the last moment, however, we shall maintain our hope that peace may be salvaged, and we are willing and ready to contribute whatever may be within our reach [to achieve that goal]. But at the same time, we are ready to face with serenity a situation which we see as very real and very imminent.

I convey to you once again the infinite gratitude of the Cuban people to the Soviet people, who have been so generous and fraternal with us, and our profound gratitude and admiration to you [personally], as well as our desires for success in the enormous task and grave responsibilities that you have in your hands.

Fraternally,

Fidel Castro

On 28 October Khrushchev sent a reply:

Dear Comrade Fidel Castro,

Our message to President Kennedy on 27 October allows for a solution to the matter in your favour and to defend Cuba against invasion, the outbreak of the war. Kennedy's reply, which, evidently, you are familiar with as well, offers securities that the United States not only will not invade Cuba with their own forces, but will not allow their allies to do so. With this, the president of the United States has replied positively to my messages of 26 and 27 October 1962. [...][3]

For the time being, however, it is not law that rules but rather the lack of sense of the militarists in the Pentagon. Since an agreement is in sight, the Pentagon is looking for a pretext to thwart it. This is why it organizes provocative overflights. Yesterday, you shot down one of them, yet previously you did not when they flew over your territory. That step will be used by aggressors to their advantage, to further their aims.

We send you, and your entire collective direction, our greetings,

N. Khrushchev

That same day, 28 October, I replied:

Dear *Compañero* Khrushchev,

Our government's position with respect to your message is contained in the statement formulated today, whose text you are surely familiar with.

I would like to clarify something with regard to the anti-aircraft measures we have adopted. You say: 'Yesterday, you shot down one of them [the spy planes], yet previously you did not when they flew over your territory.'

Before, there were isolated violations without any clear military purpose or real danger stemming from those flights.

Today, that is not the case. There was the danger of a surprise attack on certain military installations. We decided that we could not simply sit back and wait for a surprise attack. With our detection radar turned off, potential attackers could fly over the objectives with impunity and totally destroy them. We did not believe we should allow that, given the cost and effort that had been expended, and also because it would greatly weaken both our military and our morale. It was with that motive that on 24 October Cuban forces mobilized fifty anti-aircraft batteries, which was our entire reserve, to support the positions held by Soviet forces. If we wished to avoid the risk of a surprise attack, the artillery had to have orders to fire. The Soviet Forces Command will be able to provide you with further information as to what happened with the downed plane.

Before, violations of our air space were conducted on a *de facto* basis, and furtively. Yesterday, the American government tried to make the privilege of overflying our air space at any hour of the day or night official. We cannot accept that, because it is the equivalent of renouncing a sovereign prerogative. However, we do agree to avoid an incident just now which might do great harm to the negotiations, and we will give orders to the Cuban batteries to hold their fire, although only while negotiations are going on and without reversing the decision we announced yesterday to defend our air space. Both of us should, in addition, recognize the danger that in the current conditions of tension, incidents may accidentally occur.

I would also like to inform you that we are opposed, on principle, to inspections on our territory.

We are extraordinarily appreciative of the efforts you have made to maintain the peace, and we absolutely agree as to the need to fight for that objective. If that is achieved in a just, solid and definitive manner, it will have been an inestimable service to humanity.

Fraternally,

Fidel Castro Ruz

Khrushchev wrote to me again on 30 October:

Dear Comrade Fidel Castro,

We have received your letter of 28 October and the communications on the conversations that both you and President Dorticós have had with our ambassador . . .

We understand that certain difficulties are being created for you because we have promised the government of the United States to withdraw the missile base from Cuba, on the grounds of [its being] an offensive weapon, in exchange for their commitment to set aside any plans for an invasion of Cuba by troops of the US or its allies in the Western Hemisphere and to raise the 'quarantine', that is, end the [naval] blockade of Cuba. This led to the end of the conflict in the Caribbean, which was complicated, as you well understand, by a conflict between two world powers and had threatened to become a third world war involving thermonuclear weapons and missiles.

As we understand our ambassador, there is the opinion among some Cubans that the Cuban people would have wished for a statement of another kind, and at any rate would not have wished for a statement on the withdrawal of missiles. [. . .][4]

In addition, there are opinions that you and we have not sufficiently consulted with one another on these issues before taking the decision which you know. [. . .][5]

Wasn't that consultation with us? We understood this cable as a sign of extreme alarm. If in the conditions that had been created, and also taking into account the information that the bellicose and unbridled militarists in the United States wanted to take advantage of the situation and attack Cuba, we had continued our consultations, time would have been lost and the attack would have taken place.

We have reached the opinion that our strategic missiles in Cuba became a kind of obsession for the imperialists: they became fearful and, out of fear that the missiles might be used, they might have risked taking action to eliminate them, either by bombing them or attacking Cuba. And one must say that they could have taken them out of combat. Therefore, I repeat, your alarm was entirely justified.

In your cable of 27 October you proposed that we carry out a nuclear first strike against the enemy territory. You, of course, understand what that would lead to. This would not be a simple attack, but rather the beginning of a thermonuclear world war.

Dear Comrade Fidel Castro, I believe your proposal to have been wrong, although I understand its motivation.

We have lived through the most serious moment, in which a thermonuclear world war might have broken out. Clearly, in that case the US would have suffered enormous losses, but the Soviet Union and the entire Socialist camp would also have suffered terribly. With respect to Cuba, the Cuban people, it is hard to say how it would have turned out. In the first place, the fires of war would have burned Cuba. There is no doubt that the Cuban people would have fought valiantly, but that it would also have perished heroically cannot be doubted. [. . .][6]

Now, as a result of the measures we have taken, we have achieved the objective we set ourselves when we entered our agreement with you to send the missiles to Cuba. We have extracted from the United States the commitment that they themselves will not attack Cuba and that they will not allow their allies in Latin America to do so. We have extracted all that without a nuclear strike. [. . .][7]

Naturally, in the defence of both Cuba and other Socialist countries we cannot confide in the veto of the government of the United States. We have adopted and will continue to adopt all measures to strengthen our defences and gather the forces needed in case of a counter-strike. [. . .]

We believe that the aggressor has suffered a defeat. It was preparing to attack Cuba, but we have stopped that, and forced [the aggressor] to acknowledge before the world that it will not do so in the current stage. We judge this to be a great victory. The imperialists, of course, are not going to cease their fight against Communism. But we have our plans, too, and we are going to adopt our measures. This process of struggle shall continue so long as two political and social systems exist in the world, until one of them, and we know that it shall be our Communist system, conquers the entire world. [. . .]

[Comrade Fidel Castro, we wish you all possible success, and I am sure that you will achieve it. There are still machinations against you, but we intend, with you, to take every measure to thwart them and to contribute to the strengthening and development of the Cuban Revolution.]

N. Khrushchev

On 31 October – this is the last letter I'll read you – I replied to Khrushchev in the following terms:

Dear Comrade Khrushchev,

I received your letter of 30 October. It is your view that we were indeed consulted before adoption of the decision to withdraw the strategic missiles. You based [your letter] on the alarming news you say you have received from Cuba and, lastly, my cable of 27 October. I do not know what news you may have received; I am simply referring to the message I sent you the night of 26 October, received by you on the 27th.

What we did in the face of the events, Comrade Khrushchev, was prepare ourselves to fight. In Cuba there was but one kind of alarm: the alarm that called our people to arms. When in our judgement the imperialist attack became imminent, I decided that I should communicate that news to you, and alert both the government and the Soviet [military] command – since there were Soviet forces committed to fighting alongside us in the defence of the Republic of Cuba against outside attack – of the possibility of an attack that it was not within our power to halt, although we might indeed resist it . . .

The danger could not daunt us, because we have felt it hanging over our country for many years, and to a certain extent we have become used to it . . .

The eyes of many men, Soviet and Cuban, who were willing to die with supreme dignity, wept when they learned of the surprising, unexpected and practically unconditional decision to withdraw the weapons.

You may not know to what degree the Cuban people were prepared to fulfil their duty to the *patria* and to humanity.

I was not unaware when I wrote them that the words of my letter might be misinterpreted by you, and so they have been, perhaps because you did not read them slowly and carefully, perhaps because of the translation, perhaps because I tried to say too much in too few lines. However, I did not hesitate to write. Do you think, Comrade Khrushchev, that we were thinking selfishly of ourselves, of our generous people ready to immolate themselves, and not, of course, unconsciously, but fully assured of the risk we ran? . . .

We knew – do not assume that we didn't – that we might well be exterminated, as you insinuate in your letter, should a thermonuclear war break out. Still, that did not persuade us to ask you to withdraw the missiles, or ask you to give in. Do you think we wanted that war? But how were we to avoid it if the invasion had occurred? It was precisely because such an invasion was possible, that imperialism might thwart every solution – and from our point of view, their demands were impossible to accept, by either the USSR or Cuba.

And if such an event had occurred, what was one to do with the madmen who unleashed the war? You yourself have said that in the current conditions, war will inevitably become thermonuclear war, and quickly so.

It is my position that once the aggression has occurred, the aggressors must not be given the privilege to decide when nuclear arms will be used. The destructive power of these weapons is so great, and the means of transporting them so swift, that the aggressor can count on a considerable initial advantage in his favour.

And I did not suggest to you, Comrade Khrushchev, that the USSR become the aggressor, because that would be worse than wrong, it would be immoral and unworthy of me. What I did suggest was that from the moment imperialism unleashed an attack against Cuba, and in Cuba[, therefore,] against the armed forces of the USSR stationed here to aid in our defence in case of a foreign attack, a response be given the aggressors against Cuba and the USSR in the form of an annihilating counter-attack . . .

I did not suggest to you, Comrade Khrushchev, that the USSR attack in the midst of the crisis, as it seems from your letter you think, but rather that after the imperialist attack, the USSR act without hesitation and never commit the error of allowing the enemy to strike you first with nuclear weapons. And in that sense, Comrade Khrushchev, I maintain my point of view, because I believe it to have been a fair, realistic assessment of the situation at the time. You can convince me that I'm wrong, but you cannot tell me that I'm wrong without first convincing me . . .

You may wonder what right I had to do so. I approached you without concern for how thorny it might be, following the dictates of my conscience, as befits a revolutionary inspired by the most disinterested sense of admiration and affection for the USSR . . .

I don't see how I can say we were consulted on the decision made by you. There is nothing I could want more at this time than to be mistaken. I wish you were the one who was completely right. It is not several, a handful of Cubans, as you have been informed, but rather many, who are now living moments of indescribable bitterness and sadness.

The imperialists have already started talking again about invading the country, as proof of how ephemeral and little worthy of trust their promises are. Our nation's will to resist the aggressors, however, remains unshakeable, and perhaps more than ever needs to trust in itself and that will to fight.

We shall fight against adverse circumstances; we shall overcome the current difficulties; and we shall move forward – and nothing will be able to destroy the bonds of friendship and eternal gratitude towards the USSR.

Fraternally,

Fidel Castro

These letters have been published before, but I thought it was a good idea to include them in this retelling today, at your request, of the events of the October crisis, because as I told you, it's not possible to fully understand our conduct during the crisis in all its political, emotional and military aspects without them.

In September 1991, during a visit to Moscow by US secretary of state James Baker, Baker and Russian president Mikhail Gorbachev negotiated the withdrawal of the last Soviet troops from Cuba – the Mechanized Infantry Instruction Brigade. Did they consult with you this time about that decision?

Consult! They never consult. By that time, they were falling apart. Everything they took out of here they took without consultation. In the October crisis, they didn't consult and they agreed to allow the withdrawal of missiles to be under inspection, under inspection by the United Nations, and we said, 'No, nobody comes in here to inspect. We will not authorize that. If you want to leave it's none of our affair.' So they invented this new procedure – they inspected en route out, at sea. That was the cause of a pretty tense situation, the way they did it, but the USSR was still a superpower. We could talk about that for a long time – many mistakes were made; I've talked about this on other occasions.

About this, one more detail. When the Soviets withdrew, in 1991, when they withdrew the Soviet brigade from Cuba . . .

No, they negotiated that directly with the United States, without consulting us. They negotiated everything without consulting us. Now then, there was no reason to negotiate that brigade; both its personnel and its equipment had been weakened – how could it fight, when the USSR was divided and falling apart and the brigade had personnel from all the different republics? Despite the fact that the Soviet troops were technically very well prepared, they're brave, they showed that in the Second World War. But by the time of the withdrawal the political situation in the former USSR was very bad.

There, too, one might think that in exchange for withdrawing the Soviet brigade from Cuba, the Americans could have been persuaded to withdraw from the base at Guantánamo, right?

Well, I think that was possible only at the time of the October crisis, as I said. The concession could have been won easily, with a little equanimity and sang-froid, because the world wasn't willing to enter a nuclear war on a whim of the United States.

A world war.

We put five demands on the table, among them a cessation of the pirate attacks [and] the acts of aggression and terrorism against us, although they went on after that for decades; a lifting of the economic blockade; [and] return of the arbitrarily occupied land on which the Guantánamo Naval Base was located. All those [concessions] could have been easily obtained, in that dramatic state of tension [the world was in], since, as I told you, nobody was willing to march into a world war on account of a blockade, a few terrorist attacks and a naval base that was illegal and on land occupied against the will of the Cuban people. No one would have gone into a world war for that.

The presence of the strategic missiles was a very strong reason for the United States and its allies to join together. But the important thing was that there was nothing illegal about an agreement with the Soviets to bring in the missiles [against] the real threat of an invasion that was already being planned, with all the pretexts in place. American historians, in their own archives, have all the papers to prove that – the plans to invade us. So by the time the Soviets started talking about installing missiles as a way to guarantee our security, the American plan for invading Cuba after Girón was already drawn up; the pretexts for invading us had been prepared since February 1962, and the missiles, I believe, started arriving here in June.

In the summer of 1962.
That's right, in the summer – months later. It's very possible that the Soviets mentioned that, because they tended to have quite a bit of information – both superpowers had been spying on each other by every means imaginable for years. Through espionage or intelligence methods, the Soviets knew about the Americans' invasion plan. They didn't *tell* us they knew; they said they'd deduced it from Khrushchev's conversations with Kennedy in Vienna, etc., but knowing the Soviets, they knew.

There was nothing illegal about our agreement with the Soviets, given that the Americans had Jupiter missiles in Turkey and in Italy, too, and no one ever threatened to bomb or invade those countries. The problem wasn't the legality of the agreement – everything was absolutely legal – but rather Khrushchev's mistaken political handling of the situation, when, even though both Cuba and the USSR had the legitimate right, he started spinning theories about offensive and non-offensive weapons. In a political battle, you can't afford to lose the high moral ground by employing ruses and lies and half-truths.

I repeat: the act was absolutely legal, legitimate, even justified. It was not illegal. The error lay in the Soviets' lies and disinformation, because that emboldened Kennedy. Because Kennedy had real proof, which the Americans had obtained from air reconnaissance, in the photos taken from the U-2s, which had violated our air space, and was allowed to do so. If you install surface-to-air missiles, you can't let the other country fly over the territory they're supposed to defend. The United States doesn't allow any rival power to fly over its territory, nor would it have allowed a Soviet plane to overfly its missile sites in Italy and Turkey.*

There were many political and military errors, and it's essential to talk about them, in order to explain what happened back then.

In October 1962, it wasn't that we authorized the pull-out, it's that we didn't take measures to keep them from pulling out the missiles, because [if we did] we were going to have problems with both the two superpowers, and that was too much for Cuba.

It would have been too much!
We had control of the country, and no missile would have moved an inch if we'd decided they weren't going to, but that would have been stupid, it made no sense. What we refused to do was authorize inspections. We protested, expressed our displeasure, demanded those five [concessions].

But now, when the Soviets – this is what happened, just the way I'm telling it – negotiated with the Americans, within that policy, within that love affair that emerged during those difficult days, hot love in the middle of a cold war, the Soviets and the Americans agreed to inspections at sea instead of inspection on Cuban soil.

Later, in October 2001, when the Russians announced they were closing down and pulling out the Centre for Electronic Surveillance,[8] it was a *fait accompli* – they *informed* us, hoping we'd go along.

But you were opposed to that pull-out too?
We disagreed with it, because during Vladimir Putin's visit to Cuba in December 2000, we visited that centre, a large electronics base located south of Havana. Putin came to Cuba under the friendliest of terms. At the centre, I discovered a kind of ghetto, because the Soviets lived there in isolation, self-imposed isolation, mind you, with their families, so we decided to design some programmes for their children, for visits to places of cultural interest, recreational centres, that sort of thing. I hadn't known what the situation was there. When they announced they were closing it down and pulling out, it was a unilateral decision. They announced it about ten months after Putin's visit. So in neither case had there been any prior agreement.

* [(in 1st ed.:) But the Soviets did.]

*Despite the crisis in October, the so-called 'Cuban Missile Crisis', you still
maintain a positive opinion of Kennedy.*
That crisis gave Kennedy added stature, authority – he showed he had the
ability to come up with an effective response.

If we'd taken part in the negotiations, we'd have done so in, let's say, a
constructive way . . . A dialogue might have begun, an exchange of impressions and points of view, that might have allowed us to avoid many of the
problems that our two countries have had since then.

Irrespective of what happened, in judging Kennedy's policies I have to
consider the times we were living in, what doctrines prevailed, what disturb-
ance must have been caused by a government ninety miles from the United
States that declared itself to be a Socialist revolution – and declared itself
Socialist on its own, because the Soviets didn't give us one penny for the
Revolution, or one rifle.

In January 1959 I didn't know a single Soviet, or the leaders.

I believe your brother Raúl did know some Soviets.
Raúl had met one, Nikolai Leonov, a young Soviet that [Raúl] was on the
same boat with on his way back from an international conference on young
people's rights in Vienna in 1953. As I told you, Raúl had been a member
of the Socialist Youth. What a catch that was for them! No doubt about it.
And so he met Leonov – he's still alive – who was on his way to Mexico as
a diplomat. They came on the same boat, but that was it. Socialism didn't
arrive here through cloning, or through artificial insemination. It [Socialism]
was very different here, and you have to keep that in mind when you compare Cuba with the other processes or attempts to construct Socialism in
the countries of Eastern Europe, which are now attempting to construct
capitalism.

Despite the historical evolution, the development of human society and
the factors that have had the greatest influence on it, even *determined* it,
there are factors of a subjective nature that influence events, slowing or
accelerating, sometimes, the probable course of history.

In the case of Cuba, there is not the slightest doubt that a combination of
objective and subjective factors accelerated the process of revolution in our
country, accelerated the changes that revolution entailed. And all of that
led, because of the interests involved, to the confrontation with the United
States and the crisis in October 1962, which the Americans call the 'Cuban
Missile Crisis'.

But at that moment, Kennedy showed himself to be reasonable – he refused to complicate things; he gave the order to suspend the 'reconnaissance' flights, the low-level espionage flights, and also ordered that Operation Mongoose be halted.[9]

All of that created an intense hatred of Kennedy on the part of all the adversaries of the Cuban Revolution, because he didn't give the order for the fleet to step in during Playa Girón to help the mercenaries, and because he didn't take advantage of the October crisis to intervene against us as many generals and many of our enemies were advising him to do. That may be who was behind the conspiracy to assassinate him. Although I have no proof, I'm making deductions about what may have happened. I daresay that it's true, though – there are many, many reasons to be suspicious.

When Kennedy was killed, on 22 November 1963, Lee Harvey Oswald was accused of doing it, and people said he was a Cuban sympathizer. Do you think that people were trying to implicate Cuba in that assassination?
Thank goodness we didn't give that guy permission to visit Cuba. That would have been a tremendous manipulation, a tremendous provocation, because they could have used that to implicate Cuba. Actually, when the investigation was being carried out, we gave them all the information we had.

What do you think of the official version of Kennedy's assassination?
Well, it's all very strange. With the expertise I acquired in sharpshooting, I can't imagine that with a rifle with a telescopic sight such as he had you can fire, load and fire again in a matter of seconds. Because when you shoot with a telescopic sight, if the weapon moves a fraction of an inch you lose your target. You're aiming at a plate, say, that's 600 or 500 metres down the range, and with the recoil from the shot you lose the target, and you have to find it again.

If you're in a window and you fire, you immediately have to reload, reposition the rifle, cock it, find the target again and fire. And finding a target in motion in a fraction of a second with a telescopic sight is *very* difficult. Firing three times in a row, so accurately, somebody who almost certainly didn't have much experience – that's very difficult.

So you think there was more than one shooter?
Well, what I can't understand about those shots is the way they were fired. I can't formulate any other theory. There are a lot of theories. What I can talk about is just on the basis of my experience with a rifle with a telescopic sight, and what the official version says is quite simply not possible – not just like that, *bang bang bang.*

There are two things about that assassination that are just incomprehensible to me: one, the kind of shot made by a man with a rifle, which is repeated with incredible accuracy in a very short length of time. That doesn't jibe with the experience that I've had.

Second, Oswald was a prisoner, he was there in jail, and this charitable, noble soul, Jack Ruby, so consumed with grief by the assassination, right there in front of the police and the television cameras and everything killed Oswald. I don't know if anything like that has ever happened anywhere else.

You distrust the official version?
Yes, I do. I totally distrust the version of the way Oswald fired. And Arthur Schlesinger, one of Kennedy's advisers, who has been to Cuba since then,[10] wrote a 900-page book[11] in which he tells the whole story and says who that man was. This Oswald fellow tried to come here, to Cuba, and since our people had a terrible mistrust of him, we told him no.

Imagine what would've happened if that guy came here and then went back and within a few days killed Kennedy, immediately after being in Cuba for a week. There's a plan there, not just against Kennedy, but against Cuba. I knew that that version was impossible. Schlesinger gives details.

Oswald may have been a double agent. You know how it might have happened – he went to the Soviet Union and came back, and everybody knows how those people, at the height of the Cold War, kept each other under surveillance.

He had been in the Soviet Union.
That's right, he was there; he married a Soviet woman. Later he came back, and they got divorced. Schlesinger thinks there may be an almost Freudian explanation for this guy's behaviour.

What was that guy doing when he tried to come to Cuba? How in the world could this Jack Ruby get into the police station and kill Oswald? Those are two extremely strange things, which support, quite reasonably, all the suspicion, the idea of some conspiracy. But I have no evidence, all

I can do is speculate. The things that I can talk about are those two questions, and the physical impossibility of firing as Oswald is supposed to have fired – and those things lead one to question the truthfulness of the explanation that's been given.

14
The Death of Che Guevara

Che and the anti-imperialist movement – The farewell letter –
In the guerrilla conflicts in Africa – Return to Cuba –
Preparing the mission to the Andes – Régis Debray –
The last battle – Che's legacy

After the crisis in October 1962, the threat of US aggression against Cuba lessens. The Revolution continues to consolidate its gains. Che Guevara begins travelling around the world. He seems to have been very interested in international affairs, the anti-imperialist movement, right?
He was most certainly an observer of the situation in the Third World. He was concerned about international issues, about the Bandung Conference,[1] the Non-Aligned Movement and other issues. He left in 1965 – he'd travelled around the world, met with Chou En-lai, with Nehru, with Nasser, with Sukarno, because he was a true internationalist and had a great deal of interest in the problems of the developing world.

With respect to China, I recall that Che spoke with several Chinese leaders. He made contact with Chou En-lai, as I said; he met Mao, he was interested in the Chinese thinking as to revolution. He had no conflicts with the Soviets, but it's obvious that he was closer, in a way, to China, or more sympathetic to that country.

He even visited Yugoslavia, despite the [financial] self-management [being experimented with by the Eastern bloc] and that sort of thing, which, really, I didn't like very much. Because a cooperative would have hotels and all sorts of things that distracted it from its original objective, and I'd already seen some of them here in Cuba that sometimes, instead of putting their energies into agriculture, devoted them to trade and tourism.

In December 1964 Che was at the United Nations, then in Algeria, and he also travelled through Africa during the first few months of 1965.
Yes, but that was a strategy, in the final phase of the execution of his mission, when he'd already made the decision to go to Bolivia. He was fine; he had tremendous enthusiasm, and he intended to make a contribution to revolution in Argentina. He was creating the conditions [necessary for the success of a revolutionary struggle], because at that time everybody wanted to destroy us, and our response was to change the status quo – to 'revolutionize'. That was the great truth, and we always held to that principle.

You once told me: 'They internationalized the blockade; we internationalized guerrilla warfare.'
The case of Trujillo, whom a group of armed Dominicans left Cuba to fight in July 1959 – an event that was the first movement of support against a dictatorship, in this case in response to an old commitment to the Dominicans who'd fought alongside us – was an exception. Trujillo had provided weapons to Batista; Batista took refuge there when the war was over, armed actions were being launched from the Dominican Republic against our country.

With regard to other countries in a similar situation, our rule was respect, observe international law, despite the fact that none of those other countries may have had much love for us. But they all had their own subtleties, their own particularities – some of them were relatively more independent of the United States, others, less. Of course the most unconditionally loyal [to the US] broke off relations with Cuba immediately, while others resisted: Brazil resisted, Uruguay resisted, Chile resisted. Venezuela, on the other hand, didn't resist for a second, because Rómulo Betancourt[2] was there, a man who'd been a leftist early on, though he was nothing but a bundle of reactionary resentments by that time. So there was a group of Latin American countries that maintained relations with Cuba for a while – Mexico, always.

The United States admonished Cuba for spreading subversion around the world.
The United States' demands on Cuba have been different at different times; they've varied. Every so often they add a new one. First, we had to renounce Socialism. Next, we had to break all commercial and other ties with the USSR. They've always had some demand to make on us, even after condemning us and isolating us, after Playa Girón, after the October crisis, there

would always be some new problem. Then there were the revolutionary struggles in Latin America: Cuba had to cease all support for those struggles – I'm quoting some of their demands. Later it was Angola, which was attacked by South Africa in 1975. Everyone knows what happened – we had to withdraw from Angola; if we withdrew from Angola all the problems with Cuba would be over, they told us . . . And the list goes on . . .

Later, there were still more problems, because in 1974 revolution had broken out in Ethiopia, and because of the situation that was created there, in 1977 we felt we were obliged to help the Ethiopians and do our bit for other causes as well. We were a country that had been isolated, and the more the United States tried to isolate us, the more we sought out relations with the rest of the world.

But Cuba continued to be accused of 'exporting revolution'.
Back at that time, in the sixties, no one in Latin America maintained diplomatic relations with us – Mexico was the only one. At that time we observed all international rules of conduct. We did, of course, want revolution; we desired it out of doctrine, out of conviction. But we observed international law. And I maintain that revolution can't be exported, because no one can 'export' the objective conditions that make revolution possible. That has always been our premise, and we still think that way.

After the triumph of the Revolution in Cuba, in May 1959, I was in Buenos Aires. My visit coincided with a meeting of the OAS, and I presented a sort of Marshall Plan for Latin America – much like the famous plan for the reconstruction of Europe after the Second World War. I estimated it would cost about $20 billion. Of course I didn't have the experience I have now – far from it. But I did have some ideas. I didn't have much international experience, except all the things I'd read throughout my life and of course my own meditations on the subject. Nor did I have much experience with Latin America, but I presented this plan there anyway. Do you know how much money Latin America owed at that time?

No.
Five billion dollars.

Compared with its debt today – $850 billion – that's not much.
At that time, Latin America had half the population it has today, fewer than 250 million people. Today there are over 500 million. And the foreign debt

– I'm not talking about the domestic indebtedness, which is also the nation's debt to those with a lot of money – the foreign debt is the debt a country has to pay outside its borders, with interest. That doesn't include the flight of capital, unequal exchange rates, the tendency of capital to flow towards nations with stronger and more solid economies, the Bretton Woods privileges given to the United States,[3] the rights of those who print up dollars in the world ... Now the shelter is not gold, because President Nixon, in August 1971, unilaterally halted gold exchange for dollars, so all there was left was the dollar, which is the only currency that exists in this hemisphere – all the others fluctuate a great deal, all the time, and none of them is secure. So all the money of all the Latin American countries, both well- and ill-gotten, tends to flee, and it flees towards the United States.

The plan you proposed at the OAS meeting was rejected, I imagine.
That plan would've helped avoid many tragedies on this continent. And two years later, as I've said, Kennedy picked up the idea and proposed his own Marshall Plan for Latin America – the Alliance for Progress: agrarian reform, fiscal reform, housing construction, etc.

Which didn't keep him from harassing Cuba.
That's right. At the time, they freed us from all commitments. I think there were no doubt objective reasons for that, and I think that what Che did was absolutely correct – there was not the slightest disagreement. At that moment there was a great deal of talk of the United States' political interventionism, and President John Kennedy, a guy with a great deal of talent, really, had the misfortune to inherit that expedition against us, the Playa Girón invasion – he inherited it and he let it take place. He was brave in defeat, because he assumed all the responsibility for it, he put it this way: 'Victory has a thousand fathers, but defeat is an orphan.'

Kennedy got very excited about the Green Berets, the special forces, and he sent them to Vietnam. He had fought in the Second World War, he behaved honourably, they say, but he got into an irresponsible and unjustified entanglement in that horrendous, ignominious war in Vietnam – he took the first steps, and then he started sending in more and more troops. That's where it started. And the Vietnamese, who'd won a war against France in 1954, in turn – as we've been told the story by the Vietnamese – seeing the Cuban Revolution's victory at Playa Girón, were inspired by that, they've always said so, said that our army had had that effect, that influence, that it inspired them to fight to win. They may have been being polite . . . They always maintained their combat organization in the south.

Vietnam also inspired the Cubans. Che urged the Third World to 'create two, three, many Vietnams'.[4]
And he was absolutely right, in my opinion. I will say that in 1979, twelve years after his death, the war had ended in Vietnam and the Sandinista movement was seeing victory in Nicaragua with the kind of struggle that we had waged and Che had waged. And the movement in El Salvador was also emerging, with frightful strength – it was one of the struggles with the greatest experience.

Cuba helped the Salvadorans quite a bit, didn't it?
Well, we gave them some modest aid. The Vietnamese, after their victory against the United States in 1975, sent us a lot of American weapons they had recovered after the fall of Saigon. And we in turn sent them by ship around the southern tip of Africa and then sent some of them to the Salvadorans in the FMLN, the Farabundo Martí National Liberation Front.

Did you believe that the conditions were ripe in Latin America at that time for another revolutionary struggle like the one that had taken place in Cuba?
Look, there are factors of a subjective nature that can change history. Sometimes objective conditions exist for revolutionary change but the subjective conditions aren't there. It was the factors of a subjective nature that prevented the revolution, at that time, from really spreading. The method of armed struggle was proven. Nicaragua won its victory twelve years after Che's death in Bolivia. That means that the objective conditions in many countries in the rest of Latin America were better than those in Cuba. In Cuba there were many fewer objective conditions, but there were enough to make one, two, even three revolutions. In the rest of Latin America, the objective conditions were much better.

I should say that we contributed a great deal to the unity of those people in Nicaragua, in El Salvador, in Guatemala. To the Sandinistas, who were divided; the Salvadorans, who were divided into something like five organizations; the Guatemalans, who were equally fragmented. Our mission, as we saw it, was to unite, and we managed to unite, really. We have shown our solidarity, and we have given some modest aid to the revolutionaries of

Central America. But showing solidarity and giving some form of aid to a revolutionary movement doesn't mean you've exported revolution.

But you, Cuba, did help Che take the revolution to Bolivia.
Yes, we helped Che; we shared his views. At that moment, Che was right. At that moment, the struggle could have been spread, I honestly believe. We had not yet, at the time, seen the moment in 1968 when Torrijos emerged in Panama. Other phenomena were also to occur: Allende's victory in Chile in 1970, for instance, and reestablishment of relations with Cuba [on the part of some countries].

In Colombia, there had been guerrilla tactics, sporadic guerrilla skirmishes since 1948, long before we began to fight for the revolution in Cuba. But that's another story, a more complicated story, because there in Colombia for quite some time, the guerrilla forces were seen a little as the 26th of July Movement was. Then a lot of collateral issues came in. I don't want to talk about that situation; those subjects are always very delicate.

Did Che tell you, explain to you what his plans were with regard to Bolivia and Argentina? Did he share that with you?
He was impatient. What he proposed to do was very difficult. So then, because of our own experience, I told Che that better conditions could be created. We suggested that he needed more time, not to get impatient. What we wanted was for other groups, less well known than he was, to take the initial steps, create better conditions for what he wanted to do. He knew what life as a guerrilla was like; he knew you needed tremendous physical stamina, physical strength, you needed to be a certain age, and although he overcame all his own shortcomings and had a will of iron, he knew that if he waited much longer he wouldn't be in the best physical condition.

The moment came when he started to be concerned about those factors, although he didn't externalize that. There were other very weighty issues he was dealing with: almost at the very beginning of the Revolution, Che had sent an Argentine journalist, Jorge Ricardo Masetti – Masetti had been with us up in the Sierra[5] and later founded the Prensa Latina news agency; they were very good friends – to organize a guerrilla group in northern Argentina. And Masetti died on that mission.[6] [That was devastating to Che,] because when he sent someone on a mission and the tragedy of his death occurred, he would be very upset and saddened. He grieved every day, every time he remembered the *compañeros* who had died. You can see that in the diary he wrote in Bolivia, where he talks about how affected he was, for example, by the death of *compañero* Eliseo Reyes, 'Capitán San Luis': 'We have lost the best man in the guerrilla force and, of course, one of its pillars.'

Of the men who were there in Bolivia and northern Argentina in 1962, one was our current minister of the interior, Abelardo Colomé Ibarra, whom we called 'Furri',[7] who was twenty-two years old at the time. Masetti was dead by that time. Che was pondering his plan, of course, with our full support, as we'd promised him.

When Che got impatient and wanted to leave, I said to him, 'The conditions aren't ready.' I didn't want him to go to Bolivia to organize a tiny group, I wanted him to wait until a larger force had been organized. We'd been through almost the entire odyssey of the initial stages of our struggle[, so we knew what lay in store for him]. My thought was, 'Che is a strategic leader; he should go to Bolivia when a sufficiently solid, proven force is ready.' He was impatient, but the minimum essential conditions were not yet in place. I had to convince him: 'The conditions aren't ripe yet.' Because he was a strategist, with a great deal of experience and the qualities of a statesman – he shouldn't put himself at risk in those first stages.

We were aiding the Congo, Lumumba's people.[8] We had already sent aid to President Ahmed Ben Bella and the Algerians in the 1961 war against Morocco,[9] we'd done several things. But Che was impatient. Since he was very much drawn to Africa and its struggle I suggested that he go there on an important mission while the minimal conditions were being created in Bolivia for launching a [revolutionary] struggle. The basic objective of the Bolivian campaign was to extend it into his homeland, Argentina, and then for that struggle to spread throughout the region. There was a very important job that needed to be done in Africa – support the guerrilla movement in the eastern part of the Belgian Congo against Moises Tshombé,[10] Mobutu,[11] and all those European mercenaries.

The movement led by Laurent-Désiré Kabila at the time?
No, the man in charge of the movement at the time was Gaston Soumialot; he came here and we offered him aid. We also offered aid through Tanzania, with the consent of Julius Nyerere, president of the country at the time, and so Che and the men with him crossed Lake Tanganyika from there. We sent a good detachment there, in April 1965, with Che. About 150 well-armed and highly experienced men. In the African revolutionary movement nothing had been done – everything had to be started from scratch, practically:

experience, preparation, instruction . . . It was hard work. Che and his men were there for several months.

In his African diary,[12] Che was very critical of the leaders of the guerrilla movement there.

He was very critical, but not just of those leaders – of *any* [leaders]. He was very demanding. He had that trait, the habit . . . He was harsh in his criticism of people, and of himself.

He was hard on himself?

Oh yes, he was very demanding on himself. I told you about Mexico and Popocatépetl. There were even times, because of some silly little thing that upset him, that threw him off for a second, he would undertake self-criticism – all he did was criticize, self-criticize. But he was also very honest and respectful, always.

He ran up against very great obstacles in Africa when he went there in April 1965. It's a wonderful story. At a certain point all kinds of people, mercenaries started cropping up: whites, South Africans, Rhodesians, Belgians and even counter-revolutionary Cubans who were working for the CIA. The African forces weren't prepared. Che wanted to teach them how to fight, explain that there were sometimes more than one way to do something, that there were variants. Because once they get some experience, become adjusted to the culture of war, those Congolese are fearsome fighters. But they lacked that culture, although when they did finally acquire it they became extraordinary soldiers, fearsome soldiers. The Ethiopians had that, too, and the Namibians, and the others, the Angolans . . . Once they acquired the culture of war, they were extraordinary soldiers.

That culture of war hadn't been acquired yet by the combatants there in the eastern Congo. We told him. We sent *compañeros* of ours there to analyse the situation, and willing to give their support. If we'd had to send more troops, we'd have done it – there were plenty of volunteers here. But really, there was no future in the struggle there – the conditions weren't ready for the development of that sort of struggle at that time, and we asked Che to withdraw. He stayed in the Congo for about seven months. And from there he went to Tanzania and he stayed there a while, in Dar-es-Salaam.

To do all this, Che had said his goodbyes and, as is only logical, had left Cuba, you might say, clandestinely. So then the lies started – people started saying that Che had 'disappeared'.

The international press said there'd been a rupture between you and Che, serious political disagreements. There were rumours that he'd been imprisoned here, even that he'd been killed . . .

We stood silent in the face of those rumours and intrigues. But when Che left, in late March 1965, he wrote me a letter.

You didn't make that letter public?

No. I had that letter in my possession, and I made it public on 3 October 1965, at the time of the announcement of the creation of the Central Committee of the new Cuban Communist Party, because I had to explain why Che wasn't on the Central Committee. And meanwhile, the intrigues were under way, the enemy planting suspicion, causing trouble, spreading the rumour that Che Guevara had been 'purged' due to disagreements with me.

There was a whole campaign of rumours.

He wrote that letter to me spontaneously, I think even with a great deal of honesty: 'I'm sorry not to have believed enough in you . . .,'[13] and then he talked about the Cuban missile crisis and other things. I don't think he believed too much in anybody, because he was very critical.

One day he even wrote some poetry for me. I didn't know it. He was always very affectionate with me, very respectful; he always accepted my decisions. I didn't impose them on him, I certainly never 'pulled rank', as they say. I would discuss the decisions – I tend not to give orders; I tend to persuade people of what should be done. Only very rarely would I have to say [to Che], 'You're not going to do such-and-such,' forbid him to do something.

From Africa, he went on to Czechoslovakia, to Prague, in March 1966 – a complicated situation; he was there in secret, in fact. Since he'd written a letter saying goodbye, and since he was so proud, it never occurred to him, after he'd said goodbye, to come back to Cuba. But the leadership cadres for the Bolivian campaign had been chosen and were being prepared. That was when I wrote him a letter reasoning with him, appealing to his sense of duty, and to his rationality.

Asking him to return to Cuba?

That's right. I think the family has published that letter. I wrote him a letter and spoke to him in those terms – serious. I tried to persuade him to come back; I told him it was best for what he wanted to do: 'From there it's impossible to do this. You have to come.' I didn't say 'you *have to* come', as an order, you understand; I was trying to persuade him. I told him that it was his duty to come back, that it was above all other considerations; I told him [I wanted him] to wind up preparations for the Bolivian campaign. And he did come back, clandestinely. I mean nobody recognized him anywhere. Or during his trip back, either. He came back to Cuba in July 1966.

He was disguised?
I'll tell you, he was so well disguised that one day I invited quite a few *compañeros* in high-ranking positions for lunch, I told them I wanted them to meet a very interesting friend of mine. We were having lunch and none of them recognized him. Was he disguised or not?

Raúl was sitting right there across from him and didn't recognize him?
Raúl had said goodbye to him several days earlier at the centre where they were training, and the day of the lunch he was away in the USSR. But none of the people who were there realized that it was Che. There's no question about it – our people were experts at disguising him, transforming him.[14] He went to this place in Pinar del Río, a mountainous area, where there was a house, a farm called San Andrés. And that's where he organized the detachment; he spent months there training with the fifteen or so men that were going with him. He chose the men he wanted. [(inserted in 3rd ed., creating a non sequitur in the following question:) That was also where his wife and children saw him for the last time. And where I visited him.]

To take with him to the guerrilla campaign in Bolivia?
Some of them were veteran guerrilla fighters who had been with us up in the Sierra; others had been with him in the Congo.[15] He had a talk with every one of them. I expressed my reservations to some of them, I told them, 'Listen, don't do this.' He was going to separate two combatants, two brothers who'd been very close, and I told him, 'Don't separate those brothers, let them go.' They were good.[16] About another one, I knew what he was like – a very good soldier, but sometimes a little given to questioning authority.

I warned him in some cases. All the men who went to Bolivia were excellent, among them Eliseo Reyes, 'Capitán San Luis', about whom Che wrote when he was killed: 'Your little figure of valiant captain . . .' He took that line from Pablo Neruda –a very pretty line; it's in his Bolivian diary. He really loved him. Che was that man, too.

He hand-picked them all, and we discussed it; I made some suggestions, and he defended one with particularly fine qualities whom I knew and was afraid might not have the discipline required – discipline was very important. I spoke with him a great deal until the day he left, in October 1966. How excited he was when he left!

There's been a great deal of discussion about the area of Bolivia, Ñancahuazu, where Che set up his guerrilla campaign. What do you think?
When he went to Bolivia there was no alternative, because in that particular situation, with the men he took with him, in whom he had complete trust, his experience . . . I mean, he knew what he was getting into. Debray had been there, he'd given certain services as a journalist, got maps together. I gave him certain jobs to do.

You sent Régis Debray to Bolivia?
I sent him to gather information and maps of the territory, that territory. Che hadn't gone yet. When he got there, on 4 November 1966, he started organizing the people.

By the end – this is what I think, and I knew him very well – he was putting together an excellent movement and he had Bolivian leadership cadres, with Inti Peredo and others. He knew the Bolivians very well, their character, and he told me so. Initially, out of understandable caution, they set up in an area that had a *campesino* base of support. And in this place he'd chosen, while he was out on an excursion training people, which went on longer than planned, there were problems. He was out on a short raid in a more populated area and incredibly, for the third time – I've told you about the first two – Che didn't take his medication with him.

He didn't have asthma medication in Bolivia?
It ran out; it was the third time. He went out on an excursion, a long trek that went on longer than planned – almost forty days. Then he went out on a short raid, and he left his asthma medication in camp, which was overrun by the Bolivian army. And that caused serious problems.

How do you explain Che's death?
When Che returned from that long excursion, he found there were problems in the camp – a row between the leader of the Bolivian Communist Party, Mario Monje, who had some people there, and one of the leaders of an

anti-Monje faction, a man named Moisés Guevara. Monje wanted to take over the command, and Che was very upright, very rigid... I think Che should have made a greater effort towards unity – that's my opinion. His character led him to be very outspoken, and he started a bitter argument with Monje, many of whose men in leadership positions had helped to organize that mission, because Inti and the others were from Monje's group. What Monje wanted, though, was impossible: he wanted to be the commander of that force, which was a demand that was outrageous and *very* ill-timed.

So there were some problems, and something that's never been talked about but that did a great deal of harm to the revolutionary movement in Latin America: a split between the pro-Soviets and the pro-Chinese. That divided the whole Left and all the revolutionary forces just at the historical moment when objective conditions were right and there was a real possibility for the type of armed struggle that Che went there to wage.

The efforts we had to make when we learned that that rupture had occurred! In December 1966, Mario Monje came here to Cuba. Then the second-in-command in the Party came, Jorge Kolle. I invited them here and I explained to them what had happened. We also invited Juan Lechín, a labour leader – I met with him for three days in the eastern part of the island to try to persuade him to help Che, and he promised to.

You invited Lechín here to Havana?
Yes, because that rupture gave him great concern. I think there was no real reason to demand that command – all that was needed was, shall we say, a little handling. Because really, if Monje had asked for it, Che could have given him the title of general-in-chief, or whatever, with no troop command. There was a problem of ambition there; it was a little ridiculous that he should want command of the whole operation. Monje didn't have what it took to lead that action.

Was Che a bit too rigid?
The thing about Che was his super-honesty, his super-integrity. He was super-honest, super-upright, and the word 'diplomacy', I won't try to mislead you, the word 'shrewdness', probably disgusted him.

But, I'll tell you the truth, in our own Revolution, how many times have we ourselves discovered ambition in men? Who could replace so-and-so? Who had the reputation, the prestige, the talent to hold such-and-such a position? It was sometimes so juvenile. More than once we had to turn over commands and make concessions. You have to have a certain amount of tact in certain situations where if you just barge on straight ahead there's no solution. At that moment, the rupture between Monje and Che was doing the mission harm.

It was hurting the cause?
Hurting the cause a great deal. You have no idea of the efforts we made to limit the damage.

To reconcile them.
You can't imagine some of the things we tolerated even here [in Cuba] – big mistakes. Big mistakes! Made sometimes by one person, sometimes by another. But we always, above all, criticized the action, the thing, but in a spirit of unity.

Of course Monje acted badly, and later, I'll tell you, the second-in-command of the PCB came, Jorge Kolle, and I convinced him that despite party loyalty and all that he couldn't leave those people in the lurch. I called Lechín, I spoke with him, and I convinced him to back the guerrilla movement.

But then, when Che had barely got back from his training excursion – after that trek had gone on for so long, because he definitely put his men to the test; he trained them on the basis of his own experience, the experience we'd had up in the mountains – that's when he discovered those problems there, and almost immediately there were some enemy troops that came in and the guerrilla force fell into an army ambush.

At some point, there had been a betrayal.[17] So the army knew that there was a guerrilla force up in that area. That was when, you might say prematurely, the battles started. Which we'd wanted to avoid. Because we wanted a front organized before the first combat took place, a front to be organized, and for there to be enough troops to organize one.

Still, there were those political factors that came into play. In his diary, it's all explained. This is what happened: the group got separated. He kept trying to get in touch with 'Joaquín' [Juan Vitalio Acuña] and Joaquín's group; Tania was also in it.[18] He invested all that time, and a series of combats took place as he was moving, trying to meet up with Joaquín. It's strange, Che spent months trying to get in touch with him – months! He thought the news of the destruction of that group, which he'd heard on the radio, was a lie.

But at some point he became convinced that Joaquín's group really had been wiped out, and quite some time earlier. He was moving with Inti Peredo and the other guerrillas into an area where Inti had contacts and influence, and then he received that news. It grieved him terribly, and I think that at that moment he reacted with a certain degree of recklessness, rashness. Some of the men who went with him, too, weren't in the best of condition; some of them could hardly move, and that holds you back, but little by little they advanced – some of the leaders by now were Bolivian.

This group, had it reached that area, would still have been all right, but Che himself tells in his diary that he reached a little store, and he says, 'We are preceded by Radio Bemba,[19] everyone is waiting for us.' But still he went on. Around noon he reached a village, and it was empty. An empty village is a sign that something's wrong, the possible presence of troops, but he still continued his march, in broad daylight. Inti was in the lead. At that moment, some troops, a company that's been watching everything, shot and killed one of the Bolivian guerrillas, then killed some others; they're pushing back the guerrilla force, and Che had some injured men and a few *compañeros* in condition to fight, and that was when they came into some very, very difficult terrain, El Yuro creek, where they fought and resisted until the point at which his rifle was hit by a bullet and jammed.

Che wasn't a man to allow himself to be captured, but a bullet had ruined his rifle, and the enemy soldiers, very close by now, wounded him. He was wounded and weaponless, and that's when they captured him and took him away to a small town nearby, La Higuera. The next day, 9 October 1967, at noon, he was cold-bloodedly executed. I'm certain he never flinched, never trembled once, because when he was faced with a situation of danger was when he stood tallest.

Do you think he would have taken his own life?
Well, I would have, before I'd have allowed myself to be captured. He surely would have too, but he had no alternative – he was fighting, which is what you have to do. Che was a man who fought to the last bullet, and who had no fear of death.

How did you learn of Che's death?
Although I'd been aware of the danger he was in, the risks he was running for months, and the extremely difficult conditions he was facing, his death to me was incredible, something, I don't know, that you can't easily accept,

or get used to. Time passes and you still sometimes dream of the *compañero* who died, and you see him alive, and you talk to him and then you waken to reality again.

There are people who, to you, don't die; they have a presence that is so strong, so powerful, so intense that you can't manage to conceive that they are dead. Mainly because of their continuing presence in your emotions, in your memories. We – not just me, but the entire Cuban nation – were overcome at the news of his death, though it was not unexpected.

A wire report came in stating what had happened as they were crossing a river, at a creek called El Yuro, on Sunday 8 October 1967. Most of those wire reports were just simply lies, but that particular cable told about something that had really happened, because those people didn't have the imagination to invent a story that was consistent with the only way a guerrilla force could be wiped out.* To me, the conclusion was instantaneous – I realized that this was the truth.

You're always interpreting cables in which you see lies, lies, lies, with no imagination, and suddenly you realize that they couldn't invent a story of the only possible way that a group could be wiped out.

Now, what's interesting is not reading just what Che wrote in his diary, but also what the officers who fought against him wrote. It's amazing the number of firefights, and successes, that that handful of men had.

We suffered a great deal – it was natural that we would suffer – when the news of his death arrived, I mean reliable news . . . That was why, in the grief at his death, I gave a speech that day[20] and I asked, 'What do we want our children to be like?' and I answered, 'We want them to be like Che,' and that became a slogan of our Pioneers: 'Pioneers for Communism: we will be like Che.'

Later, the diary arrived. You don't know what it means to know everything that happened – his ideas, his image, his integrity, his example. A man of truly enormous modesty, dignity, integrity, that's what Che is, and what the world admires about him. An intelligent man, a visionary. Che didn't fall defending any cause or interest but the cause of the exploited and the oppressed of Latin America. He didn't fall defending any cause but the cause of the poor and downtrodden of the earth. Che's cause will triumph; Che's cause is triumphing today.

* [(in 1st ed.:) Che came to the river, crossed it, they were waiting on the other side, they opened fire when Che and his men were in the middle of the river . . .]

His image is all over the world.
Che is an example. An indestructible moral force. His cause, his ideas, in this age of the fight against neoliberal globalization, are triumphing. And then, in June 1997, how wonderful that his body and those of five other *compañeros* were found! We have to thank the men who found them – the Bolivians, the authorities. They cooperated, they were dedicated, they helped enormously.

In finding his remains?
That man, Jorge González, who is chancellor of our medical sciences school – what merit! The way they found him, it's a miracle.

What is the greatest lesson that Che has bequeathed?
What did he leave behind? I believe the biggest thing is, really, his moral values, his conscience. Che symbolized the highest human values, and he was an extraordinary example. He created a great aura, a great mystique. I admired him a great deal, and loved him. It always produces a great deal of affection, that admiration. And I explained the story of why I was so close to him . . .

There are so many indelible memories he left us, which is why I say that he is one of the noblest, most extraordinary, most disinterested men I've ever known, which would have no importance unless one believed that men like him exist by the million – millions and millions of them – within the masses. Men who distinguish themselves in a truly singular way couldn't do anything unless many millions like him had the embryo or the ability, the capacity, to acquire those qualities. That's why our Revolution has been so dedicated to fighting illiteracy and to developing the educational system. So that everyone can be like Che.

15

Cuba and Africa

The Cuban Revolution's commitments to other oppressed nations didn't end with the death of Che Guevara; they continued not just in Latin America and Central America – El Salvador, Guatemala and Nicaragua – but also, and to a perhaps lesser-known extent, in Africa. I wonder if you'd address that subject, the role played by Cuba and Cuban combatants in some of the African countries' struggles for independence.

That's an important subject. We mentioned it when we were talking about Che, but I don't think that Cuba's heroic solidarity with our sister nations in Africa has been well enough recognized. That glorious page of our revolutionary history deserves to be known, even if only to encourage the hundreds of thousands of women and men who are internationalist combatants; [it should] be written, as an example for present and future generations. Nor, in my opinion, are people sufficiently knowledgeable about the history of Europe's imperialist and neocolonial looting and pillaging of Africa, with, of course, the full support of the United States and NATO.

Ahmed Ben Bella, the former president of Algeria, told me once[1] that after the triumph of the Revolution, Cuba didn't hesitate to send aid to the Algerian freedom fighters who were fighting for the independence of their country from France. Could you confirm that?

Yes, of course. What you have to understand is that our victory in January 1959 was very far from implying the end of armed combat. Imperialist

308

treachery, imperialist perfidy, stung by every measure [of ours] that benefited the people or consolidated national independence, forced us to keep our boots on and our combat equipment ready. As part of their sacred duty, many of our compatriots continued to give their lives in defence of the Revolution, in both Cuba and other nations of the world.

And in 1961 – not two years after [that initial] victory, when the people of Algeria were still fighting for their independence – a Cuban ship took weapons to the Algerian patriots. And on its return to Cuba, it brought back about 100 children who'd been orphaned and wounded in the war.

Let me just pause for a moment to say something about another event that comes to my mind as we talk about Algeria and that I wouldn't want to forget. This story [of rescued children] would be repeated many years later, in 1978, when the survivors of the Kassinga massacre arrived,[2] the great majority of whom were children. Interestingly, the current Namibian ambassador to Cuba – she's serving today – was one of those children. Just so you can see the twists and turns that life can take.

I don't recall that episode, Kassinga. Could you tell me about it?
It took place in southern Angola. What I'm talking about is the intense, bloody battle fought by a Cuban unit defending the long line in southern Angola, at a point not far from Kassinga, which was a Namibian refugee centre – a Cuban unit advancing determinedly towards that point in order to engage South African parachutists that were carrying out the slaughter there, with the support of modern fighter planes. So our forces were advancing, with practically no armour and no cover, and under constant air attack by the enemy, and they advanced to the place where [the South Africans] were slaughtering children and women and old people. It was one of the actions in that war with the most casualties, counting both dead and wounded. But the massacre was stopped, and the hundreds of surviving or wounded children were brought to Cuba to recover. They were later enrolled in schools, where they received their primary and middle-school education. Some of them later graduated from Cuban universities.

I don't want to go on too long about this – we were talking about the days in Angola – but it isn't hard to deduce the circumstances and factors that allowed those racist and genocidal South Africans to do the things they later did in Angola, for years. In 1976, they'd been forced to fall back very quickly, and they were pursued by the Cuban forces all the way to the Angolan border with Namibia.

Going back to what we were saying about Algeria, you were talking to me about a boat . . .

Yes, I was telling you about this ship that was carrying arms to the Algerian forces fighting the French army. The French army was very close to home – you could practically see Algeria from the other coast of the Mediterranean – and they were fighting very, very hard. The arms shipment included cannons, 105-mm howitzers and lots of ammunition. It was a cruel war – no one knows the hundreds of thousands of Algerian lives it cost, and recently someone reminded us that the French have still not sent the Algerians maps of the fields where the colonial army laid millions of landmines, and that was years ago, more than forty years. And that same boat brought back children who'd been orphaned and wounded in the war, so we could treat them.

Because I should add that about that same time, despite the fact that imperialism had just lured half our doctors away, leaving us just 3,000 [for the entire population], several dozen Cuban doctors were sent to Algeria to help the people there. And that was the way we started, forty-four years ago, what is today an extraordinary medical collaboration with the nations of the Third World.

Cuba has become a sort of 'medical superpower'.

Well, I'm not sure that's the right word for it, but what I can tell you is that we now have more than 70,000 doctors, plus another 25,000 young people studying medicine, and that does, without question, put us in a very special place – an incomparable place, and I am not exaggerating in the slightest – in the history of humanity.

I don't know what other countries will do – because our neighbours to the north [the United States] can only send helicopters, they can't send doctors, because they don't have enough to solve any of the world's problems. Europe, that 'champion of human rights', can't either; they don't have even 100 doctors to send to Africa, where there are 30 million or more people infected with AIDS. They've collected tens of billions of dollars, but they can't get a group of 100 doctors together. To combat that epidemic, they'd have to have the Henry Reeve Contingent[3] and many medical forces in addition – which Cuba is putting together even now. I believe that within ten years, we'll have 100,000 doctors, and we may have educated 100,000 more from other countries. We are the largest educators of doctors [in the world]; we can now educate ten times more doctors, I think, than the United

States – that country that carried off a good number of the doctors we had and did everything possible to deprive Cuba of doctors. That's our answer to that.

In August and September 2005, when Hurricane Katrina hit New Orleans, Cuba offered medical help to the United States.
Yes, we offered 1,610 doctors, and before a second hurricane came, even more, who'd have been able to save many lives. But the American government's pride dictated that [rather than accept Cuban aid], their own citizens had to die on the roofs of their houses, or on the roofs of hospitals from which no one evacuated them, or in stadiums, or in nursing homes where some of them were given euthanasia in order to prevent a horrible death by drowning.

That's the country that portrays itself as a 'defender of human rights', that's the country that in 1959 tried to leave us without doctors but in the end was left without doctors itself – they don't have them when they need them. In the United States there are millions and millions of immigrants, Afro-Americans, tens of millions of people who don't have the means to pay for medical assistance, while here, in Cuba, any citizen has full medical service, without anybody ever asking how they think, whether they support the blockade, as some miserable mercenaries do. That has never been asked, and never will – ever, of anyone!

Today, even with almost 30,000 doctors abroad, we have no fewer than 40,000 here in Cuba, in the hospitals and polyclinics that deal with the medical needs of our people. Even in the midst of that terrible special period, we managed to reduce mortality to levels equal to those of today – we raised life expectancy and provided levels of health to our people that are nothing in comparison to what we're doing today. And [that level of health] is assured today, and much more assured in the years to come: we hope, in a very short time, to achieve a life expectancy of eighty years. Today our country, with a 0.07 per cent AIDS rate, has one of the lowest indexes of AIDS in the world. Even when we have certain difficulties that we're aware we need to resolve, the rate of the Latin American country with the next lowest infection rate of AIDS, after Cuba, is eight times higher than ours.

Recently, Cuba sent doctors to Guatemala and also to Pakistan, after the earthquake in Kashmir, isn't that right?
Yes, we sent part of the Henry Reeve Contingent to Guatemala, 700 doctors, which, with the 300 that were already there, meant that there were a total

of almost 1,000 doctors in Guatemala to confront one of the worst natural tragedies in that country's history [Hurricane Stan], perhaps the largest ever, much worse than disastrous Hurricane Mitch, which was what started our Integrated Health Programmes to aid other countries in the Third World. Those [700 or 1,000] courageous *compañeros* went off into the foothills of all those mountains, to every corner of the country that had been affected, and they stayed there for months. And that is not, by any means, the only courageous action by our doctors.

Since we've created the Henry Reeve Contingent that I mentioned, two great tragedies have occurred, by the way: the hurricane in Guatemala, of course, and the earthquake in Pakistan. Today, Cuban doctors in Pakistan are writing a magnificent page in the history of heroism, sacrifice and effective action – a page that will go down in history, like so many other great things that the Revolution has achieved.

With the Pakistan earthquake, we discovered that it's not just a question of sending in a lot of cadaver dogs or big cranes – the most important thing, the thing that's most needed after an earthquake, is doctors. Earthquakes demand doctors more than any other natural disaster. Just to give you an idea, for example – in Pakistan, the earthquake, which occurred in a remote mountainous region with millions of inhabitants, took the lives of approximately 100,000 citizens, and many more than that suffered serious injuries: broken bones, especially arms and legs ... It's hard to imagine a worse catastrophe, or a struggle like the one the government engaged in to call for aid from those immensely wealthy countries who make it a daily practice to loot the nations of the Third World, destroy the environment, which they're changing by their profligate waste of an energy source that is being rapidly exhausted, and that's becoming increasingly more scarce and more costly ... But there were the Cuban doctors, writing another heroic page in the history of human solidarity.

Forgive the digression, but this is a subject that's especially important to me.

I know you have a passion for the issue of health care, and that Cuba's internationalist solidarity, in terms of medical care, is a great source of pride for you, but I'd like to return to the subject we were talking about today. We were talking about Cuba's aid to Algeria in those first years after the triumph of the Cuban Revolution.

Yes, I was telling you that back then, in 1961, we sent thirty or forty doctors to Algeria, I'd have to find out exactly how many.[4] And after Algeria achieved its independence in June 1962, we met President Ben Bella. He came to Havana for a visit on the eve of the dramatic days of the October Crisis that year. He flew directly from Washington, where he had just had a meeting with President Kennedy. They had talked, among other things, about the developing missile crisis between Cuba and the United States. He expressed his solidarity with us. Our citizens welcomed Ahmed Ben Bella very enthusiastically because they knew about his career as a freedom fighter, as well as about the heroism of the Algerians and their historic victory over French colonialism.

Did Cuban troops take part in the war between Algeria and Morocco in 1963?

Yes, they did. A year after the October Crisis, in the autumn of 1963, an unexpected – indeed, unimaginable – situation occurred. Algeria, which was now independent after its heroic and unequal struggle, was threatened in the Tinduf region, near the Sahara desert, by aggression from Morocco, whose armed forces, with the logistical aid of the United States, were trying to steal important natural resources from Algeria, which had been bled almost to death. For the first time, Cuban troops – a battalion of tanks equipped with night-vision lenses that the Soviets had sent us for our own defence, some artillery pieces, and several hundred soldiers[5] – crossed the ocean and, without asking anyone's permission, not even of those who had provided the weapons – heeded the call of our sister nation Algeria to aid her in defence of her territory and her wealth [natural resources], which it had taken so much Algerian blood to secure against the greed of a powerful colonial power.

From very early on, the Cubans also helped insurgents in Africa who were fighting against Portuguese colonialism, which was one of the last remaining colonial powers on the African continent. Is that not correct?

Yes, quite correct. Our collaboration with the independence struggle in Angola and Guinea-Bissau began in 1965, and it consisted essentially of preparing fighting units and sending in instructors and material aid.

Guinea-Bissau was a Portuguese colony, and a fierce struggle for independence had been going on there since 1956. It was led by the African Party for the Independence of Guinea and Cape Verde (PAIGC) under its brave and heroic leader Amílcar Cabral. Finally, in September 1974, Guinea-Bissau gained its independence. At that time, about 600 Cuban internationalists, among them about seventy doctors, had been with the guerrillas for ten years, since 1966, aiding them in their struggle for independence. They had fought in the struggle for independence.

In July 1975 the Cape Verde Islands and the São Tomé and Príncipe archipelago also gained their final independence from Portugal. And in the middle of that year, Mozambique, after a difficult struggle by its people under the direction of the Mozambique Liberation Front (FRELIMO) and its leader, the unforgettable brother and *compañero* Samora Machel, also achieved its final independence. But Mozambique, even after independence, was invaded every so often by South African troops, as was Zimbabwe, which had been liberated under the command of Robert Mugabe, an intelligent, tenacious, firm leader, as well as the leadership of other fine men and women.

The last of the Portuguese colonies to win its independence was East Timor, out there in Oceania, in 1999. We were able to help that country at a very difficult moment. It was so far away, and our own country was in the midst of the special period, very isolated from the rest of the world after the collapse of the Soviet Union and the Socialist camp.

In the case of the former Belgian Congo, how did Cuba's collaboration begin there? At one point Che Guevara was there, I believe.
Remember, Che Guevara had already been in several African countries. We've talked about that. In his speech to the UN General Assembly on 11 December 1964 he had strongly denounced the American and Belgian aggression against the Congo. He said something like this – I'm quoting from memory: 'Every free man in the world must be ready to avenge the crime committed against the Congo.'

I tried at the time to calm his impatience and gain some time, while conditions were being created in the Congo [for a freedom fight].

In late December 1964, after consulting with us, Che left directly from New York on a long journey that took him to nine countries in Africa: Algeria, Egypt, Mali, Congo, Guinea, Ghana, Dahomet (today Benin), Tanzania and Congo Brazzaville. By this time the great Congolese leader Patrice Lumumba had been assassinated – that was in January 1961 – and was now considered the great martyr of the anti-colonial movement in the region.

Che managed to meet all the great African patriots: Kwameh Nkrumah in Accra, Sékou Touré in Conakry, Modibo Keita in Bamako, and Massamba Débat in Brazzaville. In Algiers he had also had long conversations with the leaders of the liberation movements in the countries that were still under

Portuguese colonialism: Agostinho Neto and Lucio Lara of Angola, Amílcar Cabral, the great revolutionary leader in Guinea-Bissau, and leaders of the Mozambique FRELIMO movement.

And was it there that Che decided to join the Congolese guerrillas?
No, after that first trip he returned to Cuba. He had become very interested in the African situation, and especially after that historic trip and his contacts with the prestigious, historic leaders of Africa, but he was still impatient to go to Bolivia at that time. And that, as I told you, was when I suggested, seeing his interest in Africa, that while the appropriate conditions were being created in Bolivia, he should go to Africa with a group of *compañeros*. The particular purpose would be to support the guerrilla movement in the eastern part of the Congo. It was a very important mission, and it also would allow him to gain greater experience and to create new military units.

On 24 April 1965 – that's the exact date – Che arrived with a large group of our Cuban combatants in a place called Kibamba, near Fizi, in the province of South Kivu, on the shore of Lake Tanganyika, in an area controlled by Laurent-Désiré Kabila's guerrillas. Kabila had received his political and military training in China; at that time, the Chinese were also cooperating with him, so he'd had several months of training at a military academy in Nanking. But his guerrillas were then in deep crisis – disorganized, under violent attack since late 1964 by units of battle-hardened white South African, Rhodesian and German mercenaries, along with fighters from other countries, commanded by Belgian and American officers.

And did Cuba send in more forces to help Che?
Yes. In July of that same year – that is, barely three months after Che's arrival in the Congo – we sent a contingent of about 250 men, hand-picked from among our best fighters, under the orders of Jorge Risquet. They arrived in Brazzaville, in the other Congo, because at that time, like today, there were two Congos: the former Belgian Congo, which was later called Zaire, whose capital is Kinshasa, and the former French Congo, whose capital is Brazzaville – two cities, by the way, that stand face-to-face across from one another, separated only by the immense Congo River. We sent [those reinforcements] in to defend the nationalist government of Massamba Débat and, from Brazzaville, to provide help to Che, who was on the eastern border of the other Congo.

But Risquet and his men, who were there in Brazzaville, also started training combatants from other guerrilla groups. In particular, they trained men from the Angola Popular Liberation Movement (MPLA). In a short while, they had trained enough men to form three columns of combatants, which set out from Brazzaville to join the Angolan guerrillas.

So in 1965, our collaboration with the independence movement in the Congo, as well as in Angola and Cabinda, which was Angolan territory, began to take clear shape. In every case, our aid consisted essentially of training troops and sending in instructors and material aid.

The Cuban intervention in Africa that's best known was in Angola. Do you recall how that started?
Yes, I remember perfectly. After what was called the 'Carnation Revolution' in Lisbon, in April 1974, Portugal's colonial empire began to fall apart. The country had already been weakened by a long reactionary, pro-Fascist, pro-Yankee government, by economic ruin and the ravages of the patriotic war that made the empire unsustainable and finally toppled it.

I mentioned earlier that in 1975, when the colonial government fell, most of Portugal's African colonies – Guinea-Bissau, Cape Verde, São Tomé and Mozambique – gained their complete independence and were recognized by the progressive government that was in power at the time in Lisbon.

But in the case of Angola, which was the largest and richest of Portugal's colonies in Africa, the situation was different. The government of the United States implemented a covert plan – this plan has been revealed now; until just a short time ago, Washington was 'innocent', it had 'had nothing to do with what happened there' – to crush the legitimate interests of the Angolan people and impose a puppet government. A key point was [a US] alliance with South Africa to train and equip certain organizations created by the Portuguese colonial regime in order to frustrate Angola's independence and turn it into virtually a condominium for Mobutu, the corrupt dictator of Zaire, the former Belgian Congo. This Mobutu was one of the biggest thieves that's ever lived – no one knows where the $40 billion he stole is now, what banks it may be in, or what government helped him to collect those tens of billions of dollars in a country where there was practically nothing left – no uranium, no copper, no supplies of lots of others products – because it had been one of the major European colonies in Africa. But so anyway, the plan was to turn Angola into a condominium for corrupt Mobutu and South African Fascism – a South Africa whose troops Washington didn't hesitate to use to invade Angola. Dictators, terrorists, thieves and confessed racists were constantly, and without the slightest scruple, incorporated into the ranks of the so-called 'free world', and not many years later, US president Ronald Reagan called them, in an incredibly cynical phrase, 'freedom fighters'.

At that time, the United States was collaborating with the South African apartheid regime.

Totally. And in that respect, there's something very important that I forgot to tell you, since we were mentioning South African Fascism and apartheid. I should tell you that while Cuba was in Angola and Angola was being invaded by South Africa, the United States made arrangements to transfer to South Africa – racist, Fascist South Africa – several atomic bombs, similar to those it exploded in Hiroshima and Nagasaki, which means that that war in Angola – this is something that people often forget – was fought by Cuban and Angolan soldiers against an army and a government that had eight atom bombs, provided by the United States through that great supporter, that eternal supporter of the blockade, Israel. And there were those who hoped that [those bombs] would be used against us – we had our suspicions, I'll tell you, and we took all precautions, [under the assumption that] the South Africans were going to drop a nuclear weapon on our troops.

The South Africans had atomic bombs supplied by the United States? I didn't know that.

Not many people do, but it's the truth. The 'democrats' – not the Democratic Party, but rather that 'democratic empire' – who *didn't* they make deals with? What act of banditry did they not carry out or countenance? They joined forces with Mobutu and turned a blind eye to his crimes. Nor should we forget that when Lumumba was assassinated, it was Mobutu, who was leading the mercenary troops armed by the Europeans, who killed so many people there, citizens of the Congo, which later became Zaire.

One day I asked Nelson Mandela: 'Mr President, do you know where the nuclear weapons that South Africa had are?' 'No, I don't know.' 'What have the South African military leaders told you?' 'They haven't told me a word.' That's a time that nobody knows about, and the world doesn't ask those questions, ever, anyone. Just like nobody asks questions about the nuclear weapons that Israel has – nobody! The news that circulates in the world is the news that interests the empire and its allies, who want to control a monopoly even on nuclear fuel, against the time when crude oil and natural gas supplies are depleted.

Right now [late 2005], they are pursuing the abusive policy of trying to prohibit Iran from producing nuclear fuel, and they're practically demanding that it burn its natural gas and petroleum reserves – the gas reserves are large – since Iran produces 5 million barrels a day of the two hydrocarbons. But Iran, with good reason and every justification, wants to produce electricity from nuclear fuel. France produces almost 80 per cent of its electricity from nuclear energy, and many other countries, such as Japan, South Korea and Canada do, too. The Iranians aren't asking for anything different [from any of those other countries] – they want to produce a large part of their electrical power with nuclear fuel, and not burn hydrocarbons.

Faced with South African forces armed with nuclear weapons, what tactics did the Cubans adopt? Because I imagine it was a military situation that was totally new for your men.

Totally new. And in fact, we had to adopt asymmetrical methods, in keeping with the fact that we were facing a South African army with nuclear weapons. We decided to form tactical groups consisting of no more than 1,000 men, heavily armed, with tanks, armoured personnel carriers, artillery and anti-aircraft weapons, because that was what there was the most of there – plus our domination of the air thanks to the audacity of our MiG-23 units, which could fly at very low altitudes and had managed to really dominate the air space in the area, even in the face of a power that had dozens and dozens of the most modern planes. It's a nice story – what a shame nobody has written about it fully.

When was that attack against Angola launched?

It was in mid-October 1975. While the Zaire army and mercenary troops backed by heavy armaments and [bolstered by] South African military advisers were getting ready to launch new attacks from northern Angola, and in fact were already in the vicinity of the capital, Luanda, the greatest danger was in the south. Armoured columns of South African troops had crossed the southern border of the country and were advancing quickly into the heart of the country. The objective was for the racist South African forces coming from the south to meet up with Mobutu's mercenaries from the north and occupy Luanda before Angola proclaimed its independence, which was scheduled for 11 November 1975. Those were difficult days!

A lot of things had happened before that – the struggle in Cabinda and other episodes that would take too long to tell about here.

And were there Cuban troops in Angola at that moment?

At that moment there were only 480 military instructors in Angola – along with a group in Cabinda, doing training there. [The group] had arrived in the country a few weeks earlier in response to a request sent us by the president of the Angolan Popular Liberation Movement (MPLA), Agostinho Neto, a famous, prestigious leader who organized and led his nation's struggle for many years. He had the support of all the African nations and was recognized worldwide. He had simply asked for our cooperation in training the battalions that would make up the newly independent nation's army. Our instructors had only light weapons. There may have been a few heavier weapons used for instruction, a mortar, say, that was at the training camp, but those men's armaments consisted essentially of light weapons.

And did these Cubans, in the face of the two-pronged invasion of Angola, take part in combat?

Yes, of course – they immediately joined in the defence of Angola. A small group of them, in early November 1975, along with their green students from the Centre for Revolutionary Instruction in Benguela, didn't hesitate to courageously face the racist army. In the surprise attack and very uneven combat between the South Africans and Angolan recruits, among whom dozens were killed, eight Cuban instructors also lost their lives in combat, and seven were wounded. But the South Africans lost six armoured personnel carriers and other equipment. They never revealed the true number of their own substantial casualties in that confrontation. For the first time, in that remote part of the African continent, the blood of Cubans and Angolans joined to nourish the freedom of that long-suffering land.

Thus, in November 1975, exactly nineteen years after the disembarkation of the *Granma*, a small group of Cubans waged the first battles of a war in Angola that would go on for many years.

And so that was when you and your advisers decided to send more reinforcements to Angola?

That's right. And we accepted the challenge without a moment's hesitation. Our instructors would not be abandoned to their fate, nor would the self-sacrificing Angolan soldiers, much less the independence of their nation, after more than twenty years of heroic struggle. At that time, Cuba, in coordination with President Neto, decided to immediately send in special troops from the Ministry of the Interior and regular troops from the Revolutionary Armed

Forces (FAR) – all fully armed and equipped for combat. They were sent in quickly by air and sea to fight against the apartheid regime's invasion.

Six thousand miles from home, Cuban troops, the heirs of the glorious [nineteenth-century] Rebel Army, entered into combat with the armies of South Africa, the largest power on the continent, and Zaire, the richest and best-armed of Europe and the United States' African puppet-regimes.

And it was at that point that Cuba launched what was called 'Operation Carlota'.
That's right. That was the beginning of what was called 'Operation Carlota',[6] a code name for the most just, long-lasting, massive and successful internationalist military campaign in our country's history.

Why did you call it 'Operation Carlota'?
The name is both a symbol and a tribute to the thousands of slaves who died in combat or were executed during the first slave insurrections in Cuba. It was in those uprisings that women such as Carlota were forged. She was a Lucumi slave on the Triunvirato sugar-cane plantation, in what is now the province of Matanzas, and in 1843 she led one of the many uprisings against the terrible stigma of slavery, and she gave her life in the struggle.

Was the operation a success? Were the Cuban forces able to prevent the taking of Luanda?
Yes, it was – a complete success. By late November 1975 the enemy aggression had been halted in both the north and south. I remember when the Cuban and Angolan forces were taking the country back town by town – we'd receive the news: 'Entered such and such a town,' 'Advanced like this,' until they reached the borders on the north and on the south, both. The empire wasn't able to achieve its goal of dismembering Angola and thwarting its independence. It was prevented from doing that by the heroic struggle of the people of Angola and Cuba.

Complete tank units, a great deal of regular and anti-aircraft artillery, armoured infantry units up to the brigade level, all transported by our own merchant-marine vessels, quickly assembled in Angola, where 36,000 Cuban soldiers launched a fierce offensive right up to the borders of the powerful apartheid nation. There, when that first offensive against the South Africans began, our pilots were flying Angolan fighters, MiG-21s and MiG-17s. When our troops crossed the bridge on the Queve River and advanced into the other side, we used those MiG-21s against the South Africans almost to the very limit of their capabilities.

Attacking the main enemy from the south, [our troops] forced them to retreat over 1,000 kilometres, some 650 miles, to their starting point on Angola's border with Namibia, which at the time was a colony of the racists. All the forces were concentrated [there]. We forced Mobutu to pull his relatively weak army back a few kilometres, but then immediately attacked the main enemy, which was the South Africans. On 27 March 1976, the last South African soldier was pulled out of Angolan territory.

Something very important: Angola was at a tremendous distance from Cuba. You look at a map and think Angola is closer than Moscow, for example. But in a plane, you reach Moscow an hour and a half before you reach Luanda. So you see how far away it is.

And a very important point: if you find yourself involved in a situation of that sort, you can't make the mistake of being weak. If you're weak with security, you're defeated. You have to be willing to send in all the forces needed, and then an additional number of forces, twice or even three times the original number. 'Forces' doesn't mean only the number of men; it depends on firepower, the number and power of your weapons, etc. We even sent planes at a later stage. I recall that we put some MiG-23s in the holds of ships.

But, well, when the offensive began, the planes hadn't been transported yet. We were flying Angolan combat fighters. They had to take Huambo, where Jonas Savimbi had his capital – he was the head of the National Union for the Total Independence of Angola (UNITA), an organization armed and financed by Pretoria and Washington. It was an area where the tribal relations tilted, supposedly, towards Savimbi, but the MPLA actually had more support in Huambo – I remember this; I was there later – many more men than Savimbi had, despite the ethnic majority in the region.

The decision to send in all needed forces was made on the night of 4 November, and by March all the troops had been sent over. They were advancing from two directions. In the south, the South Africans didn't even have time to blow up bridges.

In the north, meanwhile, in a few weeks and with a minimum of troops, Mobutu's regular soldiers and mercenaries were pushed back on to the other side of the border with Zaire. That was a decisive victory, too. I can't understand why they didn't retreat earlier, after what had happened to the South Africans.

And how do you explain the fact that the United States didn't block Operation Carlota, or Cuba's intervention in Angola?

Well, through the official documents that have been declassified in the last few years we know much more today than we knew back then about how the US authorities in Washington were thinking and acting at the time. At no time did the president of the United States, Gerald Ford, or his powerful secretary of state, Henry Kissinger, or the intelligence services, even imagine the possibility that Cuba would play a role over in Angola – Cuba in their minds being that 'little blockaded country' down in the Caribbean – even though that 'little country' had won a victory at Playa Girón and emerged from the missile crisis with honour, because no one here [in Cuba] ever trembled or lost heart. Never before had any Third World country acted in support of another nation in a military conflict outside its own geographic region.

But Cuba could, in the last analysis, count on the protection of the Soviet Union.

Listen – in Angola, when we decided to launch Operation Carlota, at no time did we count on any sort of eventual Soviet 'protection'. To tell you the truth, after its military victory, Cuba was in favour of demanding that South Africa pay a heavy price for its adventure, including the independence of Namibia. But the Soviet government put heavy pressure on us, because they were worried about possible Yankee reactions. There were letters back and forth and everything.

What did Cuba do?

After serious objections on our part, we had no alternative but to accept the Soviets' demand, though only in part. Although the Soviets were not consulted on Cuba's decision to send troops to Angola, they did later decide to provide arms for the creation of the Angolan army, and they responded positively to certain of our requests for military materiel throughout the war. There would have been no possibility of a successful outcome in Angola without the political and logistical support of the USSR after that [first] triumph.

Imagine, the USSR was the only country that could supply the armaments that the country needed in order to defend itself against the aggression of a power such as South Africa from the south, and of Mobutu from the north. There was no thought that we were going to be in Angola for ever, or even for ten years – a certain minimum set of conditions had to be created.

But I imagine that because of your two countries' very different military traditions, Cuba and the Soviets didn't have the same idea of how to wage war there.

That's absolutely right. There were differences in the way the Cubans and the Soviets conceived strategies and tactics. We trained tens of thousands of Angolan soldiers, and our advisers aided that country in both its military instruction and its fighting *per se*. We always told them: 'Our job is not to fight in an internal war, it's to defend against outside aggression,' irrespective of the fact that if a place was attacked, if some critical situation emerged, we would help them. The Soviets were advising the military at the highest levels, and generously providing the Angolan armed forces with the arms they needed. Actions that originated at that higher level of advisement caused us no end of headaches, despite our good relations, friendship and constant respect. They were issues having to do with the concepts of war: the Soviets, with their different conception of warfare, one that I would call an academic concept, because of the experience they had had of a huge war, in which so many people died; us, the other experience, which was what is now called 'asymmetrical warfare' or irregular warfare. Although there were things that had nothing to do with 'asymmetrical' at all, at all; it was a question of elementary common sense, actually.

Still, between the Cuban and Soviet soldiers there were always profound sentiments of solidarity and understanding. That is the plain truth – we got along very well with them. There was always that spirit [of cooperation].

So after that victory in 1976, Cuba withdrew from Angola.

Yes, but at the speed and in the numbers that we thought advisable [under the circumstances]. Given the delicate situation that had been created, we had to talk to the Angolans – they knew, more or less, what our position was – and explain the situation to them; in our opinion, we had no alternative but to consult with them about it. In April 1976, Raúl, who was minister of the Cuban Armed Forces, went to Angola to speak with President Neto about the inevitable necessity to proceed with the gradual, progressive withdrawal of a large number of Cuban troops. Really, we were not in agreement with the measure, because it seemed to us that it wasn't necessary. It sent a sign of weakness to the adversary, when [in fact] we controlled advantageous positions, and the adversary was super-demoralized. We thought we should stay there as long as both parties – Cuba and Angola – thought necessary for training a strong Angolan army.

323

Even so, we started to prepare to withdraw men and units. President Neto understood our arguments and very nobly agreed to the schedule for the withdrawal of Cuban troops. It was a gradual, progressive withdrawal. We reduced our presence gradually. Meanwhile, we maintained full-strength combat units up on the central plateau. But actually, we weakened ourselves, and that weakening opened the door: as soon as the South Africans saw what was happening, they started to harass, attack, penetrate, then pull back, in that immense territory between the plateau where our men were dug into the most strategic positions, approximately 250 kilometres, 190 miles, from the border with Namibia.

They took advantage – you know how imperialism and its henchmen are, always taking advantage, very opportunistically, of any situation. There's no question they knew that we were limited, that we were under pressure and were withdrawing our forces.

You visited Angola in 1977, right?
Yes, less than a year later, in March 1977, I was finally able to visit Angola and personally congratulate the Angolan and Cuban combatants on their victory. By then about 12,000 internationalists had already gone back to Cuba – that is, about a third of our troops. Up to that point, the withdrawal plan was being followed to the letter.

But the United States and South Africa weren't satisfied, and Pretoria and Washington kept conspiring – Washington, very much behind the scenes at the time. The conspiracy finally became public in the eighties with that so-called 'constructive commitment'[7] and the linkage [between South Africa and the US] established by President Reagan. The stubbornness of those two powers made it necessary for us to provide direct aid to the people of Angola for over fifteen years, despite the agreement reached in the first timetable for withdrawal.

There were two timetables for withdrawal: this one in 1976 and the last one, but the last one was an agreement with South Africa after its defeat, which is what we'd have liked to do at that time. More than 300,000 Cuban citizens volunteered [for this mission] at the beginning of that struggle. Because only volunteers went to Angola – we call it the 'reserve' here; that was a principle that could not be violated. Civil war, you know, like that dirty war in Escambray that we've talked about, cannot be fought except with volunteers. Other countries didn't do it with volunteers, and they paid dearly for it. Because by law, a man goes into combat and he can die. And an internationalist mission can't be carried out if it's not carried out with volunteers; that's another principle.

Very few people thought that we would firmly resist the attacks by the United States and South Africa for so many years, with an ally that was so very cautious.

Since Angola, has Cuba helped other oppressed nations of the region, like the peoples of south-east Africa, today Namibia, who were occupied by South Africa, or Rhodesia, now Zimbabwe, or the South African people themselves, under the racism of the apartheid regime?

In the nineteen-eighties, the decade we're talking about, the struggle waged by the nations of Namibia, Zimbabwe and South Africa against colonialism and apartheid began to grow more determined. Angola became a solid bulwark for those nations, which Cuba, indeed, also gave its fullest support to.

The government of Pretoria always acted 'with malice aforethought', as they say. Kassinga, which we spoke about earlier, Boma, Novo Katengue and Sumbe, for example, were scenes of some of apartheid's terrible crimes against the peoples of Namibia, Zimbabwe, South Africa and Angola, and at the same time are patent examples of our solidarity against the common enemy, whom we were willing to fight.

What happened in those other places?

I'll give you just one example: the attack on the Angolan city of Sumbe [formerly Novo Redondo], a particularly eloquent example of the criminal intentions of South Africa. In Sumbe there were no Cuban or Angolan troops, just doctors, teachers, construction workers and other civilian support staff, which the enemy wanted to kidnap. But these men and women resisted with militia rifles alongside their Angolan brothers and sisters, until finally the arrival of reinforcements forced the aggressors to fall back. Seven Cubans were killed in that unequal battle.

That's just one example, of the many I might give you, of the sacrifice and bravery of our internationalists, both military and civilians, who were ready to give their blood and sweat any time it was needed, alongside their brothers and sisters in the oppressed nations of Angola, Namibia, Zimbabwe and South Africa.

It was an extraordinary feat on the part of our nation, our people, especially the young people, the tens of thousands of combatants from active military service and the reservists who, with true internationalist spirit, fulfilled their duty alongside the officers and other permanent members of the FAR [Revolutionary Armed Forces].

And then there were the millions of men and women back here in Cuba who ensured the success of every mission by dedicating more hours of work for those who travelled abroad on the internationalist mission – millions who strove to see that the families of the combatants or civilian support personnel lacked for nothing.

The family members of our internationalists deserve special mention. They bore up with stoicism under the absence of their loved ones; they filled every letter with words of encouragement; they avoided talking about difficulties and worries. And the most outstanding example of those family members is the mothers, sons and daughters, brothers and sisters, and husbands and wives of our fallen heroes. They have, without exception, stood tall before the supreme sacrifice of their loved ones. They have transformed their profound pain into even greater love of country, greater loyalty and respect for the cause for which their loved one, in full awareness of the sacrifice, gave his or her life.

In 1987 a new military offensive began against Angola. South Africa attacked once again.

Yes, as we all know, in late 1987 the last great South African invasion of Angolan territory began, in circumstances that endangered the very survival of that new nation. About that time, the United States and South Africa launched the last and most threatening strike against a strong contingent of Angolan troops who were advancing through sandy ground on their way to Jamba, on the southwestern border of Angola, where the command centre of Jonas Savimbi, the leader of UNITA, was reportedly located. I should say that we had always been opposed to these offensives against Jamba, because every time it happened South Africa intervened at the last moment with its modern air power, its powerful artillery and its armoured forces able to inflict such heavy losses on the Angolan troops – and they couldn't be stopped.

We discussed this matter with the Soviets and the Angolans every year: 'Don't carry out X offensive, don't get into such wasting, costly and finally pointless offensives. And count us out if you do.'

Once in a while we'd convince them, but it was an annual exercise. One of the last times was when I paid a visit to Zimbabwe, for a Summit of

Non-Aligned Nations. It was hard, because the Soviets insisted on the theory of reestablishing the national borders, over 1,000 kilometres, 650 miles or so, from Luanda, in a distant, almost inaccessible corner of the country where the enemy commander Savimbi was supposedly located, while the UNITA gangs and the dirty war were spreading all through the country, right up to the capital. In the first stage, we had been instrumental in the programme of withdrawal, but then something unexpected happened.

At one point prior to Angola's independence, an armed group from Zaire had entered the country, the Katangans. When the war against Mobutu's invasion was over, this group, on its own but with the support of a number of Angolan officers, invaded Katanga, a wealthy province in Zaire. Boy! All the European media started an outcry! France, Belgium, everybody, sent in troops immediately. It wasn't just South Africa that had its army on the southern border; on top of that, French and Belgian troops came into the north – in one word, NATO.

In the face of that situation, we suspended the first withdrawal of our troops, as I mentioned earlier.

But the general staff of the Angolan army hadn't followed your recommen-dation. What did you do, then, in the face of the South Africans' aggression?
Are you referring to the last offensive against Savimbi's imaginary capital down there in south-east Angola?

On that occasion, once again, the same old story. The offensive, now in its last stage, was hit hard by South Africa, and the Angolans suffered heavy losses of both men and the brand-new armoured equipment that had been supplied by the Soviets for that operation, in addition to military advisers. The enemy, who became emboldened, was advancing in depth towards Cuito Cuanavale, NATO's former alternative airport, near the Menongue air base, and was preparing to launch a mortal blow against Angola. There was not a single Cuban there, as had also been the case on previous occasions, because we'd told them, 'Don't count on us.' But given the disaster that had been created – the worst of all [in this war], and one in which we bore not the slightest responsibility – we began to receive desperate calls from the Angolan government, asking for our aid.

You can imagine what a mood we were in after those previous disasters. Pretty disgusted, as is only natural. But this time the risk was much greater, because although what was left of the force was retreating in an orderly manner – because the Angolan soldier did not think of his own welfare, his own good; he was brave and disciplined – the morale of those troops had been destroyed, and the tanks and armoured transport vehicles that were left could hardly move. Our closest unit was 200 kilometres away, 125 miles.

So you wound up agreeing [to send in aid].
In a titanic effort, despite the grave danger of military aggression that we ourselves faced here in Cuba with the proximity of the United States, the military and political leaders of the Revolution decided to solve the problem once and for all – which we had proposed more than once to the Soviets: pull together the troops and materiel needed for handing a definitive defeat to the South African forces.

Our nation repeated the great feat of arms we'd pulled off in 1975. A flood of units and combat equipment was quickly sent across the Atlantic and disembarked on the southern coast of Angola, in order to attack the enemy from the southwestern part of Angola, up towards Namibia. Meanwhile, 800 kilometres, 500 miles to the east, a complete brigade of tanks, after sweeping the road for almost 100 kilometres for mines, was advancing towards Cuito Cuanavale, where the Angolan troops in retreat under the South African attack were reassembling. We used helicopters to send in tank specialists, artillerymen, and experts in repairing military technology who could press into service the tremendous amount of Angolan technology and equipment that was there. Previous to that, we'd asked President José Eduardo dos Santos to turn over command of all the Angolan troops on the southern front to us. Thus, there was one single command for all the forces in the battle against the South African racists. New reinforcements followed the tank brigade in, and for many days that forgotten name [Cuito Cuanavale] was the centre of world attention. I don't want to go on and on, so let me just say that along with the officers and enlisted men of the Angolan army that was reassembling, our combatants and their brilliant commanders prepared a mortal trap for the powerful South African forces advancing on the airport – a trap into which the racist army fell, and was overpowered.

How many troops, in total, did Cuba send into Angola at that time?
We knew very well what we were going to do. We were following two main principles. First: you have to be strong enough, or you run the risk of a defeat. A defeat there would have endangered the whole Revolution, all those years that we'd been waging battles for our own existence, our own way of life. Here [in Cuba, fighting on our home ground], nobody could

defeat us. No, we could only be killed over there in Angola. So there was a very great deal at stake, much more than some people could imagine.

Second: decide wars without big, costly battles, just as we'd done in the Sierra Maestra. We defeated Batista's huge offensive in the Sierra with no more than a few dozen casualties. Our philosophy: win battles with the fewest casualties possible. And we followed that tactic to the letter in Angola.

That time, 55,000 Cuban soldiers had been sent to Angola and mobilized. That way, while the South African troops were being bled slowly dry in Cuito Cuanavale, down in the south-west 40,000 Cuban soldiers, 30,000 Angolan troops and some 3,000 Namibian guerrilla fighters from SWAPO, backed by about 600 tanks, hundreds of artillery pieces, 1,000 anti-aircraft weapons and the daring MiG-23 air units that took over the skies, advanced towards the Namibian border, ready literally to sweep away the South African forces that were quartered in that main direction – sweep them away, but by means of many hard, unexpected hits, without any big battles; that was our principle.

Leopoldo (Polito) Cintas Frias,[8] the general who had commanded the operations in southern Angola, showed himself to be a brilliant military leader. I still remember the days when, as a boy of sixteen, he took part in the battle of Guisa, on 20 to 30 November 1958, along with the guerrilla forces. The main job we entrusted to him on the 28th of that month was to be the gunner on an armoured personnel carrier we'd captured during one of our intense combats [with the Batista forces] – we used it to attack the enemy army's main garrison, early in the morning before the sun came up. Although his T-17 APC was put out of commission by a bazooka round – not before he'd fired off fifty-five shells himself, though – Polo retreated carrying a severely wounded companion. When he saw that his companion had died, he went back to the APC's .30-calibre machine gun. It's hard to believe the bravery he showed that day. I was following it all on a PRC-10 radio that we'd confiscated from the enemy a few days earlier[, and I was amazed]. But that wasn't the only act of bravery he carried out over the next thirty-two days, until the war of liberation ended.

Twenty-nine years later, at the command of Cuban, Angolan and Namibian troops, Polo would be taking part in the battle of Cuito Cuanavale and the counter-offensive drive in southwestern Angola towards Namibia – an operation that decided the war, really.

There are so many things that could be said about all the battles and incidents in that struggle. It was a long and very complex campaign, unquestionably the largest military operation that Cuban troops have ever taken part in. And I could sit here for hours telling you about how that long, long battle unfolded, the strategy that was followed, dozens and dozens of incidents and stories, because it's still very fresh, very clear in my memory. Someday you'll have to write the complete history of that great feat.

In Cuito Cuanavale the South African forces suffered a very important defeat.
Yes, very important – I'd say decisive. The overwhelming victory at Cuito Cuanavale, and especially the withering advance by the powerful front of Cuban troops in southwestern Angola, put an end to outside military aggression against that country. The enemy had to swallow its usual arrogant bullying and sit down at the negotiating table.

How did those negotiations turn out?
They culminated in the Peace Accords for Southwestern Africa, signed by South Africa, Angola and Cuba at the UN headquarters in December 1988, and that led to our withdrawal from Angola – the same as before, in three years, very methodical, organized, down to the last man, within the timetable we'd all agreed on.

They were called 'four-party' negotiations because the Cubans and Angolans were sitting on one side of the table, and on the other side the South Africans. The United States was on the third side of the table, since the US was acting as a mediator. In fact, the United States was both judge and party to the proceedings; it was an ally of the apartheid regime – it should have been sitting over there with the South Africans.

For years, the lead American negotiator, Chester Crocker, who was Under Secretary of State for African Affairs, had been opposed to Cuba taking part in the negotiations. But given the gravity of the military situation for the South African aggressors, he had no choice but to accept us there. In a book he wrote on the subject,[9] he was realistic when he mentioned the entrance of the Cuban representatives into the meeting room. He said, 'The negotiations were about to change for ever.' That spokesperson for the Reagan administration knew very well that with Cuba at the negotiating table, there was not going to be any crude manoeuvring, any blackmail, intimidation or lying.

This time wasn't like the Treaty of Paris in 1898, when the Americans and the Spaniards negotiated the peace [after the Spanish-American War] with no representation from Cuba, the liberating army and the Cuban government-in-arms. This time our armed forces and the legitimate representatives of the Cuban government were present, along with the government of Angola.

With these accords, was it Cuba's view that it had finally achieved its mission in Angola?
Oh yes, without a doubt. The internationalist mission had been fully achieved; it was completely successful. Our combatants began their return to Cuba with their heads held high, bringing with them only the friendship of the Angolan people, the weapons with which they'd waged battle thousands of miles from home, the satisfaction of having done their duty, and the glorious remains of our fallen brothers. Our last soldiers returned from Angola in May of 1991.

Their contribution was decisive in finally bringing independence to Angola and in doing the same thing in Namibia in March 1990. It also made a significant contribution to the liberation of Zimbabwe, and to the toppling of the hated apartheid regime in South Africa.

Few times in history has a war – the most terrible, heart-rending, difficult human action imaginable – been accompanied by such a degree of humanity and modesty on the part of the victors. Let people name a single prisoner, throughout that whole fifteen years, who was executed by Cuban forces. A single one! And I will shut my mouth for the rest of my life. Unfortunately, we know what happened with some of our *compañeros* who were taken prisoner. What did the South Africans do? What did UNITA do? What did the Yankees do? – they knew about it all. Those who were finally defeated showed an almost total lack of values in their ranks. The solidity of principle and the purity of our intentions explain the most absolute transparency in every action engaged in by our internationalist combatants.

Without question, what was decisive in that humanity on our part was the tradition planted by our own *mambises* in the battles for Cuban independence – a tradition strengthened by rebels and clandestine freedom fighters during the war of national liberation, and continued by militiamen, members of the Revolutionary Armed Forces and the Ministry of Interior as they stood against foreign and domestic enemies after the triumph of the Revolution.

How do you explain that Cuba's actions in Africa, and specifically in Angola, are so little known at the international level?

Why has that extraordinary epic moment in our history never been told in its entirety? There's an explanation for that. On 11 November 2005, during the celebrations of the thirtieth anniversary of the independence of Angola, the imperialist Americans made an extraordinary effort to prevent Cuba's name from even appearing in any of the commemorative events. And to top it off, Washington is even now attempting to rewrite history: Cuba, apparently, never had anything at all to do with the independence of Angola, the independence of Namibia or the defeat of the till then invincible forces of the army of apartheid. Cuba doesn't even exist – it was all just happenstance, luck, the workings of the imagination of those nations.

And now they are also trying to claim that the government of the United States had nothing to do with the hundreds of thousands of Angolans murdered, the thousands of Angolan villages razed to the ground, the millions of landmines planted on Angolan soil, constantly taking the lives of children, women and civilians in that country.

That is an insult to the nations and peoples of Angola, Namibia and South Africa, who fought so long and so hard, and a gross injustice to Cuba, the only non-African country that fought and spilled its blood for Africa and against the odious apartheid regime.

Do you think that one of the reasons the world has 'overlooked' Cuba's actions in Africa is that the United States has become an important ally of Angola and one of the largest purchasers of Angolan oil?

It's true that Yankee imperialism extracts oil from Angola to the amount of billions of dollars, squanders its natural resources, and exhausts its nonrenewable oil reserves.

Cuba did what the famous anti-colonialist leader Amílcar Cabral said it would do: 'The Cuban combatants are ready to sacrifice their lives to free our countries, and in exchange for that aid to our freedom and the progress of our peoples, the only thing they will take away with them are the combatants that fell in the fight for freedom.'

The ridiculous Yankee attempts to ignore the honourable role that Cuba played is an indignity to the African nations. It's due, in part, to the fact that the true history of those events has never been written. Prestigious researchers are working hard to find information. And I can say that Cuba, for its part, which has never wanted to write about this, and even today resists talking about what it did with such disinterestedness and solidarity, is willing to lend its modest cooperation by opening its archives and documents to serious historians who wish to tell the true story of those events.

In all, how many Cubans took part in that long war in Angola?
In Angola, over fifteen years, more than 300,000 internationalist combatants fulfilled their mission, and almost 50,000 Cuban civilians. It was an extraordinary feat on the part of our people, most especially the young people, the tens of thousands of combatants who – voluntarily – did their internationalist duty. They played leading roles in countless acts of heroism, self-sacrifice and humanity, and all absolutely voluntarily. The great deeds in Angola, the fight for Namibian independence and against the apartheid regime did a great deal to strengthen our people – they are a treasure of extraordinary value. Although I told you that there were also millions of men and women in the rear, so to speak, aiding the cause from Cuba.

Our *mambises*, rebels, freedom fighters in the underground, our combatants at Playa Girón, during the October Crisis and the fight against bandits, our internationalists, militiamen, members of the FAR and the forces of the Ministry of the Interior – this entire combatant nation – is the fruit of the vigorous tree, with its African and Spanish roots, that grew in this land. Hundreds of Cubans went off to the Spanish Civil War in 1936–8 when the Republic was attacked by Fascism and reactionism, and not a few gave their lives in the cause. Four decades later, Cuban combatants went off to Africa with the multiplied strength of the Revolution, and there they defended a nation under aggression by those same forces. And 2,077 of our compatriots died there.

Without washing off the dust of the road, as Martí did before the statue of Bolívar, the members of the last internationalist contingent who returned home, along with the leaders of the Revolution, went to give homage before the Titan of Bronze[10] to those who had given their lives in all the battles fought by our nation.[11]

That moving tradition is continued today by tens of thousands of doctors and other professionals and health workers, teachers, sports coaches and specialists in the widest variety of fields, who do their duty, in solidarity with other nations, often in conditions as difficult as war.

What final lesson do you take from that long war in Angola?
The main lesson is that a people capable of that heroic action – what could

it not do if the time came to defend its own homeland! We have the eternal commitment to our glorious dead to carry the Revolution forward, and to always be worthy of their example; we have a commitment to all those Cubans who in the past and present have fought and died with dignity in the defence of justice; to men and women such as Máximo Gómez, Henry Reeve and Che, who have helped so much to show us, here in our own country and down through history, the immense value of solidarity.

Current and future generations of Cubans will continue on, no matter how great the difficulties may be, fighting tirelessly to ensure that the Revolution is always as invulnerable politically as it already is militarily and will soon be economically. With ever greater energy, we will face up to our own shortcomings and errors. We will continue to fight. We will continue to resist. We will continue to defeat every imperialist aggression, every lie in their propaganda, every cunning political and diplomatic manoeuvre.

We will continue to resist the consequences of the blockade, which will someday be defeated by the dignity of the Cuban people, the solidarity of other nations, and the almost universal opposition of the governments of the world, and also by the growing rejection on the part of the American people of that absurd policy which flagrantly violates their own constitutional rights.

Just as the imperialists and their pawns suffered the consequences of a Playa Girón multiplied many times over in Angola, the nation that comes to this land to wage war will find itself facing thousands of Quifangondos, Cabindas, Morros de Medundas, Cangambas, Sumbes, Ruacanás, Tchipas, Calueques and Cuito Cuanavales, and defeats such as those dealt to colonialism and apartheid in heroic nations such as Angola, Namibia and South Africa – defeats they'd never imagined would be linked to the history of this small Caribbean nation.

16

The Emigration Crises

*Agreements with Reagan – Camarioca – Mariel – The 'balseros' – The
sinking of the tugboat on 13 July 1994 – Riots in Havana on 5 August
1994 – The Cuban Adjustment Act – Emigrants and 'refugees'*

*I'd like to talk now about an almost constant problem that Cuba has, and
that's with people who want to leave – for either political or economic
reasons. On several occasions, this has caused considerable tension with
the United States, and it has been called a 'migration crisis'. I imagine that
even before the Revolution, there were always people who wanted to leave
Cuba and emigrate to the United States, weren't there?*

There were always many people – it was a sort of tradition – who wanted
to go to the United States; [the US] was idealized through the movies and
also, afterwards, by the Second World War. In 1958 the number of Cubans
officially registered in the United States stood at about 125,000, including
descendants [of immigrants]. That was before 1959,[1] not too long after the
end of the war, Fascism, the Holocaust, all those things. Each year, they
would issue 2,000 or 3,000 visas, if that many. Power, wealth – many
people brought up to worship the United States, and, above all, to idealize
(remember this, it's important) the automobile, resources, salaries, in a
Cuban population who had little or no education and in which over 30 per
cent were either illiterate or semiliterate.

That country exerted an enormous attraction. And the triumph of the
Revolution had a very, very strong impact on the issue of migration, especially to the United States. So at that time, with respect to this issue, new and
troubled relationships began to evolve between Cuba and the United States.
It's been estimated that between 1959 and 1962 more than 270,000 Cubans
migrated to the United States, among them thousands of doctors, engineers,

teachers, professors, technical personnel ... And many of the first 70,000 who left did so without filling out any migration paperwork of any kind. Remember that the United States had broken off diplomatic relations with Cuba in 1961.

The first migration agreement Cuba signed was with the Reagan administration, I believe.
That's right, we entered the first agreement with Ronald Reagan; it was signed in December 1984. He was flexible in that, because of his interest in returning the 'excludables'.[2] Reagan was interested in an agreement on the so-called 'excludables', some of the people who'd left in the Mariel exodus in 1980 and the US wanted to return to us. So we agreed, we said, 'Append a list of the excludables.' A number of 'excludables', with their names, two thousand and something, were annexed to the agreement. The American authorities would issue up to 20,000 visas a year [under the agreement], which would ensure that that number of people wouldn't have to put their lives in danger in order to make the trip.

An arrangement was reached, and we agreed to receive the 'excludables'. Some of them are still coming, from that list; there were two thousand and something – they serve out their prison sentences up there and then they're sent down here.

After those agreements, a tense situation occurred that totally paralysed application of the agreement for a while, in 1986 and 1987. That coincides with a specific action – the creation of Radio Martí. There are very few times they've acted in good faith. Afterwards, the agreements were reinstated, they began again, because the problem continued and a way had to be found to avoid illegal emigration.

The agreement wasn't a bad one, but they didn't keep it, and actually, back then people weren't fully aware of what a terrible role that Cuban Adjustment Act[3] played – it was being interpreted and reinterpreted and reinterpreted again, on and on, by the American administrations, in order to add things to it.

What things?
Well, before, for example, the people who left [the island] illegally had to wait a year to apply for permanent resident status in the United States, and there was a lot of paperwork they had to fill out in order to work there. But since then, all that has gradually changed, through interpretations

and additions and concessions to the mafia – not as law, mind you, but in practice – and they've made the problem of illegal emigration worse and worse. Now all those requirements aren't necessary; everything's done quite expeditiously, almost instantaneously, the minute they set foot on American soil.

Then later, as I mentioned, they introduced the provocation of what they call 'Radio Martí', and all that became an obstacle to the first stage of that first agreement with Reagan – it was suspended for two years, as I said, 1986 and 1987. Later, we reached an agreement, and they were sending back the famous 'excludables' and we were taking in all the people that were on the list.

And that phrase – 'up to 20,000 a year' – turned into an out-and-out deception, because the most visas they ever issued totalled no more than a thousand and something, 1,200 a year, and later they lowered it to 1,000.[4] That is, far below the [promised] 20,000. And so it was under those conditions that the migratory crisis occurred, on 5 August 1994.[5]

There was a serious disturbance that day, 5 August, in a working-class neighbourhood in Havana.
That's right. At that time, Clinton was president. Radio Martí had announced that boats were on their way to Havana to pick people up, and everybody knew that the rule we'd established from the beginning, almost from the very first, was that a boat on the open sea, hijacked, even if it was in the middle of Havana harbour, we wouldn't try to intercept it, so as to avoid accidents.

So it was that situation that provoked the events of 5 August 1994 – that disturbance.

Apparently you went yourself, in person, to calm the rioters. Is that true?
Yes, I went there myself – and there wasn't a police car, a fire engine . . . just me and my escort, with orders not to fire – that was all. When I found out what was happening, I said, 'I want nobody to move, not a police officer, not a soldier.' I took Felipe Pérez Roque[6] with me, and then Carlos Lage[7] came looking for us and joined us en route. Because when the people saw that the boats hadn't arrived, they got all upset and started throwing rocks and breaking shop windows. So that's how the disturbance started – they were smashing shop windows and breaking things, attacking people.

And was this the first time that had ever happened?
The first time. It's the only riot we've had in forty-six years, and in the conditions of the special period,[8] with the economic situation so difficult, and the lie about boats coming to pick people up, and the Adjustment Act – it all just came together at that moment. And also the failure to keep an agreement that we had signed with Reagan after the famous Mariel migration crisis, in 1980. We've [always] had to force them – the Americans closing doors and us opening them. That's been the story . . .

The Adjustment Act – when was it passed in the United States?
The Cuban Adjustment Act went into effect in [late] 1966, after the exodus from Camarioca, the little port in the province of Matanzas. In view of the Camarioca crisis in October 1965, everyone who wanted to leave the country got a free ticket. That was three years after the October crisis, because [the United States], after the October crisis, suspended all flights. There were no lines of transport [open] between Cuba and the United States.

Before the October crisis, [the US was] encouraging a lot of people to leave [Cuba]; between 1962 and 1965 we estimate that tens of thousands of people had left Cuba, illegally; the government of the United States had facilitated Operation Peter Pan, which I mentioned earlier, in which 14,000 children had been carried away.

And that accelerated after Socialism was declared in Cuba?
Operation Peter Pan happened long before that. The proclamation regarding the Socialist nature of the Revolution was issued on 16 April 1961, almost two and a half years after the triumph of the Revolution, when we were burying the men who had died in the bombardment prior to the invasion of Playa Girón by American warplanes piloted by American and Batista pilots, but bearing the colours and insignias of the Cuban air force. It was on that occasion, at the burial ceremonies for the victims, that Socialism was talked about for the first time.

You need to understand that the country became Socialist because of the Revolution's laws. It all started with events – first Batista and his tyranny toppled, then the army and police dissolved, then the confiscation of ill-gotten gains from the thieves and robbers. That [i.e., the restoration of order], thieves with ill-gotten gains [brought to justice] is what any citizenry likes, even if there's no revolution. But there was not yet a Socialist *awareness* – we could talk about that for hours, how that awareness was gradually created.

Let's continue for the moment with the issue of migration problems. You were telling me that the United States decided, after the October crisis, to halt all flights.

That's right, they halted all flights, they suspended them in 1962. So there was no longer any possibility of travel, and many families became separated. Many of the parents who'd sent their children up there were still thinking that the Revolution was going to fail, and some of them were separated for ever.

The first migration crisis occurred, you said, at Camarioca – under what circumstances was that?

Camarioca was the first [crisis] – it was in October 1965, which is why I say they cut off all flights, they didn't let people leave [the island]. So then began the illegal departures and the problems and the propaganda . . . The people who were up there [in the US] – quite a few had already left, as I said – had money, because the first people who left were the professionals, with money. The poorest people hadn't yet started leaving. As I told you, the ones who left [first] were professionals – doctors, skilled labourers, teachers and so on. And here we were, hanging on, facing the lack of all those skilled and professional personnel.

But when the October crisis came, [the US] cut off all flights, the possibility of travelling, and that's when all the problems of separation of families began to occur, and the illegal departures, with the danger and the accidents [associated with that] . . . So we said, 'There's no reason for these people to run the risks; come get them,' and we set up a little port, Camarioca, near Varadero. As many as 1,000 boats came down here, because the people in Florida trusted us completely when we said, 'You can come, and they can leave.' That time, through Camarioca, because of a migration agreement, some 300,000 Cubans left, freely and safely.

And that halted the illegal departures for a while?

That's right. They had to stop. Without a blow being struck, without the slightest problem, that dangerous and illegal traffic was halted, because those people acted in concert – even though they had other interests, such as an interest in leaving, and even though they had no sense of patriotism, they trusted the Cuban authorities. So then an agreement was reached with the United States: every person who applied, who had some notion of going to the United States, could do so legally. We ourselves obtained that permission.

We – the Revolution – were the ones to conquer the visa process so that these people could leave. For three years, from 1962 to 1965, they were carrying people away illegally and dangerously. And then, as I said, almost 300,000 people left through the window we opened in Camarioca.

What happened was that people began to accumulate up there [in the States], and then there were the hopes and dreams of the relatives who'd stayed behind and now wanted to emigrate in order to rejoin their families. They left in planes, too – safe – an airlift. There was not a single casualty. They emigrated that way, a way we ourselves had won for them, through the Camarioca operation.

I remember that they took away skilled, educated people, and a lot of them. The country bore up, though, and we overcame a considerable exodus of specialists, technical personnel and skilled workers looking for salaries and material possibilities at least twenty times what a blockaded country could pay. If you do the precise calculations, the [wages and so on] would unquestionably be higher. Not to mention that [in Cuba,] distribution [of food and other commodities] was inevitably rationed, so that things would actually go around for everyone. That was through the first six years of the Revolution, when there was still not a really strong sense of patriotism or the solid Socialist awareness that would gradually emerge in the vast majority of the island's citizens. The new state lacked experience, organization and the abilities that it later acquired in its confrontation with the most powerful empire on earth. Only the Revolution's colossal educational efforts made it possible to withstand that drain of skilled [and professional] personnel. Nor should we forget that during that same period, the dirty war, the Bay of Pigs invasion and the October crisis took place.

The Carioca exodus happened in October 1965. And shortly afterwards, in November 1966, the Americans – I honestly don't know why – passed the Adjustment Act.

That Adjustment Act, people began realizing just what it was, the conse-quences of it, as time passed. That's why at none of those times did we suggest to the US that they repeal that law.

Then, in 1980, came the Mariel crisis.
Mariel was the second crisis, and it was triggered by the empire in complicity with other countries in Latin America and Europe. After an incident in which the Peruvian embassy was forcibly broken into, the Cuban watchman was murdered inside the embassy, and the Peruvians decided not to turn

over the murderer, we gave orders to remove the guards around the Peruvian embassy. We knew what would happen. About 10,000 people, most of them lumpen who'd wanted to go to the United States but had never received a visa, stormed the embassy. We set up the port of Mariel and removed all restrictions on anyone who wanted to emigrate. We authorized boats belonging to the famous Cuban-American emigrants to come down to get them. Again, as in Camarioca, a sort of sea-bridge was created, and over 100,000 people went off to Florida.

We made the decision and solved the problem ourselves, just as we solved the problem of the hijackings of American planes later on, with a great sense of responsibility, because it had been shown that sentencing the people who committed that sort of crime to twenty years in prison in Cuba didn't stop them. And we realized that the people who hijacked planes in the United States were, generally speaking, mentally unstable. I don't remember a single case of a political nature of the hijacking of an American plane to come to Cuba. They were, more or less, people with the same kind of problem as those who do it here in order to fly there.

So as I say, we were the ones who stopped the Mariel exodus, unilaterally and unconditionally, because we didn't want to contribute to the triumph of the Right in the United States, out of consideration for President Carter. We let about 100,000 people leave, and then we closed the Mariel doors. But once again, the effects of the Adjustment Act had been felt, and the fundamental incitement to illegal emigration.

The third big migration crisis was the balseros *in 1994.*
That's right. The exodus of 1994 was brought on by the Soviet crisis, the fall of the USSR, the beginning of the special period in Cuba. And throughout that whole long period, the United States was issuing fewer than 1,000 visas a year . . . Do you see how the circumstances were changing? You can't look at them [in isolation] . . .

So that was the period in which the Adjustment Act became the accessible vehicle for going to the United States, and also an instrument for huge anti-Cuban propaganda. In 1994, during the special period, fewer than 1,000 people were allowed to leave the island legally with visas, and then about 5,000 or 6,000 who left illegally, in order to take advantage of the Adjustment Act – despite Reagan's promise to issue up to 20,000 visas a year. That was the way they went about trying to promote discontent and internal subversion. When [the US] failed to comply with the 1984 agreement, the road to emigration to the United States lay in the Adjustment Act. But the people who took advantage of that law were, as always, not the teachers or the workers or people with no police records . . . People like that didn't tend to be the ones who left illegally, by stealing boats and whatnot. The people who did that were of another sort – lumpen, people who lived outside the law, that sort. Those were the ones who caused that riot in Havana in August 1994.

The disturbances of 5 August had been preceded, on 13 July, by an incident that the international media had given a great deal of attention to – the sinking of a hijacked tugboat in which there were many casualties. The Cubans were accused of having provoked that tragedy, and that led to a very big campaign against you. Do you remember what happened back then?

Yes, of course. I'll tell you about it. Before the tugboat incident, there had been another incident in Cojímar, with a speedboat that pulled up to the shore right there in the small port of Cojímar and in broad daylight picked up people, who then migrated, illegally, to the United States. It was unheard of, an American boat right up on the shoreline. That was bad enough, because the people [witnesses to the event, bystanders] who were there, some police officers, fired several shots at the boat.

Then later there was another incident when a tractor pulling a wagon with a number of people in it who wanted to leave the island illegally – when it got down close to the shore, a police officer tried to stop it and they drove the tractor into the policeman. Those two incidents had occurred within a short time of each other. So at that point strict orders were given that no attempt was ever to be made to intercept a boat with people aboard. That rule was laid down, and it was followed.

Some time later, I believe it was 13 July 1994, the affair you're asking about took place – an event our enemies have tried very hard to exploit.

There was a dock from which the tugboats that service the ships entering Havana harbour operate – where they tie up at night and so on. A group of people got together and hijacked an old tugboat – an old wooden tugboat, which was good for nothing but short distances close in to the shoreline. They took this old tugboat away at night, they cut communications. And three or four of the crew members from other tugboats got furious – they were very upset because these people had stolen this tugboat; [the other crew members] had the spirit to want to protect their workplace, so they got into two other tugboats, on their own, without contacting anybody, because there was no phone there, and they chased down this old tugboat that by now was already out of the harbour.

No authorities were ever notified of something suddenly taking place. We have the complete report of everything that happened that night of 13–14 July. As soon as news came of what was happening – I'm not sure whether it was an hour later or a little longer – the border guards sent out a patrol boat at full speed, not to intercept the boat that had been hijacked but rather to order the crew members of the boats that were chasing it down, these men who'd gone off on their own, to order them to come back.

It was a dark night, and the seas were choppy. And those crew members, what did they do? Those tugboats move slowly, no more than five or six miles an hour; [the two pursuing tugboats] followed the hijacked old tugboat – I think in two or three hours they'd more or less caught up with it – and started manoeuvring to make it turn back. One got in front of it and the other behind, and it was under those circumstances that an accident happened: the boat that was behind, a metal-hulled tugboat, got too close and at one point a wave pushed it into the old wooden tug. When it hit, it made a breach in the hijacked tug – there were over sixty people in it – and it started taking on water, and people started falling into the water.

The metal-hulled tug, the one that hit the other one – there were three or four crew members aboard it, no more than that – had no way to rescue the people [i.e., had no rescue equipment], but they started rescuing people and they saved some of them, until the moment came when they were afraid the number of people they'd rescued meant that they might be hijacked, too. But they were trying to save as many as they could and as luck would have it the patrol boat, at full speed, comes up just minutes after the accident had taken place.

And what happened then?
The boat that had hit the other one saved some of those who'd fallen into the water, but most of those who were saved, about half, about thirty people, were saved by the patrol boat, because the patrol boat was prepared for that sort of contingency; it had life buoys, rope, all that, to pull people out of the water with, and they managed to save many of them. So most of the people who were rescued alive were saved by the patrol boat. But it was all a tragic accident, a tragedy that left some thirty people dead, and as usual, it was exploited to the maximum by the Americans, as they do with everything.

Do you and your people consider it to have been an accident? That one boat hitting the other one was not intentional?

There was not the slightest intention on the part of the boat following the hijacked tugboat to bump into it. They followed it on their own initiative, and tried to turn it. They weren't to blame – it's simply that they reacted to the hijacking of that boat, which is essential in any harbour. The ones to blame are the ones in the US government who promote and encourage acts of vandalism. We opened a complete investigation here. What took place, really, was indiscipline or disobedience, not a deliberate or intentional act.

Now then, did they know what the orders were? I think they must have, although the orders weren't given to tugboat crews. It was the Coast Guard, the commanders, the captains of each patrol boat who received and were aware of the instructions to never stand in the way of a hijacking, in order to avoid accidents and casualties.

The tugboat crew members, in their irritation, or out of honour, or for whatever reason, attempted to stop them from escaping, to bring them back, and then made the humanitarian gesture of trying to rescue them. The authorities had absolutely nothing to do with the accident and its consequences – on the contrary, they saved half the people.

You can understand that it became fuel for terrible accusations that the government of Cuba had provoked the accident and had sunk a boat in which there were civilians and women and even children, as there tend to be on that sort of adventure – the hijackers involve women and children despite the danger. That occurred in July of that year – 1994.

The sinking is still cited in criticism against Cuba.

Well, it was the cause of a great deal of publicity against Cuba. But truly, honestly, the instructions that our people have are as I've told you: a boat that's under way, when it's been hijacked, even in Cuban waters, there will be no attempt to intercept it, in order to avoid accidents.

They conducted precise investigations of that accident, and really the crews of the tugboats had not the slightest intention of sinking that boat – they even saved people's lives. It would have been demagogic, unfair, to severely punish those crews for what happened.

Do you think the sinking of that ship and the campaign it led to caused the atmosphere at the time to become even more charged, more tense, and led, perhaps indirectly, to the disturbances on 5 August?

I believe I mentioned that to you. The riot in Havana took place because 'Radio Martí', as it's so misleadingly called – it's hard for me, I'll tell you, to call that station 'Radio Martí' – started talking about a group of boats that were on their way down here to pick up people on the coast, right in the city. So people started gathering, lumpen mostly, because when you're talking about assaulting a boat in any old condition, at night, and even in heavy weather, as I said, it's people of another sort that get involved, not people with, shall we say, a political axe to grind, or disagreements with us. Over 90 per cent of the people who have left Cuba have done so, like Mexicans and so on do, for economic reasons, although not because they don't have jobs or don't have an education or don't have medical care or don't have a sure source of food for virtually free, extremely low prices.

So why do they leave?

They leave because they want a car, because they want to live in a consumer society, that society that advertising makes look so appealing. You could ask the same question of the Chinese, too: why do they leave, why do they emigrate? Everybody talks about the great progress being made by China – real, objective, substantial advances. I'm not just talking about the Revolution's achievements – [people's right to] land and many more rights and opportunities – I'm talking about a China that's growing at a rate of 10 per cent a year – and yet, every so often here comes a boat with 800 or 1,000 Chinese being smuggled out of the country.

There is a migratory pressure all over the world, just as you're feeling in Europe – people emigrate from Algeria, from Morocco, from all over Africa. According to Europe, Morocco is a wonderful place, an ally, and yet the Moroccans cross the Strait of Gibraltar, and there are accidents there, too, even though the distance is much shorter.

There are a lot of accidents.

Over there?

Yes. There are dozens of deaths every year, on the Strait.

Ah! More than here?

Probably.[9]
Despite how close it is?

Yes, that's right.
And the Mexicans, despite the FTA ...[10] On the Mexican border, about 500 people die every year. And they're not just from Mexico, they're from Central America, too, trying to get to the United States, but most of them are Mexicans; others try to get there by sea.

Over the last twenty years, more than a million people have entered the United States from the Dominican Republic. They go through the Mona Passage [between the Dominican Republic and Puerto Rico], which is extremely dangerous, and many of them die. You see? They go in through Puerto Rico. So there are over a million Dominicans who've emigrated. Today, that country's largest source of revenue is the money sent by relatives.

Sent by the people who've emigrated?
That's right. It's much greater than any other income source, more than the salaries of many of the plant workers there in the Dominican Republic.

And is Cuba not asking that the Adjustment Act be suspended because it's so inhumane?
The Adjustment Act has caused the loss of no one knows how many lives – thousands of lives. They never even report the names of the people who reach [the United States], whether anyone died [in the crossing] – never! Cuba is the only country in the world that that brutal law is applied to.

If they did that with Mexico, what would happen? I'm not asking for an Adjustment Act for other [countries], because it's a murderous law, but I do argue that if it's to be defended, on the basis of neoliberalism, the free movement of capital and merchandise, then, as happens with the Europeans in the Schengen space,[11] the free movement of people should be allowed, as well. That's what I defend, not an Adjustment Act that leads to illegal emigration and causes the death of so many people.

How many people are dying at this 'wall' between the United States and Mexico? People talked about the Berlin Wall. Everybody, if they want to, can investigate the causes, the conditions, the dangers of the Cold War, the tanks facing off against each other, the terrible ideological and propaganda war between consumerism and the most industrially backward countries in Europe. I'm not going to argue over the causes that brought about the construction of the Berlin Wall in 1961, whether other ways to stop the 'human drain' might have been found. But I just wonder – what were the causes of that 3,000-mile wall between Mexico and the United States? Five hundred people, as I said, are dying every year on the border between Mexico and the United States, on land that was once Mexican territory, and where nobody knows how many millions of *indocumentados* there may be – millions of illegals! Some even leave their families for long, long periods of time.

In addition, the highest income Mexico has, besides the income from oil, $22 billion a year, is the money sent back home by its emigrants. And the more dangerous the border is, the fewer illegals will [go back to] visit their families – they can't, because there are millions of them.

The number of people who want to go to the United States grows in direct proportion to population, unemployment, and the salary difference that exists – fifteen times higher in the US than in Mexico, at least, for the same sort of manufacturing work; twenty times more for those who work at a job that doesn't involve manufacturing – the factories, the *maquiladoras*, pay a little better – and I'm not sure but [I think] thirty times more in the United States than salaries in southern Mexico.

Those who leave Cuba, you say, are 'economic' emigrants, like the Mexicans, Dominicans and Argentines?
That's right – you asked me a question: why do they leave? And I was telling you that emigrations from Cuba are like the ones from the Dominican Republic, Mexico, Central and South America – countries that are not under a blockade, that aren't Socialist, where there are plenty of cars and other things associated with consumer societies. They have many of the things one finds in consumer societies for those who dream of a bourgeois lifestyle, and there's no Adjustment Act that gives them the legal right to enter the United States even though they have no documents. An Adjustment Act that acts as the fundamental stimulus for all the emigrants who illegally leave Cuba.

There's no Adjustment Act with Mexico. If there were, 30 or 40 per cent of the population of Mexico, and of other countries in Central America, would be emigrating to the United States. With hundreds and thousands of factories in Mexico making products for consumption in the United States, and their workers getting salaries a little higher than the national average in Mexico – if they had an Adjustment Act, around 40 or 50 million Mexicans would already be on the other side. I can't give exact figures, but I know that in Argentina, and before the crisis . . .

The crisis that occurred in December 2001?
That's right. But even before that, because of problems and economic difficulties, and a lack of jobs, in Argentina, 30 per cent of the population wanted to emigrate to Europe or the United States – 30 per cent! And Argentina isn't blockaded, and it's one of the largest producers of food in the world.

Many professionals, scientists, intellectuals, eminent professors also emigrate, because the US snatches away the best – although university-educated professionals tend to emigrate legally. The brain drain – or really, brain theft – doesn't happen on the basis of people who hijack a boat and run risks, or risk their lives crossing the border.

I think Argentina had a better economic situation than Mexico, a higher standard of living than Mexico did, but people call the Argentines emigrants just like they do the Mexicans.

And not political refugees, you mean, as they do the Cubans.
For over forty years, every person who leaves Cuba is an 'exile', an 'enemy of the Socialist regime'. Cubans have the highest educational level of all Latinos emigrating to the United States, and therefore the highest income, because many of [the Latinos] that go to the United States from other countries in the hemisphere are forced to do the hardest work because of their lack of education. Many are semi-literate, or have no trade or training, and they wind up picking tomatoes or other vegetables or doing domestic work – being a source of cheap labour, basically, and doing work that the elite doesn't want to do. The fact is, if there were an Adjustment Act for Latin America, I think over half the residents of the United States would be Latin American.

Imagine an Adjustment Act for China, for the countries of Asia, even of Europe. No one knows how many people from the poorer regions of Europe, or the unemployed, would emigrate to the United States. For every bona fide American, Americans born there, there would be at least two or more recently arrived from somewhere else . . . In short: they'd invade the United States, they'd occupy it if there were an Adjustment Act for the entire world like there is for Cuba. That Adjustment Act has been in effect for almost forty years, and it gives every right to people who hijack boats or planes. It's an incentive to crime.

According to you, then, it's the desperate who employ those methods in order to leave the country?
The people who organize those hijackings and 'boatlifts' and what have you are traffickers in human beings. They drag off citizens who have family members in the United States and are anxious to join their loved ones, people who almost always have to wait an eternity [for visas] because they aren't university-educated professionals or skilled labour. Most of the people who have some hope of leaving the country legally, by one means or another, to an intermediate country – Spain, Mexico, Canada or any other country – don't hijack boats or planes, and they don't paddle off on those rafts; they don't engage in that sort of irresponsible behaviour, they don't endanger the lives of children.

The people who commit a crime in order to emigrate aren't arrested and returned by the American authorities?
The people who leave here illegally are the only citizens in the world who, if they violate the laws of the United States and enter that country by any means, even if they land with false documents, a false passport, when they arrive at the airport, they say, 'I'm so-and-so, a Cuban citizen, and I claim refugee status under the Cuban Adjustment Act,' and that's all they have to do – the next day they have the right to live and work there.[12] Before, they had to wait a year, but no more. Objective? To destabilize. How many lives has that cost!

Anyone with a police record or who commits a crime can take advantage of that law and be declared an 'exile', an 'enemy of the Socialist regime' . . . When the special period came into effect, as I told you, there was an immigration agreement, but they didn't keep it. All of which encouraged illegal acts, because the people who don't get visas – I repeat – their family will send down a boat for them, call them to tell them when they're sending for them, the traffickers in emigrants come down with speedboats . . .

They make arrangements to pick them up in some out-of-the-way place?
They make contact by telephone, at any hour of the day or night. It's not hard to coordinate some spot on the coast, set an exact time for the arrival . . . But within that atmosphere, all those secrets, there are always people, the ones who can't leave legally, who, when they find out about one of those pick-ups, will blackmail the others and go down there to get on the boat, too. Add to that the fact that the trafficker in a boat that can carry

maybe six to eight people will, out of greed, pack in twenty, twenty-five or thirty.

Even at the risk of sinking.
Which is why nobody knows how many perish. People say 'thousands', but nobody really knows, because you never receive any information about who got there, whether there was an accident, the names of the people who drowned. The American authorities don't even give you the names of the people who die – you can see the spirit with which they enforce and apply that Adjustment Act.

The people in Miami defend the law – they put on big shows for the authorities up there, take TV reporters to where the Coast Guard are waiting, to keep them from stopping a boat and, imagine this, somebody who wants to get to the coast [i.e., dry land] will fight with the crew of the Coast Guard patrols that are trying to intercept them because they want to reach the coast and take advantage of the wet foot–dry foot rule.[13] They know they can do anything to get to American soil and that they'll be supported [by the 'Cuban mafia'] for it. The mafia has made all sorts of noise to demoralize the American Coast Guard. Sometimes they have TV shows right on the shoreline.

They film the Coast Guard?
Yes, they put everybody there on television. So then, with this pressure, they try to intimidate the Coast Guard, and even in an administration that was less hostile, such as the Clinton administration, all this that I'm telling you about would take place, because all of this is used in the electoral campaigns, the fight for votes in Florida. Clinton won in Florida. He didn't say anything, but part of the power those people have is the power of making a big fuss, the power of noise, the power of the anti-Cuba lobby in Congress. Clinton had a minority in Congress, so they had power there – the Cubans in Florida – Democrats and Republicans both, because [the members of Congress] are given a lot of money for their campaigns by that Cuban-American National Foundation, so they can count on dozens of congressional representatives who receive election funding, such as Bob Menendez,[14] for example, a very well-known congressman from New Jersey, who's backed by the Cubans, and he's a Democrat. So in the anti-Cuban lobby and with lots and lots of money, there are both Democrats and Republicans. All those things happen.

Do you think Clinton was more constructive?

Yes, he wasn't particularly demanding. But Clinton inherited that whole community, he inherited all the campaigns that have been waged against Cuba, and there was very little he could do to behave more decently [towards Cuba]. Those things happened before his administration. They happened with Reagan. But after 1989, during the special period, Bush's father was occupied with other things: the Gulf War, squeezing the maximum advantage out of the new political line of the Soviets, making strategic arms agreements – everybody knows the concessions they made to Gorbachev and especially Shevardnadze.[15] Those two negotiated without knowing very much about arms or strategy or anything else, because what they wanted to do was negotiate, and the US government got all the advantages.

Cuba can now, despite the embargo in place since 1962, buy food from the United States, right?

That's right. In November 2001, after we were hit by a devastating hurricane, Hurricane Michelle, on the basis of laws passed by a wide majority in the US Congress to exclude food and medicine from the blockade . . .[16]

The Republican [Congress]?

It was both Republicans and Democrats who, by a wide majority, passed a law authorizing the sale of food and medicine to Cuba.

In other things, such as the right to travel to Cuba, the initiative was stymied – even debate was blocked. What procedure did the [Cuban] mafia and the extreme Right use? They proposed measures inserted into essential laws – ['riders'], they call them. When a law as important as, say, the defence budget, or the budget for farm subsidies or other things like that is discussed, or the budget for the entire government, those are measures so significant that if one of those [congressional] committees allows a rider, then they hang it on [the essential bill] and any battle people want to fight against the rider becomes practically impossible, because they've hung it on that law that nobody can possibly oppose.[17] What happens, in effect, is that they modify the law that had been passed, and opposition to it becomes impracticable.

Well, we didn't like that, because you *can't* like the fact that sales are allowed to go in just one direction. But at any rate, that law was so patched and mended that for any sale to Cuba you had to ask the Treasury Department of the United States for permission – which is like when you want to buy a suit from a tailor, you have to ask the mayor of your home town.

Or my bank.

No, no, not the bank, the secretary of the Treasury Department of the United States. It's a *cabinet officer* who has to give his approval. So that was how, a few days after Hurricane Michelle, they made an offer, just as we'd made an offer to help after the September 11 disaster. They offered humanitarian aid, offered to send people to evaluate the damage. We replied that we'd already evaluated the situation, that we were helping the people who'd been affected with the food reserves that we had. We thanked them for their offer and told them it would be very useful to us if we could purchase quantities more or less equal to the [food] reserves we were going to be using to help the people affected by the hurricane. And they agreed to that, and so, in accordance with that law plastered with Band-Aids of theirs, they sold us certain food products. Of course, they had to ask for State Department permission for every shipment.

We announced publicly that for every gesture of friendship *they* made, there would be a corresponding gesture on our part. So they got permission for a full year – that was seen by us as very constructive – and so we increased our purchases of foodstuffs, not just the first purchase to restock our reserves. All the sales made under that law had to be paid for by us in cash, and we did.

There's a wide majority, in both the House and Senate, that opposes the blockade.[18] They want the administration to respect Americans' constitutional right to travel, and to pass a law that would even make it possible to buy Cuban products.

There is also a strong current of American public opinion, more than 70 per cent, that's against the blockade and in favour of the right of American citizens to travel to Cuba legally.[19] But that's illegal – only people of Cuban descent can do it, and only once every three years.[20]

US citizens can't come here?

It's illegal. But quite a few do – so many that if they were all caught, they'd have to build a lot more prisons up there. A person can be sentenced to up to ten years in prison.

For coming to Cuba?

For coming to Cuba or for any other violation of the blockade, an American citizen can be sent to prison. And if I'm not mistaken, there's a fine of up to $250,000 for visiting Cuba without permission. The fine can be as much as a million dollars in the case of a corporation. Plus, they're levying administrative fines of up to $55,000 for each violation.

17

The Collapse of the Soviet Union

The ecological disaster – The infrastructure – Computer mediocrity –
The reign of the mafias – Living without the USSR

After the collapse of the Soviet Union in 1991, and of other Eastern bloc nations, terrible things were brought to light. It was discovered that there was an enormous ecological disaster over there, that the infrastructure was in a lamentable state. You yourself told me that health care wasn't working . . .

It didn't work very well – but it was ten times better than what there is now.

People discovered that daily life was terribly hard, and then a kind of reign of mafias arose, astronomical corruption. The Party apparatchiks took over a large part of the country's wealth and resources. The fact is, seventy years of Soviet Socialism hadn't been able to build that 'new man'. All those revelations: first – did you have any suspicion of all that? And second, did it affect your own convictions?

I'm going to answer that. You've pointed out a list of issues – some of them people knew about before, but many of them have been revealed only later. You have to analyse them . . .

There were many things I wasn't happy about. For example, when I went to Moscow I'd complain because they'd have some Party apparatchik constantly accompanying me everywhere I went, making me practically their property. I'd see small humiliations, jealousies, egos . . . There was all that sort of thing, but you see that everywhere, of course, and much worse in capitalist societies, so . . . I'll admit that there were problems like that, but to a much smaller degree than in other places.

But let's look at them one by one. What's the first one?

The environmental disaster.
It's true. People didn't know that there was an environmental disaster in the world, and one can say that the West discovered it first. Marx thought that the limit on the development of wealth lay in the social system, not in natural resources, as we know today.

The Soviets didn't know about the dangers to the environment, and in a territory as huge as the USSR, it may have been hard to see it, but the ecological disasters that have been discovered there are just like in the United States and Europe.

And what about Chernobyl . . . ?[1]
The accident at Chernobyl, the only tragedy that has occurred with the kind of reactors that aren't [cooled by] water but graphite, has, indeed, created terrible, terrible damage. But before that, there were other ecological disasters: the destruction that's occurred in Mexico, in Central America, in South America; the Amazon jungle . . . there's a dispute over how to save it, if it can be saved at all . . . Ecological devastation is worldwide, it can't really be attributed just to the USSR.

But for example, the Aral Sea:[2] the Soviets made decisions to change the course of some of the rivers and now the Aral is disappearing, and it's due to a policy of increased production – overproduction, really.
But that's not a problem exclusive [to the USSR]. There was a great deal of discussion during the time of Khrushchev, Brezhnev and others. They wanted to produce and produce and produce . . . For example, in Kazakhstan they started developing wheat production, so each person, each producer tried to increase production. They also tried to put into cultivation what they call the 'steppes of hunger' in Uzbekistan, the salt steppes – I was there – so they took water from rivers that came down out of the mountains. They produced millions of tons of cotton. In my view, it was an incorrect application of technology. They didn't know . . . they never even suspected – thinking they were doing this wonderful thing – that they could trigger a huge ecological disaster. I remember Khrushchev telling me about that plan, the conquest of new lands, hyperproduction. They were determined to do the same things the United States was doing. And, well, agriculture prospered there, crops with irrigation and so on, but problems with the salt residues kept getting worse.

We, for our part, were also discovering things. The Revolution used herbicides. When sugar production reached 8 million tons, if you didn't use chemical products at a certain point [in the growing cycle], there was no way to have an agriculture industry. Fertilizers ... well, at one point fertilizers saved humanity, and humanity couldn't even think about feeding over six and a half billion people, with a large part of the Third World malnourished and starving.

On the other hand, I remember a book by André Voisin[3] titled *Hierba, suelo y cáncer* [*Soil, Grass and Cancer*] and it analysed the effect of potassium in the growth of certain cancers – I've read a lot of those books; I'm very interested in agriculture – the danger of excessive potassium. Tubers, especially, need it; for bananas or sugar cane it's nitrogen, phosphorus and also potassium ... but there's a series of food crops, among them the grains, that need the three elements.

Today, we know about so many incredible undesirable side effects of the abuse of fertilizers and herbicides. Rachel Carson wrote *Silent Spring*, which taught me so much. Today, people are studying genes; twenty years ago, not very much at all was known about genes – genetics was ruled by Mendel's laws. Those discoveries made in peas helped traditional genetics tremendously by [offering rules for the action of] chromosomes and genes. But nobody knew anything about genetic engineering, nobody had ever transferred genes from one cell into another. We worked a great deal within traditional genetics, and then later we began to see the possibilities of genetic engineering, which we also began to use. Today you have medicines produced through genetic engineering, vaccines or [other] pharmaceutical products that are not naturally occurring. Naturally occurring medications can be contaminated with other elements, so making a synthetic vaccine gives much greater safety and security than a natural vaccine.

There was a time when it appeared that science would solve all of humanity's problems. Today, we've discovered that that's not the case. The challenge becomes harder because we also can't refuse to try. Science is going to have to solve a lot of problems that science itself creates. Saving the species will be a titanic undertaking, but it will never be possible through economic and social systems in which the only things that count are profit and advertising.

That is, these are very complex and profound questions unresolved by mankind, and which can't be blamed, for goodness' sake, on the former USSR.

The lamentable state of infrastructure, means of transport – trains, highways – telephones, electricity, all in very bad shape.

Well I'll tell you, I'm not interested in defending any of the bad things that the Soviets did. I should make that clear. I came to think, and I still think this way today, that without the accelerated industrialization that country was forced to engage in, largely because of the West, which blockaded them, invaded them, and made war on them, the USSR would never have been saved from the Nazi onslaught; they'd have been defeated. In the middle of the war, they were able to transport factories and set them down right there in the snow and start production without even a roof over them – it was a great feat, maybe one of the greatest feats in that war in which so many previous political mistakes had been made. *That* is where [the political realm] I would be most critical of the errors they made.

Looking back over our relations with them, which lasted over thirty years, until the collapse, I think the Soviets had more than enough petrol because petrol is what's left over after producing the fuel oil, the diesel and all that for industry, for agriculture. They didn't develop a consumer society glutted with privately owned cars that are big consumers of petrol, as happened in the United States and Western Europe. I think they were right. My idea is that petrol was left over, and that in the sixties, the USSR wouldn't have found a market. There'd be no other explanation for the incredible expense [i.e., lack of efficiency] of petrol engines for Soviet lorries, vans, Jeeps and cars. Who could know that better than we, who purchased tens of thousands and in thirty years never missed a shipment of petrol by the Soviet fleet? Nor, for that matter, did a boat with crude oil, kerosene or diesel ever fail to arrive. Equipment with diesel engines was much more efficient.

But the fact is, [the Soviets] were technologically behind the times in several areas of the production economy, and that had its price in Socialism's struggle against imperialism and its allies. What's curious is that the USSR had more research centres than any other country, carried out more research projects, and, except in the military sphere, applied fewer of its own findings to the benefit of its own economy.

Their roads are narrow. Maybe it was due to security reasons that they didn't develop big multi-lane highways. For reasons of security, its rail lines used a different width from what the European trains did. In that method of transport, they did progress considerably. Maybe their carriages weren't very luxurious, but the Siberian train went for thousands and thousands of miles, and it was unquestionably much cheaper to transport goods and people over long distances by train than by road. Trains went to every corner of that huge country. Today, privately owned automobiles use most of the petrol that the world's refineries produce. In the United States, consumption is over 8.5 million barrels a day – really unsustainable – and that level of consumption is contributing to the rapid exhaustion of proven and probable oil reserves around the world.

Nor did they develop computers, even though they had thousands upon thousands of engineers; they had the capacity, certainly. How do you explain that?
There's no justification for that; it's a lack of vision. It's shocking, sobering, while the Yankees, on the other hand, developed computers as fast as they could. In some things the Soviets were mediocre. Not in research, however; the problem lay in the application of their research. They had more research . . . they'd gone into space first, and you don't go into space without computers.

In Cuba, have you avoided that mistake? Are you putting efforts into developing computer science, computers?
In our country there were times when computer science wasn't taught even in the universities. We moved gradually, and we started in the universities. Then we created 170 Youth Clubs for computers, and then not long ago we increased that number to 300, with twice the number of machines in each club. The essential thing is that today, in our country, the teaching of computer science starts at the pre-school level. A hundred per cent of our children, from pre-school through to university, have computer labs, and we've discovered the enormous possibilities that that opens. We also use audiovisual methods exhaustively in educating children, adolescents, young people and the whole population. For the use of these technologies, solar panels, which cost very little to buy and maintain, supply the electricity needed to 100 per cent of the rural schools that once lacked it.

And we've now entered the mass stage in other areas of information science; we're training tens of thousands of programmers and designers of programs. And we've created – it's now in its fifth year – a university for computer science with students chosen from the best from all round the country. Two thousand students are admitted every year.

Let's go back to the USSR. When the Soviet Union collapsed, a kind of reign of the mafias arose all over the country. It was revealed that there was terrible corruption; the Soviets hadn't managed to inculcate ethical values – on the contrary, what had been created was a generalized, wide-spread corruption.

I'm going to talk to you about that. Capitalism is the creator of all sorts of germs; capitalism created the mafia.[4] All those germs of corruption are present. They exist in Socialism, too, because people have needs – what you have to do is plant values, promote them. We fought – and we still fight, a lot – because a revolution begins by doing away with all laws. I remember that we discovered that there was a culture of the rich and a culture of the poor. The culture of the rich, very honest people: I buy, I pay. The culture of the poor: how can I get this here [in Cuba]? How can I steal this from the rich guy or whomever?

Many good, patriotic humble families would tell their son who was working, for example, in the hotel industry: 'Listen, bring home a sheet, bring home a pillow, bring me this, bring me that.' Those attitudes are born out of a culture of poverty, and [even] when you carry out social changes to change all that, the old habits last a long time.

If this Socialism were to disappear in Cuba, if we'd followed the advice of Felipe González[5] and all those people, then those mafias would have sprung up again here, too, and to a very, very high degree, as would all the worst parts of capitalism, including drugs and crime. There are entire sectors in our society that we haven't been able to change yet, and the enthusiasm we have is that we see very clearly how they can be changed through a real revolution in education.

In the Soviet Union, that must have been the case, too; I don't really know to what extent what you're talking about existed in the USSR, because the USSR had lots of schools, they did a great deal of research, and the universities were good.

But be that as it may, a human being is a human being; we can't idealize him. Fortunately, I work from the position of a tremendous confidence that this human being, with all his defects and limitations, has enough smarts, if you will, to preserve himself, and has enough intelligence to improve himself. If I didn't believe that, there'd be no reason to fight to the death. I'd say, 'Listen, there's no hope for this; this is going to hell in a handbasket no matter what.' So you just do all the comparisons you can, and I think that one reason or another can explain what there's apparently no justification for; there are phenomena of another nature.

In Cuba, the Cubans didn't engage in what was called, in Gorbachev's time, perestroika, *the general overhaul of the system and its functioning. Do you think* perestroika *wasn't necessary here, and that that was what helped preserve the Revolution?*

Well, what I can say is that in the Soviet Union, historical phenomena occurred that haven't occurred here. Stalinism didn't occur here; in our country, there was never a phenomenon of that nature – the abuse of power, the cult of personality, statues and all that sort of thing. Here, from the very first days of the Revolution, a law was proclaimed that forbade giving streets, or public buildings, or bridges or whatever, or statues, living leaders' names. Here, there are no official portraits hanging in public offices; we've always been very much against the cult of personality. That's something we haven't had here.

There's no reason for us to rectify mistakes that were made somewhere else. Here, there was no forced collectivization – that phenomenon never occurred in this country. We've always respected one principle: Socialism is constructed by free men who want to make a new society. There's no reason for us to rectify mistakes that were never made.

If we'd had that *perestroika*, the Americans would have been delighted, because, as you know, the Soviets destroyed themselves. If we'd split into ten factions and a huge power struggle had started here, the Americans would have been the happiest people in the world; they'd have said, 'We're finally going to get rid of that Cuban Revolution down there.' If we'd started carrying out reforms like that, which have nothing to do with conditions in Cuba, we'd have destroyed ourselves. But we're not going to destroy ourselves – that needs to be very clear.

Did you take any interest in Gorbachev's efforts to reform the USSR?

Listen, at one point of his leadership I had a terrible opinion of everything Gorbachev was doing. I liked him at first when he talked about applying science to production, making progress on the basis of intensive production that would be brought about by [increased] productivity in the workplace and not on the basis of more and more factories – that path had been tried; it had already seen its day; you had to move ahead on the basis of intensive production. Greater and greater productivity, the intensive application of technology – nobody could disagree with that. He also talked about being against income that didn't derive from labour. Those were the words of a true Socialist revolutionary.

Those were the first statements by Gorbachev, and we found him very good from the first moment – and he was also opposed, of course, to alcohol abuse, over-consumption of alcohol, and I thought that was right. I mean, I don't think it's so easy over there to handle that problem – that would take a long discussion, because the Russians have been producing vodka, homemade vodka, for a long time, in any old still. I even talked about that with him. Those things, I liked.

I also explained that the USSR needed to have other kinds of relationships with the other parties – needed to give them more space, so to speak – and not just with the Communist parties [in the various countries], but with the entire Left, all progressive movements.

With the other pro-Soviet Communist parties they had a pretty hegemonic attitude, didn't they?
Listen, I'm not one of those people that criticize historical figures who've been satanized by world reaction in order to please the bourgeoisie and the imperialists. But I'm not going to be so foolish as not to say something I have the right to say. So yes, in the Soviet Union, because of its traditions of absolutist government, hierarchic mentality, and feudal or whatever culture, a tendency towards the abuse of power emerged, and especially the habit of imposing one country's, one hegemonic party's, authority on all the other countries and parties.

For over forty years, we've been maintaining relations with revolutionary movements in Latin America – and very, very *close* relations. It has never crossed our mind to tell any of them what they ought to do. As time went on, we've discovered, too, the zealousness with which each of those revolutionary movements defends its rights and prerogatives. I remember crucial moments: when the USSR collapsed, a lot of people were left standing outside in the cold, so to speak, we among them, we Cuban revolutionaries. But we knew what we had to do. The other revolutionary movements in many places were over there fighting their fights. I'm not going to say which ones, I'm not going to say who, but we're talking about very serious movements. In the face of that desperate situation, the collapse of the Soviet Union, we asked ourselves whether we should keep fighting or whether we should negotiate with the opposing forces to try to find a peace, when a person knew what that peace would lead to.

I said to [those other movements], 'You can't ask us for an opinion; it's you who will go on to fight, it's you who will go on to die, not us. We know what we're prepared to do, but you have to make that decision for yourselves. We'll support whatever decision you make.' There you have the most extreme manifestation of respect for the other movements. And not an attempt to impose – on the basis of our knowledge, our experiences and the enormous respect they had for our Revolution – the weight of our opinion, our point of view. At that moment, we couldn't be thinking about the advantages and disadvantages for Cuba of the decisions they might make: 'You decide for yourselves,' we said. And they did – each one, at the decisive moment, adopted their own line.

Did you know Boris Yeltsin?

Yes. I met Boris Yeltsin. He was an outstanding Party Secretary in Moscow, with lots and lots of good ideas: the intention to address the city's needs, the development of that city. I laid a great deal of stress on preserving the historical parts of the city – I advised him not to destroy them. Yeltsin had the idea of creating greenhouses to supply Moscow; he was very critical, very demanding with all the Party apparatchiks, so we printed up all of Yeltsin's speeches because of the rigour with which he criticized short-comings, failures, problems. And when I was over there I told him, 'Take care of the historical buildings, because you people have almost made the old Moscow disappear; you've built a whole other city.' He had a stopover here on his way to Nicaragua for a visit; he talked a great deal with us.

So anyway, one day I was over there visiting Moscow, and it turns out that Yeltsin is assigned to be my special host, and I'm talking to him about some things, saying it's incomprehensible that some products are still sold at the same prices as they were forty years ago, so there are scarcities and that leads to other problems. Caviar – it was the same price as in the days of Stalin. So I told him: 'You people keep some products so cheap that they're wasted. Bread is too cheap,' I told him, 'and a lot of people buy bread to raise chickens with the bread and sell the chickens in the "peasants' open market".' I mean, I saw a lot of expenses, a lot of those super-cheap, anti-economic products, when so many things had changed in the country and the world – the money mass had multiplied, yet sometimes [the price-controlled products] weren't essential goods. [That policy] lent itself to all sorts of waste and diversion of resources.

There was a contradiction there: that open market, free market, that sold at the price it wanted to, but also the theory – and the Americans used this argument in defence of private property – that I don't know what incredibly large percentage of potatoes would be produced by *kolkhozniks* on small plots of land; I don't know what percentage of eggs and this and that, and what they didn't say was that the *kolkhoznik* could produce cheap eggs and cheap meat because he used grain from the state granaries, which was very cheap, and in an area of fifteen metres by fifteen metres you can raise 2,000 chickens, 3,000 chickens, even 5,000 chickens – even several high-production cows.

Have the Cubans experimented with that?
Oh, yes. Once we carried out an experiment, in a room in a house, using electric light, to find out how much milk could be produced per square metre using agriponics – the number of kilograms of biomass a square metre could produce with that method. We did that experiment because we wanted to see how much energy was used over an area of one hectare, about two and a half acres. In theory, you could build a twenty-storey building in the city and turn that hectare into *twenty* hectares, which would produce what fifty hectares would produce if you had the light, the water, the fertilizer, and the several high-production cows. Nobody knows what a cow will produce! A cow is an herbivore – it can live almost without those grains that put out juicy green shoots when they're fertilized, very rich in protein. We had to do a great deal of study on those problems in the first few years of the Revolution. So Yeltsin and I discussed that, we talked about all that. He wasn't president of Russia at that point.

About how things worked in the Soviet Union?
Listen, the trolley bus cost four cents, the metro I think five cents – and that meant that people were going back and forth between this place and that place too much. I explained to Yeltsin what happened to us with respect to that, because at one point he says to me, 'I think public transport should be free.' And I told him it should have a reasonable price, if only to cut down on the number of unnecessary trips people make when transport is free, because once, here, in Cuba, a Party secretary in a certain region – when we still had regions, which were smaller than a province but larger than a municipality – a *compañero* of ours, we'd assigned him some buses for the region, and he'd made the decision that those buses would be free.

Transport here was almost free, but instead of walking for ten blocks, seven blocks, people would take the bus – they might not even pay, there wouldn't be time, or they'd pay to ride half a mile, which multiplied usage unnecessarily. So here comes Yeltsin saying that transport ought to be free, and I had to advise him that they shouldn't make transport and other similar services free – although of course education and health care would be exceptions – and that they already had too many things almost free because the prices were fixed, which was something that we certainly knew about [in Cuba]. So I also saw Yeltsin several times on that trip, and really, back then we had a high opinion of him, because of his radicalism. This was quite some time before the disaster of the [Soviet Union's] disintegration.

How were your relations with Gorbachev?
The same thing happened. There were good relations with Gorbachev. Raúl had known him for years; he'd met him during a trip he made to the Soviet Union, and he had very friendly relations with him. I talked to him quite a bit, I met him, conversed with him often. Gorbachev was a very intelligent man; that was one of his characteristics. With us he was very friendly, he behaved like a friend, really, and one could see his respect for the Cuban Revolution. As long as he held power in the Soviet Union he did everything he could to respect Cuba's interests and not to damage those good relations. A man of great ability, with good intentions, because I have no doubt that Gorbachev intended to fight to perfect Socialism – I have no doubt of that.

But he couldn't manage to find solutions to the big problems his country had. And he unquestionably played an important role in the phenomena that arose in the Soviet Union, and in the subsequent débâcle. He couldn't prevent the disintegration of the Soviet Union; he didn't know how to preserve it, keep it a great nation and a great power. On the contrary, his errors and his later weaknesses contributed to [the collapse]. We suggested, as I said, that he should invite to those Party Congresses of theirs, those celebrations they had, not just the various Communist parties but also other forces on the Left, progressives . . . A hurricane struck, and he called us and sent us aid – everything great. They drew up an initial plan, which was a good one, as I say, on the basis of these ideas relating to intensive production, which they had to develop.

Then began the concessions in the area of international politics, the concessions on strategic arms, on everything, and one day, well, Gorbachev asked Felipe González and the PSOE for advice. He told me that himself, I think in one of the paragraphs of a letter. By then his situation was very complicated. I was astounded to read that, although I wasn't surprised. I resigned myself to the fact that Socialism in the USSR had been set back 100 years.

Did the Cubans, at any point, believe that Cuba's security was guaranteed by the Soviet Union's military power?

Never. At a certain point we became convinced that if we were directly attacked by the United States the Soviets would never fight for us, nor could we ask them to. With the development of modern technologies it was naïve to think, or ask, or hope that [the Soviets] would go to war against the United States if [the US] intervened in this little island ninety miles from American soil.

So we became totally convinced that that support would never happen. And one more thing: one day we asked the Soviets straight out, several years before the Soviet Union collapsed: 'Tell us the truth.' 'No,' they said. We knew that was going to be their answer. And so then, more than ever, we accelerated our plans and we perfected the tactical and strategic ideas out of which came the triumph of this Revolution, the military victory over an army 100 times greater in terms of number of men and who knows how many times more powerful in terms of weapons. After that answer, we relied more than ever on our own plans and philosophy, and we strengthened ourselves to the point that we can say today that this country is militarily invulnerable, and not by virtue of weapons of mass destruction.

When the USSR collapsed, many people predicted the collapse of the Cuban Revolution, too. How did the Cubans make it through that?

When the Soviet Union and the Socialist camp disappeared, no one would have wagered one cent on the survival of the Cuban Revolution.

The country took a stunning blow when, from one day to the next, that great power collapsed and left us out in the cold, all by ourselves, and we lost all our markets for sugar, we stopped receiving foodstuffs, fuel, even the wood to bury our dead in. From one day to the next, we found ourselves without fuel, without raw materials, without food, without soap, without everything.[6] And everybody thought, Well, this [Revolution] is going to collapse, too, and some idiots still think that – and if it doesn't collapse now, it'll collapse later. And the more they fantasize about that, the more they think about it, the more we have to think, the more we have to come to our own conclusions, so that defeat can never take possession of this glorious nation.

The United States intensified the blockade. The Torricelli[7] and Helms–Burton[8] acts were passed – that last one is extra-territorial. Both our markets for and our sources of commodity supplies suddenly dried up. The consumption of calories and proteins fell by almost half. The country resisted, and it made considerable progress on the social front. Today, it has recovered most of its nutritional requirements and is making rapid progress on other fronts. And even under those conditions, the work done and the awareness created for years produced a miracle. Why did we resist? Because the Revolution always had, has, and increasingly will have the support of a nation, an intelligent populace which is increasingly united, educated and combative.

18

The Ochoa Case and the Death Penalty

A revelation by Navarro Wolf – The MC businesses – Drugs and dollars –
The Colombian connection – The execution of Ochoa – The Cuban
Revolution and the death penalty – A de facto *moratorium*

The Ochoa case,[1] in 1989, aroused endless controversy. On that occasion
the Cubans imposed the death penalty, which created a tremendous
international furore, and I imagine in Cuba, too.
You're right. We had to mount a firing squad at the time of the famous Trial
Number 1, when we discovered grave acts of treason. I'll tell you, there was
no alternative, the country was put in great danger, and we had to be harsh,
and even more so with people from our own ranks who compromised the
country and the Revolution in that way. As for the minister of the interior,
it was much easier to prove that he was involved than to prove he was
innocent. It's that I knew him very well and could understand his strange
behaviour.

Are you talking about Abrantes?
Yes, that's right. I met him while he was a member of my escort service,
which he came to direct, in fact, and later when he was promoted for
outstanding service. Oh, but power is power! The most difficult, most important fight that anyone with power faces is the fight against himself, the
struggle for self-control. That may be one of the toughest ones . . .

Against the corruption made possible by power?
Against corruption and even against the abuse of one's prerogatives. One
has to have a very well-trained, strong conscience, a great deal of awareness,
because I've seen people become full of themselves and use power in the

wrong way: the tendency towards the use of power in the wrong way is something you have to be on constant watch for. I knew that *compañero* very well, as I say, but when his case was looked into fully, [it was seen that] he'd had a mental lapse.

Who are you talking about?
I'm talking, in this case, of the man who'd been minister . . .

Abrantes.
Yes, Abrantes. I ordered an investigation because I kept reading certain news stories, and information kept coming in that intrigued me . . . I asked Abrantes for an investigation into reports that were coming in on wire reports – aeroplanes landing in Varadero – and although I didn't think they were true, I said, 'Investigate this – I want to know exactly what's happening, because I keep getting reports on it.'

I sent for somebody from over there, from Colombia, a man named Navarro Wolf [2] – he's alive, he was in M-19, he was injured by a bomb over there and he received medical treatment here. He came. But I wasn't able to meet him myself. Because a lot of times, even in the case of very important matters, the burden of work keeps me from doing other things that are also important, even if [the matter is] not entirely credible. Navarro Wolf spoke with some *compañeros*, and he went back to Colombia. Nor did Abrantes tell me that Navarro Wolf was about to return to his country.

Abrantes would come to my office almost every day, he was in constant contact with us. His work against the counter-revolutionaries had been good, efficient. Unfortunately, very subtly, he began to become more and more ambitious. I don't want to talk about that. But every day, practically, he'd come over here, and he'd wait; he always had some news or some event he wanted to discuss with me, down to the smallest details, because he was very much in the habit of consulting with me about things both large and small. Sometimes he'd take time I really didn't have for him, because there have never been enough hours in my day.

But it so happened that when Navarro Wolf came over, I asked Abrantes, 'Did you and your people see Navarro Wolf? Did he have anything of importance to tell us?' And he said, 'No, nothing important.' I'd later find out whether that was entirely true. [At the time,] we were dealing with the problem of Ochoa, an officer of historic merit, a 'Hero of the Republic of Cuba', one of those who'd been in the column under Camilo Cienfuegos' command . . . Oh, but he had power . . . He came to handle funds one day. Not that I can say that Ochoa *stole* money.

Did Ochoa enrich himself personally?

What's incredible is that the people who got mixed up in that [affair] did so because they thought they were helping the Republic. Since we were a country under blockade, and every few days we would have to buy a replacement part or something blocked by the embargo, there were some small companies managed by the Ministry of the Interior that fought back against the blockade – they would buy crucial parts for some plant or factory, and they'd bring them in, as is only logical, without going through customs procedures. Yes, we refused to go along with the blockade – it's illegal, genocidal. And so these *compañeros*, sometimes, would sell Cuban cigars or other products[, and pay for the parts from the proceeds]. When they brought in the parts, they'd have to pay for them, of course, and they'd sell them to a certain company [and they'd make a profit]; those profits would then be used for the Ministry, for communications [equipment], transport [equipment]. The country has always been strict with its resources, but they had small companies for those purposes, although we'd forbidden them to create businesses strictly for profit; they had to work with the ones that already existed. They had experience.

Did they have some of those companies in Panama?

They may have. I don't know the details. They had the logical facilities for their relations with the Coast Guard, customs and other institutions.

Then one day they got the crazy idea to make contact with some drug smugglers.

With drug traffickers?

I'm not sure how it started – well, there are reports that have been published, there's all that information about the contraband, and they'd turn the money over to the ministry. The Ministry of the Interior would administer the money, invest it basically in buying spare parts, replacement parts, that sort of thing. But also, when people start handling money in that particular way, the weakness sets in – putting special tinted windows in your car, special tyres, a radio with a CD player; people start putting luxury items in their little Lada car, start dressing better . . . and not putting the money in the bank.

Ochoa had an account abroad in which he had money that came from the Sandinistas, which he'd been given so that he could try to buy [(in 1st ed.:) some weapons that they couldn't get, some kind of weapons, bazookas, or for] communications equipment they couldn't get. He'd been a consultant over there, in Nicaragua.

Had he taken part in the Sandinista war to overthrow Somoza?
The Sandinistas had already won. He went over there later to help the Sandinistas in their struggle against the dirty war. But hold on, I have to tell you something else first – I mentioned Navarro Wolf . . .

Yes, Navarro Wolf, the Colombian, the former member of the M-19 guerrilla group.
A Colombian, member of M-19, which had signed a peace accord. But I didn't tell you what he reported to us. When Abrantes told me, 'Nothing important,' that was the moment when we were investigating offences committed by Ochoa, who had an account abroad whose purpose was not particularly clear, and other irregularities he'd committed when he was leader of the Cuban military mission in Angola, and trying to persuade him to come clean so we could find a solution that wasn't the most severe, considering his history, his record with the Revolution. He never completely came clean, so we'd arrived at a situation in which you couldn't go any further with the investigation without his knowing about it. We had to speak with aides, etc., and we couldn't do that without some of it leaking out. But our investigation didn't have anything to do with drugs; it was [(in 1st ed.:) the irregularity of the bank account, and some irregularities committed over there by one of the businesses, which had used the pretext of helping the troops] the errors we've just mentioned.

In Angola?
That's right, in Angola, where he'd been posted, as I told you, as commander of the military mission. But he never came clean. Raúl, the minister of the Armed Forces, spoke to him three or four times.

Personally?
Yes, of course, but very carefully, and he couldn't persuade him to come clean. You can't go on investigating an important leader, whom you'd like to have helped, without taking stronger disciplinary measures, given the facts available to you at the time.

Did he have personal political ambitions? There was talk of a conspiracy; people said he might be a rival of yours.
No, there was no danger there. There were no political dangers. The level of discipline, the awareness, the mobilization of our armed forces is not based on any sort of *caudillismo*,[3] or personal factors, but rather on a solid political education.

It was the kind of crime that you can't categorize as political, because Ochoa never manifested anything political against the Revolution. And when he was arrested, since he refused to come clean about these problems, when we did a search and we found a captain, Jorge Martínez, who was an aide to Ochoa when he was in Nicaragua, and [in our further investigation of this captain] we turned up a card from a hotel in Medellín.

Medellín, in Colombia.
During this officer's interrogation, he was asked: 'What's this? What does this mean?' And he says he'd received orders from Ochoa to go to Medellín and make contact with Pablo Escobar.

One of the major leaders of the [Medellín] drug cartel.
The most famous drug trafficker in the world. So that was a matter of enormous seriousness. It put the country in the position of being accused of being involved in drug trafficking. It was very serious that a Cuban officer might have met with Pablo Escobar.

Why did this happen? Because in Angola, Ochoa became close friends with a high-ranking officer in the [Cuban] Ministry of the Interior, the representative of that agency in that country, so he had found out about certain operations that this official's brother was carrying out. Who was the brother? It was the officer's twin. The two of them carried out missions and other work for the Revolution for many years, both inside and outside Cuba.

The brothers Patricio and Tony de la Guardia.
Exactly. And after a number of years they'd become very close friends of Ochoa; one was the head of the department in charge of that business that I was telling you about – it was called MC – the business that carried out those operations.

For getting currency?
Not currency – for buying parts and, in passing, selling certain goods that

371

were subject to the trade embargo. They were very close friends of Abrantes. Abrantes tended, when friends were involved, not just to defend the friend but also to be incapable of imagining that they were capable of doing anything wrong.

When I gave instructions to open an investigation into what was being published on the news services about drug trafficking through Varadero, Navarro Wolf came over – we asked him for information about what was being said in Colombia about all this. And Abrantes tells me that Navarro Wolf's information isn't important. Ochoa had already been arrested, on 12 June, and it wasn't until he'd been arrested that the connections with the drug trade were discovered, through this Captain Martínez, who explained why he had that card from a hotel in Medellín.

Were you and your people surprised to discover that?
We were surprised by the fact that such a phenomenon was happening . . . Ochoa had sent his aide to commit a serious offence, while the person in charge of the business implicated in running drugs through Varadero was Tony de la Guardia. Although, as I said, there was no evidence that any of the several men implicated in all this were keeping the money – they were still involved in the initiative to buy spare parts, to get around the blockade. They *were*, however, wasting it, squandering it – there were even a series of amounts in cash that they'd put away, because there were operations in which the foreign counterpart would take its time paying, and the money was delivered days before the arrest.

But what was the key? The key was that Navarro Wolf had told the *compañero* that spoke with him that there were rumours in Colombia that Pablo Escobar's people had had contact with Tony de la Guardia, the manager of that business.

MC . . .
That's right. We'd known the de la Guardia brothers for years – they had great prestige and authority. So, in carrying out this investigation, we discovered another matter of even greater seriousness, and it became necessary to arrest important high-ranking officers and other people immediately.

I mean, money that had been recently received and stashed in friends' houses was even picked up. There was a writer, a man who'd worked on a book on Hemingway, Norberto Fuentes,[4] who'd been over there in Angola, and in Norberto Fuentes's house there was a stash of about $200,000. There was money in other places, too. It was money they'd been owed and that they'd been paid very recently. The drug traffickers paid them $1,000 a kilogram for the cocaine they transported. So of course if they transported 500 kilos, that was $500,000. And $500,000 is a lot of money.

How did they go about this? How did they operate?

The pilots of the transport planes risked their lives. They flew low, right at the level of the tree tops even at night, if they were being pursued – they didn't pay any attention to any warning [to land]. Then the pilots would 'bomb' some place – that is, they'd throw the bales out a few miles off the coast. What would happen? Somebody had to go out in a boat and pick [the packages] up. There was another way, so they didn't even have to 'drop the bombs'. A small plane would fly in from Colombia, land in Varadero, and from there the people from MC would deliver the drugs to ships that were supposedly bringing in merchandise in exchange for our selling them tobacco. The people from MC would come and go, they had tremendous authority, because of their positions within the Ministry of the Interior.

It was much more comfortable for the plane to land and the drugs to be delivered on a dock to some speedboat. And that's how Trial Number 1 came about.

But Abrantes hadn't told me something, and that to me was the key. If he'd told the truth at that moment the two things wouldn't have come together – the investigation into Ochoa and the drug-trafficking operation. Because I'd ordered an investigation into [the drug trafficking]; I'd been seeing some cables and I just had a hunch. You become an expert at reading cables, you know where a truth is, you know where people are making things up and where there may be some truth in it . . . So I'd asked for an investigation.

We'd discovered this strange situation about two months earlier, news of these flights, these landings in Varadero, and then in the midst of the Ochoa trial, that's when we found out about this Captain Martínez' trip to Medellín.

One afternoon, in the meeting we have every day in the Ministry of Armed Forces, I happened to run into a kid, Alejandro Ronda Marrero, a young officer who had an important post in the special forces. He had been the person who'd met with Navarro Wolf. I know this kid very well, he's a fine officer, and I said to him, 'Listen, what was it that you and Navarro Wolf talked about?' And he says, 'Didn't you receive the report that I gave Minister Abrantes?' 'No,' I say, 'are there any copies?' 'Yes,' he says. He had it right there in his computer. After the meeting, I talked to him on the way back to the Palacio, we went up to my office, and from there I sent him straight to his computer to find that report. He brought me the copy of what Navarro Wolf had reported. Abrantes also took part in those meetings of the General Staff of the Revolutionary Armed Forces that we held every day, in order to analyse the situation.

And that report, had this officer turned it in to Abrantes to pass along to you?
He turned it in to Abrantes, and Abrantes, who brought me every little report and consulted with me about every little thing . . .

Didn't bring you that one?
He hadn't said a word about that one, and he'd been discussing the whole operation with me, and all the investigations into drugs, which some of his people were involved in. So I sent for him that same afternoon and I said to him, 'Listen, Abrantes, I've got the report here about what Navarro Wolf said – what did you do? Don't you have a copy?' And I repeated my question: 'Don't you have a copy?' We sent for a copy of the report and he didn't have it. 'How is it possible that you didn't bring me this report, Abrantes?' There was no explanation.

There was another thing – he hardly remembered this report. 'How is it possible that you never said a word about it?' So then I say to him, 'Go and look! See if you can't find copies of it.' But no copies turned up. I should say that Navarro mentioned the name of Tony de la Guardia in contact with Pablo Escobar, according to rumours that Navarro had heard.

There was no question that the minister's subconscious had played its part in all this. That report compromised people in whom he'd had absolute faith and trust, people he'd thought were Olympic champions of business. I don't know whether George Soros, maybe – or Bill Gates – might be more brilliant than these guys at paying for parts and selling cigars . . . But these guys with MC [de la Guardia et al.] sold themselves as world champion wheelers and dealers. They even had that money stashed away so it could be turned in little by little, so that too much wouldn't turn up all of a sudden and call someone's attention to it.

With all these operations, they wound up with $3 or $4 million, maybe more, in their stash. But they weren't stealing it – I was following every detail, and I'd have known it if they were. But it was madness on their part, absolutely irresponsible, and had it been discovered [by someone outside Cuba] it would have caused the country terrible harm and endangered its security – a gift from heaven to the treacherous and aggressive empire.

And they had lots of people involved with them, among them this friend of theirs Norberto Fuentes, and some others. Not everyone was included in Trial Number 1. Norberto, for example, was a writer, he'd published books on Hemingway, he'd been in Angola as a writer, too; there were others who weren't included in Trial Number 1, but who'd held money [for the others]; they were like the MC's banks, just holding the money. Certain people were not included in that case. The main ones implicated had a lot of connections; including all the collaborators, even in all good faith, wouldn't have contributed anything. And that was the famous Trial Number 1.

I tell you, Ochoa had even come up with the fantastic idea of loading a big boat with those bales [of drugs]. What was his idea? That Escobar would send a boat with six tons of drugs and the speedboats would pick it up here, south of Cuba, and take it to the United States. A crazy idea, and they thought they were helping the country . . .

And Cuba would be taking part in the drug trade.
I mean . . . listen, a country whose exportable goods and services total billions of dollars, and whose imports exceed that amount, let's say you move, I don't know, 50,000 kilograms, and you earn what? Fifty million? You think a country is going to solve its economic problems that way, which is what those guys thought they were going to do? [But they weren't even working on that scale:] MC probably brought in from four to six tons. They'd been doing it for quite a while. And those are the reasons for the investigation and the measures we took.

But the sentences – don't you think they were too severe?
It had been many years since the death penalty had been applied for strictly counter-revolutionary reasons, reasons of a political nature, crimes of a counter-revolutionary nature. It had been applied to a number of cases of common crimes, horrible crimes, repugnant murders, but not other kinds. Trial Number 1 was a combination of crimes – that was in 1989.

Personally, for you, the decision, surely, to order compañeros *shot by firing squad . . . it must have been very hard, no?*
Yes, but it was not a personal decision. It was a unanimous decision by the

Council of State, which had thirty-one members. I'll explain how it works. Over time, the Council of State has become a judge; it's a pretty weighty prerogative, and the most important thing is that you have to struggle to ensure that every decision is made with the consensus of all its members. When there are some who don't agree, there is long discussion, and these *compañeros* are all very well educated, very serious, very concerned with the cases. It almost has to be unanimous, and almost unanimous it has usually been. Because when there have been objections, two, three, even one, well, you solve that by discussion, or you simply don't apply the [death] penalty. And that meeting of the Council of State for Trial Number 1 was public; it was broadcast live on television.

Is drug trafficking punishable in Cuba by the death penalty?
Listen, when it comes to drugs, terrible things are happening here. A Spaniard, for example, set up a mixed business, and he started looking for markets. He had technology, capital . . . He manufactured very nice little figurines. He brought in the raw materials from Colombia – he might bring in a ton of it in containers. He came over here – he seemed like a really hard-working businessman – unloaded the raw materials, loaded up the finished product and sent it off to Spain in containers. One day we read a news article – 'Seized – containers containing cocaine bound from Colombia to Cuba'. I don't know whether it was two tons or three. It looked like powdered milk being imported from Colombia, something like that. What happened? A mistake on the part of the chief of police in Colombia. He didn't report it [the seizure]. He didn't say anything to us about it. If he'd reported it, we'd have captured them, but the guys, with that news report, escaped. And do you know they're still at large?

We've sent every kind of report over there, to Spain, we've analysed the containers – they probably didn't send that many, but several containers full of stuff, and we've seen the proof. I'll have you know they're still walking around [i.e., free, on the street].

In Spain?
Yes – they haven't been sanctioned in any way, and they've stated that we – to get the heat off themselves; there were twelve or fourteen of them in on it – accused them of that [i.e., fabricated the case]. And they've got away with it, I'll have you know.

That made people pretty upset, pretty irritated. We said, 'How are they going to use a mixed business for large-scale drug trafficking!?' So we called a meeting of the National Assembly and much harsher sanctions were passed, including, in fact, up to the death penalty for attempting to use the national territory for large-scale drug transport. That sentence is on the books, and there are laws that sentence people to as much as life in prison for that crime.

And are there many drug-trafficking cases [in Cuba]?
Well, most of the cases are on a small scale. There are people who bring in [drugs] in their stomach, or in certain places in their bodies, and some of them die, they get nervous – the dogs don't smell what they've got in their intestines. But the people who deal with [this problem] acquire experience over time – some of [the mules] act suspicious, they get nervous . . . There are even people that have a [surgical] operation and carry up to a kilo. Do you know what a kilo is worth? Fifty thousand, $60,000 – who knows how much they sell it for wholesale in Europe and other places.

Once, a group – some of them were English, some from Canada – in the linings of their suits, they were carrying up to seventeen kilos. There are things that are hard to believe; some people die, others hide drugs in things with false bottoms – people keep inventing new tricks. There are about 150 foreigners in prison here for drug trafficking. A lot of people bring them in as a stopover on the way to Europe, but there's a small incipient internal market, too.

Where do the drugs come from?
Mainly from those 'bombings' I was talking about, from planes, and some of the bales wash up on shore. The Bahamas channel is very close to Cuba.

They throw the drugs out at sea?
The US Coast Guard watches out and they also have planes, and intelligence services; there's a certain amount of cooperation with us, but they've never wanted to sign the agreement to fight drug trafficking that Cuba has been proposing since 2001, along with another agreement to fight terrorism and a third one on immigration. The boats run in close to the shore and when they get in trouble they throw out the drugs.

Over in the province of Holguín, people sometimes tell me, 'Two ships have come into port.' When I hear that, what does it mean? It means two shipments of drugs have arrived. They're generally bales of marijuana, but 'coming into port' can be merchandise from a boat that's thrown out thirty or forty bales.

If they're under pursuit.
That's right – if the boat is being pursued, they throw [the drugs] out and the waves wash them in, especially there in Holguín and other places to the east.

There's another method: a big merchant ship comes along, makes contact . . . All of these boats make contact with speedboats from the United States, [which] come in and pick up the bales the ship has brought in, or that have been thrown out of a plane. Of course, these 'ships coming into port' are one of the main sources when some small incipient market arises, because of tourism and so on . . . Over 100,000 Cubans, for example, used to come down from the United States every year, they were allowed to come; most of them, of course, behave perfectly well, but there are some who bring in a little drug, plus some tourists, who bring it in for their personal use, although tourism in our country is, as a general rule, clean.

There are other methods used for large-scale drug trafficking, when the drugs are brought in on a yacht. There are thousands of tourist boats. Here there are places visited by private boats, yachts, and there are a lot of people on that kind of boat, and some of them bring in drugs. Then, too, drugs can be grown, but that's not the main source. The *campesinos* are well organized, and they have a high level of social awareness. The major suppliers are the 'arrivals', the 'boats coming into port', the 'dockings', as they're sometimes also called. We're in a successful struggle against that problem, and we have to stop it, because drugs destroy minds. There's one thing particularly bad about drugs: they destroy people's minds, they destroy your ability to think. They confront a person with very serious moral and ethical dilemmas.

Listen, the man who traffics in drugs for money takes precautions, he 'watches his back', as they say, because punishment acts as a disincentive. It's one of the few cases where I think the fear of capital punishment can act as an effective means of preventing a crime which is serious, because drug trafficking threatens people's very lives, and we must prevent drug use from becoming a problem of serious social consequence.

In many countries around the world, the death penalty is being abolished. All the countries in the European Union have abolished it, and many people

wonder why in Cuba, where there has been so much social progress, the
death penalty is still being used.

I think that's a difficult subject, and an interesting question. Like environmental and other problems, it's a subject that we've been discussing here for a long time.

Did we question the death penalty when we became revolutionaries, or when we were fighting, or when the Revolution triumphed? No, we really didn't. Did we question it during the years of invasions, the dirty war, the assassination attempts, the sabotage, all that? No, we certainly didn't question it then. We mulled over its forms, the procedures, the legal aspects of the subject, and there's also a little historical experience.

What's happened? What's happened is that political movements have had to be defended. As have the bourgeoisies . . . Both counter-revolutions and revolutions have had to be defended through procedures of one sort or another. For us, the essential thing has been to defend ourselves through laws, rules, legal procedures, and to avoid injustices, above all. And to avoid, as I explained to you, anything that might be extra-legal or extra-judicial; that was something we avoided.

It's not that we were happy to have to enforce the death penalty. There was even a time when executions were suspended, but then we discovered plans for terrorism, assassination attempts, and not just one or two . . . There came a moment during the first year of the Revolution when [the death penalty] was suspended, and I'll tell you, quite a few men's lives were saved, but there were still a lot of men yet to be tried, and a few were fugitives, and later on we had no alternative but to reinstate it. Things were in store for us that we could never have imagined.

We looked at the issue from a certain angle, from the question of life or death, and we also based our decisions on certain criteria that had been arising out of revolutionary processes, out of profound revolutions themselves, for some time. Generally speaking, the principle on which the people who take part in those struggles base their activities – and the principle is sound – is that it's a battle for life or death. So if you aren't capable of defending yourself, your cause is lost and you have to pay with your life.

That, for us, was clear. So faced with the most serious crimes, we said, 'How can we put a stop to them?' If there's a great deal of mercenary interest involved, then it's not ideological. Fortunately, we didn't have to fight against fanatics with clear ideals, or fanatics for a cause. We had the privilege of fighting against people motivated mainly by ambitions of a material nature, ambitions of an economic nature, and a social nature.

Simple mercenaries, not fanatics for a cause.
We would never have been able to free ourselves of fanatics – I would never have escaped with my life from all the plans to assassinate me. No one can escape the fanatics, but we were fortunate that it wasn't fanatics fighting against us, and the other thing was that there was that element of calculation. But if people thought killing people, murdering teachers, sacrificing the lives of *campesinos* and the lives of soldiers – when it was the labourers and *campesinos* who were our strength – thought they were going to win a prize for that, they were very much mistaken . . . [Although] that was what they were hoping for.*

And have you managed to capture many of [these mercenaries]?
We have – because we've managed to adopt all the measures, create the organizations and do everything necessary to totally wipe out action launched from outside. Methods of penetration, intelligence information, even technological methods. They aren't the only ones who can find out where someone's calling from, for example, you know. Anybody can find that out now, anyone who's technologically literate.

And have they been imprisoned?
The people responsible for the bombs in the hotels have been given the death penalty, but the decision was made not to apply it for obvious political reasons. They were young Latin American mercenaries, of whom there are many thousands, and it's possible their sentences may ultimately be commuted. There was a *de facto* moratorium for all felonies.

The laws still exist, they're still in effect, but the punishments are not being applied. That doesn't mean we'll never use [the death penalty], because you never know what terrible thing may someday be done by someone. If somebody blows up a plane with passengers aboard, this country would not accept an amnesty for the guilty parties, or a pardon, because, generally speaking, public opinion is harsh.

---

* [(In 1st ed.:) Of course under those circumstances, the most serious crimes were punished by death. That was the prevailing philosophy. And that war began to be won, the battle began to be won against people motivated by counter-revolutionary ambitions. Call it political motivation, which is what it was called for many years . . .]

Of course a government doesn't always have to do what people call for. You know that almost everywhere, capital punishment has more supporters in the population than opponents. In Europe itself, there are many countries that want to impose capital punishment.

Yes, public opinion favours it. In France, there's still a majority in favour of it.
But one has the duty not to be swept up [by public opinion], not to blindly follow a point of view, however popular, even dominant, it may be, when, of course, it may be extremist.

Here in Cuba, is public opinion mostly in favour of capital punishment?
People tend to be much more radical. Because there are situations that inspire profound indignation in our people. When someone is fired on and wounded, or shot at from the base at Guantánamo and killed, if you asked people, you can imagine how radical their answer would be . . . But you don't have to do, *have* to do, I mean, what people want.

When one of those terrible, terrible crimes occurs, you can't imagine how hard it is! But then for some reason, for example because one of the people who committed one of those crimes is very young, there's a tendency for the highest authorities to reduce the sentence, and then you get problems with the people around [the victim], the family members, public opinion. Still, that's not what determines the final decision. But to answer your question, I will tell you that it's not easy.

Wouldn't the easiest thing be, as the European countries have done, to abolish the death penalty once and for all?
We have not expunged it from the law books, but *de facto* the death penalty has not been imposed since April 2000[5] – which doesn't mean we'll never use it. I don't think we're living in the kind of world that would allow that. Have they continued to observe the Ford formula? Nobody's told us about it if they have – we haven't heard anything about it. That decision made by President Gerald Ford to prohibit American officials from organizing, planning and carrying out the assassination of opponents of the US? No one knows at this moment, when there are new and very aggressive doctrines, whether the Bush administration continues to respect that decision. Some say it does not.[6]

If they start using terrorism again against our country, committing crimes and killing children in a school, I promise you that it would be very hard, under those conditions, not to make use of one of the most severe laws, which originated in what's called – because I don't know what to call it; what name could you give setting off bombs in a school? – [being] 'in the service of a foreign power'.

Anyway, the Europeans aren't under a blockade, they aren't being bombed every day. I don't know what they did when they had those groups like the Red Brigades,[7] but I've heard stories of crimes committed against some of the members of the Red Brigades ... I've also heard about people being executed in third countries – the case, for example, of the Basques, several dozen ...

Are you referring to the GAL,[8] for example? Because in Spain capital punishment no longer exists ...
There may not be any capital punishment, but things have happened that *we've* never done – executing people for political reasons without first trying them, and in Europe, dozens of people have been executed that way.

Extra-judicially?
Let the history of the members of the Red Brigades who were executed extra-judicially be written! Or let the true history of the ETA members executed extra-judicially when there was no death penalty in Spain be written!

Here we have the death penalty, but we don't have extra-judicial executions. Just to point out appearances and the differences, and where the truth might lie and where there might be demagoguery or hypocrisy.

We guarantee that there will never be an extra-judicial execution in Cuba; in Cuba there will never be torture. You can ask the men who set off those bombs [in 1977] whether they ever said a word about torture, whether they ever received one blow. Of course, they aren't fanatics, they're mercenaries; they tell everything, immediately – all you have to do is show them irrefutable proof of their guilt ... I mean, they explain how they brought in the explosive in a little TV set, the plastic such and such a colour, so the dogs couldn't smell it, a kind of explosive that dogs pass right by and don't detect, and where the fuses were, in some small cables, and the wristwatch they had to set the bomb off with. They could leave the bomb in a hotel and set it off, if they wanted to, five minutes later, or an hour, or ninety-nine hours ... All very sophisticated.

But that type cooperates. They immediately tell everything, because they've been paid to do the job . . . And we didn't offer them money. The people I'm talking to you about cooperated like little lambs, as cool as could be. And there are potentially thousands of that kind.

After all the problems and conflicts in Central America and other places, [there are] people who'd do just about anything for $5,000 . . . And for much less. Some of them would be offered $2,000 to set off a bomb, plus their airfare and whatnot. They took advantage of how easy it is to go in and out as a tourist, and that's very dangerous, because in a plane, any oversight, any failure to be alert can be fatal for everyone. No machine is totally safe [i.e., no scanning machine is foolproof]; they'll use an explosive of a special kind, and wear a normal wristwatch, some piece of medical equipment, and a little television, if you'll let them on with it . . . I'll tell you, those are the problems the Americans have got now, after September 11, the vulnerability to the very technologies they taught to those who carried out terrorist acts against Cuba.

Posada Carriles, for example, drew up plans to blow up planes en route from Central America to Cuba and carrying American passengers. I think everyone benefits to the extent that methods of discovering a terrorist plan become more precise, and [discovering] drugs, too. Those are the two great problems, and all the technology that's being developed to combat them benefits everyone.

How many of the death sentences that have been given have not been carried out so far?
None of the people from outside the island responsible for the bombings in counter-revolutionary actions have been sent to the firing squad. I can't say since when, but it must be several years.

With respect to common crimes, [the death sentence] was being applied until April 2000, and I couldn't tell you just now what the exact number is, but we can ask – several dozen, I'd say, and sentences, I couldn't say exactly but it must be twenty or twenty-five. I can't give you an exact number because I don't have that information here.

And since then it hasn't been applied.
Not once [until 11 April 2003. – I.R.].

Since three years ago.
It's sort of what's called a moratorium. But I do want to say this: it has not

been abolished. Later, if you want, I can give you my own opinion, but it hasn't been abolished. I mean, there are so many ways of killing, and the science or art of killing is very sophisticated, and you can't just say now, 'We're going to give up the death penalty.' There are two very serious cases of murder pending trial now, among them one in which an entire family who'd had a visitor from Miami was killed – including a child. Those very serious crimes committed by common criminals create a very serious public-opinion problem, and those [two] cases have yet to be resolved. It's not that we enjoy doing it, or that we're in a hurry, or that we have desires of any kind to [impose the death penalty], but I think some time will have to pass before the death penalty is abolished completely for every kind of crime, although we'd be very glad to do so. But there is no commitment to a complete and final moratorium.

Is Cuba studying the problem?
I talked to you about the kinds of concerns we had, and about the fact that the application of the death penalty had begun tapering off for activities of a political nature; I told you about the case of those mercenaries who brought in bombs, and then I told you that it had been some time since [the death penalty] had been applied. But we have not renounced it, because we're living in a complex time.

In the case of common crimes, in fact, the death penalty has not been imposed, but it hasn't been renounced, either, as I explained to you, because I don't want to deceive anyone, and we believe that not even the people are totally prepared for that, and [abolishing the death penalty] would create a serious public-opinion problem. Although you may be sure that here, at no price, will an injustice be committed. But those who commit serious offences are also not going to benefit by generosity towards them that the people really wouldn't understand, and there's a need for education. There needs to be an educational effort among us, but the Revolution can do that, as to the minimal conditions for applying that policy.

You, personally – what do you *think about capital punishment?*
I have certain ideas about the death penalty. Yes, I have a great many ideas, and I think that the death penalty doesn't solve any problems; the influence the death penalty has is relative.

Even now we are studying crime and the causes of crime. We need to go further into the matter, and I'm happy with the work we're doing and the studies of all kinds that we're carrying out. There have been cases of crimes so horrendous that a person who studied law knows that there's a principle in law that says that a man not in full possession of his faculties cannot be tried. We're giving serious study to that question. We're studying how many cases of mentally ill persons . . . In the United States, there's a huge number of people with mental problems. And there's a legal principle: you have to prove – and how can you do that? – that a person has not committed a crime under those conditions.

How many studies have been done on the mental causes of crime? Which may be of genetic origin, or [caused by] an accident, accidents that create problems in people and make them violent . . . What are the genetic or accidental factors that affect the functioning of the human mind and practically turn certain people into monsters?

We've been keeping pace with those realities, with that experience, with those concepts, and here, no one is ever, ever punished out of revenge. Among our punishments we also have life sentences, which is an alternative to capital punishment . . .

I think we're moving towards a future in our country in which we'll be able to abolish the death penalty. So one day we will be among those countries that have abolished it. We aspire to that, on the basis not just of philosophical issues, but out of a sense of justice and reality. That is the current state of our points of view and our positions with respect to capital punishment.

19
Cuba and Neoliberal Globalization

The new capitalism – What is Socialism today? – Ideological confusion –
The tragedy of the environment – Preserving the environment –
'The battle of ideas' – Towards a general education

Some time ago, I asked you how you planned to prevent the effects of
liberal globalization from spreading to Cuba, and you answered in this
way: 'We will wait, patiently, for globalization to collapse.' Do you still
think the same way?
When I gave that answer Stiglitz[1] had not yet written any books; Soros,[2]
what you heard from him were announcements of his big speculative operations; the financial crisis in Argentina in December 2001 hadn't yet taken
place, nor had the series of crises we're seeing now.

We were becoming more and more aware of what globalization was, and
for some time before that we'd been reading materials that led us to the
conclusion that a situation more critical than that of 1929 could occur, and
that led us to study the crisis of 1929, and to reread Galbraith[3] and other
economists, and to study the theses, the fundamental ideas of the capitalist
system of production, and even ask ourselves what was left of that system,
and if there *was* still anything left, whether such a thing as free competition
still existed in the world, and free enterprise, and all those 'truths' that are
considered divine dogma.

You yourself have used another name for that globalization – I think you
called it 'the one philosophy';[4] others have talked about the 'end of history'.[5]
Still, I was fully convinced that it was the other way around, and that it had
to be resisted. That is the certainty I had then.

You asked yourself what was left of capitalism. Do you think that globaliza-
tion is destroying even capitalism itself?
There's no capitalism today, there's no competition. Today, what we have
is monopolies in all the great sectors. There is some competition between
certain countries to produce televisions, or computers – even cars have been
produced by the World Bank – but capitalism, that capitalism doesn't exist
any more.

Five hundred global corporations today control 80 per cent of the world's
economy. Prices don't stem from competition. The prices at which, for
example, medicine to fight AIDS is sold are monopolistic. Medicines continue to be one of the most abusive, extravagant and exploitative items in
the world's budgets; the price of medicine that's sold to people is sometimes
ten times what it costs to produce it. Advertising practically determines what
sells and what doesn't. The person who doesn't have much money can't
advertise his products in any way, even if they're excellent.

After the last worldwide bloodbath in the forties, we were promised a
world of peace, we were promised that the gap between rich and poor would
be closed, and that the more developed would help the less developed. All
that was a huge lie. A world order was imposed on us that cannot be justified,
cannot be sustained, and cannot be borne. The world is being driven into a
dead-end street.

At this point, none of those categories that we all thought capitalism was
based on exist, and therefore, the theory the 'Chicago Boys'[6] espouse doesn't
exist. And yet the theory and practice of Socialism is yet to be developed
and yet to be written.

On another occasion you said to me that there was no longer any 'model'
in the sphere of politics and that today no one knew very well what the
concept 'Socialism' meant. You were telling me that at a meeting of the São
Paulo Forum that was held in Havana, which all the Latin American Lefts
attended, you, the participants, had to reach an agreement not to speak the
word 'Socialism' because it's a word that 'divides'.
Look – what is Marxism? What is Socialism? They're not well defined. In the
first place, the only political economy that exists is the capitalist one, but the
capitalist one of Adam Smith.[7] So here we are making Socialism sometimes
with those categories adopted from capitalism, which is one of the greatest
concerns we have. Because if you use the categories of capitalism as an instrument in the construction of Socialism, you force all the corporations to

compete with each other, and criminal, thieving corporations spring up, pirates that buy here and buy there. There needs to be a very profound study [of this].

Che once got involved in a tremendous controversy about the consequences of using budget financing versus self-financing. We talked about that.[8] As a government minister, he had studied the organization of several great monopolies, and they used budget financing. The USSR used another method: self-financing. And he had strong opinions about that.[9]

Marx made just one slight attempt, in the *Critique of the Gotha Programme*,[10] to try to define what Socialism would be like, because he was a man of too much wisdom, too much intelligence, too great a sense of realism to think that one could write a utopia of what Socialism would be like. The problem was the interpretation of the doctrines, and there have been a lot of interpretations. That was why the progressives were divided for so long, and that's the reason behind the controversies between anarchists and socialists, the problems after the Bolshevik Revolution in 1917 between the Trotskyites and the Stalinists, or, we might say, [in deference to] the people on one or another side of those great controversies, the ideological schism between the two great leaders. The more intellectual of the two was, without a doubt, Trotsky.

Stalin was more a practical leader – he was a conspirator, not a theorist, even though once in a while, later, he would try to turn theorist ... I remember some booklets that were passed around in which Stalin tried to explain the essence of 'dialectical materialism', and he used the example of water. They tried to make Stalin into a theorist. He was an organizer of great ability, I think he was a revolutionary – I don't think he was ever at the service of the tsar, ever. But then he committed those errors that we all know about – the repression, the purges, all that.

Lenin was the genius; he died relatively young, but he would have been able to do so much had he lived. Theory doesn't always help. In the period during which the Socialist state was being built, Lenin desperately applied – beginning in 1921 – the NEP,[11] the new economic policy ... We've talked about that, and I told you that Che himself didn't like the NEP.

Lenin had a truly ingenious idea: build capitalism under a dictatorship of the proletariat. Remember that what the great powers wanted to do was destroy the Bolshevik Revolution; everybody attacked it. One mustn't forget the history of the destruction they caused in that underdeveloped country; Russia was the least-developed country in Europe, and of course Lenin, following Marx's formulation, thought that the revolution couldn't occur in a single country, that it had to occur simultaneously in the most highly industrialized countries, on the basis of a great awakening of the forces of production.

So the great dilemma, after that first revolution took place in Russia, was what path to follow. When the revolutionary movement failed in the rest of Europe, Lenin had no alternative: he had to build Socialism in a single country: Russia. Imagine the construction of Socialism in that country with an 80 per cent illiteracy rate and a situation in which they had to defend themselves against everybody that was attacking them, and in which the main intellectuals, the men and women with the most knowledge, had fled or were executed. You see?

It was a pretty terrible time, with intense debates.
There were many, many controversies. Lenin had died by then. In my opinion, during the ten years of the NEP the Soviet Union wasted time setting up agricultural cooperatives. Since individual production yielded the maximum of what could be produced under those conditions, collectivization was precipitate. In Cuba there were always, out in the country, over 100,000 individual landowners. The first thing we did in 1959 was give everyone who was leasing land or working as sharecroppers the property they were working on.

Do you think that at the present moment we're in a time of great ideological confusion?
I do. In ideology, there is great confusion. The world we live in today is very different. There are many problems that the great political and social philosophers couldn't, at such a great distance, foresee, although their knowledge was decisive in turning us into people with revolutionary ideas.

People struggle against underdevelopment, disease, illiteracy, but what we might call the *global* solution to humanity's problems has not yet been found. Humanity's problems cannot be solved on the basis of individual nations, because today more than ever before, domination is achieved on a global basis: that 'neoliberal globalization' we were talking about, which is backed by the power of the empire and its allies. The WTO [World Trade Organization], the World Bank, the International Monetary Fund establish the rules for a situation of *de facto* domination and exploitation which is equal to or worse than the most dreadful consequences of colonial slavery.

Many people are looking for ways to free themselves from that domination. You've been a witness to the number of people who attended the World Social Forum in Porto Alegre, and in Bombay in 2004. And who knows how many articles about liberal globalization I've read in your journal.[12] I've also read articles in other serious publications.

Here, for many years our *compañeros* went through journals like yours, centrist journals, right-leaning journals too, all week long, and clipped the basic articles on the world's economic problems. So yes, we can say that it's very hard for people to understand the problems, because in most countries the vast majority of the people don't receive an economic education, or a political education. And now the peoples of the world are reacting to economic and social situations that are, and will continue to be, more and more unsustainable.

And yet, don't you have the impression that liberal globalization has taken some hard knocks, and is now less arrogant than it was a few years ago?
Yes, I have that impression, too, because we've had the case of Argentina, the victory in May 2003 of Néstor Kirchner and the defeat of the symbol of neoliberal globalization that has taken place in that country at a decisive moment in the international financial crisis. It's no longer just a crisis in south-east Asia, as it was in 1977; it's a worldwide crisis, plus the war in Iraq, plus the consequences of huge debt, plus the growing waste and consequent cost of energy, plus the fatalism that currency will be devalued and flee due to an excess of issuance, plus the deficit on the part of the main economic and military power on the planet.

The problem is worldwide, and that's why a worldwide awareness is growing, too, which is why there will come a day of glory when another, better world finally becomes possible. I'll tell you, that phrase – which I think you yourself proposed – is growing stronger: 'A better world is possible.' But when we've achieved a better world, which is possible, we have to keep repeating: a better world is possible, a better world is possible, and repeat it yet again: a better world is possible. Because the world is at the crossroads – getting better or disappearing.

I believe in ideas and I believe in awareness, in knowledge, in culture, and especially in political culture. We've devoted many years to creating an awareness, and we have great faith, shall we say, in education and culture, especially in political culture. We live in a world that lacks political culture. You should know that better than anyone, because you've struggled to bring political culture to bear on problems as complicated as the new economic order and the neoliberal globalization you mentioned.

What's taught in almost every school in the world is dogmas – we even teach dogmas here.

You're irritated by dogmas?
Well, I'm anti-dogma; I'm profoundly anti-dogmatic, I've talked about that before. So that, I'll tell you, that's where our faith lies, in the tremendous strength of ideas, in what we've learned in forty-something years about the value of ideas and of knowledge. And yet there are still dangers, so we always try to educate, more and more, educate the new generations. Because today the globalized world forces you to have more and more knowledge and to look for and find global solutions.

Such as?
First, to ensure that humanity is preserved, because there's absolutely no guarantee of our survival. That's the part we know from the history, which is very short, of the survival of species. Our species is very recent; it may be no older than about a million years in its various stages of evolution.

The human of today, with all its intellectual abilities, may be about 100,000 years old. We know that the evolution of life was interrupted by a meteorite – this is a fact accepted by everyone – which fell on to the isthmus of Tchuantepec. Scientists say it was like a huge nuclear explosion that filled the planet's atmosphere with dust and covered the earth with darkness for weeks. It killed off who knows how many species of dinosaurs and other similar forms of life, while other species evolved . . . But humans did not yet exist.

Today there's a new danger for the industrialized world: a population that has 6.5 billion inhabitants and is growing by almost 100 million people a year, or 80 [million] at least. I have three clocks that keep track of more or less how fast the [world] population is growing every day. And we should note that China has made heroic efforts to limit its population growth – had it not, the planet would have over 6.7 billion inhabitants today.

Everybody knows how much the population is going to grow, everybody knows the relationship between illiteracy, lack of culture and the number of children in a family. Everybody knows that and a thousand other things about this world today. There is a true population explosion in many countries where the economy is not growing – where what's growing is debt and disaster.

And globalization continues to ignore those explosive realities. The rules of the IMF are going to keep leading many countries and many people into the abyss, because its dictates are still in full force. Meanwhile, imperialism, which likes to protect the interests of its large corporations, does exactly what it wants to, even at the cost of riling everybody else – [the United States] puts a tariff on anything it wants to; they even slapped a 30 per cent tariff on Canada for exported lumber, which affected a multi-billion-dollar market.

It's that there's a lord of the world . . . When they wanted to blast a bunch of countries, the United States put a tremendous tariff on imported steel . . . But its own small businesses, to them it gives all sorts of concessions. The American political economy has never been so self-centred with respect to the rest of the world and [even] its own allies [as it is now].

All around the world, countries are developing strong national sentiments. And that's not good; it's time that our worries and concerns be not just national, but global. Now, the world has to develop internationalist sentiments, because we wouldn't be internationalists, or possess a doctrine of worldwide solidarity if we began to blame other nations. That's like blaming the entire German people for the horrors of Nazism, and I'll tell you, at a certain point many people in Germany supported that dreadful cause.

The cause of Hitler and Nazism, you mean.
But that was the nation that had suffered the consequences of the 1919 Treaty of Versailles, which were intolerable. What gave Hitler the majority [in 1933] were the points agreed on in the Treaty of Versailles, which drove the nation into a very difficult situation. After their defeat, after a bloody inter-imperial war over a new partitioning of the world, that treaty united the Germans. And they voted. Yes, because Hitler came to power through elections that elevated him to the chancellorship, that is, the leadership of the government. There was no coup d'état. It's true that in 1923 he'd tried to carry out a putsch there in Munich, one of those crazy adventures, and was even in prison for a time . . . And he led his country, on the basis of a nationalist programme, to a racist, absurd, criminal doctrine. I visited Auschwitz in 1972, and it's hard to imagine the horrendous crimes that were committed there.

The crime of crimes.
For thousands of years, humanity will remember the Holocaust, the crimes at Auschwitz and other extermination camps, with horror and repugnance . . .

Though nothing is comparable to the horror of Auschwitz, today globalization favours the great crimes committed against the environment, which cause tremendous harm and may have dreadful consequences for future generations. Are you sensitive to the problem of environmental protection?
Thirty years ago, no one was talking about what we know today about that. There was the Club of Rome[13] – several prominent figures got together and made prophecies and talked about various things on the basis of data and the analysis of interest rates. They were criticized, some people called them utopians, doomsayers and so on. They were the first. I don't think that was much more than thirty years ago. The environment issue has grown vertically, dizzyingly, in the last quarter of a century. And the real drama may lie in our ignorance of the risks we've lived with for so long.

Do you think that people didn't know, or didn't want to know, because they had such blind faith in science and technology?
I'll tell you, I don't think a single person – twenty-five years after the end of the Second World War, in 1945, and even with the use of their right reason and knowing how to read and write – had ever heard a word about the blind, inexorable and accelerating march of humanity towards the destruction of the natural foundations of their own lives. No other generation, of the hundreds that preceded the generation of today, ever confronted such bitter perils, or ever faced such enormous responsibility.

Barely thirty years ago, I repeat, humanity had not the slightest awareness of the great tragedy [that was upon it]. Back then, people thought that the only danger of extinction lay in the colossal number of nuclear weapons ready to be fired in a question of minutes. Today, although dangers of that kind have not totally disappeared, another peril – a terrifying, Dantean peril – hangs over humanity. I'm sure that when you yourself were in college you never heard people talking about the ozone layer and climate change. Those problems began to be discussed many years after you graduated. There are many new problems.

Today we know that oil, which was a natural wonder, and which took 300 million years to form, humanity will have used up the proven and probable reserves of it in just 150 years ... That fact is as serious as the worst natural disaster imaginable, because if we're suddenly left without fuel, every car in the world comes to a halt. And there is still no substitute for oil – at one time, we thought it might be nuclear power.

Those same members of the Club of Rome talked about the necessity of who knows how many thousand nuclear-energy plants, and people were already terrified of contaminated territories because of the number of sites that continued to be saturated with radiation thirty years later.

At one point, Cuba was tempted by nuclear energy, and even started construction on a plant in Cienfuegos, I believe, although you later abandoned it.

Yes, that project was abandoned. It wasn't an open, graphite-cooled facility like the one in Chernobyl; it was closed and water-cooled – that is, the most used and safest technology in the world. The technology of nuclear energy has solved the energy problem in some countries, such as France, which in order to do its neighbours a favour built plants on its own soil and when it produces an excess of energy, sells it cheaply to the other Europeans that didn't build nuclear plants. But when the price of oil began to go up – which no one had foreseen, I might say, because everyone thought oil was as abundant as the Pacific Ocean – then that increase in prices in the seventies had one positive consequence: it forced people to develop technology that consumed less energy, in factories, in industries, etc. People used energy more efficiently, [as did] automobiles, buses, planes, etc., so that it would last, say, a few years longer. It forced people to save energy, and countries such as France and others developed their nuclear industries; that led to less pollution than there would have been if the price of oil hadn't become so expensive.

France was able to develop its nuclear industry, but, for example, today Iran wants to produce nuclear fuel and Washington won't hear of it, and a worldwide crisis has been created. What do you think about this situation that's been created with Iran?

Iran is defending its right to produce nuclear energy like any other industrialized nation, and to not be forced to destroy its reserves of a raw material that is used not just as a source of energy but also as a source to produce many products: fertilizers, textiles and countless materials that are used universally today. The empire is threatening to attack if Iran produces that nuclear fuel. Nuclear fuel is not nuclear weapons, it's not atomic bombs. Forbidding a country to produce the fuel of the immediate future is like forbidding a country to explore in search of oil, which is the fuel of the present, and set to run out. What country in the world is forbidden to look for fuel – coal, gas, petroleum?

With more than 70 million inhabitants, Iran is attempting to embark on industrial development, and it thinks, quite rightly, that it's a terrible crime to commit its natural gas or petroleum reserves to producing the potentially billions of kilowatt-hours that a Third World country needs for its industrial development. The empire wants to forbid that, and is threatening to bomb the country. Today [December 2005], at the international level, a debate is going on about what day and hour [the bombing will occur], and whether it will be the empire or whether the empire will use – as it used in Iraq – its Israeli satellite to launch preemptive bombings of research centres engaged in trying to obtain the technology to produce nuclear fuel. And we'll see what happens if they decide to bomb Iran.

The Cubans have been accused of aiding Iran with technology.
Yes, we've been accused of that – we've been accused of just about everything. We've been accused of collaborating with Iran, transferring technology with that objective. And what we're building, in cooperation with Iran, is a factory to produce drugs to combat cancer! That's what we're doing! Iran has signed the Nuclear Non-Proliferation Treaty, just as Cuba has. We have never considered the idea of fabricating nuclear weapons, because we don't need them. Even if they were technologically accessible, how much would it cost to produce them? And what's the purpose of producing a nuclear weapon when your enemy has thousands of them? It would be entering an arms race all over again. *No one* should have the right to produce nuclear weapons, much less the privileged right demanded by imperialism to impose its hegemonic domination [on the world] and take away the Third World's natural resources and raw materials. We've denounced that a thousand times. And we will defend to the last, in all the forums and courts in the world, with no fear or trepidation whatsoever, the right of countries to produce nuclear fuel. We need to put a stop to all this silliness, the abuses, the empire of force and terror in the world. More and more nations have less and less fear, more and more nations will rebel, and the empire will not be able to uphold the disgraceful and despicable system it is now upholding. One day Salvador Allende talked about 'sooner or later' – well, I think that sooner or later that empire will no longer be the lord and master of the world.

To a degree, this crisis is the first consequence of the current depletion of petroleum and the changes that that's bringing about.
Yes, because 80 per cent of the oil is now in the hands of Third World countries, since the others have used up their own – among them the United

States, which had immense reserves of oil and gas. Now there's only enough for a few years, which is why they're trying to guarantee possession of oil anywhere on the planet, and in any form. That source of energy, however, as we've seen, is running out, and within just twenty-five or thirty years all that will be left, for the massive production of electricity – apart from solar [energy], wind, biomass, etc. – will be the fundamental source: nuclear energy. Because the day is still far away when hydrogen, through technological processes that are only beginning to be developed, can be turned into an excellent source of fuel, without which humanity cannot survive – humanity at a certain level of development, at least. This is a grave problem, and it is with us now. And that's the course this world is on.

There are countless ecological problems that aren't even being recognized; catastrophes follow one upon another, and there are natural disasters even worse than nuclear energy, such as cancer.

Or AIDS.
AIDS didn't exist twenty-five years ago, and today there are no fewer than 40 million people sick or infected with the AIDS-HIV virus. And [the countries] that have the best laboratories are dedicated to treatment, not prevention, not vaccines, because a treatment – this is common knowledge – which is sold for $10,000 dollars a year and the sick person has to keep taking it, makes more profits [than a one-time vaccine]. Therapy simply produces more profit than preventive medicine. Now, too, the SARS [Severe Acute Respiratory Syndrome] virus has appeared, when no one was expecting it, and Nile fever, in the northeastern United States, clearly transported there from somewhere else in the world, and dengue fever, which has four different types of the virus, and the combination of one and another produces complex diseases such as haemorrhagic dengue. And bird flu may come and start a terrible, unimaginable pandemic. All these problems were unheard-of not long ago; today we have a clear awareness that there is a close relationship between all these things – economy, industry, population, development, ecology . . .

Generally speaking, the countries in the former Socialist camp – we've talked about this before – were not particularly concerned with the issue of the environment. Does this concern exist in Cuba?
We have seen concern with the environment grow – we have seen and measured climate change here in Cuba; the change in sea level, we've seen

and measured it here in Cuba; pollution, we've seen and measured that, too, here in Cuba. And the truth is, in our country there's a growing awareness of the environment. People are being educated; we have TV programmes constantly broadcasting information and orientation; all our children have been educated in the subject, and today they're the primary defenders of the environment.

In just 100 years, humanity grew from approximately 1.5 billion people to more than 6.5 billion, as I've said before. It will have to depend entirely on energy sources yet to be discovered and developed. Poverty is on the rise; old and new diseases threaten to wipe out entire nations; the earth is eroding and losing fertility; the climate is changing; the air and our drinking water and the oceans are becoming more and more polluted.

The authority of the United Nations is being taken away from it, undermined; the institution is being obstructed and destroyed. Aid to development is shrinking. The Third World is being required to pay a debt of $2.5 trillion, which is utterly unpayable under the present conditions. And yet $1 trillion is being spent every year on increasingly more sophisticated and lethal weapons. Why and for what?

A similar amount is being spent on commercial advertising, which produces in billions of people an urge to consume that is impossible to satisfy. Why and for what?

Our species, for the first time, is in real danger of extinction – self-extinction, due to the madness of human beings themselves, who are the victims of this so-called 'civilization'.

Fifteen or so years ago, in 1992, when almost no politicians were talking about this, in a speech to the Earth Environmental Summit in Rio de Janeiro sponsored by the United Nations, I talked about this danger. Many people thought I was exaggerating, they called me a doomsayer. What I said at the time was that one species in particular was on the verge of extinction: man. Time has proved me right, unfortunately more clearly so every day.

Would you draw some connection between liberal globalization and the acceleration of the destruction of the environment?
I think that all efforts to preserve the environment are incompatible with the economic system imposed on the world, that ruthless neoliberal globalization with the impositions and conditions by which the IMF sacrifices billions of people's health, education and social security. And with the cruel way in which, through the free buying and selling of currencies between

strong currencies and the weak currencies of the Third World, fabulous sums are being taken out of the Third World every year.

To put it succinctly, I think that preserving the environment is incompatible with the policies of the WTO, which are apparently designed to allow rich nations to flood the world with their merchandise with no restrictions whatsoever and to wipe out the industrial and agricultural development of the poorer nations, who are left with no future except to supply raw materials and cheap labour; with [the policies of] NAFTA and other free-trade agreements between the sharks and the sardines; with the monstrous foreign debt, which sometimes eats up as much as 50 per cent of a nation's budget and which is absolutely unpayable under current circumstances; with the brain drain, the almost total monopoly on intellectual property, and the abusive and disproportionate use of the planet's natural and energy resources.

The list of injustices would never end. The abyss is growing deeper and deeper; the looting greater and greater . . .

Cuba is not a 'consumer society'; consumption is, in fact, austere, and some people here even bemoan that. What would you say to those who complain of not having access to the products of capitalist consumer societies?
Well, I'd tell them that the consumer society is one of the most frightening, terrifying inventions of developed capitalism today in this phase of neoliberal globalization. It is disastrous, just awful, because I try to imagine 1.3 billion Chinese with the per capita number of cars that the United States has . . . I can't imagine India, with its more than 1 billion inhabitants, living in a consumer society; I can't imagine the 600 million people who live in sub-Saharan Africa, who don't even have electricity and in some places more than 80 per cent of whom don't know how to read and write, in a consumer society.

Under a diabolic and chaotic economic order, in fifty or sixty years at the most, consumer societies will have exhausted the proven and probable reserves of fossil fuel . . . There is no clear and coherent idea about the energy that in fifty years or so will be moving the billions of motorized vehicles that flood cities and highways in the wealthy nations, and even in much of the Third World. [The consumer society] is the expression of a completely irrational mode of life and consumption, and it will never serve as a model for the 10 billion people who will supposedly inhabit the planet when the dreadful oil age is over.

That economic order and those models of consumption are incompatible with the world's limited and non-renewable essential resources and the laws that govern nature and life. They also clash with the most elementary principles of ethics, culture and moral values created by mankind.

But citizens also need material goods, don't you think?
Yes, of course. I don't minimize, in the slightest, the importance of material needs – you always have to give them first priority, because in order to study, to achieve a higher quality of life, certain needs have to be satisfied – and those are physical, material needs. But quality of life lies in knowledge, in culture. Values are what constitute true quality of life, the supreme quality of life, even above food, shelter and clothing.

You're still an incorrigible dreamer.
There's no such thing as dreamers, and you can take that from a dreamer who's had the privilege of seeing realities that he was never even capable of dreaming.

Should we despair of the human being? Or can we still maintain a little hope for the human being's ability to stop the race towards the abyss?
Well, today we know how things stand. From my point of view, no task is more urgent than creating a universal awareness, taking the problem to the masses, to the billions of men and women of every age, including children, who inhabit the planet. The objective conditions, the sufferings of the immense majority of those people create the subjective conditions for the task of awareness-building. Everything is related: illiteracy, unemployment, poverty, hunger, illness and disease; a lack of drinking water, housing, electricity; desertification, climate change, the disappearance of forests, floods, hurricanes, droughts, erosion, biodiversity loss, plagues and other tragedies that you are very aware of.

What results have we achieved since the Rio Summit in 1992? Almost none. On the contrary. While the Kyoto Protocol has become the victim of an arrogant boycott, carbon dioxide emissions, far from falling, have increased 9 per cent, and in the most polluting country, the United States, 18 per cent! Oceans and rivers are more polluted today than in 1992; 15 million hectares of forest, a little under 60,000 square miles, almost four times the area of Switzerland, are devastated every year.

Human society has made colossal errors, and continues to make them, but I am profoundly convinced that human beings are capable of conceiving the noblest ideas, harbouring the most generous sentiments, and overcoming the powerful instincts that nature has imposed on us – we are capable of giving our lives for what we feel and what we think. That has been shown many, many times down through history.

Has Cuba taken any initiatives to help preserve the environment that you might mention?
I'll tell you, when the Socialist camp collapsed and we were forced to face an extraordinarily difficult situation, our country, under a blockade for over forty years, was able, for example, to produce – and is still producing – in spaces available within cities, over 3 million tons of vegetables a year hydroponically, using straw and other agricultural waste and employing drip irrigation or microjets, with a minimal amount of water, and giving additional employment to some 300,000 citizens – and without emitting a gram of carbon dioxide into the atmosphere.

Cuba produces tobacco, and today many consumer associations denounce tobacco, saying it produces cancer. You yourself were a famous cigar smoker, but you've stopped smoking. How do you see that problem?
Well, everyone knows that historically we've been a tobacco producer for over 500 years; it was a product native to this island, cultivated and con-sumed here when Columbus arrived and 'discovered' us, and our tobacco. We can't give it up, much less while we're under a blockade. It would be wonderful if we could. But when we give a box of cigars to a friend, we say, 'With this box, if you smoke, you can smoke; if a friend of yours smokes, you can pass it along to him; but the best thing you can do is give this box to your enemy.'

Cuba is a tobacco producer and exporter, yet it is waging a no-smoking campaign. Cuba is also the producer of rum of a certain quality, and I can't recommend it, but if someone should want to try it they should do so in moderation. What I recommend to pregnant women, almost demand of them, is that they not drink it – that they not smoke or drink at all. We do that because we know the harm that alcohol and tobacco do to pregnant women.

In Cuba, you're staking a lot on what you call the 'battle of ideas'. What is your definition of 'battle of ideas'?
The battle of ideas is what we're doing. There are new, very new things; there are things that I might call, without reservation, extraordinary. We've

learned a lot, but this has culminated, and it's been a privilege, in the last few years.

You helped, too, because your book on the issue of cultural invasion[14] and the data you gave on the transnational monopoly of the principal communications media, we studied that, we discussed it, and we brought it up in a symposium on culture. Before the battle of ideas, the first battle we undertook was how to save the country's culture. And intellectuals recall a phrase that I used during the special period, when everything was in doubt: 'We must save culture.'

We'd had a meeting of UNEAC [Unión de Escritores y Artistas de Cuba, the Union of Cuban Writers and Artists] a few months earlier, and that conference lasted for many days, and at that time we were already talking about 'cultural invasion' and there we used data from another of your books which we later published here.[15] But then journalists also had their own meeting, and later those debates were repeated almost every six months. We began to acquire awareness.

You yourself have brought to light many of the problems associated with neoliberal globalization. How long ago did the world's intellectuals, scholars and economists first become aware of this problem? I think, because I'm an optimist, that this world can be saved, despite the mistakes we've made, despite the immense and unilateral powers that have been created, because I believe in the preeminence of ideas over force.

It is ideas that have enlightened the world, and when I talk about ideas I'm only talking about just and fair ideas, those that can bring peace to the world, those that can bring a solution to the grave dangers of war, those that can put an end to violence. That's why we talk about the 'battle of ideas'.

Cuba has also put its faith in what we might call 'general education', an increase in the level of knowledge, education and culture in every citizen. A socialization of knowledge. Knowledge as a common good. Am I right?
It took us a long time to discover the following: many people think that money is the decisive factor. Wrong. The level of knowledge, of education in the social classes is the decisive factor. Tens of thousands of people belonging to the bourgeois class, or those who aspired to it, people with knowledge and education, left Cuba for Miami. The Revolution has graduated about 800,000 professionals and intellectuals from the less privileged sectors of society.

And what have we discovered? We've discovered that those people with the most knowledge and the most culture within the family go to the best schools, because you get into those schools on the basis of your academic record, and they obtain the best positions and the best jobs. And the class, or sector, that produces the leaders and managers and all the major political officials, that sector tends to perpetuate itself, while those whose families have little education also tend to perpetuate themselves – the children of the poorest of the poor, the most discriminated-against of the discriminated-against in capitalism.

I want to be clear that I'm not talking about a class difference from the strictly economic point of view; I'm talking about differences in the levels of education associated with poverty and marginalization [versus affluence and a tradition of education]. Building a new society is much harder than it might appear, because there are so many factors that stand in your way.

In our own particular Socialist society, after many years, and when there were no longer any illiterates, when everyone had at least a ninth-grade education, it so happened that the, shall we say, more privileged sector tended to perpetuate itself, and another sector, which was more marginalized, also tended to perpetuate itself.

After 1959 we changed the whole system of education. There is no illiteracy any more, there is no child who hasn't gone to school, but within the school system, and at the university, which bases admission on [an applicant's] academic record and exams, a difference has spontaneously occurred between social sectors in which one sector has clear advantages over that other one in which you find the whites, blacks and mestizos who come from the poorest sectors within the poor people from the times of capitalism. The parents' educational level, even after we've made the Revolution, continues to have a tremendous influence on the children's later outcome. Children whose parents come from the lowest economic levels, or who have the least amount of knowledge [education], don't get the grades they need to get into the best schools. And that tends to perpetuate itself decade after decade, as I've pointed out. If you leave things the way they are, you can predict that the children of those people will never be managers of corporations, or directors, or hold the most important positions, because today you can't manage anything without a university education. What awaits them, mainly, is prison.

And how do you propose to change that social determinism?

To try to correct that, we're now waging a profound educational revolution – one not even conceivable in the first stage of the [revolutionary] process. We're turning all that around. And it's not by taking opportunities away from those who do get into the best schools – young people who are also revolutionaries. No, we're extending the possibility for higher education into the whole country, which [i.e., higher education] then becomes, on the one hand, an inevitable step in educational development, and on the other hand, a formidable instrument for social levelling. For several years now, we've been taking all those young people of seventeen to thirty years old with ninth-grade educations, but who for one social reason or another did not continue their studies or go to work, and we're persuading them to keep studying. We've created relevant, varied and attractive courses for them and even given them financial assistance.

We started this in September 2001, and in September 2005 over 45,000 of those students entered our universities. They are going to be among the most revolutionary of our citizens, because these programmes represent a rebirth for them. Where would many of them have wound up without education? – no job, no social support.

Where would *they have wound up?*

I asked for an investigation into the situation of all prisoners between twenty and thirty years of age who'd been sent to prison for common crimes in a Socialist state, person by person. And we discovered – it's incredible – that just 2 per cent of those in prison because they'd committed common crimes were the children of professionals or intellectuals. You go to the best schools in the country and there, in contrast, the immense majority of students are the children of professionals and intellectuals, while very few of them are the children of people in the poor *barrios*. Well, I gave you all that data.

Now we're improving everything we've done in education. Of the 16,000 students in the art-instruction schools who attended excellent institutions with excellent reputations, the social and racial mix is much more satisfactory than the historical average, and not just in dance, where one ethnic group may have more facility for that activity, but also in music, in drama, in painting – in all areas of artistic expression. And we are very pleased with that. In the integrated courses for young people, which were designed for those who've left school and are unemployed, the application of this new concept of 'study as work' has led to over 113,000 students being now in school. There are new schools for the medical specialties in which our country is becoming better known every day. We have created hundreds of computer clubs, polytechnic academies for computer studies with tens of thousands of young people, and a prestigious university of information science that has over 8,000 students.

If we have to 'rationalize' [i.e., lay off, suspend] somebody because the number of employees is cut in X activity, we pay him his salary and send him off to school, although always on a voluntary basis. In our particular conditions, it costs more to produce something inefficiently, such as sugar cane, than it does to pay the worker 100 per cent of his salary.

How many students are there in Cuba?

At the current time there are over 600,000 students in our universities, in all the branches of science. Citizens who are qualifiable and requalifiable [i.e., those susceptible to training and retraining because of a generally positive attitude towards education] can move from one activity to another and be able to do many things. Of those students, over 90,000 used to be youngsters who were neither in school nor at work – many of them from disadvantaged backgrounds, you might say, who are getting excellent results today in their university studies. There are currently 958 university centres. There are 169 municipal centres [campuses], which are under the Ministry of Higher Education; there are eighty-four university centres on former sugar-cane *centrales*; eighteen in prisons, which is something totally new; and 169 municipal university centres for public-health studies, 1,352 in polyclinics, health units and blood banks, where people study in various degree programmes related to public health. And there are almost 100,000 teachers of higher education, counting both full-time and adjunct faculty. Many people who worked in the bureaucratic apparatus of sugar-cane *centrales* and other places are giving classes today, they're adjunct professors. Between the two categories, students and teachers – and I'm not talking about the other people who work in the universities – there are about 600,000 people.

20

President Jimmy Carter's Visit

Torrijos and the Panama Canal issue – Carter and the Mariel crisis –
First encounters – Presidents of the United States – The Varela Project –
Change the constitution? – The response

In 2002 you invited former American president Jimmy Carter, who later
won the Nobel Peace Prize, to visit Cuba. What was it that motivated that
invitation?
First, I had always had a high opinion of Carter as a man of honour, an
ethical man. His policies towards Cuba were constructive, and he was one
of that country's most honest presidents. He was ethical, moral. I was
remembering the time, back in 1976, when he had that famous interview in
Playboy magazine,[1] in which he answered in a very healthy way.

Are you a reader of Playboy?
No, but since a very interesting interview with Carter came out in it, I read
it. They asked him about everything, even whether he had always been
faithful to his wife or had ever strayed, and he answered, 'Well, in my
mind . . .'[2] He was honest enough to say that. Carter was incapable of
inventing a lie. So, I'll tell you, I sensed in Carter, even before he was elected,
a man of ethical principles based on sincere religious beliefs.

During his presidency, from 1977 to 1981, were there no particular crises?
No . . . When I realized that he was going to win the election in 1976,
there were important problems pending, such as Panama and the risk that
Torrijos,[3] who was a very determined man, a very patriotic man, might take
some action, because more than once he had said publicly that if the Canal
was not returned to Panama he was going to take it by force. I perfectly

understood the consequences that such an action might have had – I had great sympathy for Torrijos' patriotic struggle, and we were in contact. He was one of those who, with the support of several Caribbean states, fought to help Cuba break out of its isolation when all relations were broken off.

Torrijos was demanding the return of the Canal and a fair agreement on the issue. I realized from Carter's statements, his speech – I didn't know him well at all, but you get used to sizing up people from a distance, from certain traits – that the possible future president of the United States was an honourable man. But I also saw that Torrijos, with those statements of his, might find himself committed to some drastic action that would've been a disaster for a country as small as Panama ... So I took the liberty of suggesting that he wait for the results of the elections in the US, that he be patient.

Ford[4] was still the president of the United States. Gerald Ford was not aggressive [i.e., combative or anti-Cuban], but he was there temporarily, so to speak – provisionally, after Nixon. Actually, I told Torrijos two things: 'I'm convinced that Carter is going to win the election' – you could draw that conclusion from the conjunction of circumstances at the time – and also, 'He's a man who in my opinion will be capable of understanding the problem; he's somebody you can come to an agreement with over the Canal.' That's the truth. I told him that more than once ... He told that story himself; I'm just telling you something that he told one day.

That Torrijos himself told?
That's right. Or rather, he didn't tell what I said; he told what I'd told him about the idea of seizing the Canal by force, and he even expressed his thanks in a visit he made here to Cuba.

I perceived in that man, in Carter, a man of integrity. Later, he didn't just win the election, he had a better attitude towards Cuba; he was ready for change. It's to him that we owe the [American] Interests Office.[5]

That office was created at that time, during Carter's presidency?
That's right; that's exactly when. The problem of territorial waters had also come up, the 200 miles and all that. We were fishing twelve miles off the US and Canadian coastlines. We had defended the right to [control] 200 miles [of ocean waters] out of solidarity with Chile, Peru and the countries of the Third World. It turns out that once we had an excellent fishing fleet we had no ocean to fish in. One of our main fishing grounds was the waters near

the territory of the United States. So we discussed that – Carter was even willing to discuss the agreements over maritime borders, and was disposed to give permission for us to go on fishing, just as Canada had. Although, of course, those permissions were pretty thoroughly discussed, quite limited, and they had other requirements that made things difficult – raised the quotas, the cost.

The Torrijos–Carter agreements, several of the measures, the creation of the American Interests Office, all of that was positive – all those were positive steps taken by Carter. There was one difficult moment back then, which was the Angolan war, which had been going on since 1975, but Carter was a man who wanted to fix the problems between the US and Cuba.

But then came the Mariel problem, right?
Right. That happened in 1980 – we've talked about that issue. But Mariel was halted, precisely because Carter was in office; he'd behaved well, generally speaking, and we didn't want an obstinate position on our part to contribute to a win by Reagan and the extreme Right. The problem in Iran had already taken place,[6] with the unnecessary attempt to free the US embassy personnel by force and the consequent loss of life and the bloody war. And the Mariel events – well, they were due to the people that got into the embassies with total impunity and the support from outside.

Into the Peruvian embassy, no?
There were two; Peru and Venezuela. The embassies even sent everybody back home, on orders from abroad, but then they decided to recall some of them that they'd already sent away, [they decided] to pick them up and bring them back to the embassies . . . which there weren't many of back then, because there weren't many Latin American nations that had relations with us. Then, a gang of delinquents drove a bus through the fence at the Peruvian embassy, and [the embassy] took them in. A policeman was killed.

The next day we withdrew the escort that was guarding the embassy, and people immediately realized what that meant – lumpen poured into the embassy grounds. It meant they could go to the United States without a visa, with the badge of 'political refugee'. They filled the embassy. And there, propaganda fooled Carter; he was made to believe that the 'enslaved populace' was seeking the freedom and liberty of the United States, when in reality the people who had swarmed the embassy were lumpen, who would never have been given visas.

Only lumpen?
The vast majority – there's always one or two who aren't.

There were thousands of them inside, right?
About 10,000.

Ten thousand! There couldn't possibly have been space . . .
You're right – there wasn't room for another person. And that's when Carter had the bad idea of saying that they'd be received in the United States 'with open arms'. And that was the beginning of Mariel. The same thing that happened in Camarioca. [See Chapter 16, 'The Emigration Crises'.]

Carter, who'd taken a pretty hard hit with what had happened in Iran, at that point made what I consider, really, to have been an error. The Adjustment Act was in force at the time, as it still is today.

Did you remind him of that when he was here?
You can't do that. It was one more thing that caused him to lose the re-election . . . First, Iran . . . The fact is, that weakened Carter a great deal. Carter as a candidate for a second term had a failure working against him, he'd sent an expedition to Iran . . .

And that military expedition he'd sent to recover the American hostages in the Tehran embassy failed; a helicopter went down . . .
That's right, and Carter also – maybe even worse – had to deal with double-digit inflation, oil prices through the roof, and that led to a strengthening of the Right, Reagan's people.

Kennedy's brother, the senator, was a Democratic candidate and he had been sweeping the primaries – a very influential person at the time, a very good communicator.

Edward, right?
Edward. He was a legend. So despite the Chappaquiddick disaster,[7] the car accident the girl drowned in, he was picking up enormous strength within the Democratic Party. The Iran situation interrupted that process, and suddenly the people on the Right began to gain strength. Carter became the weakest candidate. I'm convinced that the only person who might have defeated Reagan at that time was Ted Kennedy. The Chappaquiddick episode was already pretty much forgotten. Clinton had a similar scandal –

not because of its nature, but in terms of people's exploitation of it – although he concluded his term.

Are you referring to the Monica Lewinsky affair?
Yes, and the most regrettable thing about it is that this one [George W. Bush] was elected Clinton's successor, and elected, on top of that, by fraud.

The Cubans stopped the Mariel exodus so as not to create problems for Carter during the re-election, then?
That's right. Listen, when we stopped the Mariel boatlift, we could have discussed the Adjustment Act, for example, but we didn't, because we didn't want to waste time and damage Carter during the election campaign. We even solved a problem created by the United States itself: the plane hijackings. Because as I told you, when hijackers came into Cuba with planes they'd hijacked in the United States, we gave them longer and longer sentences, up to twenty years in prison.

And that was when you decided to return all hijackers of American planes? . . .
The [long] sentences in Cuba didn't stop the hijackers. So, Carter was out in January 1981, and Reagan came in. The first time we had returned hijackers was 18 September 1980, under the Carter administration.

Really, with Carter we did *two* things: we stopped the Mariel boatlift and we returned the first two hijackers, who unfortunately were Cubans – some of the ones who'd entered the United States illegally. And then had come back! Because the same ones, sometimes, they'd divert a plane to come back, no matter what the sentences were . . . But we did that only with Carter, because he had a more constructive attitude.

I think they were sentenced to forty years. But we'd issued public warnings that that would be our policy, because, really, when an American plane with passengers aboard would appear, the risk of a disaster was always there. But the jail time wasn't a deterrent – it was clear that only returning the hijackers would solve the problem, but [the Americans] never returned them [to us, in reciprocity]; instead, they practically encouraged hijackers and never punished them. Despite that, we made the decision to turn them over to the American authorities. That's the real story; that's the facts.

You never felt that Carter was overly hostile towards Cuba . . .
Carter was a man who I realized, as I said, despite being the leader of a hateful empire, was a humane man; he wasn't a murderer or genocidal. The things I read by him, his statements, his interviews showed that he was a good, decent man – as decent and honourable as anyone can be who's governing a country with so many interests, so many privileges, so many prerogatives, and so much power.

And so many pressures.
Even in the middle of a Cold War. But I'd say that he was the best president of all those I've known, irrespective of the opinion I have of each of the others . . . I have an opinion about Kennedy, about Clinton. All of them I have to have some opinion about, since every day I'm reading news and cables, not to mention facing the empire's hatred and hostility.

You've had every president since Eisenhower, in fact, as adversaries, or, at any rate, as presidents of a country with the most difficult relations with Cuba.
We are very passionate people, but we harbour no hatred, which is another thing. I don't know what hatred is born out of – it might just be part of human nature. There are people who are capable of being more serene, while others are very passionate. You can feel contempt, disdain, you can have a terrible opinion about a political system, but not hatred of *people*.

Out of doctrine, we do not harbour hatred. You have to have a certain conception of what it is to be human, and the other thing is personalizing problems, blaming a man who may have been led into a certain position and can't do anything about it – may not even be able to be honest.

In that great, colossal country, in that great, colossal empire, like the Roman Empire, which had some intelligent, brilliant emperors, and others who were . . . Well, there was one who, as Suetonius tells it, made his horse a consul.[8]

The emperor Caligula.
People know more or less the entire history of Rome – or what's said to be the history of Rome, because history is also full of anecdotes.

There are presidents of the United States who are different: some of them have boasted of never reading a book, or more than one, anyway; others have read very little, and others have read a great deal. John Kennedy, for example, was a man who'd read a great deal; he was an educated man, and he wrote his famous book *Profiles in Courage*.[9] He had fought, too, in the Second World War, and commanded a PT boat in the Pacific, and he'd saved some of his buddies in action – he was decorated.

And you would include Carter among the educated, well-read presidents?
In my opinion, Carter was as honest as one could be while holding the position of president of the United States. We must remember, too, that he inherited the legacy of the Vietnam War, which had eaten up almost all the [country's] money, $500 billion dollars – gold reserves had dropped from $30 billion dollars in troy ounces to $10 billion, when gold was at $35 a troy ounce. That had led Nixon to suspend the gold standard for US currency in 1971, thereby unilaterally violating the Bretton Woods accords[10] and beginning the policy of free issuance of dollars without gold to back it up. Gold rose – that was associated with the oil crisis: people wanted gold because it was safe; they had no faith in paper money, so an ounce of gold rose to $300, or more, and the 10 billion that was in the vault turned into 300 billion, in terms of paperback dollars. At the time of Bretton Woods, in 1944, US reserves had stood at $30 billion, at the price of the time, which was $35 dollars an ounce. There have been phenomena like that that people forget about – so many are forgotten.

But I'll tell you, I always had a good opinion of Carter. You asked me what he was like. Where I met him. That was at the funeral of Trudeau in early October 2000, when Pierre Trudeau died – he'd been a close friend and an extraordinary figure.[11]

He'd been prime minister of Canada and always maintained good relations with Cuba, despite US pressure.
That's right – he was a noble man. I remember he came [to Cuba] when his son was just three or four months old, the son who as an adult died in an accident,[12] not long ago. It was tragic.

We took Trudeau out to a little key that I used to go to all the time, where the only thing there was the lighthouse-keeper's house – an old place, pretty much abandoned, over 150 years old, or almost 150. A roof had been put on it, and [Trudeau] slept there with his wife and baby. Outside the house, down by the sea, we talked a lot. He was a man I had real affection for. He came to Cuba more than once. He was an outdoorsman, a sportsman, he liked to paddle down rivers; he had a bathyscaphe, one of those things, and he took it off the coast of Greenland to look for the remains of the *Lusitania*.[13] He was the kind of man who liked nature, a very healthy man. In Canada, Carter might have been able to be like Trudeau; in the US, that wasn't possible.

You went to Trudeau's funeral and met Carter there, then?
That's right, in Ottawa, in October 2000. I'd already met [Carter]; I'm not sure whether I'd run into him at some point somewhere else. After his presidency, he continued his policies, the foundations and other academic, social and political initiatives. As I told you, his ethics were born not out of political theory, as happens with many of us, but rather from his religious beliefs.

Carter is a Protestant minister, isn't he?
Yes.[14] So, we saw each other at Trudeau's funeral, and we talked. Oh! – I'd seen him one other time, I think at an inauguration, earlier, when Carlos Andrés Pérez was sworn in in January 1989.

In Venezuela.
It was the second inaugural, because Carlos Andrés remained active and was elected president for a second time. That time I met Carter there in Caracas, and I spoke with him, we conversed a bit, and I also spoke with Robert Kennedy's widow, because the Kennedys, the family, after the assassination of John Kennedy, made contact with us and we developed really friendly relations and exchanges. That's another proof that one can't be swept along by hatred.

And did John Kennedy's son not also come [to Cuba]?
In one of his last trips, Kennedy's son came down, the one who'd been a little boy . . .

John-John Kennedy, who was two or three years old when his father was killed.
He was editing a magazine, *George Magazine*. He had dinner with me, we talked for two or three hours, and a short time later, in July 1999, there was the crash of the plane he was piloting at night – the accident in which he and his wife died. That was a sad tragedy. Well, the Kennedys have been through quite a few.

Quite a few, yes.

But on that occasion they were in Venezuela [at the inaugural], and I met Robert Kennedy's widow there; I've also met a sister, Eunice,[15] the one who was married to Sargent Shriver, the man who organized the Peace Corps in 1961, and I know some of Bobby Kennedy's children.

So that was where you first found yourself with Carter, in Venezuela?

That's right. That time, in Caracas, in a pair of twin towers where he was staying. We talked for a while, because he wanted to straighten out, to a degree, the relations between our two countries. Some of his people visited us in Cuba, but there was always a demand. There was the situation in Angola, and the revolutionary struggle in El Salvador – that is, problems and situations with regard to which we couldn't make any concessions whatsoever, but there was a man there who wanted to change the policy with Cuba, and that man was Carter.

It was the period of double-digit inflation in the US, which was a consequence of the Vietnam War, as I said, of the cost of it. Then there was the Islamic revolution that took place in 1979 – all of that had an influence afterwards, as I said, on his not getting re-elected – and the most powerful policeman in the Middle East was defeated, one might say, by a mass movement ... An extraordinary example of the fact that the people, at certain moments, can defeat the most powerful army on the basis of emotions, ideas and heroism, and practically without a shot being fired. The case of Iran is a historic example.

It was disastrous for Carter, and it cost him his re-election.

Disastrous! Well, Carter was already having a hard time. It was disastrous for the election of any Democratic candidate. I remember, as I was saying, that at the time Edward Kennedy had emerged. Given the problems that had hurt Carter – which were, I repeat, first, what had happened in Iran, the vain rescue attempt, in an operation that really, who knows how they managed to convince him to do it, because Carter was an intelligent politician, they may have talked him into a Girón[Bay of Pigs]-type operation, something like that – anyway, that military failure hurt him, and he was the man who was up for re-election, so he lost. Second, double-digit inflation combined with an explosion in oil prices; we mustn't forget that he was almost coming into office when the price rose to $35 a barrel, the same price as today [January 2003].

413

All those factors came together, then, and during the primaries, a strong candidate began to sweep the field, and that was Edward Kennedy, a man, without question, of great talent. People even said that he was the most political [i.e., politically savvy] – family members have said this – of the whole Kennedy family. So he was sweeping the field. But when the problems came up in foreign affairs that we've mentioned – every time there's a foreign policy problem – this is practically a law of physics – opinion tends to unite, and that very thing began to happen in the midst of the primaries when Kennedy was coming on very strong – so then all of a sudden, the situation changed, and public opinion unified around the president, Carter.

All those events, in general, tend to become magnified, not just because of their importance *per se* but also because they have such strong repercussions within the United States. The hostage situation was important, but it was a problem that could have been solved; it's true that it wasn't going to be solved in two days or two minutes – we're talking about a world power being humiliated, and reacting with arrogance.

It makes the superpower look a little ridiculous.
It had great repercussions, and it changed the trend in the election, the way things were moving. So then Carter, who was running against Edward Kennedy and was behind in the polls, in the Democratic Party primaries, began to gain ground, and he became the candidate. At that moment, however, Carter could not win that second election. There was a chance, though, that it could have been won by Kennedy, curiously enough – I say curious because it was Kennedy who'd nominated Carter, and it was a brilliant speech.

The man who might have been able to win against Reagan in 1980 was named Edward Kennedy. There are a lot of people who don't even talk about that, or haven't thought very much about the subject. Still, it's the thesis I maintain. I remember those days very well.

Then came Reagan, and if Nixon waged war without taxes, Reagan went about rearming the country with dollar bills fresh off the press. Public debt soared – exactly what Bush is doing now, and it's leading the world to disaster.

Later, we got to know Carter better, when he visited Cuba. We were also aware of his vast experience, his keen mind, his diplomatic skills, and I learned, too, about some things that aren't so clear for him, the points where there may be a little naiveté.

When you invited him to Cuba, what was the reason for that invitation?
Well, we'd had that encounter in Venezuela, and then in Canada; we'd talked, and I'd told him that he should visit us someday. Because really, when you know a country only by what's written about it – and then by what its *adversaries* have written about it – then you're talking about virtually dogmatic ideas about what kind of country it is . . . I said, 'Well, no, direct contact is better; let him get to know us a little.'

There was always news about him, his activities, and when I went to Canada for Trudeau's funeral, we were there at one of the ceremonies – I think at a church, or before going into the church – and I stood talking with him for a few minutes, we shook hands, I reminded him of the conversations we'd had in Caracas, and I said to him, 'We're still waiting for you to come to visit us.' I reminded him of that again. And he said, 'Yes, I'll go soon.' And sure enough, one day there came news that he'd made the decision to visit us.

And of course, as we do with all our visitors, we asked him to make his own programme, his own agenda, we asked him to decide what he wanted to talk about, we could talk about anything he wanted, and he would be able to talk to anyone he wanted, too, anybody, and at the university: 'Speak there, speak your mind, talk about your ideas,' which are not in the slightest, not at all, at all, similar to ours. They're two different concepts of life, of society, of the system of production, of the political system, ideas about the existence of parties and just about everything else.

Carter's speech at the university – I watched it live on CNN, and it struck me as quite daring, quite honest; he talked about his disagreements very directly and frankly. Did that surprise you?
At the university I was with him. He made a strong speech there at the university, and some of the students debated with him. When he finished I got up, went over, and shook hands with him. We were going afterwards to a baseball game, and the stadium was full, totally packed. So we got there and I convinced him – that was possible because I managed to first convince the head of his escort. I said to him, 'Listen, we're going out on the field.' We wanted him to throw the first ball. So I say to Carter, 'We're going to go out on the field,[16] but I'd like you and I to go out together, alone.' There were 60,000 people there.

Without bodyguards or anything.

No, no, we went out by ourselves. I'd already tested the waters, to see whether the head of his escort was a man who could be convinced [to let him]. It wasn't easy, but finally I gave my escort an order, and they had to follow it, because you say, 'That's an order!' and they have to obey it. So then we discussed it with them and I say to my escort, 'Listen, I've managed to convince Carter's escort; we're going to go out alone. When we come out of that dugout over there, we'll walk about 100 yards, 100 metres to home plate, in front of the crowd – *alone*.'

To the middle of the field.

To the pitcher's mound. There was a huge crowd of people up in the stands, and we were all by ourselves. And later I joked about it with him, because quite a few people were pretty mad about the things he'd said at the university.

Let's talk about that.

And there were debates. I kept talking with him afterwards. Everything perfectly normal, but at the end of the conversation we had here [in Cuba], a friendly, rational exchange of ideas, of opinion, I told him, 'Listen, it's a good thing all those people at the baseball stadium were in that stadium while your speech was being broadcast live and didn't hear it, because if they hadn't been, we'd have had ourselves quite a headache.' Because those people greeted us with tremendous applause, such happiness, such tremendous friendship. But I told him, 'It's a good thing those people didn't hear your speech at the university.' Because that speech caused quite a ruckus here.

Carter's speech was broadcast live here?

Live, the whole speech. It's that time after time, we've said, 'Anybody who wants to come, come . . . You're welcome to come.' We'd fill the plaza even for Bush . . . Because he goes to Miami and makes a speech . . .

You're also inviting President Bush to come down here?

We told Bush that we're willing to debate, we'll have the entire population out. We've also invited all the militants, all the leaders, all the major players.

Let me tell you that the vast majority of the people of Cuba support the Revolution unwaveringly. If it's a question of ideas, we're willing to debate, in the Plaza de la Revolución, with anybody that wants to come down here and have a debate and try to convince the people. If they need them, we'll put up every loudspeaker in the country and give them all the time they need to explain things to the people, and to debate. Because it's not a question of living by dogmas, it's a question of defending what you think on the basis of arguments, reasoning.

That is, President George W. Bush himself could come down here and set forth his arguments and debate. The Cubans would allow that?
The Cubans would. But the Americans won't let him.

No, they probably won't.
But if they want to they can. Right here, we'll fill the [Plaza de la Revolución], and they'll be safer than in Washington, because this is a people with a political culture. This is not a fanatical people; it has not been educated in fanaticism or hatred. If we were a people educated in hatred we would be nothing. There can be constant and ever-increasing strength in a cause only to the extent to which it's based on ideas and convictions, not on fanaticism.

Never has the Revolution blamed the American people, although at a certain point a vast majority of American citizens were persuaded that everything that was said against Cuba was true, that we were a threat to the security of the United States, and so on and so on. Cuba welcomes Americans with the greatest of respect and with no insults or affronts whatsoever.

And with the greatest safety and security?
With the greatest friendship. Because hatred has not been sowed here. It's stupid to blame a citizenry for what it's been made to believe, whether through the media, lies or defamation.

[We have] never preached hatred against anyone. This is not a country of fanatics. You talk about safety and security. Here, that safety and security can be offered to an American visitor because it's the entire nation, not just the security forces – it's the entire open-minded nation that cares for and respects the visitor, discusses, listens respectfully.

We have two examples: first when Pope John Paul II was in the Plaza de la Revolución in 1998. The pope gave his speeches with absolute freedom there. What he preached was not congruent with the philosophy and doctrines of the Revolution, regardless of the opinion that you may have about the person and merits of the pope, who was an extraordinary figure, no question about that. His own philosophy, he explained that to the people, the historical reasons for his very tough position against Socialism, but there he was, on Cuban soil, surrounded by consideration and respect . . .

There was also, in Santiago de Cuba, an activity with the pope, and the entire town was there, and one of the people who spoke gave a hard, hard speech . . . and people began leaving, little by little, and the plaza just emptied out, no more than 10 per cent of the people stayed. I saw it on television; the cameras had to find angles to keep from showing the empty plaza . . . Raúl was there, I asked him to go to Santiago. But not one shout, no heckling. The people had been told, 'Not one sign, not one poster, not one word, one shout against [the pope], no matter if you're against what he's saying.'

This is a nation with a political education, and the people understood that that was the way [to act on the occasion of the pope's visit]. The pope was welcomed not just by the believers, he was received by the entire nation. What's more, I myself spoke on television twice, because we had to guarantee that the people understood his personality, his history, his solidarity with the poor – in a word, who he was, and what he was.

Which is why I told Carter, 'We can fill the plaza – come down here and persuade the people. Convince them that the Revolution is no good, and why it's no good; put forth your arguments, debate us.' We brought the people together and we put every television set in the country at the disposal of the president, all the channels, so that people could hear the debate. 'Those are the conditions you may expect when you visit us, if you accept our invitation,' [we told him].

You've referred to Carter's speech at the university, a speech that was broadcast live, in which he alluded to the Varela Project,[17] and from what I've read, it's an initiative based on an article in the Cuban Constitution that stipulates that laws may be initiated not just by Parliament but also by the citizens, on the condition that it be the will of at least 10,000 people – they can introduce a bill in congress.

An initiative of that sort was signed apparently by over 11,000 citizens, and President Carter alluded to that case in your presence; the print media published his speech in its entirety and so I, about that, wanted to ask you: do you consider President Carter's allusion to that Varela Project a lack of tactfulness, a discourtesy, an insult on his part?

Not in the slightest. He came to Cuba, as I say, he decided what his programme was to be, he met everyone he wanted to meet, in absolute liberty – there was no insult. How are we supposed to tell Carter to come down to Cuba and then impose limitations on him, here and there, about what he can say? So no, in no way was it offensive.

What is your opinion of the Varela Project?
You can either analyse that initiative politically or you can analyse it legally. I want to talk about it with no passion of any kind.

We might say that that was the latest 'brilliant idea' in a series of dozens the United States has had, or the policy of the United States. The latest – just another in a long series – which consisted of taking Félix Varela, who was a Cuban priest, a progressive, advanced thinker[, and using him for their own purposes]. Varela was an enemy, for example, of slavery, he had a series of ideas that we might call, for the times in which he lived, very humane, very humanistic. He was one of the first to talk about [Cuban] independence, because back then people didn't talk much about independence – I'm talking about the early nineteenth century. He was a prestigious intellectual, back in the times when Cuba was a colony, a noble man, one of those men who harboured patriotic sentiments among the very isolated groups of citizens who shared those views, because I'll tell you, we had a slave society, with hundreds of thousands of slaves.

In that century there emerged in Cuba a number of brilliant thinkers – José de la Luz y Caballero, for example, who was a great pedagogue. Among that group there were several figures who spoke out for certain changes, or autonomy,[18] or certain improvements within the colonial system that our country was suffering under. Varela was one of those Cuban intellectuals.

Later, Varela emigrated to the United States. [He was] a very respected, revered figure there among the great thinkers. Martí was the culmination of that thinking, and there were many more – but Varela was one of the first. In the Grand Hall at the University of Havana we have the ashes of Varela, one of the precursors of a philosophy that then gradually evolved into abolitionism and a struggle for independence. That is the story of Varela, a beautiful human story.

But recently, the idea has emerged that Varela should be canonized. We respect and admire Varela, but we see him as a civic figure, a lay figure. Since there were certain conflicts with the Catholic Church – we talked about this – at the beginning, in the early years of the Revolution, the United States tried to use that to create religious opposition [to the Revolution], present the image of a revolution opposed to religion. There was an attempt on the part of the empire, too, to use the Church.

I didn't know that the Church wanted to canonize Padre Varela.
When the idea of canonizing Varela came up, many of us were suspicious; we began to see an attempt to turn a respected, admired lay figure into a religious figure, into a saint. I mean, I wouldn't necessarily object to that, but – and I say this with all respect – a lot of other Cubans would have to be canonized, too.

For example, they'd have to canonize Che, because if you're going to sanctify patriots because of their goodness, their spirit of sacrifice, their ability to be a martyr in the cause of humanity and die for a cause, then there would be a lot of people to sanctify. Many of the combatants at the Moncada barracks also were of one religion or another and died fighting against tyranny, died fighting against a repressive regime, and others died fighting for their country against the imperialist attack at Playa Girón.

I don't want to stick my nose into the Church's business, but I was a little suspicious, as you may imagine, and yet we never made the slightest protest, we never questioned a thing about it. Really, Varela is a lay figure, a patriot, and he should remain that way. Are we going to turn Varela, who is a figure that belongs to all of us, into a saint that belongs to just one church, however respected and respectable it may be? That wouldn't make us very happy.

But to return to your question, the Varela Project thing, the attempt to use him against the Revolution, was just another brilliant idea, as I say, a *cynical* idea, the latest in a series, although every one of them has been given tremendous publicity.

I've had to go on a bit – to say things that people need to hear. I thought I needed to let people know who Varela is, which is why I've taken some time [to talk about him]. Now I can give you details that have more to do with your question about that so-called Varela Project.

Are you very upset when the opposition uses the name of figures such as Padre Varela, or José Martí?
What you're calling the 'opposition', if you're referring to the people in Miami who've used Martí's name, is actually a terrorist mafia. As for Varela, this historical figure, respected by all Cubans, has been used for this latest manoeuvre. Just as the name of José Martí, our country's most admired,

most sacred personality, has been used for no less than the name of an illegal, subversive, destabilizing radio station.

The station headquartered in Miami?
The biggest lie factory that's been built in modern memory. And that same name has been used for an equally illegal TV station that used to broadcast from a balloon about 10,000 feet up in the air, and now from a plane that flies almost into Cuban air space, trying to poison international public opinion. And these are official organs of the United States.

Getting back to the Varela Project: what's the Cuban parliament going to do with that petition signed by 11,000 people? Is it going to have any response?
You were talking about a legal aspect, about the fact that 10,000 signatures could initiate the law-making process.

A bill.
A bill. Our constitution, I imagine like all the others, establishes who can begin an initiative to propose something. So then, there are a lot of people who have initiatives. For example, people's organizations, unions, women, young people, students, members of congress, government officials, ministers . . . That is, there are countless people who are able to propose a law, an initiative aimed at passing a new law. Almost all constitutions make allowances for that. I can't tell you what that process is like in the United States, for example, or in Mexico, or in the other Latin American countries, but our constitution says that 10,000 people can propose a new law. All right, so that constitutional mechanism is the legal instrument on which the manoeuvre is based.

So what happened? People have been talking about this for a year now – it must be at least a year that they've been talking, trying to gather the 10,000 signatures. And there's a story about that that I'm not particularly interested in talking about, but I should add that there was a little bit of everything there.

In collecting the signatures?
I'm telling you, promises of visas for travel to the United States for people whom visas aren't given to for one reason or another. And all of that backed by organizations in the United States, with financial resources . . . There was

money there, just like in regular election campaigns, which is something that disappeared in Cuba a long time ago.

You're saying that some of those signatures were bought?
There was a little of everything – bribes, too. And what's more, some of the signatures have to be checked, because you have to check to make sure that what's-his-name has the right to vote; you have to verify . . . Eleven thousand – that's not many, is it? Eight *million* [signatures] were gathered for the revolutionary initiatives.

In an official election?
No, not an election – but after Bush's speech in Miami on 20 May 2002, when he practically demanded that we change our constitution and abolish the Socialist system in Cuba, and change our laws, conditions of all kinds – a real harangue for his friends in Miami, who are the voters that made the difference in his presidential election, as the entire world knows, just as they know how that fraudulent election of 2000 was decided – dirty tricks, political dirty tricks, because even the dead voted to elect Bush. Whole neighbourhoods of Afro-Americans couldn't exercise their right to vote because they weren't allowed to get to the polling stations . . . There were technical tricks – they changed the order of names on the ballot, so one of the candidates who hadn't got 100 votes in one precinct, got thousands, just because of the technical change in the order of names on the ballot. There were people who tried to change their vote when they realized what had happened, and their ballots were nullified. It's been calculated that there were no fewer than 40,000 or 50,000 votes that weren't cast, or weren't counted, because of all this.

Which would have given the victory to Al Gore.
When Bush won by just a few thousand votes. After that colossal fraud, new cabinet secretaries and key positions in the State Department, even on the National Security Council, were given to figures associated with the Miami terrorist mafia that gave Bush his spurious victory. That same gentleman who was appointed for a while to be under-secretary for Latin America . . .

Otto Reich?
That's right. A man – we've already talked about him – linked to the dirty war in Nicaragua when the US flouted the decisions of the International

Court in The Hague, which had condemned the United States in 1987 for its constant aggressions against the Sandinista Revolution, when the United States violated its own laws, when the Irangate scandal occurred, and all those other iniquities that Reich was complicit in. History cannot overlook all these things.

Really, it was those things that decided the presidential election in the US. It just so happens that it's not totally that they have so much power; it's that luck also played a role in making Florida the state where the election was decided. And it was decided by no more than about 1,000 votes, a thousand and something, because later the military votes came in, from soldiers overseas, and Bush won.

There was not even an intelligent strategy on the part of his opponents. At no time did it occur to them to call for a repeat of the election [a second election], even when they had every legal basis for doing so, and no one could have said that that wasn't democratic.

They did ask for a recount.
What they asked for was a recount, but what they should have called for was a second election in those [precincts] where there had been irregularities, which everybody in the world knew had happened. Is it possible that a political system as 'perfect' and as 'brilliant' as the American democracy can't repeat the elections in some district? – not in the entire United States. How much would that cost?

All it would take is for a few districts [to revote] and the difference in favour of Al Gore would have been tens of thousands of votes – when they could finally vote. Not to mention the fact that the vote is very restricted [in the US] for the poorest people, the Afro-Americans, because they're the ones who are sent to prison most, for one reason or another, and that deprives them of their right to vote. It's the poorest people, who have the fewest opportunities to go to college and advance into important positions in private corporations or state governments. And once you've been in prison once . . .

You lose the right to vote.
In many countries, a person in prison has no right to vote; you lose your right for a period of time. In the United States you lose it for life, in many states – I can't say that it's in all of them, but in a lot of them you lose it for life. But in Florida, in the 2000 election, they didn't even let the people who had the right to vote, do so.

And that's the way the election was decided in the United States. Those who went from here to Miami, in 1959 to 1961, had been world champions in electoral fraud back in the time of Batista; they introduced things [into the US] they hadn't ever had in the United States, such as getting the dead to vote . . . And that's the way Bush won the election.

But what, specifically, have the Cubans done with the Varela Project?
Leaving aside questions about the signatures, the legitimacy of X number of signatures – leaving all that aside and assuming that what we actually have is 11,000 people with the legal and constitutional right to sign a petition, that petition was processed: the request was received, it was analysed by the pertinent committee in the National Assembly, and a response was given.

And what was the response?
I don't have the document here.

But in summary.
To give a short answer, the initiative was rejected. We rejected the idea of proposing a constitutional change,[19] with much more logic, I think I mentioned, if you take into account that a few weeks earlier, more than 8 million people, 99.05 per cent of all people eligible to vote, had signed a document and presented it to the National Assembly declaring that the Socialist nature of the Revolution was 'irrevocable'.

All the National Assembly's established rights would be respected except the right to revoke the Socialist nature of the Revolution, which is contained in that constitution. It was the response to the demand made by United States president George Bush in his speech on 20 May 2002 in Miami – I mentioned this earlier. The amendment was presented by all the people's organizations, signed by that number of citizens, in their own handwriting, because here everyone knows how to read and write.

So that, specifically, is the official response to the Varela Project.
That was the response not to the Varela Project, but to George Bush's insolent demand, which is more or less the same thing.

Do you think that that response, that type of response, is going to be accepted by your opponents?
We carried out an enormous mobilization as a response to those statements

by the president of the United States. It had nothing to do with the Varela Project – that would be killing butterflies with cannons. In a single day 8 million people marched, all across the country, in the largest mobilization the country had ever seen, and there's filmed proof of it.

Of course, the international media ignore that, with all the problems there are in the world . . . But for our people it was very important. What does it take in France to amend the constitution?

Well, at least two-thirds of both legislative chambers, meeting jointly, must approve it.
Who has the legal initiative in France, who can propose a change?

The government can propose an amendment and there can be a referendum, but nowhere does it say that citizens, signing a petition, can amend the constitution.
Well, so our constitution is more democratic than yours. Here many organizations, the unions, even citizens can propose, but 'propose' doesn't mean the law *has to be* passed along for debate in the National Assembly. It doesn't mean that the constitution of the republic has to be amended, much less when what's proposed is a change in the Socialist nature of the Revolution.

So, quite simply, the Varela Project was received by the [parliamentary] committee, the committee studied it, responded to it, and what happened is that [the project's] promoters refused to receive the response. It was all fodder for publicity. What they get for free, and in great abundance, is the possibility that the international media talk about them, but they're a virtual reality.

Any person can come to this country and see what happens in Cuba, what strength the mass organizations have and what strength the small groups of so-called dissidents have – who are, by the way, divided. This counter-revolutionary, pro-Yankee project has been more clever, more skilful in the sense that it calls for no terrorism and asks that the change be peaceful.

And it also denounces the blockade.
Of course. Today, really, there's nobody in this country who could get ten people to support the idea that the blockade should be continued, when for some time now, even in the United States, it's been fashionable to oppose the blockade.

But if you support all the rest, if you sign your name to every libellous statement, all the lies, and all the campaigns on which the blockade is based, and the justification of the blockade, you can oppose the blockade *in words*, while doing exactly what they need to try to justify the blockade, even if nobody in the world can justify it any longer. That's what I know, because I've asked . . .

What I mean to say is that this country is in the midst of a great battle, a decisive battle over fundamental issues. Other things are important only in relation to that one great battle. The magnification of this project has everything to do with a media campaign – something about which you know a great deal.

A campaign not just in the media, because the person who initiated this project, Osvaldo Payá,[20] was given the Sakharov Prize [for Freedom of Thought] for human rights, and he came to France to receive it, to Strasbourg. Many political analysts and some intellectuals, too, said he wouldn't be able to leave Cuba to receive his prize, but he did, and he went back pretty normally. And the Project also has the support of many political, union and religious sectors. Do you think that Europe is taking part in a campaign against Cuba?
Europe doesn't know anything about this – that's what I can say about that. The president of France even sent a message, because people had said that Payá wasn't going to go, that he hadn't been given permission and I don't know what other kind of things. That makes no sense, because as a general rule we let people travel. It's not important, but what *is* important is that all the leaders and all the ringleaders of all the counter-revolutionary groups, groups against the Revolution, are organized by the American Interests Office.

You can't imagine to what extent that American Interests Office intervenes in the internal affairs of our country – they call [the dissidents] in for meetings, they send them literature, they send them money, and with a dollar, you can buy a hundred litres of milk, which [one litre] is a child's daily quota [ration]. For one dollar, at the exchange rate of twenty-five pesos to the dollar, and at four litres of milk per peso.

All those so-called dissidents don't go to Miami, to be cured up there. If they can buy 100 litres of milk for a dollar – within certain limits, $100 will get you 2,500 pesos – and they don't pay rent, they don't pay taxes because they're not the owners of the places they live in; what they pay for rent is symbolic in those housing units in which occupants haven't been given title because the property is needed by factories or industries; their children receive the best educational services in the world for free, and excellent health services; their children are guaranteed a very, very long life expectancy, any kind of medical treatment, even heart surgery, open heart surgery or cardiovascular surgery, which might cost $50,000, or a heart transplant, which might cost $100,000, or a kidney or liver transplant, and the dissidents receiving Yankee dollars to buy whatever they want – that's a pretty sweet life.

No one has ever been asked, when they enter a hospital for treatment, whether they're a revolutionary, whether they're a supporter or not, whether they're a dissident or not. There may be cases in which someone is favoured because they've got dollars they get from up there, and that might cause a certain degree of corruption in the case of a product there's a scarcity of. But there's never been discrimination against this or that social category – never! I defy you to find proof of that! The so-called dissidents have all those guarantees, and those organizations [in Miami, etc.] send them $100. The Americans have reported how many millions of dollars they're going to send down here to help a handful of dissidents live a virtual, absolutely virtual life.

What one has to ask each and every one of them is what they've produced, where they work and what they work at, and how much money they receive from rewards. They write any old article – libellous articles – send them off to those media, to anti-Cuban Yankee broadcasters . . . Which is against the law – there are laws in force against that, but they're quite simply not enforced, because the state, the state's attorney, has the power to enforce them or not.

Nowhere in the world can you put yourself at the service of an enemy power; nowhere in the world can you work under the orders of a foreign government, whether you disguise it in one way or another or not. We have mountains of proof.

All those so-called dissidents are a virtual reality; as I've said, they don't exist – it's an insignificant number and, what's more, they're run by the American Interests Office.

There are divisions between them, because some of them say they want to negotiate with the government and others won't hear of it. But we aren't obliged – they'd have to throw us out, declare us imbeciles and incompetents if we sat down to listen to every complaint they had or opened a parliamentary debate just because a handful of people want us to – or it might even be 10,000 . . .

But 10,000 is what the constitution stipulates.
You're right. They have the right to present a law, and we, in this case, have rights [given us by] many millions of Cubans. But they refuse to take into account details [i.e., information] about irregularities: signatures repeated; sometimes surnames missing, etc. We all know this, but that's not the subject under discussion.

Our assumption has been that those signatures exist, that they're real, that every one of [the signatories] had the right to sign, that all [the signatures] were given freely, that there was no [monetary] interest involved, no favours, no quid pro quo, no visas for entry into the United States. We overlooked all that. Our assumption was that it was honest and above-board. They [the signatures] were treated in the appropriate legal manner and the parliamentary committee exercised its right, the absolutely legal and constitutional right that a committee exercises.

If Europe analyses its entire history and its constitutions and what's happened over there, then it won't be so astonished when a committee of the Cuban National Assembly makes a decision. There are many, many committees, and it was analysed by the appropriate committee, and not just two or three assembly members – it was dozens . . . We've observed our laws to the letter. Why so much surprise over these things?

That's all that's happened in this case – that's it. That's what's happened, that's the situation, since you were interested in knowing.

Señor Payá left and came back. Is he free?
He has his ways of attracting the attention of the international broadcast media: every day he finds some pretext. Often he didn't even submit the appropriate paperwork. They even look for any little pretext that will serve as fodder for publicity, and statements of all sorts. Each of them has his techniques.

The Cuban Commission on Human Rights published a document in January 2003 that said that as of that date there were 223 dissidents in Cuban jails.
Well listen, then, it appears that there are a little over 1 per cent of the 15,000 there once were, [after the Playa Girón invasion,] whom we set free. But there's more – we guaranteed them passage to the United States, every single one that passed through our prisons, more than 95 per cent, are up there, because that was the equivalent of a visa to enter the United States.

They were the ones that introduced them to all that – that inspired them . . .

Back then there were that many in prison, as I say. If they say there are now 203 in jail, then we ought to raise a monument to the Revolution.

Two hundred and twenty-three.

We could make a list of the thousands we've set free, including some, such as Rolando Cubela, for example, who'd received all those weapons to use against the Revolution; he was a student, he'd distinguished himself during the Batista era, I think he'd executed one of Batista's military officers; he'd been a guerrilla fighter for a while; we were all friends. But he was persuaded, at a certain point, and he started conspiring. He was arrested and sent to prison, but he wasn't there long.

Now – what was he tried and sentenced for? Up there [in the US], under a pretext, they trained him, they gave him a telescopic sight, they gave him everything – it was official, it wasn't forced or anything of the kind – for an attempt on my life. He wasn't in jail long; we set him free.

Dozens of individuals who've taken part in plans to assassinate me were set free, were sent out of the country, and a lot of them are still in the business, because it turned into a business, like a travel agency – they had an agency to plan assassination attempts. That's been the story. How many do they say – 202?

Two hundred and twenty-three.

Now, be assured that those people have broken laws – and another thing, if we'd tried every person who, in a conspiracy, in complicity with the American Interests Office and paid by the United States, had gone into the business of 'dissidence', if we'd sent all those people who've broken laws to prison, it wouldn't be 223, it would be a lot more. That number is really proof of the Revolution's generosity. There really aren't many – when the pope came there were more.

Did John Paul II ask you to free some prisoners?

Somebody gave the pope a list, unfortunately a very badly compiled list, because there were a lot of people on it who'd already been released. He was given the list at the end. The pope, in all the plans for his visit, never talked about the subject, and at the end, he presented a list, a terrible list, unfortunately. The people who presented us with it had no consideration for him – sometimes we'd have just a [first] name, [or] a surname, by which to identify the person on the pope's list and try to satisfy his request. But a lot of them had already been set free, and there were even some who'd already emigrated. The pope was given a bad list – and he'd never talked about any list.

We said, 'Well, we're willing . . .' The Vatican foreign secretary said, 'No, it doesn't matter, it doesn't have to be just prisoners who have motivations of a political nature.' We ourselves call them counter-revolutionaries, but we don't deny that counter-revolution is a political act, even if Jiménez de Asúa,[21] the great Spanish jurist, said it wasn't. He said that 'political prisoners' were those who were arrested for promoting revolutionary changes and advances in a society, and that those who fought to move the society backward were not political prisoners. I'd agree with him, but concepts are concepts. We've always used the word 'counter-revolution', but they've all insisted on being called political prisoners or prisoners because they were 'dissidents'. I maintain that they all broke the law, and that there are more of them yet. The Revolution has its laws, but out of generosity it doesn't always apply them, so it almost deserves a monument.

As we've been talking, an idea has come to me: ask the *compañeros* to get out the lists of all the people who were set free when they'd barely served half their sentences. And not just that – they were given the opportunity to work, almost without restriction, building social or economic facilities, and were paid a salary without deducting a thing, when there were thousands of them.

Right at the beginning of the Revolution, back in the days of Playa Girón and other terrorist actions, there were a tremendous number of counter-revolutionaries in prison. I met them, when a lot of them were on the Isle of Youth [formerly Isle of Pines]; I went by, they were there with picks, shovels, working; I went over to them, I practically mingled with the whole group. I've talked with a lot of them; we would even aid their families.

I'm going to ask that a study be done, a list, how many and through whom they were set free, sometimes through the Catholic Church in the United States. We'd say to [the Church], 'Get them a visa.' Because you'll understand that in this environment, it was hard for a counter-revolutionary to find a job and a place to live; people can be very hostile. So we decided, 'Let's let them leave Cuba,' and they'd get a visa for them. And there must have been tens of thousands of those cases, because there were some who'd served out their sentences, but some of the sentences had already been reduced; and later all of them, since they knew that they were owed favours, insisted.

The ones who were in prison – did the Cubans let them leave Cuba and go to the United States?

When there was no migration agreement with the United States, all the people who'd been in prison had the right to request a visa, and very few of them were rejected. The best dossier you could present for getting a visa to go to the United States is having been a counter-revolutionary and having been in prison in Cuba. Today there's a lottery, a draw – I find that a little strange, the idea of a lottery – and there's a quota of 20,000 people a year.

The answer I give – there may be 223; there may be 250 or 300 – is that none of them are in jail if they haven't broken a law . . .

There were four famous 'dissidents'.[22] The things they did . . . I, honestly, I almost complained to the Ministry of the Interior when they published the list of everything they'd done against the country: sabotaging investments, sending letters to investors, telling them their investments were going to be confiscated . . . I was indignant that they could do all those things. Then one day they were arrested . . . I mean, four people arrested, and they were given light sentences – don't think they were harsh, because the acts they were guilty of were serious; they were felonies.

During the height of the special period there were people who were very deliberately sabotaging the country's efforts. When they reached a certain extreme and there was no alternative, they were arrested, but the Ministry of the Interior didn't act out of fear, nor was it guided by a policy of repression – it has its powers, and it doesn't use severity, not at all.

Now, this is a Revolution that defends itself, and has always defended itself, and if it didn't it wouldn't be here, and it's not here, still existing, because we've got nuclear weapons, or because we're rich. We've resisted a blockade that's lasted forty-six years – the hostility, the aggression, the economic warfare, and on top of that a very difficult special period. No country would have been able to bear up under all that without the support of its people, without the consensus of its people, without political aware-ness. That's what I can say to those who accuse us of violating human rights, and of keeping what we call counter-revolutionaries and they call 'dissidents' in prison. That's my reply.

21

The Arrests of Dissidents in March 2003

James Cason in Havana – Meetings in the Cuban Interests Office in Washington – War against Cuba? – The Raúl Rivero case – The Valladares affair – The death penalty

To continue for a bit with what we were just talking about, I'd like to look back at the arrests of dozens of dissidents in March of 2003 and the execution of three men who hijacked a boat in April of that same year. I read Felipe Pérez Roque's statement and [a transcript of his] press conference,[1] and also your own speech on 1 May of that year, so, in a general way, I'm familiar with your explanations of those events.

The question is: why was the decision made to arrest the dissidents just then? I mean, before the boat hijackings and before the beginning of the Iraq War? What was it that motivated the Cuban authorities to arrest them at that particular moment? The first arrests came on 15 March, I believe.

None of that was discussed or planned previously on the part of the Cuban [government]. The United States government's macabre plans started coming one after another. The war in Iraq hadn't yet broken out, but Cuba was one of the possible targets of the surprise preventive attack announced by Bush, because they had classified Cuba as a terrorist state. Not long before, we'd heard the outrageous accusations by [John] Bolton[2] that we were carrying out research aimed at producing biological weapons, not to mention other shameless lies against us.

In the American Interests Office in Havana, people were working at full speed, complementing the plans laid out by Bush and his cronies to destabilize the country and the Revolution and find some pretext for an aggression [against us].

One of the factors that triggered [our action] was the arrival in Cuba in

November 2002 of James Cason – [whose appointment had been] announced in September of that same year – as head of the Interests Office in Cuba. He'd already made several prior scouting trips to Cuba.

Cason was one of Otto Reich's men. This sinister figure [Reich] had played an important role, a leading role, in the bloody dirty war against Nicaragua – he was a theorist, and he wrote proclamations and manifestos for the leaders of the armed counter-revolutionary bands that were waging war against the Sandinista revolution. The statements published in the name of the counter-revolution were formulated by Otto Reich. As we now know, the dirty war led to a huge international scandal, because the people who were pushing it in the White House, under Reagan's presidency, violated congressional mandates, traded weapons for money, and took part in drug trafficking.[3] Congress was so furious with this double-dealing by the administration that when Bush tried to name Otto Reich under secretary of state for Latin America, and even despite the Republican majority in both houses of the legislature, the Senate refused to approve the nomination. Taking advantage of a congressional recess, Bush appointed him anyway, to an interim term, and later made him his adviser on Cuba, a position that doesn't require congressional approval.[4]

So this man they sent down, James Cason, as head of the American Interests Office, was one of Reich's men. He replaced Señora Vicky Huddleston, who was very hostile towards us, as was only to be expected given the policy followed by the government of the United States; she'd been there even before George W. Bush took office, but she hadn't been sent precisely to carry out a mission. Then came Cason, whose brief was well defined. We knew that a replacement was coming; we figured whoever they were would be more or less similar to [Huddleston], with the same hostile policies. But we were mistaken – [(in 1st ed.:) he was worse.] Cason had been specially chosen; Otto Reich chose him and gave him all his instructions.

When did Señor Cason arrive in Havana?

As I said, he'd made several trips to [Cuba] to explore, under the cover of being a guest in the country and the future head of the Interests Office. A cynical action. He took office in November. He'd already shown his true nature in a series of statements made previously. He came with a pre-conceived plan, and it was extremely provocative.

At the time, the region was going through a very tense period. On 11 April of that year there'd been a military coup against President Hugo Chávez that had been promoted and supported, to all appearances, by the Bush administration. [Castro seems to be ticking off events on his fingers:] Loyalty to the elected, constitutional president and revolutionary leader by his troops and by the commanders and newly promoted officer corps. Popular uprising and return of the president. December: oil coup, also in Venezuela, serious consequences, production falls to almost zero, three months of battle, the miracle of recovery under the firm and decisive leadership of the Bolivian leader. 'Not one barrel for Cuba!' shout the imperialists and Fascists. Prices double, the agreements between Venezuela and Cuba are interrupted for months, we had to pay surcharges to third parties, our country was bleeding to death financially, the counter-revolutionary action in Venezuela prevented the exchanges and was a hard blow to Cuba.

While all this was happening, Otto Reich's lieutenant, sent by Bush, landed in Washington's Interests Office in Havana on 19 March 2003, just after the attack had been launched against Iraq – four months and a few days afterwards. And taking into account the whole chronology, the evolution of the situation, I felt I was forced to make three important trips abroad: [counting off again:] late November 2002, trip to Quito for the inauguration of the Chapel of Man, created by renowned painter Oswaldo Guayasamín;[5] late December, visit to Brazil to attend the 1 January inauguration of Lula, a tenacious and fraternal fighter for the rights of labour and the Left, and a friend of our people; 19 January, a second trip to Quito for the inauguration of Lucio Gutiérrez, who'd been elected president of Ecuador by a coalition of social forces and leftist parties.

I should point out that if one looks at those December and January dates, [it will be seen that] Venezuela had not yet emerged from that cunning and most dangerous oil takeover. Our profound exchanges in moments of great importance for our two countries, both of which were under a threat of outside aggression, were essential, and they were, each time I made one of these three trips, a profound motivation. It was [out of this concern] that there emerged some ideas about what would become a close collaboration [between the two countries] and also the foundations of what would later be the Bolivarian Alternative for the Americas.

And to all this, one must add the meeting of the Cuban National Assembly of Popular Power in the last week of December 2002, and the general elections that took place on 19 January.[6]

While I was personally engaged in all this intense domestic and foreign-affairs activity during those two months, Cason was going about his dirty tricks with feverish determination, under the mantle of his diplomatic immunity and the imperialistic habit of doing exactly what he pleased, in utter contempt for the other nations of the world. Apparently, he knew absolutely nothing about all those times the empire's actions had come to naught when faced with the steely will of the Cuban people.

All those [domestic and foreign] activities kept you from paying too much attention to what this Señor Cason was doing here in Cuba?
I'm not the only person who concerns himself with the empire's counter-revolutionary actions and its aggressions against our people, because it's a struggle that's waged on many fronts. As is only natural, I tend to pay special attention to the Revolution's strategic affairs. You've been asking me questions related to those affairs.

Since we were so used to the dirty deeds of the Interests Office, we weren't paying too much attention to Cason's absolutely anomalous behaviour. He had been meeting with the Miami mafia and making statements before he took office. Once he was in place officially, he'd go back and forth between Miami and Havana constantly, receiving instructions and support not just from the White House but also from the terrorist mafia in Miami, which had been the decisive element in Bush's election. He would use his diplomatic pouch to bring in thousands of portable radios [pre-]tuned to subversive broadcasters, pamphlets, flyers, instructions for his operations and other similarly repugnant things.

These were serious matters – he went considerably beyond normal operating procedures for that office. The days passed quickly. Came 24 February 2003, a holiday, a festive day, a patriotic day in Cuba, commemorating the beginning of the last War of Independence against Spain in 1895. And on that day, Cason called a big meeting.

In the Interests Office?
No, in a private residence, the home of one of the best-known counter-revolutionary ringleaders. He went to this place, where the meeting was held – several dozen people, twenty or thirty counter-revolutionaries, I don't recall the exact number now – to what they called a 'party'. The holiday was the pretext – he invited some friends.

What was the importance of that meeting?
The importance was the public statements he made there. On 24 February

he made some very insolent, very offensive remarks – public statements. Cason talked, too, about his schedule for a 6,000-mile jaunt around the country, as though he were running for the presidency of the United States. None of the diplomats from other countries he'd invited were there, he was the only one, and when he was asked whether he wasn't afraid to be there ... he said terrible things, even insults of a personal nature, personal attacks, insulting, really intolerable.

Insults against you?
Yes. I was involved in so many things and in so many programmes that I didn't pay too much attention, but a few days later, on 6 March, the National Assembly met and at that point I began to carefully analyse his statements.

The days between 24 February and 6 March passed, and I hadn't spoken in public, but I'd read all his statements, the ones he'd made here and the ones he'd made in Miami,[7] because as I said, he'd go back and forth, very openly, very provocatively. It was obvious. I didn't know whether he was crazy and thought he'd be allowed to do that, or as many people think, what he wanted to do was deliberately create a conflict. All this worried our friends in the United States and other places very much – they kept telling us not to allow ourselves to be provoked.

Because it could be a trap?
Well, but what sort of dilemma are you put in? – a man who starts driving all over the island; he was even organizing ... The pretext was that he was monitoring people whom the Americans had captured at sea and sent back here. Not all of them [were sent back], but some of them [were], because the United States doesn't observe the migration agreement I was talking to you about, they never have – they always let some of [the people intercepted at sea] stay. A number of those they're able to capture at sea are returned. But these people often, out on the open sea and knowing that they have the support of the groups in Miami, don't even obey orders. And they look for conflicts with the American Coast Guard, which is accused by the anti-Cuban lobby in Miami of 'persecuting Cuban patriots'. I explained to you that most of the people who have left Cuba have nothing to do with politics, because the ones who wanted to leave for political reaons were given visas, in keeping with the migration agreement.

The sense of the question I was asking you is this, regardless of the technical answer: at that moment, the world was on the eve of the Iraq War . . .
Well, it wasn't all that close yet. The war in Iraq started on 19 March and the most provocative things Cason did happened on 24 February, almost a month before, when no one knew what day the Yankees would hit Iraq.

I'll explain. He made that statement. That, in itself, was unacceptable. Other diplomats received an invitation to that meeting on 24 February, but they didn't go. At this affair, Cason gave an interview to the press. When a reporter asked him whether his presence didn't confirm the Cuban government's accusation, Cason said, 'No, because I believe the whole diplomatic corps was invited here [tonight], and we as a country always support democracy,' etc., etc., 'and I was invited to come here.' Then he says, 'I'm not afraid.'

He gave a very short answer to another question – very rude . . . Then he added, in perfect Spanish: 'Unfortunately, the Cuban government *is* afraid – afraid of freedom of conscience, freedom of expression, human rights. Groups are showing that there are Cubans who aren't afraid,' etc., etc. – a whole harangue. And Señor Cason ended his statement like this: 'I'm here as an invited guest and I'm going to go around to the whole country, visiting everyone who wants freedom and justice.'

Well, I don't know what the French or the Europeans would have done if somebody made statements like that. Any citizen can understand that this was a provocation. This crisis began taking shape completely independently of the plans for the war against Iraq, which no one knew about with any certainty.

And the crisis with the European Union – did that have anything to do with some international problem, or did it have to do with a decision that was made? We had a lot of things to do, important activities; we weren't interested in making any additional trouble. But could we allow the European Union to make that statement it made[8] after the Iraq War had started and when we were on a list of 'terrorist nations' and therefore must have been among the top countries of the 'sixty or more' that Señor Bush was saying might be subject to preventive surprise attacks? Can anyone reproach us for seeing a tremendous threat in that? Are we supposed to get down on our knees and have diplomatic discussions with the European Union? All we need [as justification] is that exactly that sort of felony has been perpetrated against us [in the past] – we respond as one has to respond. Those who don't respond, those who don't fight, those who don't combat [that sort of threat], those people are lost from the beginning, and in us, you'll never find that kind of person.

So that was the situation with Cason – such a thing had never been done by any officer in any embassy, and he did it in the house of a counter-revolutionary ringleader, and meeting with a group there, celebrating the date of our independence – because if there's a nation that's defended its independence, it's this one. But they want to annex Cuba to the United States, turn this country into an appendix of the United States. You tell me – what would Cuba become if people like that, associated with *bandidos* like the ones above this gentleman, Otto Reich and company, the extreme Right in the United States, had their way? What would become of Cuba? And another thing – how can this group of traitors be celebrating the nation's independence day?

So I said: 'It's so strange, that any reasonable person might well ask himself just how much alcohol was drunk at that "patriotic" activity.' And – this is the irony – I said, 'Since Cuba is really so very frightened, we'll take all the calm we need to decide how to deal with this very strange official. Maybe the numerous members of American intelligence who work in that Interests Office will explain to him that Cuba can very easily do without that office, which is an incubator of counter-revolutionaries and a command centre for the crudest sort of subversive activities against our country. The Swiss officials who represented the US for a long time did an excellent job for years, and they weren't carrying out espionage or organizing subversion.' Then I said, 'Well, bring in the Swiss and let them represent the US again.'

'If that's really what they're trying to provoke with all these insolent statements, they should at least have the courage to say so. Some day, sooner or later, the people of the United States will send a real ambassador . . .' That's what I said on 6 March, when confirmation came that our five heroes[9] detained in the United States had been transferred to special units. The [US authorities] had taken harsh measures against them, and that was a very sensitive matter here – the five of them were popular idols, they'd been named 'Heroes of the Republic of Cuba', and up there they were locked up in the 'hole',[10] for nothing, 'just because' – out of vengefulness, hostility, as an offence [to Cuba]. We were indignant that they'd been stuffed into a coffin in the most cruel, pitiless way. The next day it was confirmed that they'd been sent there [to the hole]. Us giving speeches, and them doing that.

On 10 March MINREX [the Ministry of Foreign Relations] delivered a diplomatic note to the head of the Interests Office. You have it.

I do have it, and I've read it.
But the important thing is what came next. This Señor Cason, who says he's going to be travelling all over the island, we tell him two things: first, monitoring of the returned *balseros*, [rafters, as they call them in English] is not a part of the migration agreements, it's a courtesy we've shown [the Americans], and there's not a single case, in ten years, of violation of those agreements by us.

Those agreements state that the balseros *sent back by US authorities will return to their normal lives, to their jobs?*
That's right. And sometimes it's not easy; sometimes we've had to give these *balseros* other jobs, because the people who worked with them refuse to have them just walk back into their old jobs. In the case, for example, of one particular university, one of the *balseros* who used to work there, you're not going to take over a university and occupy it, you're not going to war with people to make them accept a returned *balsero*, so you try to find him a job that's more or less the same.
And Cason was actually travelling around the island, because some of them, the *balseros*, had organized a group of former *balseros*.

There's an organization of former balseros?
Returned *balseros* out there that Cason was meeting with – he's practically got them organized. He organizes groups with the *balseros* and he calls it 'monitoring'. It's not an obligation on our part [to allow him to do that], it was a courtesy, the same as with a large number of *balseros* they had in Guantánamo, during the crisis in 1994 – they had over 10,000 over there; they were OD'ing on them. We offered to let them [the American authorities] use some of the 20,000 visas so they could start sending them out. Afterwards, they gave us a few more [visas], but we were talking about a few visas more or a few visas less. The point was, they had no right to monitor. We told them so – told them it wasn't in the agreements.
And second, we told them that American diplomats could not travel. They were restricted. Before, they'd been under the obligation to notify us that they were travelling for this or that reason, they were to give us seventy-two hours' notice. It was an obligation for our diplomats, too, up there in

Washington, but this is a tiny island, that's an enormous country, and they have something like ten times more people in their Interests Office here than we have up there. In that [respect], there was no reciprocity whatever. There's no comparison. The number of our people up there, with the size of that country, and the number of people they have down here, with the size of this country . . . To visit someone, you don't just have to inform us, you have to ask permission, seventy-two hours ahead and, of course, we were *not* going to give that gentleman permission.

They [the US authorities] applied that up there too, but, I mean, the situation was not comparable. What did we do? We informed him that he was not allowed to travel. So then Cason had two meetings. After the one on 24 February, again . . . They had two more meetings, one on 12 March and the other on the 14th.

Did you consider those meetings an answer to your statement on 6 March and the decision to limit his movements?
Listen, I spoke on the 6th, I said this, I said we could live without the Interests Office, the world wasn't going to come to an end or anything . . . And on 12 March 2003, in Cason's residence, there took place that activity with a group of eighteen counter-revolutionaries. He gave them the run of the house – this man who can no longer make the 6,000-mile counter-revolutionary tour of the country, this meddler now is using his house for a meeting with eighteen so-called 'dissidents'. All those people organized, egged on and paid by [the Americans] – because I'll tell you, we've got all the papers. We have all the proof, and we could have been a lot stricter with respect to all this.

I've read the book* Los disidentes[11] *that Cuba published.
They met again on the 14th, in Cason's house. The note says: 'March 14. Once again in the residence of the head of the American Interests Office in Havana, a meeting takes place with ringleaders.' It was practically every other day by now. This was an 'ethics workshop' for people who style themselves 'reporters', and of the thirty-four of them, there are just four who've ever studied anything resembling journalism, but all of them are 'reporters' who've been given the title by Cason and propaganda.

That day, 14 March, I had a meeting at about eleven that night, asking for details. What happened? What happened that day? Because we couldn't tolerate any more of it. What were we waiting for? A war that might last six months? No one knew how long that war was going to last. This was something that simply could not be tolerated any longer. Our friends up there, in the United States, saying, 'Listen, don't let yourselves be provoked.' They were worried.

Why didn't Cuba expel Señor Cason?

We've never expelled an American diplomat. They, on the other hand, have used expulsion. Besides, Cason wasn't committing any crime, he was just violating international rules. You can't go to the International Criminal Tribunal because there was nothing criminal involved . . . He was creating the conditions for genocide, but he wasn't yet taking part in genocide.

Could we allow that? And you aren't going to hold a man legally, diplomatically responsible when he has [diplomatic] immunity. But he can't do [what he was doing]. And these people [the dissidents], filled with encouragement, were now openly, brazenly organizing. I don't know what the French would have done – I know them well; the French have a very well-developed sense of dignity.

Well, so no one knew what day the war in Iraq was going to start, so we said, 'We have to move against the main ringleaders.' Because they were very active. Among them was Señora Martha Beatriz Roque, who'd already opened her house for the meeting on 24 February. Total impunity? We couldn't allow it! Nor could we allow it for a man who represented a country whose plans we knew all too well, because they commit a great many indiscretions. We knew what they were thinking, what they wanted to try. We already knew what he was intending to do, and statements had been made, for example about the idea of triggering massive emigration, which would be the pretext for an aggression against the country [Cuba]. We were worse off than in the days prior to that 5 August 1994, with respect to the climate of . . . So anyway, that open conduct was linked to ideas of aggression – they were provocations.

You say 'provocations'. Don't you think that Cason's behaviour was precisely a provocation, and that responding with these arrests was falling into the provocation?

What is the concept of 'provocation'? You'd have to look it up in a dictionary, but the one I have says that it's actions carried out in search of an objective. There are provocations that might be an insult – sometimes gratuitous. Sometimes people provoke other people so the other person will start a fight. The world is full of provocations, but there are provocations and then there are provocations. We understood what our friends in the United States and other places were asking of us – not to allow ourselves to be provoked. They didn't want us to expel Cason.

If somebody's about to shoot you and they're creating all the conditions to start shooting at you, how can you prevent that? Letting yourself get shot and killed?

But there was a context. Those provocations, to a certain extent, have been seen by many people as carefully calculated, within the international context of the eve of American intervention in Iraq. There was a rejection of President Bush and his allies among many social movements. There was a context in which, internationally, Señor Bush seemed to be the most criticized political figure [in the world]. And at that moment, when the arrests occurred here [in Cuba], a diversion was created; the American administration was given an argument: 'Look what's happening in Cuba, too, where they arrest non-violent opponents.' Then, the very friends of Cuba who'd protested against Bush found themselves in a spot, and many of them, as you know, found themselves pressured, and they were forced to say, 'What Bush is doing [in Iraq] is wrong, but what's happening in Cuba is, too.' As though they were the same thing. That context contributed to the weakening of support for Cuba.

Correct, and we understood that. But when you're doing something, you're doing it out of total and absolute conviction. A person doesn't act without profound convictions; one has to defend the country, the country is in danger, the country is being threatened, all this is unfair.

We were thinking of our American adversary. Our problem was not with the Europeans, it wasn't with anybody [but the Americans]; we were thinking about this one, which was the one that was directly threatening us, the one that was directly provoking us, the one that was directly creating a danger to us. And there are many people up there in the United States who are struggling, and under conditions even worse than those in Europe, because a European is in no danger even if he's a progressive; he defends his arguments, of course, he argues on the basis of a series of principles.

Now then, in the case of our friends in the United States, they themselves told us, 'Don't expel him,' but we really didn't see expulsion as a way out. Because the battle was being fought not in Europe, not in Japan, not in any other part of the world – the battle was being fought here, ninety miles from a neighbour who's spent the last forty-six years harassing us.

So we'd come to a situation that was intolerable. If we'd expelled him it would have simply been a diplomatic action. But I don't think, I have to tell you in all honesty, that we were obliged to think any further afield [about what we did]. It's much easier to analyse things in hindsight. So, basically, we said, 'We've got to put a stop to this,' and we did that.

They've got [our] five heroes up there and the people are indignant down here because they're being held prisoner, after a totally unfair trial – that, in the first place. Second, they have all the plans I've been mentioning; they're doing these things here and nobody's stopping them – there's no way to stop them. You think about . . . you even think, Will I be committing a crime? No. Who are the ones that are committing a crime? Right – all those people.

Up there they have unjustly imprisoned five people who were looking for information, because we've been getting hit with bombs, pirate attacks, acts of sabotage, assassination plans and attempts, bombs in hotels . . . And those five people jailed not now, but since 12 September 1998.

In the midst of the terrorist offensive – because after September 11, 2001, there was a tremendous campaign against terrorism and all that. And at the moment they arrested those five *compañeros*, on 12 September 1998, it was also in the midst of an anti-terrorist campaign, because on 7 August 1998, there had been those terrible attacks on the American embassies in three East African countries, with almost 300 people killed. And the fundamental role of those *compañeros* of ours was to penetrate and collect information on terrorist activities.

They were trying to stop terrorist acts against Cuba?
That's right. A tremendous paradox in the mind of our people here, a contradiction between those five prisoners up there who have been crammed into a coffin and, on the other hand, all these friends of Cason's enjoying total impunity here. And not to mention that the very stringent laws we'd passed here, under perfectly normal conditions, weren't being applied. Why, one of the times we imposed long sentences there was tremendous pressure against us, but we didn't yield to the pressure; they served out their sentences according to their behaviour, like now.

I'll confess to you that under those conditions, no argument would have prevailed over sheer necessity . . . because you're being threatened with war, you can't allow a fifth column to be organized against you in which [the actions to be taken] involve potentially criminal activity. Which is what they were doing. There are theorists who don't agree. Jiménez de Asúa, as I believe I mentioned, one of the great Spanish criminal jurists, didn't agree that people committing acts of that kind, people fighting against a progressive process, could be accused of committing 'political crimes'. We call them 'counter-revolutionary crimes', but they are unquestionably associated with politics and, in this case, international politics.

Those people know that even though there are problems that may produce a certain amount of suffering among the people, the Revolution has, and always has had, the almost unanimous support of the population, and we also know the motivations [the dissidents] have. So then I said, 'Well, gentlemen, that's the end of the tolerance and the impunity – we have to make a response.' We weren't going to throw them out – if they wanted to leave they were welcome to do that – but we had to arrest the main actors, and not even all of them, just the ones who'd been taking the most active part in those concrete actions: the meeting in the house of Señora Martha Beatriz [Roque] when Cason made his statements on 24 February, those courses in 'journalistic ethics', and the other meetings of that nature.

I was [meeting] with the *compañeros* until eleven o'clock at night analysing all the information, all the news, the confirmation that [the five heroes] were in those conditions, and we said, 'Well, the only decision to be made is this one, despite its cost.' We take responsibility for what we do.

Did you and your advisers calculate the cost it was going to have in terms of Cuba's image?
The cost, but mainly to the enemy that was provoking us and organizing all that. The response was for them, it wasn't for anyone else.

We were in a political conflict with the United States, and at risk of a military conflict with them. Our mind was on nothing else – for us the main thing, the essential, fundamental thing, the vital thing, a question of life and death, really, was the conflict with them.

No one in Europe was going to attack us, unless it was some crazy, so we were concentrating on that [the threat from the US], and I'm convinced – not just me, but the other *compañeros* who were there analysing the situation, too – that there was no alternative to that response. Because we were thinking that there was something much more worrisome: the possibility of war. There had not yet been even an ultimatum to Iraq, but you could see from the propaganda and the discussions that it was coming. Now then, you couldn't know whether it was coming within a month or . . .

A war against Cuba?

Yes. Our decision would have been made earlier if I had looked more closely into this material relating to 24 February, plus what Cason had been doing. But as I say, I was involved in so many activities; papers like that came in every day, but suddenly you see one that doesn't look like any of the others, and at an extreme that's absolutely intolerable, and not because of any personal insult or offence. I don't care what sort of things people say about me – I'm used to that kind of attack, and sometimes attacks of all kinds are made, some of them so disgusting they make you nauseous.

The struggle took that road, and we had to respond. There's a moment when they're disembarking on your coasts – you say, 'It's a provocation,' but you still have to shoot. At what point do you contain a provocation that seeks that objective, and where do you reach the point at which it can no longer be contained? They were determined to do whatever it took to provoke a situation . . . So there came a moment at which, in our opinion, if it went any further it couldn't have been contained. That's the factor that determined our reaction, and the rest is coincidence.

Did you and your advisers really think that the United States was setting a trap in order to start a war against Cuba?

Listen, that war hasn't come, nobody knows what's going to trigger it, although we do know, because we've thought a lot about what an aggression against this country would be like, how much destruction there would be. Dante couldn't imagine what an aggression against Cuba would cost [the aggressor] today – many times greater than in Iraq. We've thought about it a lot, because there was a war in Vietnam, we know what happened there; there was a war in Kosovo; there was a war before, in the Gulf, in Iraq . . . If you're faced with a situation in which the country's life, the lives of millions of people, is in danger, you can perfectly understand that this country is worried by that much more than by anything else, that we put it at a higher priority than anything that interests you.

The defence of the country?

Yes. Let me tell you that there are millions of Cubans here ready for a war – the entire nation. I've sometimes said that we have reached 'military invulnerability', that that empire [the US] can't pay the price in lives – unimaginable, perhaps higher than in Vietnam – if they try to occupy us. And besides, the American people aren't ready to give their rulers leave to sacrifice tens of thousands of lives for some imperial adventure. Don't think they have large reserves of soldiers. As we're seeing with the war in Iraq, fewer and fewer Americans are enlisting. Enlisting in the army has become a source of employment – they hire the unemployed, and often they try to hire the most blacks they can for their unjust wars. But there's been news that fewer and fewer Afro-Americans are willing to enlist in the army, despite unemployment and the marginalization they're subjected to, because they're aware that they're being used as cannon fodder. In the ghettos in Louisiana, when Hurricane Katrina hit, in late September 2005, the government yelled 'Every man for himself!' and abandoned hundreds of thousands of citizens – among them many Afro-Americans – some of whom drowned, or lost their lives in nursing homes or hospitals, and some were even euthanized out of fear on the part of the medical staff that they'd have to watch them drown . . . These are true stories that are indisputable, well publicized, and one does well to meditate on them.

For their wars, they try to find Latinos, immigrants who, seeking to escape hunger, cross the border, that border where more than 500 immigrants die every year, many more than died during the twenty-eight years the Berlin Wall lasted. The empire talked about the Berlin Wall every day; the wall they've put up between Mexico and the United States, where hundreds of people die each year as they try to escape poverty and underdevelopment – they don't say a word about *that* wall. That's the world we're seeing.

A world in which one has to be able to defend oneself.
The enemy also engages in psychological warfare. If the enemy thinks that you're going to tolerate it, if the enemy thinks that you're not going to do anything, you trigger what one might call, biologically speaking, a pursuit instinct.

Lion tamers sometimes turn their backs on the lions, they use their whip, crack the whip so it makes noise, and sometimes they bow, wave, there's applause – and they move this way [turning towards the lion], because if they don't, the lion reacts, out of an instinct of pursuit, a predatory instinct. Even a little lapdog, one of those tame little things, starts barking if you run away, it'll run after you and even bite your trousers. But if you turn around, the little dog will back off. That same thing has happened to me in the ocean with barracudas, sharks – when you face them down, then their instinct of preservation kicks in and makes them back away. There's nothing worse than turning your back on your enemy, and an empire is much greater, much larger and more dangerous than a wild animal, and the psychology of the people who lead an empire and manage its weapons is like a wild animal's.

And the Cubans didn't want to be any wild animal's dinner.
That's right. You have to face wild animals down. First, the empire has to know that there's going to be a fight and that the price will be high. Second, they should suspect that it can all turn out the way this sort of adventure has always turned out, and how I'm sure one would turn out here. But, I'll tell you, we don't want that, at all – a person would be crazy to want that.

So, that was our fight, you see, and that was our response, and they will always find the same response, not in the way they might imagine, because another thing that the weaker party has to do is use his intelligence, psychology, cunning. I mean, I'm talking about a clean fight, because never, within the means taken in the struggle, have we contemplated anything immoral. Means will never be used that go against our principles, that are contrary to our ethics. Because how long did their plans to assassinate me go on? And yet the thought of assassinating the president of the United States never crossed a single Cuban's mind. And that lasted for years, and it was the reason some people wondered whether Cuba might have had something to do with the death of Kennedy, or other people. You know the story. That is not in keeping with our ethics. Nor is it our policy to do that. In the face of problems, you defend yourself.

The way you win that battle is by making it hard for them to achieve their objectives politically; the other way can be a mistake. I mean, what it comes down to is that we're in the midst of that battle.

About that, I'd like to ask you two questions. First, it has been a surprise, I'd say even to Cuba's friends, that those dissidents were sentenced to such long prison terms when they were, without question, non-violent opponents and you and your advisers so often have talked about the 'battle of ideas'. Second, among the dissidents arrested there was one poet, and there is unanimity even in Cuba in considering him a great poet – Raúl Rivero.[12] Don't you think it's negative, as an image, for a country to imprison a great poet?
It's regrettable. It's regrettable, but, in terms of justice, a person's occupation shouldn't be grounds for impunity. I, quite honestly, haven't read or heard that he was a great poet. They say that we all have a little of the poet and a

little of the madman in us. But in my opinion, for example, Federico García Lorca[13] is a great poet.

You'd have to define, even, what a 'great poet' is. If a great poet can be someone who is divorced from ethics, who's divorced from his native country, who lives on the money of those who blockade his country, those who want to starve his country to death, those who make plans to destroy it, then there may be somebody who technically organizes and arranges words but in my opinion, he'll never be a great poet. In my opinion, a great poet is José Martí, who gave his life; Antonio Machado,[14] Federico García Lorca, Miguel Hernández,[15] men who died when they were hunted down or stood before a firing squad by Fascism, because more is necessary than just beautiful, harmonious phrases.

I haven't read Raúl Rivero; I cannot give an opinion on the effect of his words.

You haven't read Raúl Rivero?
No, but really, I've got a lot of poets to read! In this country there are thousands of good poets, although they haven't had the fortune of worldwide publicity or the favour of having a statue erected to them as a 'great poet'. Technically, I can't judge; ethically I can, and so I have the right also to say that there is no poetry where there is no ethics. Because poetry is a more ethical thing – more ethical, even, than the novel. The novel is a plot, a story, while I associate poetry with an emotion or sentiment. I recall, for example, the case of Valladares,[16] who suddenly emerged as this 'poet in the world' . . .

Armando Valladares, a cause célèbre; he was imprisoned here.
That's right; he was imprisoned for acts of terrorism, pure and simple, for setting off bombs. There were two [people] involved; one was younger and we didn't try him for it, because he wasn't old enough, but Valladares was sentenced. It was during the days right after Playa Girón, when that famous Operation Mongoose was still in effect, which included dozens of plans for assassination attempts,[17] acts of terrorism by the thousands – thousands! – and then Valladares, at one of those acts, was arrested, tried and sent to prison. At one point he passed himself off as paralysed, he fooled the whole world, because there was a huge propaganda campaign orchestrated by the empire [to free him].

There was a huge commotion all around the world because the Cubans had somebody in prison that the media were presenting as a poet, who was also paralysed, supposedly as a consequence of mistreatment in the jails.

This book of poetry comes out, *Desde mi silla de ruedas* ('From My Wheelchair'), published by a 'poet-prisoner' – a terrorist, with explosives and dynamite; he wasn't a terrorist that hurt the economy, he was a terrorist [that used] explosives and dynamite, that harmed people's lives – and Valladares becomes this world-renowned figure, with books written [about him] abroad, and 'paralysed' to boot. Listen, you know Régis Debray, just as I know him – he was working in those days as an adviser to French president François Mitterrand. He came to Cuba to argue in support of Valladares; he told me the Mitterrand government was practically going to collapse if the 'poet-prisoner' wasn't released.

Quite a responsibility for you . . .
So then, what happened? I asked an eminent doctor, 'Listen, my friend, what is it really that's wrong with him?' Because there was all this brouhaha and campaigning, and he says to me, 'There's nothing wrong with him.' I say, 'What do you mean, nothing wrong with him? That's impossible.' And he insisted: 'There's nothing wrong with him.'

Valladares was in a wheelchair.
That's right. And he says to me, 'Test him.' So that was easy: you use audiovisual means to check on his activities. That had never been done here, nothing of the sort. So we did that, we checked, and we received a film of everything he did. Because you've got to give Valladares the Olympic prize for faking; he managed to pull the wool over the eyes of the whole world. As soon as he was alone, he'd look around – we've still got the films – stand up, go into the bathroom, and there in the bathroom he'd do all sorts of exercises. He was in better shape than you are, than I am – than an athlete! Perfectly healthy.

He was faking.
I told you what Régis Debray told me. We called Debray in and we showed him the film. We showed it to him, too.

Showed it to Valladares?
That's right. Before we gave our answer, we called Valladares in and we

449

showed him the film we had of him doing wonderful exercises – he could write a manual of exercises to keep people in excellent shape while pretending to be paralysed – and his reaction, when he saw it? He stood straight up, like a shot, out of his chair.

Then we showed it to Régis Debray, and then we told Valladares, 'Listen, you're going to be set free' – he'd served a large part of his sentence and had been the instrument of a fierce campaign – 'and we have just one condition: you have to board the plane walking on your own two feet and you have to leave the plane walking on your own two feet.' Debray already knew that the only condition we were putting on Valladares' release was that he walk on and off the plane, that he give up on that ruse of paralysis. I'm not criticizing him, because a prisoner [has the right to] invent anything to get out.

He has the right to do that.
Yes; I'd say that he has the right to invent things, but we caught him at it. Oh, he was clever – he fooled a lot of doctors. I couldn't believe it. We sent in an eminent specialist, and he said, 'There's nothing wrong with him.'

You, personally, thought that he was paralysed, really . . . ?
I thought there was something wrong with him, some problem, and I wanted to know what kind of problem it was and why he had it, whether or not there was any solution from a medical point of view.

We will never give in to pressure. That is a principle as unwavering as respect for the human person, as the principles that have guided our Revolution. One of them is this: by force, one obtains nothing in this country; by other means, one obtains many things.

Going back to Raúl Rivero, who was set free in November 2004 – he hadn't used force, hadn't set off bombs, not to mention that he was one of Nicolás Guillén's favourite disciples, and you do consider Guillén a great poet.
Vladimiro Roca was Blas Roca's favourite son, and Blas was the head of the Communist Party for a long time.

But Vladimiro Roca, in the opposition, wasn't arrested – nor was Osvaldo Payá, for example, or Elizardo Sánchez. Why has there been that difference between some who were engaged in the same activities and others?
There really aren't any differences.

But these [the ones I named] weren't arrested.
There's been a difference in the treatment. [The ones you named] have been breaking laws for some time, and seriously so – we have exhaustive dossiers on them. But here, the action was directed, basically, against recent events, and that was what determined which ones had the most responsibility. And some of [the ones you mentioned] might be cause for just as much scandal as any of the others, I admit.

There are two events that might answer the first question you raised, about the fact that the measures had been harsh, and I was going to tell you that they weren't so harsh given that the sentences approved by the National Assembly for this type of crime, 'high treason', make [the crime of treason] in our penal code subject to the death penalty, a life sentence or thirty years, and some of the sentences have been in keeping with the seriousness of the circumstances, and others have been minimum, five years. The sentences have ranged from five years to twenty-eight years.

There are people with grave responsibilities [for crimes], and not just those whom we've mentioned, who, however, were not brought to trial but who have more than enough reason to be – and of course, no one can think they have the right to do what they're doing or that the state is going to sit idly by. If it should become necessary to take action against those you've mentioned and quite a few more, then we will take action. We do not go to extremes, because their actions were relatively moderate.

You ask and I explain: no one's impunity is guaranteed, and everything depends on the way events evolve, and when it becomes necessary to take action we will take it, given that the things we're defending are, for us, above all other things. When it becomes essential to take action, we will do so, whatever happens and whatever the cost.

I tell you this because you've asked me, you've almost forced me to answer, as the friends we are. You ask logical questions, but what I want to say is that [what I've said] shouldn't be taken as a threat. I won't lie to you, I have to answer you and I've answered in all honesty, but I want very sincerely to be certain that no one takes this as a threat, but rather under the terms, the conditions, and within the circumstances that I've explained. It's a right, a power that can be exercised. We've had patience for a long, long time; those laws have been on the books for many years now.

And they hadn't been applied until now?
Those laws had not been applied; they're there, on the books, everybody is

aware of them, they were passed unanimously by the National Assembly of Cuba. Those who think that the National Assembly is a bunch of idiots, unconditional [supporters of our ideas and initiatives], and so on – let them think what they like! But we have a very high opinion of the women and men who are in the National Assembly, and we respect their judgement.

For example, there is a group of religious persons in the Assembly who are against capital punishment. They do not support any law that specifies that sentence, which is why some of these laws under which capital punishment might be applied haven't been passed unanimously. There are some exceptions there, and we totally respect them, because they express the will of the immense majority of the National Assembly and, generally speaking, what's even more difficult in this question of the death penalty, public opinion.

Let's talk about that, then.
If you think we're done with this . . .

Yes. The logic of the question is this: in Europe, no country belonging to the European Union any longer has the death penalty. What's the maximum sentence that replaces the death penalty and is applied for the worst crimes? A life sentence. Which corresponds, in practice, generally speaking, to a maximum sentence of about twenty years in prison. So, clearly, some percentage of public opinion in Europe asks itself: why give opponents who, without question, are not violent, have not committed bloodshed, such long sentences?
I didn't know that was the maximum sentence.

The maximum. In Europe no one can, in principle, be in prison for more than twenty years.
Including military codes?

In the military codes, in Europe, there's also no death sentence in peacetime.
There's no death sentence, but they put a limit of twenty years as the maximum sentence even in the case of an act of treason against the nation, in the military code? In the case of war, what are the laws?

I don't know. The maximum sentence is life in prison; for example, a person can't be extradited if he faces the risk of being sentenced to death or more than twenty years in prison, as the actual term of imprisonment, in his own country. So that's why there's such commotion in Europe to see that some of these peaceful opponents [of the Cuban government] have been sentenced to up to twenty-eight years . . .

Well, and what about the ETA members killed over there in France – was that with the knowledge of the authorities or without their knowledge?

That's another problem – we've talked about that. The last time we talked about capital punishment, you expressed your philosophical opposition to it, and you said you thought that Cuba might be able to move towards eliminating it.

Yes, and I say it again. I understand, and I'm grateful for the piece of information you've just given me, that Europe has not just eliminated capital punishment, but that they either don't have life sentences or can't give more than twenty years.

In principle, although there may be exceptions, no one can be held in prison for more than twenty years.[18]

You know that at a certain point we had to make and modify laws, because they were inspired a bit by the illusion that international law existed, by the belief that no country would take upon itself to invade another one, although there was one, an exception, our neighbour to the north, which one day in 1983 invaded Grenada, because there were some American students there – who, I might add, were in no danger – and as payback for an action that had been taken against the United States somewhere else, and which invaded Panama in 1989 . . . At that time it was not just a one-pole world, with one hegemonic superpower – there were two.

Cuba's situation, from the point of view of security, seemed much better. The economic situation, even with the blockade, was bearable in the sense that raw materials, fuel, a large amount of foodstuffs and other vital goods were assured, our sugar was being sold at a reasonably good price . . . But all that changed.

Now then, I think that there was some sleight of hand going on among the *compañeros* who worked back then, in 1976, preparing the draft of the constitution and formulating all those laws,[19] so that capital punishment always existed and was never discussed, precisely because of a history of thirty years of acts of aggression, threats of war, the danger even of nuclear war, a blockade, thousands of people killed, like the victims of the terrorist acts that had been perpetrated over a period of years and that continued to be committed until just a short time ago, officially, by the government of the United States and then later unofficially – that is, tolerated, allowed and even encouraged, depending on the circumstances, by the US authorities.

We took into account, for example, the more than 600 plans to assassinate me, some direct, others incited, which I've talked to you about. People are naïve, they tend to simplify things, but it's still killing, no matter how you look at it, whether you organize a conspiracy to kill someone or you create all the conditions and all the psychological circumstances to incite people to kill. I'm talking about the plans in which people were persuaded, all this propaganda of incitement – inciting, inciting, inciting.

I'm sure that in Europe, you people wouldn't allow, I don't think, propaganda to be broadcast on all the mass media inciting people to kill. Or that said, 'Listen, kill anyone that tries to steal something from your house, kill anyone that insults a child, kill anyone that insults a woman, kill any woman who has not fulfilled her marital obligations.' You people would say, 'We can't allow this; this has to be prohibited.' But the United States, or let's say the people responsible for that country's policies, has spent years inciting people to murder. I'm trying to make the whole background clear.

So far as I'm concerned, I'm not worried, I assure you. Proof of that in the first stage of the Revolution was the invasion of Playa Girón, when they attacked the country with planes bearing the insignia of Cuba when they were from another power – that's one of the worst violations of international law.

The death penalty was unconnected to anything that had to do with criminal sentencing; one might say that from the beginning there was a suspension [of it] and it had to be started again, because we began to discover such horrendous, outrageous crimes . . . a serious political situation was being created. But the fact was, there was a suspension of the application of the death penalty at the beginning of the Revolution.

Because I imagine that since you Europeans aren't at war, you don't have cases like the ones we have; no one wants to subvert order in Europe, the Cold War is over, your existence is not threatened, the death of millions of Europeans . . .

Is not foretold.[20]

Is not foretold, is not foreseen. There's NATO, super-NATO, the disappearance of the so-called 'Cold War' – nothing is threatening you. Although there have been terrible terrorist actions, in Madrid, in London ... I ask you: what year did you [the Europeans] do away with capital punishment?

In France, more than twenty years ago, in 1981, it was abolished by President François Mitterrand. Public opinion was in favour of the death penalty, but President Mitterrand held firm, and we, I mean as intellectuals, as citizens, were militant in supporting him in abolishing the death penalty. It was eliminated, in particular, because there was a trial in which two prisoners, Buffet and Bontemps, who were in jail in 1971, took a guard and a nurse hostage and cut their throats. Both prisoners were tried for murder and they were both sentenced to death and sent to the guillotine in 1972. But an enormous controversy arose over that, because one of them had slit their throats but the other one hadn't. So people said, 'How can you sentence someone to death who hasn't killed anyone?' One of them had, and the other one may have been his accomplice but he hadn't killed, so he shouldn't be sentenced to death. There was a tremendous controversy, and there were also two or three other very controversial cases, and those controversies led to a movement against the death penalty. And finally, in 1981 Mitterrand made the decision to abolish it.
This happened in France first and then in the other countries?

No, other countries had already eliminated it; I don't recall the chronology.[21] Spain is the most recent country to abolish it.
When was it eliminated?

In Spain, in practice, it was suspended with the adoption of the democratic constitution in 1978. Officially, in 1995.
And what countries in Europe have the death penalty today?

None of them; as full members of the European Union, none of them.
What about the ones that are about to enter?

The ones that are about to enter, if they have it they can't keep it, because Protocol 6 of 28 April 1983 of the European Convention on Human Rights requires the elimination of the death penalty.
But do they have it?

I don't think they do, but if they do, even just officially, they have to do away with it in order to join the EU.
Does the Czech Republic have it? Does Hungary have it? Does Poland have it?[22]

The Council of Europe in Strasbourg[23] requires, on the basis of respect for human rights, that it be abolished. So to become a member of the European Union [a country] has to abolish the death penalty. That's one of the problems that Turkey has. Turkey has the death penalty, but since it wants to become a member of the European Union it was asked to eliminate it. For example – do you remember? – when Abdullah Öcalan, the head of the PKK, the Kurdistan Workers Party, and who'd been the leader of a group that had committed many terrorist attacks,[24] was arrested, Europe requested that Turkey not sentence him to death.[25]
I just finished explaining to you that the question of capital punishment during all that period was always there, because it was so closely associated with the history I told you about.

In our country [the death penalty] wasn't associated with political activities, it was associated basically with common crimes of a civil nature. The death penalty was no longer applied for things linked to counter-revolutionary activities.

That must have been for ten, or many more than ten years – maybe twenty, twenty-five years.

You told me that it was virtually never applied.
I'd have to see exactly . . . It was applied in one case, something [our enemies] have tried to present as political, but wasn't really political.

The Ochoa case?
That's right, the Ochoa case. I told you that that was a matter of criminal activity of a common [i.e., not political but civil] nature. It was just that those activities were carried out by people who had very important responsibilities, people even of great merit, because Ochoa was a man who had shown great merit in missions for the Revolution, in internationalist missions – it became an act of *de facto* treason, and the country was exposed to extremely delicate, and even surprise, actions, which might be of a political, destructive nature, or might be of a military nature, albeit limited. It was decided that in our country, under those conditions, [for] people with that sort of great

responsibility, not to mention the nature of those responsibilities, who carried out an act of that kind, it would be categorized as an act of treason; it did not have a political meaning, but it was an act that was equal to or worse than treason against the nation. That was why it was classified as treason.

And also why he was tried by a military tribunal?
That's right, because he and the others were officers in the armed forces and the state security agencies. I think few people were as hurt by what happened, the execution of Ochoa, Tony de la Guardia and the other two, as all of us were. You know that enemy propaganda, US propaganda, tried to present the affair as a problem of rivalry, a struggle for power. Every time something happens here, it's inevitably associated with lies, ambitions, fears, rivalries. So, for forty-six years, every one of the things that's happened, of any kind, has been used for political ends.

So the Cubans, for political causes, don't apply the death penalty?
Not for counter-revolutionary acts. I don't know what would have happened here if we'd captured Posada Carriles or one of those men who set off bombs and carried out so many terrorist activities. I want you to know that we've come up against the disagreement of many people due to cases of counter-revolutionaries who disembark with weapons, cases in which there has even been loss of life – and we've been extremely tolerant so as not to apply the death penalty.

Those acts had not only X degree of intentional gravity, they were serious, grave acts in themselves – that is, not just immoral, cynical, base[, but criminal as well]. I don't think those people had to disembark – they earned the death penalty, according to the law and according to the opinion of the immense majority of our people, and we've even had political problems because we didn't apply the death penalty to those who had earned the death penalty because of the mercenary nature of their acts, because they were at the service of an imperialistic, genocidal power.

But what I wanted to say was that there are acts which, independent of the [perpetrator's] intentions, have more or less importance – when they have more importance, the difficulties in adopting one option or the other are much greater. That's the detail that should be remembered.

Because really, a sentence of death is, by law, taken up to the Council of State, which convenes as the nation's Supreme Court. That responsibility could be discharged by one person, one person might have it in Europe, but in our case it's collective – there are thirty-one members of the Council of State. Crimes meriting the death penalty are precisely those common crimes that are repugnant, monstrous: premeditated murder, a little girl raped. Raping a little girl and then killing her, too, is terrible – not applying the death penalty in a case such as that might create a serious problem, of a political nature, in the court of public opinion.

You know that here no publicity is given to crimes of violence; there is no publicity, here there's no such thing as the 'police blotter', sensational reporting of murder and so on – we do not allow reporting crimes of violence that may induce other similar crimes. Before, that was common: somebody cut up into pieces, a huge commotion, and then a little while later, another person cut up into pieces by even more horrific methods – crazies, people totally out of their minds, which do exist, and reporting on all those events incites them, encourages them, to a relatively extreme degree, to commit that same kind of crime.

Since 1976, when our constitution was adopted, all sentences of capital punishment must go to the Council of State for appeal. You see the thirty-one members of the Council of State racking their brains over every case, looking in detail at the facts before handing down their decision – out of a sense of responsibility, and also because, like the guerrilla commanders in the war, no one likes the death penalty, however repugnant the crime committed. They also look at public opinion in each case.

There's not a case, even if the monstrous details of the crime haven't been publicized, that people don't know about. People talk – a lot; even when there's no 'police blotter' or 'yellow journalism', the facts become known, the news spreads, and [public] rejection is often unanimous.

And you should see the complaints. It was always a headache – a double or sometimes triple one: first, one's repugnance for the crime; second, making what seemed to be the best decision within the idea that punishment is justified because it's a way of containing crime and protecting society.

But does the Council of State see a difference between a crime of a political nature and a common crime?
They have been making that distinction, between one type of crime and another. For those who've opposed the death penalty, there's the argument, among others, that [the death penalty] doesn't prevent that kind of crime from being committed – it isn't a deterrent.

Seeing all these situations, the process, the analysis, took a long time at first, and later there was a conscious move to draw the process out[, the process of actual execution]. It was an incipient movement down through the years.

There's also the awareness that opposition by those who oppose the death penalty has been growing more and more widespread in the world; there's a natural rejection, if you will, a rejection by people who are not educated in hatred, passion or the spirit of vengefulness – that's inconceivable in a political leader. I, at least, can't conceive a spirit of vengefulness; we have the experience of war – I told you about when an outbreak of banditry took place in the Revolutionary Army, and the Revolution's laws had to be applied – the firing squad, executions. There were only a very few cases. But that nipped it in the bud. It never happened again.

This is independent of one's emotions, one's feelings, which may be philosophical, may be religious, and they're arguments that in my opinion are much stronger than the debatable argument as to deterrence. I think there are types of crime in which the death penalty really has no effect, and I also think there are certain circumstances in which a drastic punishment of that kind does have an effect, even a lasting effect.

22

The Hijackings in April 2003

*Air piracy – Heading for a new migration explosion? – The hijacking of
the boat in Regla – The negotiations – The attitude of the American
authorities – Revolution, Socialism and crime –
Execution of three hijackers – A statement by José Saramago*

**Speaking of all this, I'd like to ask you about those three executions that
took place in April 2003. People were surprised that the three hijackers
were sentenced to death and executed when they had really not killed or
injured anyone. So there was real surprise that the death penalty was given
these people.**[1]

This hijacking is one of those cases [we were talking about]. There was the
real risk that a wave of hijackings would be triggered by it, and that that
would be a pretext for aggression, war against this country, within that
whole [US] philosophy of waging 'preventive war'.

The terrorist acts of September 11 2001 had taken place in New York
and a militaristic philosophy had been declared, which we call Nazifascistic.
I'm glad we talked about 5 August 1994 – I remember that case because
we'd arrived at a situation back then that triggered a wave of emigration,
because there wasn't a boat, a vessel in Havana harbour, a tourist ship, a
fishing boat, *anything*, that was safe [from hijacking].

We faced a difficult economic situation; we were about three years into
the special period in 1994, with very serious shortages. The clear majority
of the people wanted to defend the Revolution, but a great number of people
had been incited to go to the United States – I told you that there was a
migration agreement that hadn't been kept. I told you that those who wanted
to emigrate by other means were able to do so and that in general the ones

who took this route to the US were the lumpen, criminal types, and in many cases people with criminal records.

So what did [the US] want to provoke this time, in April 2003? A situation like the one created in August '94, when the Americans, after reducing the number of visas [they issued] to fewer than 1,000 a year, announced that they were sending boats to pick up people that wanted to emigrate.

A situation resembling a pressure cooker.
That's right. They were supposed to have given out 10,000 visas by then, and they'd given out about 500. In the new situation, the Bush administration, its most extremist [advisers and officials], the Otto Reichs, the Roger Noriegas and all those bandits had come up with the idea of provoking a wave of emigration in order to justify a conflict.

That was what we knew, although we still weren't aware of many of the details; we didn't know how they were going to provoke the crisis. But they did have a plan of that sort. In my view, the crimes committed by the so-called 'dissidents' who conspire with the United States and receive a salary from up there are more serious, morally, than the crime committed by those people who were given the death penalty – which is what you want to know, and why [we sentenced them to death], when you allege there'd been no bloodshed, there'd been no deaths.

The hijacking of that ferry at that moment was linked to the situation I'm explaining to you; it was very serious, extremely serious. But [it would not have been] as serious, I might tell you, not as serious if something that happened earlier hadn't happened. Two hours before the war started in Iraq, at 7.00 p.m., something happened that hadn't happened in ten years, almost since those migration agreements had been signed.

There had not been a hijacking in ten years?
For a long time we'd had boats stolen, crimes, people stealing crop-dusting planes, planes associated with production, fishing boats. But it had been ten years, since the 1994 accords, since there had been a hijacking of a plane with passengers aboard. And – very strange – about two hours before the war in Iraq started, on Wednesday, 19 March 2003, a passenger plane departing from the Island of Youth, which is between eighty and 100 kilometres, fifty to sixty-something miles, south of Cuba, making the last trip of the day, announced as it was making its approach to the Boyeros airport,

near Havana, that it had been hijacked. Six individuals with knives had penetrated the cabin and put knives to the pilot's and co-pilot's throats; they hijacked them exactly the way the planes that flew into the Twin Towers in New York were hijacked. That's pretty strange.

And they wanted to go to the US?

That's right. But they had only enough fuel to get them to Key West, United States. [The plane] had fuel to get to the island [of Youth] and back; these are planes that hold forty-something passengers. There were several hijackers; they'd been planning it for months – they'd taken flights, come down here, gone back, observed ways to get around surveillance, get around the security measures, even taken photos. There was a little carelessness [on the part of security] – that was normal; routine, you know, because it had been ten years, as I say, since there had been anything like this.

They were met in the United States, and what did the authorities do? They arrested the six people with knives, but they immediately gave residency to the accomplices, on the basis of the Cuban Adjustment Act. They started an investigation, detained part of the Cuban crew while they did their investigation. They left the plane there, and that created all the conditions for that whole Miami terrorist mafia up there to confiscate the plane, which they did. There was a lot of mistreatment of the rest of the passengers, who wanted to return [to Cuba] – rudeness, incitation for them to stay. All the abuses they could commit with respect to that plane, they did.

American planes hadn't been hijacked since Cuba put a measure in place over twenty years earlier, which put an end for ever to the hijacking of American planes. American planes would often arrive here with 200 or even 300 passengers. They'd hijack them with a bottle of water; they'd stick a wick in it and call it a Molotov cocktail – often mentally deranged people, they weren't even doing it for political reasons . . . people fleeing justice, or doing it for the thrill, or the mentally ill. Sometimes several weeks would pass without anything happening and then all of a sudden there'd be three or four in one week, like some kind of psychological contagion among people that had some tendency towards that sort of adventure.

We tried to take care of the planes, and the hijacked passengers, too. We'd provide them with fuel if they needed it and then immediately turn the plane and passengers back over to them. There were dozens and dozens of cases. It was them [unclear 'them': the US, or the 'Miami terrorist mafia'] that came up with this type of hostile activity against Cuba, during the first few years of the Revolution: they'd take the hijackers and make them out to be patriots, and then make a big media fuss over them, to provoke imitators. And that's how the phenomenon of hijacking Cuban planes began.

Cuba had solved that problem for them. In return, they wouldn't punish the person who'd hijacked one of our planes or boats. Quite the contrary – they'd exonerate them completely. It had never occurred to anyone that in 2003, while we were under the 1994 migratory agreement, a passenger plane would be hijacked on the eve of a war.

The hijacking of that plane created a great deal of indignation in Cuba, but the worst part was that within a few days, a judge in Miami set the six hijackers free. Oh! because they weren't considered dangerous; they didn't pose a threat to society. In addition, there was the belief [in Miami] that they were 'dissidents', when [in fact] their motivation had nothing to do with politics. They exploit the political situation, but they usually aren't political activists. You try to analyse the motivation of people who do things like that and you find that in almost every case, they have criminal records, or legal problems, or [they do it] because they're lazy or because some-body's reprimanded them, maybe for fighting or something – not all of them, but they tend to be people who've been sanctioned in one way or another. They're the kind of people who don't work, that live off anti-social activities – and that's the ideal place for them. They're thrill-seekers, adventurers . . .

And still we're trying to do something about that; for several years now we've been working on this problem, with social workers, to ensure that people getting out of jail, out of prison, can be reinserted into society, find a job – we're working to see that people give them jobs, and are told what the situation is, because the fact is, if somebody's been in prison for this crime or that crime, has such-and-such a criminal record, it's hard to find them a job . . . Still, this case in particular was so strange that one couldn't be sure these individuals hadn't been used by the enemy. There was just too much coincidence, and it was just too unusual that they'd be set free almost immediately, despite the extreme seriousness of their actions.

What happened here when people found out that the six hijackers had been released up there in Florida?
The news of their release came on 29 March – the war in Iraq had been going on for ten days at that point – and very quickly, on the 31st, another plane was hijacked, with even more passengers. It was also making a direct

flight from the Isle of Youth, but this second one had slightly greater capacity, forty-five passengers.

An individual with a grenade – he pretended to have a grenade – said he was going to blow up the plane; he was in the rear. He wanted to be taken to Miami, but there wasn't enough fuel so the pilot landed – he didn't want to take the plane [to the US], he said he'd do anything but lose the plane, and he landed at the airport in Havana – but he landed in the middle of the runway, so that runway was shut down for the rest of the night.

So we found out that there were people in the US [in the government] who didn't want the plane to go to Florida. They were showing some interest, they were moving; we informed them immediately of what was happening, and they sent a statement saying they didn't want it [to fly to the US], they even asked that we make [the hijacking] public – they spoke with us.

This second plane was hijacked at more or less the same time as the other, during the last trip from the Isle of Youth. But [we] began to look into the situation and an attempt was made to persuade the individual; the State Department was notified in Washington, the person in charge of the Interests Office was woken up. And [Washington] sent a fairly positive message; they were opposed to the plane's landing in the US, they were against that.

When they said that, we asked them to send someone to tell the hijacker. So right away they sent the head of the Interests Office, that James Cason, with instructions to tell the hijacker [what the US position was], and to our surprise, despite everything we knew about Cason, he followed orders. He was met at the airport and he contacted the pilot. The only way to communicate was by way of the pilot; the hijacker – the man with the grenade – refused to talk; he said no way, how could he be sure it was really Cason, and Cason told him he was willing to send him his passport as identification – he did everything he could to identify himself and stop this thing.

There was even some discussion of the idea of the plane landing not in Florida, but in some other state instead – they knew the problem it would create [if the plane landed in Florida], because the anti-Cuban mafia runs everything there. But the problem was that the plane didn't have enough fuel, and the fuel that could be added still wasn't enough to let it reach another state. So it was a long fight – it took all night.

Were you personally in on the operations?
Well, I wasn't near the plane when Señor Cason came, because I didn't want to see that gentleman even from a mile away. I went to the air-control centre.

But the *compañeros* from the IACC (Cuban Civil Aeronautics Institute) were there, the people in charge of aviation, doing all they could to resolve the complicated situation. People from Foreign Relations came in, too; an official from Foreign Relations accompanied Cason when Washington told him to go to the airport – I think he'd been asleep; it was like one o'clock in the morning, or one-thirty. He went up to the side of the plane, because from that point there was a possibility of direct contact, not through the pilot, [but] the hijacker, the man with the grenade, refused to talk to him – he just simply refused, flat refused.

It was clear that there were two tendencies [i.e., two opposing pulls in Washington as to the handling of this situation; Castro clarifies this statement later]. The head of the American Interests Office went home to sleep about two-thirty, and I stayed there, trying to persuade the man.

You didn't speak to the hijacker?

No, the hijacker would only allow us to speak with him through the pilot, as intermediary. At a certain point I told the pilot to put me on the plane's speakers and I spoke to the crew; I told them not to panic, because [at that point] the guy was threatening to blow up the grenade, and I accused the guy. I said, 'He's being totally irresponsible.' Because he was doing things you could see by now, and that helped to get to know him psychologically. The hijacker had sent the men [passengers] forward, to a cargo compartment, and he took the women and children to the back. He was back in the back.

And was he alone or did he have accomplices?

He was alone, but he was carrying two grenades; he was squeezing them back there and making threats. He'd say, 'In so many minutes, if you don't get fuel in the plane, I'm going to blow it up.' I gave the pilot instructions: 'Tell him this, tell him that.' When he'd make a threat, I'd make a strong response: 'You are absolutely crazy if you do this,' things like that. All our questions were aimed at probing how dangerous the individual was.

So anyway, finally the sun came up. Cason was at home asleep, but meanwhile the plane had to fly to Florida when we released it; it couldn't go anywhere else. A long battle. There came a moment when a door opened so the men [hostages] could come out, but since there were women still inside and [the men] were determined to be 'gentlemen', they wouldn't leave the plane. We also had to see how we were going to bring in the fuel, find a way to fill the plane when it suited us.

So the discussions went on. We were trying to protect the passengers, trying to find a way to get them out of the cabin even if the plane took the hijacker to Florida. The pilot himself was refusing to fly, because he said he wasn't going to let them confiscate the plane up there. I, of course, told him, 'Listen, you're going to obey the orders you're given,' as forcefully as I could. He wouldn't say anything, so I repeated my orders – 'You'll do as you're told' – because the pilot was like on strike.

At a certain point – I'd been studying the individual closely, the things he was doing – when he had the women and the son [sic] go back there, and the others up here, I said to Rogelio Acevedo [head of the IACC], who was standing beside me, 'Acevedo, get on the loudspeaker and talk to those people, tell them this guy is a criminal.' I gave him instructions to explain [to them], tell them to be calm, although to aim his message especially at attacking the hijacker.

Of course Acevedo's message probably lasted no more than half a minute, and when he finished I told him, 'Listen, everything you said and the way you said it was just perfect to make him do exactly the opposite.' So at that point I had to make the decision to talk to the crew, everybody, the passengers – I had to talk to them myself.

You spoke to the passengers?
Yes, I said, 'You people know my voice, you've heard it,' – calmly, of course, very quietly. 'This individual,' I said, 'is putting the lives of women and children at risk, and he's persisted in doing that. There is that risk.' And I urged them, if they saw he was about to throw the grenade, to take it away from him, to keep him from doing it. So I was talking to them, urging them [to be calm but to act if necessary], giving them instructions – I told them we weren't promising the hijacker anything, but that we *were* discussing a solution; I told them the Americans didn't want the plane up there, everything they'd said about that so far; I even told them that the hijacker was refusing to talk to the head of the Interests Office, and that he was taking a miserable position. Oh, I was tough, to soften [the hijacker] up and [at the same time] alert the passengers that at the last minute, given the danger, they should act. The whole problem lay in studying this individual, in order to make the right decisions.

To [persuade him to] turn the people loose, right?
That's right, turn the people loose – put in some fuel and let the plane land

somewhere else [not Florida]. At that hour of the night, we even had to call in geographers to look at some other maps, because aviation maps don't include that information. We called: 'Find maps and call to see exactly how far it is to such-and-such a place, to the airport,' to find out how far [the plane] could get. There was fuel for at least 100 kilometres further, sixty miles further, so it would reach the very border of the place where there was another airport. There was no way to solve the problem safely; we did all the calculations.

There came a moment when the guy, desperate, said to Acevedo, 'Tell them to let the plane go.' And [Acevedo] answered: 'There's not enough fuel to get to the Bahamas.' They actually could have reached the Bahamas, and we could have called the authorities there. We didn't know how they'd react, but the Bahamas are very vulnerable, and an agreement we have about illegal immigrants means a lot to them . . . They return them, but there are so many islands, and smugglers have no respect for any country's sovereignty . . .

So, we could have telephoned [the Bahamas] – a meeting of Caribbean leaders had taken place not long before – and it wasn't hard to ask them to arrest the hijacker and return him, but why was that not a good idea? First, locating the prime minister, seeing whether he was there, persuading him and so on. Second, what we were doing really made no sense, because what really would have counted was for the Americans to respect the agreement, for them not to confiscate the plane up there, for them not to detain the crew – we didn't want the plane confiscated, and we didn't want some accomplice, if there was one, to stay up there. Of course, we ourselves were imposing all those conditions, we were raising [those issues], and they seemed to be willing for what had happened not to happen again.

In the Bahamas there was another issue – in the Bahamas they could fill the plane with fuel and it still wouldn't reach [the US]. Because the problem could have been solved in the Bahamas; we could have said, 'Give them fuel so they can keep going and get to one of those other states,' but what were we afraid of? We were afraid that despite filling the tanks in the Bahamas the plane still wouldn't be able to reach one of the other states and it would fall into the ocean. Somebody suggested that it might possibly be able to reach Jamaica, pushing it, because pilots always have a little [fuel] in reserve; [the plane] could just barely make it to Jamaica, and the problem then would've been in the Jamaicans' court, so we decided not to do that. We told [the hijacker] that was out, because a problem had to be solved in the Bahamas and it wasn't a problem that could be solved in a few minutes, and they couldn't go to Jamaica because of the risk of dropping into the ocean.

But anyway, we had the tank truck out on the runway, and the fire engines, too, all the equipment, in case he set off the grenade.

Had you been able to identify the hijacker?
Well, we'd been trying to find out who this guy was from the passenger list, because there was a woman and a little girl . . . But unfortunately, there was an initial error: a reasonable suspect showed up, a doctor with his wife coming back from a trip, and for a minute our idea of who the hijacker was was wrong. For three or four hours we worked on the theory that it was this other man, and then in the morning [i.e., after the sun was up] we got information that it wasn't him, it was this other one.

We identified his residence. And we discovered that he had some moulds for grenades in his house, for making plaster grenades, but that could have been a step prior to actually pouring a metal grenade, and we didn't know whether the guy had done that or not . . . And I also think they discovered some things such as some plastic that he had, which might lead one to suspect that he actually had a real grenade, although we weren't 100 per cent sure about it. I increasingly tended to think that he didn't, taking into account all his answers, all his reactions, all the circumstances.

We discovered that the hijacker's brother worked in the Ministry of the Interior, so we located him – in the province of Matanzas – and he also came to the airport and helped. I said, 'Have him come, too, to see whether he can convince this guy.' He came to see whether he could make some sort of deal with him, tell him that if he'd give it up he'd receive a punishment in keeping with that [i.e., a reduced sentence for cooperating, for not causing loss of life, etc.]. We told them both that he'd be punished, and with his brother there, we might have found a solution. We were trying hard to do that. Meanwhile, we were waiting for word from the United States.

In the meantime, had Cason come back to the airport?
We'd told Cason, right about dawn, that there wasn't enough fuel to get to any state but Florida, and we asked him to think about some place, maybe an air base, where it could be flown, where there'd be more facilities and the plane with its pilots and passengers could be returned to us. They studied the situation for a long time – apparently there was quite a bit of discussion that morning at the State Department or somewhere else.

We kept pushing those arguments, but we were also negotiating with the guy so he'd give himself up and come out, after all those remonstrations and whatnot. We began our negotiations on the basis that we'd give him fuel so he could keep going, but we explained various difficulties to him, trying to buy time while we waited for the State Department's answer, and that had to be about eleven. Meanwhile, we were buying time [to try to get] some people off the plane and refuel it. In the midst of that battle, the time passing, the guy's exhaustion and all that, we managed to send in water for the children and at a certain point we convinced him to let twenty-two people off the plane. And when those twenty-two people got off, with the lowered weight, there was enough fuel.

At that point, we called Cason again. 'Any word?' 'No.' We called again: 'Any word?' 'No.' There still had been no decision about the place where they were going to authorize the plane to land. We informed him that we'd managed to get twenty-two people off the plane, so now it could go to any of the states [apparently under discussion (?)].

'Check with your people,' we told him, 'it can get to wherever, there's no risk any more.' We gave him quite a bit of time, because that arrangement – the release of the twenty-two passengers – came at around nine in the morning, and we gave him two hours, and still nothing . . . We waited: 'Any answer?' 'No.' 'Any answer?' 'No.' Came eleven, and we'd negotiated with the guy to let us bring in the tank truck and fill the plane – we'd calculated the time it took to refuel, which might be twenty minutes or an hour or an hour and a half, all the time it took – so as to eliminate the risk of the grenade and get him off to another state, and to see whether there was really any disposition on the part of the American authorities to change their policy. I think it was clear that there were two policies up there.

Two opposing tendencies in Washington?
That's right. There were two different lines up there, no doubt about it, and we didn't know which one they were going to take.

Meanwhile, the man said he wanted to take off at eleven – we had to find pretexts and whatnot: the brother who was coming, he'd already been called, everything's under way . . . The plane the brother was coming in took off from Varadero – a plane or a helicopter, I don't remember – and me looking impatiently at my watch; they took a little longer than expected but they finally got there, I think the brother got there at almost [eleven]. Oh, and the hijacker was asking for water, everything necessary for him and the people on board – and money, boy!, what a mentality! He needed for us to lend him $1,000 to give to some people up there when he got off the plane ... And us waiting for an answer from Washington. It helped that the brother's plane was delayed, and so finally the brother arrived. He talked to him, but the [hijacker] didn't trust him at all. But we were buying time, and those Americans – at 10:55, 'Any answer?' 'No.' Where are they going to land? We didn't know.

Did the Cubans keep Cason informed of this whole process, of the way the situation was developing?

Every step we took, we explained it to Cason: 'Listen, we've done this and that, we've talked to this person and that person, we've managed to persuade [the hijacker] to let so many people off, the brother's arrived now,' etc. All the information. So now comes the departure time. 'We're going to buy some more time,' we told him, with the brother, with this and that, some sandwiches that had to be made, the money. The head of aviation, Rogelio Acevedo, wasn't too happy with the situation, or the handling of it ... So I said to him, 'Have you got the money there?' He was in open rebellion. Well, not exactly in open rebellion, but he was suffering. I said to him, 'Listen, have you got the cash there?' 'Yeah.' So I said, 'Okay, well, we're going to send in $500. We're not going to give him 1,000, we're going to give him 500.' But [the hijacker] is saying, 'Are you done? When do we leave?' He was pretty determined. 'Right away,' we said.

So we told the guy out on the runway, 'Go nice and slow.' They were moving slowly. We sent in two pilots, two copilots. They went in through the door up front, the one the pilots disembark through, so he couldn't see them. The case was, there were two pilots that had been there all night and during the trip [from the Isle of Youth]. And the answer hadn't come. So we told the pilots, 'Get ready,' and they started the engines at about 11:54, an hour after the flight was supposed to take off, and the people in the Interests Office still hadn't received any answer. So I told the pilots, 'Take it easy up in the air, wait for the answer.' And when the plane was in the air, Cason got the answer: the plane was to land in Key West – the worst possible place! It was worse than any run-of-the-mill air base.

[In Key West] they mistreated our people again, terribly. They arrested [the hijacker]. Oh, also – he was taking a woman and a son, which wasn't his, [it was] the lady's son, but the next day they released the lady and the little boy. She shouldn't have been released; she wasn't clean, because she'd been an accomplice, she'd helped get the grenade on board, or certain plastic components of it, the non-steel mechanisms.

So it wouldn't be detected?
That's right. But [the Americans] turned her loose the next day. The hijacker is still up there. Open investigation, mistreatment of all the passengers, efforts to persuade some of them to stay in the US, pressure. Some of the crew were waiting for the investigation to be completed, they left the plane – and it was confiscated. They [the Americans] did the exact opposite of what they promised.[2]

The next day, 1 April 2003, a boat full of passengers and even some tourists on board was hijacked in Havana harbour.
Yes, that was very strange – the next day, word came in the morning: The boat to Regla had been hijacked by some guys with a pistol and knives . . . So, we applied the principle: nobody was to try to intercept it. So they leave the bay and head into the open sea. They would communicate over the ship-to-shore, and when they were about six or seven miles out they demanded a boat to take all those people to Florida. They said, 'We've got fifty passengers' – they said fifty but it wasn't quite that many – 'and we've got so many children, we've got . . .'

The leader of the hijackers said they had so many children and so many foreign tourists. From six to eight children and five to six tourists. They exaggerated a little bit: children, actually, in the end, there was just one. It's strange there weren't more, in fact, because there's always a group of children.

And where was this boat going?
It was a ferry, a motor boat; it has about a hundred seats, and it takes people who live in the area of Old Havana or in other municipalities in and around the city across the bay to the other side.

To Regla?
That's right. It's a boat for quiet water. Those boats have flat bottoms, they can't be used in heavy seas. So they hijacked it, said they had fifty passengers on board, they hijacked it early in the morning. I didn't find out about it until sometime mid-morning; they'd already made their first threat. They were asking for a faster boat, and they threatened, if they didn't get it, to

start throwing hostages overboard. That was the first threat, then they repeated it – they were talking on the ship-to-shore, the marine band radio. I asked the Coast Guard and was told that as always, the US Coast Guard had been notified.

That was how long after the plane hijacking we were talking about?
Twenty-four hours.

You'd just finished dealing with the other negotiations.
The plane was hijacked on 30 March, on the 31st all the negotiations took place, and early on the morning of 1 April this hijacking of the ferry took place, using almost the same methods ... The plane hijacking had been made public by that time, possibly on the 31st, to the Cuban people. It's likely that when the news first broke that the hijackers of that first plane had been released on bail up in Florida – the ones with the knives, on 19 March 2003 – this new group had started planning to hijack the ferry. Because they'd all had a meeting the night before, in a certain house. [Although] they improvised quite a bit. I can't tell you exactly, but I'm pretty sure that the news of that second plane encouraged them, although this time they hijacked the ferry to Regla.

There were nine of them, I think.
It was a big group, really, all accomplices. It may have been eleven or twelve; some of them were women. The woman travelling with the son was in on the conspiracy.

And you thought these events – the hijacking of the ferry, added to the two previous hijackings of planes and so on – might trigger a new wave of migration, a second migration crisis?
It was obvious; it was a proven fact, because when they stole the Regla ferry, that's the sign that people can't leave, and the American authorities encourage that.

The first hijacking was on 19 March, and the Americans met the hijackers and did what they always do, but then they said, 'Let's turn them loose.'[3] And while the judge was making that decision [to free them], the prosecutor – unless it was incredible hypocrisy – was insisting that they not be released; he went to the [circuit] court in Atlanta, which has jurisdiction over Miami, but Atlanta upheld the judge's right [to release the hijackers]. That meant

that now, after the terrorist attacks of September 11, you saw *some* efforts
– because they were in a very embarrassing situation – to keep the hijackers
from being released [i.e., a double standard was at work for terrorists]. But
in the end, they couldn't stop [the judge] . . .

Here, as I've told you, 90 per cent of those who left illegally were people
that other people, up in Florida, came down to get. Just 10 per cent of them
made or stole a raft, or stole a boat. And that practice has cost many lives,
because, as I said, the boats are overloaded – they're operated by traffickers
in illegal emigrants . . . and when they arrive up there [in the US], the
American authorities don't do anything about it. We had to take harsh
measures, hand down heavy sentences. Of course later, the US, the presidents, have gradually changed their methods, they've adopted different
positions with respect to the subject of migration.

With President Bush, has the migration problem worsened again?
What did they do? They suspended the issue of visas, just as they'd done in
Reagan's time, under pretexts – there are always pretexts – but under whatever pretext, the point is, they suspend them. And not long afterwards James
Cason came [down here] and that strange event occurred on 19 March –
two hours before the war in Iraq started – when a plane full of passengers
was hijacked at knifepoint. And a whole series of very similar things started
happening: [Castro seems to be ticking the events off on his fingers:] on
1 April, early in the morning, the Regla ferry. And several days later, a
soldier was assaulted and his weapon was taken . . . A third hijacking was
thwarted, and over thirty projects, undertaken by people who weren't alleging any political motivations. Every case, every one, was as serious, as
criminally serious, as the events of 5 August 1994, when riots broke out in
Havana and a situation occurred that virtually forced us to tell the Americans, 'We're not going to guard our borders,' and we declared that we were
on strike. Which is when the massive exodus of *balseros* took place – which
they were afraid of. Now, in the circumstances of that moment [i.e., 1 April
2003], with the Iraq War starting, they've used [hijackings] as the pretext to
create a situation that would justify aggression.

How did the hijacking of the Regla ferry end?
Well, the people who hijacked the boat, at a certain point their fuel ran out.
What did we do in response? We sent the minister of the interior down
there, Abelardo Colomé Ibarra. The head of the border patrol went down

there, too. I spoke with an aide, and I told him, 'Listen, locate a fuel transport and send it down there, and X number of more boats . . .' To prevent any tragic sinking like the one on 13 July 1994.

Because a situation had taken place that same day that had to be taken into account. The Coast Guard in Florida said they were sending boats, as usual . . . They did that every time we informed them that a boat was leaving illegally. But then all of a sudden they informed us that they've given orders for their boats to turn back, that there's a law in I don't know what year – I'm not sure but I think they said 1988 – that says that in these cases, it's the country under whose flag the boat is sailing that has to solve the problem. They said Cuba had to solve it.

They knew there was a boat that had been hijacked, with hostages, and dangerous guys on board, and they could have said, 'Well, we're not going to let them in; we'll send a boat and return them, with the guarantee that we've returned them all.' Despite the fact that they've never kept the bargain, when they feel like it they let 20 per cent or more [of the illegal emigrants] stay in the US, in order to halfway satisfy the mafia up there, which is opposed to returning *anybody*.

They sent us a message informing us that they weren't going to do what they usually did: wait, approach the boat, escort them, and once they were in American waters, make a decision. They're supposed to observe an agreement, but what they did was say, 'You deal with it.' So we had to deal with the matter ourselves.

So – citizens have been hijacked; there are children, there are foreigners. My instructions were, 'Send in more men and equipment.' The sea at force 3 [4] and worsening. Before they'd reached twenty-two miles out, more or less, I said, 'Send in several boats, a rescue team, a tugboat and everything.' Naturally, we weren't going to attack the boat, nothing of the sort, that was stupid; we had to ensure that it didn't sink. That's why we sent in the minister of the interior. The instructions were – we had about three boats out there – 'Position one on the right, 100 metres from the hijacked boat; another one 100 metres to the left; and a third one behind, about a kilometre behind, and escort [the hijacked boat] so if there's an accident you can go to its aid immediately. And maintain those positions, escort the boat until it reaches the jurisdiction of American waters. Watch them and be sure nothing happens to them till then.'

The American authorities, pretty cynically, declared that we were to deal with this, that they'd take over when the boat got up there – that's what they replied after telling us that they were sending boats, as usual. When the boat's fuel ran out, it hove to.

The hijackers kept threatening a group of women they were keeping close, as hostages; they had knives to their throats. They'd keep knives at the throat of some of the women, and the tourists, too; they knew very well, they were aware that they were doing damage with all that. And when their fuel ran out, they agreed to be towed.

It was a miracle that boat didn't sink – you should have seen it . . . It was a flat-bottomed boat, for inland waters; the [Americans] knew that, too, and yet they refused to accept them. When the fuel ran out, the hijackers contacted us and finally said they'd let a tugboat throw a line to the boat, in the bow, but their attitude didn't change, they tied up to the pier with a line several metres long.

Of course they'd come in for fuel, like the plane that had asked for fuel, with this completely distrustful attitude.

Were you following this one personally, too?
I took charge of this one, too. I'm going to explain why. In the midst of all my work, it was getting to be eleven o'clock at night, more or less, and all the forces, the Coast Guard, all of them were out . . . You know what they do in Europe and everywhere else when there's a plane hijacked – they impose no limitations of any kind on themselves: they may even assault [the plane], shoot, kill.

We had special forces troops there, and the Coast Guard, and their idea was to liberate the boat. The first thing *I* did was tell them not to take any action.

You went personally to Mariel?
I gave instructions by phone, and when I finished with other activities I had to attend to, I went quickly [to Mariel], before the time [the security forces] said they were going to take measures to free the hostages. So as I was arriving – it was about midnight – they asked me to stop; we were almost coinciding with the moment [the security forces] were going to strike.

They had the instructions I'd given them – to stand by, stay beside the boat, but the boat was already very close to the dock. There was some hope that once the hijackers had come up to the dock they could be made to see reason. Which is why I went – I was worried . . . I gave orders that [the security forces] weren't to carry out any of those actions, because of the consequences [these actions] generally have for the passengers, the hijackers and everybody else.

A little before midnight, the boat had been stopped. And in the middle of all this, I was communicating via a mobile phone – for my communications I have to be very careful; the minute I make a call, the United States knows everything.

They listen in on everything.
I said, 'Tell them not to do anything.' They were preparing for what they were going to do, the measures to take, how they were going to free the hostages – planning, you know – and I arrived and observed the situation, and I recommended that they not do anything right away. The boat hadn't arrived yet – I think there was even a merchant ship tied up to that dock, and I said to them, 'Don't take any action,' because it's dangerous . . . You have to find a solution that doesn't involve bloodshed, that won't injure or kill people.

All through that night, through the radio on one of the police cruisers, we studied the individual that was acting as the leader – the individual was really dangerous, unlike the other one, the one with the grenade in the aeroplane.

The authorities had learned their identities?
You never know at first, you have to send people to investigate. There [on the scene] what you're analysing is the behaviour – how he talks, what he says, how he argues, how intelligent he is. And this guy seemed to be pretty primitive. The position he had the pistols in, pointed straight at the hostages' heads, was very dangerous. He chose, by the way, the French women; there were two from Scandinavia and two from France, four women.

Four tourists.
The leader was dangerous, that's the conclusion we reached, so that's how we approached the problem. I was there observing everything; the people [i.e., government authorities] were exhausted, they hadn't slept since one o'clock the previous morning, twenty-four hours had passed and it was hard to tell who needed more rest, the hijackers or our own people. I said, 'Everybody go take a break, rest.' We reached a kind of truce so they could get some sleep. We sent water to the children – there were 'four or six little children', they told us; we sent in milk, some water for the hostages,

and we managed to get them into a negotiation situation, trying to find a solution.

I left and slept for a few hours. The leader of the hijackers had agreed to send one of his men to the pier. And the negotiations started.

The man he sent came in with this very insolent attitude – he was acting very tough, when we'd managed to soften them up at least a little. They'd turned tough, demanding, threatening. They gave an ultimatum. Given that situation, we changed tactics – we didn't answer their calls any more, and we started thinking about how to solve the problem, because now there was no way to even negotiate. We had to find alternatives, because the hostages were really suffering.

So at that point we started using a series of tactics of a more psychological nature. There were tactics using force that we could have used, but we rejected some of them, despite the fact that the main leader, the most dangerous of them, was vulnerable . . .

Were you thinking about an intervention?
Yes. He had a gun to the tourists' heads, the hammer was cocked and the safety was off. We learned that afterwards, because when the pistol was later found in the water, it went off as the diver was bringing it up. The whole situation was dangerous, really – this was an individual who was ready to use the weapon. But it wasn't a question of making him pay, that wasn't the problem. It was a really dangerous situation, and we had to look into all the alternatives.

We didn't use any sort of violence, we used psychological methods of various kinds. We had created all the conditions so that the risk would be reduced to almost zero. Remember that it was noon by now, twelve hours after the truce, or break, the night before. But it worked. There was a contingent of troops on the side of the dock in front of the boat, as one psychological element, and one of the French women managed to make a barely perceptible sign to the troops that were there on the pier, very close by. She had a gun to her head. The guy, too, was pretty exhausted, agitated, because we had cut our communications with him; it had been an hour since we'd spoken to him in any way, or replied in any way.

In order to study his behaviour, we made contact again . . . I said to the minister, 'Tell him the only guarantee we'll give him is if he releases the hostages.' There came a moment that afternoon, and at a point when we were about to use one of the other possible methods, to guarantee a non-violent solution, when this French woman ... she made a sign to a squadron of special forces troops that were over there, and they consulted [with us] and we said, 'Yes, that would be the smartest thing to do. Encourage her to jump in the water.' So the two French women jumped into the water. One of them was more determined than the other – she was the one who was in the most danger; the other one was more scared, terrified, really. But both of them were very brave, very daring. I don't know what pretext they used, but one of them jumped in and then the other one, and immediately one of the men that was with [being held by?] the leader of the hijackers opportunistically jumped into the water. The leader moved with the pistol to see what was happening in the water. One of the hostages was a member of the Ministry of the Interior, and he grabbed the guy, got him in a bear hug, and they were struggling and they both fell in the water – the pistol, in fact, fell in first – which was why we had to dive for it later. They pulled it up about thirty hours later. And the pistol went off in the water. It was loaded, and the hijacker had taken off the safety. It was dangerous to wrestle with him that way, but he fell into the ocean and then everybody on the boat did the same thing – into the water.

No one was injured?
No, no one. Of course, we'd been employing several psychological tactics. The leader, for example, was pretty intimidated when the [Coast Guard] launch pulled in close out there at sea. But he had nothing to complain about – the [Coast Guard] boat was just going around in circles ... We did a little of everything, all the things you do to keep him under pressure, keep things tense; he was being worn down and he was beginning to be pretty exhausted; but the French girl was what triggered the outcome, and they all jumped into the water, the hijackers, too – everybody jumped into the water and then were picked up.

I saw them all later – I spoke with the French women, I asked them the essential questions; I spoke with the hostages. I didn't talk to the leader of the hijackers, but I did talk to the others, just generally asking them things. Among the forty passengers there were several accomplices – there were around twelve of them, some of them women; that lady with the little boy was an accomplice, but at least twenty-eight of the passengers weren't implicated in any way.

In their negotiations with them, did the authorities promise anything – freedom, a visa to go to the United States, anything like that, if they released the hostages safe and sound?

Look, they were the ones who'd created the problem. Even the attempt to persuade them was very complicated. I didn't like it, and I said, 'Tell them they'll be punished on the basis of their behaviour,' if they cooperated in solving the problem, and we sincerely talked to them about the priority of resolving the concrete situation, while we also looked for some way to resolve the problem created by the cynical position taken by the US authorities.

In that situation, it was essential to find a solution, like the one we adopted for the hijackers of US planes when we sent back to the Americans what turned out to be the last plane hijacked in the United States. There hadn't been a hijacking in twenty-four years, because now everybody – crazies, half-crazies – knew they weren't going to achieve their objective, because we'd return them, but that's what the American authorities refused to do with any of these cases of hijackings of boats or planes – which, if they'd just been returned, hopefully would have solved the problem.

Even a drastic sentence wasn't enough, it didn't do the trick; we had to assume additional risks, warn them that under no circumstances would a hijacker of a boat or plane receive one drop of fuel – no petrol and no cooperation, for boat or plane.

The third thing was that anybody doing such things would be subjected to the same procedure, and that the Council of State would offer no clemency.

So in fact because of the attitude on the part of the American authorities, we were exposed to the risk here of eventual hostages. So I said, All right, whose responsibility is it if a commercial plane, a plane with 100 passengers, is blown up in the air? Who's responsible for those deaths? The ones who from up there [in the US] are encouraging that kind of action. Which is why I tell many of our friends who sometimes criticize us that they should try to understand the circumstances under which this country has to defend itself.

But even in those circumstances, the hijackers could have been given stiff sentences. In any other country they would have been, but why the death sentence and such a quick execution?

In fact, not even the exemplary sentence was enough. It would have been very complicated for us, and yet we were willing to deal with him, the one who was the leader – if in fact he was actually the leader – and make some compromise on the sentence, and we'd told him, 'You will all be punished, but the sentence will depend on whether or not you cooperate.' Honestly, we made great efforts to persuade the man to cooperate. But no matter what, he had put us in a very difficult situation, because while the trial was going on there was an attempt to steal a weapon in order to hijack another plane – there were dozens, more than thirty plans; word came in from everywhere of attempts to hijack planes and boats, and it was that kind of person, who's very daring, very audacious, and totally without fear.

At that point, the problem had been created by the Americans. And a person knows, because of the circumstances under which they operate, that that's proof that the problem isn't going to be solved. All it would have taken is for them to say they were going to return every plane that was hijacked. The day they return the first hijackers, the problem's solved. We solved the problem for them, but they didn't, and won't, solve it for us. There was still the Cuban Adjustment Act, there were still hijackings of ships, thefts, piracy of crop-dusting planes, but not passenger planes. No one even thought it could happen – honestly, it was a total surprise.

And consider something: the hijacking of the plane took place just before the Iraq War started, which shows the urgent need, from our point of view, to stop them [the hijackings], so in our view they had to be stopped, and we saw no other way to stop the wave of hijackings. We had to speak [to the nation] later and explain; we had to say, 'Policy: not a drop of petrol.' So they could land one way or another but there would be not one drop of petrol; that meant that no one would get any petrol no matter what they did. And of course there were other measures, too.

So, if there was no possibility of achieving their objective – even if they did manage to steal a boat somewhere – by hijacking boats and planes, and taking hostages, that possibility was taken off the table at this moment, there is no possibility of that.

Now then, think about the facts I've given you: since September 2002, the Americans had been breaking the agreement that they'd been keeping for ten years. This wasn't after we talked to them about the monitoring, it was six months before we imposed the ban on travelling, six months before – who knows why; they stopped issuing visas and thereby created the same situation as in August 1994. We'd have had chaos here if people had started stealing boats and planes. Consider the importance that we had to give that – almost more than anything else.

So that first plane was hijacked in such a strange way that nobody could understand it – the war against Iraq hadn't even started, and [the hijacking] had been planned beforehand, because they [the perpetrators] had made several trips. No one knew who these guys were, what they knew, whether they were induced, incited, to do what they did, which was possible and I think even probable, because all it takes is one, all it takes is a leader, it wasn't going to be a huge coincidence. They [the US authorities] had it all planned, they'd been holding up visas for months and months – they had plans to do that [hijack a second plane, set off a wave of hijackings]. They'd got one plane hijacked, and they knew as well as we did what the potential was.

When Oliver Stone[5] came back to Cuba, we met Oliver and the people who came with him – Felipe Pérez Roque was there, too, and the eight guys who assaulted a soldier and stole his rifle so they could take over a plane and hijack it. Those hijackers were tried and convicted, although the hijacking was foiled. They were already at the airport, they had it all planned and they were carrying the plan out. Of course, none of them acted out of political reasons. They all told their story, each one, their motivations. We were all talking, almost like you and I are talking now: 'Why did you people do this?' 'Because of so-and-so.' All of them with ninth-grade educations, one with a little more ... because this is a literate population, and the criminals here, most of them, have ninth-grade educations. They're all there, filmed, and a conversation with Oliver and his team, Oliver also asking questions, and I also asked them, and even explained to them: 'You will have to be punished, but fortunately you didn't manage to pull off the hijacking.'

They explained, one by one, why they'd decided to hijack this plane and when. One day we said, 'Let's go see them.' They were here, because the crime scene was within the jurisdiction of the Havana court. None of this has been made public, and they talked like you and I are talking now.

And did they say why they wanted to leave?
Everything, they explained it all. But it's that there were, also, over thirty cases ...

Which were taking place at the time.
Yes, thirty hijack plans, and now they've almost dropped to none.

Do you think, then, that the use of the death penalty was effective in this case?
This is a case in which I say that a measure of this nature nips the problem in the bud. And the antecedent can be found in the fact that in twenty-five

years, from that country, the United States, where there are so many crazies and all kinds of mentally deranged people, no one has hijacked a plane, when before, dozens of planes full of passengers were hijacked despite any sanctions we imposed on the hijackers. It was the one sanction, returning them, that solved the problem. If [the US] would return them, the problem would be over. If they'd take away their Cuban Adjustment Act, there'd be no problem of this kind. That's the story, I've told you the whole story – I almost forgot we were in an interview.

What are your feelings when you see all the people who've protested against those three executions?
We totally respect the opinions of those people who for religious, philosophical or humanitarian reasons oppose the death penalty. We Cuban revolutionaries also abhor it, for reasons more profound than those that have been dealt with by the social sciences on crime, under study today in our country. The day will come when we'll be able to accede to the desire of all those friends, you among them, who advise us to do away with capital punishment. I should say that we have suffered, in particular, because we haven't been able to respond positively to the noble intervention of Pope John Paul II.

I felt a sincere and profound respect for that pope. I understood and admired his noble efforts on behalf of life and peace. No one opposed the war against Iraq as tenaciously and as constantly as he did. I'm absolutely certain that he would never have advised the Iraqis to allow themselves to be killed without defending themselves, nor would he have advised the Cubans to. He knew perfectly well that this is not a problem between Cubans; it's a problem between the people of Cuba and the government of the United States. Not even Christ, who flogged the money-lenders out of the temple, would deny the right of a people to defend itself.

Were you surprised by José Saramago's statement? [6]
Yes. We were hurt by it. I think he acted a little precipitously. Without fully knowing the situation, or the circumstances. But I respect his convictions. Many of our friends were upset by those executions. We respect their principles. But there's been a great deal of propaganda, and it's created a great deal of confusion.

23

Cuba and Spain

Felipe González – José María Aznar – The Spanish Socialists and the Cuban Revolution – The Spanish Left – The break with Felipe González – Franco and Aznar – King Juan Carlos I – Prince Felipe of Spain – Manuel Fraga

After the arrest of the dissidents in March 2003, Felipe González, former Spanish prime minister,[1] made some very harsh statements about you.[2]
Some very stupid things. He's mad about what I said about the extra-judicial executions of the Basque ETA members in Spain. Because I said that under the mandate of the head of the Spanish government, Felipe González, dozens of ETA members were extra-judicially executed without anyone uttering a word of protest or filing a denunciation with the United Nations Human Rights Commission.[3] And I also said that another head of government, José María Aznar, advised the president of the United States at a difficult moment in the war in Kosovo to ratchet up the war, increase the bombing and attack civilian targets, especially television [stations], which would have caused the death of hundreds of innocent people and immense pain to millions of people. All the press said was, 'Castro attacks Felipe and Aznar'. They said nothing about the real content [of my remarks].

And I've said it absolutely clearly: The [Felipe González] government was implicated in those executions [assassinations]. And Felipe González, as its leader, as the prime minister of the country, had to know about it. That nonsense that he didn't know anything, nobody can believe that – anyone with the slightest idea of the way a government works knows that an operation of that kind can't be carried out without the complicity of the government. His closest advisers, the minister of the interior, the chief of police obviously were following orders. Those advisers were tried and found guilty,[4] but he wasn't. The first thing any leader has to do is take responsibility for what happened. If I behaved that way, I wouldn't be able to give another order to another soul in Cuba.

You'd had a long friendship with Felipe González, right?

I've known Felipe since the days of the opening of democracy in Spain, in 1976, long before the Spanish Socialist [Workers] Party (PSOE) became a force in the country. Before the first elections in 1977, when he was elected to the Spanish parliament. He visited Cuba in June 1976 and we talked for a long time. Later, when he was touring Latin America, he would often stop over in Cuba. He went to Panama, he had good relations with Omar Torrijos; he visited several places, because he was always very interested in Latin America. He would come here – he liked the ocean, he liked to fish, he was really passionate about sport fishing. Once we spent two days out on a boat. And we had many very friendly conversations with him. García Márquez came along, and Guayasamín, the Peruvian writer Alfredo Bryce Echenique and also Javier Solana, who was later minister of culture, I think, and then afterwards became 'grand marshal', the secretary-general of NATO; today he's some sort of minister of foreign relations for the European Union. We invited several personalities and we were like family, talking about all sorts of things – very positive, very constructive.

Later, the press attacked him in Spain because the man who'd been head of a terrorist organization was being held in prison here, a man originally from Spain.

Eloy Gutiérrez Menoyo?[5]

That's right. Gutiérrez Menoyo, whom we decided to free. He'd already served almost his whole sentence. We didn't want that to cause any problems for Felipe. He'd talked to us, very cautiously, very respectfully, about the issue. And we took the initiative of freeing Gutiérrez Menoyo.

Did you have good relations with Felipe González when he came to power in October 1982, when he was named prime minister?

We'd been hoping that Felipe would win, because despite his faults, he was an individual you could discuss things with, talk to; he observed the forms, he was honest. Once he became prime minister it was another thing, and some differences arose [between us], because in our view, during the Cold War Spain's role had been positive in its relations with the whole world, because it was a privileged situation, it was a situation of trade and peace, and we didn't like the idea of Spain entering NATO; it was that simple.

At the time, there was a great deal of discussion of that, because I made some statements to a Spanish news agency. He'd already won the elections. I perfectly understood the economic issues behind joining the European Union, which Spain did in 1986, because that was to Europe's benefit and, consequently, Spain's. But we totally disagreed as to the issue of NATO, and I made some open, frank anti-NATO statements, about the role I saw for Spain in terms of diplomatic openness and the role Spain could play in the world, within that situation, instead of joining NATO, which Felipe González had said he wouldn't do, and I gave my opinion: you can find it all in a long interview I did about Spain entering NATO in May of 1982.

The issue of NATO, then, cooled relations between you and him?
Well, Felipe changed quite a bit. But we supported him in the 1992 elections against Aznar. I followed the debates, I watched Aznar: he was a robot, a machine whose head had been filled with a series of data, figures. He had a televised debate with Felipe, and Felipe didn't come out too well in that first debate. I saw Aznar's tactics, his psychology, his method of attack, the way he accused, repeated like a machine, and despite that, Felipe was over-confident, he didn't pay enough attention to that first debate, and really, the results of those surveys they do after the televised debates were pretty bad. I even made certain comments to him, and I warned him a bit of the need to take the second debate seriously, to prepare for it well. Since he has more education and general culture than Aznar, more experience, more skill, he was better that [second] time. So in the second debate Felipe had a big win, and that disconcerted Aznar; Aznar didn't have a script, he had no script, because Felipe pulled him off his script, and he won.

But, well, everybody knows the things that happened in Spain during the government of Felipe González: there was corruption, people became millionaires, even the story of that house that one of them built that had I think forty bidets – a lot of people got rich, doing business deals of all kinds. There was a gradual increase of corruption, of enrichment, of loss of moral compass.[6]

I remember that during the first few years after Felipe came to power, at a dinner in the Spanish embassy in Havana, there was a discussion as to how long the Socialist Party could remain in power, how many years, you see, and I said it could remain in power for ever with honest politics, a minimally sincere sort of politics. I couldn't see what possibility there could be in Spain of grabbing power from the Socialists.

The right turn that Felipe's politics took led, in my view, to a loss of support, political decline, corruption and all those things. Our relations at one point were good and then they started going downhill. At one point the Latin American summits began to be held and Felipe would go to the summits and everything would be normal, respectful between us. But he became more and more committed to the policies and politics of the United States and NATO and all that. He squandered his political support; it became completely eroded, and at that point Aznar won.

When the USSR collapsed, did Felipe González have any advice for you as to the reforms that would have to be made in Cuba to avoid a similar collapse?

I remember very well, when the USSR collapsed, the number of people who kept insisting that we do the same stupid things that everybody else was doing. You'd go to a meeting, an inauguration, for example, an investiture of some kind, and some of them would always get together – Carlos Andrés Pérez,[7] Felipe González and other Latin American figures – they'd meet to give me advice on what we had to do in order to ensure Cuba's survival.

With all the respect in the world, I'd listen to them; I'd argue, to the extent it made any sense to argue about it, but I remained inflexible. So Felipe said I was taking a 'Numantic position',[8] as much as to say 'Well, this leads to that,' but we prefer *this*.

We argued a bit over the subject – I told him I was a great admirer of those people, the Numantians, for their valour, their bravery, and for the attitude they had. But [I reiterated] my complete opposition to making the concessions they were demanding, concessions that had sunk all of them, one by one, among them Felipe, Carlos Andrés and, in the first place, the USSR.

I believe the man who'd been Felipe González' minister of economy, Carlos Solchaga, came [to Cuba], too, didn't he?

That's right, because back then Felipe González wanted to help us – imagine, as though we were halfwits and didn't know what was going on in Spain. But he wanted to 'help us' so much that he offered us an adviser, and as calm as could be we thanked him. I said: 'Thank you very much'; that is, we didn't refuse his offer.

You listened politely.

Felipe hadn't yet said who he was going to send, but we knew very well that the PSOE had been advising Gorbachev. Gorbachev's first advisers had been Felipe's people, and one day Gorbachev told me – we were talking on the phone, or in a letter, I don't remember – and he was talking about how much he admired Felipe González. 'Felipe, a Socialist,' he said. For a long time I'd known by memory [*sic*] that Felipe was no Socialist – there was nothing Socialist about him. And Felipe as happy as could be, sending his people off to advise Gorbachev over there.

There ought to be a monument to the PSOE for its contributions to making the USSR what it is today! Even, a bit, for the people who died when the health services – which were never optimum – all disappeared, for the rise in infant mortality, the reduced life expectancy: [the PSOE should get a monument for bringing about] the terrible situations that ensued.

So from your point of view the PSOE has a degree of responsibility for that?

Yes, the PSOE has [some responsibility for] it because it sent in those advisers. Later, the Americans arrived in Moscow. There were more and more of them, and more and more concessions, and, quite simply, the USSR fell apart.

And the advisers that Felipe González sent you at some point – they were the same advisers [he sent to Gorbachev]?

That's right. What I want to say to you is that I knew perfectly well what advice they were going to give me. Felipe's ideas were nothing like the concepts we hold – I'll tell you a story: once there were thousands and thousands of doctors without work in Spain and I told him: 'Why don't you do what we're doing, educating doctors and creating family doctors for communities, tremendous services that can be offered in every village and hamlet, all over the country?' The cost was such-and-such; I even discussed the cost of giving jobs to several tens of thousands of doctors and what those services were worth to the population.

And what was his answer?

Well, he listened, and he was very interested. In November 1986 Felipe came [to Cuba] again, we went out on the ocean fishing, we spent a whole day out at sea, we came back; we went to the Tropicana. Raúl Alfonsín was there, too, the president of Argentina. Felipe wanted to go to the Tropicana, so we had them do the whole big show for him. With very beautiful women, almost all of them Afro-Cubans, and very good singers and dancers, in that show.

I remember we went up on stage with Felipe to congratulate the performers, and people took all the photos they wanted, everybody very warm and welcoming. And there was a particularly attractive girl, a singer, whose name was Linda Mirabal, who later stayed over there in Spain, because you Europeans steal brains . . .

And apparently bodies, too, if I'm following what you're saying . . .
Yes, you fix on the body first, but I'm talking about the artistic mind. The artistic mind is often housed in very beautiful bodies, depending on which art it is.

They took a picture of Felipe standing like this: the woman, very beautiful and very revolutionary, has Felipe like this, by the neck, and he's looking at that mulatto woman like this, apparently in awe. And some magazine, I don't know which one, one of those you people spend so much money on, for glossy paper and whatnot, with all the European society gossip, this magazine has a big headline that says 'Castro and Felipe: The Big Blowout', 'Night on the Town with Dictator in Havana'. It was funny, because Linda was looking at Felipe with her best smile and Felipe was just drooling. That photo was something!

I think it was that same newspaper [*sic*] that published [an article] on King Juan Carlos' son, when he was sailing around the world as a cadet – there were two pages devoted to the king's son. About Felipe and me, but mainly about Felipe, the magazine said 'Night on the Town with Dictator', because he'd gone to the famous Tropicana.

We were going through that period we've talked about before, after the fall of the USSR – we'd fallen into the special period, and they met with me to advise us [to do] things that had brought down that revolution over there in six months. I mean, it was a joke, really – to us, down deep . . .

And the Cubans didn't follow that advice, although you did carry out some reforms, didn't you?
Yes, of course, we had to take measures. We had to agree to allow foreign-currency shops, which we hated, because we knew what it meant: people who had the possibility of receiving foreign currency sent by many of those

who'd left Cuba legally or illegally [would be shopping there; they would be 'privileged']. But certain circumstances forced us to consider them.

I mean, we'd had the idea of mixed businesses before – or, rather, for the development of tourism.

You'd had the idea of tourism since before that?
Yes, and the idea of some mixed businesses also, but basically what we did was take some moderate economic measures – you can't suddenly leap into that sort of venture. We created several mixed businesses with foreign capital, we studied their characteristics, where it was advisable, could be helpful, where it wasn't, or wouldn't be. We gritted our teeth and instituted foreign-currency shops. We knew what the disadvantages of tourism were. And there *are* disadvantages, because certain customs can be introduced . . . You have to fight against corruption; drugs can come in, although fortunately the tourism we've had has been wholesome people, Canadians and people from many European countries, that's what we've promoted – people who come down here mainly to rest and relax.

Almost all the hotels have been built by us – we've done it ourselves – and then there appeared [advertising saying]: 'A such-and-such corporation . . . Hotel Such-and-Such in Havana'; it looked like this foreign corporation spent the money, built it. That's not so. We built many of them ourselves, and since [foreign businesses] have experience in tourism and its techniques, well the hotel was ours, with a contract for its administration by foreign corporations. There are very few hotels built with mixed capital; several, partly with our money and partly with theirs.

In addition, in the construction of those hotels we use many materials that we produce here in Cuba, so we don't have to pay out-of-pocket in foreign currency. Then, as [the hotels] gradually increase in quality, better and better quality, you have to gradually incorporate imported elements. But 80 per cent of the hotel capacity, at least, has been created by Cuba with our own resources.

There were foreign businesses, even, which afterwards ran out of money and we had to finish [the hotels] ourselves. Now, it's by lease contract, but 80 per cent is Cuban. The country has been saved basically by the sweat of its own brow. And by its resources, its sacrifice, although we've reached some positive agreements with some good companies – I mean, solid, serious companies. Of course, you have to discuss things, you have to know what you want, because otherwise, they'll buy out the republic for a dollar.

We had very clear ideas with respect to the fact that you have to retain 100 per cent control, and we entered agreements on electricity, oil, everything, but we didn't privatize a single hospital or school or economic service or basic social service.

How did the rupture with Felipe González come about? Why is he so critical [of you and Cuba] now?
Well, because everything started out very well at a time when there was the Socialist camp, the USSR and so on, and Cuba was not in straitened conditions. At that time there was a certain degree of friendship. Later, when the USSR disappeared, as I said, Felipe and his friends wanted to 'save' us with advice that sunk everybody that followed it – advice like [following the tenets of] neoliberal globalization. Everybody who followed that advice has been ruined. All that advice, in the sphere of politics and the economy, has brought many countries to the verge of ruin. We had very solid, very firm convictions as to our own ideas, our own goals, our own objectives, where we could make a concession and where we couldn't, and we were gaining more and more experience.

For example, with the mixed businesses that [you and I] were talking about, sometimes you find that some machine costs a million dollars, or a million and a half, and you can pay it off in a year or a year and a half. You shouldn't start any mixed business in which somebody brings in a machine, you bring in something else, and what can be amortized in a year and a half is going to be draining money out of the country for twenty years.

Now, if you have to drill offshore, if you have to drill for oil, do the study, all that – that's a place where because of monopolistic phenomena and other reasons, the market prices are many times the cost value – you can do risky contracts if you don't have the technology or the capital that's needed. What you have to know very well are all the international laws and regulations that govern those contracts, discuss them in detail and very firmly. Here, businesses are approved centrally; it's highly advisable and advantageous to do that. We've known of some highly advantageous mixed businesses. And we've also known of some *timbiriches* [fly-by-night operations] that haven't solved a thing.

What do you mean by timbiriches?[9]
I told you the story of those two Spaniards who came in with an investment of a hundred and something thousand dollars and set up a drug-trafficking

operation. They'd buy their raw materials in Colombia and their market was Spain. They seemed like the most efficient kind of administrators; when a container came in for them, they were waiting for it on the dock, they'd take it over there to their factory; when they made a shipment to Spain, in those same containers, they'd accompany them right down to the dock. And as I told you, we later discovered that these were containers that had false walls . . . they filled them with drugs! They produced little figurines or something; they had twelve or thirteen employees – oh, they were so friendly with people, we learned all this later – and the container would go off to Spain with the figurines inside, and the drugs behind a false wall, to be sold over there in Europe or be sent from Spain to the United States.

So at some point this scheme was discovered, over there in Colombia, and what happened was that [somebody in Colombia] warned these guys, and they stayed in Spain. They were charged over there, but they alleged that [none of it was true], that what was happening was a problem with Cuba, because what Cuba wanted was to 'take over their factory, their production' and they were innocent investors. And they're free, as I told you, despite the fact that everybody knows, in Colombia and Cuba, that this was large-scale drug trafficking. Listen, we feel truly insulted, and those guys are walking around free in Spain, without any consequences – everybody knows this.

On television,[10] I've seen you be very angry with Señor Aznar. I have the impression that you aren't enormously fond of the former Spanish prime minister.

Fortunately. [sic] But I don't think I was so irritated, because I was calm – there may have been some indignation at that inopportune statement by the Europeans when everyone's seen the bombings in Iraq, the bombs falling, when they know that millions of people have been traumatized for the rest of their lives. Often you have to envy the ones who died more than the ones who survive, especially when they're mutilated. And when I talk about mutilations, you also have to think about the mental mutilations: people mutilated mentally, people traumatized for the rest of their lives, those children five, six, seven years old, the people thirty, sixty, eighty if they're going to live to be ninety, millions of people with psychic traumas from those bombs – there is no way to measure the [number of] victims, because there have been so many people wounded, so many people killed. The psychological trauma of seeing it all lost – all that wealth, the culture, the museums.

People had just seen all that, which led to 92 per cent of the citizens of Spain opposing the war in Iraq, and France and everywhere in the world against the war. Our country saw that, too, and it's threatened with the same thing happening to it. And at that point there appeared a declaration by the European Union[11] feeding the arsenal of arguments with which the government of the United States was trying to impose its will on the world and crush our country, [and the United States was] offended, insulted, its pride wounded because we resisted, we refused to obey its orders – it's inevitable that there would be a sense of repugnance . . . There was tremendous indignation.

Later I saw the broadcast you're talking about. And there was, well, indignation. But losing my temper, anger, no.

I found you to be pretty hard, pretty stern.
I was stern, my expression may have been stern, but I also used a lot of humour, irony. I prefer irony and humour to ranting and raving, or frowning. At the time, in that broadcast, I wasn't really irritated. I didn't think so, at least. You got that impression; the others [i.e., my advisers] – maybe because they were angrier than I was, or more indignant than I was – didn't. I always ask them, and they tell me; and I know that being calm is much more effective.

Naturally, sometimes I have to say things with a certain degree of passion. I thought I spoke with a certain degree of passion, a certain degree of vehemence, more than fury, or rage. But the whole country's reaction – which was seen the next day[12] – was triggered, really, by the indignation [that statement] caused, the danger that that kind of statement entails – a statement none of those European countries was able to justify.

I mean, that we have one party, that we have dissidents, that we have prisoners – we're not the only party or the only country in the world . . . Can we not have one party? Do we have to have dissidents anyway? Can we not enforce any law? . . . There are a number of questions that no European government can answer, with regard to a double standard, to discrimination against a small country.

During that programme, you called Señor Aznar a 'little Führer' and, among other things, you called him a coward. Do you think that Señor

Aznar's attitude, in particular, was what led the European Union to take measures against Cuba?
He was the ringleader. Listen, Aznar is a friend of that Cuban-American terrorist mafia in Miami; they gave him money for his electoral campaign, he travelled around in planes belonging to those people.

The friends of Jorge Mas Canosa[13] and the Cuban-American National Foundation?
That's right. Although I have to say that Felipe González had already started making economic concessions. But Aznar was a close friend of all those people, and it was Mas Canosa's personal plane that he flew all over Central America in; they also aided him in the general elections in 2000, which is how he beat Felipe.

Aznar came to power in 1996 – full of prejudices, reactionary hatred, because Aznar is a genetic reactionary. Aznar is a conservative, reactionary man.

There was another factor that helped him – the assassination attempt in April 1995, just before the elections,[14] which really helped him to win victory. He did act well, one has to give him that, he behaved – according to what I've read – very bravely. He immediately went to visit all the people who'd been injured, and the people always appreciate that. He acted generously – that is, he exploited that assassination attempt for all it was worth, and if you add that to the mistakes, contradictions, incongruities, and divisions within the Left, well . . .

Which is why, I think, he thought he could exploit the horrendous terrorist attack in Madrid on 11 March 2004, at the Atocha station. But that idea backfired on him, and his party lost the elections. José Luis Rodríguez Zapatero won, and he pulled the Spanish troops out of Iraq – we were glad about that.

Is the Spanish Left overly divided, in your view?
I have to be honest – I'm no apologist for the Spanish Left; we've had relations with Izquierda Unida [the United Left], but they've been very divided. I can't blame [the Izquierda Unida] for the division, because the party that was most intransigently opposed to finding any kind of accord with the rest of the Left was the PSOE.

As for how Aznar and his party thought, everybody knew. And of course, we had no sympathy for him, nor did we want him to win the elections, because we knew more or less what the consequences would be, based on the way he thinks and his relations with the Miami mafia – he was the mafia's man; I mean he received a lot of support, and those people had great hopes for Aznar's policies.

Very soon after he came to power in 1996, he started pretty systematically criticizing Cuba.
There were heated debates in the parliament in Madrid over his policies [towards Cuba], because he named an ambassador, José Coderich, which usually should come after we'd agreed to [the person], and that ambassador started making statements about what he was going to do and undo here in Cuba, and we simply withdrew our agreement to the appointment. We said, 'We do not accept this gentleman as ambassador, and we withdraw our agreement – find somebody else.' All this led to heated debates in the parliament in Madrid.

During that television programme we were talking about, when you criticized Señor Aznar's position, I think – this is from memory – you said something like 'even Franco, finally, had a more respectful attitude towards Cuba'.
At least more honourable.

More honourable? In what sense?
Let me tell you. Doctrinally, at the time of the triumph of the Revolution, we were rabid anti-Franquistas. Then the Yankees started taking all sorts of measures against us, and all of Europe did, too. Once the Revolution went on without Europe, and it could be shown that it could go on perfectly well without Europe – because back then, in 1960, it hadn't been long since the war, and there was NATO, the Cold War, the Yankee blockade and all that – the United States imposed its rupture with Cuba on almost all the countries in Latin America and demanded the same thing of its European allies. We were criticizing Franco and attacking Franco, yet he was the only one who didn't bend to Washington's demand. Ours was a position that was absolutely doctrinaire. There wasn't a place where I didn't attack Franco.

Once – I think it was in January 1960 – a Spanish ambassador, Juan Pablo de Lojendio – he was a *marqués*[, a real *toro*, a fighting bull, he had a very short fuse, you might say . . .]. Back then we hadn't taken a great many measures towards organization, and our security measures weren't particularly impressive, either. It was twelve o'clock at night and in the Telemundo building, where I was on TV talking to the country, criticizing Franco, there was this snorting and bellowing, and this huge bull, as if from some bullfight, storms into the studio like a tank – because he was hefty, you know, too, chunky – and made this huge scene, insults and the whole thing . . . I don't know what exactly I said to him, really because I felt I had to protect him from that sort of provocation, which could create violent reactions, so finally I said, 'Get this so-and-so out of here!' Which was not easy. He was brave, I'll say that for him. And I wasn't all that offended, I have to say, because, I mean, afterwards I had to laugh. But we had to expel him, we had no alternative.

But relations weren't broken off, were they?
No, [Cuba's] relations with Franco, there was nobody who was going to [make me] break them off. Cuban tobacco – who bought it? Spain. Cuban sugar – Spain. Cuban rum – Spain. And yet, really, we were rabidly against Franco, criticizing him constantly. Plus we had obvious relations with Spanish Communists – Santiago Carrillo,[15] La Pasionaria,[16] everybody.

Some of those who'd been in the Spanish Civil War and later gone to the Soviet Union were military men, such as General Enrique Líster, while others, lower-ranking, came to Cuba to help us organize the militias. And Franco didn't break off relations.

That was a praiseworthy attitude that deserves our respect and even, at that point, our gratitude. He refused to give in to American pressure. He acted with real Galician stubbornness. He never broke off relations with Cuba. His attitude in that respect was rock-strong.

How do you explain that?
Well, there are several explanations. Franco was from El Ferrol; the Cervera squadron was made up of people from there, from El Ferrol.

The Admiral Cervera who was commander during the battle in Santiago de Cuba in 1898.
[completing the thought] . . . that battle that was a colossal mistake, a futile sacrifice. Cervera should have got off those boats and sent the sailors in to fight as infantry. Use the cannons to defend the city, the infantry to defend the city. He was given a stupid order – one of those orders that politicians who don't know anything about war give, as is happening today in the war in Iraq, because Aznar didn't know a thing about war, or Bush either.

Over there in Madrid, some politician gave the squadron the order to sail out of the harbour in Santiago, and it was shot dead, boat by boat. One of the cruellest things . . . it hurts you – [although] the bravery of those Spanish sailors was admirable. What was demonstrated there was the Spaniards' Quixote-like bravery and heroism to a high degree. We honour them, we pay tribute to those men. So anyway, they say that Franco was from there, from El Ferrol, from the same place as that squadron, and that [its defeat] was a terrible trauma for him – what happened in Cuba was a terrible trauma for the whole Spanish military.

Under those circumstances, the United States carried out a very unequal, opportunistic war against Spain, and inflicted on them one of the worst humiliations in history. It destroyed a whole naval squadron in an easy battle. It was a terrible blow to the military's pride, and to all of Spain's pride. And it happened when Franco was a boy in El Ferrol. Franco must have grown up and read and heard all about that bitter experience, in an atmosphere of despondency and a thirst for revenge. He may even have been present when the remains of the defeated fleet were returned, the soldiers and officers who'd been humiliated and thwarted. It must have left a profound mark on him.

And what the Cuban Revolution did, beginning in 1959 – resisting the United States, rebelling against the empire, defeating it at Playa Girón – may have been seen by [Franco] as a way to secure Spain's revenge. We Cubans, in the way we had faced the United States and resisted its aggressions, had definitely restored the Spaniards' [patriotic] sentiments and honour. That historical, almost emotional, element must have influenced Franco's attitude. I don't think there were economic reasons, or reasons of some other kind.

Later, in the twenties, Franco took part in a colonial war, in Morocco, in which the army had massive casualties. There was one battle, at Annual,[17] in which Spain lost over 3,000 men. I've read the whole history of that war. Franco distinguished himself as a military leader there; he won fame as a brave man, he had a certain degree of prestige among the military class. In Asturias, in 1934, he was sent in to repress the miners' strikes, and he began to be noticed among the reactionary classes. He was, unquestionably, shrewd, cunning – I don't know whether that came from his being Galician; the Galicians are accused of being shrewd – and, well, everybody knows the story, there's no reason to repeat it: Mussolini's and Hitler's part in the Spanish Civil War, Guernica,[18] the battle of Guadalajara,[19] where the Italians were badly defeated. Everybody knows how it happened. Franco was shrewd, because later they wanted to involve him in the world war.

Mussolini entered the war after the Germans defeated the French; [after they'd] successfully invaded France and expelled the English, Mussolini declared war, but Mussolini thought he could count on the Roman legions. He'd forgotten that in the end, the Roman legions were made up of barbarians, and that the Rome of olden days, of the age of Julius Caesar, no longer existed. The Italians were a peaceable people, with another culture, another mindset; they no longer had those militaristic traditions that the Romans always had – [whereas] the Germans had maintained them – so Italy entered the war and you know what happened: defeat after defeat. In Ethiopia they were crushed, in Libya they were crushed, in El-Alamein they were crushed – the Italians turned out to be a hindrance to the Germans in the war, and they had to send Rommel to North Africa. Rommel became famous, he didn't have a reputation for being repressive; he was, apparently, a gentlemanly sort of general.

But anyway, there's Hitler at the peak of his power, and in October 1940 he met Franco in Hendaya and he couldn't persuade him [to enter the war]. Franco was shrewd.

Prudent – he didn't get involved in that war.
He did promise to send a division – the Blue Division – but he didn't get involved in the world war, as I said, and he held his ground until the end. Later, the Americans, following their tradition of 'profound convictions' that had led them to join the war, became allies with Franco, who from 1953 on was protected by the United States.

If you analyse Franco's life, I mean the number of people he killed, the repression he imposed on Spain, his name is associated with a tragic period in Spain's history. In fact, he brought in from Morocco those same Moors, as they were then called, [the Berbers] whom he'd fought against; he brought them in, they were the first troops to arrive, and he kept them as his personal guard the whole time.

I don't think Aznar, in Franco's place, would have been any less cruel; he'd probably have got into the Second World War the way Mussolini did. Without actually having to in any way, Aznar turned himself over to the Yankees and became a lackey of the United States.

You think he had less political vision than Franco?

Listen, he was *far* beneath Franco, as a personality, in ability, as a statesman – that's what I'm trying to say. Aznar wouldn't come up to Franco's knees in terms of political ability. Franco clearly showed what he was made of. Aznar would have been less flexible and, in addition, probably more cruel, because he is a man with all these complexes, all these hatreds.

Franco was an individual with reactionary ideas ... Throughout his life he acquired a place, and Aznar is an heir of Franco, because it's clear that the Popular Party arose out of those ranks, not the ranks of the Socialist Party. Aznar didn't come from the ranks of the followers of Karl Marx, he came from the ranks of the Franquistas, and his mindset was Franquista.

Now then, I never heard anyone say that Franco seized as much money as others have. It was the rich who supported him, but apparently it was not a particularly corrupt administration. If we were to make a kind of *Parallel Lives* and put Franco on one side and that 'little gentleman' on the other . . .

Franco had the newspapers; Aznar did, too, more or less, but by actually *buying* them. In Spain, the fundamental national media, the big TV channels, were controlled by Aznar and his group. What's the difference?

On the other hand, I don't think Franco was a man – although he was a short fellow – with a lot of complexes. Aznar, on the other hand, was a man of very short moral and political stature. The first time I met this individual, Aznar, in Santiago de Chile, I noted some strange behaviour – a man of little self-confidence, a little befuddled – always changing his ties and things, silly, ridiculous.

There was a very bad period at first in the relations between Cuba and Aznar's government, when the debates in the Cortes took place.[20] Then one day, they made an agreement with Cuba's minister of foreign relations and came to an arrangement: Aznar [sent a message that he] was going to call me. I waited for an hour one morning, and Aznar finally called; his tone was very friendly – at that moment there was still quite a crisis, because we hadn't given our agreement to their ambassadorial appointment, so there was that debate going on – and he started talking, he was using a very friendly tone – apparently he can use it when he wants to, although he doesn't always want to – and he started talking about the problem: [Spain] wants to improve relations between our two countries, he says, they're going to name a new ambassador, and out of that conversation came a normalization of relations between the two countries. I thought, 'Well, he's thought about it and changed his mind; maybe he's realized that he can't just kick Cuba around and impose conditions on us.' And we were more accessible after that, we received the new ambassador, Eduardo Junco Bonet. Naturally, [Aznar] sent us a Franquista, he couldn't send anything else, a man of absolute Franquista thinking,[21] so [this ambassador] came.

All this time, but before, too, the Spanish embassy in Cuba was functioning as a kind of double agent, an instrument of conspiracy with the [American] Interests Office. I can't say that this happened under Felipe González, but Felipe himself, at a certain stage, as his ideas, his thoughts, his philosophy began deteriorating, was already collaborating with the Yankees.

The Spanish embassy was cooperating with the United States; they were in on that conspiracy with James Cason and the so-called 'dissidents', etc. And the European embassies, more than one of them was pretty fed up. I won't mention the Czech embassy, because I don't consider it European, or the Polish one. The Scandinavians, the so-called Left, the Social-Democratic Party is not the party of Olaf Palme any more – he was an excellent man, a good friend, with a sincere concern for the problems of the Third World, which is not the case today, far from it. They've all started moving towards the right, almost as far as Señor Blair, the man with the 'new way', the leader of the Labour Party in the post-Thatcher era, which was the period of liberalization of the economy *par excellence*, and now he turns out to be a fire-breathing militarist.

Have you ever met Tony Blair?
I saw Blair one time, in Geneva, at a meeting of the WHO. I observed him: he had a swagger, he was haughty, as though he were looking down his nose at people. We had a few words, brief but sharp. Really, I was thinking with a good deal of abhorrence of [Blair's] 'understanding' with the United States; this was back in the days when the Europeans had reached an agreement, in exchange for their cowardly positions, that the Yankees would not apply certain parts of the Helms–Burton Act [to England], and in exchange the Yankees would give [the British] permission to make some investments in oil in Libya, or some other places, the Middle East, or maybe Iran. They made a pact of convenience, absolutely immoral.

The Brits and the Yankees?
All of them – the Europeans, too – but an American ambassador was discussing all this with Blair. When I saw him there [at the WHO meeting],

I was not very happy, really. I rejected what they had done, I considered it an act of treason, an agreement that was immoral and unprincipled.

He had been talking about child labour and I said to him, 'Listen, I saw that you were talking about child labour throughout the world, but I understand that in England there are 2 million children who are working.' I said it very calmly. I think he thought it was a piece of insolence from a nobody, a nit, a Third World know-nothing, but I was speaking the truth.[22]

Blair was the first to arrive there [at the meeting], a lot of people coming and going, all acting very natural. Clinton had left the building, but Clinton wouldn't have done what Blair did. [Blair] looked arrogant, haughty, but that was all. I can like a person or not like him much – that's irrelevant. No, what I'm interested in is what a person thinks, what a person does.

I read Anthony Giddens' book, which contains the theory out of which arose the so-called 'Third Way.'[23] There's nothing of a third way in it – it's the 'way' taken by every turncoat in this world. Oh, I could see that it was aimed against the social-security state achieved by the Europeans: fewer resources for the retired, less aid to the unemployed, because [aid] turns [the unemployed] into a bunch of lazy bums – according to this theory – who then won't work, you have to force them in some way. Well, I admit that you have to educate people, but you don't have to force them through economic means – and I could see that he belonged to that school.

Blair saw Clinton as an *alter ego*. Of course Clinton is an educated man, an intelligent man, a man who thinks about things. I seemed to see in the Brit somebody who worshipped Clinton, but I could never have imagined that one day Blair would turn *Bush* into another *alter ego*. Which is what Blair has done.

I've been careful – I don't like to go around attacking people unnecessarily, but telling the facts and talking about these things, I remember that.

However, Blair seems to me a more open, frank sort of man than that Franquista Aznar, that heir of Franco. Plus, England never had a Franco. Everyone knows that down through history many mistakes have been made, abuses committed, all sorts of things, but I see differences between Blair and Aznar. I see in Aznar and in Silvio Berlusconi two great lackeys, two great heirs of Fascism, because that's what they are.

Berlusconi, too, is an owner of all sorts of media, and he uses them, which is why he was [in power]. It's perfectly well known that a media owner can create opinions, impose opinions – the mass media are powerful. Berlusconi owns all those media over there, and it was with those media that he got to where he got; he was the lord and master, he could make people and he could destroy them.

To continue with Spain and Spanish politics: you, on the other hand, have been very complimentary about the king of Spain. Is it your view that he's taken the correct position, generally speaking, in his relations with Cuba?
I do. I think [he has] in everything. To begin with, I like King Juan Carlos, a king who, you know, was educated during the Franco period. Some of the credit for the king's upbringing can be attributed to Franco; at least he established a method by which the king could be educated. [Juan Carlos] was given training in the military, in the navy. [Franco] employed a good method for educating and training a king in Spain, and a king who is, without question, a gentleman.

In his relations with you personally?
I think he is a gentleman generally – because, I'll tell you, no one was particularly fond of him, there was no reason to be. He was put in there as king and everyone knew the reasons he'd been put in there, but he rendered an extraordinary service to Spain when that coup took place over there.

The coup attempt on 23 February 1981.
And the conspiracy. The king, with the support of several intelligent military leaders – I don't recall all their names now – managed to impose discipline and stave off a coup that would have had dreadful consequences. And he did that after Greece, because there had also been a coup in Greece, in 1967, launched by the generals – it was a disaster. It couldn't have been sustained.

It cost his brother-in-law, King Constantine of Greece, his throne.
Who?

The king of Greece who backed that coup in Athens – Constantine. He's Queen Sofía's brother, the king of Spain's brother-in-law. Afterwards [Constantine] tried to topple the military junta but failed, and he lost the throne, and in 1973 the colonels declared a republic. Apparently it was there that Juan Carlos learned what not *to do under those circumstances – you don't back the military in a coup.*
I was in a meeting, I think at a congress in Moscow – that was where I learned about Tejero's attempted coup in Madrid.[24] Later, I read quite a bit

501

about it, the whole history of the role played by all the participants and I must say that the king demonstrated character, conviction; he demonstrated ability and authority. He did a tremendous service to Spain, because no one knows what he saved that country from. We never had any reason to have anything but a good opinion of him, but from that point on, everyone began to respect and admire the king, and to be fond of him.

That day, Juan Carlos became king of Spain; before, he'd been *installed* as king, but at that moment, he became king in his own right, and he has always been a real gentleman, respectful – I've never seen him overstep his authority, despite his enormous prestige. He has been super-respectful with the laws, the constitution . . . He's an honest, decent person. I might say, too, that at certain points people have tried to blackmail him.

Blackmail him?
I won't say any more, but there are those who've tried to pressure him, to reduce his authority, his prestige. I mean, they don't like a king with authority, with prestige, and so respectful.

I'll tell you, when he was asked, 'Are you going to Cuba?' he said, 'Well, I'd like to go back,' but he hasn't come back to Cuba because . . .

. . . Señor Aznar won't let him.
Clearly. That's the rule, and Aznar doesn't want him to, because his answer was, 'He'll go when it's his turn, when it's time.' That's a pretty nasty way of putting it.

I've met [the king] since then – we've spoken many times. He's a very likeable person – he tells stories, he has charisma. He's educated his son. Because the monarchy in Great Britain is criticized for not educating the prince; you can't say that about the king of Spain, because at least he's tried to educate and train Prince Felipe. [The prince] went through school, he knows about the military, the navy – he's a very polite and well-brought-up young man. I've seen him at meetings, too, summits, inaugurations I've attended. And I'll say that King Juan Carlos has that merit, too – he's educated his son; he sends him on his behalf to all sorts of international activities. That's another reason I have such a high opinion of the king.

I see in those Spanish soldiers who died in May 2003 in that tragic plane crash in Turkey[25] that Spain had no business being in that war, unless it's so Señor Aznar can play the lackey [to the US] and pretend he's important on the world stage.

That's like Argentine president Carlos Menem sending a warship to the Persian Gulf in 1991 so he could see the war in Iraq on television. Aznar sent [those soldiers] over there to Afghanistan to die, instead of Bush's invading troops.

You see how that was: the Yankees were determined to get everybody involved in their dirty business – there were soldiers from Honduras, Nicaragua, El Salvador, the Dominican Republic, under the command of Spanish officers, acting as policemen, or cleaning up [land] mines, or who knows what over there in Iraq. It's just incredible! I mean, honestly, it's the seventeenth century!

The Spaniards commanding Latin American soldiers – that's like something out of the Arabian Nights, isn't it? – over there as policemen in Iraq, to see how many Spaniards and Latin Americans can get themselves killed. Those people had no reason to be over there, in the first place. In the second place, [the Spanish authorities] put them on planes that everybody knew belonged to companies created just to make money, and I think Spain has enough resources and planes . . .

Aznar must shoulder a large part of the blame for the loss of those lives, because an accident can happen despite all the precautions, but it's clear, for example, that in the fifteen years that we transported hundreds of thousands of combatants to Africa by air, we didn't have a single accident. In large part that was due to the measures we took to make sure those trips were safe.

Leasing planes from any old company . . . companies that everybody ought to know what they were like, ought to know that what they wanted was to save money – if they could save on parts, they'd save on parts, because they were driven by a desperate desire for money. [The Spanish] leased them and sent their soldiers on those planes . . . So there's a responsibility there somewhere, I have not the slightest doubt about that.

You sent a telegram of condolence to the king of Spain, but not to Señor Aznar.

That's right, because I see those officers and enlisted men as victims. They went over there because they were ordered to; they didn't ask to go. All of our people who went on internationalist missions did so as volunteers. So long as those Spanish soldiers were following orders . . . And what were they doing in Iraq? What did Iraq ever do to Spain?

No, the soldiers in the plane crash had been in Afghanistan.
Sorry, I meant to say Afghanistan. That's even further away. I doubt whether
many of them even knew where Afghanistan is, because really, when American young people were asked where Afghanistan was, I think barely 12 per
cent of them knew – that means that American young people are sent off to
fight countries that they don't even know where they are, if they've ever
heard of them at all.

That's why it seemed to me the right thing to do to send my condolences.
I wasn't going to send a telegram to that fraud Aznar, who was to blame for
the death of those soldiers, so I sent it to the king. Fortunately, they have a
king, because otherwise I wouldn't have had anybody to send a telegram to.

*In Spain you also have very good relations with Manuel Fraga, the former
president of the Xunta in Galicia.*
Yes, he's an intelligent, shrewd Galician. And don't think I [maintain good
relations with him] because I'm half Galician myself – no, Fraga has taken
a sincere interest in his friends, he tries to involve all Galicians. He's made
changes, he's worked for Spain, he's been a good administrator. I do have
family over there in Galicia, too, and I talk to them.

Of course, he's not totally well-mannered, because, for example, he'll be
very friendly on one side and then do things that aren't right.

In what sense?
Fraga is one of those people, along with Felipe González and others – I don't
want to mention them all – who were part of the group that was so insistent
about giving me [economic] advice when the USSR collapsed. He took me
to a very elegant restaurant over there one night – this was in 1992, during
the Barcelona Olympics – and he tried to give me formulas, too. You know
what he suggested? – I hope don Manuel Fraga will forgive me – you know
how he defined the formula for Cuba that he gave me? 'The formula for
Cuba is the formula in Nicaragua,' he said – that's verbatim. Despite the
fact that I like him, and respect him.

And what does that phrase mean?
Well, it means that everything they did in Nicaragua after the Sandinistas
had to be done in Cuba ... All the things that have led Nicaragua into a
bottomless abyss of corruption, theft, negligence ... terrible! That was the
formula[26] ... Imagine what sort of formula – they wanted me to follow the

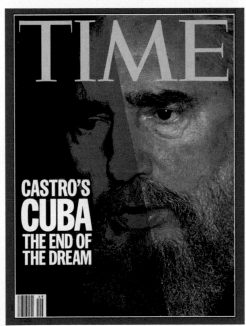

Castro on the cover of *Time* magazine: 1959, 1965, 1993, 1995.

/TIME LIFE PICTURES/GETTY IMAGES

With Vice President Richard Nixon in Washington, April 1959.

With writer Ernest
Hemingway in late
1959, Cuba.

AFP

With friend Salvador Allende, president of Chile, in Santiago de Chile, 1971.

SLAVA KATAMIDZE COLLECTION/GETTY IMAGES

With Leonid
Brezhnev during
a period of good
relations, 1965.

With Indian Prime Minister Indira Gandhi.

BETTMANN/CORBIS

In Yugoslavia with Prime Minister Josip Broz Tito, March 1976.

DIRCK HALSTEAD / TIME LIFE PICTURES / GETTY IMAGES

Soviet president Mikhail Gorbachev's state visit to Cuba, 1 April 1989.

AFP

Fidel Castro with Sandinista president Daniel Ortega of Nicaragua.

NOGUES ALAIN/CORBIS SYGMA

With French president François Mitterrand in Paris, 13 March 1995.

PPO/GETTY IMAGES

With Palestine leader Yasser Arafat in Durban, South Africa, during a recess in the UN-sponsored World Conference Against Racism, 31 August 2002.

AFP PHOTO/ADALBERTO ROQUE

Giving a speech, 30 August 2002.

ODD ANDERSEN / AFP

With South African president Nelson Mandela.

AFP PHOTO/MICHEL GANGNE

With Pope John Paul II at José Martí Airport in Havana, January 1998.

AP PHOTO/JOE CAVARETTA

AFP/ADALBERTO ROQUE

With Nobel Prize winner Gabriel García Márquez in Havana, 4 March 2000.

AP

In Portugal, at the 1998 Ibero-American Summit in Oporto, with Nobel Prize winner José Saramago.

RAFAEL PEREZ / REUTERS

Playing baseball with former US president Jimmy Carter, May 2002.

With American intellectual Noam Chomsky in 2004.

ANDREW WINNING / REUTERS

With Spanish King Juan Carlos I during the Sixth Ibero–American Summit in Chile, 1996.

AFP PHOTO/CRISTOPHE SIMON

With José María Aznar, president of the Spanish government, in Havana, 14 November 1999.

AP PHOTO/JOSE GOITIA

With Hugo Chávez, president of Venezuela, in Pampatar, near Caracas, 11 December 2001.

AFP/NIURKA BARROSO

idel Castro and Lula da Silva, president of Brazil, during the playing of the national anthem in Havana, 7 September 2003.

AFP/ADALBERTO ROQUE

With Bolivian president Evo Morales during a public ceremony in Cuba, 30 December 2005.

AFP PHOTO/HO-ISMAEL FRANCISCO-AIN

Castro at a gathering of *trabajadores sociales*, 'social workers', volunteers pledged to combat corruption in certain economic sectors, Havana, 1 January 2006.

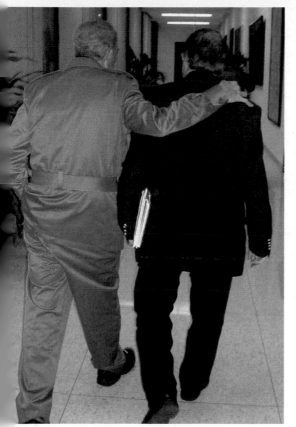

Fidel Castro with Ignacio Ramonet after more than a hundred hours of interviews:

'I think I've taken far too much of your time.'
'No, we've been working seventeen or eighteen hours a day and we're fine. Clearly, you're in very good shape, because I think you've worked harder than I have.'

'I'm very interested in what you've been saying.'
'I am, too. I'm interested, as you are, in all these subjects, and the doors of our country will always be open to any interest, any question.'

A picture released by Cuban newspaper *Juventud Rebelde* on 13 August 2006 shows Fidel Castro recovering after his gasterointestinal surgery.

AFP/GETTY IMAGES

Russian formula, the one that Felipe and his elite advisers urged Gorbachev to follow, and that other people were advising other people over there to follow, and there's nothing left. All those men whose advice was [to follow the tenets of] neoliberalism to the death – privatization, strict compliance with the International Monetary Fund rules – have driven many countries and their inhabitants into the abyss.

When do you plan to visit Spain again?
Well, it wasn't possible while that little gentleman Aznar was in office . . . But now that he's not there any more, there'll be some likelihood.

The first time I was in Spain was on a stopover in February 1984, returning from Moscow with Daniel Ortega from the funeral of Yuri Andropov.[27] Felipe González was the prime minister. We landed in Madrid and there was terrible fog. Despite the fog, we were taken to Moncloa[28] by helicopter. I spoke to King Juan Carlos by telephone. We were met by Felipe, a fine host, and since he's from Seville we were served sherry, *jabugo* ham, manchego cheese.[29] . . . Then we went to the residence, which is close by, for lunch, and the sherry had made me hungry . . . I remember they served lunch, some vegetable, a little breast of quail that I thought was the appetizer, and then all of a sudden – dessert! It was funny. That was the first time I'd ever been in Spain. I saw almost nothing of Madrid; we were just there a few hours. Later I went back and spent more time, and at that point I went up to Galicia.

24

Fidel and France

You told me[1] that when you were a boy, living in the house of that teacher of yours, Eufrasia Feliú, in Santiago, you were given a 'French education'. Do you think that period left some lasting mark on your behaviour?

Of course; it must have. As I told you, Eufrasia Feliú and her family were originally from Haiti; at any rate, her father had lived a long time in Haiti, which is a neighbouring island that had once been a French colony, so before the slave insurrection in 1791 it had had a bourgeoisie of French descent and also actually had a small aristocracy that descended *directly*, and with no admixture of other blood, from France. Remember, for example, that Josephine de Beauharnais was a member of the bourgeoisie, though she wasn't from Haiti – she was from Martinique – and she couldn't resist Napoleon's desire to make her his empress. Napoleon became emperor when he strayed – strayed very far – from the ideals of the French Revolution in 1789, although in the eyes of Europe's established aristocracy he would always be an impostor.

Both the teacher and her sisters, the music teacher and the doctor, had gone to France to study, or to Haiti, and they'd received a very strict French education. They observed the codes and rituals of that education, which they were very attached to. They all spoke French to one another. And some of that language stuck with me, because at that age, children learn foreign languages very quickly. I still remember some of the words I learned back then – I'll never forget them: *bonjour, bonsoir, fourchette, merci beaucoup*

... Later on, in high school, I studied French, and I was crazy about the French Revolution, so I learned that political motto the revolutionaries of 1789 gave the world: *Liberté, egalité, fraternité*. For the first time in history, class struggles were foreseen and theorized about by philosophers and intellectuals, and it was also the first time that people ever talked about those three beautiful, and very revolutionary, concepts. They considered them an ideal for humanity [to aspire to]. No one could argue against them. The theorists, however, couldn't foresee that the objective development of the new society would make applying those three principles impossible.

Besides words, do you think some of that 'French education' remains in your behaviour, your habits?
My godmother, Belén [the piano teacher], made a great effort to teach us good manners. In particular, she insisted that at mealtimes – although we ate very little in that house! – we behave correctly at the table. We were supposed to behave just so, according to the rules of the bourgeoisie. Know how to use the different knives and forks and spoons, not talk with our mouths full, not chew with our mouths open, not make a slurping sound when we ate our soup, not put our elbows on the table, not raise our voices – all those basic things that didn't seem so basic in Birán.

Out there in the country, as I told you, I lived in almost complete freedom, without laws and without any great impediments of any kind – always outside, playing, running, making mischief. My parents were very busy, engaged in agriculture and trade, and didn't spend their days watching us, or making us mind our manners, and there were very few things we weren't allowed to do. Which is why the limitations and obligations in that teacher's house seemed such a harsh, traumatic experience to me.

Here you can see the result of those contradictions. I, who came from the country, didn't usually eat vegetables. It's been in the course of my life that I've learned the immense value of vegetables in our diet and our health.

I realized later that that 'formal French education' was very useful. And even up in the Sierra, later, despite the thousand and one hardships of war and life in a campaign, we always tried to maintain good behaviour, with good manners, out of respect for ourselves as individuals and for others. Never, not even under the pretext that life was very hard up in those mountains, did we behave like savages.

In your intellectual development, and in the construction of your political ideas, has French culture had any influence?
Oh, no doubt – a very important influence. I told you that the first elementary school I attended was a school run by French Catholic brothers, the La Salle order. Although the fact is, most of the time I attended Catholic schools where almost all the teachers were Spaniards, very nationalistic, and the basic literature they taught was fundamentally Spanish literature and a little – too little – Cuban.

But on my own, since I was very young, I've read many French authors who've been decisive in my intellectual development and helped me understand the world and human passions. For example, one author who's had a considerable influence on me is Victor Hugo. A giant – of literature, of philosophy, of politics. With very advanced ideas for his time. A humanist and a revolutionary. He defended the insurgents of the Paris Commune, demanded amnesty for them. He defended the right to vote for women.

I read his novel *Les Misérables* when I was still a teenager, and it made a great impact on me not just because of the eloquence of its words, but also because of its strong social and political content. Without a doubt, that novel had an indirect influence on my way of looking at the world, its injustices, and the need to fight to correct them. I say 'indirect influence' because authors of political works, such as Marx, have had a direct, very direct, influence, while literature influences you differently. At any rate, *Les Misérables* may, along with Cervantes' *Quixote*, be the novel that's made the greatest impact on me. I remember in particular how impressed I was by its detailed description of the Battle of Waterloo.

Not long ago, Chávez, the president of Venezuela, who reads a lot and is coincidentally named Hugo, like Victor, was reading [*Les Misérables*], or rereading it, and he's referred to a lot of episodes from it in his speeches and public appearances. We've been talking, and we've talked a lot about that fabulous novel that continues to be so relevant today, if you consider certain social and political situations in Latin America that are similar to those that existed in France at the beginning of the Industrial Age in the mid-nineteenth century.

Have you read, for example, Honoré de Balzac, another great French author of that period?
Quite a lot. I read him especially during the years I was in prison [1953–5]. I'm almost nostalgic for those years in prison, because that's the time in my

life when I had the most time to read. I read constantly, fifteen hours a day. Although it was mostly political essays, history books, a lot of Martí – but all sorts of literature and novels, too. That, for me, was a real cultural university. A 'fertile prison', as one historian has put it.[2]

There, I remember reading several Balzac novels, such as *Père Goriot*, *Eugénie Grandet* and *Le Colonel Chabert*, his very famous series *La Comédie humaine*. Before that, I'd already read *La Peau du chagrin* [The Wild-Ass's or Onager's Skin], a fascinating story of a man who becomes involved in a diabolic pact with a strange animal skin that grants him three wishes but, at the same time, shrinks.[3]

According to some scholars, Karl Marx liked Balzac's realistic style. He admired Balzac immensely, as he also admired – one should emphasize – Cervantes and *Quixote*. Apparently Marx intended to write a critical study on *La Comédie humaine* after he finished his works on economics and politics. In *The Communist Manifesto* one can see the influence of Balzac's style – the clarity of the prose, the effectiveness and elegance of the simple expression. Balzac wrote his novels serially for popular newspapers with large readerships; he knew how to write for large audiences, for the masses. Had it not been for Balzac, the *Manifesto* might not have had the success it had, the enormous readership. A paradox, eh? Because Balzac was not Marxist at all, and although he was one of the first novelists critical of the bourgeoisie that was beginning to become so powerful in society, down deep he was a monarchist. His greatest desire was to obtain a title, to become part of the nobility – although with what he was paid, he almost starved to death. That was the great dream of his life, and it has nothing to do with his literary merits, because Balzac is unquestionably – with Dostoyevsky, Tolstoy, Galdós[4] and Victor Hugo – one of the nineteenth-century European novelists I most admire.

You also admire another French novelist, Romain Rolland.[5] Isn't that right?
A wonderful writer. Romain Rolland was a great humanist, a pacifist, and his prose is of incomparable quality. He met Gandhi and became an apostle of non-violence; he opposed the First World War. He defended the emerging Soviet Union. He loved music. I read all ten volumes of his immense *Jean-Christophe* with great pleasure. A masterpiece. It's an extraordinary story, a vindication of the human being, a lesson in humanity. It's a shame he's a bit forgotten now. He's not read as much, probably even in France.

No, he's not read much today. I wanted to ask you, since you're so passionate about history books, are you familiar with the French historians of the French Revolution?
I've read the *Socialist History of the French Revolution* by Jean Jaurés, the great leader of the French Left who was murdered just on the eve of the First World War.[6] And another history of the French Revolution. I remember I read it when I was preparing for the examinations for my undergraduate degree. The only version I could find was Thiers's, another ten volumes, though not as thick.[7] Thiers, as I learned later, had put down the insurgents of the Paris Commune in 1870 with the support of the German army, which had occupied Paris. I've also read Lamartine, another conservative, who wrote a *History of the Girondists*, the right wing of the Revolution.[8]

I'm interested in anything that has to do with that tremendous shock to the political system that occurred in 1789, the first victorious people's uprising in modern history. For decades, France was the only republic in a nineteenth-century Europe of monarchies, a truly retrograde continent. And that political uniqueness earned it all sorts of attacks and sieges. [Other countries] wanted to strangle that insurgent nation. Because France had fought a revolution and now stood as a lighthouse of freedom, for many years the French were encircled by a siege of hatred laid by the neighbouring monarchies.

Later, and one must keep this firmly in mind, the Revolution, like Saturn, devoured its own children.

In addition, the French gave the world the 'Marseillaise', one of the most beautiful and universal anthems. I don't recall the name of the composer right now.

Rouget de Lisle.[9]
Right. And we mustn't forget that the 'Internationale', another moving, mobilizing, revolutionary anthem – the heritage of the proletariat and every rebel in the world – is the work of the French.[10]

Are you familiar with the new French historians – for example those of the Annales school, who give greater importance to long periods and to the events and situations of the daily life of simple people than to the great deeds of a few mythified heroes?
I like history, I've always liked it, especially – and of necessity – the history of warfare, of military affairs. I've read almost everything that's been written

about the Second World War. But I'm not in any sense a specialist in historiography, and I'm not familiar with all its different schools. I've read many very excellent Soviet historians who approach history that way, though – the daily, concrete lives of people, the slow evolution of customs.

And a fascinating work I read a few years ago may belong to that school you mention – a book by a contemporary French historian, Georges Duby is his name, a wonderful *History of Private Life* in several volumes,[11] translated into Spanish – an incredibly rich book that tells, beginning in Greece and Rome and coming down to the present time, how relations within the family have evolved, the rights of children, the role of the father and the mother, the status of women, laws and regulations governing marriage and divorce, domestic matters, the question of death and inheritance, and so on. A collective work by historians, most of them, I believe, French.

What memories do you have of the French philosopher Jean-Paul Sartre?
I met Sartre when he came through here in 1960. He came with Simone de Beauvoir. I saw them very little; I met them, we talked, I'd have liked to have had more time to talk with them. He wrote a friendly book about Cuba, *Huracán sobre el azúcar*,[12] a warm report for a Paris daily [*France-Soir*] on the early years of the Revolution.

One of the men who's made the greatest mark on the history of France in the twentieth century is General Charles de Gaulle. When the Cuban Revolution triumphed in January 1959, de Gaulle had been in power only a few months in France and he was about to found the Fifth Republic. One might say that the Cuban Revolution and the Fifth Republic in France are contemporaries – they're both about to celebrate their fiftieth anniversary.[13] What opinion do you have of de Gaulle?
Although relations with him were not very good because of the war in Algeria, in which we were supporting the Algerians, de Gaulle was a great man. [But even] with all his prestige and all his power, it was very, very difficult for him to find a solution to the problem in Algeria, because of the presence there of so many French colonials.

I remember one quality of de Gaulle as a military man: he conceived the idea of bringing together all the tanks and creating an armoured division. He foresaw that the French could be defeated by the Germans, because although the French had more tanks, the Germans massed them into armoured divisions.

Second, I admire his intransigence, his defiance of the United States and the English and the whole world. He saved France after that terrible war in which France could have wound up lower than Spain or Italy. He saved its traditions, its national pride, the French defiance. Then, in 1958, there came that moment of very grave crisis because of the war in Algeria, the danger of a coup, threats and so on, so they called de Gaulle: 'Come, please, and help us get out of this situation.' And who could do that? He could, because he had great prestige.

In 1971 he opposed the Americans when President Nixon decided to end the convertibility of the dollar into gold. He knew that printing currency without any support from gold was an exorbitant privilege.

De Gaulle did great things for France – with his struggle against Nazism at the end of the war he assured France a place among the five permanent members of the United Nations Security Council. With the prestige France won during the war, thanks in part to the role de Gaulle played, France made a great effort and produced an atomic bomb. No one could forbid them from doing that at the time, the way everybody's forbidden to do it today. Of course, a country such as Israel, which is closely allied with the United States and an enemy of all the Arab nations, received aid to become a nuclear power.

De Gaulle was a genius, and he never changed his spots. That's what I can say about de Gaulle, a brilliant historical figure. You can agree with him or not, but he played a very great, historic role in France. People who have read the history of France – and we've had to read the history of France for one reason or another, given the role it's played down through the centuries – and is still playing – an extraordinarily important role . . . That de Gaulle of the Resistance, that de Gaulle who founded the Fifth Republic, that de Gaulle who saved France once again . . . Although I'm not sure what he saved, or what he saved it from, because you people [in France] have always had political crises, and there was a time when you had a different government every six months.

During the Fourth Republic, from 1944 to 1958.

I mean, errors such as those that occurred during Hitler and Fascism, allowing the occupation of the Ruhr and 20 million other things, the annexation of Austria, when Hitler didn't have enough power and his General Staff was opposed, the annexation of the Sudetenland after that defeatist Treaty of Munich in 1938. All that, Hitler was allowed to get away with.

And then he attacked France with his tank formations, just as de Gaulle had feared.

De Gaulle theorized about that in a book.[14]

About the armoured divisions. The French had their tanks dispersed as support for the infantry; the Germans broke through those formations, and there's nothing more terrible for that mentality than the news that you have tanks in the rear! The Russians, now, they already had tank divisions; their errors, from a military point of view, were other.

But de Gaulle was able to command the Resistance from London, despite his Yankee allies, whom he refused to bow down to. It was thanks to de Gaulle that France achieved the role of major power that it later played, and de Gaulle wasn't a leftist, he wasn't a Socialist, he was a French patriot, a soldier who had strategic ideas.

But what happened in 1968 when there were threats of destabilization? De Gaulle went over there to Germany, where the French troops were stationed, in order to ensure the support of those troops and put down any attempt at popular rebellion. That's the way it looked to me, and I can't agree with that.

The French person you've known best is probably Régis Debray, isn't that right?

I've known a lot of French people, people of great merit such as the agronomist André Voisin, an expert on grasses, pasture, whom I mentioned earlier. We were very fond of him in Cuba. He died here during one of his visits. For us, he was a wonderful teacher; I read all his books on pasture for cattle, and on fertilizers. A scientist who gave an early warning about the danger of pesticides. The books by this French scholar, whom we knew very well, were published here – tens of thousands of copies have been distributed. Our country owes him a great deal.

Another French personality I knew well was Commander [Jacques-Yves] Cousteau, the great oceanologist. He came here a lot, and explored our coasts in that famous ship of his, the *Calypso*. He liked Cuba, and he was always very friendly to us; he showed us great solidarity. I had many conversations with him, on several occasions. I had the exceptional privilege of sharing his concerns about the dangers threatening the environment. We learned a great deal from him. He shot several of his popular documentaries here in Cuba. He was an ardent defender of humanity's natural heritage. A great ecologist. His death, in 1997, was an immense loss for our planet.

Early on, another French agronomist who came here was René Dumont, but he wrote some very critical things about the agrarian reform in Cuba.

Well, Dumont criticized everybody, and especially the whole Third World. He claimed that all agrarian reforms everywhere had failed. He was here during the first years of the Revolution; I talked with him quite a bit because at that time I was very, very interested in the problems of agriculture. He was a very self-assured person, and also bad-humoured, although he had some intuitions that today we'd called ecological – quite advanced for the time. But he wasn't constructive. In practice, his diagnosis, which was too pessimistic, was not useful to us.

Let's go back to Régis Debray. How did you meet him?

Apparently, he'd been here during the literacy campaign, in the early sixties. He'd been a volunteer in that campaign and travelled all over the country. Then he went back to France, where he was, I think, a professor of philosophy, and he wrote a document analysing the revolutionary process in Cuba that interested some of the *compañeros*.[15] It was translated and distributed widely in Cuba. I read it with great interest. Then he came back, we talked with him, and he remained here, helping.

Was he given military training here?

That was done regularly with many [of our] friends who, voluntarily, wanted to receive some type of [military] training. But he was an intellectual above all, a typical French intellectual, very rational – he wasn't going to fight. I talked with him a lot. He was very well educated, very cultured. He wanted to help. As I said, we sent him to Bolivia to prepare for the arrival of Che, to gather information, maps on the area where the general headquarters were going to be set up. Then, as everyone knows, he was taken prisoner. We mobilized, and mobilized our friends all around the world, to obtain his freedom. And he was freed.

Later, he went to Chile to follow the evolution there of the Unidad Popular. And then – at that point as an adviser to President Mitterrand – I told you that he came here to ask us to release that fake poet and fake paralytic Armando Valladares.

Did you meet President Mitterrand?

The first time I spoke with him I think was in Chile, as a matter of fact, in

November 1971, with Salvador Allende. They'd known each other no doubt from the Socialist International.

A few months earlier Mitterrand had been elected first secretary of the French Socialist Party, and he'd started moving towards closer relations with the Communist Party, which was very powerful at that time in France, and he'd mobilized the Socialists to join the international protests against the Vietnam War. He had clearly expressed his solidarity with Cuba.

What was your impression of him?
He was a man with an indisputable personality. Cultured and intelligent. You could see that he was a leader with great political experience, and great astuteness. At that time he was beginning the long political march that would lead him to the presidency ten years later. We formed a good relationship.

Did you see him other times?
We invited him to come to Cuba, and he came, with his wife, Danielle, in 1974. They were visiting the country, seeing what we were doing here: the educational programmes, the health programmes, the social initiatives. We talked for dozens of hours. The tragedy in Chile had taken place the year before, as had the Carnation Revolution in Portugal. He'd run an excellent electoral campaign in France and won 49 per cent of the vote against the candidate of the Right [Valéry Giscard d'Estaing]. I think at the time he was thinking about a common platform for all the French left-wing groups and parties.

He did that, and in 1981 he was elected. Did you see him after that, while he was president?
Well, when he was elected president the relations between the two countries grew closer. That was very positive. A proof of trust and friendship is that he sent his daughter, Mazarine, whom he'd had from another relationship. She came here in late 1991, I think; I met her, spoke with her at the residence of the French ambassador [Jean-Raphaël Dufour], a courageous diplomat, by the way, who had saved the life of Haitian president Aristide during the coup in Haiti in September 1991.

I saw Mitterrand again especially during my visit to France in March 1995. I was returning from the World Summit for Social Development in Copenhagen and UNESCO, whose headquarters are in Paris, had officially invited me. But Mitterrand, despite opposition from the Right – at the time there was what they called 'cohabitation', which meant that his prime minister [Edouard Baladur] belonged to the opposition – treated me as a guest of the Republic.

That was less than a year before his death. How did you find him?
You could see that he was ill, and very tired. But he faced his fate with tremendous integrity and great dignity. Despite all the criticism from the press, he welcomed me very warmly, and he held a luncheon for me in the Élysée Palace; it was very nice, very friendly. [But even then, Mitterrand was] resisting the torments of his illness.

It was at the end of that luncheon, as we were saying our goodbyes on the stairs of the Élysée, that Danielle, breaking protocol, turned and embraced me and kissed me on each cheek. Boy, was she criticized for that display of friendship! The press was merciless.

Danielle very kindly also welcomed me to the Mitterrands' private residence, on historic rue de Bièvre, in the Latin Quarter, and from there we walked through those enchanting little streets down by the Seine, around Notre-Dame Cathedral, to the nearby offices of France-Libertés.[16]

And was that the first time you'd ever been in Paris?
The first time. And I wanted to see everything – the Bastille, the Tuileries, the Place de la Concorde – because I remembered the events of the French Revolution . . . And, of course, all the eternal monuments in Paris: the Eiffel Tower, Notre-Dame, the Arc de Triomphe, the Champs Élysées. I was taken to the Louvre by the man who'd been Mitterrand's minister of culture.

Jack Lang.
Yes, who's also a friend of García Márquez. I was taken to meet the man who at that time was the president of the National Assembly [Philippe Séguin]. And I had a meeting with businessmen, and also, at the Maison de l'Amérique Latine, a meeting with many of Cuba's friends in France.

François Mitterrand died ten months after your visit, on 8 January 1996. Did you go to his funeral?
I was invited to attend and I did. I was able to give my personal condolences to Danielle, who, as one might imagine, was distraught. I attended the religious ceremony in Notre-Dame Cathedral. Impressive. There were dozens of heads of state or government. There was the new president of France,

Jacques Chirac, and Boris Yeltsin, King Juan Carlos, Norodom Sihanouk of Cambodia, and then vice president Al Gore, from whom Bush stole victory in the 2000 elections.

For reasons of protocol I was seated in the front row, not far from German chancellor Helmut Kohl, who wept during the entire ceremony. Although he was a man of the Right, a Christian-Democrat, he had had excellent relations with Mitterrand, and they had cemented relations between Paris and Berlin – they'd managed to put behind them the old hatreds of so many cruel wars fought between the two countries.

You know Danielle Mitterrand quite well, don't you?
She's a wonderful person. Enthusiastic, generous, a tireless defender of just causes throughout the world. I admire and respect her a great deal. For all the things she's done and all the things she's doing. She's come to Cuba countless times. She's familiar with our process and with other processes in Latin America. She follows what's happening in Venezuela, Brazil, Bolivia with great interest. And like you, she's been in Chiapas; she was drawn to go there because of the indigenous cause, and she's talked with [Sub-] Comandante Marcos.

Has she ever asked you to look into the case of anyone held in prison here?
Yes. And we authorized a mission composed of representatives of international associations, headed by her, to come here and look into any cases – there were several dozen – they might be concerned about, with total freedom, and even to visit any prisons they wanted to visit. We didn't put any obstacles in their way, because we knew they were acting without any prejudgement, but rather out of truly altruistic motives.

And in some cases they were able to get satisfaction. You'd have to ask for the list of all the people who were able to benefit from that visit. Afterwards, they published a very objective, very fair report that contradicted most of the arguments and attacks that are constantly being made against us in that regard.

Danielle has always shown herself to be very supportive of Cuba – she's shown great solidarity.
The foundation she directs [Fondation France-Libertés] has made many concrete gestures of solidarity towards us. We have spoken a great deal with her. And I can assure you that she has a strong personality. Well, you know

her – she always says what she thinks. No beating about the bush. She's sometimes expressed certain differences with us. She voices her disagreements very frankly. And we always listen with respect, because she's a sincere, honest person.

You also knew Georges Marchais, the secretary-general of the French Communist Party, didn't you?
Yes, Georges Marchais came to Cuba often. Almost every year he'd take a holiday here with his wife, Liliane, and their children. Back then I still liked to hunt, so I'd invite him to go hunting on the south coast, not far from the city of Trinidad. That enabled us to talk to him about all sorts of things. Every time he came, he'd bring me several bottles of excellent French wine, wonderful cheeses, and sometimes *foie gras*, whose producers he knew personally. French wines, cheeses and *foie gras* are the best in the world. How delicious! And what variety! What flavour!

One day I asked him, 'What do you people intend to do when you come into power?' And he said, 'We're going to nationalize a number of banks and large corporations.' Well, I said, don't even *think* about nationalizing agriculture. Leave the small producers alone, don't touch them. Otherwise, you can kiss good wine, good cheese and excellent *foie gras* goodbye!

Another person who likes good wine is your friend the actor Gérard Depardieu, right?
As a matter of fact, Depardieu likes everything in life that's pleasurable. He's an enthusiast. I don't know anyone who can recognize a good wine as quickly as he can. He has an exceptional nose and palate. He's a producer of wine himself; he owns vineyards in southern France and produces a white wine, 'President' I think it's called. Sweet, although I personally have always preferred red.

Since 1992 Depardieu has come here quite often, with his friend [Gérard] Bourgoin, a businessman who likes aeroplanes and the Paris-Dakkar rallies, which he was an expert in. He's miraculously survived several accidents. We convinced him, Depardieu and some others to invest in oil exploration [here]. That was during the special period. Although neither we nor they knew very much about the subject, some of us have learned, and there have been several successes. We're still associates in that venture.

When you were in France in 1995, you visited Bourgogne with Gérard Bourgoin, right?

Yes, we went with him to a little town, Chailley, near Auxerre. We visited his business and that whole wonderful Burgundy region. Then we drove around the area of Chablis, where they make the best white wines in the world, we talked with farmers there. It was a quick visit, but very warm, very nice.

To end these reflections over France and the French, I wonder if you would talk to me about Jean-Edern Hallier, a contemporary writer, now deceased, who was very sympathetic towards you, and wrote a very original book on you and Cuba.[17] Do you remember him?

Of course I do! I remember him very well – he was here in 1990. Before that, he'd written a book I'd liked, *El evangelio del loco* [*The Madman's Gospel*] or something like that.[18] He was a very talented polemicist, a fierce pamphleteer. With an incredible imagination. A real agitator. We had our Celtic background in common – mine by way of my father, who was born in Galicia. He was very proud of his ancestors. He was a rebel who wouldn't make peace with anyone. I was struck by his personality. We talked for hours, all one night. He was very friendly, showed great solidarity with us. When we learned that he'd lost his sight, it made us very sad. And then we learned that he died in 1997. It was a pity – he was young and exceptionally talented.

25

Latin America

Subcomandante Marcos – The indigenous peoples' struggles –
Evo Morales – Hugo Chávez and Venezuela – The coup against Chávez –
Progressive military leaders – Kirchner and the symbol of Argentina –
Lula and Brazil

Comandante, I want to ask you a question about Subcomandante Marcos. January 2004 marked ten years since the Zapatista uprising in Chiapas on the occasion of the implementation of the Free Trade Agreement between Mexico, the United States and Canada [NAFTA]. I'd like to know what you think about that very peculiar figure, who's become so popular in the alter-global movement.[1] Do you know him, have you read his texts?

I can't judge him, but I have read some of your pieces on Marcos,[2] and what you say about him is really very interesting; it helps understand his personality, including why he gave himself the rank of *subcomandante* . . . Before, everybody who started a war or a campaign in Latin America was a general. Since the Cuban Revolution there's been a custom – the leaders are '*comandantes*'. That's the rank I had when we came back on the *Granma*. Since I was the head of a small rebel army, and up in the Sierra we had to have a military organization – we couldn't very well say 'secretary-general of the guerrilla columns' – I began to be called the *comandante en jefe*. *Comandante* was a more modest rank in the traditional army and it had one advantage – you could add *jefe*, and we did.

Never, since that time, has any revolutionary movement used the rank of general. Yet Marcos styled himself '*subcomandante*'. I'd never understood that very well; I'd thought it was an expression of modesty.

Yes, he says, 'The comandante *is the people; I'm the sub*comandante, *because I'm at the orders of the people.'*

It has to be explained: he is the *subcomandante* of the *comandante*-people . . . All right. From your book of conversations with him, I learned many details, ideas of his, concepts . . . his struggle for the cause of the indigenous people. I read him with great respect; I was very glad to be able to have information of that sort about his personality and the situation in Chiapas.

There was daring, no doubt about it, when he later went on that journey. There's some discussion as to whether it was the right thing to do or not, but at any rate I've followed it with great interest . . .

You're referring to the 'march for peace' through Mexico that Marcos made in April 2001.[3]

That's right. I've been observing all that. In Marcos I see integrity; he is unquestionably a man of integrity, ideas, talent. He's an intellectual, whether or not he's the person people thought he was when little was known about him. I'm not well enough informed, but that's not important; what's important is a person's ideas, his constancy, the knowledge that a revolutionary combatant has.

I understand how a Marcos – or two, or 100 – can emerge, because I know, I've been aware of the situation in which the indigenous people have lived down through the centuries; I've known about them in Bolivia, Ecuador, Peru, and other places, and I'll tell you the truth, I feel a sincere political, human and revolutionary respect and sympathy for the indigenous peoples of our hemisphere.

Have you been following the fight waged by the indigenous peoples in Latin America?

Yes, with a great deal of interest. As you know, I was a close friend of the painter Guayasamín. I had great admiration for him; I talked with him a great deal, and he often talked to me about the problems and the tragedies of the Indians. In addition, as history tells us, there's been a centuries-long genocide, although now there's beginning to be a greater awareness. And the struggle being waged by Marcos and the indigenous people of Mexico is yet another testimony to that new combativeness.

That's what I can say about Marcos. We observe, with great respect, the line he is taking, just as we respect the line of every organization, every progressive party, every democratic party. I haven't had the opportunity, there's never been the possibility, to speak with Marcos personally – I don't know him personally; I know him only from all the news reports and references to him I've seen, and I also know about many people, among them intellectuals, who feel great admiration for him.

In Ecuador there's also a strong indigenous movement, is there not?
I admire – yes, of course – the organization [of] the Indians in Ecuador – the Confederation of Indigenous Nationalities (CONAI) and Pachacutik [Our Land] – their social organization, their political organization, and their leaders, both men and women. I've known very brave leaders in Bolivia as well, where there is a formidable combativeness, and I know the main Bolivian leader, who is Evo Morales today, an outstanding man, a very outstanding person.

I imagine you were happy about Evo Morales' victory in the Bolivian presidential elections on 18 December 2005.
Yes, very. The election of Evo Morales – [his] overwhelming, indisputable [victory] – was very moving to the whole world, because it was the first time an indigenous person had been chosen to be president of Bolivia, which is extraordinary. Evo possesses all the qualities [needed] for leading his country and his people in these difficult times, which are like no others.

Located in the heart of the Americas, Bolivia takes its name from the Liberator, Simón Bolívar. Its first ruler was Grand Marshal Antonio José de Sucre. It is a country rich because of its peoples and its mineral resources, but today it is ranked as the poorest country in the region, with a population of about 9 million inhabitants distributed across an essentially mountainous territory of over 1 million square kilometres, around 400,000 square miles.

That is the framework, and within that framework Evo Morales is looking towards the future, and he represents hope for the majority of his people. He embodies a confirmation of the bankruptcy of the political system traditionally applied to the region, and the determination by the masses to achieve true independence. His election is the expression of the fact that the political map of Latin America is changing. New winds are blowing in this hemisphere.

Initially, people weren't certain of the lead Evo would have in the elections of 18 December, and there was some concern, because there could have been some manipulation in the congress. But when he won almost 54 per cent of the votes cast in the first round [of the elections], and also in the Chamber of Deputies, that eliminated all possibility of controversy.

It was a miracle election, an election that shook the world, that shook the empire and the unsustainable order imposed by the United States. It has demonstrated that Washington can no longer turn to dictatorships as in the past – imperialism no longer has the instruments it once had, nor can it apply them.

Cuba was the first country Evo Morales visited; that was on 30 December 2005, just after he'd been elected president, and even before his inauguration on 22 January 2006. Do you think that visit has created problems for him in Washington?

The visit of friendship paid us by our *hermano* Evo, president-elect of Bolivia, takes its place in the series of historic and profound relations of brotherhood and solidarity between the Cuban and Bolivian people. No one can be upset about that. Or by the agreements that have been signed.[4] They are pro-life, pro-humanity agreements, not a crime. We don't think [they are a crime] even in the Americans' view. How could it offend the government of the United States if Cuba helps increase the life expectancy of newborn Bolivian children? Can anyone be offended by a reduction in infant mortality or the eradication of illiteracy?

Do you think other Latin American countries will now have to deal with the indigenous element?

There are pretty critical social situations in three countries where there is great indigenous strength and a large indigenous element: Peru, Ecuador and also Bolivia. There is a large element in Guatemala, too, but there the course of events has been different from that in the other countries. As to the indigenous element, the Mexicans, of course, have quite a lot. I can simply say that in this hemisphere, you can perfectly understand how a Marcos has emerged to fight for the rights of the indigenous peoples – just as there might well be ten, or 100. I am impressed particularly by the seriousness of the indigenous leaders whom I know. I've spoken a great deal with the Ecuadorians. They speak with great seriousness. They inspire respect, trust; they have great integrity. And in Ecuador, as in Peru, and in other countries, they will have to be dealt with.

You've said that you are also a great admirer of Hugo Chávez, the president of Venezuela.

Well, yes, there you have another Indian, Hugo Chávez, a new Indian who is, as he says, a 'mixture of Indian and mestizo'; he actually says he's a little black, a little white and a little Indian. But you look at Chávez and you see an autochthonous son of Venezuela, the child of that Venezuela that was a mixture of races, with all those noble features and exceptional talent. I often listen to his speeches, and he is proud of his humble origins and of his mixed ethnicity, in which there's a little of everything, mainly the autochthonous Indians and slaves brought over from Africa. He may have some white genes – and that's not bad; a combination of so-called ethnicities is always good, it enriches the human race.

Have you followed very closely the evolution of the situation in Venezuela, in particular the attempts to destabilize President Chávez' government?

Yes, we've followed the events with great concern. Chávez visited us in 1994, nine months after he got out of prison and four years before his first election as president. It was very courageous of him, because he was strongly criticized for coming to Cuba. He came and we talked. We discovered an educated, intelligent man, very progressive, an authentic Bolivarian. Then he won the elections. Several times. He changed the constitution. With formidable support from the people. His adversaries have tried to get rid of him by both force and economics. But he has faced all the oligarchy's, all of imperialism's assaults against the Bolivarian process.

In Venezuela, in those famous forty years of democracy that preceded Chávez, according to calculations we've made with the aid of the most experienced staff of the banking system, some $300 billion were taken out of the country. Venezuela could be more industrialized than Sweden and have Sweden's education if there had only been a true distributive democracy, if those mechanisms had worked, if there'd been any truth or credibility in all that demagoguery and its colossal publicity.

In Venezuela, from the time the administration of Chávez took over until the exchange rate was controlled in January 2003, we calculate that another $30 billion or so fled the country, a flight of capital. As we have said repeatedly, all those phenomena make the currently dominant order of things in our hemisphere unsustainable.

On 11 April 2002 there was a coup in Caracas against Chávez. Were you following those events?

At noon on 11 April, when we saw that the demonstration by the opposition had turned and was approaching Miraflores,[5] I immediately realized that serious events were about to take place. Actually, we were watching the march on [cable channel] Venezolana de Televisión, which was still broadcasting. The provocations, the shooting, the victims came one after another almost immediately. Minutes later, the broadcasts from Venezolana de Televisión were cut off. News began to be fragmentary; it was coming in from various places. We learned that some high-ranking officers were speaking out against the president. It was being reported that the presidential guard had withdrawn and that the army was going to attack Miraflores. Several Venezuelans were calling friends of theirs in Cuba to say goodbye, because they were ready to resist and die; they were talking specifically about sacrificing their lives for their country.

I was in a meeting that night in a room in the Palacio de las Convenciones with the Executive Committee of the Council of Ministers. An official delegation from the Basque Country, chaired by the *lehendakari*,[6] had been with me since noon – we had invited them to a luncheon before anyone could have imagined what was going to happen on that tragic day. They were witnesses of the events [that took place] between 1 and 5 p.m. on that 11th of April.

Beginning early that afternoon, I kept trying to phone the Venezuelan president. I couldn't get through! After midnight, at 12.38 a.m. on 12 April, I received news that Chávez was on the line.

I asked him what the situation was at the moment. He replied: 'We're dug in here in the Palacio [Miraflores]. We've lost the military guard that would have decided the issue. They've cut off our television feed. I have no forces to move [as on a chessboard or in battle], but I'm analysing the situation.' I quickly asked him, 'What forces do you have there with you?'

'Between 200 and 300 exhausted men.'

'Any tanks?' I asked.

'No. There were some, but they withdrew them back to their base.'

I asked again, 'What other forces do you have?'

And he answered: 'There are some that are far away, but I have no communication with them.' He was referring to General Raúl Isaías Baduel and the paratroopers, the Armoured Division and other forces, but he'd lost all communication with those loyal troops.

I tried to be as delicate as possible when I asked him, 'Can I give you my opinion?' He said I could, so I said with as much persuasion in my voice as I could muster:

'Lay down the conditions for an honourable agreement and save the life of the men you have, which are the men who are most loyal to you. Don't sacrifice them, or sacrifice yourself.'

He answered emotionally: 'Every man is ready to die here.'

I immediately said back to him, 'I know, but I believe I can think about this more calmly than you can at the moment. Don't resign, demand honourable conditions for surrender, guarantees that you won't be the victim of a felony, because I think you should preserve yourself. Besides, you have a duty to the men with you. Don't sacrifice yourself!'

I was very conscious of the difference between Allende's circumstances on 11 September 1973 and Chávez' situation on 12 April 2002. Allende didn't have [the support of] a single soldier. Chávez had most of the soldiers and officers in the army [behind him], especially the younger ones.

'Don't resign! Don't resign!' I kept telling him.

We talked about other things: the way he should leave the country temporarily, get in touch with some officer with real authority among the ranks of the coup members, assure them of his willingness to leave the country but not to resign. From Cuba[, I told him,] we'd try to mobilize the diplomatic corps in our country and Venezuela; we'd send two planes with our foreign minister and a group of diplomats to pick him up. He thought about it for a few seconds, then finally agreed to my idea. It would all depend now on the enemy military leader.

In their interview of José Vicente Rangel, then minister of defence and now vice president of Venezuela, and who was with Chávez at that moment, the authors of the book *Chávez nuestro* ('Our Chávez') recorded these words: 'Fidel's call was decisive in preventing [mass] self-sacrifice. It was the determining factor. His advice allowed us to see better through the obscurity. It helped us a great deal.'

You were encouraging him to resist with weapon in hand?
No, quite the contrary. That was what Allende did – quite rightly so under the conditions he was facing – and he heroically paid for it with his life, as he'd promised.

Chávez had three solutions: barricade himself in Miraflores and resist to the death; leave the Palacio and try to meet with the people in order to trigger national resistance, which had virtually no possibility of success under those circumstances; or leave the country without resigning, in order to fight another day, which would have a real chance of rapid success. We suggested the third way.

My final words to convince him were, in essence: 'Save those brave men who are with you now in that unnecessary battle.' The idea came from my conviction that if a popular, charismatic leader such as Chávez, toppled in that deceitful way and under those circumstances, wasn't killed, then the people – in this case with the support of the best members of his armed forces – would demand his return, and that return would be inevitable. Which is why I assumed the responsibility of proposing what I did.

At that very second, when there was the real alternative for a quick and victorious return, there seemed no reason to die fighting, as Salvador Allende had done, and quite rightly so. And that victorious return was what happened, although much more quickly than even I had imagined.

Did the Cubans at that point try to help Chávez in some way?

Well, at that moment we could only act by deploying the resources of diplomacy. In the middle of the night we called together all the accredited ambassadors in Havana and suggested that they accompany Felipe [Pérez Roque], our minister of foreign relations, to Caracas to peacefully rescue Chávez, the legitimate president of Venezuela – get him out alive.

I had not the slightest doubt that Chávez, in a very short time, would be back, and this time carried on the shoulders of his people and his troops. Now, what I had to do was save him from death.

We proposed to send two planes to bring him back, should the coup leaders agree to his leaving the country. But the officer at the head of the coup rejected the formula; he also said that he'd be court-martialled. Chávez put on his paratrooper's uniform and went, accompanied only by his loyal aide, Jesús Suárez Chourio, to Fort Tiuna, the coup's headquarters and command centre.

When I called again, two hours later, as he and I had agreed, Chávez had been taken prisoner by the officers of the coup and all contact with him had been lost. Television was broadcasting the news of his 'resignation' over and over again, in order to demoralize his supporters and the rest of the country.

Hours later – it was now broad daylight on 12 April – at one point arrangements were made for a telephone call, and Chávez spoke with his daughter María Gabriela. He told her that he hadn't resigned, that he was a 'prisoner-president'. He asked her to contact me so I could tell the world.

His daughter called me immediately that same day, 12 April, then, at 10.02 in the morning, and repeated her father's words to me. I immediately asked her, 'Are you willing to report this to the world in your own words?' 'I'd do anything for my father,' she said to me.

Without wasting a second, I contacted Randy Alonso, the host of [the TV show] *Mesa Redonda* (Round Table). On the phone, with tape-recorder in hand, Randy called the mobile phone number María Gabriela had given me. It was almost eleven by then. The clear, emotional and persuasive words of Chávez' daughter were recorded, transcribed immediately and broadcast by our national news station at 12.40 p.m. that day, in María Gabriela's own voice. [A copy of] the tape had also been given to all the international television agencies accredited in Cuba. CNN en Español broadcast the news from Venezuela exactly as fed them by coup sources, and with great delight; in Havana, however, the CNN reporter quickly reported, at noon, the clarification by María Gabriela.

And what consequences came of that?
Well, it was heard by millions of Venezuelans, mostly opposed to the coup, and by the soldiers loyal to Chávez, who were being brazenly lied to about the alleged resignation in order to confuse and paralyse them.

That night, about 11.15, María Gabriela called again. Her voice sounded terrible. I didn't let her finish what she was saying, I just asked her, 'What's happened?'

'They took my father away tonight in a helicopter,' she told me. 'No one knows where they've taken him.'

'Quick,' I said, 'you've got to report this at once, in your own voice.'

Randy was with me – we were in a meeting with leaders of the Youth and other organizations on the programmes for the Battle of Ideas. He had his recorder with him, so the same thing that had happened at noon happened again. That way, Venezuela and the world would be informed of that strange middle-of-the-night removal of Chávez to points unknown. This all happened between the 12th and the early morning of the 13th.

On Saturday the 13th, very early, an Open Tribune had been scheduled in Güira de Melena, a city in Havana province. As I was en route back to my office, before ten, María Gabriela called again. 'Chávez' parents are uneasy,' she said – they wanted to speak with me, make a statement. They were in [the state of] Barinas.

I told her there'd been a cable from an international news agency reporting that Chávez had been transferred to Turiamo, a naval base in Aragua, on the north coast of Venezuela. I told her that from the kind of information it contained and the details, it seemed to be accurate. I recommended that she find out as much about that as she could. She told me that General Lucas Rincón, inspector-general of the armed forces, also wanted to speak to me, and that he also wanted to make a public statement.

Chávez' mother and father spoke to me: everything was normal in Barinas. Chávez' mother told me that the head of the military detachment there had just spoken to Chávez' father, Hugo de los Reyes Chávez, who was the governor of Barinas. I tried to be as calm and optimistic as possible.

The mayor of Sabanetas also came on the phone; this was the town in Barinas where Chávez had been born. He wanted to make a statement. He told me in passing that all the army detachments there were loyal to Chávez. He seemed very optimistic.

I then spoke with Lucas Rincón. He told me that the Parachute Brigade, the Armed Division, and the F-16 base were all against the coup and ready to take action. I suggested that he do everything possible to find a solution without pitting soldier against soldier. Obviously the coup was over. There was no statement from the inspector-general, because the call was interrupted and we couldn't re-establish contact.

Minutes later, María Gabriela called again; she told me that General Baduel, the head of the Parachute Brigade, needed to speak with me, and that the loyal forces in Maracay wanted to make a statement to the people of Venezuela and the world.

An insatiable desire for news led me to ask Baduel three or four questions about the situation before we continued our conversation. He answered my questions to my fullest satisfaction; his voice was filled with combativeness. I immediately told him: 'Everything is ready for your statement.'

'One moment,' he told me. 'I'm going to give the phone to Major General Julio García Montoya, permanent secretary of the National Council on Security and Defence. He's here to offer his support for our position.' This officer, with much greater seniority than the young military officers in Maracay, was not at the moment in command of any troops, but Baduel, whose paratroopers were one of the main elements of the powerful tank forces, armoured infantry and fighter-bombers stationed at Maracay, in the state of Aragua, was respectful of rank, so he put the general on the phone. García Montoya's words were really intelligent, persuasive and perfect for the situation. In essence, he said that the Venezuelan armed forces were loyal to the constitution. That said it all.

Using a mobile phone and a recorder held by Randy, I'd become a kind of news reporter, receiving and broadcasting news and public statements. I was a witness to the formidable counter-coup mounted by the people and the Bolivarian armed forces of Venezuela.

The situation at that point was excellent. The coup that had begun on 11 April now had not the slightest chance of success. But a sword still hung by a thread over the country. Chávez' life was in the gravest danger. Kidnapped by the leaders of the coup, Chávez was the only piece the oligarchy and imperialism had left in their fascistic adventure. What would they do with him? Would they assassinate him? Would they satisfy their hatred and their thirst for revenge against that rebellious, daring Bolivarian, friend of the poor, indomitable defender of Venezuela's dignity and sovereignty? What would happen if, as in Bogotá after the death of Gaitán, the people were given the news of Chávez' assassination? I couldn't get the idea of that tragedy and its bloody, destructive consequences out of my mind.

After those calls, as the hours of midday went on, news began coming in from everywhere about the people's indignation at what was happening. In Caracas, the centre of all these events, a sea of people were marching along the streets and avenues towards Miraflores and the coup leaders' headquarters. In the desperation I felt as a friend and brother of the imprisoned president, a thousand ideas were running through my head. What could I do with my little mobile phone? I was about to call General Vázquez Velasco himself.[7] I'd never spoken with him, and I had no idea what sort of person he was. I didn't know whether he'd answer or not, and what he'd do if he did. Nor, in that unique mission, could I count on María Gabriela's valuable services. I had second thoughts. At 4.15 that afternoon, I called our ambassador in Venezuela, Germán Sánchez. I asked him whether he thought Vázquez Velasco would talk to me or not. He told me he might.

'Call him,' I told Sánchez; 'tell him you're calling on my behalf, on my orders. Tell him I'm afraid there's going to be a river of blood in Venezuela if this goes on. Tell him there's just one man who can keep that from happening: Hugo Chávez. Urge him to free Chávez immediately, to forestall that very likely course of events.'

General Vázquez Velasco took the ambassador's call. He said he had Chávez in his power and that he guaranteed his life, but that he couldn't agree to what we were asking. Our ambassador insisted – he argued, tried to persuade him. Finally the general got angry and hung up on him.

I immediately called María Gabriela and told her what Vázquez Velasco had said, especially his promise to guarantee Chávez' life. I asked her to put me in contact with Baduel again. At 4.49 [that afternoon], the call went through. I told him in detail about our ambassador's conversation with Vázquez Velasco, and I gave him my view of how important it was to make Vázquez Velasco aware of the gravity of the fact that he was holding Chávez. That fact made it possible to exert maximum pressure on him.

At that moment in Cuba, we didn't know for a certainty whether Chávez had actually been transferred or not, and if so, where. Hours earlier, there had been rumours that he'd been sent to the island of Orchila. When I spoke with Baduel, around 5.00 that afternoon, he was choosing the men and preparing the helicopters for a rescue. I could imagine how hard it was for Baduel and the paratroopers to obtain accurate details for such a delicate mission.

All the rest of that day, until midnight of the 13th, I spent all my time talking to anyone I could about the subject of Chávez' life. And I talked to a lot of people, because all that evening, the people, with the support of army officers and enlisted men, were controlling everything. I still don't know what time and how 'Carmona the Brief'[8] left Miraflores. I learned that the escort, under the command of Chourio and the members of the presidential guard, were already occupying strategic positions in the building, and that Rangel, who had stood firm throughout the whole crisis, had gone back to the Ministry of Defence.

I even called Diosdado Cabello,[9] as soon as he assumed the presidency. When our phone call was interrupted due to technical problems, I sent him a message through Héctor Navarro, the minister of higher education, to suggest that as president he should order Vázquez Velasco to free Chávez, reminding [Vázquez Velasco] of the seriousness of the consequences should he refuse to do so.

With almost everyone I spoke, I felt that I was a part of that drama that María Gabriela's phone call had involved me in on the morning of the 12th. It was only when the details came out of the experience that Hugo Chávez had been put through since his transfer on the night of the 12th that we realized what incredible danger he had been in – danger that required all his mental agility, all the calm and sang-froid he could muster, and all his instincts as a revolutionary. More incredible yet was the fact that the coup members had, until the last moment, kept him absolutely uninformed of what was happening in the country, and until the last moment they'd insisted that he sign a resignation, which he consistently refused to do.

A private plane that was said to be owned by a well-known oligarch whose name I won't mention, since I'm not completely sure that it's true, was waiting to transfer him somewhere else, into someone else's hands – we haven't been able to find out where, or who was to be involved.

That's all I know; one day someone else will write the story in all its details.

Chávez is an example of progressive military leaders, but in Europe and also Latin America, many progressives criticize him precisely because he has a military background. What is your opinion as to that apparent contradiction between the military aspect and the progressive aspect?

Omar Torrijos, in Panama, was another example of a military man with a profound awareness of social justice and patriotism. Juan Velasco Alvarado,[10] in Peru, also instituted important progressive measures. Nor should we forget, for example, that among the Brazilians, Luiz Carlos Prestes was a revolutionary officer who carried out a heroic march in 1924–6 that was almost like the one carried out by Mao Zedong in 1934–5.

Among his magnificent literary works, Jorge Amado[11] wrote a moving story about the march by Luiz Carlos Prestes – *El caballero de la esperanza* ['The Knight of Hope']. That was a truly impressive deed; the march lasted over two and a half years. He marched through immense territories in his country without ever suffering a defeat.

There have been many heroic revolutionary feats on the part of military men in the twentieth century. One of those leaders was Lázaro Cárdenas, a general in the Mexican Revolution, the man who nationalized oil, instituted agrarian reforms, and totally won over his people – his name is still alive.

Among the first to rise up in Central America in the twentieth century was a group of young Guatemalan officers around Jacobo Arbenz in the 1950s. Arbenz was a high-ranking officer in the Guatemalan army, and this group took part in historical revolutionary activities, among them the noble and courageous agrarian reform that led to the mercenary invasion which, like the Playa Girón invasion, and for the same reason, imperialism launched against that very government which well deserved the title 'progressive'.

There are quite a few cases of progressive military men. Juan Domingo Perón, in Argentina, was also from a military background. You have to look at the moment he emerged: in 1943 he was appointed minister of labour, and he made such a number of laws that favoured the workers that when he was taken to prison the people themselves rescued him.

Perón made some mistakes: he offended the Argentine oligarchy, humiliated it – he nationalized its theatre and other symbols of the wealthy class – but the oligarchy's political and economic power remained intact, and at the right moment it brought Perón down, with the complicity and aid of the United States. Perón's greatness lay in the fact that he appealed to that rich country's reserves and resources and did all he could to improve the living conditions of the workers. That social class, which was always grateful and loyal to him, made Perón an idol, to the end of his life.

General Líber Seregni, who up until a few years ago was president of the Frente Amplio, or Broad Front, in Uruguay, is one of the two most progressive and most respected leaders in the history of Latin America. His integrity, his decency, his firmness and tenacity aided in the historic victory of that noble people which elected Tabaré Vázquez, Seregni's successor, president of the Republic of Uruguay and brought the Left into power in that country at a time when it was on the verge of an abyss. Cuba is grateful to Líber Seregni for the solid bases which he and other eminent Uruguayans laid for the fraternal relations of solidarity that exist today between our two countries.

Nor must we forget Francisco Caamaño, the young Dominican military officer who for many months heroically fought against 40,000 US soldiers that President Johnson had sent into the Dominican Republic in 1965 to prevent the return of constitutional president Juan Bosch. His tenacious opposition to the invaders with only a handful of soldiers and civilians – an opposition that lasted for months and months – is one of the most glorious revolutionary episodes ever written in this hemisphere. After a truce that he won from the empire, Caamaño returned to his homeland and gave his life fighting for the liberation of his people.

Without a man like Hugo Chávez, who was born in humble circumstances and educated under the disciplined eye of military academies in Venezuela, where so many ideas of Latin American freedom, unity and integration were taught by Bolívar, there would never have emerged at this decisive moment in our hemisphere a process of such historical and international transcendence as the revolutionary process in that country. I see no contradiction whatever.

[(in 1st ed.): There's also the case of a civilian who had influence on the military – he studied in Italy, where Perón had also studied; that was Jorge Eliécer Gaitán, and they were popular leaders. Perón was an embassy attaché, he was there in Rome in the thirties, during the days of Mussolini, and some of the forms and methods of mass mobilizations that he saw made a huge impression on him, there was influence there even in some [political] processes, but in these cases I've mentioned, Gaitán and Perón used their influence in a positive way, because you have to recognize that Perón carried out social reforms.]

In Argentina, Perón and Peronism continue to be quite influential politically – and this in an Argentina where, to a certain extent, the neoliberal model collapsed with a bang in December 2001. What do you think about the recent events in Argentina?

In May 2003, when the news came of the results of the elections in Argentina, with the victory of Néstor Kirchner and the defeat of Carlos Ménem, I was delighted. Why? Well, there's one important reason: the worst of savage capitalism, as Chávez would say, the worst of neoliberal globalization had been defeated in the Latin American country that had become a symbol *par excellence* of neoliberalism.

The Argentines, though far from fully achieving their most desired goals, have no idea of the service they did to Latin America and the entire world when they sank that important symbol of neoliberal globalization into the deepest trench in the Pacific, which is almost 30,000 feet deep. They have given tremendous inspiration to the growing number of people who are becoming more and more aware of what a terrible, mortal thing this phenomenon of neoliberal globalization is.

If you want, we could remember that Pope John Paul II, who was universally respected, spoke about the 'globalization of solidarity' when he came to Cuba in 1998. Could anyone be against the globalization of solidarity in the fullest sense of the word – that means including not just relations between the men and women within a country, but across the *planet*, and that solidarity should also be exercised tomorrow in a world of true liberty, equality and justice by those who today are spending vast amounts of money and destroying and squandering natural resources and condemning the inhabitants of the earth to death.

You don't get to heaven in a day, but believe me, the Argentines have struck a tremendous blow against a symbol, and that has enormous value.

Latin America continues to have the problem of foreign debt.

That debt, worldwide, has grown in direct proportion to the population. Now the total foreign debt has reached $2.5 or 2.6 *trillion*! This year, the developed countries will offer the countries of the Third World official aid towards development totalling about $53 billion. In return, they will collect, as interest on those countries' foreign debt, more than $350 billion! So at the end of the year, the foreign debt in [the Third World] will have become even larger . . .

In Latin America, that debt has been steadily growing, and now it totals some $800 billion. Nobody can pay that, and it makes any serious development policy impossible. Hunger can't be eliminated in Latin America so long as the governments have to keep sending one-fourth of their export income off to pay a debt that's been paid twice over, almost, and is now almost double what it was ten years ago . . .

Now the United States is proposing FTAA as the solution – the Free Trade Area of the Americas. What do you think of FTAA?

It's a disaster. But a disaster that can be avoided. Because we were witnesses to the battle waged down there in Mar del Plata on 4 and 5 November 2005, at the so-called 'Summit of the Americas'. It was a grand battle against the FTAA – actually there were two, one on the street and in the stadium and the other inside, where the heads of state were meeting.*

In Mar del Plata, that disastrous FTAA project was defeated once and for all. The FTAA sought to open the borders of all the countries that have a very low level of technological development to the products of those

---

* [(in 1st ed.:) In the first one, a whole force of Cuban revolutionaries took part, the *crème de la crème* – Abel [Prieto, Cuban minister of culture] led it, and Diego Maradona was there, and Adolfo Pérez Esquivel, the Nobel Peace Prize winner,[12] and many intellectuals and prestigious figures, all in that glorious march with tens of thousands of citizens from around the world and basically Argentines, whom the emperor [George W. Bush] offended by bringing an army of escorts and hiring thousands of bodyguards.

Nobody was going to confront him physically. That was exactly what he wanted – for somebody to throw a rotten egg at him. No, he doesn't deserve such 'high honours' in any way . . . It was a peaceful demonstration – not a tomato, not even a tomato skin was thrown at him, and when so many people started to march in that cold misty rain, marching for hours to the stadium and filling that stadium with an enormous mass of people, they gave an unforgettable lesson to the empire, because they showed it that they were nations that know what they're doing and know that they're marching towards a great victory – they were absolutely sure of that. And those who don't know what they're doing are crushed by the nations, by the people.]

535

countries that have the highest level of technological development and productivity, those who build the latest-model aeroplanes, those who dominate worldwide communications, those who want to get three things from us: raw materials, cheap labour, customers and markets – a new form of ruthless, savage colonialism.

Do you think that it could increase Latin America's dependency on the United States?
If Latin America were devoured by the empire, if we should be swallowed up by it, then like that whale that swallowed the prophet Jonah and couldn't digest him, it would have to spit us out one day; we would be born again in our hemisphere. But I don't think we'd be easy to swallow, and I have hopes that [the empire] won't be able to swallow us. Events in the last few years have been demonstrating that: a world of 6 billion 400 million inhabitants can't be governed with a soldier and a bayonet in every school, in every house, in every park.

I've always said that we have to rely on the North Americans themselves – the intellectuals, and the American people. The American people can be fooled, tricked, deceived, but when they learn the truth . . . as in the case of little Elián:[13] more than 80 per cent of them believed that he should be returned to his father.

[The American] people today are opposed to the blockade of Cuba. In increasing numbers, they are opposed to the doctrine of a surprise, interventionist war, despite their having received that cunning, terrible blow to New York on September 11, 2001. We must rely on them.

We must also rely on the European intellectuals, because men like you have been making enormous efforts to create awareness, and have made notable contributions to the creation of that necessary awareness.

Now there are also a number of governments – in Venezuela, in Brazil, in Argentina, in Uruguay and in other countries – that are applying progressive measures. How do you view what Lula is doing in Brazil, for example?
Obviously I view the reforms that Lula is implementing very positively. He doesn't have a sufficiently large majority in parliament; he's had to find support in other places, even among conservatives, in order to implement certain of his reforms. The media have given a great deal of publicity to a corruption scandal in the parliament. But they haven't been able to implicate him. Lula is a popular leader [i.e., a populist leader, leader of the masses].

I've known him for many years; we've followed his career, we've spoken with him many times – a man of conviction, intelligent, patriotic, progressive, a man from a very humble background but who hasn't forgotten that background, a man of the people, who have always supported him. And I think everyone sees him the same way. Because it's not that he's making a revolution – he's meeting a challenge: to do away with hunger. He can do it. He's trying to do away with illiteracy. And he can do that, too. [(in 1st ed.:) He's trying to give land to the landless. And he can do that, too.] And I think we should all support him.[14]

Comandante, *do you think that the age of revolutions and armed struggle in Latin America is over?*
Listen, no one can guarantee that revolutionary changes are going to occur in Latin America today. But no one can guarantee that they're not, either – at any time, in one or a number of countries. If one analyses the economic and social situation in some countries objectively, there's not the slightest doubt that it's an explosive situation. The infant mortality rate in several of those countries, for example, is 65 per 1,000 babies born; ours is less than 6.5. That means that ten times more children die in some countries in Latin America, on average, than in Cuba. Malnutrition is sometimes over 40 per cent in Latin American, illiteracy and semi-literacy continue to be too high, unemployment affects tens of millions of adults throughout the hemisphere, and there is also the problem of abandoned children, millions of them. The president of UNICEF told me one day that if Latin America had the level of medical and health care that Cuba has, 700,000 children would be saved every year.

If a solution is not found for these problems quickly – and the FTAA is not a solution, and neoliberal globalization is also not a solution – more than one revolution may occur in Latin America when the United States least expects it. And there'll be no one to blame [i.e., Fidel Castro], for promoting that revolution.

26

Cuba Today

Human rights – The economic embargo – The press and information –
The terrorist attacks on September 11, 2001 – President Bush's
aggressiveness – The Iraq War – A 'preventive war' against Cuba? –
On terrorism

What are the main concerns that you, as head of state, have at the present time?
Today, our attention is focused on the fight against terrorism, the fight against espionage. Our country is focused on the fight for the liberation of the Five Heroes who are being held prisoner in the United States. Domestically, we are engaged in a fight against several manifestations of corruption and in a vigorous campaign to promote energy saving and transform the entire system of energy production in the country – what we've called a true energy revolution – in order to even further improve the quality and efficiency of our systems of education and health. We have devoted a great deal of attention and energy to the development of new programmes of internationalist cooperation, such as the presence of thousands of Cuban doctors and health personnel in many places around the world. In Pakistan, for example, after the earthquake that caused so much death and destruction. Or Operation Miracle, which has already yielded spectacular results.[1]

The country is concerned with the international financial crisis, the country is concerned by the problems of oil, concerned with countering all the measures [taken against it] in the economic and political war; the country is focused on the battles, over there in Geneva, in the UN Human Rights Commission, where the entire world is aware of the show that takes place year after year, the lies and calumnies that are spread about us. The world

538

has not been told that 80 per cent of the measures in defence of human rights passed by that commission have been proposed by Cuba.

By the Human Rights Commission, in Geneva?
That's right. Proposals introduced by Cuba, supported sometimes by every country except the United States, and always by thirty, thirty-five, forty votes. There's just one subject that the United States insists on, pressures, threatens.

Cuba.
Cuba. It's constantly condemning Cuba for 'violations of human rights'. And every year there's a fierce diplomatic battle over that.

Another battle takes place in the United Nations General Assembly, where Cuba is gaining more votes against the blockade every year; this year [2005] there were over 180. Only four countries voted against the resolution condemning the blockade: the United States, of course; Israel, its unconditional ally; and two of the tiny island states in the Pacific, whose very livelihood depends entirely on the United States. That is, over 90 per cent of the members of the United Nations condemn the blockade.[2]

Ninety per cent of the countries in the UN support Cuba's denunciation of the economic embargo?
That's right. There are a few that abstain, but, as I said, only three support the United States: the Marshall Islands,[3] a few small islands – I respect the size of any country, but these are some little Pacific islands that were a Yankee protectorate – Palau, another little island in the same situation, and Israel, which, unfortunately, plays the inglorious role of US partner, supporting the blockade against Cuba against the opinion of the immense majority of the world's countries. The few that abstain do so really not because they support the blockade, but rather because of the problems [that denouncing it] would cause them with the United States.

You have to admire the dozens and dozens of countries that have credits pending with the Monetary Fund, or the World Bank, or that have some financial need, that depend on the United States, and that still vote against the blockade. It's not a secret ballot; it's public – if the voting were secret, if the voting in Geneva were secret, they'd never win any [initiative] on any subject.

Of course, one must say 'with all due respect to Europe', that Europe votes with the United States in Geneva like a mafia, always. I have to say that, it's my duty. But that's never been questioned. All of NATO votes, and countries not in NATO, too. When the Socialist bloc was still in existence, none of those ploys passed in Geneva, but they changed jerseys, changed teams, they went over to the other side, and even so, five years ago they got a little careless and became a minority.

What happened to the United States had never happened before: the countries that elected the members of the Human Rights Commission didn't elect the United States. Months have been spent trying to find out who in the world it could have been that, in secret balloting, voted against [the US], but [the US] is now in the minority, and they don't dare risk a secret ballot – instead, they found a candidate that would resign so that the candidate they wanted would win. That is, they had to ask one of the candidates to withdraw.

And that's how things are done over there, and all those campaigns have been carried out, a lot of them – for forty-six years, one after another after another after another.

The criticism most often made against Cuba is that it imprisons its political opponents.

Who has freed thousands and thousands of counter-revolutionaries, even before they'd served out their sentences? The government of Cuba. Not the government of the United States. The United States has used any arrest made here, in enforcement of the law, for their propaganda campaign against us.

You people over there in Europe have very strict, very harsh laws, much more severe than ours, against political crimes. In England, the jails are full of Irish prisoners who had political, patriotic motives. I remember there was a hunger strike once in which the English let several Irish prisoners die. The Spaniards use very harsh laws against the Basque prisoners who are fighting for political rights over there. The Italian government still has members of the Red Brigades in prison, from thirty years ago. We know how harsh the German government was with the members of the Baader-Meinhof group[4] – almost all of them died in prison. In France, how many dozens of Corsican prisoners are there who were in a struggle for political reasons?

In the United States, why don't they free the Puerto Ricans who fight for the independence of Puerto Rico?[5] Why don't they free the journalist Mumia Abu-Jamal,[6] who's been in prison for over twenty-two years? Why don't they free the American Indian leader Leonard Peltier,[7] who's been in prison for more than twenty-five years?

I told you earlier that after [Playa] Girón, we took 1,200 prisoners, and freed them. At that time, in the first years of the Revolution, there were about 300 counter-revolutionary organizations, and it was a time of wholesale terrorism and sabotage, and at one point there were as many as 15,000 prisoners in the country.

Fifteen thousand political prisoners, after the Revolution?
You can call them political prisoners if you want to. Yes, I told you about those years – [Playa] Girón, the October crisis, Operation Mongoose. There were dozens of plans for operations against us, which led to thousands of acts of sabotage and terrorism – there were armed bands, a dirty war, which cost us more lives than the war itself.

There was also that terrorist act in 1976 – a Cuban civilian airliner was blown up in mid-air.
And everyone died. Photos of the time show a million people protesting [that]. And the person who committed that crime, an international terrorist who's confessed to the act and been convicted of it in a court of law, Luis Posada Carriles [see Chapter 11, note 13, p. 685] was taken in by the United States in March 2005. In the middle of their supposed 'war against international terrorism' they've given asylum to one of the biggest international terrorists! Are there two terrorisms? A good one and a bad one? Many times, we've asked President Bush, the younger one, 'Shrub', a very simple, straightforward question: where did Posada Carriles enter the United States? On what ship? Through what port? Which of the heirs to the throne authorized it? Might it have been the chubby little brother in Florida [Governor Jeb Bush]? I apologize for calling him chubby – it's not a criticism, just a suggestion that he get a little more exercise and watch what he eats; I'm saying it for the gentleman's own good. Who met Posada Carriles [when he entered the country]? Who gave permission [for his entry]? Why is the person who so shamelessly brought him into the United States strolling along the streets of Florida and Miami today? And the shameless little 'Shrub' hasn't deigned to answer so far – he's keeping his mouth shut. The authorities in our sister country Mexico also haven't had time – apparently they're very busy – to answer the question.[8]

They're absolutely brazen – they tell all the lies in the world, and when somebody asks them an innocent little question, a simple little question, months pass and you don't hear a word from them. So here in Cuba, in the face of all those aggressions, and all that complicity, down through all these years, what can we do? And there were laws [here in Cuba]; the laws were strict. But what's *never* happened here is the death of a prisoner, an extra-judicial execution. But we *have* had to defend ourselves. I don't think it's a crime to defend yourself, and there's no historical process that hasn't defended itself, one way or another. It's the most legitimate thing you can do, because if you don't, you should resign and get the hell out – go somewhere and become a preacher, become a pastor, preach the gospel, which I'm not against, because it has a lot of positive things in it, but we didn't choose the career of pastor or preacher, we chose to be a revolutionary politician, and to act ethically.

President Chávez of Venezuela has also been attacked.
You know, and the world knows, that the state that doesn't defend itself is cut to ribbons. Look what's happening in Venezuela – we've already talked about that. There's not a man who's respected democratic and human rights as much as Chávez. They mounted a coup against him, they kidnapped the president, his life has been in constant danger. The leaders of the coup put in a man who within a few hours had trampled on all political rights, all human rights, all freedoms – he'd dissolved the parliament, abolished judicial power, closed down radio stations, arrested patriots. A Fascist, Carmona, who was the president of Fedecámaras, the oligarchy's federation of chambers of commerce . . . Then they orchestrated an oil strike. And yet there's not a single political prisoner over there.

Are you particularly irritated by the accusations of violations of human rights that are regularly levelled against Cuba?
Listen, I think there's not a country with a cleaner history with respect to human rights than Cuba. What the Revolution has done for our population can be expressed in numbers that no other state is able to claim. In these forty-six years since the triumph of the Revolution, the lives of at least 450,000 children have been saved – children who would have died without the advances achieved by the Revolution. The life expectancy of Cuban citizens is now almost eighteen years longer than in 1959, when the Revolution came to power.

We have made universal literacy possible, made it possible for every child to go to school, made it possible for every citizen to get an education. In the fields of education and health, there's no country in the Third World, or even in the developed capitalist world, that's done what we've done in those areas, for the good of the people. Begging and unemployment have been eradicated. Drug use and gambling have also disappeared. You won't find children begging in the streets; we don't have homeless beggars here, or children sleeping in the street, or barefoot, or malnourished, or not going to school.

And I won't go on too long about the aid we've given dozens of countries in the Third World. There are Cuban doctors in over forty countries, and they've saved thousands of human lives. We've given free treatment to thousands of children from Chernobyl that no other country took in. I don't think any place else in the world has equalled the generosity to human beings that's been shown by Cuba. And this is the country that people want to condemn for violations of human rights? Only through lies and calumnies can such profoundly dishonest accusations be made.

I don't think Cuba is criticized for its health policy; on the contrary, that policy is generally applauded. Although I do think that people don't know the figures, and they don't know about what you just mentioned, the aid to Third World countries. Could you give us more information about that?

With respect to its health policy, Cuba has an infant mortality rate under 6 per 1,000 live births in their first year of life, behind Canada by a slight margin – we're on the way to fewer than 5, and maybe fewer than 4 in the near future, to take first place on the continent. In turn, it will take [us] half the time it took Sweden and Japan to raise life expectancy from seventy to eighty years of age – today, we're at 77.5. Our medical services have increased life expectancy to that level in just under eighteen years, from the sixty years that it was in January 1959, at the triumph of the Revolution.

Today our people can call on the services of at least fifteen doctors for every doctor that was left here in Cuba in 1959, and they're much better distributed. We have tens of thousands of other doctors abroad lending their expertise, in solidarity with the peoples they serve. Cuba now has more than 70,000 doctors. At this moment – I'll give you the exact number – we have 25,000 medical students. And that's not counting the tens of thousands who are studying in other branches of health science. If we include all those who are studying for their degrees in nursing, and all those in health-related studies, we find that in the health area we have around 90,000 students.

There will be many medical schools in other cities in Cuba with 400 or

450 students, and their psychological profile has been studied, as has their student profile and their family profile – a new and unique experience. Schools with excellent physical facilities, the equipment needed for classes, audiovisual equipment, interactive programmes. This means that in six years of study, a doctor is going to have the knowledge that traditional methods would have needed twenty years to impart.

We are making efforts to create the best medical capital[9] in the world. And not just for us – for the peoples and nations of Latin America and other places in the world. There are over 10,000 students registered in the ELAM [Escuela Latinoamericana de Medicina, the Latin American School of Medicine] now, among them 2,000 young Bolivian university graduates. Many countries are now requesting that we educate and train their doctors; we have the resources to do that, and no one can do it better. We have developed pedagogical methods that we never even dreamed of before. You'll be seeing the results, and soon. We will have tens of thousands of Latin American students in medical schools. Over the next ten years our country will be educating some 100,000 Latin American and Caribbean doctors, under the ALBA principles [the Alternativa Bolivariana para las Américas, or Bolivarian Alternative for the Americas] that have been signed between Cuba and Venezuela, which will provide an equal number, in a determined march towards the integration of our nations.

With President Hugo Chávez, on behalf of the two nations, we have made a commitment to important social and economic programmes that will make a great human impact and bring our two countries closer together – specifically, support for literacy, education, Petrocaribe, Electrocaribe, the fight against the HIV-AIDS virus, and health.

You've also decided to launch Operation Miracle.
That's right. We launched Operation Miracle, the enormous task of preserving and restoring sight to no fewer than 6 million Latin Americans and Caribbeans, and educating and training 200,000 health professionals in ten years – [an achievement] unprecedented anywhere in the world. We began in Venezuela, and we decided to expand Operation Miracle into the Caribbean countries. In September of 2005 there was a total of 4,212 Caribbean citizens who'd had eye operations here in Cuba, along with 79,450 Venezuelans – a number that's growing every day.[10]

And Cuba is also sending brigades of doctors to places where disasters have occurred, aren't you?

Yes, we are. We've created a team – the International Contingent of Doctors Specializing in Disaster Situations and Serious Epidemics, the Henry Reeve Contingent. [See Chapter 15, note 3, p. 690.] No other country can send 1,000 doctors to a sister nation in Central America struck by a devastating hurricane, as we did to Guatemala in the autumn of 2005. Or as we have at this moment [winter 2005] on the other side of the world, an eighteen-hour flight from Havana, in Kashmir, Pakistan, in the midst of pain and death, to aid with the worst natural tragedy that has occurred in our world in many years. I don't recall a worse natural disaster, given the place in which it happened, the humble community it has affected, a community of shepherds who live high up in the mountains, and just before winter, over there where there is such intense cold, and such terrible poverty.

One by one, I spoke to each of those brigades; I saw them off. We know what our compatriots are doing everywhere around the world; we're in constant contact with them, the men and women of the Henry Reeve Contingent and the others. There's a whole wonderful story being written at this very moment, like no other that's ever happened in the life of our Revolution.

You showed me the impressive stack of documents you read and consult every morning so you can closely follow world events – dozens of cables [wire stories] and articles translated from the international press. And in that regard, I wonder if we could talk about information in Cuba. The impression people have is that although there are excellent journalists, there is very little information critical of what's happening in Cuba. What is your opinion of that?

Well, sincerely, our press organs are not in the hands of enemies of the Revolution, or in the hands of agents of the United States. They're in the hands of revolutionaries. Our press is revolutionary; our journalists – on radio, on television – are revolutionaries. We have many newspapers; every organization has its own press organ: workers, young people, the Party, *campesinos*, the armed forces. There are dozens of newspapers, and all of them are revolutionary.

The impression one gathers when one reads them, or when one listens to the radio or watches the news on television, is that everything's going swimmingly, that all there are are successes, victories, that there are no problems, that nobody's discontent. It's a little strange, because I imagine that in the Party, in Party meetings, there must be debates and disagreements, even arguments, that are more critical.

I'll tell you, for a pretty long time, there's been a tendency here to assume that criticism, denunciations of things not done right, play into the hands of the enemy, aid the enemy, aid the counter-revolution. Sometimes there's a fear of reporting on something because people think it might be helpful to the enemy. And we've discovered that in the struggle against negative events and actions, the work of the press is very important. And we've encouraged a critical spirit. I have been stimulating [that critical spirit] to the maximum, because it's fundamental to perfecting our system.

Of course we know that there are drawbacks, but we want responsible criticism. And despite the possible consequences, anything is better than the absence of criticism.

Of course one has to be extremely responsible in the way one handles the issues, and not give the enemy sensitive information that can be useful to their plans to destroy the Revolution. Therein lies the difficulty of the revolutionary's job.

That desire for responsible criticism – could it go so far as authorizing the freedom of the press that many are calling for?

If what you call freedom of the press is the right to mount a counter-revolution and allowing Cuba's enemies to speak and write freely against Socialism and against the Revolution, to write slanders and lies and create conditioned reflexes, I'd have to say that we are not in favour of that 'freedom'. So long as Cuba is a country blockaded by the empire, the victim of iniquitous laws such as the Helms–Burton Act and the Cuban Adjustment Act, a country threatened by the president of the United States himself, we can't give that 'freedom' to our enemies and their allies, whose objective is to fight against Socialism's very existence.

Free media would be considered incompatible with the Revolution?

In those 'free' media, who speaks? What do they speak about? Who writes? What's spoken about is what the owners of the newspapers or television stations want. And the people who write are the people they choose. You know that. People talk about 'freedom of expression', but actually what's being defended, basically, is the right of private property belonging to the mass media. Here in Cuba, I'll tell you quite frankly, there is no private property as it applies to the mass media. But the various mass organizations do have their own media: the students have theirs, the workers, the unions, the *campesinos*, even the military. Everyone has his own organ of inform-ation, and believe me, they very freely publish everything they think it's necessary to publish.

Instead of questioning our ways [of dealing with this], which are the result, the consequence, of more than forty years of resisting our powerful neighbour, the question that should be asked of our citizens is whether they feel free or not.

There are foreign newspapers that are also censored and not distributed in Cuba.

Listen, there are a lot of foreign newspapers distributed here in Cuba, both American and European. Important, serious newspapers. In that, we're more tolerant than people say we are. They can be found at many points of sale, and they can be bought with foreign currency. Tourists buy them, and any Cuban who has foreign currency can buy them and even pass them around. That's not a crime. No one here is afraid of what those newspapers may say against the Revolution – those newspapers or information channels, such as CNN, which many people here pick up without any problem.

But we can't spend our resources – because we have other priorities, such as energy conservation, nutrition, health – on importing foreign publications. That type of import is absolutely not a priority for us. And it's possible that the circulation of this or that publication might be restricted because it's waging a systematic campaign against us, a counter-revolutionary cam-paign; it's publishing lies and libels and falsehoods, it's trying to divide us, create conflict. That, we won't tolerate. Why should we allow a counter-revolutionary publication to circulate here?

Because I'll tell you, those media that are always talking about freedom of the press, when they don't want some of the things that Cuba denounces known publicly – and the lines are drawn by the people who control them – they don't publish them. Because you know that every organ toes a certain line, and the lines are drawn by the people who control them, the owners of those media, and some are drawn more freely, some less, although there are, I can't deny it, a lot of independent people, too.

Are you satisfied, then, with the degree of criticism in information published here?

Well, I don't know whether you've been able to follow in detail our organs of information, but I can tell you that my most important source of information on what's happening in this country – better than the reports sent to me by the Party or other state agencies – the [source] I think most highly of, is the newspapers. They keep me up to date on everything that's happening. And I read them every day, at the end of the day.

You talk about a critical spirit, but I wonder: where's the critical spirit in the press of so many countries that consider themselves so much more democratic than we are? Where's that critical spirit in those journalists and those TV channels in the United States that have supported – like honest-to-goodness propaganda spokespersons – President Bush's war against Iraq?

Truth, ethics, which should be the human being's first right or attribute, occupy less and less space in those media. The wire services, radio, television, mobile phones, the internet spew out a torrent of news from everywhere all the time. It's not easy for a citizen to follow the course of events. The human intelligence can barely find its bearings in that whirlwind of news.

I say to those organs of information that call themselves free and critical but depend on advertising and never criticize their advertisers: why does the political and social system you defend spend so many billions of dollars on advertising? So much could be done with just one billion of the dollars that are wasted on advertising! Here you have a country in whose GDP [Gross Domestic Product] you won't find one penny for advertising – not in newspapers, or on television, or on the radio – in Cuba not one cent is spent on commercial advertising.

What role have those mass media played, unfortunately, in the United States and many other places in the world? And I'm not attacking them. Those like you who know the effect those mass media have on people's minds can understand that here in Cuba, those media are used to educate, to teach, to create values. I am totally convinced, from my own experience, that values can be sown in the souls of men, in their intelligence and in their hearts.

We hold no brief for hypocrisies of any kind when people talk about that European 'freedom of the press'. Our dream is of another freedom of the press, of a country that is educated and informed, of a country that has a holistic general culture and can communicate with the world. Because those who fear free thought don't educate their people, don't give them anything, don't try to encourage them to acquire the highest possible level of culture, the broadest and deepest possible knowledge of history and politics, and to value things for their intrinsic value, and to encourage them to use their own heads, to reach their own conclusions. In order to do that, to use their own heads, they need the facts on which to reach those conclusions.

When the mass media first emerged, they took over people's minds, and they govern on the basis not just of lies, but also of conditioned reflexes. A lie is not the same thing as a conditioned reflex. Lies have a negative effect on knowledge; a conditioned reflex has a negative effect on the ability to think. And it's not the same thing to be uninformed, or disinformed, as to have lost the ability to think because your mind is full of reflexes: 'This is bad, this is evil; Socialism is bad, Socialism is evil; it'll take away the guardianship of your children, it'll take your house away, it'll take your wife away.' And all the ignorant people in the world, all the illiterates, all the poor people, all the exploited people repeat in chorus, 'Socialism is bad; Socialism is evil.' That's the way parrots are taught to speak, and bears are taught to dance, and lions to crouch down respectfully.

The masses are not taught to read and write, while a billion dollars is spent every year to pull the wool over the eyes of the vast majority of humankind, turning human beings into people who, apparently, don't even have the ability to think, because they're led to buy the same product under ten different brand names, and they have to be fooled, because that billion dollars isn't paid by the corporations, it's paid by the people who purchase the products because of the advertising, which is basically brainwashing. This guy buys Palmolive, the other guy buys Colgate, the other one another brand, just because they've been told to a hundred times, and they associate [a certain brand] with a pretty image and it's been drummed into their brains. Those people who talk so much about brainwashing are in fact the ones who hammer things into people's heads, who brainwash people until they've taken away their ability to think.

Are people going to talk about 'freedom of expression' in countries where 20 per cent, 30 per cent of people are wholly illiterate and 50 per cent are functionally illiterate? With what criteria, with what knowledge, do they give an opinion, and where do they give it? If when many educated, intelligent people want to publish an article there's nowhere to publish it, and it's ignored, trampled upon and discredited? The big media have been turned into instruments of manipulation.

We have media, and we use those media to educate, to develop our citizenry's knowledge. Those instruments play an important role in the Revolution; they've created awareness, concepts, values, and we haven't always used them to best advantage. We do know, however, what they can do, and we know what a society can achieve in knowledge, in culture, in quality of life, and in peace by using those media for the social good.

We're not going to believe the story that in the West those media are used to create values such as solidarity, brotherhood, justice. They put forth the values of a system that is by its nature selfish, self-centred and individualistic. The more education a person has, the better he can understand that the increasingly complex problems of this world cannot be solved through means that strip a society of its ability to think, or its ability to reason.

Although you are hostile to the cult of personality, and have often denounced it, the media in Cuba often talk about you and publish photographs of you – you occupy an important place in the media's content. Does that upset you?

Listen, I'm going to say this to you: contrary to what many people think, I don't appear that much in public. I'm not in the habit of appearing on the news on TV every day, and two weeks may go by without any news about me appearing in the newspapers. I appear when there's some commemorative celebration in which I have to take part, or when some visitor, some head of state, visits Cuba, or when some extraordinary event has occurred, such as a devastating hurricane, for example.

I assure you I don't much like appearing in the newspapers, or on television or radio. Here, there's no worship of news about the head of state – nothing of the kind. The writing is quite natural. I'd say that the media talk about me with respect, but familiarity. Nobody sees me as a figure standing up on Mount Olympus. Many people treat me like a neighbour, they talk to me.

By nature, I'm against anything that might appear to be a cult of personality, and you can see for yourself, as I've said, that in Cuba there's not a single school, factory, hospital or building that's named after me. Nor are there statues, or practically any portraits of me. Here we don't even produce official portraits. It's possible that somebody may have put up a photo of me in some office, but that's by personal initiative – in no way is that photo an official portrait. Here, no state agency spends its money and wastes its time taking and passing out official photographs of me, or any leader. That [practice] does not exist in this country.

It's common knowledge that I do everything I can not to appear in the press or on the nightly news. I resign myself to [appearing] only when it's strictly necessary. You'll observe that I'm one of the heads of state who least often appears in his country's media. Nor do I like it when they attach titles and posts to my name. Fortunately, the people call me Fidel.

Those who know me and are familiar with my speeches and my ideas know that I'm very critical, very self-critical about that, and that I've fought adamantly against any manifestation of the cult of personality, or idol-worship.

Mass media in the hands of the state have often been used to broadcast propaganda.
Apart from informing the public about events taking place in the country and the world, we want to use the media to raise the level of general culture, to fight against lies, and to respect the truth. To do that, we've created new educational channels. And through them, the programme 'University for All' is giving language courses and lots of other kinds of courses, apart from curricular courses. In 2003 we inaugurated our third TV channel, which is for education, and in 2004 we also launched a fourth educational channel. Television is a wonderful, though not very well utilized, way of making knowledge available to the masses.

Using audiovisual methods, and using them exhaustively, we've entered the stage of mass education and mass information not to sow venom or broadcast propaganda, not so that somebody else can think for you; because if media are used in that terribly wrong way, as happens in capitalist societies, they repress the citizen's ability to think, because somebody else is thinking for you and telling you what colour suit to wear, whether skirts should be short or long, whether this kind of fabric is 'in' or 'out', absolutely everything you have to do from the minute you get up until you go to bed at night, including the brand of toothpaste to use and the pill to take for a good night's sleep. Advertising is propaganda, and it's often dehumanizing and harmful. Nobody wants their children to be entertained by learning to drink alcohol or eat junk food, or watching violence and stupid things that poison children's minds.

Do you think, then, that in this modern world of new technologies, states can still control information?
Less and less. Today there are new ways of transmitting and receiving messages. There are satellites that can send down a signal; there's the

internet, which allows you to send a message to any corner of the world, because really, generally speaking, the people who have internet also have electricity, telephones and the possibility of communicating.

Nor should we underestimate those intellectual sectors of our societies – there are millions and millions of [intellectuals] around the world – that do not necessarily constitute an exploitative, wealthy class. Remember, for example, up there in Seattle; remember Quebec, remember Geneva, Florence, Porto Alegre . . . Remember the demonstrations, the mobilizations against neoliberal globalization that have taken place all around the world; those demonstrations were organized through the internet by educated, cultured people. There are many phenomena that threaten the planet today besides war: there's climate change, the destruction of the ozone layer, global warming, the poisoning of the air we breathe, the poisoning of rivers and oceans – these things threaten our lives. And against all that, the peoples of the world are mobilizing, they are finding common cause with Latin Americans, with North Americans and with Europeans.

Today there are ways of communicating with the world that make us less victims, less dependent on the big mass media, whatever they may be – private or state-owned – because today, having that internet in the world, every person with an aspiration, a dream, a cause, whether they live in underdeveloped countries or rich countries, can make common cause with others. The internet can also be used with the worst of intentions, as the CIA and the Pentagon use it, or as apparently happened with those who carried out the terrorist attacks on September 11.

Did the Cubans condemn those attacks?
We condemned the crime committed on September 11 in no uncertain terms. And we have reiterated our condemnation of terrorism in all its shapes and forms. The United States has cynically included Cuba among the 'countries sponsoring terrorism', but Cuba will never allow its territory to be used for terrorist actions against the people of the United States or any other country. And we also condemn state terrorism. We have proposed that the United States adopt a programme to fight terrorism in our region, but they have rejected our proposal.

Do you agree that terrorism is the biggest threat to the world today?
I agree that terrorism is a serious threat to the world today, but I believe humanity is facing other threats of equal or greater seriousness: the acceler-

ating destruction of the environment and of the very conditions for the survival of our species; the deepening of poverty; the lack of health care; hunger among countless millions of human beings around the world ... There are many other serious problems facing this planet today besides the problem of terrorism. To all of which one would have to add the hegemonic designs of the only superpower that aspires to become the ruler of the planet, and its arrogant policy of domination.

With respect to terrorism, the American administration is constantly talking about the 'worldwide war against terror', but I myself would be very careful about how I used the concept of terrorism. Because the terrorist attacks on New York are one thing – or the terrorist attacks in Madrid and London and so on, and the necessary fight against those abominable attacks – that's one thing, and the dubious extrapolations that are made on the basis of that legitimate concern are another.

Since September 11, 2001, we've seen that many national struggles – in Iraq, for example, or in Iran, for the peaceful use of nuclear energy – have tended to be categorized as 'terrorist' struggles. Back in the eighties, in the time of Reagan, the Americans used the word 'terrorism' indiscriminately. They called the combatants in the ANC, such as Nelson Mandela, fighting against apartheid in South Africa, 'terrorists'. And those who were fighting for the independence of Namibia; or the Palestinians fighting for their own independent state, or the Salvadoran patriots. Reagan would compare the counter-revolutionaries in Nicaragua with the founding fathers of the United States, or with Lafayette's volunteers, or with the French Maquis that fought in the Resistance against the Nazi occupiers of their country.

But when the Israeli armed forces bomb civilian neighbourhoods in Gaza, causing the deaths of innocent people, they don't call that terrorism; or when the American army itself shoots off missiles indiscriminately, killing women and children, that's not called terrorism, either.

In our war against Batista – you know about that, we talked about it – to the best of our ability we always avoided all those accidents in which non-combatants might be killed or injured. We were violent, but let me tell you that within our revolutionary violence, we never, ever used those methods.*

Although I should add that the constituted authorities sometimes use quite

---

* [Methods specified in 1st ed: the suicide bombings of civilians, the kidnapping and beheading of non-combatants, bombs in schools.]

a bit of violence, quite a few repressive methods, in many places, very bloody repressions, and nobody calls them terrorists, no matter what they do.

Does President Bush's attitude worry you?
Well, we're living in difficult times . . . Not long ago, we heard some chilling, frightening words and ideas. In a speech at West Point in June 2002, the president of the United States said the following to the military graduates, and I'm quoting him: 'Our security will require transforming the military you will lead – a military that must be ready to strike at a moment's notice in any dark corner of the world.'[11] That same day he proclaimed the doctrine of 'preventive, surprise war', a thing which no one in the political history of the world had ever done before. Months later, referring to the military action against Iraq, he said, 'If we are forced to go to war, we are going to fight with the full force and power of our armed forces.'

The person who made those statements was not the leader of some small state, he was the head of the most powerful military force the world has ever seen, the possessor of thousands of nuclear weapons, enough to eliminate the entire population of the world several times over, and of other fearsome military weapons systems, both conventional and of mass destruction.

According to Señor Bush, that's what we are: a 'dark corner of the world'. That's how some people see the countries of the Third World. No one has ever defined us that way before, or done it with more contempt. Former colonies of powers that divided the world up among themselves and pillaged it for centuries, today we are 'the underdeveloped countries of the world'. None of us has our full independence, none of us is treated fairly and justly and as equals, none of us has any national security whatsoever; none of us is a permanent member of the UN Security Council, none of us has veto power or the power to decide anything in the international financial agencies; none of us can retain our finest talents, or protect ourselves from the flight of capital, from the destruction of nature and the environment brought on by the profligate, egotistical and insatiable consumerism of the developed countries.

In the Security Council, the United States once again announced that it reserved the right to decide, on its own, whether to attack other nations. And in violation of the spirit and letter of the United Nations charter, they're talking now about 'preventive war'.

The United Nations couldn't prevent the war in Iraq. Do you think the UN should be reformed?

Yes, urgently. A real reform must be undertaken without further delay, and especially a profound process of democratization of the United Nations. The situation is no longer tolerable, and the proof of that is the shameful inability of the Security Council to prevent the war in Iraq.

I think that the outcome of the international crisis created by the Iraq War will decide the future of the United Nations. The most serious danger to all of us today is that we are all still living in a world in which the law of the jungle prevails, in which the strongest rule, and in which the great majority of people are exposed constantly to aggression, underdevelopment and despair. Are we going to see a worldwide dictatorship imposed on our peoples, or will the United Nations and multilateralism be preserved? That's the question.

I believe that the role of the United Nations in 2005, fifty years after its founding,[12] is irrelevant, or at least on the road to becoming so. But some of us say that with concern and want to strengthen the organization, while others say it with secret satisfaction and have hopes of imposing their own designs on the world. I ask this with all honesty – what role does the UN General Assembly play today? Almost none – and that's the truth. It's a forum for debate – without any real influence or practical role at all.

I ask: are international relations governed by the purposes and principles set down in the United Nations charter? No. Why now, when philosophy, the arts and sciences are reaching unprecedented heights, do we hear the proclamation of the superiority of some nations over others, why do we hear some nations, which should be treated like brothers, being called 'dark corners of the planet' or 'the Euro-Atlantic periphery of NATO'?

Why do some countries feel they have the right to launch a war unilaterally when the United Nations charter says that armed force shall not be used 'except in the service of the common good' and that to preserve the peace, 'collective means' shall be employed? Why are we no longer talking about using peaceful means to resolve controversies?

When the charter was approved at the San Francisco Conference in 1945, the principle of the sovereign equality of the states was established. Are all the member-states truly equal, and do we share similar rights? The charter says we are and we do, but crude reality says we're not and we don't. Respect for the principle of the sovereign equality of states, which should be the cornerstone of contemporary international relations, can only occur if the most powerful countries agree to respect the rights of the others, even though [these smaller states] do not have the military strength and economic power to defend [those rights]. Are the most powerful states ready to respect the rights of the others, even though that might, even minimally, infringe on their privileges? I fear they aren't.

The Iraq War – did you see it as inevitable?

In February 2003, a few weeks before the war, I was in Malaysia at the Non-Aligned Summit, and there in Kuala Lumpur I spoke for a long time with the members of the Iraqi delegation and with then vice president Taha Yassin Ramadan. I told them, 'If you really have chemical weapons, destroy them, in order to facilitate the work of the UN inspectors.' That was their only chance to prevent an attack. And I think they did that, if they ever had any. But the decision to attack had already been made, even if they didn't possess such weapons.

What opinion does Saddam Hussein deserve?

*In 1991, after the invasion of Kuwait, he locked himself into a logic that led to a serious crisis. We voted for the UN resolution that condemned the invasion. I sent him two letters via personal emissaries[13] advising him to negotiate and withdraw from Kuwait in time.

In the first letter, dated 2 August 1990, I wrote the following:

I am writing with great sadness, due to the news today of the entry of troops from your country into the territory of Kuwait.

Regardless of the motives that led to this dramatic decision, I feel I must express our concern over the grave consequences it may entail for Iraq and Kuwait, in the first place, and for all the countries of the Third World. Cuba, despite its bonds of friendship with Iraq, must oppose a military solution to the conflict that has arisen between Iraq and Kuwait.

The immediate reaction by international public opinion, as reported by transnational news agencies and media, creates a very dangerous and vulnerable situation for Iraq.

I believe it quite probable that the United States and other allies may take advantage of this occasion to intervene militarily in the conflict and strike a hard blow against Iraq. Washington, in addition, will seek to consolidate its self-proclaimed role as international policeman – including, of course, in the Gulf.

* [in 1st ed: Well, how shall I put it – a disaster. An erratic strategist. Cruel to his own people.]

In this situation, time is of the essence, and I appeal to you to employ the good offices of the Arab League or the Movement of Non-Aligned Nations, to whom we have written for this purpose, to express your willingness to withdraw Iraqi troops from Kuwait and seek an immediate negotiated political solution to the dispute. These steps will help strengthen the Third World countries' international position opposing the United States' role as international policeman, and will at the same time strengthen Iraq's position in the eyes of the world.

What is essential at this time is to avoid any imperialist intervention under the pretext of defending the territory and sovereignty of a small country in the region. That precedent would be most lamentable for both Iraq and the rest of the Third World.

A clear position on the part of Iraq and firm, immediate steps taken by your country towards a political solution will help us forestall and frustrate the United States' aggressive interventionist plans.

Cuba is willing to cooperate in any step that may aid all involved in arriving at this solution.

I am certain that these points of view express the feelings at this moment of dozens of countries around the world who have always held your country in respect and esteem.

And that was how our exhortation for a just and reasonable solution ended.

Not long after that, on 4 September that same year, 1990, in response to a message we received from Iraq, I reiterated the principles I'd set forth and called for a political solution at this terrible juncture, which at any moment could turn more complex, more dire, and have even greater consequences for the world.

So we repeated our plea. One of the paragraphs of my second letter went like this:

I have decided to send you this message, which I beg you to read and consider. Although I feel I am obliged to share with you my reflections on these undoubtedly bitter circumstances, I do so with the hope that they may be useful in this moment when you must make dramatic decisions.

Then I went on to say:

In my opinion, war will inexorably come if Iraq is unwilling to reach a negotiated political solution on the basis of withdrawal from Kuwait. This war may be extremely destructive for the region, and especially for Iraq, regardless of the bravery with which the people of Iraq are willing to fight.

The United States has managed to forge a large military alliance, which in addition to NATO includes Arab and Muslim forces, and, in the political sphere, it has painted an extremely negative picture of Iraq to world opinion, due to the succession of events mentioned above, each of which has caused a profound reaction, indeed hostility, in the United Nations and most of the world. That is, ideal conditions have been created for the United States to carry out its hegemonic plans for aggression. Iraq could not fight a war under worse military and political conditions. In these circumstances, war will divide Arabs for many years; the United States and the West will maintain an indefinite military presence in the region, and the consequences will be disastrous not just for the Arab countries, but for the entire Third World.

Iraq is exposing itself to an unequal battle, without solid political justification and without the support of world opinion, with the exception, of course, of the sympathy shown it in many Arab countries.

That was our perception of the affair, and we continued to urge Saddam to change his position:

It should not be allowed that everything the people of Iraq have built over many years, including the great possibilities for its future, be destroyed by the sophisticated weapons of imperialism. If there were justified, irrefutable reasons for it, I would be the last to ask you to avoid that sacrifice.

Yielding to the demand of the vast majority of member nations of the United Nations who are calling for a withdrawal from Kuwait should never be considered dishonorable, or a humiliation for Iraq.

Regardless of the historical reasons that Iraq believes apply in this confrontation with Kuwait, the case is that the international community, almost unanimously, is opposing the methods being used. And it is to that broad international consensus that the forces of imperialism are appealing in their design to destroy Iraq and take over the energy resources of the entire region.

But none of those efforts bore fruit.

Did you know Saddam Hussein personally?
Yes, I met him in September 1973. I had been in Algiers, at a Non-Aligned Summit, and was en route to Hanoi, at the invitation of the Vietnamese government. Vietnam had not yet been completely liberated. Saddam Hussein came to meet me at Baghdad airport. At the time he was vice president; he was not yet president of Iraq; he was the head of the Ba'ath Party. He seemed to me a very correct man, he was friendly; we toured the

city, a very beautiful city with broad avenues, the bridges over the Tigris and Euphrates. I was only there one day. It was in Baghdad that I learned about the military coup in Chile against Allende . . .

From a military point of view, how would you judge the system of defence used by the Iraqi forces in that war?
We followed that war with great attention, from March to May 2003. Why didn't Iraq resist? It's a mystery. Why didn't they blow up the bridges to slow the advance of the American troops? Why didn't they blow up the munitions deposits, the airports, before they could fall into the hands of the invaders? All that is a great mystery. There were undoubtedly some leaders that betrayed Saddam.

Every country but Cuba closed its mission in Iraq just before the war – how long did [the Cuban delegation] stay in Iraq?
Our embassy was the last one left in Baghdad. I mean, along with the Vatican's. Even the Russians left. Only after the American forces had entered the capital of Iraq did we give the order to leave Baghdad. We couldn't ask the five people in our embassy to defend the buildings against two armies . . . They were willing, but we asked them to evacuate. We had to prevent the embassy from becoming an eventual refuge for officials of the [Saddam] regime. And the US would have used the pretext to pressure us. It would have put us in a very delicate situation. Our diplomats obtained safe-conduct passes and were able to leave Iraq with no problems. The documents were delivered by an international organization, not by the Americans.

How do you see the situation in Iraq evolving?
In my view, the popular resistance is going to continue to intensify so long as the occupation of Iraq continues. It's going to be an inferno, and that's not going to change. That's why the first objective should be the immediate turn-over of real control of the country to the United Nations, and the commencement of a process to recover Iraq's sovereignty and establish a legitimate government, one that obeys the will of the Iraqi people – but their authentic will, expressed through a legitimate decision, not by elections held in the middle of a neocolonial military occupation. And the outrageous dividing-up of Iraq's riches should be stopped immediately.

*In its 'worldwide war against terrorism', President Bush's administration
uses the Guantánamo base in Cuba as a high-security prison for 'prisoners
of war'. What reflection does that inspire in you?*

It's been over a century, and the United States is still occupying that piece
of Cuban soil by force – and it causes the world shame and horror when we
hear the news that since January 2002 [Guantánamo] has been turned into
a torture chamber where hundreds of people, picked up anywhere in the
world, are held. They don't take them to American territory because [on
American soil] there are laws that create difficulties for holding those men
illegally, by force – men kidnapped, and [held] for years, with no charges
filed, no news of them, no law governing them, no trial. And in addition, to
the planet's horror, those men have been subjected to sadistic and brutal
torture.

The world learned of this when [the news broke that] over there in a jail
in Iraq, Abu Ghraib, they were torturing hundreds of prisoners from the
invaded country with all the power of that colossal empire, and when
hundreds of thousands of Iraqi civilians had lost their lives. In Guantánamo
some 500 men – from teenagers to old men – are imprisoned with an absolute
and total contempt that no one, ever, should be forced to endure. They have
been stripped of all the protections guaranteed them by international law
and locked up in cruel, inhumane and degrading conditions.

And every day new things are being discovered. A short time ago information was revealed indicating that the government of the United States has
secret prisons in satellite countries in Eastern Europe – those countries that
vote against Cuba in Geneva and accuse us of violations of human rights.
They send kidnapped men to those secret prisons under the pretext of
the war against terrorism. Now it's not just in Abu Ghraib, not just in
Guantánamo, it's all over the world that you'll find these secret prisons
where the 'defenders of human rights' are carrying out torture.

But that's not all. There has also been news about the use of white phosphorus in Fallujah, when the empire discovered that a nation, virtually
disarmed, couldn't be conquered. The invaders found themselves in a situation where they couldn't leave and couldn't stay – if they left, the combatants would return; if they stayed, they'd need those troops at other
points. White phosphorus in Fallujah! When that crime was reported, the
government of the United States said white phosphorus was a 'normal
weapon'. If it was so normal, why didn't they reveal that they were using it?
But didn't anybody know they were using that weapon, which is in fact

prohibited by international conventions? If napalm is prohibited, white phosphorus is much more so.

Already, over 2,000 young American soldiers have lost their lives,[14] and some people are asking themselves how long they will go on dying in a war that is unjust – justified, in fact, by crude lies?

Even high-ranking American officers are recognizing that the war is lost, and that they should withdraw. That will be the best thing for the United States, whose young people are dying over there while fighting an unjust and inglorious war with shameful, immoral acts such as torture; it will be the best thing for Iraq, whose people will be able to begin a new stage of their history; it will be the best thing for the United Nations, which has also been the victim of that war; and it will be the best thing for all our countries, which have had to suffer an international economic recession and the growing insecurity that threatens us all.

Do you fear there may be an invasion, or 'preventive war', against Cuba?
If President Bush should decide to invade Cuba, there would be a terrible war. They would have to face our entire population, organized and armed, an interminable popular resistance. Such an invasion would cost us a great deal, but to invade Cuba and maintain an occupation of our country, we calculate that millions of soldiers would be needed. In Iraq, they have about 150,000 men and you can see that they control very little. If you analyse the proportion of forces that existed when we faced Batista – 80,000 men against 3,000 – you'll see that they had over twenty-five times the men we had. So that's why I say that they'd have to invade us and occupy the island with millions of soldiers. Which they don't have.

We have the means to make life very hard for an invader. Besides the regular army and the reserves, we have the territorial militia – millions of people, men and women, all ready to fight without respite in defence of their country. Calculating that the Yankee army, to liquidate this country, would have to deploy two soldiers for every combatant of our own, they would need a force of no fewer than 5 million soldiers. And they'd have lots of casualties, I assure you. We can guarantee them that all the conditions are in place here to turn Cuba into a hell for them, a mortal trap.

They know that, because they'd be entering a hand-to-hand fight, man against man – not one with mechanized divisions against mechanized divisions, or air force against air force, or fleet against fleet. In a conventional war, they would have many advantages. But in a war of popular resistance, organized throughout the country, where there's no front or rear, all their technology would be reduced to nothing. Look what's happening in Iraq. What good is the Americans' superiority in heavy, sophisticated weaponry? Any man or woman in Cuba prefers death to living under the boot of the United States.

Would you call the foreign policy of the George W. Bush administration militaristic or dangerous for the world and for Cuba?
Cuba, which, as I told you, was the first country to express its solidarity with the people of the United States on September 11, 2001, was also the first to warn that the policies of the extreme Right in the United States – which assumed power fraudulently in January 2001 – was a danger to the world. This policy on the part of President Bush didn't emerge as a consequence of the terrorist attack against the people of the United States by members of a fanatical organization which in earlier times had served other American administrations. I'm convinced that it was a policy coldly formulated [beforehand], which explains the rearmament and the colossal weapons spending when there was no longer any Cold War and when the events of September 11 were still far in the future. The events of that black September 11 served as an ideal pretext for setting that policy in motion.

On 20 September that year President Bush said so openly in Washington before a Congress shocked by the tragic events of just nine days earlier. Using strange words, he talked about 'infinite justice' as the objective of an apparently infinite war: 'Americans should not expect one battle, but a lengthy campaign unlike any other we have ever seen'; '[we will use] every necessary weapon of war'; 'every nation in every region now has a decision to make: either you are with us or you are with the terrorists'; 'I have asked the armed forces to be on the alert, and there is a reason: the hour is coming when we will act'; 'this is civilization's fight'; 'the achievements of our time and the hope of all times now depend on us'; 'we don't know the course this conflict will take, but we do know what its outcome will be . . . [,] and we know that God is not neutral.'[15]

Was this a statesman talking, or some uncontainable fanatic? Two days later, on 22 September, Cuba denounced this speech as the designs of a worldwide military dictator under the aegis of brute force, without laws or international institutions of any kind.

Months later, on the 200th anniversary of the West Point Military

Academy, at the graduation ceremonies for 958 cadets on 1 June 2002, President Bush, as I mentioned, expanded upon his thoughts in a fiery harangue to the young officers who were graduating that day: '[Our] security will require [us] . . . to be ready for preemptive action when necessary to defend our liberty and to defend our lives'; 'We must uncover terror cells in sixty or more countries'; '[We] will send you, our soldiers, where you're needed'; 'We will not leave the safety of America and the peace of the planet at the mercy of a few mad terrorists and tyrants. We will lift this dark threat from our country and from the world'; 'Some worry that it is somehow undiplomatic or impolite to speak the language of right and wrong. I disagree . . . We are in a conflict between good and evil, and America will call evil by its name. By confronting evil and lawless regimes, we do not create a problem, we reveal a problem. And we will lead the world in opposing it.'[16]

But the objective of these statements was, in the name of the war on terrorism, to prepare for military interventions against Afghanistan and Iraq. Why do you think that Cuba is threatened?
Listen, the policy of the government of the United States is so provocative that on 25 April 2003 – after the hijackings, the hijacking of the Regla ferry, and the arrests of the 'dissidents' we were talking about – Señor Kevin Whitaker, then head of the Cuba Bureau at the State Department,[17] told our head of the Interests Section in Washington that the National Security Council's Office of Homeland Security[18] considered the 'continuous hijackings from Cuba' a 'serious threat to the national security of the United States', and requested that the Cuban government take all necessary measures to prevent actions of that kind.

As though it weren't [the United States] itself that provoked and encouraged those hijackings! And as though we weren't the ones who in order to protect the life and safety of the passengers, and knowing for years of the extreme Right's criminal plans against Cuba, have taken drastic measures to prevent them. Leaked by [the Americans], this contact on 25 April created a great deal of commotion among the terrorist mafia in Florida. In Miami and Washington today, discussion is going on with regard to how and when Cuba is to be attacked, or how the problem of the Revolution is to be solved.

In the short term, they have taken economic measures to even further intensify the brutal blockade.[19] If the formula were to attack Cuba like Iraq,

I would be very sorry for the cost in lives and enormous destruction that it would entail for Cuba, but that might be [the Bush] administration's last attack, because the struggle would last a very long time, as I said, with the aggressors facing not just one army but thousands of armies, constantly reproducing and making the adversary pay such a high price in casualties that it would take many more of their sons' lives than the American people would be willing to pay for the adventures and whims of President Bush.

The American administration has made statements accusing Cuba of preparing biological weapons. How have the Cubans answered?
Those accusations are all the more cynical, all the more nauseating when you realize that we have known first-hand the results of viruses and bacterias used to attack our agriculture and even our populace. I assure you, and I am not exaggerating, I wouldn't have an iota of shame if I told you a single lie. We know some things, and we have proof of almost all of them, when we talk about those problems.

Our country does not have nuclear weapons or chemical weapons or, obviously, biological weapons. The tens of thousands of scientists and doctors in our country have been educated in the ideal of saving lives. It would be in absolute contradiction of that ideal to employ a scientist or doctor to produce substances, bacterias or viruses capable of causing other human beings' deaths.

There have been, it's true, reports that Cuba is doing research on biological weapons. In our country we do research to cure diseases as terrible as meningococcal meningitis, hepatitis, with vaccines produced through genetic engineering, and, of utmost importance, searching for vaccines or therapeutic formulas through molecular immunology – I hope you'll forgive me for using that technical word; it means through methods that directly attack the malignant cells – some that can prevent and some that can even cure, and we are moving forward in those directions. It is the pride of our doctors and our research centres.

Tens of thousands of Cuban doctors, as I've told you, have gone as internationalists to lend their services in the most distant and inhospitable places. One day I said we couldn't, and wouldn't ever, launch preventive surprise attacks against any 'dark corner of the world', but that our country, rather, was able to send doctors to those 'dark corners' whenever they were needed. Doctors, not bombs; doctors, not intelligent weapons, or at least weapons that always hit their marks, because when all is said and done, a weapon that kills so stealthily and treacherously is not 'intelligent'.

Do you think that the United States, under the Bush administration, may drift into an authoritarian regime?
Just over sixty years ago, humankind underwent the tragic experience of Nazism. Hitler had an inseparable ally – you know this – and it was the fear he was able to inspire in his adversaries. Once he possessed a fearsome military force, a war broke out that caused a conflagration around the world. The lack of vision and the cowardice of the leaders of the strongest European powers at that time led to a great and terrible catastrophe.

I don't think a Fascist-type regime could ever emerge in the United States. Within their political system, grave errors and injustices have been committed – and many of them still survive – but the American people have certain institutions, traditions, educational, cultural and political values that would make that virtually impossible. The risk is in the international sphere. The powers and prerogatives of an American president are so great, and that country's network of military, economic and technological strength is so immense, that in virtue of circumstances that have absolutely nothing to do with the will of the American people, the world is threatened.

Do you fear an attempt on your life?
In 2003 a man with the unfortunate first name of Lincoln, Díaz-Balart is his last name, a close friend and adviser of President Bush, said to a television network in Miami, referring to me, the following enigmatic words: 'I can't go into details, but we're trying to break that vicious circle.'

Which methods for 'breaking the vicious circle' are they referring to? Physically do away with me, as Señor Bush promised in Miami before the elections?[20] If that's it, I'm not worried in the slightest. Although I do think that they're going to start the attacks again. Everybody knows they want to assassinate Chávez. And they think that if they can assassinate me too, they've solved the problem. But the ideals for which I've struggled all my life cannot die, and they will live on for a long, long time. Precautions have been strengthened. I'm here talking to you . . . well, we've taken measures, but I mix with everyone everywhere.

As for an invasion of this country, today, against that, you can't wage war, no way, as you might have done in 1959 or 1961, or during the October crisis or after that, when the fight was divisions against divisions. We've been thinking about all that back then, and we've arrived at the concept of a 'war of the entire country', because with the old academic concept [of warfare], you've got six divisions and the American army has 100, all they want. And in that type of classic confrontation, the people watch the fighting the way they watch wars today on CNN, without taking part in it. Those up there have more divisions, they destroy yours; they have more technology, air superiority, etc., etc., so try applying academic tactics to the defence of your country and you're lost.

It's one of the things we know best – and I've talked to you about it before. We went back to those ideas a lot, because we learned a long time ago, after the October crisis, that faced with an invasion of Cuba we'd have to fight alone, and that not one bullet would be able to be brought in. That's a truth that we've been conscious of for a long time, and that's what led to the 'war of the entire country', the organization of the whole country, because it's also been proven that a people that fight can't be defeated by anyone . . .

Are you referring to Vietnam?
Well, there are even more remarkable examples, like the western Sahara, for example: the Saharans out there in the middle of the desert, where there weren't even any woods or jungle, and no one ever defeated them.

You can see that in Chechnya today, too.
Yes, there's also that other situation that we see in Chechnya. You can't agree with their methods, their procedures, because they have been merciless with the noble Russian people, but a very powerful, experienced army such as Russia's has not been able to defeat the Chechnyan extremists.

Look at what happened in Kosovo. [(in 1st ed.): Faced with a Milosevic – another disaster as a leader; nationalistic, racist, corrupt and trusting nothing but force –] the Serbs were admirable in their resistance, and their forces were practically intact when the war ended.

Has Cuba analysed these recent wars?
We've studied them all. And very closely. From the Vietnam War to the latest war in Iraq, from the Gulf War to the Bosnian conflict to Kosovo, and so on.

In these latest wars, the people resisting an occupation – in Palestine, in Chechnya, in Afghanistan, in Iraq – have made frequent and often criticized use of terrorist actions. Could Cuba ever resort to that type of method?

No. As I've told you, and I repeat, we will never abandon our ideals as soldiers, and as I've said, we will never apply methods that sacrifice innocent people. In the struggle against the adversary, against soldiers, against the military fighter, we will follow the policy we have always followed, but never against a citizen of a country from which the invaders come. We will always fight fundamentally against combatants.

Although there is one weapon we haven't renounced, the only weapon we have, which is our people. We will not renounce the 'war of the entire country', as I call it.

On the other hand, as I told you and repeat now, we are not going to be swept up in the madness or stupidity of starting to manufacture biological weapons. What we've taught people is to manufacture vaccines and to fight against illness, disease, and death. We have educated those scientists in an ethics; we're not going to tell them now, 'Listen, start manufacturing small-pox' or whatever. Besides, what on earth for?, against an adversary that has 100 times more of it?

Nor are we going to start manufacturing a chemical weapon. How are you going to transport it? Who are you going to use it against? Against the American people? No! that would be unfair and absurd! Are you going to make a nuclear weapon? You'll ruin yourself – a nuclear weapon is a good way to commit suicide at a certain point, all right: 'Gentlemen, the time has come, we're going to immolate ourselves, and this atomic bomb is just the thing.' Make an atomic bomb to destroy the country with? Against a country that must have at least 30,000 of them? And I'm not talking about strategic weapons – [I'm talking] tactical weapons, nuclear weapons. The United States must have [tactical weapons] in briefcases, because during the Cold War both the Soviets and the Americans even manufactured briefcases with atomic bombs in them, for sabotage . . . There was no horror they *didn't* invent.

Portable atomic bombs?

That's right. So – you're going to manufacture three of them. You're going to ruin yourself – you're going to do that against the entire world's public opinion. [For a long time] we didn't sign . . .

The Nuclear Non-Proliferation Treaty.
But it's that we didn't feel like renouncing a right – we never, never thought of manufacturing nuclear weapons, but we did say, 'Well, but why that inequality? Why do some people reserve the right to have those weapons?' And now we've just forgotten about it.

But now you've signed it.
Yes, we've signed it. As a clear sign of our commitment to an effective disarmament process that will guarantee world peace, and we hope someday all nuclear weapons will be totally eliminated – under strict international verification. We've also signed and ratified the twelve international agreements relating to the fight against terrorism up there in the United Nations. And we've also decided to ratify the treaty prohibiting nuclear weapons in Latin America and the Caribbean, the Treaty of Tlatelolco, which we'd signed in 1995 . . .

But you haven't signed the treaty prohibiting the use of anti-personnel mines.
No, the landmine treaty, we haven't. We waged war with mines and rifles; they had planes, artillery, tanks, everything . . . But ours were anti-tank mines, or mines used for advancing troops, set off electrically; they weren't automatic.

But mines can kill civilians . . .
I don't remember a single civilian wounded by our mines – we used them against troops that were moving.

Let's hope you never have to use them again. And at any rate, should an invasion of Cuba occur, I imagine that Cuba will be able to count on the support of thousands of people around the world, who will mobilize.
The Cuban Revolution has many friends in many countries; many people support us, and they have expressed their solidarity after the threats against us announced by President Bush. On the other hand, we'd like to know how many of those who, from their supposed leftist and humanist positions, have attacked our people recently because of the legal measures which we were forced to adopt – in an act of legitimate defence – how many of those people have read those threats against us, woken up, and denounced and condemned the anti-Cuba policy announced in the speeches given by Señor Bush . . .

But nobody will fight for us. Only we ourselves, with the support of the peoples of the Third World and millions of manual labourers and intellectuals in the developed countries – who are also seeing the catastrophe of neoliberal globalization looming over their countries – sowing ideas, creating awareness, mobilizing public opinion around the world and among the American people, will be able to resist [the invasion].

27

Summing Up a Life and a Revolution

*Eloquence and speeches – Love and hate – On treason – A dictator? –
Attachment to the uniform – Regrets – The end of the sugar
monoculture – The Revolution's successes – The judgement of history –
Memorable personalities*

*You're famous for being an extraordinary political speaker, but I've noticed
a difference between your more or less improvised speeches, where your
eloquence is impressive, and the speeches you read, which are, let's say,
less brilliant. How do you prepare your speeches?*

Well, sometimes I don't even have time to revise my speeches, and spoken
language, I'll tell you, is not the same as written language – the accent, the
tone of voice when you speak. When you see it written down, repeating a
word throughout a paragraph may look unnecessary. But it's correct when
you're speaking – you're emphasizing. In a written text, repetition looks
unnecessary; people don't like it. I tend to look back over my improvised
speeches and revise them. Sometimes a phrase can be brought out a little
better.

*But your speeches – do you write them yourself or do you have collaborators
who prepare them for you?*

Every time I've ever asked someone to write a speech for me, or at least do
a draft for me, it's almost always been a disaster – empty, ineloquent. I've
had to rewrite it entirely. I've talked to several advisers to American presidents, who've written hundreds of speeches. But it's still a mystery to me.
I've never been able to give a speech that I haven't prepared myself, haven't
written myself. How do the French presidents do it?

It depends on the president – but in general, they have a staff of advisers who write their speeches for them. Some work on the content, others the form, and others polish and perfect it. Then the president reviews it and adds his personal touch – a phrase, a word . . . That's the way almost all of them do it.
Is it true that Régis Debray wrote Mitterrand's speeches?

Yes. He wrote the famous Cancún speech in 1981, a call to support the Third World.
But the ideas – were they Mitterrand's or Régis'?

I think they were Régis'.
Ah!

To go on to another subject, you're a man who's admired and beloved not just in Cuba but in other countries as well – we saw that in late May 2003 when you visited Argentina.
I'd limit it to Cuba.

It was clear in Argentina, and I saw it myself in Ecuador, in January 2003, in the popular demonstrations of affection for you. But at the same time, you're one of the men most hated by many adversaries and many enemies, who accuse you of being a 'cruel dictator'. How do you experience that duality – love and hate?
You know, I've never even stopped to think about that. I live a life that's totally, absolutely, completely calm and peaceful. I don't really understand that hate. I can understand hating someone for ideological reasons, out of frustration with the failure of [one's] attacks [on him], or frustration with the ability of a small nation to resist forces as powerful as those that have tried to destroy us. But, for example, the Japanese have no reason to hate me – I didn't drop any bombs on Hiroshima or Nagasaki, no Japanese person anywhere in the world has ever died because of me, and the Japanese don't hate me – they're pretty much indifferent, I'd say.

Hatred of the Cuban Revolution happens in Latin American countries, or in the United States – and it's understandable on the basis of frustration, the propaganda that stops at nothing. I've told you about some of the cases. Listen, there was even an imputation in a document recently, with incredible brazenness, the inclusion of Cuba in the category of 'countries that engage in the trafficking of persons' because [Cuba] supposedly exploits children sexually in order to obtain income. Can you imagine anything more disgusting, more nauseating and irritating?

I also don't understand why I'm called a 'dictator'. What is a dictator? It's someone who makes arbitrary, unilateral decisions, who acts over and above institutions, over and above the laws, who is under no restraint but his own desires and whims. And in that case, Pope John Paul II, who always opposed war, could be accused of being a dictator, and President Bush considered a defender of peace, a friend of the poor and the most democratic of rulers. That's the way the industrialized countries in Europe treat him, without realizing that Bush can make terrible decisions without consulting the Senate or the House of Representatives, or even his cabinet. Not even the Roman emperors had the power of the president of the United States! Any American president has more possibility of giving orders, and decisive, dramatic orders, than I have.

Look, I don't make unilateral decisions. This isn't even a presidential government. We have a Council of State. My functions as leader exist within a collective. In our country, the important decisions, the fundamental decisions are always studied, discussed and made collectively. I can't appoint ministers or ambassadors. I don't appoint the lowest public official in this country. I have authority,[1] of course, I have influence, for historical reasons, but I don't give orders or rule by decree.

As for cruelty – I really think that a man who has devoted his entire life to fighting injustice, oppression of every kind, to serving others, to fighting for others, to preaching and practising solidarity, I think that all of that is totally incompatible with cruelty.

There are also lots of people who love and defend Cuba.
Yes, there are, especially in Africa and Latin America – lots of people who love our country, because who has ever shown more solidarity with Africa than Cuba has? What is the only country that has spilled its blood fighting against Fascism and the racism of apartheid, helping to eliminate that hate-filled system? We've created a culture of internationalism in the face of chauvinism, and this is a country that has an internationalist culture. More than half a million Cubans have gone on internationalist missions as technicians and as combatants.

Who has sent more doctors, more teachers, and given more free help, while being a country as poor as we are? What small country – and we do this not out of luxury but because we are moved to – has 10,000 Latin American young people studying medicine here for free, and more every day?

So that hatred may be ideological, a poison that has gradually spread. If people tell you somebody's worse than Satan himself, then you tend to hate that person. Now then, I know that all that propaganda is based on hate, and on lies. How can people say that even one man has been tortured in Cuba? Or that I've ordered a man tortured? How can they say that?

Here, no one has ever been imprisoned for being a dissident or because they see things differently from the way the Revolution does. Our courts sentence people to prison on the basis of laws, and they judge counter-revolutionary *acts*. Down through history, in all times, actions by people who put themselves at the service of a foreign power against their own nation have always been seen as extremely serious [crimes].

The idea that in Cuba we send people to prison for having a belief that's different from the Revolution's is ridiculous. Here, we punish acts, not ideas. There are tens of thousands of people with different beliefs and different ideas from the Revolution's, and who still enjoy all the guarantees and all respect.

Furthermore, I've told you that we have followed a line of absolute respect for the physical integrity of the individual. Even though our enemies spread lies and slander us, there is not a single case of physical maltreatment or torture in the entire history of the Revolution. No one can give a single case of torture, a single person assassinated, a single person 'disappeared', which is so common in Latin America.

Nor has there ever been a state of emergency or state of siege declared here. There has never been a demonstration broken up by public law enforcement. No police officer has ever, in forty-six years, beaten a citizen during a demonstration, or shot tear gas, or sent in dogs against our citizens – things that happen every day in many parts of Latin America and in the United States itself.

And why is that? Because this Revolution has the support of the people; it is defended by the people, because the entire nation defends the Revolution.

Despite that, those who criticize the Revolution blame you entirely – they talk about 'Castro's Cuba'.

Those people tend to personalize, to make me the representative, as though the people didn't exist. All that exists is the leader. The millions of people who have struggled, who have defended [the Revolution]; the hundreds of thousands of doctors, of professional people; those who farm, produce, study – those people don't exist. All that exists is this evil guy named Castro, who thinks up ways to bring more culture to his people.

Here, the more education people have, the more revolutionary they are, the more they admire [the Revolution], because there's also an accumulation of events and achievements down through all these years – they see a constant line, they appreciate the dignity, the serenity. We have been through very difficult times without having made unnecessary mistakes.

If there's a war here someday, it'll be because it's forced on us. If we're put in the position of either surrendering or fighting a war, there will be war, because we can't even conceive the other choice.

But there are lots of accusations, I tell you, of all kinds. Now they're saying 'Castro is using children,' but they don't say that we're educating teachers, that we're creating conditions to limit class size to twenty students in elementary school, fifteen in secondary school, they don't talk about all the things we're doing in health care. And it's all for the people, because doing all that is part of the nature of any one of us. On the other hand, they've had the nerve to put us in the category of 'trafficking in persons' or 'commercially exploiting sex to raise money [for the state]' . . . If you tell somebody that and they get used to hearing it and used to believing it, they might think: 'Heavens, what kind of monster is this! What a hypocrite this man is!' People say lots of terrible, slanderous things, it's true, but reality disproves [those slanders] one by one.

I know it does harm. But we've also been through some very difficult moments, and we've recovered. We've climbed up one step and backed down one, although we've climbed two in terms of respect, international opinion.

The number of times I have to sign things – autographs – you can't imagine. When I meet with Americans who come here and talk to me, and we speak very seriously about all sorts of subjects, all sorts of things, well, I can hardly speak. Sometimes there are fifty people at a meeting, they give me a bouquet of flowers or something, and the number of books, cards, things I have to sign, the number of pictures I have to let them take and so many flashbulbs that you can hardly see, it's hardly to be believed. So I guess I'm some kind of strange, unreal figure . . .

A star.

Yes, somebody you have to get quick, so you can say – people like to tell their family – 'Look, I got a picture with so-and-so.'

Some people think that we aren't what we are. Only we know what we are – we're the only ones who can judge ourselves and you can believe me when I tell you that I'm very hard on myself, self-critical with myself. When I say too much or something comes out of my mouth that might sound a little vain, listen, you can believe I'm hard on myself, really hard. You have to keep a watch on yourself. I like actions; I'm not interested in glory.

I'm also a witness to the fact that throughout the years, influence, power, rather than gradually making me conceited, vain and all that – every day, I think, I'm less conceited, less pretentious, less self-satisfied. It's a struggle against your instincts, you know. I believe that it's education, or sincere and tenacious self-education, that turns a small animal into a man.

One thing I see quite often: when men have a little power, they get all puffed up and want to use it; sometimes it's almost like a drug. You see all those things, and it's a constant struggle. And I know that as the years pass, it's possible to have not less enthusiasm, but more; not less energy, but more – energy stems from conviction.

But your question, what effect does it have on me? I swear to you that I don't think about it, I never lose spirit, and I believe in people; I've never had any sense of ingratitude. And men don't like to recognize what they owe to other people – it's a universal law.

I'd like to ask you another question of the same kind. You've had friends, extremely close friendships, of great solidarity, but you've also been betrayed by a number of compañeros. *What feeling does betrayal give you?*
Well, I must say I've known only a very few betrayals – a very, very few. At one point, the betrayal of one of our guides.[2] He was arrested [by Batista troops], he was in the hands of the Batista army, he could see the difference between how small and ragtag our troops were and theirs, which had some impressive weaponry and forces, and they made him promises and offered him money. That was an important betrayal, and not the only one in the course of our struggle.

Were there political betrayals? Yes. For example, I'm trying to remember the big ones . . .

For example, Carlos Franqui,[3] Huber Matos,[4] Manuel Urrutia . . .
Look, Carlos Franqui wasn't a friend of mine. I met Carlos Franqui, really, up in the Sierra Maestra. After the unsuccessful strike in April 1958, which was the result of a tactical error on the part of the 26th of July Movement,

which we've already talked about, Carlos Franqui was sent [up to us]. After that tremendous failure, they sent him up to us. Franqui had been publishing a little newspaper created by the organization; he'd been a Communist; the leaders of our movement at one point were recruiting ex-Communists, and there's nothing worse than a renegade, that's for sure.

So then, some of those ex-Communists hated the Communists worse than anybody – not that the Communists were perfect; they made a lot of mistakes, but they did fight for the workers. Their battle was economic; you couldn't ask more of them because this was the time of the Cold War and McCarthyism. Being a Communist was a disgrace, yet in Cuba, despite that, there were more than 100,000 registered, known, respected [Communists]. The difficulties they had were of another kind – sectarianism, opportunism in a way, because of the sectarianism. The thesis some of them held was: let those petit-bourgeois in the 26th of July Movement fight; after the war, we'll have our chance to run the country.

At the beginning of the Revolution, what were the methods used to fight the rabid anti-Communism rooted in some people? An anti-Communism that led to desertions [from our ranks] as a pretext used by some people who were actually petit-bourgeois in thought, who were poisoned, because there was no awareness here in the masses, no Socialist culture. It was laws, it was speechmaking, it was example that created that awareness. Ninety per cent of those who were with us in the struggle weren't Communists, they didn't belong to the Communist Party; there weren't many fighters or leaders from the Party, they didn't send them to us, and the ones we had, such as Che, or me, were Communists of our own making, although some of the ones the Party sent [us] were very good, very tenacious. The 26th of July [Movement] had 90 per cent of the leaders [i.e., 90 per cent of the leaders came from that organization], and almost none of those people betrayed [the cause]. Ninety per cent remained with the Revolution and died with the Revolution.

So I, personally, have known very little, I tell you, betrayal. Huber Matos was an individual who joined when the war was well under way. It didn't hurt me a bit. I did know him, I met him, you could immediately see the pro-capitalist stripe in him, tremendous vanity. What happened is that we lost a lot of troops at the end, in the last offensive, and Huber Matos came to be given a squad during the offensive, because he had a certain degree of education and we had to reinforce ourselves. At the end, we had to give him a column of several dozen men, well armed, but you could already see that he was arrogant, ambitious . . . Almost out of necessity I assigned him that column during the last phase of the war. What I mean is that he hadn't been with us at Moncada, or on the *Granma*. All those people who'd been at Moncada or on the *Granma* were people who were solidly with us, such as Che, Camilo, Raúl, Almeida and so many others. But Huber Matos wasn't a part of that old guard.

Manuel Urrutia wasn't a traitor, either. Urrutia was a good judge and in our eagerness to show that we weren't going to fight for positions, or out of ambition, we offered him the presidency; [it was] at the point, in fact, when the 26th of July [Movement] was about to make an unconsidered pact with the former government. He wasn't a traitor, he was an opportunist, a mediocre individual – more mediocre than anything else.

General del Pino?[5]

Well, yes, that was a kind of betrayal because he had distinguished himself at [Playa] Girón, he was a good combatant, and we never expected . . . But it's not that I experienced what could be categorized as an important betrayal by that combatant, who joined the ranks of those who were guilty of the deaths of their own companions at Girón. I knew him as I knew them all; I admired the ones I admired in their moment, the heroes. I explained the Ochoa case, when that officer fell into corruption.

So, listen, I don't remember any person of a truly revolutionary character that has committed a betrayal. If you said: Che committed a betrayal, then *that* would be terrible; Raúl committed a betrayal, Juan Almeida committed a betrayal, Ramiro Valdés committed a betrayal, Guillermo García committed a betrayal . . . All those *comandantes* of the Revolution, all those extraordinarily valuable people, the ones who survived, were at Moncada, were on the *Granma*, were up in the Sierra, and they lived through those decisive times without ever once showing any sign of weakness or irresolution.

There's a bunch of new values, there are many new values. You look at Felipe Pérez Roque, for example. Felipe hadn't been born, many of these people hadn't been born on the day of the triumph of the Revolution. There's a bunch of new people who were born from the blood of many heroes.

There are also some military leaders who distinguished themselves in war, in military actions, and we haven't had any real betrayals there. We had that embarrassing Ochoa case, which was actually corruption, degeneration, he wasn't a *compañero* with a great deal of knowledge, a great deal of culture; he was courageous and he had merits as a combatant. I don't deny him any

577

of those qualities; we were hurt by the damage he did. What we've had is a lot of exploitation by our enemies of the slightest incident.

Now, look at those boys who are in prison up there in the United States, the Five Heroes – what men those are! What integrity!

Several times, the Cubans have punished very highly placed leaders. Recently there have been Carlos Aldana,[6] Roberto Robaina[7] . . .
Well, they haven't been found guilty. There were some serious offences on their part, but they haven't been found guilty and sent to prison; what's happened is that our enemies have given those cases a great deal of publicity, [there's been] a political spin to the problem. We're just sorry they lapsed in that way. They did this to themselves.

They were just removed from their posts?
There was no act of betrayal, or of treason, let's say. There were serious, grave errors.

Of behaviour, of ethics?
Let's say of ambition, of creating conditions seeking power, a little bit of 'things going to their heads'.

In recent years, especially in your appearances at international events, you've been seen in a civilian suit and tie, but here in Cuba you're almost always dressed in a uniform. Why that attachment to the olive-green uniform?
Well, more than anything, for practical reasons, because with the uniform I don't have to put on a tie every day . . . It avoids the problem of what suit to wear, what shirt, what socks, so everything goes together. I only put on a suit for very special circumstances, some international conference, or when the pope came, or a meeting with some head of state, although even that protocol has been simplified here in Cuba.

If I remember correctly, I think the first time I appeared dressed in civilian clothes was at the Ibero-American Summit in Cartagena de las Indias in 1994, because our Colombian hosts asked all participating heads of state and government to wear a *guayabera*. Since then, as you say, I've worn civilian clothes at other international meetings, but also on special occasions here inside Cuba.

But this uniform I've always worn, since the Sierra, is what I ordinarily wear; I'm used to it and I feel perfectly comfortable in it. It's not a sophisticated uniform. It's very simple, almost like the one I wore in the war. We've just made a few modifications to it, that's all. I also have a uniform for receptions that I wear for some occasions, with a shirt and tie, a little more formal. But the one I feel most comfortable in is this one.

You were once a great smoker, and for a long time, in the early years of the Revolution, you were almost always seen smoking a very impressive puro habano. *Are you sorry you smoked so much?*
It was my own father who gave me my first cigar, back in Birán. I must have been fourteen or fifteen. And I remember that I smoked that first *puro*, and I didn't know how it was done. Fortunately, I didn't inhale the smoke. Although you always absorb a little of the nicotine, even if you don't inhale at all.

Yes, you're right, I've smoked too much in my life. Until one day, over twenty years ago, I decided to stop. Nobody made me. I just decided to make myself stop smoking. I believed that giving up that habit was a necessary sacrifice, for the good of the country's and the people's health. Listening to people [talk] so much about the necessity of a collective fight against obesity, the sedentary lifestyle, smoking, I became convinced that the ultimate sacrifice I should make on behalf of public health in Cuba was to quit smoking. Teach by example. I gave up tobacco, and I've never missed it.

At the age of seventy-nine, when you look back over your life, what are you sorry not to have done?
Not to have discovered earlier all the things we know now – knowledge with which, in half the time, we could have done much more than we've done in forty-six years.

What are you sorry that you did *do?*
Let me think . . . what do I have to regret, something to be sorry about?

I've made mistakes, but none of them were strategic – just tactical. A person regrets a lot of things, sometimes even in a speech . . . But I have not one iota of regret about what we've done in our country and the way we've organized our society.

Do you, for example, regret your approval of the entrance of Warsaw Pact tanks into Prague in August 1968,[8] [an approval] that caused so much surprise among admirers of the Cuban Revolution?
Look, I can say that we believed – and history has proved us right – that

Czechoslovakia was headed towards a counter-revolutionary situation, towards capitalism and the arms of imperialism. And we were opposed to all the liberal economic reforms that were taking place there and in other places in the Socialist camp, a series of measures that tended increasingly to accentuate mercantile relationships within the heart of the Socialist society: profits, earnings, enrichment, material stimuli, all those factors that stimulate individualism and egos. That was why we accepted the bitter necessity to send forces into Czechoslovakia and didn't condemn the Socialist countries that took that action.

Now then, at the same time, we maintained that those Socialist countries had to be consistent, they had to commit themselves to adopting the same type of attitude in the case of threats against a Socialist regime some other place in the world. And furthermore, we said we thought that the first issues raised in Czechoslovakia were unobjectionable, because they tended to improve Socialism. The denunciation of the methods of governance, the bureaucratic policies, the divorce of the masses, all those denunciations were unquestionably correct. But from fair slogans there had been a move towards an openly reactionary policy. And we – bitterly, sadly – had to approve that military intervention. The preservation of the unity and strength of Socialism in the face of imperialism was for us vital, of first priority.

Another example: the 'battle for the ten million'.[9] Do you think that was an important economic battle, or do you regret having made the demand on the country for that colossal effort in 1970?
That battle was a great feat. In some sectors, we've been able to achieve many things that we could never even have dreamed of, and in other spheres we've managed to achieve two-thirds, three-fourths or half. But all those battles have been inspired by a desire to spur the economy, for the good of the people. There may have been errors, I don't deny that, but they were never errors of principle.

Recently, Cuba has decided to reduce the amount of land devoted to growing sugar cane and also close down many centrales. *That's leaving thousands of people without a job . . . Isn't that going from one extreme to the other?*
The sugar industry reached a stable production of 8 million tons, while today it barely produces one and a half. We had to cut back radically the ploughing and planting of land, because fuel was at $40 a barrel, which was

running the country into bankruptcy. Especially when you add in factors such as increasingly frequent hurricanes and more prolonged droughts and the fact that land for sugar cane barely lasts four or five years – before, it was fifteen or more, when the cutting was manual and people didn't use heavy machinery – and the fact that the price of sugar on the world market had fallen to seven cents [a pound]. One day I asked a question about the price of sugar and another about the cost of production by a commercial sugar producer. And they didn't even know how much sugar the *centrales* were producing! And when I asked the cost in foreign currency of a ton of sugar, nobody could give me an answer. It was only about a month and a half later that they came up with the answer. So imagine . . .

Yes, we did, quite simply, have to close *centrales*, or we were going to wind up in the Bartlett Deep [Cayman Trench[10]]. The country had a lot of economists, a lot, and I don't mean to criticize them, but as honestly as I talk about the errors made by the Revolution I want to ask: why didn't we discover that keeping that production going was absolutely about to bankrupt us – at a time not long after the USSR collapsed, when oil was at $40 a barrel and the price of sugar was at rock bottom? Why didn't we 'rationalize' that industry? Why did we have to plant 20,000 *caballerías* that year – almost 270,000 hectares, about 650,000 acres? For which we had to plough with tractors and heavy plough machinery, plant sugar cane that then had to be weeded with machines, fertilized, sprayed with expensive herbicides, etc., etc., etc.

No economist, apparently, realized this. And we simply had to give instructions, practically an order, to stop ploughing. It's as though they tell you, 'The country is being invaded' – you can't say, 'Wait a minute, I need to have thirty meetings with hundreds of people so I can decide what to do.' It's as though back at Girón, when the empire was bombing air bases and its mercenaries were attacking, we'd said, 'Let's have a meeting and talk for three days about the measures we're going to take against the invaders.' I assure you that the Revolution has been, throughout its history, in a real war, and the enemy constantly lurking, the enemy ready to strike, and striking as many times as we give it the chance to.

Really, I called the minister and I said, 'Listen, how many hectares do you have ploughed, please?' Answer: 'Eighty thousand.' So I told him, 'Don't plough another hectare.' It wasn't my usual role, but I had no choice – you can't let the country go under.

How many sugar centrales *has Cuba closed?*

We've stopped using seventy sugar-production facilities, the least efficient ones, whose cost in convertible currency was far above the income produced by sales of their sugar. And with what we've saved by closing *centrales* that cost more convertible currency than they bring in, using part of that we've been able to keep paying workers in those industries the salary they'd been receiving up till then. Those are possibilities that exist in our society. But the most daring decision adopted recently may have been the decision to make going to school a form of employment, to the benefit of many people who'd been working at those plants. When we reduced personnel, almost 40,000 of those workers are now going to school as their job.

And over 100,000 young people between seventeen and thirty who before weren't at school or in a job are today enthusiastically attending classes where they can refresh and increase their knowledge, and they're paid for that. Our blockaded country has now managed to achieve practically full employment, which is what it's called when unemployment is below 2 per cent. We must be very close to that now, or will be soon.

In addition, approximately 70,000 active workers in the sugar-cane industry who weren't affected by the restructuring in that area have been offered the chance to attend classes at the end of every working day. That is extraordinary, really – such a large number of active sugar-cane workers attending those classes, and not as their regular job; they're workers linked to production, working in the industry, in agriculture.

You were asking whether I had anything to regret. Something I can regret is that I did not go on to further studies. When I was studying law, social science and diplomatic law – three interrelated subjects – I planned, I intended, to go deeper into other disciplines, especially economics. That is, I'm sorry I didn't go further in my studies. But if I had, I'd have lost the chance I had before me, to make a revolution – a chance that was much closer than I imagined.

It pains a person not to have lived at a time of better education; it hurts, really, not to have had a preceptor, and to have had to make decisions from a very early age on one's own. My family lived out in the country, you know; I went to a boarding school – those are things that hurt one, but one's not to blame for them. But I don't regret anything.

Looking back from half a century on, did you ever think everything was going to be so hard, that you were going to meet so many obstacles?

I knew, of course, that it was going to be very difficult. I thought the fundamental difficulties were going to lie in seizing the power to make the Revolution. First topple Batista, but not topple Batista so that everything would be the same – no, to change things. Because when I went to Moncada, my essential ideas were already formed, all of them, the question was developing the tactics and strategy to carry them out.

If we'd won on that 26 July 1953, we wouldn't be here today. The alignment of forces in the world in 1953 was such that we wouldn't have been able to withstand them. Stalin had just died – he died in March of 1953 – and the troika that succeeded him[11] would never have given Cuba the support that Khrushchev did, let's say, seven years later, when the Soviet Union didn't, perhaps, equal the United States but did at least have great economic and military power.

Do you see the dreams you had when you set off for the Moncada barracks now realized?

That's what I was just going to say, because you mentioned several issues. I told you, I had to solve certain problems; governing is harder, and I was aware of that because that's what I said on that 8 January when I entered Havana, the day of the doves.[12] I felt a bit of nostalgia, even, the day the victory was won, a little like the nostalgia I felt that day, after our defeat of that great enemy offensive in summer of 1958, when we almost won the war. I felt that we'd learned to do something, but everything was different.

On 1 January 1959, I felt that sensation. I said, 'Well, we've learned to do this this way, and now we have a job that's going to be much bigger,' and when I got to Havana and saw some of the problems, I realized that everything was going to be much harder after the triumph.

We were very ignorant; we had a lot of very good ideas, but very little experience. We'd had experience of men, some ideas without which we'd never have been able to conceive a strategy that led us to victory ... I mean, I was able to survive. Surviving is a privilege, not something you can claim as your own, because you can't ignore experience, the weight of the accumulation of experience.

And I can say now, after forty-six years since the triumph and over fifty since Moncada, that what we've achieved is far greater than the dreams we could conceive back then, and we were pretty good dreamers from the start!

Some prosecutors continue to make accusations against the Cuban Revolution, and continually accuse it of all sorts of things. You, as a lawyer, what arguments in defence of the Revolution can you offer them?

Well, this is going to take a while, I warn you. I'm going to go over some arguments I made in my speech on the fiftieth anniversary of Moncada.[13] Because, let's see, what is Cuba blamed for? What honest man has any reason to attack us?

With its own blood and weapons seized from the enemy, the people of Cuba brought down the cruel US-backed Batista tyranny, with its 80,000 men under arms. It was the first territory free of imperialist domination in Latin America and the Caribbean, and the only country in the hemisphere where, throughout post-colonial history, torturers, murderers and war criminals, who had taken the lives of tens of thousands of people, were tried and exemplarily punished.

The Revolution recovered land and turned it over entirely to the *campesinos* and farm workers. Natural resources and fundamental industries and services were put in the hands of the only true owner: the Cuban nation. In less than seventy-two hours, fighting tirelessly day and night, Cuba destroyed the mercenary invasion at Girón organized by a government of the United States, thus preventing a direct military intervention by that country and avoiding a war of incalculable consequences. By that time the Revolution had the Rebel Army, over 400,000 weapons and hundreds of thousands of militiamen. With honour, and with no concessions whatsoever, the country faced the risk of attack by dozens of nuclear weapons in 1962. It defeated the dirty war carried out across the country, at a cost in lives exceeding that paid in the war of liberation. It has implacably withstood thousands of acts of sabotage and terrorist attacks organized by the government of the United States. It has frustrated hundreds of assassination plans and attempts against the leaders of the Revolution.

In the midst of a strict blockade and economic war that has lasted for almost half a century, Cuba has been able to eradicate illiteracy in one year, a phenomenon that the rest of Latin America – with the notable exception of Venezuela, thanks to the Bolivarian revolution there – and, I might add, the United States, have not been able to do in over four decades. [Cuba] has taken free education to 100 per cent of its children. It has the highest retention rate for students in school – over 99 per cent between pre-school and ninth grade – of all the nations in the hemisphere. Its primary-school students are first in the world in their knowledge of language and mathematics. It is also first in the world in teachers per capita and lowest number of students per classroom. All children with physical or mental difficulties study in special schools. Computers and computer science are taught to all children, adolescents and young people in both the countryside and the city; intensive use is made of audiovisual methods in all schools.

All young people from seventeen to thirty who were not in school and did not have a job are now entitled to study, with financial compensation by the state – the first time in the world a nation has provided its citizens with this opportunity. Any citizen has the opportunity to pursue studies leading from pre-school to a doctorate in science without spending a cent. Today the country has over thirty times the number of university graduates, intellectuals, and professional artists that there were before the Revolution. The average education of a Cuban citizen today is at least ninth-grade. There is not even any functional illiteracy in Cuba.

Schools to educate and train artists and art teachers have been expanded into every province in the country, so that over 20,000 young people are able to pursue their studies and develop their talent and their vocation. Tens of thousands of other young people study in vocational centres, which then feed into our professional art schools. University campuses are now being expanded into every municipality in the country. In no other country in the world has such a colossal educational and cultural revolution taken place, making Cuba, by a wide margin, the country with the highest knowledge level and highest cultural level in the world – a manifestation of Martí's profound conviction that 'without culture, freedom is not possible'.

Our infant mortality rate has dropped from 60 per 1,000 live births to a figure that ranges between 6 and 6.5, the lowest in the hemisphere, with the exception of Canada, from the United States to Patagonia.[14] Life expectancy has increased more than fifteen years. Infectious and transmittable diseases such as poliomyelitis, malaria, neonatal tetanus, diphtheria, measles, chicken pox, mumps, whooping cough and dengue have been eliminated; others, such as tetanus, meningococcal meningitis, hepatitis B, leprosy, Haemophilus meningitis and tuberculosis are totally controlled. Today, people die in our country of the same diseases as in the most highly developed nations: cardiovascular disease, cancer, accidents and so on.

A profound revolution is being carried out to take medical services to the population, in order to facilitate access to clinics, preserve lives and relieve pain. Profound studies are being carried out to break the chain, mitigate or reduce to a minimum genetic, prenatal and postnatal problems, including those associated with childbirth. Today, Cuba has the highest number of doctors per capita [in the world], almost twice as many as the country in second place.

Scientific centres are working tirelessly to find preventive or therapeutic solutions for the most serious illnesses. Cubans will have the best health system in the world, whose services will continue to be provided absolutely free. Social security covers 100 per cent of the country's citizens.

Eighty-five per cent of the population owns its own home, tax free. The other fifteen per cent pay an absolutely symbolic rent – barely ten per cent of their salary.

Only a tiny percentage of the population use drugs, and we are resolutely fighting against that problem. Lotteries and other forms of gambling were prohibited after the first years of the Revolution so that no one would stake his or her hopes of personal progress on chance.

Our television, radio and press have no commercial advertising. Any promotion is aimed at issues related to health, education, culture, physical education, sport, recreation, defence of the environment, directed at the fight against drugs, against accidents or other problems of a social nature. Our mass media educate; they do not poison or alienate. No one worships or praises the values of the rotting consumer societies.

There is no cult of personality with respect to any living figure associated with the Revolution – no statues, official photographs, street names, institutional names. The men and women who lead the country are people, not gods.

In our country there are no paramilitary forces or death squads, nor has violence ever been used against the people; there are no extra-judicial executions, no torture. We cultivate fraternity and solidarity between men and nations, inside and outside the country.

The new generations and the entire country are educated to protect the environment. The mass media are used to create ecological awareness. Our country firmly defends its cultural identity, assimilates the best of other cultures and resolutely struggles against any distorting, alienating and degrading material. The development of healthy non-professional sport has led our people to the highest percentages of world-class medals and honours.

Scientific research, at the service of our people and humanity in general, has been increased hundreds of times over. One result of this effort is important medicines that save lives in Cuba and other countries. We have never done research towards any biological weapon, nor have we formulated any – this would be in absolute contradiction to the training, education and conscience with which our scientific personnel have been inculcated.

In no other country has the spirit of international solidarity been so deeply rooted. Our country aided the Algerian patriots in their struggle against French colonialism, even at the cost of damaging our political and economic relations with a European country as important as France. We sent weapons and combatants to defend Algeria against Moroccan expansionism when King Hassan II of Morocco attempted to take over the Gara Djebilet iron mines near the city of Tinduf in southwestern Algeria.

At the request of the Arab nation of Syria, a complete brigade of tanks stood guard on the Golan Heights from 1973 to 1975 when that part of Syrian territory was unfairly occupied.

The leader of the then recently independent Republic of the Congo, Patrice Lumumba, hounded by foreign powers, received our political aid. When he was assassinated by the colonial powers in 1961, we helped his followers. Four years later, in 1965, Cuban blood was spilled in the western area of Lake Tanganyika, where Che, with over 100 Cuban instructors, supported the Congolese rebels in their fight against white mercenaries led by the West's puppet Mobutu, whose stolen $40 billion are in unknown European banks in unknown hands.

The blood of Cuban instructors was also spilled training and supporting combatants belonging to the African Party for the Independence of Guinea and Cape Verde (PAIGC), who, under the command of Amílcar Cabral, were fighting for the independence of those two former Portuguese colonies.

The same thing went on for ten years as Cubans gave aid to Agostinho Neto's MPLA [the Movement for the Liberation of Angola]. Once independence was won, and for fifteen years thereafter, hundreds of thousands of Cuban volunteers took part in the defence of Angola in the face of attacks by racist South African troops who, in complicity with the United States and using the tactics of a dirty war, laid millions of landmines, wiped out whole villages and murdered more than half a million Angolan men, women and children. In Cuito Cuanavale and on the Namibian border, in southwestern Angola, Angolan and Namibian forces, along with 40,000 Cuban soldiers, struck a decisive blow against the South African troops, which at that time possessed atomic bombs supplied or helped to produce by Israel with the full knowledge and complicity of the government of the United States. This battle meant the immediate liberation of Namibia, and it speeded the end of apartheid by perhaps twenty to twenty-five years.

For almost fifteen years, Cuba held a place of honour in its solidarity with the heroic people of Vietnam in a barbaric and brutal war waged by the United States, which killed 2 million Vietnamese, not counting the number of wounded and mutilated, and which flooded [Vietnam's] soil with chemical products that caused incalculable, and ongoing, damage.

Cuban blood was spilled along with the blood of the citizens of several Latin American nations, and along with the Cuban-Latin American blood of Che, who was murdered on instructions of US agents in Bolivia when he was lying wounded, his weapon disabled by a bullet in combat.

The Cuban blood of construction workers about to complete an international airport of vital importance to the economy of a tiny island dependent on tourism was spilled as they fought in the defence of Grenada, a country invaded by the United States under cynical pretexts.

Cuban blood was spilled in Nicaragua when instructors from the Cuban armed forces were training brave Nicaraguan soldiers as they faced the dirty war organized and armed by the United States against the Sandinista revolution.

And I have not cited all the examples. Over 2,000 heroic Cuban internationalist combatants have given their lives in pursuit of their sacred duty to support the fight for the independence of our sister nations. In none of those countries does Cuba own or occupy any property. No other country of our times has ever written such a brilliant page of sincere and disinterested solidarity.

Cuba has always preached by example. It has never given in, never backed down. It has never sold out another nation's cause. It has never made concessions. It has never betrayed its principles. Not for nothing was it re-elected, in July 2003, by acclamation, in the United Nations Economic and Social Council, to an additional three-year term on the Human Rights Commission, a membership it has held uninterruptedly for fifteen years.

Over half a million Cubans have carried out internationalist missions as combatants, as teachers, as technicians, or as doctors and health workers. Over a period of more than forty years, tens of thousands of these health workers have given their services and saved millions of lives. Today, over 3,000 specialists in holistic general medicine and other health workers are in the farthest reaches of eighteen Third World countries, where, using preventive and therapeutic methods, they are saving hundreds of thousands of lives every year and preserving or returning health to millions of people without charging one cent for their services.

Without the Cuban doctors offered to the United Nations, should the UN receive the necessary funds – without which entire nations and even whole regions of sub-Saharan Africa are in danger of perishing – essential, urgent programmes aimed at preventing and treating AIDS could not be carried out.

Cuba has developed a technique for using the radio to teach people to read and write, with texts produced now in five languages: Créole, Portuguese, French, English and Spanish. And these programmes are being put into practice in other countries. We have now completed a similar programme for teaching Spanish literacy through television – an exceptionally effective programme. These are programmes created and designed by Cuba, and they are genuinely Cuban. We are not, however, interested in patenting or trademarking them. We are willing to offer them to all the countries of the Third World, where most illiteracy is to be found, and absolutely free of charge. In five years, the 800 million people who are illiterate today could be reduced, at minimal cost, by 80 per cent.

I'll stop here, so as not to exhaust your patience, but I could go on . . .

That's an impressive record – how do you think history will judge you?
That's something it's not worthwhile worrying about. You know why? Because this mankind has made so many mistakes, there've been so many stupidities, that if it manages to survive – which is yet to be seen – if it manages to survive, in 100 years people will look back on us as tribes of barbarians and uncivilized cavemen who aren't worth remembering.

They may remember a period in history when mankind almost disappeared, when terrible things happened, when we were still uncivilized barbarians. That's the idea a future generation may well have of us in 2100. They'll look back on us the way we looked back at primitive man until just a short time ago – I'm convinced of that. Every decade that passes in this decisive twenty-first century will be the equivalent of almost 1,000 years.

So it doesn't make any sense to talk about the judgement of history. That's the way I think, honestly; I think that. I'm more interested in the prestige a country might have for its struggle, its battles, but not necessarily linked to *me*.

Listen, I've read a lot about prominent figures, eminent men who talked about glory . . . Napoleon talked about *la gloire*, he was constantly concerned with glory. Well, in lots of countries today, the name Napoleon is known more for the cognac that bears his name than for all the things done by the real general and emperor. I'm sure if I asked teenagers of practically any country who Napoleon was, they'd know the name Napoleon more because of the cognac of that name than for all the things he did on the battlefield. So I say, why worry?

Men such as Bolívar also talked a lot about glory. I've always been a great admirer of Bolívar, and once, in a speech at the Universidad Central de Venezuela, I said, 'Bolívar talked about glory, but Bolívar wasn't a conqueror of nations, he was a liberator.' Alexander was a conqueror of nations, and a creator of empires. There have also been great men whom the world has admired down through the centuries: Hannibal, Julius Caesar – they were all conquerors, they were warriors.

If you think about it, it's only recently that young people have been taught that Shakespeare was a great writer, a person of great value, that other people did great paintings, that others were brilliant philosophers, others brilliant poets, unsurpassed today. That is, those with great intellectual merit, the great creators of music, painting, drama, literature and all that, were known by very few, and the history we were taught hardly mentioned those cases; all it talked about was Christopher Columbus; Hernán Cortés; Pizarro; Magellan, the guy who circumnavigated the globe; Napoleon; the pirate Drake; Xerxes, the Persian emperor who fought Leonidas at Thermopylae; Julius Caesar; Hannibal – all those warriors – and Westerners, because the warriors of the East, nobody even knew who they were.

Except for the 'bad guys' – Attila, for example.
Well, but he came into the West. If Christopher Columbus had been right and there hadn't been a continent in the way, he'd have reached China and then, if he'd wanted to, he could have tried to conquer it with twelve horses, as I believe they did in Cuba, and a few harquebuses. But he'd have met up with Mongol armies of hundreds of thousands of soldiers on horseback – Columbus would never have been heard of again as a guy who had the bad luck and crazy idea of reaching China – he'd have disappeared within fifteen minutes of getting there, if he'd really tried to take possession. You see, if he'd gone like Marco Polo, he'd have been welcomed; if he'd taken possession in the name of the King of Spain, with cross and sword, he'd have lasted about fifteen minutes, and Cortés and all the others, likewise.

But other figures, history doesn't usually talk about. The great scientists, the great inventors, researchers who have made such important contributions to mankind ... History, you can say, doesn't talk about them;

maybe a few people remember them . . . but political leaders haven't made enough contributions to be remembered.

What political leader do you remember – of all those you've known – who's made the greatest impression on you?

Let me think. Che – I always remember him as one of the most extraordinary personalities I've ever known. One of the noblest, most extraordinary, most disinterested men I've ever known. And Nelson Mandela is one of the men I admire most, because of his merits and his history, his struggle. Contemporary foreign leaders . . . one of the ones I've most appreciated is Jiang Zemin.[15] Because I've come to know him over a period of many years; it wasn't the first day, or the second, but over the years, on the basis of contact and time – he's a very capable man.

In the contemporary period, in the Western world, I'd say that one of the most capable statesmen was German chancellor Willy Brandt. I met him, spoke a lot with him. He was a man of vision, of elevated thought, a man concerned for peace and for the problems of the Third World.

Speaking of the West, another leader I knew well and also consider to have been a responsible, honest, capable statesman was Swedish prime minister Olof Palme. I had deep admiration and respect for him, and his death, his assassination under strange circumstances, was a terrible loss.

You never knew President Kennedy personally.

No. And I think Kennedy was a man of great enthusiasm, very intelligent, with personal charisma, who tried to do positive things. He may have been, after Franklin Roosevelt, one of the United States' most brilliant personalities. He made mistakes: he gave a green light to the Playa Girón invasion in 1961, but that operation hadn't been prepared by him – it was put together by the previous Eisenhower–Nixon administration. He wasn't able to stop it in time. He also tolerated the activities of the CIA; during the period he was president, the first plans to assassinate me and other international leaders were formulated. There is no unequivocal proof of his personal complicity, but it's really hard to think that somebody in the CIA could have made the decision to undertake actions of that kind on his own, without the approval, at least tacit approval, of the president. He may have been tolerant, or have allowed his own ambiguous words to be interpreted by the CIA in its own way.

But at the same time, I find – because I see very clearly that although

Kennedy may have made mistakes, some of them ethical mistakes – [that] he was a man who was able to rectify [them himself], a man courageous enough to introduce some changes into United States policy. Among his mistakes is the war in Vietnam. With his enthusiasm, his obsessive sympathy for the Green Berets and overestimation of American power, he took the first steps to take his country into the war in Vietnam.

He made mistakes, I repeat, but he was an intelligent man, sometimes brilliant, brave, and it's my opinion – I've said this before – that if Kennedy had survived, it's possible that relations between Cuba and the United States would have improved.[16] Because after Girón and the October crisis, he was quite impressed. I don't think he underestimated the Cuban people; it's even possible there was some admiration there for our people's courage and strength of character.

The day he was killed I was talking to a French journalist, Jean Daniel,[17] whom Kennedy had sent to me with a message, to talk to me. So communications were being established, and that might have favoured an improvement in our relations.

His death touched me and grieved me. He was an adversary, of course, but I was very much saddened by his death. It was as though I'd lost a very capable, worthy opponent. I was also saddened by the way he was killed – the cowardly assassination, the political crime. I experienced a sense of indignation, of repudiation, of sadness, and in this case for an adversary that I didn't think deserved such an end.

His assassination worried me, too, because when he was taken from the stage he had enough authority in his country to impose an improvement in relations with Cuba. And that was palpably demonstrated in the conversation I had with that French journalist, Jean Daniel, who was with me – bringing me very important words from Kennedy, because of the terrible days he'd lived through during the October crisis, as he himself said – with me the very instant we heard the news of Kennedy's death. 'Talk to Castro,' he said, 'and then come back and talk to me and tell me what he thinks.' That's what Jean Daniel had just said to me.

Did you know Ernest Hemingway very well?

I'd have liked to know Hemingway better. He liked Cuba, he loved this island. He lived here; he left us many things – his library, his house, which is a museum today. During the first year of the Revolution I was able to talk to him twice, quite briefly. If Hemingway had lived a few years longer, I'd have liked to have time to talk much more with him. To become a little closer friends.

I've read some of his novels more than once. And in a lot of them – *For Whom the Bell Tolls, A Farewell to Arms* – he always has his main character talk to himself. That's what I like best about Hemingway – the monologues, when his characters talk to themselves. Like in *The Old Man and the Sea*, the book he was given the Nobel Prize for.[18]

As a person, in the little I knew him, he seemed to me, in his habits, his practices, his things, a very humane person. I always liked his literature a lot. His books paint a portrait of him, himself, the adventures he had throughout his life and the [adventures] he'd have liked to have had but couldn't, or didn't. I sincerely admired his zest for adventure.

Did you know Mao Zedong?

No, I didn't know Mao. Nor did I have the privilege of meeting Ho Chi Minh, whom I see as a leader with some of the purest, clearest philosophy.

Mao Zedong has great historical merit. He was, without question, the organizer and inspirer of the Chinese revolution, one of the great revolutions of the twentieth century. A man of political and military talent who promoted, pushed and achieved the victorious struggle against Japanese imperialism, against the puppet government of Chiang Kai-shek, and who undoubtedly wrote brilliant pages in history.

But at the same time, I am absolutely convinced that in the final stage of his life he made great political errors. They weren't errors of the Right, they were errors of the Left, or rather, the extreme Left. The methods for putting those ideas into practice were harsh, unjust, as during the so-called 'Cultural Revolution', and I think that as a consequence of an extreme-Left policy, what followed was a turn to the right within the Chinese revolutionary process, because all those great mistakes produce reactions: errors of left-wing extremism at some point are going to produce right-wing inclinations and policies.

I don't mean to say that the revolution is lost in China. The country is looking for the right road. Mao was a great revolutionary, with great historical merits, great talent, but he made grave errors in the final phase of his life. It was truly shocking to see the degree the cult of personality reached.

You knew Marxist leaders who, while in power, behaved abominably, criminally. I'm thinking, for example, of Hafizullah Amin of Afghanistan[19]

and of Ieng Sary of Kampuchea,[20] *one of the two men responsible for the genocide in Cambodia in 1975. What memories do you have of them?*

In Afghanistan, in 1979, Amin, who was the prime minister, led a secret group that was conspiring against the president, Muhammad Taraki, as a matter of fact while Taraki was in Havana, and within a few days, in July of that year, a palace coup took place that ended with Taraki's death – he was secretly assassinated [the death attributed to 'unknown causes'] and Amin took office as president. That assassination, which Brezhnev disapproved of, was what led to the Soviet intervention in December 1979.

Amin was a person in a way very much like Pol Pot. We'd had the opportunity to meet Amin in April 1978, after the triumph of the revolution in Afghanistan. You can't imagine a pleasanter, friendlier person! Exactly like Ieng Sary, who also paid us a visit after the revolution in Kampuchea.

I have, it's true, had the odd privilege of knowing some figures who appeared to be perfectly normal, perfectly well mannered, with a Western education, who'd studied in Europe or the United States and then later did horrendous, abominable things. It's as if, at some point, people went crazy. Apparently there are people whose cerebral neurons aren't adapted for the complexity of the problems that arise during a revolutionary process. And they commit ignominious acts of madness that I never cease to be amazed at.

Did you know Deng Xiaoping?

No; I'd have liked to.

At the beginning of this survey you asked me which leaders had made the greatest impression on me. I started by mentioning Che, a Latin American, but I forgot to mention another eminent Latin American who impressed me greatly from the first moment: Hugo Chávez.

Is there any leader in the second half of the twentieth century that you regret never having personally met?

I mentioned one, Ho Chi Minh. And I'd also like to have met Mao. That wasn't possible because of all those problems and differences that came up because of the Sino-Soviet conflict. Among the great political strategists, great military leaders of any era, one would have to include Mao Zedong. I can't forget the posthumous letter from Mao asking China and the USSR to put their rivalries aside and join forces.

28

After Fidel, What?

'Critic Number One' – Corruption – The single party – Fidel's salary –
Socialism: no turning back? – The succession – Raúl Castro –
Can the Revolution be brought down? – The future of the Revolution

I'd like us to talk now about the domestic situation in Cuba, if we could.
In every country, there are people who aren't happy, and that includes
Cuba, and apparently you've been in the habit, regularly, of sensing the
problems in people's daily lives and being the first to express them in your
own speeches – such and such is not working, this other thing needs to be
worked on – and people found in your speeches an expression of what they
themselves were feeling. But apparently for some time now you haven't
been mentioning what's not working in Cuban society, and a lot of people
miss your role as this country's 'Crítico Número Uno'.

It's the truth, I've been critic number one, not of the country but of mistakes,
things that aren't done right. But we now have methods that allow us to
know – as with a microscope – the state of [public] opinion. You must
recognize that in our country, people express themselves quite freely – that
trait is part of their tradition, expressing their points of view.

For several years we've been collecting the country's spontaneous opinions
after every event, and among the opinions, some are adverse. There's also
the instruction, as I've said, that every adverse opinion has to appear. I never
read any opinions that have to do with me, because they can be very
complimentary, and it would be unpleasant, vain, to read them. I worry
even when it's just a few thousand who aren't happy among the millions of
my compatriots. It is enough, for example, that 16,000 people have an
adverse opinion, for you to have to worry, not because of the percentage,
really, but because they can be reasonable, fair opinions or they can be the

opinions of people who are openly hostile, people who are not friendly to the Revolution.

You know which is which because when they say, 'This must have been very expensive,' or 'Such and such a TV broadcast should be done this way or that,' those aren't the opinions of enemies. Although your enemies also express themselves: 'They're talking about X but not about food'; 'They're talking about such and such a problem, but not about this other one.' That is, our information on the state of [public] opinion is complete, total, broad; it's driven by a concern that it reflect [people's] true opinions. All the negative things are included. You have to worry, be concerned, and often those adverse opinions help; they're very spontaneous.

Now then, I'm really the most critical, the most implacable [critic]. You should hear the things I say. And that I've said publicly.

Speaking of that, in a speech on 17 November 2005, you declared an 'all-out war' on certain problems the country is facing – petty corruption, theft from the state, illicit enrichment [misappropriation of funds] – which up until now hadn't been denounced quite so harshly in public.
That's right. We've invited everyone, the entire nation, to take part in a great battle, a battle against any and all offences, whether petty thievery or grand larceny, any kind at all, in any place, any offence that takes place because of a lack of a deep economic awareness that we've failed to inculcate in the people.

We think about that more than anything else: our failings, our mistakes, our inequalities, our injustices. We are involved in a battle against vices,[1] against the diversion of resources, against certain widespread habits. Yes, we are facing a great battle that we're just beginning to fight, with greater strength and experience than ever before – and that we're going to win.

Because here – and we have to say this – we have several tens of thousands of parasites that don't produce anything yet are getting rich. For example, buying and stealing fuel. A lot of people go around with a little piece of hose, rubber tubing, putting petrol in the [American cars from the twenties to fifties] and getting paid by the nouveau riche who doesn't even pay for the petrol he uses. There's a widespread mess there, among other things, that entails the loss of tens of millions of dollars . . .

How do you explain that you've had to intervene personally in that? Why has the usual recourse to collective criticism and self-criticism not worked?
We trusted criticism and self-criticism, it's true. But that's become practically

fossilized. That method, as it was being used, hardly worked any more, because the criticisms tended to take place within a little group, and to stay there; criticism never went to a broader forum, a theatre, for example, with hundreds or thousands of people. If a public health officer, to cite just one case, falsified data on the existence of the *Aedes aegypti* mosquito, he'd be reprimanded, he'd be criticized. Which is fine. But I know some people who say, 'Yeah, I criticize myself, I self-criticize,' and that's it – they're cool as cucumbers with that. Happy as clams. But what about all the harm you did? What about all the millions that were wasted as a result of that negligence or the way you acted?

You have to have self-criticism in the classroom, in the nucleus [the workplace or group meeting], and after that, outside the nucleus, in the city or town, and in the whole country. We have to use that shame that people surely have, because I know a lot of people quite rightly called 'shameless',[2] who, when a local newspaper published what they did, were filled with shame. In this battle against vices there will be no quarter given anyone, we're going to call a spade a spade, and we are going to appeal to the honour of each sector. In the end, those who refuse to understand are going to self-correct, but in another way; yes, they're going to be smeared with their own offal. One thing we're sure of: in every human being there is a high sense of shame. And a revolutionary's first duty is to be extremely harsh with himself.

We are going to fight this battle, and use the highest-calibre weapons we have. The Revolution has to use those weapons, and it *will* use them if need be. The Revolution is going to establish all necessary controls. We are not a capitalist country, where everything is left to chance.

Do you think that the hardships and shortages of the special period have led in some way to the habits of corruption and theft?
Yes, I do. Although the theft of materials and resources is nothing new; it didn't start with the special period. The special period worsened it, of course, because it created a great deal of inequality and made it possible for some people to make a lot of money. But it's not new. I remember that back in 1990 – the Soviet Union hadn't self-destructed yet – we were building a very important biotechnology centre in Bejucal [outside Havana]. And near there, there was a little cemetery. I'd drive out there, and one day I went by the cemetery, and I found a clandestine market where that whole building crew, the bosses and a large number of builders, had organized the sale of things:

cement, rebars [steel reinforcing rods for concrete], timber, paint, everything that is used in construction . . .

How much has been stolen here, even sometimes from important factories that manufacture products in great demand? Factories that produce medicines, for example? I know of one out in La Lisa [a Havana neighbourhood] where they had to remove the administrator and a lot of employees, dozens of people . . . The management and a bunch of people were involved. Dozens of people had to be removed – go get this one and that one and replace them. Firing them isn't enough, nor will it be the only solution. You should see how deep-rooted some of these vices are, how much pilfering was going on, how people were diverting resources, the way things being stolen.

How do you explain all that?
Here, the special period gave rise to profound inequalities. How I rue the day foreign-currency shops were created, just to pull in a little of the money that some people were receiving from abroad and spending on highly desirable goods in stores when there were tremendous scarcities across the island – which meant that the prices of those goods were, and will inevitably be, high – and then taking that money and investing it in the essentials for those who *weren't* receiving anything at all from abroad.

In addition, some people were charging high prices for things they did 'off the books', so they were earning several times as much per month as one of our doctors who's up in the mountains of Guatemala or some distant place in Africa, or Kashmir, at altitudes of thousands of feet, in the Himalayas, saving lives. And those doctors were earning 5 per cent, 10 per cent of what some crook selling petrol to the nouveaux riches was, or a guy diverting resources from the docks in lorries, by the ton, or the guy stealing things from the foreign-currency shops, or from the state in a five-star hotel, maybe bringing in a bottle of rum he's bought in a dollar store and pocketing all the money he takes in for the daiquiris and mojitos he makes. How many ways are there of stealing in this country?

Apparently it was in the petrol stations that most of the stealing was going on.
I'll tell you, we started in Pinar del Río [province] to see what was happening at the petrol stations that sold petrol for foreign currency. And we soon discovered that what was being stolen was as much as what was coming in! Almost half the money was being stolen! And in other places, more than half!

In Havana, a lot of people had learned to steal like crazy. If I tell you about all the petrol stations in the capital, you'd be shocked; there are over twice as many as there should be, it's chaos. Every ministry decided to put in its own, and distribute fuel all over the place. In the Popular Powers [the local governments], disaster, chaos is universal. Plus, all the oldest lorries, the ones that use the most petrol, were given to the Popular Powers. When it looked as though the use of lorries was being brought into some sort of rational order, what was actually happening was that the country's entire future was being mortgaged. Because one thing that people know is that state-owned lorries are driving around doing things that have nothing to do with their normal work – a guy going to see some relative, some friend, his girlfriend.

Soon, technology is going to allow us to know where every truck is,[3] just as they're doing in many developed countries – the exact street, the exact place. No one will be able to run off in a lorry, go see their aunt, some friend of theirs, their girlfriend. Not that going to see your relatives or your friend or your girlfriend is a bad thing, but not in a lorry that's supposed to be used for work.

I remember once, several years before the special period, I saw a brand-new Volvo front-loader, which back then must have cost $50,000 or $60,000, speeding along right down Quinta Avenida in Havana. I wondered just where it was going at that speed, so I had my escort stop him and ask: 'Stop, ask that guy where he's going – I want an honest answer.' And the driver confessed that in that Volvo tractor, which was going as fast as it could down the middle of Quinta Avenida, he was going to see his girlfriend ... As I sit here before you, my friend!

So things like that are going on. And, generally speaking, we know about it, although a lot of people are thinking, 'The Revolution can't fix this; no, there's no way in the world *anybody* can fix this. There's just no fixing it.' Well, they're wrong – the people themselves are going to fix it, the Revolution is going to fix it.

How?

First of all, it's a question of ethics. I've thought a lot about the role of ethics. What is a revolutionary's ethics? All revolutionary thought begins with a little ethics. But it's also a question of life-or-death economics. This is one of the most wasteful, spendthrift countries in the world when it comes to fuel. Nobody here knows what petrol costs, nobody knows what electricity costs, nobody knows the market price of it. Why, even houses – we wind up giving people houses for free. Can Cuba solve its housing problem by giving away houses? Some people used to buy them. They were the owners, they'd paid fifty pesos a month, eighty pesos – which, if you sent it off to Miami, would be worth like three dollars! After years passed, they'd paid less than $500, and some then sold them for $15,000, $20,000 . . . And who bought those houses? Was it the proletariat? The poor? Many poor people got their houses free and then sold them to one of the nouveaux riches. Is that Socialism?

What's paradoxical, although legal, is that the Cubans who receive dollars or other foreign currency from abroad have greater advantages than citizens who don't have anybody outside Cuba. And that's created some discontent. Yes, but look at the inconsistency: people have those advantages above all because of subsidies provided by the state. For example, what do people living out there [i.e., outside Cuba] do with a dollar? They send it here . . . I have relatives they send money to. I have nothing to do with that. One day we asked and [we discovered that] there are provinces where 30 to 40 per cent of the people receive some amount from the outside, even if it's just a little. But it's such good business to send a dollar – such good business! – we could be ruined if everybody sent in dollars. Because of the huge buying power those dollars have in a country under a blockade, in which rationed products are heavily, heavily subsidized, and where most services are free or extraordinarily cheap.

How much money do the people of Cuba spend because of that dollar people send down here? Because that's not a dollar that you earned with the sweat of your brow. It was sent to you – somebody who left here healthy, with a good education paid for by the state since the day they were born, they're not sick; they're the healthiest citizens who reach the United States. So anyway, to subsidize that dollar sent down here from the United States, Cuba spends, in exchange, on average, about forty-four dollars. We've got the studies that show that.

This is a noble country – it subsidizes the dollars held by people who live here, people who say to you, 'Listen, I'm going to send you dollars to buy subsidized electricity with. Listen, I'm going to send you a refrigerator, too, or I'm going to give you the money to buy a refrigerator at the *shopping*.'[4] Then the generous sender of dollars goes on: 'Don't worry, I'm going to send you whatever you need; I'll guarantee you the 300 kilowatts of that idiotic Socialist state's subsidized electricity that you're using.' We're good to them, but there may be one or another citizen who might think, quite rightly, that we're stupid. They'd be about half right, you know!

I remember when, as we were analysing the issue of electric usage, we discovered that one *paladar*[5] was using 11,000 kilowatts a month, and this idiotic state was subsidizing the owner, who was so beloved by the bourgeoisie that brought visitors there to sample the lobster and shrimp, as a miracle of private enterprise. All of it stolen by someone who took [the seafood] from Batabanó [a Caribbean coastal town almost exactly due south of Havana] and four or five little plastic chairs! No! Of course this 'totalitarian, abusive state' is 'an enemy of progress', because it's an enemy of looting.

So the state was subsidizing this *paladar* to the tune of over $1,000 every month. I found this out because I asked what he was paying versus what it actually cost, and he was paying for electricity at a subsidized rate – 11,000 kilowatts! I think after the first 300 kilowatts, he was paying thirty centavos per kilowatt. He was paying 3,000 Cuban pesos, which is about $120. But that electricity cost the state – that time I calculated it at ten cents in American dollars per kilowatt – $1,250 every month. That's free trade, that's progress, that's development, that's getting ahead . . .

So what are you going to do? Are you going to do away with subsidies?
No, but we've raised electricity rates for the people who use the most. To discourage excess usage among those who waste it, whatever their current financial status. And also, little by little, we've got to let go of these subsidies, which may be acting as a brake [on the economy] today.

Which is why, from now on, only essential, vital things will be subsidized or free. We won't be charging for medical [or health] services, or educational services, or things like that. But we're going to have to charge rent. We'll see how much. There may be some subsidy, but what a person pays in rent over a number of years has to be close to the cost of the house or apartment. Everything is within our reach, everything belongs to the people; the only thing that's not permissible is wasting or squandering riches selfishly and irresponsibly. Zero waste.

We are also gradually creating the conditions that will make possible the disappearance of the coupon [i.e., rationing] book. We are gradually creating conditions that will take that coupon book, which was essential under given conditions, and which now just gets in the way, and change it. Without committing abuses, without starving anybody to death; just on the basis of the simplest principles: the coupon book has to disappear. On the other hand, some salaries and pensions, the lowest ones, have been raised. People who work and produce will be getting more, they'll be buying more goods and services; people who worked for decades [i.e., retirees] will be getting more and having more things. Many abuses will be ended. Little by little, the culture medium [as in a Petri dish] will be removed, the conditions that allowed many past inequalities will be done away with. Once nobody has to be subsidized, we'll have made considerable progress in our march towards a just and decent society.

You're recognizing certain errors, then, made by the Revolution. Some people outside Cuba are going to be delighted at that, and some others here inside Cuba may consider your criticism too harsh.
It *is* harsh, but I stand by it. And I'll repeat it as often as I have to. I have no fear of assuming the responsibilities I have to assume. We get nowhere by mollycoddling or pulling punches. Let people attack me, let them criticize me. Yes, a lot of people will probably be a little bruised ... We must be daring, we must have the courage to tell the truth. No matter what those bandits outside Cuba say, the news reports that come in tomorrow or the day after with all their sarcastic reports ... He who laughs last laughs best.

And this isn't saying bad things about the Revolution. This is saying very good things about the Revolution, because we're talking about a Revolution that can face these problems and grab the bull by the horns, better than a bullfighter in Madrid. We must have the courage to recognize our own errors for that very reason, because that's the only way we can achieve the objective we set out to achieve.

In order to combat theft and pilferage, particularly in petrol stations, you're turning to the young 'social workers', right?
That's right. These problems are being dealt with in a very decided way – you can't imagine how enthusiastically – by the young social workers. They've already taken on lots of responsibilities. I've never in my life seen such enthusiasm, such seriousness, such integrity, such pride, so much awareness of the good they're going to do the country. Today social workers are in refineries – they get into a 20,000- or 30,000-litre (5,000 to 8,000 gallon) tank-truck, and they see, more or less, where the tank-truck goes, which one takes detours ... And that's the way we've gradually discovered private petrol stations – supplied with fuel provided by the tank-truck drivers!

We're going to be using, if needs be, the [entire cadre of] 28,000 social workers in the country. Some of them are already working to create anti-corruption cells. Around each observation point, a cell. There are also members of the [Revolutionary] Youth, the mass organizations, revolutionary combatants . . . and those people who are diverting petrol better get their act together, so we don't have to find out who they are and discover, point by point, how much petrol each one of them has stolen.

Sometimes the brigades of social workers have had to take surprise actions, with speed, discipline and efficiency. Stunning action. In Havana, for example, there were several thousand, and we mobilized several thousand more, as reserves. So they came in, and suddenly in Havana the petrol stations started reporting that sales had doubled. Why hadn't the employees who'd been there before reported more income? The social workers had to step in. I said, 'Will it be possible to avoid making object lessons here, will they correct their errors?'

Havana has become a spectacular school where people are learning what has to be done, and the social workers know more and more. We're willing to use the 28,000, and the 7,000 who are still in school. If that's not enough, I'll tell you right now that we'll meet with the students in the University Student Federation and we'll find 28,000 more students, and we'll pair them up with the social workers, who are gaining more and more experience every day, and we'll mobilize them. And if 56,000 aren't enough, we'll find 56,000 more.

We're going to show the corrupt element what progress is, what development is, what justice is, what bringing theft and pilferage to an end is. With the determined support and aid of the people. Our society is truly going to be an entirely new society. There won't be many people any more who say, 'This can't be fixed; this is going to go on for ever.' In concert with the people, we're going to be showing that it *can* be fixed. We must be determined: either we defeat all these diversions, or we die.

Speaking of political organization in Cuba, I'd like to ask you whether you think that the one-party structure isn't ill-adapted to an increasingly complex society such as the Cuban society today.
You're asking about a single party, right? The more culture they acquire and the more they know about the world, the happier our people are about unity and the more they value it. Really, I see the spectacle of what happens in some countries with 100 or 120 parties . . . I don't think you can idealize

that situation as a form of government, or a form of democracy. It's madness, a manifestation of madness. How can a Third World country organize itself and develop with 100 parties? That doesn't lead to any healthy formula for government.

In many countries, the classical, traditional electoral system with multiple parties often becomes a popularity contest and not, really, a competency contest – a race to demonstrate the competency, honour and talent [that makes a person capable of governing]. In an election of that kind, people wind up electing the most likeable person, the person who communicates best with the masses, even the person who has the most pleasant appearance, the best advertising on television, or in the press or on radio. Or, in the end, and this is practically a rule, the person who has the most money to spend on advertising.

As you well know, because you've discussed this in some of your books, in certain countries in our hemisphere that I prefer not to mention, electoral campaigns cost tens and sometimes hundreds of millions of dollars, in the American style, and image consultants teach candidates how to comb their hair, how to dress, how to talk to the electorate, and what they should and shouldn't say. It's a carnival, a farce – totally staged . . .

Sometimes the only people who take part are people with money who can use it for advertising. People with the most access to the media are almost always the ones who are finally elected. If an opposition candidate can't call on enough money to carry out an effective campaign – what American publicists call a 'scientific advertising campaign' – he can lose the election. That's the reality. The results of that kind of election are very strange, due essentially to the presence of factors that have very little to do with the candidate's ability to govern.

In Cuba, the party doesn't exist to nominate candidates and elect [parliamentary representatives], as in almost any other place . . . For example, in Spain, in the PSOE, president Felipe González decided who would make up the parliament under the banner of the PSOE. A method as simple as a simple survey – calculate the money the guy has, the advertising he can use . . . but never mind, if you calculate that he has 15 or 20 per cent in a province or department or region, he knows exactly how many representatives to parliament he'll have, he names the candidates and then the citizens vote for a party. Because a party is abstract, an organization, and the voter votes for that abstract thing; who actually elects, or chooses, the parliamentary deputies, who chooses them is the party.

Others, like the English or the Jamaicans, have the constituency; the constituency method is a little bit better, because there's one candidate per party, and there are usually two parties, and [over time] the representative acquires a great deal of experience in Parliament. As a general rule, the political candidates and elected officials in the Caribbean islands are more efficient and better prepared and educated than the officials in a presidential system.

For us, in Cuba, one of the first principles is that here, the Party doesn't nominate candidates – candidates are nominated by the people; the people who live in each electoral district meet in an assembly and nominate – that is, they appoint, they choose the candidates who are going to represent them in parliament; the Party has no say in it. That's strictly prohibited.

It's pretty hard to believe that the Party has no say in the matter.
Our Party neither nominates nor elects. The delegates in the electoral district, which are the base of our system, are proposed by the people, as I say, in assembly, in each district. There must be at least two, and there can't be more than eight, candidates in each electoral district, and those district delegates, who make up the municipal assembly in each municipality across the country, are proposed and elected by the people, in an election in which [candidates] must receive more than 50 per cent of the votes. The Cuban National Assembly, with just over 600 delegates, is made up, almost 50 per cent of it, by those district delegates, who have not just the role of serving on the municipal assemblies, but also of nominating candidates to the provincial assemblies and the National Assembly.

I won't go on, but really, I'd like you to learn a little more one day about Cuba's electoral system, because it's shocking that up there in the north, sometimes people ask us, 'When are you going to have elections in Cuba?' If we Cubans asked that question, it would be, 'How much of a supermillion-aire do you have to be to become president of the United States?'; or, I mean, the candidate doesn't necessarily have to be a supermillionaire, but we might ask, 'How many billions does a candidate need in order to be elected president?' and 'How much does each office cost – even a modest city councilship?'

In our country, that doesn't happen – nor _can_ it happen. We don't plaster our walls with posters or handbills, we don't use mass-coverage television with those subliminal messages, I think they're called.

There may be two, three, even eight candidates – usually there are two to three, almost always two; sometimes it's hard to choose [between them] because what's important is their record, their past history, and usually they campaign together and they're both very excellent candidates. And almost half the Cuban parliament is made up of those people chosen there in the popular assemblies.

And those people are not Party members?
They don't have to be, no, not at all. It so happens that a very high number of them *are* Party members. And what exactly does that show? Just that many of the best people are members of the Party. And the Party may have, for instance, Catholics, Protestants – a person's religious belief is no obstacle. At first it was, as I told you. But the Party has opened itself today to people of various religious beliefs.

And the fact that those people who are nominated, some 13,000 or 14,000 of them, by the population, and elected by the population, in elections in which the candidates have to receive over 50 per cent of the votes in order to be elected, are, in the vast majority of cases, members of the Party shows that the women and men chosen by the Party are not corrupt, they're good, honest people, among them lots of new people, lots of people with higher education. I can assure you that every day that passes in the history of this country, its struggles, its confrontations, its battles, this nation has more and more culture, and it values and appreciates unity as a thing that is essential and indispensable.

In many of the countries of the former Socialist camp, being a member of the Party was a way of obtaining privileges and favours. People did it [became members of the Communist Party] more out of self-interest than conviction and a spirit of self-sacrifice or a dedication to public service. Does the same thing not happen in Cuba?
This Party doesn't exist so people can obtain privileges. If there's any duty to be done, the one whose duty it is to do it is the Party militant [member]. And [the Party] doesn't nominate or elect; it's the people who do that, through the over 10,000 electoral districts. The Party does lead, in an ideological way, I'd say; it formulates strategies, but it shares that responsibility with the parliament, with the mass organizations, and with the people. It's a different concept from the one the other Socialist countries had, where it was a source of privileges, of corruption, and a source of abuse of power.

But we've seen that there's corruption here, too. Do you think that in Cuba there's no corruption among the leadership?

It's happened with some officials who were negotiating with powerful foreign businesses, and, well, sometimes they'd be invited to a restaurant, or they'd be invited to go to Europe and be put up in the owner's house, or a luxury hotel . . . The bottom line is, some of our officials bought and sold millions, bought millions on the one hand and on the other the art of corrupting that many capitalists tend to have – more subtle than the serpent and sometimes worse than rats. Rats anaesthetize [their victims] as they gnaw on them, and they're able to pull off a hunk of a person's flesh in the middle of the night. That's the way [those corrupt officials] gradually anaesthetized the Revolution and pulled off chunks of its flesh.

Not a few of them made a show of their corruption, and many people knew about it, or suspected, because they could see their lifestyles, and sometimes because of stupid little things: this one got a new car, painted it, put this on it, or painted some pretty little stripes on it, because they got vain. We've heard these stories twenty times here and there, and we've had to take measures. But it's not easy to fix.

We've worked hard, and we've been lucky enough to avoid almost completely – I don't know of any other case – those phenomena of corruption and abuse of power. It never crosses people's minds here. There may be corruption, we've talked about that; there are a lot of people here who've engaged in it, but it can't occur within the Party leadership cadre or within a national administrative leadership cadre – it simply cannot be permitted in [those bodies] . . .

Although I've been put on a list of the richest men in the world. I mean, that takes the cake. I'm not going to sue them or anything, but . . . I, honestly, don't own a thing. I have a few pesos, because after you've paid the amounts that have been in place since the first year of the Revolution for each service, which are pretty reasonable, you may have some left over. I'm paid the same salary I always was, and out of that I have to pay the Party dues, so much per cent for housing, you pay that every month . . . And it's been quite a few years since I've had a holiday, a good many years since I've had a day of rest – not even Saturday or Sunday. But I lack for nothing, materially speaking. I have what I need. I don't need much . . .

I'll explain to you the most basic, fundamental thing about ethical conduct. Let people try to find any leader of the Revolution who has an account in some foreign bank; we'll give anybody that manages to find such a thing whatever they want. We who are the leaders of the Revolution don't have a centavo – I mean, we may have a few pesos, we may still have a little money, because almost all our expenses are paid . . .

Could you tell me what your salary is?
My salary, at the exchange rate of twenty-five pesos per dollar, is thirty dollars a month. But I'm not dying of hunger. I pay the Party dues, this, that, the other, a percentage, since the very first, for rent, I think we were paying 10 per cent.

You should understand that a man harassed and pursued from every direction can't sleep every day in the same place. I mean, all those conditions have been changing; we've gained experience.

I help out an aunt of mine on my mother's side, one of whose sons died in the war, back before we had retirement [pensions], because the Rebel Army wasn't paid for like six months.

What's more, now that we're talking about this problem, I can tell you that a lot of gifts that people gave me were stacking up. I have no idea how many millions of dollars all those gifts might have been worth, not least because people like to buy things that belong or used to belong to this one or that one . . . So one day I turned over about 17,000 gifts to Eusebio Leal, the city's historian. I've never told anybody this, I didn't want people who brought me a gift to think I didn't appreciate it. Quite the contrary: that was precisely why I turned them over to the city historian. I put just one condition: 'Leave me the books; when I die, those will be public' [i.e., I'll leave them to the state]. But the other gifts, I gave them all away. There's lots of stories there, you could laugh about a lot of them, because I turned over pyjamas, even clocks worth $6,000 or $7,000, art works, all sorts of things – I mean, good paintings, objects of value, antiques.

I'm not defending myself against a thing, I'm simply telling you things that you have to laugh about. But I've been put on that list of the world's richest people twice now – I have no idea why they do it, what they're trying to achieve; it's ridiculous. I don't have a cent of my own; I don't administer a cent. What I mean is, the state Office of Administration, in general, administers the expenses associated with the presidency. As it would in any country. Really, when I travel, I have to stay in a hotel, I have to eat some place, but I never carry a penny.

I can say that a formula has been applied: from each according to his abilities, to each according to his needs. And so my needs, my personal needs, are really very few, and I've never had an increase in salary. I'll have the glory of dying without a penny of convertible currency. I've been offered millions to write memoirs and books, but I've never done it. I've always said, 'If I do it, it's for schools.' And a person is at peace in his own mind, really happy, strong, with that sort of rule. No injustice is conceivable to any revolutionary – none.

I said that vengeance can find no place in a revolutionary's heart. You can fight with all the determination and strength of will in the world, but you can't do it out of hate. There was a moment, when we were up in the Sierra Maestra, when I said something. I was watching a bombardment by some missiles that the Americans had given Batista's bombers, and I wrote a message to Celia:[6] 'When I saw the rockets they shot at Mario's house I swore that the Americans are going to pay for what they're doing, and pay a heavy price. When this war is over, it will be the beginning, for me, of a much wider and bigger war: the war I'm going to wage against [the Americans]. I realize that that's going to be my true destiny.'

It was a premonition when I saw those bombs.

But I've seen so many things since then . . . I've seen 2 million Vietnamese die, I've seen millions of invalids, I've seen the jungle that belongs to that refined, delicate people with a culture that goes back thousands of years, I've seen that jungle sprayed with napalm – 20,000 kilometres, over 12,000 miles, from the United States, those bombings were carried out. I've seen the things they've done, the tortures in Abu Ghraib prison, the use of white phosphorus in Fallujah . . . Look at the dictatorships they put in place, the torturers by the tens of thousands educated in institutions created for just that purpose in the United States, those [torturers] who 'disappeared' 10,000 or 20,000 or 30,000 Argentines whose children were stolen from them; I've seen those people who 'disappeared' over 100,000 Guatemalans – 'disappeared'! If you add it to the repression in Chile and add to that all the horrible things that have happened, to a Dominican Republic that's been invaded more than once, with that Trujillo regime supported by the United States, *created* by them, just like the Somoza regime in Nicaragua . . .

I've seen so many horrors since I wrote that message to Celia that I think the words I wrote were fair. And it wasn't against the Americans as a people; on the contrary, an American citizen is welcomed in Cuba more warmly than in any other country in the world. There are no prejudices or complexes here; complexes create hatred and contempt. Here there's no contempt for American citizens. The Cuban people have not been brought up to be chauvinists, or fanatics, they have been educated in ideas, in fair and reasonable ideas; we'd never have lasted if that weren't true. You can only sustain a revolution on the basis of that sort of ideas.

What would you say to those who were friends of Cuba in the beginning but who, in the face of so much criticism of the Revolution, now doubt you [Cubans], or even condemn you?
What I'd say to many of those who doubt, or who condemn us because they have certain ideas, is that they should ponder on the ability of this small country to resist, for almost half a century, the constant attacks of the most powerful nation in the world. That can't be done except on the basis of principles, on the basis of ideas, on the basis of ethics. It's the only way.

We believe in the human being, in his ability to acquire an ethics, a conscience, in his ability to make great sacrifices . . . [Sacrifices] even for a bad cause, because in the First World War, for example, you see the battlefields of the Marne, Verdun, where even day-labourers went off to fight because of the French national anthem, which is really beautiful, and the French flag . . . Men have gone off to die en masse for symbols, believing that those were things to give their lives for, when in fact they were defending the interests of empire, the great capitalists, the great colonial powers in Africa, Asia and other parts of the world.

Throughout history, one sees men die for honour, values that they can hold dear. Somebody inculcated [those values] in them. [I say,] inculcate the best values from the human point of view, from the point of view of justice, fraternity.

I'm very fond, as I've said, of that phrase from the French Revolution: 'Liberty, equality, fraternity.' Which was a forecast of things to come. Today, in this world, you can't talk about any one of those three things – not even liberty, after we've seen what's been happening all over the world, up there in the United Nations, in the Security Council, the way the United States reigns supreme. And it's impossible to talk about equality, whether between men or between nations. And fraternity is very hard to talk about – it's very hard to imagine fraternity prevailing in the world. Yet liberty, equality and fraternity *will* prevail, because those sentiments are springing forth everywhere.

And that's why I tried to explain that the role of intellectuals is very important, because only people of a certain intellectual level, whom we call intellectual workers, the professors, all those who organize strong, powerful movements through the internet, such as the protest before the war in Iraq, which arose out of the World Social Forum in Porto Alegre, and like the protest in Seattle[7] and many other places, which are now beginning to terrify the lords of the world.

I am convinced that no one will ever be able to establish a lasting Fascist-type regime in the United States, because there are traditions, there are ethical values, there are institutions . . . Generally speaking, Americans, when they do something, they think they're doing good; that's why the first thing some rulers do is try to fool them. But as Lincoln said, you can fool some of the people all the time and all the people some of the time, but you can't fool all the people all the time.

We consider ourselves fortunate to have been aware that hatred and prejudice are not political weapons. There are political weapons and, in addition, we have the experience to know that principles are the best possible political weapon.

Cuba has recently inscribed into its constitution that Socialism is an option . . .
It is irrevocable.

Do you think writing that into the constitution is sufficient guarantee to maintain Socialism in Cuba for ever?
No. But there's a reason for it. It's that on 20 May 2002 Señor Bush demanded that Cuba change its social and political system, that we establish capitalism here, a democracy resembling Nicaragua's or other countries', whose names there's no need to mention. And there was a response. The mass movement lasted for two months. There were big demonstrations, and a proposition to the National Assembly came out of them, which I've already talked to you about, with 8 million and something signatures, real signatures, because except for some people who may have a problem with their eyesight, or their arm, everyone who wanted to, signed it. Eight million signatures! And [there were] protests in many places because if you weren't within your own electoral district you couldn't sign. Nobody from Santiago, for example, who was out of the city at that moment could sign somewhere else, so there were big fights, lots of people saying, 'I want to sign!' Because for the election of national representatives, you *can* vote [outside your place of residence], but this time, it was decided that you wouldn't be able to.

[People who wanted to sign would have] tremendous arguments – it all happened in four days – because they didn't understand why they weren't allowed to sign. It might be an ambassador, who was in the country he'd been posted to, some other guy who was working, somebody on a trip – we don't have any idea how many thousands of signatures *weren't* collected because people weren't in their places of residence.

So then, I'll finish explaining it to you. Since a demand had been made on us to establish a capitalist system here on the island, we fought a great battle on behalf of our own Socialist system. For the first time, we brought together all the representatives of all the mass organizations, they discussed the responses one by one, and those millions of signatures unanimously supported this step.

A person may wonder how [the Socialist nature of the Revolution] can be irrevocable. Everything is revocable. In our constitution we established the way the National Assembly can modify the constitution; as a constitutional power, the Assembly could approve a modification almost without restrictions – though following certain procedural requirements, of course. Then we decided to declare that the Socialist nature of the Revolution was *irrevocable*. What does that mean? It means that in order to revoke the Socialist nature there has to be a revolution – or rather a *counter*-revolution. That is, you have to have a revolution, and that's not very easy to do with an educated, united populace. So it took on the character of a worthy response to what Bush was demanding up there in the United States. And that's the way it is now.

And that means that the enemies of the Revolution can take over the government legally – there's still a theoretical clause: they can go to the Assembly and be a majority; if they nominate delegates in the electoral districts and win a majority, if people vote for them and . . . I mean, through elections they might be able to take power. So, alongside that 'irrevocability' they *could* take power, and once in power [they could mount] a counter-revolution, through legal means. It's happened. And then do the same thing, collect so many millions of signatures, which they'll never be able to do, and declare it by decree, revoke Socialism by decree.

I say 'counter-revolution' because they'd have to take power to do that, and that doesn't mean by force; they are perfectly able, according to our electoral system, to take power with the legal mechanisms that are in place in the country today and that govern our electoral process. When we wrote it like that – *irrevocable* – it means *irrevocable*. It means that not even the Constituent Assembly can revoke it. That's the amendment to the constitution.

Now then, they [the opponents or enemy] could amend it through an electoral victory. They take power – it's a bit longer road – one is as hard as the other.

Are you optimistic about the future of Cuban society?
I can tell you one thing: we're optimistic; we know what our destiny is: a very hard but very heroic and very glorious one. This nation shall never be defeated, that's what I can say. This nation will achieve levels of knowledge and culture, on average, that will be, if you look at it as a marathon, several laps ahead of any other country in the world behind us, and I say this without chauvinism. I detest chauvinism – I like criticism, and constant criticism. Every time I talk about what we've done, I express shame and embarrassment for not having done more; every time we use things we've discovered, I express shame and embarrassment for not having discovered them earlier; every time we take advantage of new possibilities, I confess my sadness at not having been able to have those experiences earlier. Now, at least, we've created experience.

I'll tell you, this is a society that is increasingly cultured, increasingly knowledgeable, a society moving ahead at an increasingly swift rate, swifter than ever, towards the multiplication of its knowledge in every field: philosophy, politics, history, science, the arts . . . Everything is moving forward, because in recent years we have been able to acquire an awareness of the possibilities of modern technological methods for multiplying knowledge.

Let me cite the example of using the radio to teach people to read and write, or programmes broadcast on television for teaching people to read and write, for example, or the example of solar panels for constant electricity, which is never interrupted, to every little nook and hollow in the countryside, so that for very little cost we can take that knowledge, that culture, that learning, through television, anywhere.

Ignorance is the root of many ills. Knowledge must be the fundamental ally of nations that aspire, despite all their tragedies and problems, to become truly emancipated, to build a better world. I cite these examples, but the possibilities we've discovered go much further than people imagine; it's in our hands, in [the hands of] a united people, a united nation.

You've had several activities today. This last meeting between us is taking place very late at night, past midnight, despite the fatigue all these activities must have caused you . . .

Besides my usual responsibilities, at the end of the day I had two important activities: a television appearance, and a meeting with a delegation of ours that's leaving for an important international forum. Two important issues. That's why I'm a little late in resuming – with great pleasure – this conversation.

You continue to work long, intense days, and 13 August 2005 was your seventy-ninth birthday. I'd like to ask you – how is your health?

Well, I'm fine. Generally speaking, I feel fine; above all, I feel full of energy, I have great enthusiasm for things. I feel quite, quite well both physically and mentally. I'm sure the habit of exercise has contributed to that; in my opinion, physical exercise helps not just the muscles, it also helps the mind, because exercise has an effect on blood circulation, on the delivery of oxygen to all the cells, including the brain cells.

On 23 June 2001 you fainted during a public speech, and on 20 October 2004 you had a fall, in public that time, too, and fractured your knee. How have you recovered from those mishaps?

Well, I'll tell you, as usual there's been a lot of speculation about that. It's true that on 23 June 2001, in El Cotorro, a neighbourhood in Havana, on a day of intense heat, and during a speech that lasted more than three hours, broadcast live on television, I had a slight loss of consciousness. Something perfectly excusable. It was a slight fainting spell that lasted no more than a few minutes – due to the heat and the terrible sun. A few hours later, those people up there in Miami were already celebrating – what a surprise when they saw me reappear on a television programme and give people, live, the true version of what happened. [That episode] was no big thing. It could have happened to anybody that stood that long in such hot sun.

And what about the fall in Santa Clara?

About what happened on 20 October 2004 I wrote in a letter I sent to the people [of Cuba] the next day. At the end of a speech in Santa Clara, I tripped and fell. Some [news] agencies and other media reported several versions of the causes of the accident. As the person involved, I can explain what happened very precisely.[8]

I'd finished my speech – it was around ten at night. Several *compañeros* came up on to the dais to shake my hand. We stood up there for several minutes and then we started down some little wooden steps that we'd used to go up on to the stage. I was on my way to sit down in the same seat I'd been assigned before my turn on stage, and I was walking across the granite pavement and at the same time looking up and greeting people who'd been invited to the event, shaking hands, and so on from time to time.

When I came to the area of concrete, about fifteen or twenty yards from the first row of seats, I didn't see that the granite pavement was raised. When I stepped out with my left foot, there was no pavement there, my foot found no purchase, and the law of gravity, discovered some time ago by Newton, combined with my forward motion, made me, as I stepped out, lurch forward and fall, in a fraction of a second, on to the pavement. Out of instinct I put out my arms to catch myself; had I not, my face and head would have hit the pavement.

It was my own fault. The emotion of that day filled with creations and symbolisms[9] explains my carelessness. About eleven that night they took me to Havana in an ambulance, on a stretcher. Some analgesics helped the pain to an extent.

I remember that President Hugo Chávez called almost the minute he heard the news. He asked to speak to me, and we were able to talk thanks to wireless communications.

We arrived at the Palacio de la Revolución [in Havana] and I was immediately taken to a little facility they have there that's equipped, though minimally, for emergencies. The doctors confirmed that the complications were in my left knee and my right upper arm, where there was a hairline fracture of the humerus. My kneecap was broken into eight pieces. The specialists and patient agreed to operate on the knee and to immobilize the right arm in a sling.

The operation lasted three hours and fifteen minutes. The orthopaedists put each of the fragments in place and, like weavers, proceeded to sew them back together with a fine stainless-steel thread. They worked like jewellers, or clockmakers.

I asked the doctors not to sedate me, and they used a spinal anaesthetic, which numbs the lower half of the body but leaves the rest of the organism intact. Given the circumstances, it was necessary to avoid general anaesthesia so I would be able to deal with any important matter that came up. So the entire time I continued to receive information and give instructions on managing the situation that had been created by the unforeseen accident.

Once the surgical procedure was completed, the doctors proceeded to immobilize my leg with a cast, while at the same time doing much the same thing to my right arm.

The process of rehabilitation has been relatively brief; I've been doing a lot of swimming and exercise to recover the normal use of my leg and arm. I haven't ceased for a moment to see to all the country's affairs. And here I am, as you can see – I'm walking, moving around, and I'm living a normal life now, without a problem.[10]

Following up on just that, I'd like to address the issue of the future. Have you ever thought about retiring?

I'll tell you, we know that time passes and that human energies fade. But I'm going to tell you what I told our *compañeros* in the National Assembly on 6 March 2003, when they elected me president of the Council of State. I told them: 'Now I see that my fate was not to come into the world and rest at the end of my life.' And I promised them to be with them, if they wished, as long as necessary – so long as I knew myself to be useful. Not a minute less, or a second more.

Every year, I devote more time to the Revolution, I think; I give it more of my attention, because one has more experience, one has meditated more, thought more. Plato said in *The Republic* that the ideal age for occupying ruling positions is after fifty-five. In my opinion, according to him, that ideal age should be sixty. And I imagine that sixty in Plato's day would be somewhere around eighty today . . .

You ask me how long I'm going to be around. I tell you the truth – the National Assembly must decide that on behalf of the nation; the people must decide.

In November 2005 the CIA announced that you have Parkinson's disease. What comment do you have about that 'information'?

They're expecting a natural and absolutely logical phenomenon, which is someone's death. In this case they've done me the considerable honour of thinking about me. It must be a confession of what they haven't been able to do for so long: assassinate me. If I were a vain man, I might even be filled with pride by the fact that those morons now say they'll have to wait until I die. Every day they invent some [new story] – Castro's got this, Castro's got that, this disease or that. The latest thing they've come up with is that I have Parkinson's. The CIA says it discovered that I've got Parkinson's. Well, it doesn't matter if I get Parkinson's. Pope John Paul II had Parkinson's and he travelled all over the world for I don't know how many years – he had great strength of will.

As I said, I took a tremendous fall, and I'm still rehabilitating this arm, and getting better. Two units of blood were lost inside my shoulder and upper arm, which didn't appear in the X-ray. I didn't fall on my head – if I had, by all rights I wouldn't be here today. Those people that have 'killed me' so many times are probably almost glad, but they've had one disappointment after another.

I'm very grateful for the circumstances in which I broke my arm, because it forced me to be even more disciplined. I feel better than ever; I'm more disciplined and I do more exercise. I've also been forced to work hard on the issue of rehabilitation of my knee, so the kneecap will work better. I've made a real effort, and I'm still at it. I've learned that until my last second I'm going to be doing exercises. I don't neglect anything now, and I've got more willpower than ever with respect to eating what I should, and not eating a bite more than I should.

When you're doing exercise, you have to strengthen the arm gradually muscle by muscle, of course. How many people's hands have I shaken? Thousands! And some of them come up and try to pull your arm off; you can't exactly get even with them . . . You have to do like some people do – when you touch them there they tighten up their shoulder so people will think they've got lots of muscle, they're made of iron. Every time I shake somebody's hand I do that.

You almost always carry a pistol, but as a consequence of that fall, you've lost, I imagine, the use of your right arm and [thus] the possibility of using your weapon. Does that worry you?
Since those people in the CIA are always thinking things up – assassination attempts and so on – you can imagine that in all circumstances I would be carrying a weapon, and a weapon ready to be used. I follow that principle. I have a 15-shot Browning. I've shot a lot in my life. I've always been a good shot – it was just luck – and I still am. In any case, I have no fear of the enemy. The first thing I wanted to see was whether my arm was strong enough to handle the weapon I've always used, that's always been by my side. I [picked up] the clip, locked it into place, put on the safety, took it [the safety] off, pulled out the clip, took out the bullet, and said, 'All right. I can rest easy.' That was the next day. I felt I had the strength to fire it.

Because the day after the accident, they sent you to a hospital, took you out of that one, carried you somewhere else, you don't protest but you know everything they're doing to you, because they had to discuss the operation with me. Because if I honestly don't feel that I'm in condition to do something, I call the Party and say, 'Listen, I don't feel I'm in condition.' That's why I've criticized the doctors, because they've downplayed the seriousness of some things a little. And for my arm, I preferred rehabilitation. It was much more dangerous to undergo an operation with pins and so on. A person twenty or twenty-five years old, they can do those things to. But I said, 'Well, when all's said and done I'm not going to be pitching in the next baseball championship, I'm not going to be taking part in the Olympics.' I mean, I had to do the right thing.

If you think you're not in condition to carry out your responsibilities, you say, 'This whatever it is is happening to me – will someone please take over, assume command, I can't do it under these circumstances.' If I'm going to die, I'll die. If I don't die and I recover my faculties, then I assume command again. I'll step aside if they show me that's the best thing, the most useful way to go, or if I'm doing [the country] harm. Anyway, a person has some experience . . .

I had to worry about those things at that moment. We're not going to describe, we're not going to talk about what measures we had in place. We've taken measures and we have measures planned so there won't be any surprises, and our nation has to know exactly what to do in every case. Our enemies should not delude themselves; I die tomorrow and my influence may actually increase. I said once that the day I really die, nobody's going to believe it. I may be carried around like El Cid – even after he was dead his men carried him around on his horse, winning battles.

In several of your speeches and interviews, you yourself have brought up the question of your eventual succession – what will happen in Cuba the day you're no longer leading the country. How do you see Cuba's future without Fidel Castro?

Well, I'll try to be brief about that. I've told you about our plans concerning [my] physical elimination. Early on, my role was more decisive because we had to fight a very important battle of ideas, we had to do a lot of persuading. I told you that there were prejudices and that the Revolution's laws evolved over time. There were racial prejudices, anti-social prejudices, all the poison sown for such a long time.

You mean that for a long time, you've been thinking about the eventuality that you might be assassinated, and that you've had to think about what might happen . . . ?
Now you're almost asking me about the succession.

Yes, that's exactly what I'm asking about – the succession.
Well, I'll tell you, at first, with all those assassination plots, I had a decisive role, a decisive role that I don't have today. Today I may have more authority and more trust from the population than ever.

As I've told you, we study all the states of public opinion. We follow the state of public opinion with a microscope. And we can tell you the state of public opinion in Havana, for example, and in the rest of the country, and I can present you with all the opinions. Even the adverse ones. The vast majority are favourable.

The level of authority, after forty-six years of struggle and experience, is higher than it was. The authority of those of us who fought and waged the war, who led to the toppling of the tyranny and to the independence of this country, is very high.

Another privilege: age. Chance plays a role, too, because a person can come [into life] condemned to die an early death, due to natural factors, or die because of plots to kill you. And neither of those things has happened.

There's no great merit in having accumulated the experience that we've accumulated. If there *is* any merit, it's in the fact of being constant in our loyalty to ideas and principles, of not letting ourselves become all puffed up by power, or tempted to engage in abuses of power, which is quite frequent among human beings.

Back in those days, of course I realized what an assassination could mean, so I brought up the question of my replacement, and it was natural . . . Raúl was perceived as being more radical than I was. I mean, I don't think he was more radical than me, though I admit that he was *as* radical as I was. But since he'd been in the Young Communists, people saw Raúl as more radical. I knew they were afraid, that it worried them. That was one circumstance.

Second, in my opinion, and I can reiterate this, the person who had the most authority, most experience, and most ability to fill the role of replacement was Raúl. I told you how he fell prisoner at Moncada and how he turned the situation around, how he organized the column that got separated up there in the Second Front and then really did an excellent job as a military organizer and politician. Later, his mission in the armed forces . . . he's been an educator, a trainer of men, and with a great deal of equanimity and seriousness. He's the person who has the most authority today, and people have great trust in him.

Back in those days you could talk about men replacing men. At the time of the triumph of the Revolution, I was thirty-two years old; on 1 January 1959, at the triumph of the Revolution – Raúl's birthday is in June, he was twenty-eight – we all had a lot of life ahead of us.

There were assassination plans for Raúl, too, although I was a more attractive target because of the command chain and my responsibilities. He's the second secretary of the Party and first vice president of the Council of State – that gives him moral and political authority.

If for some reason you should die, Raúl, then, would be your undisputed successor?
If something happens to me tomorrow, [I'll tell you] with absolute certainty that the National Assembly would meet and elect him – there's not the slightest doubt. The Political Committee would meet and elect him.

But he's catching up to me in years, so it's also a generational problem. We've been fortunate that we who made the Revolution have brought up three generations. Nor can we forget those who came before us, the old militants and leaders of the Popular Socialist Party, which was the Marxist-Leninist party – with us, you see, a new generation came in. Then later, the generation that came after us, and immediately after, the men and women in the literacy campaign, the fight against the bandits, the struggle against the blockade, the fight against terrorism, the fight at Girón, those who lived through the October crisis, the internationalist missions . . . a lot of people of great merit. And many people in the sciences, in technology, heroes of labour, intellectuals, teachers . . . That's another generation. Add to that the youngsters that are now in the Youth, university students and social workers, with whom we have very close ties. There have always been close ties with young people and students.

That is, you think that your real replacement, more than a person, more than Raúl, will be an entire generation, the current generation . . .
That's right – already some generations are replacing others. I'm confident, and I've always said this, but we're aware that there are many dangers that can threaten a revolutionary process. There are the errors of a sub-

jective nature . . . Certain errors existed, and we're responsible for not having discovered certain tendencies and errors. Today, they've simply been overcome.

I told you what will happen tomorrow, but now there are new generations, because ours is passing. Now the youngest [of our generation] – I've mentioned the case of Raúl, for example – is barely four years and something younger than I am.

This first generation still cooperates with the new generations that recognize the authority of the few of us who are still around . . . Then there was the second, and now there's the third and fourth . . . I have a clear idea of what the fourth generation is going to be like, because you see those kids in the sixth grade giving their speeches. What talent we've discovered!

We've discovered thousands of talents – these kids are impressive, striking. Who knows how much genius, how much talent there is among the people. I harbour the theory that talent is everywhere, if not in one thing then in another – for computers or for music or for mechanics. Genius is common and some have it in one thing and some have it in another. Now, you develop and educate a complex society – that's what we're doing – and we'll see what comes of it. Those are the 8 million people who after several years of the special period declared, 'I am a Socialist.'

I have a great deal of hope, because I see clearly that these people I call the fourth generation are going to have three or four times the knowledge that we in the first generation had, and more or less, over three times the knowledge of the second. And the fourth should know, with everything that's being done now, at least two and a half times what the third does.

Let me tell you this: more people will come here to see the social development of this country, the social achievements in this country, than Cuba's beaches. Our country is doing impressive things. A small country like ours is able to send the personnel needed by the United Nations for the campaign the secretary-general proposed for wiping out AIDS in Africa. Today that can't be done without Cuban doctors. Between the United States and Europe, they can't bring together 1,000 doctors to go where our doctors are. I say 1,000 because I'm exaggerating; no one knows how many. After the sixth Non-Aligned Summit, we offered the United Nations several thousand doctors to work in aiding the social development of the poor nations. Now, in Africa alone, there are more than 3,000 of them. And that produces a certain satisfaction in this country under a blockade, in this country that has suffered over forty years of blockade and ten years of a special period. It has created human capital, and human capital is not created with egoism, or by stimulating individualism in society.

Are you saying that the Revolution is not exhausted, not spent?
We aren't done by a long shot. We live in the best time in our history, with the greatest hope ever, and you see it everywhere.

It's true, it's correct, I'd be willing to agree with the charge that we committed some errors of idealism, maybe we tried to go too far too fast, maybe we underestimated strength, the weight of habit and other factors. But no country has faced any adversary so powerful, so rich, its publicity machinery, its blockade, combined with the sudden disintegration of its point of support – the USSR disappeared and we were left alone, and we never wavered. Yes, we had the support of most of the people – I won't say all, because some became discouraged – but we have witnessed things that this country has done, how it has resisted, how it has advanced, how unemployment has fallen, how awareness has grown.

You don't have to measure our elections by the number of votes. I measure them by the depth of sentiments, by the warmth that I've been seeing for so many years. I never saw faces so filled with hope, with pride. And all that has been coming together.

So you think the baton can be passed on without problem now?
Right away there wouldn't be any problem of any kind, and there won't be later, either. Because the Revolution is not based on *caudillista* ideas, or the cult of personality. In Socialism, the idea of a *caudillo* is inconceivable; it's inconceivable in modern society, as well – people doing things just because they have blind faith in the leader or because the leader asks them to. The Revolution is based on principles. And the ideas that we defend have been, for quite some time, ideas shared by the entire nation.

I see that you aren't worried about the Cuban Revolution's future, yet in recent years you have been witness to the collapse of the Soviet Union, the collapse of Yugoslavia, the collapse of the Albanian revolution, North Korea in such a sad situation, Cambodia, which spiralled into horror, even China, where the revolution has taken a very different turn. Don't all those things distress you?
I think that the experience of the first Socialist state, the USSR, a state which should have repaired itself and never have destroyed itself, has been very

bitter. Don't think we haven't thought a great deal about that incredible phenomenon whereby one of the most potent powers in the world, which had managed to bring its strength up to that of the other superpower, a country that smashed Fascism, collapsed as it did.

There were those who thought that capitalist methods would allow them to construct Socialism. That is one of the great errors in history. I don't want to talk about that, I don't want to theorize, but I have countless examples of times when the people who were supposed to be theorists failed to interpret correctly the philosophy of Marx, Engels and Lenin, and made major errors.

I said once that one of our own greatest errors in the beginning, and many times down through the years of the Revolution, was to believe that somebody knew how Socialism ought to be constructed. Today we have ideas that are, in my opinion, quite clear about how Socialism should be built, but we need many very clear ideas and many questions about how the future of Socialism can be, or will be, preserved.

As for China, that's another thing, a great power that emerged and a great power that did not destroy its history, a great power that held to certain fundamental principles, that sought unity, that didn't fragment its forces.

I shouldn't be a judge of that, but I'd say that China is a great economic and political power that must be reckoned with, and, of course, every period and every nation will need increasingly well prepared, increasingly able leaders. It's a new world that's emerging now. We have adapted to this world, we continue to adapt, and we're learning what to do. We've developed sentiments of solidarity, revolutionary awareness, values that have immense power.

So I can tell you, and it's something that's a continual source of curiosity, that when huge powers such as the USSR, when so many regimes that you cite and so many things are destroyed, this country under blockade and still not having fully emerged from the special period can share [its wealth], give aid, educate thousands and thousands of Third World university professionals – without charging a cent – and advance, really, on every front, in every field.

We will survive by our human capital. With that human capital we can help many people, with our experience we can do that, and with that experience we can help ourselves.

I'm not worried, because what we've done is observe, observe, observe. And I told you that there are dangers – watch out! – I've sometimes seen errors. If they're not caught in time . . . You have always to be on your guard against the dangers. You have to be almost clairvoyant, think and think and think, but think about alternatives. The habit of looking for alternatives and choosing from among the best of them is a very good habit.

But the question that some people ask themselves is whether the Socialist revolutionary process in Cuba may not also collapse.

Is it that revolutions are bound to collapse, or is it that men cause revolutions to collapse? Can men prevent revolutions from collapsing or can't they? Can society prevent revolutions from collapsing or can't it? I've often asked myself those questions. And this is what I have to say about [those questions]: the Yankees can't destroy this revolutionary process, because we have an entire nation that's learned to handle weapons, an entire nation that despite our errors, has such a high degree of culture, knowledge and awareness that it will never, ever again allow this country to become a colony of theirs.

But this country can *self*-destruct, can destroy itself. This Revolution can destroy itself. We, we can destroy it, and we would be to blame. If we are not capable of correcting our errors. If we don't manage to put an end to many vices – a great deal of theft, a great many diversions [of funds and goods], a great many sources for providing money to those who have become rich in the special period – and never return to them.

And that's why we are acting, we are marching towards a total change in our society. We must change yet again, because we've had very difficult times – inequalities were created, injustices. And we're going to change that without committing the slightest abuse. I can assure you today that resolving these problems is a perfectly achievable goal.

There will be greater and greater participation and we will be a nation with a holistic, unified general culture. Martí said, 'Being cultured is the only way to be free.' Without culture, freedom is not possible.

That is why I also have strong reservations, strong criticism of neoliberal globalization, a system that causes people to go hungry. Living in self-delusion, in lies, sowing egotism, creating consumerism – what for? So that people can reach this condition, when they haven't even been able so far to guarantee their survival?

We can't erect a statue to ourselves for our political abilities – the world is menaced by literally countless dangers. We still have to show whether we're capable of surviving. Since I'm an optimist, I do have hope that this world will survive, because I see it react, I see that humankind, despite its errors and its millennia of history – several millennia, three or four – in one century has multiplied its knowledge. But many aspects of that progress have served to sow poison, served to transmit false ideas, transmit erroneous information.

I try to analyse where we made progress and where there were setbacks, where we fell into routine and where we fell into the habit of copying. A few qualities like the habit of not copying, trusting in the country itself, combating chauvinism ... One country is not better than another, one people is not better than another – they all have their national, cultural characteristics. You can see that in Latin America – we are a whole range of nations who speak the same language; we have almost identical cultures, the same religion, the same idiosyncrasies – we're the same mix.

One sees that in Europe the Finns, the Hungarians – people who speak languages that are really, really hard to learn – are all coming together; the Germans, the Italians and all the rest, a continent that was at war with itself for 500 years ... Well, they should be congratulated, despite my sometimes critical opinions, for the degree of unity they've achieved. And I must say that it will be to the benefit of the entire world if they're successful. Now then, we have to see how it goes, because the problems, in this period of neoliberal globalization, are very complex, as you know very well.

Thank you for your interest. I've been very stimulated by your interest, because I've read many of your articles, and your books have been useful to us, and what we want is for you to keep writing books – we'll benefit from them; we still have a lot to learn. You help us to create a holistic general culture, because how can a person live in this world without that holistic general culture? The world could not be saved.

I also have hope that most of the programmes that we are engaged in will be experiences that others can benefit from. We don't aspire to paternity, we want no patent; on the contrary, we are proud when someone does something useful that's been inspired by what we do here.

[You and I] have worked many hours and I've enjoyed it – it's been a great pleasure, and in a few minutes we'll take our leave of each other.

I think I've taken far too much of your time.
No, we've been working seventeen or eighteen hours a day and we're fine. Clearly, you're in good shape, because I think you've worked harder than I have.

It's been very interesting, listening to you.
I feel the same way about your questions. I'm as interested as you are in all these subjects, and our country's doors will always be open to any interest, any question. We will never tell you a lie.

Thank you, comandante.

A Note on the Text and the Translation

The original text for this translation was the proof pages for the first edition, in Spain,[1] of *Fidel Castro: Biografía a dos voces*, supplemented with corrections to the book as it went to press. These corrections were not substantive; they were the usual changes associated with spelling errors, awkward phrasings, small errors of fact or date and so on, found by the copy-editor and author in proof pages before book publication. My English translation of that edition was completed and delivered to the English publisher, Penguin UK, in early February 2007.

In May 2007 a new set of proof pages was sent me, and I was informed that they belonged to a new, completely revised and restructured edition, which Penguin wished to use as a basis for the English-language version. This second Spanish-language edition was some 100 pages longer than the first. As Ignacio Ramonet indicates in his introduction, a new chapter had been added, as had some comments on Castro's mother, letters dealing with the Cuban missile crisis, new information on Cuba's response to the coup in Venezuela in 2002, an extension to the Chronology and so on, and the introduction had been expanded to address Castro's fall and his recent more severe health problems. But those additions accounted for only some fifty to sixty pages; the other forty to fifty pages were scattered throughout the book, in snippets here and there. I learned, in response to queries made to Ramonet and Pedro Alvarez Tabío, the Cuban editor of the book and one of Castro's closest associates, that the pages sent to the press with these additions and changes, in both Spanish and French, were not available. Given that we had nothing to go on, my editor and I consulted as to how to set about revising and expanding my already existing translation, and we decided that what was needed was a full set of second-edition pages marked up with every change (from the minutiae of punctuation and the transposition of words and phrases, to additions and cuts, to the macro-changes involved in chapter rearrangement and restructuring) that had been introduced into the first edition.

To produce that set of pages, I turned to Waldemar Burgos, Romina Iglesias and Olga Uribe, who, over a period of about three weeks and hundreds of hours, compared the published first edition with the final but unbound pages of the second Spanish edition and marked up those unbound pages. I then took those marked-up pages and proceeded to revise my translation. Ramonet says that the book was 'totally revised [and] amended'; in my view, the key word there is 'totally'. Every page was covered with markings; as I've told people, the annotations looked like ants at a picnic. Tens of thousands of changes had been made to the book, and although not all of them produced parallel changes to the translation (for instance, the word-order of a sentence in Spanish might already have been recast to conform to English usage, making any change to the word-order in English unnecessary), most did. Thus, the English translation that the reader is now holding parallels, insofar as humanly possible given the scope and number of modifications, the second and definitive Spanish edition of the book.

But for me as the translator, this total revision presented a problem of what might be seen either as fidelity to the book or loyalty to the end-reader. Consider: the first Spanish edition was 'out there'. It had been extensively reviewed and commented on, not to mention that judging by book sales it had been read by tens of thousands of readers. Thus, especially with regard to the *cuts* made to the first edition, there were two clear and distinct versions available in Spanish and able to be compared. Readers of the English translation, however, would have only the revised and amended version, and for English-speaking Cuba-watchers and Castro-watchers and other interested but monolingual readers, no comparison between the two editions would be possible. Why was this problematic? In dozens of cases Castro made subtle and sometimes not-so-subtle changes whose effect was not, of course, to censor anything he might have said, in the sense of to suppress a truth, but rather to soften a judgement, or to avoid a 'politically incorrect' statement, or to be more diplomatic. Castro will often be seen in these pages to be surprisingly, I think, outspoken; for the second edition, some of his more direct and uninhibited statements wound up on the cutting-room floor. Of course many of the cuts made were clearly intended to reduce repetitions, a quite understandable (even, perhaps, laudable) goal in a book of this size and complexity, but many, too, seemed to have been made only in order to present a less 'outspoken' or 'unbuttoned' image. Those changes, I thought, were 'interesting': historically interesting, that is, because they were words spoken by Castro and recorded for posterity; but also interesting in that they revealed Castro's mind at work during moments *before* the super-ego of hindsight and counsel kicked in. I thought it important that readers in English have some of the 'bi-ocular' experience that readers in Spanish, comparing the two versions, might have, and so, by way of example, I have left some cuts with the indication '(in 1st ed.)'. I have not wished, and do not now wish, to categorize these changes – that task is one for historians and social scientists – but I have wished to allow interested readers to see the *pentimenti* of a fascinating mind.

Regardless of cuts or 'self-censorship', to my mind there is no question that the second edition of the book is superior to the first, in both fullness of historical detail and accuracy of transcription – that is, fidelity to Castro's words. In the first Spanish edition, there were many ellipses, those three editorial dots that say 'something's not here', and in his introduction Ramonet says early on that 'Fidel answered [questions] calmly, sometimes in a voice so low that it was just a whisper, almost inaudible.' As I came upon instance after instance of uncompleted sentences, hanging verbs, uncertain direction of the thought in the first edition, I believed that at those moments Castro's voice had tapered off and become inaudible, or that he had simply become vague, or lost his train of thought. Now I think how little credit I gave his eighty-year-old mind, for in the second edition, someone has either gone back to the recordings and listened more carefully and retranscribed many passages (and that, I think, is the most probable scenario), or has reconstructed the words spoken by Castro (this, I think, would probably have been done by Castro himself) and inserted them. For this, all readers of the book can be grateful, and I count myself among the first in gratitude, because I now see that my guesses as to where the thought was going were sometimes mildly, sometimes wildly off, and thus misleading to my readers. Since often a clause in Spanish can begin with a verb, with the subject coming later, I would try to guess at where that hanging verb was headed and what the grammatically plural or singular subject was – where I thought Castro was going. Now that I see what he was actually saying, I can report that the results of my guesswork were not always what I might have wished. So now, all those ellipses have been filled in, no one need any longer trust the translator's mind-reading skills, and Castro's thought is completed in a way that will leave no one in any doubt as to his lucidity and strength of reasoning and ability to craft a complete thought. In addition, misunderstandings on the part of the original transcriber(s) have been corrected in several instances. Anyone who has ever transcribed a deposition knows how difficult that work is; in the haste to publish the first edition, it may be that not enough time was budgeted for rechecking the recordings, but now those lacunae and mishearings have been corrected.

I would like to address that issue of 'transcribing oral discourse' for a moment. From the first, given that this book consisted of one long interview with Fidel Castro, I translated it as though it were, in fact, a legal deposition. By that I don't mean that I tried to produce a

word-for-word, 'literal' translation; such a creature is a figment of the imagination, impossible in art or nature. Rather, I did not put words in Castro's mouth; I let him speak for
himself. What this has meant in practice is that where Castro used pronouns rather than
nouns or names, and where the Spanish was clear but, due to differing rules as to the
pronoun-antecedent relationship, the resulting pronoun (he, they) would not be clear in
English, I have specified the noun or name in brackets. Likewise, where an assumption or
subtext in a Spanish speaker's or interlocutor's mind was implicit but clear, yet would not
be clear to an English reader, I inserted that assumption or subtext in brackets in the text.
Third, where the words were clear but might be misinterpreted by an English reader, due to
differences between English and Spanish in the conventions of 'shorthand' expressions, I
sometimes inserted an 'i.e.' explanation in brackets. Thus, throughout the text, brackets will
always indicate to the reader those places where I have taken 'editorial licence'. Less often,
I have used [sic], generally for numbers, where there is a clear contradiction with a verified
footnote figure or previous figure in the text itself.

Not a few of the changes made to the original Spanish version of this book were aimed at
reducing some of the orality of the text, taking out some of the 'filler' words and hemming and
hawing that we all use as we form our thoughts and speak. There again, I perceived a problem:
at the point where letters exchanged between Castro and Khrushchev during the Cuban missile
crisis were inserted, Castro is made to say, roughly, 'Let me read you these letters.' Thus,
some attempt was made to preserve the illusion that this book is a straightforward interview,
when in fact Ramonet has told readers in his introduction that those letters were inserted
long after the book had gone to print, and that Castro never actually read them to him. That
is, we know from the introduction that the text has been 'edited', yet it is still presented as
an uninterrupted interview. Taking my cue from the addition of the letters and other similar
sections, I decided not to limit the orality of the text so greatly as the editor's (or Castro's)
cuts might have led me to; instead, I have tried to maintain some sense of Castro's eloquent
speech patterns and expressiveness, including those introductory words and phrases that all
Cubans use. This is the only place I have been wilfully, and silently, 'unfaithful' to the cuts
of the first edition, and it was in the service of a higher loyalty – to Castro's speaking voice.

Both Spanish versions of this book have many endnotes, most providing biographical and
historical information on figures mentioned by Castro. I was struck as I began translating,
however, that many figures who were part of the modern history of Spain (the country of
original publication) or France (Ramonet's country of residence and the book's second
publication venue) were not noted – Ramonet's assumption being, I imagined, that readers
would be familiar enough with the figures as to need no footnoted explanations – and so I
began to add notes for those personages, under the complementary assumption that my own
English-speaking readers would not be so familiar with them as their European counterparts
would be. I have also added notes for virtually every other figure mentioned but unnoted in
the original, in an attempt at simple thoroughness and so as not to presume too much on
my readers' familiarity with all of the dozens of figures that Castro mentions. In the case of
culturally grounded facts, objects, dates, etc., I have added explanatory notes, thereby, I
hope, 'cross-culturing' the text. All the notes added by me, as well as my expansions of
existing notes, are bracketed and bear the annotation ' – Trans.'

The reader will note one word in particular used throughout in untranslated Spanish: the
word *compañero*. It is clear from the context surrounding virtually every use of this word in
the Spanish that Castro has a clear meaning in mind. It is not the Russian Communists'
'comrade' (or 'Comrade', capitalized), although it shares some nuances with that word.
Rather, it indicates those closest to Castro: most often it refers to a member of his group of
advisers today; sometimes it refers to a member of that original group that made the attack
on the Moncada military barracks complex; sometimes it refers to one of the original
members of the 26th of July Movement. In every case where I have left the word untranslated,
the reader may be sure that the context makes clear that this is one of the 'in-group' with
Castro at the time he is speaking about, his closest and most trusted associates and colleagues
and advisers. Often, one senses great affection when Castro uses this word.

When I was approached about my availability to do this translation, I thought it only fair that Ignacio Ramonet and Fidel Castro be apprised of who their translator-to-be might be. Over the more than twenty-five years of my career as a translator, I have translated books by quite a number of anti-Castro figures or *personae non gratae*, including Armando Valladares, Heberto Padilla, Reinaldo Arenas and Jorge Edwards. But my ideology as a translator has never had anything to do with anti-Castroism. Rather, I believe that translators have the duty and obligation to translate voices that would otherwise not be heard, simply on the basis of language. I believe that while popular voices, voices that ratify our beliefs and worldviews should be heard, it may in the long run be more important that unpopular or unexpected or challenging, defiant voices, voices that have a viewpoint wholly different from our own, be heard – especially by our often complacent and self-centred English-language (and more especially, in that regard, American) society, and thus in my work I take somewhat the position of a defence lawyer: I commit myself first of all to the authors and cultures I translate, rather than to my readers' or my 'home culture's' comfort, so that I may give those authors a voice and secure for them a fair hearing. In the case at hand, I saw, and see, Fidel Castro as one of the most 'censored' world figures in English-language publishing, English-language society. Spanish-language readers can access his thoughts and words online and in print, but in English Castro is 'represented', as Ramonet himself says, almost invariably by his enemies. I explained my career and my position to my editor and asked him to take it to Ramonet and Castro, and I see it as a mark of their self-assurance and sense of realpolitik that neither of them objected to my taking on their project and this once being a conduit for the words and thoughts of 'the great devil', as Castro admits his adversaries think of him. I hope I have proved myself deserving of their trust as I have tried to let Castro speak his own mind in his own words, though translated.

I want to make public my deep gratitude to Waldemar Burgos, Romina Iglesias and Olga Uribe for their painstaking and eye-crossing work comparing the first and second versions of this book, and for the excellence of the pages they produced. I literally could not have done this without them. I am indebted, too, to my brother, John Hurley, lifelong hunter, for help with the nomenclature and functioning of firearms, about which I know very little. And I thank my editor at Penguin UK, Will Goodlad, for his constant advocacy for publishing the best book we possibly could – with all the delays, redoings, postponements and frustrations that entailed; he was always perfectly steadfast, and I'm grateful. My wife, Isabel, was particularly understanding throughout this project – more, even, than she usually is, which is a lot – and I am almost inexpressibly grateful to her for that.

Andrew Hurley
San Juan, Puerto Rico

Some Key Dates in the Life of Fidel Castro and the Cuban Revolution (1926–2007)

13 August 1926: Fidel Alejandro Castro Ruz is born in Birán, Mayarí, in the former province of Oriente (now Holguín), on his father's farm 'Manacas'.

On 25 March 1911 Fidel's father, Ángel Castro Argiz (b. 5 December 1875) married María Argota Reyes, a Cuban woman from Banes, in the province of Oriente, and the couple had two children: Pedro Castro Argota (b. 1914) and Antonia Castro Argota (b. 1915). After a divorce from María, Angel entered into a relationship with Lina Ruz González (b. 23 September 1903), twenty-eight years younger than he. They married on 26 April 1943, after she had borne seven children: Angela (1923), Ramón (1924), Fidel, Raúl (1931), Juana (1933), Emma (1935) and Agustina (1938).

14 June 1928: Ernesto Guevara de la Serna is born in Rosario de Santa Fe, Argentina; he will later be known throughout the world as 'Che'.

24 October 1929: 'Black Thursday': the New York Stock Exchange collapses, triggering a profound financial depression in the United States, with repercussions in Cuba; tens of thousands of Cuban workers are left without jobs.

September 1930: Fidel enters first grade in the little school in Birán.

14 April 1931: The Republic is proclaimed in Spain. King Alfonso XIII goes into exile.

3 June 1931: Raúl Castro is born in Birán.

23 January 1932: The government of the Republic of Spain dissolves the Company of Jesus. The Jesuits are expelled and a number of them take up residence in Cuba.

8 November 1932: Franklin Delano Roosevelt is elected president of the United States.

Late 1932: Fidel Castro is sent by his parents to Santiago de Cuba, where he lives in the house of his teacher Eufrasia Feliú; financial conditions are straitened.

30 January 1933: Adolf Hitler comes to power in Germany.

12 August 1933: Cuban dictator Gerardo Machado is toppled by a general strike; a provisional government assumes power.

4 September 1933: The provisional government of Cuba is overthrown by the 'Sergeants' Uprising', one of whose leaders is Fulgencio Batista. Ramón Grau San Martín assumes the presidency.

14 January 1934: Fulgencio Batista, head of the Army General Staff, overthrows president Ramón Grau San Martín. For the next ten years, with the complicity of the United States, Batista will dominate the political life of Cuba in one way or another, first naming puppet-presidents – Carlos Mendieta (1934–5), José A. Barnet (1935–6), Miguel Mariano Gómez (1936), Federico Laredo Bru (1936–40) – and then having himself elected president (1940–44).

21 February 1934: In Nicaragua, Augusto César Sandino, the 'General of the Free', who had fought in the American occupation, is assassinated by followers of Somoza.

29 May 1934: Under the 'Good Neighbour' policy, the Roosevelt administration abrogates the Platt Amendment, which had been imposed by the US on the new Cuban republic and which allowed the United States to intervene in Cuba as it wished.

5–19 October 1934: In Spain, the 'Asturias revolution' takes place, a bloody workers' insurrection that is soon put down by colonial troops sent in by General Franco.

18 October 1934: The 'Long March' begins in China. Mao Zedong leads some 86,000 Communists to Yenan over a route that covers, according to most estimates, between 10,000 and 13,000 kilometres, or 6,200 to 8,000 miles; only about 3,000 of those who begin the march survive.

January 1935: Fidel Castro is baptized in Santiago de Cuba and enters the Catholic Colegio de La Salle in that city, where he begins the second semester of first grade.

March 1935: A general strike is called against Batista's policies; the strike is put down violently.

3 October 1935: Benito Mussolini's Italian Fascist troops invade Abyssinia, now Ethiopia.

18 July 1936: The Spanish Civil War begins. The Republic is embattled and finally defeated (see below, 1 April 1939) by Nationalist forces backed by Fascist Italy and Nazi Germany.

19–24 August 1936: In the Soviet Union, the Moscow show trials and Stalinist purges begin. Grigori Zinoviev and Lev Kamenev, among many others, are sentenced to death and executed. Stalin's objective is to 'purge' the Communist Party by eliminating the first Bolsheviks, who are very popular; he uses show trials to discredit the Bolsheviks in the eyes of the general population before sending them into the Gulag or executing them.

17–23 January 1937: In the Soviet Union, the second round of show trials takes place in Moscow. Georgy (Yuri) Piatakov, among others, is sentenced to death and executed. Karl Radek is sentenced to ten years in the Gulag.

June 1937: In the Soviet Union, the third round of trials takes place – this time, secret military tribunals for generals in the Red Army. Marshal Mikhail Tukhachevsky, among others, is sentenced to death; he is executed on 11 June. During this period, 60 per cent of the marshals and one-third of the lower-ranking officers in the Red Army are arrested and sent to the firing squad.

2–13 March 1938: In the Soviet Union, fourth and last series of trials. Alexei Rykov, Nikolai Bukharin and Genrikh Iagoda, among others, are sentenced to death and executed.

23 September 1938: In Spain, the International Brigades, composed of volunteers from fifty-four countries who have enlisted to defend democracy against Fascism, retreat.

1 April 1939: End of the Spanish Civil War. The Republic has been defeated by the Nationalist forces; the dictatorship of Generalísimo Francisco Franco begins.

27 May 1939: The SS *St Louis* arrives in Havana from Hamburg carrying 1,000 German Jews fleeing Hitler's repression. The exiles have Cuban visas issued by the Cuban consulate in Berlin, but Batista and Cuban president Laredo Bru organize anti-Semitic protest demonstrations and refuse to let the exiles disembark. The ship is forced to set sail again with all its passengers, but neither the United States nor Canada will accept them; the ship finally returns to Nazi Germany, where most of the passengers will be taken off to extermination camps.

23 August 1939: In Moscow, Germany and the Soviet Union sign a non-aggression agreement, later to be known as the Molotov–Ribbentrop Pact.

September 1939: Fidel Castro enters the Colegio de Dolores, run by the Order of Jesus, the Jesuits, in Santiago de Cuba.

1 September 1939: The Army of the Third Reich invades Poland. The Second World War begins. Germany and the Soviet Union partition Poland.

22 June 1941: Germany invades the Soviet Union. Beginning of Operation Barbarossa.

1 July 1941: In the US, commercial television is born. CBS and NBC broadcast fifteen hours of live programming a week.

September 1942: Fidel Castro enters the famous Colegio de Belén, the Belén Preparatory School, another Jesuit school, in Havana.

4 June 1943: In Argentina, a coup is launched by the United Officers Group (Grupo de Oficiales Unidos, GOU), one of whose members is Colonel Juan Perón, who in November will be made secretary of labour and social security and soon become very popular with the country's workers.

10 October 1944: Ramón Grau San Martín, the 'Authentic' Cuban Revolutionary Party candidate for president in the island's first free elections, once again becomes president of the Republic. There are high hopes for his presidency, but they are soon dashed by the extreme corruption of his administration.

4–11 February 1945: In the Crimea, the Yalta Conference, attended by Stalin (USSR), Churchill (UK), and Roosevelt (US), takes place. The 'Big Three' divide the world into zones of influence.

8 May 1945: End of Second World War in Europe with the defeat of Nazi Germany.

June 1945: Fidel Castro graduates from the Colegio de Belén.

26 June 1945: At a conference in San Francisco, representatives of fifty countries, among them Cuba, sign the charter founding the United Nations (UN).

6 August 1945: The United States drops the first atomic bomb on the Japanese city of Hiroshima; 100,000 are killed. Several days later, another atomic bomb is dropped on Nagasaki. The Nuclear Age begins.

2 September 1945: Japan surrenders. Second World War ends in Asia and the Pacific.

4 September 1945: Fidel Castro enters the University of Havana, enrolling in the faculties of law and social sciences.

24 February 1946: In Argentina, Juan Perón is elected president.

5 March 1946: Former English prime minister Winston Churchill (he has failed to be re-elected) delivers an anti-Soviet speech at small Westminster College, in Fulton, Missouri, where he is receiving an honorary degree. It is in this speech that Churchill uses the phrase 'Iron Curtain' for the Soviet partition of Europe; many see this as the beginning of the Cold War.

3 July 1946: The Philippines, ceded to the United States by Spain, along with Cuba and Puerto Rico, in 1898, at the end of the Spanish-American War, become an independent nation.

12 March 1947: US president Harry Truman defines his Communist 'containment' doctrine; it will come to be known as the Truman Doctrine.

26 July 1947: In Washington, DC, President Harry Truman signs the National Security Act, creating the Central Intelligence Agency (CIA).

July–September 1947: Fidel Castro takes part in preparations for the frustrated Cayo Confites expedition to topple the Rafael Trujillo dictatorship in the Dominican Republic.

25 February 1948: In Czechoslovakia, the 'Prague coup' occurs; the Communists, with Klement Gottwald as leader, take power.

17 March 1948: In Europe, the Treaty of Brussels is signed, prefiguring the creation of the North Atlantic Treaty Organization (NATO), a military–political alliance dominated by the United States and created to fight the 'Communist menace'.

24 March 1948: Under the auspices of UNESCO, the Havana Charter is adopted, which calls for the creation of an International Trade Organization. Rejected by the US Congress, the Havana Charter never goes into effect.

31 March 1948: As part of a trip through several Latin American countries leading up to a large student conference, Fidel Castro arrives in Bogotá, capital of Colombia.

9 April 1948: Colombian populist leader Jorge Eliécer Gaitán is assassinated in Bogotá, triggering a popular uprising known as the 'Bogotazo'. Fidel Castro takes part in these riots and demonstrations.

30 April 1948: In Bogotá, the Ninth Pan-American Conference, which Cuba attends, adopts the charter creating the Organization of American States.

10 October 1948: Carlos Prío Socarrás, of the Cuban Revolutionary Party, becomes president of the Republic and deepens the rift with the 'Authentics'.

12 October 1948: Fidel Castro marries Mirtha Díaz-Balart, daughter of a wealthy, politically influential Cuban family (they will divorce in 1955). They honeymoon in New York City.

4 April 1949: In Washington, DC, the North Atlantic Treaty is signed and NATO is created.

1 September 1949: Fidel Castro's first child is born, Fidel Félix Castro Díaz-Balart, 'Fidelito'.

1 October 1949: Mao Zedong, whose forces have occupied Beijing since 1 January, proclaims the People's Republic of China.

14 February 1950: In Moscow, Mao Zedong and Stalin sign the Sino–Soviet Treaty of Friendship and Alliance.

June 1950: Fidel Castro graduates from law school with a degree in law and is admitted to the bar.

15 June 1950: In West Berlin, Michael Josselson, a CIA agent, creates the Congress for Cultural Freedom, which for almost thirty years, with the participation of many prestigious intellectuals and artists, will organize cultural activities 'to expose Communist cultural oppression and oppose all forms of totalitarian rule', as his biographical sketch for the Harry Ransom Center at the University of Texas says.

25 June 1950: The Korean War begins.

April 1951: In Tehran, Iranian prime minister Mohammed Mossadegh nationalizes the oil reserves.

June 1951: In Bolivia, the presidential election, won by Nationalist Revolutionary Movement (MNR) candidate Víctor Paz Estenssoro, is annulled by the military. MNR members organize for an armed defence of the election results.

16 August 1951: Days after shooting himself in the abdomen at the end of a radio programme, Cuban senator Eduardo Chibás dies. In 1947 Chibás founded the 'Orthodox' Cuban People's Party, with which Fidel Castro was politically linked.

10 March 1952: Second coup by General Fulgencio Batista, three months before the general elections, which the Orthodox Party candidate had been expected to win. President Carlos Prío Socarrás is overthrown and Batista institutes a repressive far-right, pro-American dictatorship.

9 April 1952: After three days of fighting in La Paz, Bolivia, with several hundred people killed, MNR militants, *campesino* militias, and the country's miners take power. Universal suffrage is instituted. The country's tin mines are nationalized in October, and August of 1953 brings agrarian reform and a reform of the educational system, making elementary education free and compulsory.

20 January 1953: In Washington, DC, former general Dwight D. Eisenhower is inaugurated president of the United States.

5 March 1953: Joseph Stalin dies in Moscow.

17 June 1953: In East Germany, workers demonstrate against the Communist regime in East Berlin.

26 July 1953: Fidel Castro, leading a group of 165 young people, attacks the Moncada military barracks in Santiago de Cuba. This action, which Castro hopes will trigger a popular insurrection against the Batista dictatorship, is thwarted by a series of chance incidents.

27 July 1953: End of the Korean War; the Korean peninsula is divided between the Communist North, allied to the USSR and China, and the South, under US influence.

1 August 1953: Fidel Castro, who has retreated into the mountains after the failure of the assault on the Moncada barracks, is surprised by a military patrol and taken prisoner.

3 September 1953: In Moscow, Nikita Khrushchev is elected First Secretary of the Communist Party of the USSR.

16 October 1953: Trial of Fidel Castro, who undertakes his own defence with a famous speech titled 'History Will Absolve Me', which denounces the crimes committed against those who attacked the Moncada barracks, declares the illegality of the Batista regime, justifies the violent actions taken to overthrow it, and sets forth his political and revolutionary programme. Castro is sentenced to fifteen years in prison.

4 May 1954: In Paraguay, a coup is launched against the government. General Alfredo Stroessner, who takes power on 8 July, will govern the country with an iron hand for thirty-five years; he is backed by the United States.

7 May 1954: In Dien Bien Phu, Vietnam, French colonial forces suffer a severe defeat by Vietnamese insurgents under General Vo Nguyen Giap; this historic event marks the awakening of colonized peoples around the world.

17 June 1954: In Guatemala, a group of mercenaries organized and equipped by the CIA overthrows the constitutional government of President Jacobo Arbenz, who has announced a sweeping agrarian reform. Ernesto 'Che' Guevara is a witness to this event. Colonal Carlos Castillo Armas, a pro-American army officer, institutes a military dictatorship on 15 August. Che Guevara seeks refuge in Mexico.

28 July 1954: In Venezuela, Hugo Chávez is born in the city of Sabanetas.

24 August 1954: In Brazil, President Getulio Vargas, who has nationalized oil reserves and carried out sweeping social reforms, is overthrown by a military coup; he commits suicide in the presidential palace.

1 November 1954: Algerian war of independence begins.

27 November 1954: Forces crossing the border from Nicaragua invade Costa Rica. A group of Cuban students under the leadership of José Antonio Echeverría, president of the University Student Federation (FEU), goes to the defence of the government of President José Figueres.

18–24 April 1955: The Asian-African Conference in Bandung, Indonesia, is attended by Nehru of India, Chou En-lai of China, Nasser of Egypt and Sukarno of Indonesia. The 'Third World' is born.

14 May 1955: The Warsaw Pact is signed, creating a military alliance dominated by the USSR as a counterweight to NATO.

15 May 1955: With his brother Raúl and others who took part in the assault on the Moncada barracks, Fidel Castro is released from jail on the Isle of Pines (today Isle of Youth, Isla de la Juventud), having been granted amnesty by Batista in the face of overwhelming popular pressure.

12 June 1955: Official founding of the 26th of July Movement, up until now an underground group, with the creation of its first national directorate, headed by Fidel Castro.

7 July 1955: Given the impossibility of continuing the fight against Batista by legal means, Fidel Castro goes into exile in Mexico, where he intends to organize an armed popular insurrection.

July 1955: In Mexico, Fidel Castro and Ernesto 'Che' Guevara meet for the first time.

16 September 1955: In Argentina, a military uprising topples President Juan Perón.

November 1955: Fidel Castro and Juan Manuel Márquez hold a series of fund-raising events in the United States. In New York, they meet with Cuban émigrés in the Palm Garden, at Eighth Avenue and 52nd Street. As he leaves the meeting, Castro is questioned by New York police. Castro and Márquez also visit Tampa, Key West and Miami, Florida.

14 February 1956: In Moscow, during the Twentieth Congress of the Communist Party of the Soviet Union, Nikita Khrushchev, Party first secretary, presents a report in which he reveals the purges ordered by Stalin and denounces Stalin's policy of repression. China does not join the denunciation.

19 September 1956: In Africa, Amílcar Cabral founds the African Party for the Independence of Guinea and Cape Verde (PAIGC).

21 October 1956: Fidel Castro's father, Ángel Castro Argiz, dies in Birán.

23 October – 13 November 1956: Uprising in Budapest, Hungary, against the Communist regime, leading to intervention by the Soviet army.

25 November 1956: Fidel Castro, his brother Raúl, Che Guevara, and seventy-nine others sail from the Mexican port of Tuxpan for Cuba on the *Granma*. Their intention is to begin an armed struggle from the mountains of the Sierra Maestra.

30 November 1956: In Santiago de Cuba, Frank País leads the 26th of July Movement militia in an uprising against the Batista government. The action is a failure, but it marks the beginning of a popular armed insurrection against the Batista tyranny.

2 December 1956: Fidel Castro and the other eighty-one members of the *Granma* expeditionary force reach the eastern coast of Cuba, in the area of Los Cayuelos, near the city of Manzanillo, in Oriente province. The Revolution begins.

5 December 1956: In Alegría de Pío, the expeditionary force from the *Granma* is surprised by the Batista army and completely dispersed.

18 December 1956: Fidel Castro, Raúl Castro and six other survivors meet in Cinco Palmas. Two days later, they are joined by Juan Almeida, Che Guevara, Ramiro Valdés and four others.

17 January 1957: The revolutionary forces, which have been joined by other survivors of the *Granma* expedition and a number of *campesinos*, achieve their first victory with the capture of the military barracks at La Plata Abajo. Five days later, in Los Llanos del Infierno, the small force achieves another victory against elite Batista troops under the command of then-Lieutenant Angel Sánchez Mosquera.

17 February 1957: Herbert Matthews, of the *New York Times*, goes up into the Sierra Maestra to interview Fidel Castro. That same day, the first meeting of the National Directorate of the 26th of July Movement since the beginning of the war takes place and traitor Eutimio Guerra is captured and executed.

13 March 1957: A commando unit from the Revolutionary Directorate, an armed association of university students, assaults the presidential palace intending to kill Batista. As part of the action, another commando group under José Antonio Echeverría, president of the University Student Federation (FEU), assaults Radio Reloj, but all attackers are killed.

28 May 1957: The rebels attack and capture the enemy's barracks in El Uvero, a battle which Che Guevara considered 'the Rebel Army's coming-of-age'. A few weeks later, Castro promotes Che to *comandante* and Che takes command of his own guerrilla column, the first such column created in the Rebel Army.

20 August 1957: Combat takes place in Palma Mocha and the town is liberated by the forces of the 'José Martí' Column (Column 1) under the leadership of Fidel Castro.

17 September 1957: First combat in Pino del Agua.

October 1957: The Rebel Army battles and puts down several manifestations of banditry, which have begun to occur in the region of Caracas, in the Sierra Maestra.

4 October 1957: The Soviet Union launches Sputnik, the world's first artificial satellite, and takes the lead in the 'space race'.

November–December 1957: Columns 1 and 4 of the Rebel Army, under the command of Fidel Castro and Che Guevara respectively, turn back the 'winter offensive' by Batista's army. There is heavy fighting in Mota, Gabiro, El Salto, Mar Verde and other places in the Sierra.

23 January 1958: Formula 1 world champion racing driver, Argentinian Juan Manuel Fangio, is kidnapped in Havana by members of the 26th of July Movement. Twenty-eight hours later he is freed unharmed. The news travels around the world; the objective is to call the world's attention to the situation in Cuba. This is the first political kidnapping for media purposes in history.

16–17 February 1958: Rebel troops win a significant victory in the second battle of Pino del Agua.

1 March 1958: The nine columns of the guerrilla army, under the command of Raúl Castro and Juan Almeida, leave the Sierra Maestra. This action will create the second and third fronts in other mountainous regions of Oriente province.

9 April 1958: Failure of the 26th of July Movement's attempt at creating an island-wide strike.

25 May 1958: Batista's army launches a heavy offensive against the Rebel Army, but is defeated in seventy-four days of intense combat. During this offensive, the most important battles fought in the Sierra Maestra take place, among them Jigüe, Santo Domingo and Las Mercedes, all commanded by Fidel Castro. The defeat of Batista's forces during this offensive signals a real strategic turnaround in the war.

Late August 1958: Guerrilla columns under the command of Che Guevara and Camilo Cienfuegos set out to invade Cuba's central provinces. In October the two columns will open a new front in the central Cuban province of Las Villas.

15 November 1958: Fidel Castro leaves the Sierra Maestra en route to Santiago de Cuba, from where he will lead the Rebel Army's final offensive.

30 November 1958: The battle of Guisa ends in a victory for the rebel forces, opening the road to Santiago de Cuba.

1 January 1959: In the face of the military defeat of his forces, dictator Fulgencio Batista flees Cuba and the rebels take power.

8 January 1959: Fidel Castro enters Havana in victory. The Revolutionary Government is officially installed; its president is magistrate Manuel Urrutia and its prime minister is lawyer José Miró Cardona. Fidel Castro becomes commander-in-chief of the Revolutionary Armed Forces.

8 January 1959: In Paris, General Charles de Gaulle is inaugurated as the first president of the Fifth Republic.

23–27 January 1959: Fidel Castro visits Venezuela. Over 300,000 Venezuelans crowd the Plaza del Silencio in Caracas to cheer him and listen to his speech.

16 February 1959: Fidel Castro becomes prime minister of the Revolutionary Government.

15–27 April 1959: Fidel Castro tours the United States under the auspices of the American Society of Newspaper Editors. In New York, 35,000 people crowd Central Park to hear him speak. On 19 April, Castro meets with Vice President Richard M. Nixon.

17 May 1959: In fulfilment of the Moncada Programme, the Agrarian Reform Act goes into effect in Cuba.

21 October 1959: Two aircraft from the United States strafe the streets of Havana with machine-gun fire, killing two people and injuring fifty.

28 October 1959: The small plane on which Camilo Cienfuegos is travelling as a passenger en route to Havana goes down over the ocean. Cienfuegos is returning after dismantling a conspiracy led against the Revolution in Camagüey by Huber Matos.

Late October 1959: US president Dwight D. Eisenhower approves a programme proposed by the State Department and CIA to take covert action against Cuba, including air and sea piracy attacks and direct support to counter-revolutionary organizations within Cuba.

26 November 1959: Che Guevara is named president of the Banco Nacional de Cuba.

11 December 1959: President Eisenhower approves a CIA-proposed plan whose objective is 'toppling Castro in one year and replacing him by a junta friendly to the United States'. This plan includes 'attacks by clandestine radio', internal interference with Cuban radio and television, support for 'pro-American opposition groups' so that they can 'forcibly establish a controlled area within Cuba', and the elimination (assassination) of Fidel Castro.

February 1960: Soviet first deputy premier Anastas Mikoyan visits Cuba, grants a trade credit of $100 million on behalf of the Soviet Union, and signs a treaty to buy sugar in exchange for oil.

February–March 1960: French philosophers Jean-Paul Sartre and Simone de Beauvoir visit Cuba and meet with Fidel Castro. They stay at the famous Hotel Nacional in Havana and also meet Che Guevara.

March 1960: President Eisenhower and Secretary of State John Foster Dulles launch a third plan against Cuba, called 'Operation Pluto'. The intention is to create a paramilitary force made up of Cuban exiles and send it into Cuba to topple Castro and replace him with a 'moderate' leader.

4 March 1960: The French ship *La Coubre*, carrying military equipment and supplies, explodes in Havana harbour as a result of sabotage [Cuba claims, though evidence is never forthcoming], killing 101 persons (among them six French sailors) and wounding more than 200.

5 March 1960: During the mass demonstration in Havana against the failed attack the previous day, Cuban photographer Alberto Korda takes the iconic photograph of Che Guevara and immortalizes the figure of the 'guerrilla hero'. The photo will not be published until 16 April 1961, in the newspaper *Revolución*, on the eve of the Bay of Pigs invasion.

8 May 1960: Diplomatic relations are reopened with the Soviet Union after being broken off by Batista in 1952.

29 June 1960: Cuba confiscates refineries belonging to Texaco, Shell and Esso when their executives refuse to process Soviet oil.

July 1960: The USSR withdraws its expert advisers from China and suspends aid to Beijing. This is the beginning of the Sino–Soviet conflict.

6 July 1960: President Dwight D. Eisenhower signs into law a bill suspending US purchase of Cuban sugar. This is the first important action in the US's economic war against Cuba.

6 August 1960: Fidel Castro announces the nationalization of American-owned oil refineries, sugar refineries, and electricity and telephone companies.

2 September 1960: First Havana Declaration, approved in a mass meeting in Havana's Plaza de la Revolución: 'The National General Assembly of the people of Cuba condemns both the exploitation of man and the exploitation of underdeveloped nations by imperialist financial capital.'

9 September 1960: At least eight conspiracies to assassinate Fidel Castro in the Hotel Teresa are uncovered.

26 September 1960: Speech by Fidel Castro before the United Nations General Assembly in New York City: 'Do away with the philosophy of plunder and you will have done away for ever with the philosophy of war!' According to the Guinness Book of World Records, this is the longest speech ever given by the leader of a country at the UN: four hours, twenty-nine minutes. While in New York City, Castro stays at a hotel in Harlem, where he has meetings with Egyptian president Gamal Abdel Nasser, Indian prime minister Jawaharlal Nehru, black leader Malcolm X and Soviet premier Nikita Khrushchev, whom he meets for the first time.

28 September 1960: Creation of the Committees for the Defence of the Revolution (CDR).

13 October 1960: Cuba's principal banks and some 105 sugar companies are nationalized.

14 October 1960: The Cuban Revolutionary Government passes the Urban Reform Act.

30 October 1960: Washington bans all exports to Cuba except food and medicine.

November 1960: Operation Peter Pan begins, the secret transport of 14,000 Cuban children to the United States by anti-Revolutionary forces. This operation has been preceded by an intense propaganda campaign claiming that Castro's Revolution is planning to strip parents of custody of their children, or alternatively that the Revolution is planning to send children to the Soviet Union.

16 December 1960: President Eisenhower reduces imports of Cuban sugar to zero.

3 January 1961: The United States breaks off diplomatic relations with Cuba and closes its embassy in Havana.

11 January 1961: National literacy campaign begins in Cuba.

20 January 1961: In Washington, DC, President John F. Kennedy is inaugurated.

21 February 1961: Che Guevara is named to head up the Department of Industry within the National Institute of Agrarian Reform (INRA); later, this agency will become the Ministry of Industry.

13 March 1961: As part of a programme to step up acts of sabotage and terrorism in Cuba, the Hermanos Díaz oil refinery in Santiago de Cuba is attacked by a pirated boat, leaving one person dead and several injured.

13 March 1961: In Washington, DC, President John F. Kennedy proposes the 'Alliance for Progress' as an alternative to the Cuban Revolution's influence in Latin America.

12 April 1961: In the spaceship Vostok-1, conceived by engineer Sergei Koriolov, Soviet cosmonaut Yuri Gagarin orbits the earth for the first time in history.

13 April 1961: Fire set by agent of the CIA at the El Encanto department store in Havana kills one, injures many, and completely destroys the store.

15 April 1961: In Cuba, [military] airports at San Antonio de los Baños, Columbia, and Santiago de Cuba are bombed by planes with false Cuban insignias flown from CIA camps in Central America and piloted by Cuban and American mercenaries; eight people are killed.

16 April 1961: At the funeral services for the victims of the attacks the day before, Fidel Castro states that this has been the prelude to an all-out invasion and declares that the Revolution is a Socialist one: 'This is a Socialist and democratic Revolution of the humble, by the humble, and for the humble.'

17 April 1961: Some 1,500 Cuban counter-revolutionaries organized, trained and equipped by the CIA land on Playa Girón and Playa Larga, in the Bay of Pigs. They are defeated in less than seventy-two hours and over 1,200 are taken prisoners; they will be exchanged later for $53 million in medicine and foodstuffs. American ships, aboard which is a heavy contingent of troops, remain in waters near the Bay of Pigs for three days, ready to intervene.

28 May 1961: A terrorist bombing at the Riego movie theatre in Pinar del Río during a children's matinée causes dozens of injuries.

30 June 1961: Fidel Castro speaks 'a few words for intellectuals' to state the government's policy in cultural matters: 'Within the Revolution, everything; against the Revolution, nothing.'

July 1961: The Integrated Revolutionary Organizations (ORI) are created. These organizations merge the 26th of July Movement, Blas Roca's Popular Socialist Party (Communist) and Faure Chomón's '13th of March' Revolutionary Student Directorate. Aníbal Escalante, former leader of the PSP, is elected secretary-general.

17 July 1961: Assassination of Patrice Lumumba in the Congo.

12 August – 20 November 1961: Construction of the Berlin Wall by East German authorities.

22 December 1961: Culmination of the national literacy campaign, with Cuba declared an 'illiteracy-free territory'.

22 January 1962: At the insistence of the United States, Cuba is excluded from the Organization of American States (OAS).

3 February 1962: President Kennedy orders a complete economic and trade embargo of Cuba. This embargo is still in effect today, in 2007, in an attempt to strangle Cuba economically and foment popular discontent.

4 February 1962: Second Havana Declaration, approved by over a million citizens in a mass meeting in the Plaza de la Revolución: 'The duty of every revolutionary is to make the Revolution.'

7 February 1962: Washington bans all imports from Cuba.

12 March 1962: In Cuba, adoption of Law 1015 establishes the equitable distribution of a family's supplies according to the availability of food in the country; the *libreta* (ration booklet) is created.

13 March 1962: Fidel Castro publicly denounces 'sectarianism' within the ORI. Aníbal Escalante is removed from office.

14 March 1962: After the failure of the Bay of Pigs invasion, the Kennedy administration approves a vast secret plan for operations aimed at 'helping Cuba bring down the Communist regime'. This programme of dirty tricks will be called 'Operation Mongoose' and is also known as 'the Cuban Project'. The operation, directed by General Edward Landsdale, a counter-insurrection specialist, includes over thirty plans, several of which are carried out: propaganda, attacks against the Cuban government and the Cuban economy, the use of American Green Beret commando units within the island, destruction of sugar-cane harvests, destruction of factories, the mining of ports, assassination attempts against the island's top political leaders, the arming of opposition groups, and the construction of guerrilla bases throughout Cuba, at which preparations are made for an invasion of the island in October.

26 March 1962: The ORI will now be known as the Cuban Socialist Revolution United Party (PURSC).

5 July 1962: End of the war in Algeria; Algeria proclaims its independence.

22 October 1962: The beginning of the October crisis ('Cuban missile crisis'). President Kennedy orders a naval blockade of Cuba in order to force the Soviets to remove nuclear warheads installed secretly at the request of the USSR and with the consent of the Cuban government; the missiles are intended to be used to frustrate new plans for direct US aggression against the island. After a few days, and without consulting the Cuban authorities, who do not agree with the secrecy of the negotiations, Moscow agrees to withdraw the missiles and Kennedy privately promises not to invade Cuba.

23 December 1962: The American merchant ship *African Pilot* arrives at the port of Havana bringing part of the merchandise demanded by Cuba as compensation for the material and human losses caused by the Bay of Pigs invasion. The invaders who have been captured and tried by Cuban courts are returned to the United States.

27 April – 3 June 1963: Fidel Castro's first visit to the Soviet Union.

6 August 1963: Death of Castro's mother, Lina Ruz González.

28 August 1963: In Washington, DC, after a march against racial discrimination, and before a crowd of 250,000 people, Reverend Martin Luther King gives his famous 'I have a dream' speech.

October 1963: At the request of Algerian president Ahmed Ben Bella, Castro sends a battalion of twenty-two tanks and several hundred soldiers, under the command of Efigenio Ameijeiras, to Algeria to help the Algerian armed forces repel an attack by Morocco in the Tinduf region. This is Cuba's first internationalist military operation in Africa.

4 October 1963: Hurricane Flora devastates the eastern region of Cuba. Fidel Castro declares that 'a revolution is more powerful than nature.'

22 November 1963: Assassination of President John F. Kennedy in Dallas. Kennedy has recently been exploring the possibility of a *rapprochement* with Cuba.

1 April 1964: A military coup topples the reformist president of Brazil, João Goulart, who has just announced an agrarian reform, control of the monetary exchange rate and other measures aimed at increasing the nation's sovereignty.

3 April 1964: Cuba withdraws from the International Monetary Fund (IMF).

14 October 1964: In Moscow, Nikita Khrushchev is deposed. Leonid Brezhnev is elected first secretary of the Communist Party of the USSR.

3 November 1964: In Bolivia, a coup is launched by generals Barrientos and Ovando. Bolivia enters an eighteen-year period of military dictatorships.

21 February 1965: In Harlem, New York City, Afro-American leader Malcolm X, who had met with Fidel Castro on 9 September 1960, is assassinated.

22–27 February 1965: Afro-Asian Conference in Algiers; speech by Che Guevara.

April 1965: In a letter to Fidel Castro that will be made public in October, Che Guevara officially takes leave of Cuba and secretly goes to Africa to support the guerrilla forces in the Congo. 'Other lands demand . . . my modest efforts.'

28 April 1965: US Marine troops disembark in the Dominican Republic to battle the pro-reform *Constitucionalista* forces commanded by Colonel Francisco Caamaño and loyal to President Juan Bosch, who has legalized the Communist Party. 'We will not tolerate a second Cuba in the Caribbean,' President Lyndon B. Johnson declares.

11 August 1965: In the black ghetto of Watts, Los Angeles, a violent riot by residents takes place against discrimination, traffic stops by police, and living conditions in the ghetto. Thirty-four people are killed and 800 injured; the area is devastated by fire and looting.

October 1965: First 'migration crisis': the port of Camarioca is readied to facilitate transfer to the United States of all Cuban citizens wishing to leave the island.

3 October 1965: The Cuban Communist Party (PCC) is created. Fidel Castro is elected first secretary of the Central Committee. At the ceremony celebrating the Party's creation, Castro explains the reason for Che Guevara's absence and reads his letter of farewell. Castro also announces that the newspapers *Revolución* and *Hoy*, the organs of the 26th of July Movement and the PSP, respectively, will no longer be published; instead, a new daily newspaper, *Granma*, will be the official organ of the PCC.

29 October 1965: In Paris, Moroccan Socialist Mehdi Ben Barka, opponent of the government of King Hassan II and one of the organizers of the First Tricontinental Conference in Havana, is kidnapped and murdered.

January 1966: Tricontinental Conference in Havana, attended by liberation movements from approximately seventy Asian, African and Latin American countries.

15 February 1966: In Colombia, guerrilla-priest Camilo Torres is killed by the army in San Vicente.

16 May 1966: The 'Cultural Revolution' begins in China.

2 November 1966: The US Congress passes the Cuban Adjustment Act, which is still in force in 2007. This act, by giving exceptional privileges to Cubans who arrive by illegal means in the United States, encourages illegal emigration and will be the cause of countless fatalities on the high seas.

25 April 1967: In Bolivia, Régis Debray is arrested by the army.

9 October 1967: Che Guevara is murdered after being captured in combat by the Bolivian army as he leads a guerrilla movement in that country.

18 October 1967: Fidel Castro announces the death of Che Guevara to the Cuban people.

17 November 1967: In Camiri, Bolivia, Régis Debray is sentenced to thirty years in prison.

9 December 1967: In Romania, Nicolae Ceauşescu is elected president of the State Council.

January 1968: Trial of thirty-five members of the 'pro-Soviet microfraction' led by Aníbal Escalante takes place in Havana.

March 1968: The Cuban government expropriates virtually all private businesses on the island, with the exception of small agricultural properties.

4 April 1968: In Memphis, Tennessee, a racist assassinates Reverend Martin Luther King on the balcony of the Lorraine Motel as Revd King prepares to lead a march supporting the local union of Afro-American workers.

20 April 1968: In Canada, Pierre Trudeau becomes prime minister. The new leader will seek to improve relations with Fidel Castro.

May 1968: Worldwide student protests against Western capitalist society. In California, Germany, France, Italy, tens of thousands of young people, often carrying posters with the image of Che Guevara, demand changes in political systems and ways of life.

5 June 1968: In Los Angeles, in the kitchen of the Ambassador Hotel, Senator Robert Kennedy is assassinated.

21 August 1968: Intervention of Warsaw Pact troops in Czechoslovakia, at Moscow's urging, in order to put down the 'Prague spring'. China protests against the invasion. In a speech on 23 August Fidel Castro approves the intervention, although with reservations.

19 January 1969: In Prague, student Jan Palach immolates himself in protest against the invasion of Czechoslovakia.

20 January 1969: In Washington, DC, President Richard Nixon is inaugurated.

1 February 1969: In the Near East, Yasser Arafat is elected president of the Palestine Liberation Organization (PLO).

20 July 1969: Astronauts Neil Armstrong and Buzz Aldrin land on the moon; Armstrong takes 'one small step for a man, one giant leap for mankind'.

1 September 1969: In Libya, Colonel Muammar al-Gaddafi topples King Idriss and takes power.

14 October 1969: In Sweden, Social-Democrat Olof Palme is elected prime minister. The new leader opens relations with Cuba and Fidel Castro.

21 October 1969: In West Germany, Social-Democrat Willy Brandt is elected chancellor. He, too, opens relations with Cuba and Fidel Castro.

17 April 1970: A group of Cuban exiles, armed and financed by the United States, disembarks near Baracoa, kills four militia members, and gravely wounds two others.

18 May 1970: Announcement is made that the 10-million-ton sugar harvest that had been the goal for this year has not been achieved.

26 July 1970: In a speech, Fidel Castro acknowledges his responsibility in the failure of the 10-million-ton harvest.

4 September 1970: In Chile, Salvador Allende is elected president.

8 October 1970: Alexander Solzhenitsyn, Soviet dissident and author of *One Day in the Life of Ivan Denisovich* (1962), *The Cancer Ward* (1968) and other works, is awarded the Nobel Prize for Literature.

23 December 1970: In Bolivia, after three years of imprisonment, Régis Debray is released.

20 March 1971: Poet Heberto Padilla, author of the controversial book of poetry *Fuera del juego* ('Out of the Game', 1967), is arrested and accused of 'acts against state security'. His arrest triggers a storm of international protest, and dozens of intellectuals mobilize to demand his release. The author will be freed after being forced to read a statement of self-criticism in public in Havana. [This episode is called the 'Padilla affair', and no good comes of it: Padilla is scorned by some for having 'apologized' for his poetry, even while Cuba and the Castro regime are harshly criticized for abridging the freedom of speech of artists and poets. In 1980 Padilla goes into exile in the US, and for several years teaches at Princeton and Auburn universities; he dies in Alabama in 2000. – Trans.]

10 May 1971: A group of Cuban exiles attacks two boats belonging to the Caibarén Fisherman's Cooperative, hijacks eleven crew members, and abandons them on a small island in the Bahamas.

12 July 1971: In Miami, a group of Cuban exiles claims responsibility for an act of terrorism in Guantánamo: causing a train crash that kills four people and injures seventeen.

19 July 1971: In Sudan, a Communist coup attempt fails. Fourteen Communist leaders are hanged in public in Khartoum.

12 October 1971: A gunboat launched from Miami attacks the settlement of Boca de Samá (in Banes, Oriente province), kills two people (Lidio Rivaflecha and Ramón Siam Portelles), and injures four, two of whom are minors.

25 October 1971: After a trip by US Secretary of State Henry Kissinger to Beijing, Taiwan is expelled from the UN and the People's Republic of China takes its place among the five permanent members of the Security Council.

10 November – 4 December 1971: Fidel Castro visits Chile, then under the Popular Unity administration of Salvador Allende.

15 February 1972: Cuba ratifes an international convention eliminating racial discrimination.

21 February 1972: President Richard Nixon goes to Beijing and meets with Mao Zedong.

4 April 1972: In Montreal, a bomb destroys the Cuban Trade Office and kills employee Sergio Pérez del Castillo. In Miami, an organization called Grupo de Jóvenes Cubanos (Young Cubans Group) claims responsibility.

22 May 1972: President Nixon visits Moscow and meets with Leonid Brezhnev. The two leaders sign an agreement mutually limiting nuclear arsenals.

July 1972: Cuba joins the Council for Mutual Economic Assistance (known in Cuba as COMECON; known in English-speaking countries as CMEA), the Socialist nations' 'common market'.

January 1973: Treaty of Paris between North and South Vietnam; the United States, which has been gradually withdrawing its troops since June 1969, promises not to intervene militarily.

20 June 1973: Juan Perón returns in triumph to Argentina: on 23 September he will be elected president for the third time.

3 August 1973: In Abrainville, on the western outskirts of Paris, a member of the [anti-Castro] organization Cuban Action is killed when a bomb he is about to throw at the Cuban embassy in France explodes.

6 August 1973: Former Cuban dictator Fulgencio Batista dies in Spain.

5–10 September 1973: Fidel Castro takes part in the fourth Summit of Non-Aligned Nations in Algiers.

11 September 1973: Military coup in Chile, with the death of Salvador Allende. General Augusto Pinochet takes over and institutes a brutal dictatorship, which is backed by the United States.

December 1973: Soviet author Alexander Solzhenitsyn publishes *The Gulag Archipelago*, a description of the Soviet system of concentration camps. The book is published in Russian by the YMCA Press in Paris, which was founded in 1921 by Russian émigrés.

February 1974: In Moscow, Solzhenitsyn is detained and expelled from the USSR.

13 February 1974: In Madrid, a package sent by mail to the Cuban embassy in Spain explodes in the central post office in Cibeles and injures a Spanish officer.

25 April 1974: The 'Carnation Revolution' takes place in Portugal; the dictatorship falls.

1 July 1974: Juan Perón dies in Buenos Aires.

8 August 1974: In Washington, President Richard Nixon resigns in the aftermath of the Watergate scandal and is replaced by Vice President Gerald Ford.

12 September 1974: In Ethiopia, a coup takes place in Addis Ababa: a group of Marxist

military officers, among them Mengistu Haile Mariam, depose and assassinate the *negus*, or king, Haile Selassie.

November 1974: Cuban and US officials begin conversations aimed at finding a solution to the migration crises.

April 1975: The US withdraws in chaos from Saigon. End of the Vietnam War, with Vietnamese victory.

17 April 1975: In Cambodia, the Khmer Rouge take Phnom Penh and genocide begins against the urban population and ethnic minorities.

30 April 1975: In Vietnam, the forces of the FLN enter Saigon, which has been renamed Ho Chi Minh City.

25 June 1975: The new Portuguese government that has come to power as a consequence of the Carnation Revolution announces that it has granted independence to Angola.

29 June 1975: Swedish prime minister Olof Palme visits Cuba.

11 November 1975: Operation Carlota begins: Cuba establishes an airlift and sends thousands of volunteer soldiers to Angola. This volunteer force halts the advance of South African and Zaïrean troops moving into Luanda to prevent Angola's independence.

20 November 1975: In Spain, Generalísimo Francisco Franco dies; King Juan Carlos I ascends to the throne.

15 February 1976: The first Socialist constitution of Cuba is approved by referendum; the vote is overwhelmingly in favour.

22 April 1976: In Lisbon, a bomb explodes in the Cuban embassy and kills two Cuban officials: Efrén Monteagudo and Adriana Corcho.

9 July 1976: In the airport at Kingston, Jamaica, a bomb placed in a suitcase explodes as it is about to be loaded on to a Cuban Airlines plane.

9 August 1976: Famed Cuban author José Lezama Lima dies in Havana.

9 September 1976: Mao Zedong dies in Beijing.

6 October 1976: A Cuban civilian plane is blown up in mid-air off the coast of Barbados; seventy-three passengers die. Venezuelan and Barbadian authorities determine that Cuban exile terrorists Luis Posada Carriles and Orlando Bosch are responsible; both are arrested.

20 January 1977: In Washington, DC, President Jimmy Carter is inaugurated.

11 February 1977: In Ethiopia, Colonel Mengistu Haile Mariam takes power.

1 September 1977: The United States, under President Jimmy Carter, and Cuba open diplomatic offices (Interest Offices) in their respective capitals.

March 1978: With the aid of Cuban troops, Ethiopia claims victory against Somalian invasion forces in the Ogaden campaign.

28 July 1978: The Eleventh World Festival of Youth and Students opens in Havana.

9 September 1978: Spanish prime minister Adolf Suárez arrives in Havana, the first Spanish head of state to visit Cuba officially since 1959.

16 October 1978: In the Vatican, Polish cardinal Karol Wojtyla is elected pope, taking the name John Paul II.

November 1978: In Cuba, the first contacts with moderate exile leaders take place; over 3,000 political prisoners are released.

24 December 1978: The Vietnamese army invades Cambodia, ruled by the Khmer Rouge. The Vietnamese take Phnom Penh on 7 January 1979.

16 January 1979: Islamic Revolution in Iran. Shah Reza Pahlevi is overthrown and Iranian spiritual leader Ayatollah Khomeini returns to Tehran on 1 February.

19 July 1979: Triumph of the Sandinista revolution in Nicaragua.

3–9 September 1979: Sixth Summit of Non-Aligned Nations Movement in Havana. Fidel Castro becomes president of the movement.

27 December 1979: Soviet troops invade Afghanistan.

11 January 1980: Celia Sánchez, one of the first members of Castro's anti-Batista guerrilla group and one of Castro's closest allies, dies in Havana.

February 1980: Fidel Castro marries Dalia Soto del Valle, a teacher from the city of Trinidad with whom he has had a relationship since 1961 and with whom he has had five children:

Alexis (1963), Alex (1965), Alejandro (1967), Antonio (1968) and Angel (1974). The marriage is not made public.

16 March 1980: Poet Heberto Padilla goes into exile.

April 1980: Second 'migration crisis': the Mariel exodus begins when the Cuban government announces that it will allow anyone to leave the island who wants to. Some 125,000 Cubans leave Cuba between April and the end of September.

4 May 1980: Marshal Tito dies in Belgrade.

17 May 1980: In Peru, the 'popular war' waged by Maoist organization Sendero Luminoso begins; this war will cause thousands of casualties.

18 July 1980: In Managua, Nicaragua, Fidel Castro attends acts commemorating the first anniversary of the Sandinista victory. He promises to aid the Sandinista government in its war against the 'Contras' and their US supporters.

14 August 1980: In Poland, a strike by the Gdansk dockworkers begins, and it soon extends to the whole country. The strikers win a great victory when agreements are signed between the Polish government in Warsaw and the Solidarity union led by Lech Walesa.

11 September 1980: Cuban diplomat Félix García is assassinated in New York by members of the anti-Castro terrorist organization Omega 7.

20 January 1981: In Washington, DC, President Ronald Reagan is inaugurated.

June 1981: In China, Mao Zedong's successor, Hua Guofeng, is removed from the presidency of the Communist Party and reformist Deng Xiaoping assumes power.

18 October 1981: General Wojciech Jaruzelski is elected first secretary of the Polish United Workers' Party (the country's Communist Party).

22 October 1981: North–South Summit in Cancún, Mexico. Twenty-two heads of state pledge to begin global negotiations between rich nations and poor nations. Washington exerts pressure to exclude Cuba despite the fact that Cuba presides over the Group of 77.

22–23 October 1981: In Cancún, Mexico, an international conference on the new world economic order is held; French President François Mitterrand has called the conference.

2 April–13 June 1982: England and Argentina go to war over the Malvinas, or Falkland Islands. The British retake the archipelago claimed by the Argentines.

21 August 1982: In Mexico, a foreign debt crisis occurs. The country declares a moratorium on debt repayment; the financial crisis spreads through all of Latin America and the Caribbean.

18 October 1982: At the request of French president François Mitterrand, alleged poet Armando Valladares, who has been faking paralysis, is released from prison in Havana after serving a sentence of twenty-two years for terrorist activity.

10 November 1982: In Moscow, Leonid Brezhnev dies; Yuri Andropov succeeds him as head of the Soviet Union.

25 October 1983: The US military intervenes in Grenada after the assassination of Prime Minister Maurice Bishop. Cuban civilians working in Grenada take a stand against the invasion, and some die in combat or are murdered. Some 600 Cubans are taken prisoner and repatriated to Cuba.

11 February 1984: In Moscow, Yuri Andropov dies; Konstantin Chernenko replaces him as head of the Soviet Union.

16 February 1984: Fidel Castro makes a brief stopover in Spain on his way back from Moscow; this is Castro's first visit to Spain. He meets with Prime Minister Felipe González.

December 1984: The first immigration agreement is signed between Cuba and the United States.

10 March 1985: In Moscow, Konstantin Chernenko dies.

11 March 1985: Mikhail Gorbachev takes power in the Soviet Union and begins to question the country's political and economic functioning. He announces his new policies of *glasnost* (transparency) and *perestroika* (restructure).

11 April 1985: In Tirana, Albania, Communist leader Enver Hodja, who has been head of state since 1945, dies.

August 1985: American magazine *Playboy* publishes an interview with Fidel Castro on 'Reagan and the Revolution'.

3 August, 1985: Fidel Castro takes part in an international conference in Havana on Latin American foreign debt, part of the battle undertaken by Cuba against debt repayment by poor countries: 'Must debts to the oppressors be paid by the oppressed?'

February 1986: Fidel Castro visits Moscow and has a cordial meeting with Mikhail Gorbachev.

19 April 1986: In Cuba, a 'Rectification Campaign' begins: Fidel Castro denounces errors in the conduct of the Party, the conduct of the economy, and bureaucracy, egoism and corruption in the government. [Basically, this marks an end to private enterprise, the 'free farmers' markets and material incentives to labour, and the beginning of the 'micro-brigades', which are 'volunteer' groups under 'moral incentives' working double shifts with no increase in compensation (1st ed.).]

25 April 1986: Explosion of the Chernobyl nuclear plant in Ukraine. Cuba will provide aid in the recovery of thousands of children affected by the accident.

November 1986: Spanish prime minister Felipe González pays a state visit to Cuba.

June 1987: Luis Orlando 'Landy' Domínguez, former leader of the Communist Youth, member of Fidel Castro's team of assistants and president of the Institute of Civil Aeronautics, is arrested as he tries to leave Cuba with his family. He will be sentenced to twenty years in prison for embezzlement.

19 October 1987: In New York, Wall Street crashes. The Dow Jones index plunges more than 22 per cent in one day. The financial crisis spreads to the markets in Hong Kong, London, Brussels and Paris.

26 July 1988: Fidel Castro rejects Gorbachev's *perestroika*, which Castro calls 'dangerous' and 'opposed to the principles of Socialism'.

20 January 1989: In Washington, DC, President George H. W. Bush is inaugurated.

27 February 1989: In Venezuela, the neoliberal 'shock therapy' announced by President Carlos Andrés Pérez leads to a popular uprising and the largest disturbances in the country's history. Between 300 and 3,000 people die during the bloody repression that follows. Hugo Chávez, an officer in the presidential guard, will be profoundly marked by these events.

3 April 1989: Mikhail Gorbachev visits Cuba.

June 1989: Diocles Torralba, minister of transport and vice president of the Council of Ministers, is removed from his post. On 24 July, he will be sentenced to twenty years in prison for abuse of power, embezzlement and falsification of public documents.

June 1989: Mikhail Gorbachev visits Beijing and meets with Deng Xiaoping. End of the Sino–Soviet rift. The 'Beijing spring' begins, leading ultimately to the events [bloody repression (1st ed.)] in Tiananmen Square.

14 June 1989: Trial of General Arnaldo Ochoa, Colonel Antonio de la Guardia, and other high-ranking officers in the Cuban armed forces and state security forces implicated in drug trafficking. Ochoa, de la Guardia and two other officers are sentenced to death and are shot by firing squad on 13 July.

26 July 1989: In a speech, Fidel Castro announces that even if the Soviet Union should disappear one day, the Cuban Revolution will go on.

5 October 1989: Chilean president General Augusto Pinochet loses the plebiscite which would have allowed him to extend his term in office.

9 November 1989: The Berlin Wall comes down. Regimes in the Socialist camp all over Eastern Europe begin to fall, one after another.

20 December 1989: [Bloody (1st ed.)] popular uprising in Romania; the [Communist] regime falls. President Nicolas Ceauşescu is shot by firing squad a few days later.

26 December 1989: Bloody military intervention by the United States in Panama. Panamanian president General Manuel Noriega is taken prisoner by the US army.

April 1990: Sandinistas lose elections in Nicaragua. End of the Sandinista revolution.

29 August 1990: Cuban authorities declare a 'special period in times of peace' and announce fourteen measures restricting the consumption of petrol and electricity.

21 May 1991: In Ethiopia, Colonel Mengistu Haile Mariam is overthrown and flees the country.

25 May 1991: The last Cuban troops withdrawn from Angola after the peace accords reach

Cuba. The war in Angola has cost some 2,000 Cuban lives, and almost 10,000 troops have been wounded. Without Cuba's military intervention, the Luanda regime would have fallen to South African troops. The defeat of South Africa allows Namibia to be fully independent and precipitates the fall of South Africa's racist apartheid regime.

11 September 1991: Mikhail Gorbachev announces the withdrawal of 7,000 Soviet troops, advisers and technical personnel from Cuba.

December 1991: The fall of the Soviet Union ends that country's economic and trade relations with Havana. The Cuban economy slides 35 per cent over the next three years.

1 January 1992: Year 1 of the 'special period'. Many around the world predict the collapse of the Cuban Revolution.

14 January 1992: In Mexico, the Salvadoran government and the Farabundo Martí National Liberation Front sign what come to be known as the Chapultepec peace accords, bringing to an end twelve years of civil war in El Salvador.

20 January 1992: In Washington, DC, President Bill Clinton is inaugurated.

4 February 1992: In Venezuela, Hugo Chávez leads a group of military officers in a coup against President Carlos Andrés Pérez. The coup fails and Chávez is jailed for two years.

5 April 1992: In Peru, President Alberto Fujimori, who is committed to a neoliberal shock-therapy economic policy, suspends his own government, dissolves Congress and grants himself the power to rule by decree.

June 1992: Fidel Castro takes part in the Earth Summit in Rio de Janeiro.

July 1992: Fidel Castro takes part in the Second Ibero-American Summit in Madrid. Castro accepts Galician president Manuel Fraga's invitation to visit Galicia, and in particular the village of Láncara, the birthplace of Castro's father, in the province of Lugo, where Castro still has relatives.

12 September 1992: In Peru, Sendero Luminoso is dismantled when its leader, Abimael Guzmán, is taken prisoner; a year later he will be sentenced to life in prison.

October 1992: Carlos Aldana, member of the Political Committee (the entity charged with setting the ideological direction of the Party) and the man considered to be the third-highest-ranking figure in the Cuban government, is removed from office due to 'shortcomings in his work and grave errors of a personal nature'.

October 1992: The US Congress passes the Cuban Democracy Act, also known as the Torricelli Act, which strengthens the US economic and trade embargo against Cuba.

24 February 1993: First direct legislative elections for 601 deputies to the Cuban National Assembly. The Communist Party per se does not submit candidates. Fidel Castro wins election as the representative of Santiago de Cuba and is ratified by the Assembly as president of the Council of State and Council of Ministers.

27 July 1993: Small-scale farmers' and fishermen's markets are authorized; ban is also lifted on self-employment and, in the case of farmers and other agricultural workers, keeping back part of the production and selling it in the markets. The ban on the use of dollars is lifted and citizens are now allowed to receive money from abroad. Tourism is encouraged and, beginning in September, small-scale private business is allowed.

22 November 1993: Chinese president Jiang Zemin visits Cuba.

December 1993: Alina Fernández Revuelta, Fidel Castro's 'rebellious daughter' who was born on 3 March 1956 as the result of a relationship with Naty Revuelta, secretly leaves Cuba and moves first to Spain and then to Miami, where she joins the ranks of opponents of the Cuban Revolution.

15 April 1994: In Marrakesh, Morocco, an agreement is signed creating one of the main instruments of neoliberal globalization, the World Trade Organization (WTO). The WTO supersedes the GATT (General Agreement on Tariffs and Trade) and becomes effective on 1 January 1995.

May 1994: Fidel Castro attends the inauguration of President Nelson Mandela in Pretoria, South Africa.

13 July 1994: The accidental sinking of a tugboat hijacked by illegal emigrants kills approximately thirty people off Havana.

5 August 1994: Riots triggered by disinformation spread by anti-Cuban broadcasting stations in Miami take place in Havana. Fidel Castro goes in person to calm tempers.

11 August 1994: In the face of the continued failure of the United States to honour its migration agreements with Cuba, Fidel Castro announces that he will no longer prevent Cubans from leaving the island. Several thousand *balseros*, 'rafters', launch small craft in attempts to reach the US.

9 September 1994: A new immigration agreement is signed between the US and Cuba in New York City. The United States agrees to issue 20,000 visas per year but insists upon returning all *balseros* intercepted at sea, who can then apply for visas in Cuba and wait their turn to emigrate.

14 December 1994: At Havana airport, Fidel Castro greets Venezuelan parachute officer Lieutenant Colonel Hugo Chávez with special military honours. Chávez was released from prison eight months earlier after his participation in the 1992 coup attempt against the government of Carlos Andrés Pérez.

24 February 1996: Cuban military planes down two small planes operated by the counter-revolutionary exile group Brothers to the Rescue, who have repeatedly violated Cuban airspace.

5 March 1996: The US Congress passes the Helms–Burton Act, which is signed into law by President Clinton on 12 March. This law further tightens the economic blockade against Cuba and threatens reprisals against all foreign investment on the island and sanctions against foreign companies that use properties nationalized in Cuba that once belonged to US citizens.

1 May 1996: Cuban authorities officially warn the United States government that any foreign aircraft that penetrates Cuban airspace and approaches Havana during the May Day ceremonies will be shot down.

15 June 1996: Fidel Castro takes part in the UN conference on human settlements held in Istanbul. On his return flight, he stops over in the Canary Islands and visits Tenerife.

27 June 1996: The International Civil Aviation Organization (ICAO), an agency of the United Nations, publishes a report stating that the two Cessna-337 planes belonging to Brothers to the Rescue were shot down over international waters. Havana maintains that they were shot down within Cuba's twenty-mile territorial limit.

April–September 1997: A series of bombings and other acts against hotels in Havana and Varadero are carried out by Miami terrorist groups. [Hotels affected are the Meliá Cohiba, Capri, Nacional, Sol, Palmeras, Tritón, Château-Miramar and Copacabana. At the Copacabana (1st ed.)] Fabio di Celmo, a young Italian tourist, is killed.

10 September 1997: Arrest of Salvadoran Raúl Cruz León in Havana. Cruz León confesses to six of the hotel bombings and says that Cuban exiles living in Miami promised him $4,500 for each attack. Cuban-born terrorist Luis Posada Carriles is implicated in the organization of these bombings.

October 1997: The Cuban Communist Party holds its Fifth Party Congress, at which Fidel Castro is ratified as first secretary and Raúl Castro as second secretary.

17 October 1997: The remains of Ernesto 'Che' Guevara, found in Bolivia after a long search, are laid to rest in the mausoleum dedicated to him in Santa Clara. In his eulogy Fidel Castro says, 'You are anywhere there is a just cause to defend; you are a prophet for all the poor people of the world.'

21–25 January 1998: Pope John Paul II visits Cuba.

6 May 1998: Author Gabriel García Márquez delivers a message from Fidel Castro to President Bill Clinton in the White House. In his letter, Castro informs Clinton of terrorist acts against Cuban tourist sites and planes, orchestrated by Cuban counter-revolutionaries living in the United States.

16–17 June 1998: As a result of efforts made by García Márquez, Cuban authorities invite two high-ranking officers of the FBI to Havana and give them many files documenting the terrorist activities of several activists living in Florida.

12 July 1998: In an interview in the *New York Times*, Cuban-born terrorist Luis Posada

Carriles admits to organizing the terrorist campaign against tourist sites in Cuba in 1997 and states that the campaign was financed by Jorge Mas Canosa and the Cuban-American National Foundation. Posada Carriles admits that he paid Raúl Cruz León to carry out the hotel bombings.[1]

August 1998: The FBI accidentally foils a conspiracy by Cuban exiles to assassinate Fidel Castro when he attends the Eighth Ibero-American Summit.

12 September 1998: Five Cuban agents who have infiltrated Cuban exile terrorist organizations in order to combat terrorism against Cuba are arrested in Miami.

16 October 1998: In Spain, Judge Baltasar Garzón signs an international arrest warrant for Augusto Pinochet. The former Chilean dictator is arrested nine hours later in London.

20 October 1998: Fidel Castro takes part in the Eighth Ibero-American Summit in Oporto, Portugal; while he is in Europe he visits the Spanish province of Extremadura and the city of Mérida.

30 October 1998: Manuel Fraga, president of the Xunta in Galicia, arrives in Cuba for an official visit and meets with Fidel Castro.

6 December 1998: In Venezuela, Hugo Chávez is elected president of the country, with 56.5 per cent of the votes cast.

17 January 1999: Hugo Chávez makes his first visit as head of state to Cuba.

27 February 1999: In New York, the UN-sponsored Guatemalan Commission for Historical Clarification (CEH) publishes a report titled 'Guatemala: Memory of Silence', which accuses the government of the United States of playing an essential role in supporting genocide and state terrorism in Guatemala.[2] The CEH documents the systematic torture and murder of 200,000 people, most of them Mayans, during the repression lasting from 1978 to 1983.

28 May 1999: Roberto Robaina, Cuba's minister of foreign relations, is removed from office. In May 2002 he will be expelled from the Party.

14–16 November 1999: For the Ninth Ibero-American Summit, King Juan Carlos I of Spain visits Cuba.

25 November 1999: Six-year-old Elián González is rescued off the coast of Florida after his mother and ten other Cubans trying to reach the United States die. American authorities give in to pressure from the counter-revolutionary Cuban community in Miami and allow the boy to be held in Miami despite his father's demand that he be returned to Cuba. In Cuba, the battle to bring the boy home begins.

30 November–3 December 1999: World Trade Organization (WTO) meeting in Seattle, Washington, gives rise to huge demonstrations. The international protest movement against neoliberal globalization is born.

21 January 2000: In Ecuador, president Jamil Mahuad is toppled by a popular insurrection and a mobilization by indigenous peoples supported by a group of military officers, among them Colonel Lucio Gutiérrez.

28 June 2000: Elián González returns to Cuba after the failure of Cuban exiles to keep him in the United States. One million people, with Fidel Castro at their head, march along the Malecón in Havana to celebrate the boy's return.

September 2000: Fidel Castro attends the UN's Millennium Summit and is party to an unprecedented event when he has a brief encounter with US president Bill Clinton. Fidel and Clinton shake hands and exchange pleasantries – it is the first time in forty years that a US president has spoken directly to Fidel Castro.

26–30 October 2000: First state visit to Venezuela by Fidel Castro since 1959 (with the exception of his brief visit in 1989 for the inauguration of Carlos Andrés Pérez); Castro is given a hero's welcome.

29 October 2000: In Peru, President Alberto Fujimori, immersed in a scandal involving corruption and abuse of power, leaves the country and takes refuge in Japan. On 21 November he will be stripped of his office.

30 October 2000: Agreement between Cuba and Venezuela by which Venezuela will provide Cuba with 53,000 barrels of crude oil per day at preferential prices and under a payment plan. (At this time, Cuba consumes 150,000 barrels a day, of which it produces only

75,000.) Cuba, in turn, will supply Venezuela with generic medicines and medical equipment and will set up a vaccination-production centre there. Today, almost 15,000 Cuban doctors, dentists, optometrists and other health professionals are taking part in the ambitious mission called *Barrio Adentro*, or 'Inside the Barrio', which is designed to ensure health care for 17 million of the 25 million Venezuelans of limited means. In addition, thousands of Cuban teachers and university professors are helping in literacy programmes, and there are also thousands of sports coaches in Venezuela.

November 2000: Cuban intelligence services discover a conspiracy led by terrorist Luis Posada Carriles to assassinate Fidel Castro in Panama at the Tenth Ibero-American Summit. Posada Carriles and three other terrorists are detained by Panamanian authorities.

13–17 December 2000: Russian President Vladimir Putin visits Cuba.

25–30 January 2001: In Porto Alegre, Brazil, the first World Social Forum takes place; its motto is 'Another world is possible'. More than 30,000 young people from around the world gather to propose alternatives to neoliberal globalization.

23 June 2001: Fidel Castro has a brief fainting spell in public in the Havana neighbourhood of Cotorro during a three-hour speech broadcast live on television. He is unconscious for only a few minutes, and the fainting spell is attributed to heat and excessive sun. Eight hours later, Fidel appears on a television programme to explain what happened.

11–13 August 2001: On his seventy-fifth birthday, Fidel Castro celebrates with President Hugo Chávez in Ciudad Bolívar, Venezuela.

11 September 2001: Terrorist attacks on the twin towers of the World Trade Center in New York and the Pentagon in Washington leave almost 3,000 people dead. Fidel Castro condemns the act in the strongest of terms, expresses his grief over the victims and his sorrow for their families, and offers US authorities logistical aid (access to Cuban airports). He also states that wars will not end terrorism in the world.

19–21 December 2001: In Argentina, hundreds of thousands of people take to the streets in protest against neoliberal economic policies. The government declares a state of siege and gives orders allowing demonstrators to be fired upon. The result is dozens of deaths and even greater anger and outrage on the part of the demonstrators. President Fernando de la Rúa is overthrown on the 21st.

7 January 2002: Washington informs Cuba of its intention to create a prison facility on the Guantánamo Naval Base (occupied by the US under constant protest from Cuba) to receive prisoners from Afghanistan suspected of having taken part in international terrorist activities. Conditions under which the prisoners are treated will soon create an international scandal.

11 January 2002: In Camp Delta on the Guantánamo Naval Base, the first twenty prisoners accused of terrorism and of being linked to the Al-Qaeda network arrive.

11 April 2002: In Caracas, a coup is mounted against President Hugo Chávez. Fidel Castro follows events closely. The coup is unsuccessful and Hugo Chávez returns to power in the early morning hours of 14 April.

6 May 2002: President George W. Bush makes the unfounded accusation that Cuba is carrying out research on biological weapons.

12–17 May 2002: Former President Jimmy Carter visits Cuba and gives a speech at the University of Havana that is broadcast live on Cuban television.

21 May 2002: President George W. Bush includes Cuba on his list of countries 'sponsoring terrorism'.

27 October 2002: In Brazil, Luiz Inácio 'Lula' da Silva, a union leader and founder of the Workers Party and a friend of Fidel Castro, is elected president.

11 November 2002: James Cason, new director of the American Interests Office, arrives in Havana. Cason immediately begins intense activity aimed at undermining the Cuban government.

25 November 2002: In Ecuador, Colonel Lucio Gutiérrez, with the support of native peoples' organizations and popular forces, is elected president.

March 2003: In Cuba, over seventy dissidents are arrested, tried and sentenced to prison[, among them the poet Raúl Rivero (1st ed.)]. The Cuban government present proof of their financial and political ties to the government of the United States through the American Interests Office in Havana.

20 March 2003: US planes bomb Baghdad and the Iraq war begins.

April 2003: A group of hijackers of a ferry attempting to pilot the boat illegally to the United States are arrested, tried and sentenced. Three are sentenced to death and executed.

27 April 2003: In Argentina, running on a platform radically opposed to neoliberalism, Néstor Kirchner is elected president.

13 May 2003: Washington expels fourteen Cuban diplomats.

26 May 2003: In Buenos Aires, Fidel Castro attends the inauguration of President Néstor Kirchner. At the university, Castro gives a speech to an audience of tens of thousands.

June 2003: In reprisal for the imprisonment of seventy-five so-called 'dissidents' and the execution of three young hijackers in Cuba, the countries of the European Union decide to invite the Cuban dissidents and their families to their embassies during the celebration of those countries' national holidays. The Cuban government responds by isolating the European embassies in Havana that go along with this plan, leaving the European diplomats incommunicado.

14 June 2003: Cuban authorities close the Spanish Cultural Centre in Havana due to its 'having instigated the sanctions adopted by the European Union against Cuba'.

18 June 2003: Over 1 million Cubans sign a petition to amend the constitution to declare Socialism 'irrevocable'.

26 June 2003: The National Assembly votes to amend the Constitution and declare Socialism irrevocable.

[13 July 2003: At the age of ninety-five, Máximo Francisco Repilado Muñoz, better known as Compay Segundo, famed singer and musician, dies in Havana. He had been born in Siboney on 18 November 1907. Wim Wenders and Ry Cooder's film *Buena Vista Social Club* (1997) had made Compay Segundo and the other musicians of that group the most famous Cuban musicians in the world (in 1st ed.).]

16 September 2003: Felipe Pérez Roque, Cuba's minister of foreign affairs, states that the economic blockade imposed by the United States and in place for four decades has, thus far, caused the island financial losses of some $72 billion.

19 September 2003: In the first instance of a conviction in forty years, the Cuban who hijacked an airliner and forced it to fly to Miami in April 2003 is sentenced by a Florida court to twenty years in prison.

24–27 September 2003: Brazilian president Lula da Silva visits Cuba and signs twelve cooperation agreements.

October 2003: In the aftermath of Hurricane Michelle, which severely damaged much of Cuba, the government of the United States authorizes the sale of food and agricultural products to Cuba, although with heavy restrictions. With this act, the United States becomes, despite the economic blockade that has been in place since 1962, the largest supplier of food and agricultural products to the country.

10 October 2003: Speaking in Florida, President George W. Bush promises to intensify pressure against Cuba and announces the creation of a Commission for Assistance to a Free Cuba, headed by Secretary of State Colin Powell and charged with 'preparing for democratic transition' on the island. Bush also decides to 'reinforce controls to prevent banned trips' to Cuba. In 2002 some 230,000 US citizens visited the island, more than 40,000 of them illegally [that is, without the permission of US authorities], exposing themselves to fines of up to $250,000.

17 October 2003: In Bolivia, widespread demonstrations demand the nationalization of oil companies. Police and other authorities shoot into the crowds and kill many demonstrators. President Gonzalo Sánchez de Losada is overthrown.

[29 October 2003: The Socialist International, meeting in São Paolo, denounces the US trade embargo on Cuba. It also asks Havana to free its 'political prisoners' and adopt 'democratic reforms' (in 1st ed.).]

31 October 2003: In Uruguay, Tabaré Vázquez, leader of the Frente Amplio (Broad Front, a coalition of left-wing parties), is elected president.

1 November 2003: In Bogotá, Cuban singer-songwriter Pablo Milanés says, 'In Cuba, there are errors that we have the right to criticize.'

[**December 2003:** All the high-ranking officials of the Cuban government tourist agency Cubanacan are removed due to 'grave errors' and 'lack of strictness and control' (in 1st ed.).]

[**5 December 2003:** First meeting of the Commission for Assistance to a Free Cuba, co-chaired by Secretary of State Colin Powell and Secretary of Housing and Urban Development Mel Martínez, of Cuban descent (in 1st ed.).]

14 December 2003: In Havana, Cuban dissident Oswaldo Payá makes public a 'political transition programme' for Cuba.

1 January 2004: On the forty-fifth anniversary of the triumph of the Revolution, Cuba finds itself engaged in a 'battle of ideas' to raise the level of overall culture of the Cuban people, in ongoing struggles to eliminate the US economic embargo and repeal anti-Cuban migration laws in the United States, and in a campaign to free five Cuban agents, 'Heroes of the Republic of Cuba', who have been sentenced to long prison terms in the United States.

3 January 2004: Speech by Fidel Castro in the Karl Marx Theatre in Havana on the occasion of the forty-fifth anniversary of the triumph of the Revolution. Castro denounces the FTAA, a project defended by Washington, as a 'final assault on the independence of Latin America'.

[**15 January 2004:** 'For reasons of infrastructure', the Cuban government adopts restrictive measures on internet access. In Cuba, there are approximately 270,000 computers, 65 per cent of which are connected to the Web (in 1st ed.).]

21 January 2004: Ecumenical patriarch Bartholomew I, spiritual leader of 250 million Orthodox Christians, visits Cuba.

22 January 2004: Fidel Castro meets Robert Redford, who has come to present a film about Che Guevara, *The Motorcycle Diaries*, which he has produced. The meeting takes place in Havana in the Hotel Nacional.

29 January 2004: Fidel Castro accuses US President George W. Bush of planning to assassinate him.

[**5 February 2004:** The Havana Book Fair begins. In protest against the trial and imprisonment of seventy-five dissidents in March 2003, Germany, the country of honour at this year's fair, decides not to take part officially (in 1st ed.).]

[**11 February 2004:** Cuba's minister of tourism, Ibrahim Ferradaz, is removed from office (in 1st ed.).]

[**24 February 2004:** UNESCO gives the World Freedom of Press Prize to Raúl Rivero, the Cuban journalist sentenced in April 2003 to twenty years in prison (in 1st ed.).]

April 2004: Diplomatic crisis between Cuba and Mexico: after Mexico's vote at the UN Human Rights Commission to condemn Cuba, Fidel Castro says that President Vicente Fox's administration has turned Mexico's foreign policy to 'ashes' by bowing to US interests. [Cuba's ambassador in Mexico, Jorge Bolaños, is expelled and the Mexican ambassador in Havana, Roberta Lajoux, is called home (in 1st ed.).]

14 April 2004: In the United States, HBO broadcasts director Oliver Stone's documentary *Looking for Fidel*, the second version of the documentary *Comandante*, which he filmed in February 2002 but which HBO refused to broadcast, considering it pro-Cuban.

24 April 2004: Judge James L. King of Florida sentences six Cubans to over twenty years in prison for hijacking a Cuban Aerotaxi DC-3 passenger plane after takeoff from the Isle of Youth on 19 March 2003.

29 April 2004: In a report by the State Department, Washington accuses Cuba of 'maintaining links to international terrorism'.

8 May 2004: The American government makes public a plan to 'speed up the transition to democracy in Cuba'; this plan restricts trips to the island by Cuban residents in the

United States, strengthens the trade embargo and promises $36 million to finance internal opposition groups.

[10 **May** 2004: Cuban dissidents Eloy Gutiérrez Menoyo, Oswaldo Payá and Elizardo Sánchez criticize the new measures taken by Washington against Cuba and reject the plan to 'speed up the transition' (in 1st ed.).]

14 **May** 2004: In Havana, before hundreds of thousands of demonstrators against Washington's attitude, Fidel Castro reads his 'First Epistle to George Bush'.

18 **May** 2004: Cuba sponsors a meeting in Havana with moderate exile leaders [and invites former political prisoner and leader of the opposition group Cambio Cubano, Eloy Gutiérrez Menoyo, to take part (in 1st ed.)].

10 **June** 2004: Cuban authorities free five dissidents, among them Miguel Valdés, who had been one of the seventy-five activists sentenced in April 2003.

21 **June** 2004: In a speech before [some 200,000 people (1st ed.)] over 1 million people, Fidel Castro reads his 'Second Epistle to George Bush' and says that the United States' new sanctions may provoke another grave migration crisis, or even war.

[23 **June** 2004: The Cuban government frees two more dissidents. Manuel Vásquez Portal and Roberto de Miranda, of the group of seventy-five dissidents sentenced in April 2003 (in 1st ed.).]

July 2004: Measures adopted in February by the US government to 'pull the rug out from under Cuba' go into effect: visits to the island by Cuban exiles are limited to fourteen days every three years, and only for direct family members; the $3,000 in cash that visitors had been allowed to take is reduced to $300; daily expenses are reduced from $164 to $50; luggage weight, formerly unlimited, is now limited to sixty pounds (twenty-seven kilos); and remittances are limited to $1,200 and may only be sent to direct family members. Estimates show that the flow of dollars from the United States to Cuba that results from aid and travel to Cuba by some 1.3 million Cuban exiles or US residents has been totalling $1.2 billion per year.

17 **July** 2004: President Bush, in a stump speech in Florida, accuses Fidel Castro of having turned Cuba into 'a main port of sexual tourism'.

[22 **July** 2004: Cuban authorities free dissident Martha Beatriz Roque, the only woman in the group of seventy-five activists imprisoned in April 2003 (in 1st ed.).]

26 **July** 2004: In Santa Clara, Cuba, on the fifty-first anniversary of the assault on the Moncada barracks, Fidel Castro, in response to President Bush's accusation that Cuba promotes sexual tourism, links George W. Bush's religious fundamentalism to alcohol.

15 **August** 2004: In Venezuela, President Hugo Chávez wins a recall vote with 58.25 per cent of the votes, consolidating his hold on power. Earlier, more than 10,000 young Venezuelans had travelled to Cuba as part of 'Operation Hope' to take forty-five-day courses to become 'participants in the social struggle', what is known in Cuban shorthand as 'social workers'. On their return, these young people join the Francisco de Miranda Front, which plays a key role in voter registration in the run-up to the recall election.

[19 **August** 2004: In a meeting held in Rio de Janeiro, Mexico, Uruguay, El Salvador, Nicaragua and Costa Rica oppose Brazil's request to allow Cuba to join the Rio Group, comprised of nineteen Latin American countries (in 1st ed.).]

26 **August** 2004: Cuba breaks off diplomatic relations with Panama as a consequence of outgoing President Mireya Moscoso's decision to grant amnesty to Luis Posada Carriles and three of his accomplices, all of whom had been accused of acts of terrorism and found guilty of planning the assassination of Fidel Castro.

10–13 **September** 2004: Hundreds of thousands of people are evacuated under the threat of Hurricane Ivan, the strongest tropical storm in fifty years. On television, Fidel Castro takes part in organizing the civil defence response. Ivan turns at the last minute and misses the island, with the exception of the extreme western tip. No casualties are reported.

30 **September** 2004: The Cuban government adopts strict measures to conserve electricity after a problem at the country's main thermoelectric plant. One hundred and eighteen businesses close as well as forty hotels in Havana and Varadero. [Blackouts lasting six

hours a day, four times a week, trigger popular discontent, but they last until February 2005 (in 1st ed.).]

[6 October 2004: In Miami, Andrés Nazario Sargén, one of the main anti-Castro leaders in Florida and founder of the Alpha 66 group blamed for numerous acts of terrorism in Cuba, dies (in 1st ed.).]

[14 October 2004: Fidel Castro removes the minister of basic industry, Marcos Portal, from office, blaming him for the problem with production of electricity. Portal was a member of the Politburo of the Cuban Communist Party and is married to one of Castro's nieces (in 1st ed.).]

20 October 2004: Fidel Castro fractures his left knee and suffers a stress fracture to his right arm when he trips and falls at the end of a speech at the tomb of Che Guevara in Santa Clara. A few hours later, Castro reappears on the screen sitting in a chair; he announces, 'in order to prevent speculation', that he has fractured his knee and hurt his arm.

26 October 2004: Fidel Castro reappears on television; he is sitting down and his right arm is in a sling. He announces the end of the 'dollarization' of the Cuban economy. Beginning on 8 November, the dollar will no longer circulate in any business, hotel or shop on the island, and will be replaced by the convertible peso, a currency valid only in Cuba.

16 November 2004: The European Union recognizes that the breakdown of dialogue with Cuba 'is not positive'.

[17 November 2004: The European Parliament, in a vote of 376 to 281, demands that Cuba free its political prisoners as a condition for resuming dialogue. The Socialist European deputy Miguel Angel Martínez disagrees: 'There are fifty countries in the world, from China to Sudan and Libya, in which the human rights situation is much worse than in Cuba, and the European Union maintains normal relations with them. Why, then, this exceptional attitude towards Cuba?' (in 1st ed.).]

[18 November 2004: Spanish prime minister José Luis Rodríguez Zapatero, in an interview with the EFE news agency before leaving for Costa Rica to take part in the fourteenth Ibero-American Summit (in which Fidel Castro will not take part), urges 'quick steps toward the democratization' of Cuba (in 1st ed.).]

23 November 2004: The president of China, Hu Jintao, visits Cuba. Agreements are signed for more than $500 million in Chinese investment in the Cuban nickel industry, credits for education and health, and the purchase of 1 million Chinese televisions.

25 November 2004: After more than a year without official contact, Cuba normalizes diplomatic relations with Spain.

[30 November 2004: Cuban authorities free dissident writer Raúl Rivero and four other dissidents: Oscar Espinosa, Margarito Broche, Marcelo López and Osvaldo Alfonso Valdés (in 1st ed.).]

[6 December 2004: The Cuban government frees journalist Jorge Olivera, founder of the dissident news agency Habana Press, who had been sentenced to eighteen years in prison in the summary trials in April 2003 (in 1st ed.).]

13 December 2004: The entire island is the setting for the huge military manoeuvres dubbed 'Bastion 2004', in which 100,000 soldiers and hundreds of tanks will take part. These manoeuvres are organized in response to 'continuous threats and aggressions by the United States'.

14 December 2004: In Havana, Fidel Castro and Hugo Chávez sign a cooperation agreement broadening already existing accords between Cuba and Venezuela. The agreement eliminates import tariffs between the two countries, opens facilities for investment, sets a 'minimum price of $27 a barrel' on petroleum sales, and promises Venezuelan financing for projects in the Cuban energy sector and electricity industry. This agreement takes place within the spirit of the Bolivarian Alternative for the Americas (ALBA), a counter to the US-backed FTAA.

[14 December 2004: The European Union's working group on Latin America recommends that European Union countries suspend invitations to Cuban dissidents to receptions organized by their embassies in Havana (in 1st ed.).]

16 December 2004: Fidel Castro meets in Havana with more than 300 US businessmen and women, mostly farmers and ranchers.

[17 December 2004: A minor diplomatic crisis between Cuba and Argentina takes place when Cuban authorities, despite a letter from Argentine president Néstor Kirchner to Fidel Castro, deny a visa to Cuban physician Hilda Molina Morejón, sixty-one years old, who is considered a dissident by the Havana government (in 1st ed.).]

[22 December 2004: Several groups of moderate Cuban dissidents found a digital journal, *Consenso* (consenso.org), and, with the consent of the authorities, present their publication in a storefront belonging to a state business (in 1st ed.).]

[23 December 2004: Two months after fracturing his left knee, Fidel Castro walks for the first time in public (in 1st ed.).]

26 December 2004: Fidel Castro announces the discovery by Canadian firm Sherritt-Peberco of a new oilfield off the north coast of Cuba near Havana. The field is believed to contain reserves of 100 million barrels of crude oil.

3 January 2005: Cuba re-establishes official contact with eight countries in the European Union: Germany, Austria, France, Greece, Italy, Portugal, the United Kingdom and Sweden, and a few days later normalizes relations with all the countries of the European Union.

[10 January 2005: The Cuban Commission for Human Rights and National Reconciliation (not recognized by Cuban authorities) publishes a list of 294 'political prisoners' held on the island. The Commission accuses the Cuban government of refusing to cooperate with the International Red Cross and the United Nations Commission on Human Rights (in 1st ed.).]

13 January 2005: In an article in the *New York Times*, editorial writer Nicholas D. Kristof says that 'If the US had an infant mortality rate as good as Cuba's, we would save an additional 2,212 American babies a year.'

15 January 2005: The United States Supreme Court declares that the continued detention in US jails of more than 700 Cubans who, despite having served their sentences, are still in the legal limbo of indefinite detention because Cuba will not agree to their being deported to the island, is illegal. Most of these Cubans had reached the coast of Florida in 1980 during the Mariel boatlift.

8 March 2005: In a speech given on International Women's Day, Fidel Castro announces that Cuba is about to achieve 'economic invulnerability'. He asserts that in 2006, the problem of the energy deficit will be solved, housing construction will double, the national railway recovery project will go into effect, and equipment will be made available to improve bus transport between provinces. He also announces that within a short time, 5 million pressure cookers and Chinese rice cookers will be distributed among the population.

17 March 2005: Fidel Castro announces a 7 per cent revaluation of the peso due to the 'excellent behaviour' of the Cuban economy.

18 March 2005: Amnesty International requests that Cuba free seventy-one prisoners of conscience.

2 April 2005: In Vatican City, Pope John Paul II dies.

13 April 2005: Fidel Castro accuses the United States of giving refuge to Luis Posada Carriles, the Cuban terrorist found guilty of blowing up a Cuban airlines plane in 1976 in which seventy-three people were killed.

14 April 2005: In Geneva, after strong pressure from the US, the UN Commission on Human Rights votes by a narrow margin to condemn Cuba's human rights record.

19 April 2005: In the Vatican, Cardinal Joseph Ratzinger, prefect of the Congregation for the Doctrine of the Faith and dean of the College of Cardinals, is elected pope. He takes the name Benedict XVI.

21 April 2005: In a television appearance, Fidel Castro announces that to save energy, traditional incandescent light bulbs will no longer be sold in Cuba. He asks for 'a little bit of patience' and says that the blackouts will end in the second half of 2006.

28 April 2005: Hugo Chávez and Fidel Castro take part in the Fourth Hemispheric Meeting of opponents of the Free Trade Area of the Americas (FTAA).

2 May 2005: Chilean Socialist José Miguel Insulza is elected secretary-general of the Organization of American States, although Washington has opposed his candidacy. This is the first time that the United States has not managed to impose one of its own candidates to that strategic position.

17 May 2005: More than 1 million Cubans, with Fidel Castro at their head, march in Havana to denounce US President George W. Bush's double standard for terrorism, which protects Luis Posada Carriles, guilty of terrorist attacks against Cuban civilians, while denouncing other countries' harbouring of terrorists. That same day, Posada Carriles is arrested on an immigration violation.

[**20 May 2005:** In the Havana neighbourhood of Río Verde, the largest dissident meeting ever held in Cuba takes place: some 150 representatives of opposition groups meet to talk about democracy and suggest actions that might lead to political transition on the island. The government does not prevent the meeting, which is marked by shouts of 'Down with Fidel!' (in 1st ed.).]

27 May 2005: The UN's task force on arbitrary detentions denounces what it calls the 'arbitrary imprisonment' of five Cubans in the United States, and underscores that the imprisonment violates international law.

6 June 2005: In Bolivia, mass demonstrations backed by indigenous organizations which are in turn supported by Evo Morales demand that oil and gas reserves be nationalized. President Carlos Mesa is overthrown.

29 June 2005: In Puerto La Cruz, Venezuela, Fidel Castro takes part in the First Meeting of Caribbean Heads of State and Energy Ministers, convened by President Hugo Chávez, at which the officials of the CARICOM (Caribbean Community) nations join in a regional oil alliance to be called Petrocaribe, aimed at cheaper and more efficient oil distribution in the region.

[**13 July 2005:** A group of dissidents demonstrate on the Malecón in Havana in memory of the sinking of the tugboat *13 de Marzo* in which forty-one people trying to flee Cuba were drowned on 13 July 1994. The demonstrators are dispersed by members of the rapid response brigades (in 1st ed.).]

[**22 July 2005:** Thirty-three dissidents are detained when they attempt to demonstrate in front of the French embassy in Havana to demand the release of political prisoners. Most of the demonstrators are freed a few hours later (in 1st ed.).]

24 July 2005: In Caracas, the Latin American TV channel Telesur is inaugurated. This project stems from a five-party alliance of Venezuela, Cuba, Argentina, Uruguay and Brazil.

26 July 2005: During activities celebrating the fifty-second anniversary of the assault on the Moncada barracks, Fidel Castro calls dissidents and opponents of the regime 'traitors and mercenaries', and declares that the American Interests Office in Havana is the main instigator of opposition groups and that its activities are 'provocative'.

[**28 July 2005:** To save energy on the island, Cuba imposes a ban on the import of conventional electric light bulbs (in 1st ed.).]

28 July 2005: US Secretary of State Condoleezza Rice appoints Caleb McCarry to be the first Transition Coordinator in Cuba; his job is to 'hasten the end of tyranny' on the island.

[**6 August 2005:** Ibrahim Ferrer, the singer made famous by the Buena Vista Social Club after decades of obscurity during the Revolution, dies in Havana (in 1st ed.).]

9 August 2005: The US Federal District Court in Atlanta orders a new trial for the five Cubans (Gerardo Hernández, Fernando González, Ramón Labañino, René González and Antonio Guerrero) sentenced in 2001 to long prison terms for espionage. Fidel Castro calls this decision a 'legal triumph' in the battle to free the five 'Heroes of the Revolution'.

[**13 August 2005:** Fidel Castro celebrates his seventy-ninth birthday. The newspaper *Granma*, in an open letter published on the first page, says that the celebration is carried out 'with the immense affection and admiration that children feel for the noblest, wisest, and most courageous of fathers'; the letter is signed 'Your people' (in 1st ed.).]

20 August 2005: In the Karl Marx Theatre in Havana, Fidel Castro, Hugo Chávez and other Latin American and Caribbean heads of state attend the graduation of 1,610 doctors from the Latin American School of Medicine, created in 1988, in which over 10,000 young people from twenty-eight Latin American and Caribbean countries study free of charge.

20 August 2005: During a visit to Cuba by President Martín Torrijos, Cuba and Panama reopen diplomatic relations.

3 September 2005: After the humanitarian disaster caused in New Orleans by Hurricane Katrina, Fidel Castro offers to send 1,100 doctors specializing in emergency medical care to Louisiana. The US government does not respond to Cuba's offer.

[8 September 2005: Coinciding with the festival of the Virgen de la Caridad del Cobre, Cuba's patron saint, authorities forbid twelve Catholic processions. This is the first such prohibition since Pope John Paul II's visit to the island in 1998 (in 1st ed.).]

15 September 2005: James Cason resigns as head of the US Interests Office in Havana and is replaced by Michael Parmly.

28 September 2005: The US government decides that 77-year-old former CIA agent Luis Posada Carriles, who escaped from a Venezuelan jail in 1985 on the eve of his trial for blowing up a Cuban plane with seventy-three people aboard in 1976, and who had illegally entered the United States, will not be deported to Venezuela or Cuba. The government's rationale is that Posada 'might be tortured in those countries'.

October 2005: The United States Senate confirms the nomination of Thomas Shannon to the position of assistant secretary of state for western hemisphere affairs. Shannon, who succeeds Otto Reich and Roger Noriega, was formerly a political adviser in the US embassy in Caracas, and in April 2002 had expressed his satisfaction at the fleeting 'victory' of the coup against President Hugo Chávez.

[2 October 2005: The European Union requests that Cuba improve the conditions under which its 'political prisoners' are held, in particular three prisoners on hunger strike – Víctor Rolando Arroyo, Félix Navarro and José Daniel Ferrer – who have been held since March 2003. Of the group of seventy-five people sentenced on that date, fourteen have been freed for health reasons (in 1st ed.).]

[3 October 2005: On the occasion of German Unity Day, the German embassy in Havana invites several dissidents – Martha Beatriz Roque, Vladimiro Roca, Elizardo Sánchez – to a 'German evening'. Ambassador Hans-Ulrich Lunscken states that the reunification of his country was possible 'because of the failure of Socialism and the work of the peaceful dissident movement'. The Cuban Foreign Ministry protests, and relations between the European Union in Brussels and Havana grow tense once again (in 1st ed.).]

14–15 October 2005: Ibero-American Summit in Salamanca, Spain. Fidel Castro does not attend. The heads of state of the Ibero-American nations condemn the 'blockade' of Cuba and demand that US authorities bring terrorist Luis Posada Carriles to justice.

15 October 2005: In Havana, young 'social workers' take over the city's petrol stations as part of the campaign against corruption[; the government discovers that over half the income of gas stations was 'lost' under the old management (in 1st ed.)].

22 October 2005: The threat of Hurricane Wilma forces the evacuation of half a million people in Cuba. The World Meteorological Organization (WMO) recognizes the effectiveness of the Cuban system of early alerts for natural disasters and commends the island's 'high efficiency' in minimizing the human and economic toll taken by disasters.

24 October 2005: Hurricane Wilma causes severe flooding in Havana.

28 October 2005: Fidel Castro criticizes the 'new rich' and launches an offensive against the accumulation of illicit wealth, the 'sybaritism' of some leaders, corruption and theft.

[28 October 2005: The European Parliament in Strasbourg gives the Sakharov Human Rights Prize to Las Damas de Blanco, a group comprised of the wives of the dissidents arrested in March 2003 (in 1st ed.).]

[29 October 2005: The Brazilian weekly *Veja* states that Cuba helped underwrite the election campaign for President Lula in 2002. Havana strenuously denies the story (in 1st ed.).]

[30 October 2005: Six of ten Cuban *balseros* intercepted by the Coast Guard and the

Immigration Service a week earlier off Haulover Beach in Florida, an operation broadcast live on Miami television, are repatriated to the island, while the other four, who have requested political asylum, are sent to Guantánamo while their requests are being processed (in 1st ed.).]

4–5 November 2005: The Summit of the Americas, meeting in Mar del Plata, Argentina, refuses to approve the proposed Free Trade Area of the Americas (FTAA). The FTAA has been put forward by US President George W. Bush as a way of consolidating the US's economic hegemony in the western hemisphere.

7 November 2005: According to the census taken in 2002 and made public now, the population of Cuba that year totalled 11,177,743.

8 November 2005: For the fourteenth consecutive time, the UN condemns the United States' trade embargo against Cuba; 182 countries vote against the blockade, while only four votes are cast in favour: the United States, Israel, the Marshall Islands and Palau.

17 November 2005: In an important speech lasting five hours, Fidel Castro says that the widespread corruption and theft committed against the state endanger the Revolution, and he announces a new offensive against corruption.

23 November 2005: Thus far this year, Cuba has welcomed 2 million visitors, which brings it close to the 2.3 million tourists hoped for in 2005, which will be the highest in its history.

7 December 2005: The Henry Reeve Emergency Medical Contingent, which provided aid to isolated communities in the high plains of Guatemala after that country was hit by Hurricane Stan in October, returns to Cuba.

8 December 2005: Fidel Castro takes part in the Second Cuba–CARICOM Summit in Bridgetown, Barbados.

8 December 2005: The new head of the American Interests Office in Havana, Michael Parmly, says, 'I don't know when a change is happening, I just know that a change is happening,' and he says he believes that the Cuban people will lead the change.

12 December 2005: Cuba and the US state of Virginia sign an agreement for the sale of agricultural products to Cuba totalling $30 million over the next eighteen months.

14 December 2005: The US Treasury's Office of Foreign Assets Control announces that it will not authorize the Cuban baseball team to enter the United States to play in the World Baseball Classic. The decision is reversed after strong international protest.

16 December 2005: 'Peace conversations' between the Colombian National Liberation Army (ELN) and representatives of the Alvaro Uribe government begin in Havana, with the presence of author Gabriel García Márquez.

18 December 2005: Evo Morales, leader of the Movement Towards Socialism (MAS), is elected president of Bolivia.

20 December 2005: In Havana during the regularly scheduled broadcast of the programme *Round Table* on Cuban radio and television, activities with so-called 'dissidents' and recent declarations by Michael Parmly, new head of the American Interests Office in Havana, are called 'provocative and cynical'.

23 December 2005: In the Cuban National Assembly, foreign relations minister Felipe Pérez Roque refers to 'after Fidel Castro' and says that the 'vacuum' can only be filled under three conditions: that the 'leaders' austere conduct and absence of privileges set an example [for the people]', that they have the support of the people, and that they prevent the appearance of a class of property owners that would be, in his opinion, 'pro-American'.

30 December 2005: In Havana, Fidel Castro welcomes Evo Morales, president-elect of Bolivia, with full state honours. The two heads of state sign an important cooperation agreement.

31 December 2005: Cuban authorities announce that according to government estimates which include the value of social services, the island ends 2005 with economic growth of 11.8 per cent. This is the highest growth rate achieved by the island in its forty-six years under Socialism.

January 2006: Within the framework of the battle against corruption, Party officials take control of hundreds of production centres. Dozens of sackings are expected.

6 January 2006: In Havana, Fidel Castro inaugurates a 'forest of black flags' symbolizing the 3,478 Cuban victims of 'US-backed terrorism'. The 'forest' is planted in front of the building housing the American Interests Office and, in response to Michael Parmly's decision to use the façade to display information hostile to Cuban authorities, is intended to hide the building's façade.

15 January 2006: In Chile, Socialist candidate Michelle Bachelet is elected president.

20 January 2006: In Brazil, presidents Lula, Chávez and Kirchner agree to construct a 10,000-kilometre oil pipeline between Venezuela and Argentina.

22 January 2006: In Bolivia, Evo Morales takes office as president.

3 February 2006: In Mexico, the Sheraton María Isabel Hotel expels a sixteen-member Cuban delegation staying there during negotiations with a large delegation of American businessmen and women. The expulsion comes under pressure on the hotel from the US Department of the Treasury in application of the Helms–Burton Act of 1996, which forbids foreign businesses from having any economic relationship with Cuban businesses or citizens; this act is in clear violation of international law.

5 April 2006: In an operation aimed at stopping the illegal trafficking of emigrants that is centred south of Pinar del Río, Cuban border guards open fire against a speedboat from Miami that has come to pick up a group of people. One of the traffickers is killed and two are arrested.

28 April 2006: The Political Committee of the Communist Party removes one of its members, Juan Carlos Robinson, for 'abuse of power and influence-peddling'. On 21 June he will be sentenced to twelve years in prison. No member of the Political Committee has ever before been tried and convicted.

1 May 2006: In Bolivia, Evo Morales signs a decree nationalizing the country's petroleum producers.

24 May 2006: Lina Pedraza, minister in charge of the government's central accounting office, is relieved of her position.

3 June 2006: On the occasion of the seventy-fifth birthday of Raúl Castro, *Granma* publishes an eight-page supplement about him.

11 June 2006: The Cuban government states that in future, Cuba will accept no foreign aid if the donor country imposes conditions on the aid.

12 June 2006: The American Interests Office in Havana reports that the authorities have cut off its electricity.

14 June 2006: In a speech, Raúl Castro says that the Communist Party is the true guarantor of Cuban unity and that after Fidel Castro, the Party will assume leadership of the country.

4 July 2006: The Communist Party re-establishes the Central Committee Secretariat, which had been suspended during the nineties, and names three women to serve on the twelve-member Secretariat.

10 July 2006: In Washington, DC, President George Bush makes public a report by the Commission for Assistance to a Free Cuba and says that 'the United States is actively working to encourage change in Cuba and will not be content to wait'. Eighty million dollars will be sent to 'support Cubans who want change'.

26 July 2006: At the end of the ceremonies commemorating the fifty-third anniversary of the attack on the Moncada barracks in Santiago and on the Cespedes barracks in Bayamo, Fidel Castro suffers a 'severe intestinal crisis' and a severe haemorrhage. He undergoes emergency surgery on 27 July.

31 July 2006: Fidel Castro's personal assistant, Carlos Valenciaga, goes on television to read a 'proclamation from the commander-in-chief to the population'. Castro turns over his responsibilities, 'on a provisional basis', to a team of seven men headed by Raúl Castro; the other six members are José Ramón Balaguer, José Ramón Machado Ventura, Esteban Lazo, Carlos Lage, Francisco Soberón and Felipe Pérez Roque.

1 August 2006: Fidel Castro says that because Cuba is besieged and threatened by the United States, his health is to be a 'state secret'.

3 August 2006: In Washington, DC, President Bush exhorts Cubans to 'work toward change'.

9 August 2006: An appeals court in Atlanta reverses its decision, handed down exactly a year earlier, to revoke the sentences of the five Cubans convicted of espionage by a court in Miami on 2 April 2003.

13 August 2006: Fidel Castro's birthday. The press publishes the first photographs of Castro during his convalescence. Birthday celebrations are postponed until 2 December.

14 August 2006: A new series of photographs is published and a video is broadcast on television showing Fidel Castro accompanied by Raúl Castro and Hugo Chávez.

16 August 2006: In Brazil, former Paraguayan dictator Alfredo Stroessner dies.

23 August 2006: Washington proposes to raise the embargo if Cuba begins a democratic transition, with the additional condition that 'no Castro have political responsibilities'.

31 August 2006: Ramiro Valdés, veteran revolutionary *comandante*, is named minister of information technology and communications.

1 September 2006: Cuban television broadcasts a video of the meeting between Hugo Chávez and Fidel Castro. Chávez says, 'This is my third visit, and the patient is greatly improved.'

5 September 2006: In a written message, Fidel Castro says that 'the worst is past' and that he is 'recovering satisfactorily'. He reveals that he has lost 18.5 kilograms, some forty pounds, and says he is in no hurry to assume the reins of power again, since the government is 'in good hands'.

11–16 September 2006: Non-Aligned Summit meeting in Havana. Fidel Castro, who is still recovering and does not take part in the summit, is elected president of the movement. Castro has a private meeting with Kofi Annan, Evo Morales, Hugo Chávez and [Algerian president] Abdelaziz Bouteflika.

9 October 2006: Raúl Castro denies that Fidel Castro is suffering from 'terminal cancer'.

17 October 2006: In Washington, President Bush signs a law authorizing the torture of any person who represents 'a danger to the nation'.

25 October 2006: Two opponents of the Cuban government, Ricardo Medina and Francisco Moure, are released from prison.

26 October 2006: The World Wildlife Fund (WWF) states in a report published in Beijing that 'Cuba is the only country that meets conditions for sustainable development.'

28 October 2006: After forty days without any news or images of him, Fidel Castro reappears on Cuban television, which broadcasts a six-minute video in which Castro says, 'Since the beginning I have said repeatedly that my recovery will be a long one, and not without risks.' He also states, 'I am taking part in important government decisions.' This will be his last public appearance in 2006.

29 October 2006: In Brazil, Lula is re-elected president.

5 November 2006: In Nicaragua, Sandinista leader Daniel Ortega wins the presidential elections; he dedicates his victory to Fidel Castro.

7 November 2006: In the United States, the Republican Party loses the midterm elections, thereby losing control of the House and Senate.

8 November 2006: For the fifteenth consecutive time, the UN General Assembly condemns the embargo of Cuba unilaterally imposed by the United States; the vote is 183 to 4.

14 November 2006: In Cuba, three government opponents are released from prison.

16 November 2006: In San Francisco, California, economist Milton Friedman dies at the age of ninety-six. Friedman was the main theorist of neoliberalism, which was exported to Chile in the seventies and which inspired the ultra-liberal policies of General Pinochet.

26 November 2006: In Ecuador, leftist candidate Rafael Correa is elected president.

28 November 2006: Celebrations commemorating Fidel Castro's eightieth birthday begin. Castro sends a written message to the people in which he says, 'I am still not ready, according to the doctors, for such a colossal event.'

28 November 2006: In London, Channel Four broadcasts a documentary by Dollan Cannell titled *638 Ways to Kill Castro*, detailing the assassination attempts on Castro backed by the CIA.

2 December 2006: Fidel Castro fails to attend the military parade held in Havana on the fiftieth anniversary of the *Granma* landing. In his speech, Raúl Castro says, 'I take this opportunity to reiterate our willingness to resolve at the negotiating table the prolonged disagreements between the United States and Cuba.'

3 December 2006: In Venezuela, Hugo Chávez is re-elected president.

7 December 2006: One member of the group of seventy-five individuals arrested in March 2003, Héctor Palacios, is released from prison. He is the sixteenth member of that opposition group to be set free.

10 December 2006: In Santiago de Chile, former dictator Augusto Pinochet dies.

12 December 2006: In Washington, DC, the office of Foreign Assets Control fines film director Oliver Stone for going to Cuba in 2002 and 2003 and filming two documentaries on Fidel Castro.

12 December 2006: In Addis Ababa, Ethiopia, the Supreme Court declares former president Mengistu Haile Mariam, who is currently in exile in Zimbabwe, guilty of genocide and sentences him to life in prison.

13 December 2006: Famed Brazilian architect Oscar Neimeyer offers Fidel Castro a 9.5-ton sculpture to be installed at the University of Information Science in Havana.

15 December 2006: The *Washington Post* publishes a statement by John Negroponte, director of national intelligence, predicting Fidel Castro's imminent death.

15 December 2006: A ten-member delegation from the US Congress favouring an end to the economic embargo arrives in Havana for a three-day visit. They are welcomed by Raúl Castro on 17 December.

20 December 2006: Raúl Castro once again states that the only replacement for Fidel Castro is the Communist Party, and that the younger generations must be encouraged.

21 December 2006: Cuba requests the help of Spanish surgeon José Luis García Sabrido in assisting Fidel Castro's medical team. Back in Madrid, on 26 December Dr García states that the Cuban president is suffering from a 'benign illness'; that is, it is not cancer, as some American officials have claimed.

22 December 2006: The Cuban parliament meets; Fidel Castro neither attends the meeting nor sends a written message.

23 December 2006: In Paris, the newspaper *Le Monde* publishes an international survey indicating that Fidel Castro is more popular in France, Germany, the United Kingdom, Italy and Spain than US President George W. Bush.

28 December 2006: In Caracas, President Hugo Chávez announces that his government will not renew the licence of private TV channel Radio Caracas Televisión (RCT). 'No medium at the service of destabilization will be tolerated,' Chávez states.

30 December 2006: In Baghdad, former dictator Saddam Hussein is hanged.

31 December 2006: Cuban minister of the economy José Luis Rodríguez announces that Cuba's Gross Domestic Product (GDP) grew 12.5 per cent over the last year, 'the highest in all of Latin America'. The UN's Economic Commission for Latin America and the Caribbean (ECLAC) confirms this figure.

3 January 2007: In Oslo, Norway, a delegation of fourteen Cubans is denied rooms in the Scandic Edderkoppen Hotel (a member of the Hilton Hotel chain) for the same reasons alleged in Mexico on 3 February 2006.

5 January 2007: In a short programme, Cuban television channel Cubavisión pays homage to Luis Pavón Tamayo, former president of the National Council of Culture, the man considered responsible for the country's dogmatic cultural policy of repression and purges against many intellectuals (among them, José Lezama Lima, Virgilio Piñeira, Antón Arrufat, Pablo Armando Fernández and César López) during the so-called 'grey years' of 1971–6. Dozens of these figures, in both Cuba and abroad, immediately mobilize in protest. On 17 January the Cuban Union of Writers and Artists (UNEAC) publishes a statement attempting to relieve the situation, but the protests and dissatisfaction continue.

8 January 2007: In Caracas, President Hugo Chávez announces the renationalization of certain corporations that had been privatized before he came to power in December 1998. Chávez mentions the telecommunications corporation CANTV, which had been privatized in 1991, and also the electric company. He also proposes to withdraw the central bank's autonomy.

10 January 2007: A statement by the Cuban minister of foreign relations reports that on 27 November 2006, for the fourth time, there occurred 'a theft of Cuban funds illegally frozen' in US banks after the triumph of the Revolution. According to the minister, accounts belonging to the Banco Nacional de Cuba and the Empresa Cubana de Telecomunicaciones totalling some $170.2 million had been frozen and now part of that money, $92 million, has been given to US citizens Janet Ray Weininger and Dorothy Anderson McCarthy, who have sued Cuba in US courts.

16 January 2007: In the United States, Luis Posada Carriles, accused of organizing the bombing of a Cuban airliner and causing seventy-three deaths in 1976, is transferred to a jail in New Mexico after being detained for over a year and a half in El Paso, Texas, for an immigration violation.

17 January 2007: In Madrid, the newspaper *El País* states that 'Fidel Castro chose to undergo a surgical procedure that led to complications and caused him to be subjected to two further operations.'

17 January 2007: In Washington, DC, US Attorney General Alberto González announces that he is ending the 'terrorist-watch program' that since October 2001 has allowed the National Security Agency to intercept telephone conversations and e-mails to foreign countries without the need of informing a special court created in 1978, the Foreign Intelligence Surveillance Act (FISA) Court. Furthermore, the press reveals that since December 2006, President George W. Bush has authorized officials to open mail without a court order and that the Pentagon and the CIA can obtain details on citizens' bank accounts in the name of national security.

18 January 2007: In Moscow, the Russian vice minister of foreign relations, Sergei Kisliak, states that the suspension of relations between his country and Cuba is now in the past. Havana 'has always been and will continue to be' Russia's foremost partner in Latin America, the vice minister goes on to say.

24 January 2007: In Miami, Howard Hunt, famous former CIA agent who took part in toppling Guatemalan president Jacobo Arbenz (1954) and organizing the Bay of Pigs invasion of Cuba (1961), dies.

29 January 2007: Cuba's minister of foreign investment and economic cooperation, Marta Lomas, reveals that Cuba has 236 'mixed' associations and corporations. In 2005 there were 258 such entities and in 2004 there were 313, generally in areas such as tourism, nickel and light industry. Among Cuba's partner corporations are several large international companies, such as Sherritt International (Canada), Altadis and Sol Melía (Spain) and Pernod Ricard (France).

30 January 2007: For the first time since 28 October 2006, Fidel Castro appears, looking much better, on television. He is accompanied by Venezuelan President Hugo Chávez, who says, 'There's Fidel, on his feet, right as rain!'

31 January 2007: Two US congressmen introduce a bill that would make the embargo against Cuba more flexible and eliminate restrictions on travel to Cuba by US citizens and legal Cuban residents in the United States.

31 January 2007: In Caracas, members of the Venezuelan legislature, in an extraordinary meeting in Plaza Simón Bolívar, in the historical centre of the city, unanimously pass an 'enabling' law giving Hugo Chávez the power to rule by decree for eighteen months.

[**18 June 2007:** Vilma Espín (b. 7 April 1930), wife of Raúl Castro and long the unofficial 'first lady' of Cuba, dies in Havana. For over forty years, Espín served as president of the Federation of Cuban Women; before that, she had protested and fought against the Batista dictatorship and been one of the leaders of the Revolutionary movement in eastern Cuba.–Trans.]

[**26 June 2007:** The CIA releases some 700 pages of documents, dubbed the 'Family Jewels', detailing semi-legal and illegal CIA operations through the 1970s and 1980s. Pages 12 to 19 of this document discuss a government–Mafia plan to assassinate Fidel Castro.–Trans.]

[7 July 2007: Former Cuban general Fabián Escalante reveals that the CIA came very close to assassinating Fidel Castro by administering botulism toxins in the 1960s at a hotel in Havana; the poison was to be slipped into a milkshake by Juan Orta, a Cuban official who had been receiving kickbacks from the Mafia. At the last minute, Orta seems to have got cold feet. The CIA acknowledged that the assassination attempt was personally approved by John F. Kennedy's CIA director Allen Dulles.–Trans.]

Notes

A Hundred Hours with Fidel

1. Where information for figures and personalities does not appear in notes here in the introduction, those figures will be found in the chapters that follow or are, the translator believes, sufficiently well known as to need no explanatory notes. Notes by the translator are enclosed in square brackets ([ ]) and contain the notation '– Trans.' Almost all other notes are by the author, although some have been supplemented, especially with bibliographical information on English-language texts, by the translator; those additions have generally been made silently, although from time to time, where the information is substantial or in some way controverts material in the notes, the translator's hand will be noted. Most errors in the notes, as for example, in note 13 of this introduction, which in the Spanish states that the 2006 UN resolution opposing the US embargo on Cuba was the 'fifth consecutive year' such a resolution had been passed, when in fact it was the fifteenth, have been corrected silently; one exception to this translatorial-editorial silence occurs in the case of the misspelling of Huber Matos's name in all Spanish editions, where the translator notes this discrepancy, and others. In a few cases, the 'Cuban editor', Pedro Alvarez Tabío, adds a note; these additions are so indicated.
2. [José Antonio de Sucre (1795–1830; Venezuela) was an exceptionally able military officer during the wars of independence in South America. He fought alongside Miranda and other leading generals, rising rapidly through the ranks of command, and by the age of twenty-seven was chief of staff under Bolívar himself. He won great victories at Pichincha and Junín and the final, decisive battle for Latin American independence at Ayacucho. As the organizer of Peru and Alto Perú, which became the Republic of Bolivia, he became Bolivian president and served two years in that position, although he had been proclaimed president-for-life. He was assassinated in 1830 under circumstances, and for reasons, that have never been entirely clear. – Trans.]
3. *Marcos, la dignidad rebelde. Conversaciones con el subcomandante Marcos*, Valencia, Spain: Cibermonde, 2001.
4. [Carlos Marighela (1911–69) was a Brazilian Marxist, guerrilla leader, and theorist whose ideas on the city as the locus of guerrilla activity contrasted with, or complemented, Che Guevara's ideas on a revolution fought in the countryside. Marighela began as a Communist, but was expelled from the Party when he opposed its reformist tendencies; he then allied himself with Fidel Castro. He was founder and main leader of the ALN, or National Liberation Action group. – Trans.]
5. [Camilo Torres Restrepo (1929–66) was born into a well-to-do Colombian family in Bogotá. He studied law but then entered the seminary and became a priest; he is known as the 'guerrilla priest'. His interest in social causes led him to do studies of urban and rural poverty in Colombia and, later, to found the People's United Front. He published a weekly newsletter and became active in politics, but also allied himself with the National

Liberation Army. Harassed and persecuted, he decided to launch a guerrilla struggle, and he was killed in the first battle, on 15 February 1966. – Trans.]

6. [Mehdi Ben Barka (1920–disappeared 29 October 1965) was a Moroccan politician in the opposition party who in 1962 was accused of plotting against the king. He went into exile, and in Algiers he met Che Guevara, Amílcar Cabral and Malcolm X. From there, he continued his travels, coming eventually to Havana, where he helped with planning for the Tricontinental Conference (of Third World nations) that was to be held there in 1966. Ben Barka was one of the main leaders of the Third World movement that began to emerge during this period. In 1965, he was 'disappeared' by the French police and never heard from again. – Trans.]

7. [Miguel Ydígoras Fuentes (1895–1982) was president of Guatemala from 2 March 1958 to 31 March 1963.

At the height of the Cold War, in May 1954, the United States decided to overthrow President Jacobo Arbenz, with the aid of Nicaragua and Honduras. A series of military officers headed the governments of Guatemala from that point on, with Ydígoras, a general, taking office in 1958.

At the urging of the United States, Ydígoras allowed anti-Castro Cuban exiles to train in Guatemala for the Bay of Pigs invasion in 1961.

Because of Ydígoras's strong-man tactics, the country grew restive, and he himself was overthrown by right-wing military officers in 1963, who installed an even more repressive president, Enrique Peralta Azurdia, who allowed right-wing death squads to operate in the country. – Trans.]

8. [Marcos Pérez Jiménez (1914–2001) was president of Venezuela from 1952 to 1958. From late 1948 to 1952, Venezuela had been ruled by a military junta that included Pérez Jiménez. In 1950, the junta-elected president was murdered and a new junta member became president, although Pérez Jiménez was the power behind the throne. In 1952, general elections were held, but when it became clear that the opposition candidate was about to win, the junta suspended the elections and installed Pérez Jiménez. Although Pérez Jiménez is recognized as making many improvements in Venezuela, his government was ruthless in its pursuit and suppression of all opposition. In 1963, after being extradited from the United States for allegedly embezzling $200 million during his term in office, he was convicted and imprisoned until 1968. He died in Spain in 2001 at the age of eighty-seven. – Trans.]

9. As of December 2006, King Bhumibol Adulyadej of Thailand, crowned 5 May 1950, and Queen Elizabeth II of Great Britain, who came to the throne on 6 February 1952, had held their offices longer than any other head of state, including Fidel Castro, but neither of them can be said to be their country's *political* leader in the way Castro is. Both Thailand and Great Britain have prime ministers.

10. [Olof Palme (1927–86) was the leader of Sweden's Social Democratic Party and prime minister of that country from 1969 to 1976, then cabinet minister until his death by assassination. – Trans.]

11. [Houari Boumedienne (1927 [or 1932?]–78) was born Mohammed Bou Kharrouba in eastern Algeria. In 1954 he joined the Algerian National Liberation Front (FLN) to aid in the guerrilla struggle against the French. Upon Algeria's independence, he became minister of defence under Ahmed Ben Bella, but in 1965 he led a coup against Ben Bella and set up an Islamic socialist government. – Trans.]

12. [Eduardo Galeano (b. 1940) is a Uruguayan journalist and novelist. His best-known work of history is probably *The Open Veins of Latin America* (1971), a powerful story of the exploitation of Latin America from the arrival of the Spaniards to modern American capitalist and political domination. – Trans.]

13. In November 2006, for the fifteenth consecutive time, in a vote of 183 to 4, the United Nations asked the United States to lift the economic and trade embargo unilaterally imposed on Cuba.

14. The new measures adopted on 6 May 2004 by the Bush administration are extremely severe. For example, any Cuban resident of the United States who visits a sick relative in Cuba without having obtained authorization from the Treasury Department, or who spends more than fourteen days every three years on the island, or who spends more than $50 per day during a fourteen-day stay, or who sends financial aid to any member of his or her family who is a member of the Communist Party of Cuba, risks a ten-year prison term and as much as $1 million in fines. See Salim Lamrani, 'Cuba et l'espoir d'un monde meilleur', 28 December 2006, http://www.cmaq.net/fr/node/26391?PHPSESSID= 02f4d0b7e31dcddc4ff7d224d1c3d9f6.

15. Between 1961 and 2006, the damages done to the Cuban economy by the American embargo have been estimated at more than $70 billion (about €53 billion).

16. See, for example, Laura Wides-Muñoz (Associated Press), 'US Sends Foreign Aid to Third Countries to Promote Change in Cuba', originally published in the Bradenton (Florida) Herald, 22 December 2006. The article may now (June 2007) be found at http:// archives.econ.utah.edu/archives/marxism/2006w51/msg00158.htm

17. See Wayne S. Smith, 'Bush's Dysfunctional Cuba Policy', Center for International Policy, Washington, DC, 6 November 2006: http://www.ciponline.org/cuba/Op-eds/110606_ Dysfunctional.htm

18. See Abby Goodnough, 'US Paid 10 Journalists for Anti-Castro Reports', New York Times, 9 September 2006.

19. See Philip Agee (former CIA agent), 'Terrorism and Civil Society: The Instruments of US Policy in Cuba', in Counterpunch, 9 August 2003: http://www.counterpunch.org/ agee08092003.html

20. [See http://www.cafc.gov/cafc/rpt/2006/68097.htm (as of 5 June 2007). – Trans.]

21. The expression 'fifth column' dates back to the Spanish Civil War, when Franquista general Queipo de Llano stated that rather than the four columns of his army that were advancing on Madrid, it would be the *fifth* – made up of militant Franco supporters inside the city – that would take the city. In 1938, Ernest Hemingway (1899–1961) published a play, the only one he wrote, titled *The Fifth Column*, which popularized the expression.

22. See Maurice Lemoine, 'Demain, Cuba', in Le Monde diplomatique, September 2006. http://www.monde-diplomatique.fr/2006/09/LEMOINE/13923

23. BBC World, London, 13 July 2006.

24. See http://web.amnesty.org/report2006/cub-summary-eng

25. In fact, since April 2003, there has been a moratorium in Cuba on the death penalty; the result is a virtual suspension of the practice. In its 2006 report Amnesty International notes that in December 2005, 'More than thirty prisoners remained on death row; no one was executed.' Op.cit.

26. In its 2006 report Amnesty International notes that in Colombia, 'At least seventy trade unionists and seven human rights defenders were killed in 2005. At least 1,050 civilians were killed or "disappeared" in non-combat situations during the first half of 2005.' In addition, the report states that 'more than 2,750 killings and "disappearances" were attributed to paramilitaries between the announcement by the AUC [Autodefensas Unidas de Colombia; United Self-Defence Forces of Colombia] of a ceasefire in 2002 and the end of 2005.' These flagrant violations of human rights have not prevented the United States from granting the Colombian government financial aid totalling $781 million (some €659 million) in 2005. (For quotations from the AI 2006 report, http://web.amnesty.org/ report2006/col-summary-eng#4.)

27. In 2006 the infant mortality rate – that is, the number of children born alive but dying before reaching one year of age – stood at 5.3 per 1,000 in Cuba, the lowest rate in Latin America and the second-lowest in the Americas, after only Canada.

28. In its 2006 Human Development Report the United Nations Programme for Development (UNPD) puts Cuba in the first third of the 177 nations studied; that is, among the

'countries of high human development'. Cuba was in fiftieth place, behind Argentina, Uruguay and Costa Rica, but ahead of Mexico, Brazil, Colombia and the other countries of Latin America.

29. See 'Amérique latine rebelle', *Manière de Voir*, num. 90, December 2006, and 'Amérique latine, le tournant à gauche?' in *Mouvements*, num. 47–48, November 2006, Paris: La Découverte.

30. 'Victory obtained by arms raises the victor above all other men,' said Alexander the Great, one of the historical figures that Castro admires most.

31. The other six officials are José Ramón Balaguer, José Ramón Machado Ventura, Esteban Lazo, Larlos Lage, Francisco Soberón and Felipe Pérez Roque.

32. Reported by the France-Presse news agency on 3 August 2006.

33. [This is a book of reconstructed conversations between Goethe and his secretary, Johann Peter Eckermann, and although the title seems to present it as Goethe's work, it is in fact the work of Eckermann. The book is available in English in a translation by John Oxenford (San Francisco: North Point Press, 1984). – Trans.]

34. See Horace Greeley, 'Two Hours with Brigham Young', in Christopher Silvester (ed.), *The Penguin Book of Interviews*, London: Penguin, 1993.

35. *Moi, Fidel Castro*, six fifty-two-minute episodes in a two-DVD edition, published by Editions Montparnasse, Paris, in September 2004.

36. See Hernando Calvo Ospina, 'Nouveaux médecins aux pieds nus. Une Internationale de la santé', *Le Monde Diplomatique*, August 2006.

37. [Quoted in *Granma International*, 13 December 2006, at http://www.granma.cu/ingles/2006/diciembre/mier13/51oliver-i.html – Trans.]

38. [The Note on the Text and Translation addresses this same question for the English version. – Trans.]

39. [Not a list, but the pages of the Spanish proof sheets marked up for the additions and changes to this now revised English edition will be available in the Andrew Hurley Archives at the University of Texas Humanities Research Center, in Austin, Texas, after the English translation goes to press. These mark-ups have been done in great – in fact, exhausting – detail by Waldemar Burgos, Romina Iglesias and Olga Uribe, and should exactly parallel (or as closely as humanly possible) the now unavailable mark-ups sent to the press in Spanish and French. Despite repeated queries, neither the translator nor the UK publisher have been able to determine why these important documents seem no longer to be in existence, for either the Spanish edition or the French edition, both of which were published prior to this English edition. – Trans.]

1: The Childhood of a Leader

1. [A *central* (plural *centrales*) was a sugar-cane plantation on whose property there was also the machinery for processing the cane into sugar: the mill and grinders to squeeze the liquid from the cane, the boilers and vats to reduce the liquid to molasses and then to sugar. It would have been unusual to have the processing equipment to bring the brown sugar to the white form in which sugar is mostly found today, but all the prior steps would have been taken on the *central* (also called an *ingenio*). It was called a *central* specifically because it was a 'centre' to which the sugar cane would have been brought; outlying plantations that did not have the processing equipment (and the manpower it took to run it at this time) were generally called *colonias*, 'colonies', which supplied the *central* with the raw cane it needed to keep its machinery busy. A *central* was sometimes virtually a city, with hundreds of workers during the harvest living and working on the grounds. There would be a central plaza, roads, a great deal of traffic as the wagons and carts brought in the cane, etc., unlike the sugar-cane *plantation*, which was just where sugar cane was grown. – Trans.]

2. At the time, this was a relatively widespread practice in Western countries; young men recruited into the army could pay a certain amount of money to avoid serving; those paid

tended to be the poor. In the United States, for example, this unjust system was instituted by the administration of President Abraham Lincoln in July 1863, in the midst of the Civil War, and the act triggered a riot in New York; Martin Scorsese evoked this riot in his film *The Gangs of New York* (2002). [The book on which the movie is based, also titled *The Gangs of New York*, is by Herbert Asbury and can be found in a number of recent editions, due in part to Scorsese's film. The book was originally published by Alfred A. Knopf Company in 1927. – Trans.]

3. Antonio Maceo Grajales (1845–96), known as the 'Bronze Titan', was one of the most notable participants in the Cuban wars of independence. Maceo attained the rank of lieutenant-general of the liberation army and took part in countless battles and skirmishes during the two main wars, among them the invasion of the western part of the island. A man of lucid political thought, Maceo fell in combat in San Pedro on 7 December 1896.

   Máximo Gómez (1836–1905) was born in Santo Domingo. In 1865 he came to Cuba with the Spanish army and in 1868 he changed sides and entered the fight for the island's independence. In 1895 he returned to the island with José Martí as a general in the liberation army. A brilliant strategist, Gómez led the invasion of the western part of the island. He died in Havana.

4. [The 'dead time', the period after the harvest and before the next cycle of planting and cultivation, when there was nothing, or very little, for sugar-cane workers to do and no way, therefore, to earn a living. Many families were in desperate straits during this time of the year, and near-starvation was not at all uncommon. – Trans.]

5. [Literally, 'adjustment'; here, something much freer, along the lines of 'take care of, deal with, on a *quid pro quo* basis', and with the added meaning 'contract, agreement, setting of price'. – Trans.]

6. A *caballería* is a peculiarly Cuban land measure, equivalent to 13.4 hectares, or about 33 acres. If, as Castro remembers, there are eighteen *rozas* per *caballería*, then a *roza* is equivalent to .75 hectare, or about 1.85 acres. [The word *roza* is generally used to refer to a field cleared and prepared for planting; in Cuba, it seems to have been a common measure for a 'plot of land'. – Trans.]

7. [Here, the *person employed* would be speaking: 'I'll deal with this plot for you for twenty pesos.' – Trans.]

8. [A *batey* is the 'village' organization of the native inhabitants of the islands of the Caribbean, consisting of a central communal area, a sort of plaza, its dirt packed hard, surrounded with no great orderliness by the houses (*bohíos*) of the group, usually a large extended family, that lived together. Thus, Castro is saying that it was a loose sort of aggregation of buildings grouped within an accessible area. – Trans.]

9. [The custard-apple, or *anón*, is not related to the apple; its scientific name is *Annona squamosa*. There is a related fruit tree, the *Annona reticulata*, which also produces a sweet fruit, the *corazón*, or custard-apple. Because the names of these trees and fruits vary from country to country, island to island, and area to area across Latin America, the fruit Castro is referring to might be either of these. – Trans.]

10. Giovanni Guareschi, Italian author of a series of humorous novels, very popular in the fifties, whose hero, a village priest named don Camilo, had constant fights – very fierce, but friendly – with the Communist mayor, Peppone. The 'don Camilo' novels were made into several popular movies in which the main character was played by the famous French comic actor Fernandel.

11. The Abyssinian War (1935–6). On 2 October 1935 Italian Fascist dictator Benito Mussolini launched an offensive to conquer Ethiopia, and on 2 May 1936 Italian troops entered Addis Ababa, at which point the *negus*, or emperor, Haile Selassie, fled the country. In 1941 the British put an end to Italy's adventurism and Haile Selassie was returned to the throne.

12. Eusebio Leal, historian and leader of the architectural restoration of the old colonial centre of Havana.

13. [Here, there is an ambiguity in the form of the question, which in Spanish is 'Decidida-mente, *la guerra* le interesaba.' The use of the definite article *la* is required in Spanish, but *la guerra* can refer to either war in general or the specific war Ramonet and Castro have been talking about. This ambiguity is the cause of the next two exchanges, when Castro takes the question to mean war in general but Ramonet is talking about the Abyssinian War. – Trans.]

14. Genesis 9:18–27. Noah curses Canaan, the son of his son Ham, and condemns him and his descendants to slavery.

15. Captain Joaquín Barberán y Tros and Lieutenant Joaquín Collar y Serra flew more than 4,000 miles over water in thirty-nine hours, fifty-five minutes, the longest voyage over ocean up until that time. On 10 June 1933 at 4.45 a.m., Barberán and Collar took off from Tablada airport in Seville, Spain, in a biplane, the *Cuatro Vientos* (Four Winds), destined for Cuba. At 3.40 p.m., Cuba time, on 11 June, they touched down in Camagüey. From Camagüey they flew to Columbia airport in Havana. A few days later, flying between Havana and Mexico City, they disappeared.

16. On 3 February 1932, when Castro was five and a half years old, a powerful earthquake shook the entire eastern region of the island, which of course included the area of Birán. The city of Santiago suffered severe damage.

17. Gerardo Machado (1871–1939) was president-dictator of Cuba from 1925 to 1933. He is known for his pro-American stance and for his brutal repression of any opposition to his regime. He fled Cuba in August 1933 in response to a general strike that was the culmination of what was called the 'Revolution of '33'. One month later, on 4 September 1933, the 'Sergeants' Uprising', led by Fulgencio Batista, took place.

18. [A *guajiro/guajira* is the Cuban *campesino*; the noun is equivalent to Puerto Rico's *jíbaro/jíbara*, the US's 'hick' or 'hillbilly', if those latter terms are understood affectionately, with no pejorative connotation – an innocent, simple-hearted, unsophisticated person of rural background. – Trans.]

19. [A *cantinita* was a series of round metal containers, stacked one on top of another, with metal or leather straps to hold the entire 'tower' of containers together, and a handle on top for carrying, for delivery of food to homes – a common method of meal-delivery in many Caribbean towns and cities. If the women (who were the 'cooks') worked, as in this case, or if household chores, such as taking care of sick parents, etc., meant that there was little time for cooking – one must remember that this was a time of wood- or charcoal-burning stoves, home-killed chickens, home-shelled peas and beans, extremely time-consuming tasks related to food preparation – then food would be ordered in from a service or, perhaps, a relative who could be persuaded to cook larger quantities for the needy family. – Trans.]

20. In 1923 Julio Antonio Mella (1903–29) founded the Federación Estudiantil Univer-sitaria (the University Student Federation, or FEU) and in 1922 he founded the Cuban Communist Party. His real name was Nicanor MacFarland. During the Machado dictator-ship (May 1925–August 1933), he was sent to prison, where he went on hunger strike. Once he was freed, he went into exile in Mexico, where he was assassinated on 10 January 1929.

21. [Ramón Grau San Martín (1887–1969) was the son of a prosperous tobacco-growing family who became a physician and, as Castro says, a professor of physiology at the University of Havana. In the late twenties he supported student protests against dictator Gerardo Machado, and in 1931 he was imprisoned for these actions. After release from jail, he left Cuba, but when Machado was overthrown Grau returned and was soon serving as the president of the new government. Grau was very liberal, and his liberalism aroused the hostility of the US government, which refused to recognize his regime. This allowed Batista to force Grau to resign. Even in 'failure', however, Grau had sufficient influence to organize the Partido Revolucionario Cubano (Auténtico), which sent him to the consti-tutional convention of 1940, which he later chaired. He was defeated in the 1940 presiden-tial elections by his old rival Batista, but triumphed when he ran again in 1944. His

administration soon became corrupt, however, and Grau began to face increasing opposition. Finally, in disgrace, he did not run again in 1948, and faded from public sight. Upon the triumph of the Revolution in 1959, Grau returned to Havana, where he died in 1969. – Trans.]

22. Antonio Guiteras (1906–35) was born in Philadelphia, where he spent his early childhood. In 1914 his family moved to Pinar del Río, Cuba, where his father taught English. Guiteras was one of the leaders of the Revolution of '33. As a member of the provisional government, he implemented reform measures including a minimum wage and an eight-hour workday. After the coup in January 1934, Batista unleashed a campaign of fierce repression and on 8 May 1935, Guiteras was killed.

23. The United States, whose military had occupied Cuba since 1898, forced the Cubans to add an amendment to the Cuban constitution of 1901 – the 'Platt Amendment', named after the senator who proposed it. This amendment put significant limitations on the new Cuban republic's sovereignty; gave Washington the right to intervene in the island's internal affairs, even militarily; took jurisdiction over the Isle of Pines; and forced the Cuban government to give up several naval bases where American ships could take on fuel and supplies. On 2 July 1903 one of those supply bases became the Guantánamo Naval Base, which the United States occupies even today, against Cuba's wishes. In recent days, Guantánamo has been the object of considerable press attention because of the George W. Bush administration's use of it as a military detention facility for alleged Islamic terrorists, some of whom have been, according to repeated denunciations, subjected to torture and other inhumane treatment.

24. [The US Army Appropriation Act of 1901, Article VI, stated that 'the Isle of Pines shall be omitted from the proposed constitutional boundaries of Cuba, the title thereto being left to future adjustment by treaty.' – Trans.]

2: The Forging of a Rebel

1. [A dish made of minced meat with tomato sauce, peppers, onion, garlic and spices. – Trans.]

2. [A *durofrío*, 'hard-cold', a fruit-flavoured ice, sometimes made commercially, more often made artisanly and sold in private homes. – Trans.]

3. José María Heredia (Santiago de Cuba, 1803 – Mexico City, 1839), Cuban pre-Romantic poet, author of the *Himno del Desterrado* ('Exile's Anthem') and other essential poems in the nineteenth-century Cuban canon, and Cuban poet laureate; his most famous poem, the *Ode to Niagara*, was written in 1824. He should not be confused with the French Parnassian poet of the same name (1842–1905).

4. This political group was formally organized in 1955 by Castro and other revolutionaries. It was named in honour of the date of the assault on the Moncada barracks complex in Santiago de Cuba and the Carlos Manuel de Céspedes barracks complex in Bayamo on 26 July 1953. This group and the Revolutionary Directorate were the two major organizations leading the war against Batista. The 26th of July had two sections: the Sierra (a guerrilla group in the mountains) and the Llano (Flatlands, subversive activities in cities).

5. Frank País García (1934–57) was a young revolutionary from Santiago de Cuba who strove to bring student groups into association with *campesino* and workers' groups in Oriente province. He joined the 26th of July Movement upon its creation in June of 1955, and became a member of its directorate and was its national action commander. País played a main role in the underground support of the guerrilla struggle against Batista until he was killed by Batista forces in July 1957.

6. [A 'mestizo' is, literally, any child of mixed-race parents, but the word is used much more commonly to denote specifically the offspring of Indians (pre-Columbian natives of South and Central America) and whites. It is highly unlikely that the Haitians to whom Castro is referring were, in fact, mestizos in this latter sense; more probably, they were light-skinned

mulattoes (the children of blacks and whites). Castro later seems to be using this meaning when he talks about the racial composition of schools he went to. – Trans.]

7. [Through more or less mid-century, perhaps a little later in some places in Latin America, it was common for children to be given names on the basis of the Catholic Church's calendar of saints: the child's name would be the name of the saint who was venerated on the date of the child's birth. – Trans.]

8. St Fidel (or Fidelis) of Sigmaringen was born in Hohenzollern-Sigmaringen, in southern Germany, in 1577. He was a lawyer who defended the poor and downtrodden, earning him the sobriquet 'lawyer to the poor'. At the age of thirty-five, he joined the Capuchins in Friburg, Switzerland. He became a famous orator and preacher and was sometimes called the 'Demosthenes of the People'. He was killed in Seewis on 24 April 1622; Pope Benedict XIV canonized him in 1746.

9. That is, St Hippolytus (d. c. 325). Not much is known of Hippolytus' life, but he was the most important writer of the church at Rome in the third century. He seems to have written against the bishops of Rome and to have been 'framed' as being a rival to bishop Callistus, making Hippolytus the first known 'antipope'. He was banished to the rock quarries in Sardinia and died in captivity.

10. [6 January, Epiphany, which is traditionally the day gifts are given (brought, that is, by the Three Kings, the Three Magi or Wise Men) to children. Even today, when Christmas Day is often celebrated in Latin America, Three Kings' Day is even more important, and the Christmas holidays do not end until after 6 January. – Trans.]

11. Harriet Beecher Stowe's *Uncle Tom's Cabin* (1852).

12. Iñigo Óñez de Loyola (1491–1556), a noble from the Basque country, entered the military at a very young age. During the French siege of Pamplona in 1521, he was gravely wounded. His readings in religious literature during his long convalescence caused him to abandon his worldly life, and in 1539 he founded the Company of Jesus in Rome, dedicated to teaching and militant apostolicism and structured like a military order. He was canonized in 1622.

13. [The translation of a few lines of these lyrics is: 'Founder art thou, Ignatius, and general of the Royal Company, which Jesus honoured with His name. The legions of Loyola, with faithful heart and fearless, raises the Cross as its emblem. Lances, lances, to the fight against fierce Luzbel and his hordes of monsters!' – Trans.]

14. *La forja de un rebelde* is a trilogy – *La forja, La ruta, La llama* – published between 1941 and 1946 by Spanish novelist Arturo Barea (1897–1957); it is the semi-autobiographical story of a Spaniard from early in the twentieth century to the Spanish Civil War of 1936–9.

15. [What Castro is saying is that half the courtyard was raised some ten feet, one storey's height, to accommodate the cistern, where rainwater would be collected. The lower half of the courtyard, the part not raised, was surrounded on three sides by a two-storey part of the building. – Trans.]

16. Joe Louis, the 'Brown Bomber' (1914–81), world heavyweight champion boxer, fought German Max Schmeling (1905–2005), who had won the world championship in 1930. The first fight took place on 19 June 1936, and Louis was defeated. The second, to which Castro is referring, took place on 22 June 1938, in Yankee Stadium before more than 60,000 spectators; it was broadcast on radio in four languages: English, German, Portuguese and Spanish. This fight was especially significant because of the tensions between Germany and the United States on the eve of the Second World War – a black man and an 'Aryan', democracy and Nazism, were disputing for primacy. Joe Louis ko'd Schmeling in the first round.

17. *El Gorrión* ('The Sparrow') was a comic book founded in Buenos Aires in 1932. Its most popular story came out in 1938; it was titled 'El Vengador' (The Avenger) and its eponymous character was a superhero. This comic was drawn by Alberto Breccia (1919–93), who in 1968 produced an album on the life of Che Guevara.

18. Novel (1880) by Spanish author José María de Pereda (1833–1906); its name is equivalent to 'a chip off the old block' or 'the apple doesn't fall far from the tree'.

19. [The letter reads as follows, with all spelling and punctuation *sic*:

Santiago de Cuba
Nov 6, 1940

Mr Franklin Roosvelt,
President of the United States

My good friend Roosvelt,
I don't know very English, but I know as much as write to you. I like to hear the radio, and I am very happy, because I hear in it, that you will be President for a new (período) [Here, young Fidel's English fails him and he includes the Spanish word in parentheses.]
I am twelve years old. I am a boy but I think very much but I do not think that I am writting to the President of the United States.
If you like give me a ten dollars bill green american, in the letter, because never, I have not seen a ten dollars bill green american and I would like to have one of them.
My address is:
    Sr. Fidel Castro
    Colegio de Dolores
    Santiago de Cuba
    Oriente. Cuba.
I don't know very English but I know very much Spanish and I suppose you don't know very Spanish but you know very English because you are American but I am not American.
Thank you very much.
Good by.
Your friend,
Castro [very ornate]
Fidel Castro
If you want iron to make your ~~SHEAPS~~ ships I will show to you the bigest (minas) of iron of the land. They are in Mayarí Oriente Cuba.

A copy of this letter may be seen here: http://history1900s.about.com/library/photos/blycastro.htm, and a facsimile, along with the text of the letter, is also contained in *Dear Mr President: Letters to the Oval Office from the Files of the National Archives*, ed. Dwight Young, Washington, DC: National Geographic, 2005. – Trans.]

3: Entering Politics

1. Eduardo Chibás (1907–51) emerged out of the student uprisings against Machado; he had been a prominent member of the Partido Auténtico. In May 1947, disillusioned by Authentic Party president Ramón Grau San Martín's betrayal, Grau's willingness to compromise his 'principles', and his administration's corruption, Chibás founded the *Orthodox* Cuban People's Party (Partido del Pueblo Cubano Ortodoxo), which Castro joined a short time later. Chibás was a charismatic leader, an able communicator, and a defender of the nationalist agenda and its denunciations of corruption and other problems; he became his party's candidate for the presidency of Cuba in the elections of June 1952, and he was predicted to win. On 5 August 1951, at the end of his radio broadcast, he shot himself in the stomach and died several days later.
2. Until 1952, the main political forces in Cuba were associated with the Authentic, Orthodox, Liberal, (Cuban) Democratic and (Cuban) Republican parties and, to a lesser extent, the Popular Socialist, or Communist, Party. In elections, the Republicans usually allied with the Authentics, while the Democrats and the Liberals formed coalitions in which, to a greater or lesser degree, the Action Unitarian Party also joined; this last party had been founded by Fulgencio Batista.
3. On 29 and 30 September 1938, in Munich, Germany, representatives of France (Daladier),

Great Britain (Chamberlain), Italy (Mussolini) and Germany (Hitler) signed a series of accords whose practical effect was the democracies' capitulation to the expansionist designs of the Fascist powers. For fear of a war, which was nonetheless inevitable, London and Paris allowed Hitler to annex the Sudetenland in Czechoslovakia, and this encouraged the Third Reich in its expansionist agenda. This action also led the USSR to seek an agreement with Germany.

4. Rubén Martínez Villena, poet, intellectual and revolutionary, was born in a town near Havana called Alquízar in December 1899. Linked from an early age to the political struggles against the ills and abuses of the neocolonial republic, in 1923 he and other progressive liberals engaged in what was called the Thirteen-Man Protest. In 1927 he joined the Communist Party, rising to become one of its officers, and from whose ranks, despite his delicate health, he distinguished himself in the workers' and people's confrontation with the bloody dictatorial regime of Gerardo Machado (whom Martínez Villena famously called an 'ass with claws'). Martínez Villena died of tuberculosis in Havana in January 1934. In Cuban history, he is one of the great symbols of the *engagé* intellectual. [Note by Cuban editor.]

5. Carlos Rafael Rodríguez (1913–97) had been involved in politics since 1930, fighting against the dictatorship of President Gerardo Machado. From early on he had been an active member and leader of the Communist Party, whose name was changed in the forties to Popular Socialist Party. Rodríguez was minister without portfolio (as was Juan Marinello, another Communist Party member) in the coalition government formed by Batista in 1940. After the triumph of the Revolution in 1959, Carlos Rafael Rodríguez held several posts in the Cuban Communist Party, where he was a member of the Politburo, and in government. He died in Havana.

6. [Full title: *The Eighteenth Brumaire of Louis Bonaparte* (*Der achtzehnte Brumaire des Louis Bonaparte*, 1852). – Trans.]

7. [With an introduction by Carl Sagan, New York, London, etc.: Bantam, 1988. – Trans.]

8. Original title: *Tecnica del colpo di Stato* (1931). Malaparte (1898–1957) was an Italian author whose other major works include *Kaputt* (1944) and *La Pelle* ('Skin', 1949).

9. Abel Santamaría Cuadrado (1927–53) was a militant member of the Orthodox Youth and later one of the leaders of the movement founded by Castro. He was second-in-command of the assault on the Moncada barracks complex, where he was captured, tortured and murdered that same day: 26 July 1953.

10. Jesús Montané (1923–99) was born on the Isle of Pines and was one of the founding leaders of the Cuban Revolution. As a member of the Orthodox Youth he was one of the leaders of the attack on the Moncada barracks complex. He was captured and spent time in prison with Castro. He was a founder and member of the first directorate of the 26th of July Movement. He went into exile in Mexico and joined the group that returned on the *Granma*; like many of them, he was captured at the battle in Alegría de Pío. After the triumph of the Revolution, he held important Party and government posts, such as deputy to the National Assembly, and he served for some time as minister of communication. He died in Havana.

11. [It is possible that here Castro is making a little joke. The Spanish is *eran más educadas*: the girls were better educated; but *mejor educadas* can also mean 'more polite', so Castro may be laughing at himself a bit, saying the girls sat and listened, politely, while the boys, less polite, would either ignore him or get up and walk away. – Trans.]

12. Rafael Trujillo (1891–1961) was dictator of the Dominican Republic from 1930 to his assassination in 1961; he was an ally and protégé of the United States. In 1946 he decreed an amnesty for Communist exiles from the country, but when they returned he had them executed, and this triggered the planning for the Cayo Confites expedition. Trujillo's long dictatorship was one of the most reactionary and repressive in the entire history of Latin America.

13. For a full description of this conflict, see Gabriel García Márquez, *Living to Tell the Tale* (trans. Edith Grossman, New York: Vintage, 2004), 303–33.

14. In September 1981, Castro gave a long interview to Colombian journalist Arturo Alape about Castro's experience in the 'Bogotazo'. See Arturo Alape, *El Bogotazo: Memorias del olvido*, Havana: Casa de las Américas, 1983.

15. On 18 October 1945 a coup d'état in Venezuela toppled dictator-president Isaías Medina Angarita, and a Revolutionary Junta was created; it was presided over by Rómulo Betancourt until 15 February 1948, when Rómulo Gallegos, winner of the elections in December 1947, assumed the presidency. That 'revolutionary' period lasted only until 24 November 1948, when a military coup toppled Gallegos.

16. Rómulo Gallegos (1844–1969) was, in addition to a statesman, a fine author, whose novels include *Doña Bárbara* (1929) and *Canaíma* (1935).

17. The Falkland Islands.

18. The course in History of Social Doctrines was given by Raúl Roa García, who also wrote its text. Roa (1907–82) was an intellectual and writer linked to the revolutionary student movement that stood up to Machado. During the Batista dictatorship, he had to leave Cuba. For many years, Roa was the Revolutionary Government's minister of foreign relations, and in that position he became known as the 'Chancellor of Dignity' due to his impassioned defence of Cuba's foreign policy. The text in Labour Legislation, which was also part of the curriculum in the law school, had been compiled by Aureliano Sánchez Arango, the minister of education in the Prío Socarrás government that had been denounced by Chibás. [Note by Cuban editor.]

19. [A *bohío* is a dwelling generally constructed of wood with a dirt floor and palm-thatch roof, which was the typical housing construction employed by the poor Cuban *campesino* class until, perhaps, mid-century. – Trans.]

20. After the assault on the Moncada barracks on 26 July 1953, Castro was arrested and brought to trial. He acted as his own defence counsel, and his allocution, published not long after, has come to be known as 'History Will Absolve Me'. (One English edition still sometimes available is *History Will Absolve Me: The Moncada Trial Defence Speech, Santiago de Cuba, October 16th, 1953*, London: Jonathan Cape, 1967.) This text was at once a manifesto against Batista and his crimes, a philosophical, legal and moral argument for the legitimacy of a struggle against the Batista dictatorship, and an explanation of Castro's programme for radically transforming the economy and society of Cuba. (See also Chapter 6, note 7.)

4: The Assault on the Moncada Barracks

1. José Antonio Echeverría (1932–57) was born in Cárdenas, Matanzas province, Cuba. He was an outstanding student leader at the University of Havana and in 1955 became president of the FEU. The next year he created the Revolutionary Directorate, the FEU's armed-action group. He organized the assault on the presidential palace on 13 March 1957, in an attempt to assassinate Fulgencio Batista and trigger a popular insurrection, but he was killed during the action.

2. Franz Mehring, *Karl Marx*, ed. Ruth Norden (trans. Edward Fitzgerald), New York and London: Routledge, 2003.

3. Haydée Santamaría Cuadrado (1922–80) was, like her brother, a militant in the Orthodox Youth and later in Castro's 26th of July Movement. She was one of the two women who took part in the assault on the Moncada barracks, where she was captured and sent to prison. She was key in the printing and distribution of the first edition of *History Will Absolve Me* (in Spanish, of course), and was a member of the national directorate of the 26th of July Movement in its struggle against Batista. She founded the important cultural institution Casa de las Américas and served as its director until her death.

4. [Here, Castro is referring to the very common practice of 'clubs' made up of emigrants from certain areas or even certain cities; thus, there might well be a 'Galician Club of Santiago de Cuba' or a 'Galician Club of Havana', where emigrants and their descendants would meet socially. Today in Florida and Puerto Rico, the Cuban community carries on

this tradition with clubs from Cuban cities and provinces; these clubs print newsletters, have social activities of many kinds, and generally revisit the 'good old days'. – Trans.]

5. Raúl Martínez Ararás was one of the members of the small group that planned the assault on the Moncada barracks and the other actions of 26 July 1953, and he led the group that was to take the Carlos Manuel de Céspedes barracks in Bayamo; this action was also unsuccessful.

6. This is the building once occupied by the Army Corps of Engineers. [Note by Cuban editor.]

7. Pedro Miret Prieto, b. 1927, was one of the organizers of the detail that attacked Moncada. He was wounded in that action and taken prisoner. He is currently vice president of the Council of Ministers.

8. [Generally, however, throughout this book Castro does use the word pejoratively, usually to mean 'delinquent', 'member of the criminal class' or 'unsavoury characters', etc. – Trans.]

9. On 12 September 1943 Otto Skorzeny, commander of the German special commandos, rescued Mussolini, who had been held prisoner after his defeat in June 1943; Mussolini was being held in the Gran Sasso, in the Apennines, after his overthrow in June 1943. See Otto Skorzeny, *My Commando Operations: The Memoirs of Hitler's Most Daring Commando*, trans. David Johnson, Atglen, PA: Schiffer Books, 1995.

10. Renato Guitart Rosell was born in Santiago de Cuba in November 1930. He was the only person from Santiago who knew the plans for the actions of 26 July beforehand, and he had a decisive role in the planning of those actions. He was part of the detail that took Post 3 at Moncada, although he was killed during the raid.

11. Melba Hernández Rodríguez de Rey was born in 1921. A lawyer by profession, she was the only other woman besides Haydée Santamaría to take part in the actions of 26 July 1953. She was captured and imprisoned. She, too, played a key role in the printing and distribution of *History Will Absolve Me*. During the war she was the auditor for the rebels' Third Front. Since the triumph of the Revolution she has held several important posts, including chairwoman of the Cuban Committee for Solidarity with Vietnam and ambassador to Vietnam and Kampuchea. She holds the title 'Heroine of the Republic of Cuba'.

12. [That is, four shells in the magazine and one in the chamber. – Trans.]

13. [A peculiarly Latin American genre, *testimonio* is a memoir of a particular event or period of time, very seldom of a whole life, told generally from the limited point of view of the author-participant and with that personal focus. It is an individual's view of a historical moment, period, or event; a 'boots on the ground' sort of narrative, as the current media slang would have it, rather than a historian's, or more synoptical, view. – Trans.]

14. For a very detailed and accurate description of the attack on Moncada, see Robert Merle, *Moncada: Le Premier Combat de Fidel Castro*, Paris: Robert Laffont, 1965. Cuban historians such as Mario Mencía and José M. Leyva have also reconstructed the events of 26 July 1953 in detail. See in particular Mencía's book, *El grito del Moncada*, Havana: Editora Política, 1993.

15. The attack on the Carlos Manuel Céspedes barracks complex in Bayamo, led by Raúl Martínez Ararás at the head of twenty-five men, also failed; ten of those taking part were later captured and murdered.

5: The Backdrop of the Revolution

1. Carlos Manuel de Céspedes (1819–74), born in Bayamo, Cuba. In 1840 he began law studies in Spain. From 1842 to 1844 he travelled through Europe, Turkey, Palestine and Egypt. In 1844 he returned to Bayamo, where he began practising law. He took part in the Pozas rebellion in 1852 and was imprisoned for it. On 10 October 1868, on his sugar-cane plantation La Demajagua, to the cry 'Long live free Cuba!', he took up arms, freed his slaves, and signed the Declaration of [Cuban] Independence. On 20 October he

took Bayamo. On 27 December he signed a decree denouncing slavery. In 1869 he was acclaimed president of the Republic at Arms. In 1873 he was deposed by a meeting of representatives in Jijagual. He died in combat, in the Sierra Maestra, on 27 February 1874. (See also p. 185.)

2. In 1791, on the island of Hispaniola (in the western, French section called at the time St-Domingue), there were some 100,000 Frenchmen, who among them owned 7,800 sugar-cane plantations and more than 500,000 slaves. On 14 August these slaves, citing the ideals of the French Revolution, began an uprising under the leadership of Toussaint L'Ouverture, the 'black Spartacus'. The war lasted thirteen years. Napoleon (who was married to Josephine, the daughter of Créole parents from the French island of Martinique) sent an expedition of 43,000 veteran soldiers to put down the rebellion. On 18 November 1803, in the battle of Vertières, the rebels dealt a final defeat to the French. The war took a terrible toll: 150,000 slaves and 70,000 French soldiers dead. On 1 January 1804, in the city of Gonaïves, the French side of the island of Hispaniola was declared free, and the new nation took the old Indian name Haiti.

3. [This number has been changed in the text of the 3rd edition from 500,000 to 400,000, but the number in note 2 was not changed; thus the discrepancy in the figures. – Trans.]

4. From 1779 to 1781, Francisco Miranda (Caracas, Venezuela, 1750–Cádiz, Spain, 1816), a Venezuelan patriot, took part as an officer in the Spanish army in the English colonies' War of Independence, the American Revolution, from 1779 to 1781. Made a general in France, he served in the Napoleonic campaigns. In 1806 he organized an expedition to Venezuela in order to proclaim the Republic there, and in Caracas, in 1811, he voted for the Venezuelan Declaration of Independence. Defeated in 1812 by the Spanish, he was taken to Spain and imprisoned in Cádiz, where he died in prison.

5. One of the best known of these was Bernardo de Gálvez (1746–86), who during the campaign of 1779 occupied the ports of Manchac, Baton Rouge and Natchez. He also occupied Mobile (1780) and Pensacola (1781), thereby preventing the British fleet in the Caribbean from coming to the aid of Cornwallis in the Battle of Yorktown, where Cornwallis and the British met their final defeat.

6. José Tomás Boves (1782–1814) was born in Oviedo, Spain, and became the leader, or *caudillo*, of the Venezuelan *llaneros* in the service of the Spanish crown; he defeated Bolívar at the battle of La Puerta (1814) and occupied Caracas.

7. [These are the 'cowboys' of Venezuela and Colombia, similar to the *gauchos* of Argentina. *Llano* is the Spanish word for 'plain', so the *llaneros* are the men who live on the plains, in this case breaking wild horses, tending cattle and living life in the open with almost no human comforts. In terms of horsemanship and proud independence, one might think of them almost as the Mongols of South America. When Castro refers to their being 'mestizos', the word should be understood as being men of mixed Indian and Spanish blood. As the text indicates only sketchily, the *llaneros* at first were the natural enemies of the aristocratic criollos and landowners, who looked down on the rough-and-tumble plainsmen; the pro-Spanish forces were able to exploit the *llaneros*' hatred of the criollos in order to put down the pro-independence uprising. Later, though, Bolívar convinced the *llaneros* that Spain, not the native-born criollos, was the *llaneros*' real enemy, and with that, the tide changed and the *llaneros* became fierce allies of the Bolivarian independence struggle. – Trans.]

8. Arturo Uslar Pietri (1906–2001), Venezuelan master of the historical novel, author of *Las lanzas coloradas* (1931; trans. *The Red Lances*, 1963), *El camino de El Dorado* (1947; 'The Road from El Dorado'), *Oficio de difuntos* (1976), *Samuel Robinson* (1981) and *La visita en el tiempo* (1990), as well as many books of political and social commentary.

9. Alexandre Pétion (1770–1818), Haitian general, important figure in the French defeat in 1803, president of Haiti from 1807 until his death.

10. Máximo Gómez Báez (1836–1905) was born in Santo Domingo. In 1865, he went to Cuba with the Spanish army and in 1868 he changed sides and entered the fight for the island's independence. In 1895 he returned to the island with José Martí as general in the

Army of Liberation. A brilliant strategist, in the course of the two wars Gómez engaged in countless campaigns and battles, decisively defeating the best colonialist forces; among his victories was the conquest of western Cuba, which is considered by many European military historians one of the great military feats of the nineteenth century. He died in Havana.

11. [One might more accurately say that saints' names, and to an extent their 'qualities' or 'characteristics', including special colours, etc., were used as 'camouflage' within the African religions; African deities would be called by the Western names. Thus, Santa Bárbara was 'code' for Chango (Shango, Django), an African deity or *orisha*; the leper Lazarus (not the man restored to life by Jesus) was Babalú Ayé; either Jesus or Our Lady of Mercy, depending on the area of Cuba, was Obatalá. In that way, the slave population could allege that they were worshipping in 'accepted' ways while in fact pursuing and keeping alive the worship of their ancestral deities. This 'translation' (or the syncretic result after decades of such worship) became known as *santería*, 'the worship of saints', and today it is a religion with probably millions of followers (it has only recently begun to be seen as 'socially acceptable', or, because of animal sacrifice, even legal, so its followers' numbers are difficult to assess) in Cuba, Florida, New York, and other large Cuban-community centres around the US and the world. – Trans.]

12. [A *caudillo* is, in its most basic sense, a Latin American political and military leader, but that bare definition cannot convey the loyalty a *caudillo*'s men feel for him, or the strength of his political power among men and women alike. *Caudillos* are strong, charismatic leaders, always able to stir the people's emotions, and so are generally populist, rather than cerebral or 'theoretical' politicians. They tend not to be associated with any particular ideology or political philosophy, but are rather motivated by power. Though they promise to overturn 'the great' and restore equity to the people, they inevitably end up as the oligarchs they set out to overthrow. In the nineteenth century they tended to come from the landowner class, and so had enough wealth to begin their careers with private armies. They are immune to their opponent's logical arguments, and lead by demagoguery. They are 'strongmen', dictators, but they tend to be fanatically beloved by their followers. They are, of course, hated by their detractors and enemies, whom they almost always terrorize. They are invariably polarizing elements in a country. Every country in Latin America has had its *caudillo* or *caudillos*. It should be noted that Bolívar was a 'leader', 'the father of the independence movement in Latin America', whereas Juan Perón of Argentina, or Juan Manuel de Rosas, before him, was a *caudillo* – the word is almost always pejorative. – Trans.]

13. Narciso López (1799–1850), born in Caracas, Venezuela, to a Spanish family. As an officer in the Spanish army, López fought against Bolívar. In Spain, he took part in the first Carlist war. He arrived in Cuba in 1841 as an aide to the governor, but in 1848 he took the side of the Cuban criollos opposed to Spanish domination and seeking US annexation of the island. He had to flee to New Orleans, where he organized several expeditions to Cuba. He designed Cuba's new flag (taken in part from that of Texas). He was arrested and executed in Havana by garrotte on 19 May 1850.

14. [*Mambí*, plural *mambises*, is a word coined in Cuba, most probably by Afro-Cubans, whose etymology is unclear, though there are several colourful explanations of its derivation. What is clear is that this was the name given the fighters (both men and women) who made up the army that fought against Spain, mostly with fearsome machetes, in the two wars of Cuban independence (1868–78 and 1895–8), and that the army was called the Mambí Army. It is estimated that Afro-Cubans made up as much as 92 per cent of the army, and certainly some of its most distinguished generals, Antonio Maceo being the most famous, were black-skinned, so there is also an association with strong, powerful blackness. – Trans.]

15. Benito Juárez (1806–72). Of native Mexican descent, Juárez was president of Mexico in 1858 when he refused to pay the foreign debt of his country, which was then invaded by the forces of Napoleon III. Napoleon installed Maximilian as emperor of Mexico

and, in response, Juárez conducted a guerrilla war of resistance, captured and executed Maximilian, defeated the French, and once again served as president of the republic until his death.

16. Jorge Eliécer Gaitán (1898–1948), leader of the Colombian Liberal Party and legendary orator. Gaitán was assassinated on 9 April 1948, and his death set off a popular insurrection, which the authorities brutally suppressed, causing thousands of deaths – the reprisals were called the 'Bogotazo'. (See also Chapter 3, notes 13 and 14.)

17. [Manuel Mercado (1838–1909) was at the time under secretary of the interior in the Mexican government. Mercado and Martí had been dear friends since 1875, when Martí lived in Mexico City in a house next door to Mercado's. This information, and the translation of the letter that follows in the text, is taken from *José Martí: Selected Writings*, ed. and trans. Esther Allen, New York: Penguin Classics, 2002, pp. 346–9. – Trans.]

18. [There is some controversy as to whether Martí and his thought can reasonably be seen as precursors of Socialism in Cuba, or as supporting the tenets of Socialism at all. For an interesting and polemical 'short course' on this controversy, see Raymond Carr's review of three books – all edited by Philip Foner, all translated by Elinor Randall, and all anthologies of the writings of Martí: *Inside the Monster: Writings on the United States and American Imperialism*; *Our America: Writings on Latin America and the Struggle for Cuban Independence*; and *On Art and Literature: Critical Writings* – in the *New York Review of Books*, Vol. 35, No. 12 (21 July 1988) (also at http://www.nybooks.com/articles/4354) and the follow-up letter to the editor by Carlos Ripoll (*New York Review of Books*, Vol. 35, No. 19, 18 December 1988; www.nybooks.com/articles/4231), to which is appended a reply by Raymond Carr. Foner's books allege the Martí–Socialism connection in two hefty volumes, while both Carr and Ripoll dispute it much more briefly but in no uncertain terms. – Trans.]

19. [An imposing, very strong fortress built by the Spaniards; there are others very much like it – built, in fact, on the same plan – in Havana and San Juan, Puerto Rico, and Santo Domingo, Dominican Republic. – Trans.]

20. [In the Spanish-American War,] the naval battle of Santiago de Cuba took place on 3 July 1898; the Spanish fleet, under the command of Admiral Pascual Cervera, was destroyed by an American armada of twice the tonnage and carrying twice the armour of the Spanish ships. The American ships were under the command of Admiral William Sampson. Three hundred and fifty Spanish sailors lost their lives.

21. The exact quotation, in English, is: 'He deserves to be honoured, for he has put himself on the side of the weak' (*José Martí: Selected Writings*, op.cit., 'Tributes to Karl Marx, Who Has Died', p. 131). Martí's original 'Letter from New York, March 29, 1883' was published in *La Nación*, Buenos Aires, on 13 and 16 May 1883. In this letter, Martí renders homage to 'that silken-souled and iron-handed German, the hugely famous Karl Marx, whose recent death is honoured'. See José Martí, *En los Estados Unidos: Periodismo de 1881 a 1892*, ed. Roberto Fernández Retamar and Pedro Pablo Rodríguez, Madrid/Paris/Havana: ALLCA, 2003.

22. [According to the editor of Martí's *Selected Writings*, 'In the twenty-seven volumes of Martí's *Complete Works*, he mentions Karl Marx only twice outside of "Tributes to Karl Marx, Who Has Died," op.cit.: once as a citation from a French author that he copied into Notebook 8 and a second time in an article discussing the formation of trade unions in the United States, published in *La Nación* on 20 February 1890. There he wrote, 'Each nation finds its own cure, in keeping with its nature, which either requires varying doses of the medicine, depending on whether this or that factor is present in the ailment – or requires a different medicine. Neither Saint-Simon, nor Karl Marx, nor Marlo, nor Bakunin. Instead, the reforms that are best suited to our own bodies' (op.cit., p. 130). – Trans.]

23. [Castro is here referring to the killings at the 'Haymarket Riots' in Chicago, which actually took place on 4 May 1886. On 1 May the Chicago Knights of Labor, led by labour activist and organizer Albert Parsons, marched to demand an eight-hour workday;

they were soon joined in a general strike. On 3 May strikers met at the McCormick Harvesting Machine Company plant in Chicago, where disturbances occurred and the Chicago police killed two people and wounded several others. This action triggered a call by Chicago anarchists for a mass demonstration the next day at Haymarket Square in Chicago; the anarchists alleged that the police had been in the service of 'big business' and had murdered the strikers to intimidate the labour movement. At the Haymarket rally, things were very quiet until near nightfall, when the police began dispersing the demonstrators. Someone – it has never been learned who – threw a bomb (which, over the next few days, took the lives of eight police officers), and the police began firing indiscriminately into the 'mob', killing eleven and wounding a large but unknown number. (People were afraid to go to hospitals for fear of reprisals by the authorities.) In the aftermath, eight anarchists were arrested and tried; all were found guilty of inciting to riot. There has never been any really convincing proof of their guilt in the bomb-throwing. – Trans.]

24. The idea for a Free Trade Area of the Americas was put forth on 1 June 1990 by then-president George Bush and has been defended by his successors, Bill Clinton and George W. Bush. Its purpose is to integrate all the countries in Latin America and the Caribbean – except Cuba – in a free-trade zone of 800 million inhabitants. The FTAA extends the North American Free Trade Agreement (NAFTA), which included Canada, Mexico and the United States and went into effect on 1 January 1994, throughout the hemisphere. The strong opposition in Latin America to the FTAA, which is considered both an attempt to consolidate the United States' economic hegemony to include the entire western hemisphere and a deathblow to the economies of most Latin American countries, has so far prevented the signing of the agreement, and this, in turn, represents a significant defeat, at a strategic level, for the US government. The most recent setback for the agreement occurred at the Summit of the Americas in Mar del Plata, Argentina, in early November 2005, when President Bush was unable to secure passage of the agreement in the face of opposition by several Latin American delegations.

25. Matthew 5–7. The Sermon on the Mount contains the essence of Jesus' teachings and is at the core of Christian doctrine.

26. Water into wine: John 2:1–11. Loaves and fishes: Matthew 14:14–21; Mark 6:34–44; Luke 9:12–17; John 6: 5–14.

27. Matthew 20:1–16. This is the 'parable of the vineyard'. In the English Bible, the rich man's name is not specified; he is called only a 'householder'.

28. Matthew 21:12–13; Mark 11:15–16.

6: 'History Will Absolve Me'

1. Oscar Alcalde Valls (1923–93), a member of the group that attacked the Moncada barracks, was one of those who joined Fidel Castro in the Gran Piedra mountains after the assault. He was taken prisoner, tried and sentenced to thirteen years in prison. After the amnesty granted the Moncada group in 1955, he went into exile. After the triumph of the Revolution, he held several important governmental posts. He died in Madrid on 5 January 1993.

2. José 'Pepe' Suárez Blanco (1927–91) was one of those assigned to take Post 3 at Moncada. He, too, went with Fidel Castro up into the Gran Piedra mountains after the assault; he was taken prisoner, tried and sentenced. After the amnesty in 1955, he went into exile. He died in Havana on 15 June 1991.

3. [See Chapter 3, p. 86, in reference to the 'Palmacristi and Escape-Act colonels', for insight into Castro's state of mind in this situation. – Trans.]

4. Andrés Pérez Chaumont, chief of operations of the Rural Guard's 1st Regiment, whose headquarters were at the Moncada barracks complex. Pérez Chaumont was directly responsible for the murder of many of those who attacked the barracks.

5. For further details on this episode, see Lázaro Barredo Medina, *Mi prisionero Fidel, Recuerdos del teniente Pedro Sarría*, Havana: Editorial Pablo de la Torriente, 2001.

6. Spanish edition: *La historia me absolverá*, Havana: Publicaciones del Consejo de Estado, 1993. There have been several English editions; the first publication was, in fact, in Havana, in 1959, in a translation by Oscar Rodríguez Estrada. There appears to be no English edition now in print (mid-2007), but secondhand-book dealers and the internet booksellers always have used copies available.

7. The title 'History Will Absolve Me' is taken from the last words of the long speech read by Castro in his own defence on 16 October 1953, during the next-to-last session of the trial in Santiago de Cuba of those accused of having taken part in the assaults on the Moncada barracks complex in that city and the Carlos Manuel de Céspedes barracks complex in Bayamo, both of which took place on 26 July of that year. This document is a manifesto, a programme, an accusation, a denunciation and a legal, moral, philosophical and political defence of the revolutionary struggle against tyranny. It is, in its own right, the foundational document of the Cuban Revolution, and one of the major texts in the history of political philosophy and revolutionary action in Cuba and Latin America. See Fidel Castro, *La historia me absolverá*, with notes by Pedro Álvarez Tabío and Guillermo Alonso, Havana: Oficina de Publicaciones del Consejo de Estado, 1993. [Note by Cuban editor.]

8. Augusto César Sandino (1895–1934), a Nicaraguan revolutionary and one of the great precursors of the armed independence and anti-imperialist struggles in Latin America in the twentieth century. Sandino led an uprising in 1926 and the following year began a guerrilla war against the conservatives then in power, who were backed by American forces within the country. In 1928 the Salvadoran Communist leader Farabundo Martí joined the Sandinistas' struggle. In 1933 the Americans withdrew and Sandino's cause claimed the victory, but Sandino himself was assassinated on 1 February 1934, at the orders of Anastasio Somoza, then head of the Nicaraguan National Guard and soon to be dictator of the country, a man famed for his violent and brutal pro-US stance. He was finally toppled by the Sandinista revolution on 19 July 1979.

9. Vo Nguyen Giap (b. 1911) is a Vietnamese general who joined the Communist Party in the thirties, where he met Ho Chi Minh. He organized the Vietnamese resistance forces against the Japanese during the Second World War. In 1946 he launched an offensive against the French colonial forces in Vietnam, whom he defeated in Dien Bien Phu in 1954, leading to the French withdrawal, and was the main strategist in the Vietnamese people's victorious war against the United States from 1961 to 1975. Though self-taught, he is considered one of the great theorists and masters of war in the twentieth century.

7: Che Guevara

1. Castro has often – in texts, speeches and interviews – spoken about Ernesto 'Che' Guevara; his main recollections are gathered in the book *Che: A Memoir by Fidel Castro*, ed. David Deutschman, Melbourne: Ocean Press, 1998. See one of the longest and most moving reports in *Un encuentro con Fidel*, an interview by Gianni Miná, Havana: Oficina de Publicaciones del Consejo de Estado, 1987, pp. 311–49, and published in Spain under the title *Habla Fidel* (introd. by Gabriel García Márquez), Madrid: Mondadori, 1988, pp. 345–71; in English, see *Encounter with Fidel*, trans. Mary Todd, Melbourne: Ocean Press, 1991.

2. See 'Recorrido por el interior de Argentina (1950), Fragmentos de su diario', in Ernesto Guevara Lynch, *Mi hijo el Che*, Madrid: Planeta, 1981.

3. See Ernesto 'Che' Guevara, *The Motorcycle Diaries*, Melbourne: Ocean Press, 2003 and *Back on the Road: A Journey Through Latin America* (trans. Patrick Camiller), New York: Grove Press, 2002.

4. On 9 April 1952 the popular uprising that would become the Bolivian revolution began. It was spearheaded by Víctor Paz Estenssoro's Movimiento Nacionalista Revolucionario (MNR) and Juan Lechín's Central Obrera Boliviana (COB). Within days, the three great families who owned the mines and controlled much of the country's wealth were

overthrown, the armed forces were disbanded, the labour unions were armed, and land, businesses and prefectures (regional governments) were taken over, thus creating a parallel government. The uneducated indigenous peoples, who were a majority in the country, were given the vote, the mines were nationalized, and land belonging to the *latifundios*, or large estates, was redistributed.

5. Alberto Granado, *Con el Che por Sudamérica*, Havana: Letras Cubanas, 1986.

6. Jacobo Arbenz (1913–71), at the time an officer in the army, was one of the leaders of 1944's 'October Revolution' that overthrew the dictatorship of General Jorge Ubico, who had been kept in power by the army for some fourteen years. In 1951 Arbenz was elected president in democratic elections and his government passed an agrarian reform act. This law hurt the US fruit companies, which owned much of the agricultural land, and led the CIA to accuse Arbenz of being a 'Communist'. With the support of several Central American dictators and the approval of President Dwight Eisenhower, the CIA organized a military coup against Arbenz, who was removed from power on 27 June 1954.

7. Antonio 'Ñico' López Fernández (1930–56) was one of those who attacked the Moncada barracks on 26 July 1953. He avoided being captured by seeking asylum in the Guatemalan embassy in Havana. After the amnesty in 1955, he returned to Cuba and became a member of the directorate of the 26th of July Movement. He was also among the group who returned from Mexico on the *Granma*. He was killed in Boca del Toro on 8 December 1956.

8. [An 'empty' word like 'gosh' or 'cool' or 'wow', indicating, like those words, amazement, surprise, agreement, etc., and sometimes puzzlement or disappointment; it is, indeed, used a great deal by Argentines in daily speech. – Trans.]

9. In an interview with the Argentine journalist Jorge Masetti in April 1958, while still in the Sierra Maestra, Che said, 'I talked with Fidel all night. And by dawn I was the doctor for his future expedition.' See Jorge Masetti, *Los que luchan y los que lloran (El Fidel Castro que yo vi)*, Havana: Editorial Madiedo, 1960. In another place, Che wrote, 'It is a political event, to have met Fidel Castro, the Cuban revolutionary. He is young, intelligent, self-assured, and has extraordinary audacity – I think we liked each other' (*Notas del Segundo Diario de viaje*, 1955).

10. Alberto Bayo, *Mi aporte a la revolución cubana*, Havana: Imprenta del Ejército Rebelde, 1960. Bayo settled in Cuba after the triumph of the Revolution and died in Havana in 1967, at seventy-five years of age.

11. [Abd el-Krim (1882?–1963) was the leader of the Rif tribes of Morocco; his full name was Muhammad Ibn Abd al-Karim al-Khattabi. He had been a high-ranking administrator in the Spanish Zone until 1920, when he took up arms against Spain. In 1921 he and his guerrilla forces defeated the Spanish colonial forces, and over the next three years he strengthened his position and in 1924 drove the Spanish back to Tétouan. He was eventually defeated by a Franco-Spanish force and deported. Late in his life, he presided over the Liberation Committee for the Arab Maghreb, and he lived to see the last country in that region, Algeria, independent. The guerrilla tactics he employed in fighting the Spanish inspired Ho Chi Minh, Mao Zedong and Che Guevara. – Trans.]

12. Miguel Angel Sánchez was known as the 'Korean' because he had been in the Korean War. He was a US citizen of Cuban descent whom Castro met in November of 1955. In December Sánchez joined the group of future revolutionaries in Mexico to help with tactical training. In late 1956, he parted ways with the Cubans.

13. During the Twentieth Communist Party Conference in Moscow, held from 14 to 25 February 1956, Nikita Khrushchev presented a 'secret report' denouncing Stalin's crimes and the errors made in agriculture.

14. Lázaro Cárdenas (1895–1970) was a general who fought in the Mexican revolution and served as president of Mexico from 1934 to 1940. He was the force behind an important agrarian reform in that country, and he nationalized the oil industry in 1938.

8: In the Sierra Maestra

1. [*Dichrostachys cinerea*, an invasive shrub with sharp thorns that forms thick, almost impenetrable stands, especially in fields left fallow or used for pasture. This plant presents a considerable problem for agriculture in Cuba, and it has recently been introduced into the United States, though it seems not to have spread beyond Florida. – Trans.]

2. [Though Castro does not give this mechanism a name, in English it is called a 'double-set trigger'; pulling the back trigger first 'sets' the front trigger, making it a 'hair trigger' – the 'touch of a hair' will detonate the rifle. In this mode, the rifle is used for sharpshooting, or by snipers. The front trigger can also be pulled independently, with normal, heavier pressure. There are very few US gun manufacturers who use this type of trigger, leading one to assume that Castro's weapon was probably European-made. – Trans.]

3. Herbert Matthews was the first non-Cuban journalist to go up into the Sierra Maestra when all the media in Cuba were censoring information on the rebels and Batista's propaganda proclaimed that Castro had been killed in the fighting at Alegría de Pío. At the time, Matthews was fifty-seven years old and was head of the Latin American desk at the *New York Times*. He had been a *Times* correspondent in Ethiopia when Italy invaded that country in 1935; in Spain during the Spanish Civil War; and in Europe during the Second World War. He interviewed Castro on 17 February 1957, and published three articles in the *New York Times*. The first was on the front page on 24 February, and the headline read 'Cuban Rebel Is Visited in Hideout; Castro Is Still Alive and Still Fighting in Mountains'; the other two were published on the 25th and 26th of that month. On the 28th the *Times* also published a photo of Matthews with Castro as a way of verifying that the interview had actually taken place, as the Batista government was denouncing it as a fraud. The photo was soon being published around the world. It was thanks to Matthews, then, that Castro's guerrilla war became known internationally and its leader acquired the image of a romantic freedom fighter.

4. After this first service to the guerrilla forces, José Isaac [*sic*] continued collaborating with the Rebel Army. He died in Havana in the late nineties. [Note by Cuban editor.] [It is unclear whether the Cuban editor intends to correct Castro's citation of the man's name as 'Isaac' or whether, perhaps, as is quite possible, the man whose full name was José Isaac was generally called Isaac. It should be noted that a couple of paragraphs later, Castro himself calls him 'José Isaac'. – Trans.]

5. Guillermo García Frías, a *campesino* born and raised in the Sierra Maestra, played an important role in the preparations to receive the *Granma* expedition and in recovering weapons and regrouping the dispersed expeditionary forces after Alegría de Pío. Early on, he joined the guerrillas, taking part in the first two victories. For his outstanding merit during the entire war, he was awarded the rank of Honorary Comandante of the Revolution. Since 1959 he has held several high-ranking military and civilian posts, and he is currently head of the National Directorate of Flora and Fauna.

6. In the Sierra Maestra, the 'Maestra' is the name generally given the ridge line, or watershed area, of the cordillera, the longitudinal axis that runs from west, at the Toro River, to east. This is the line that divides the northern watershed from the southern. Minas del Frío, the point mentioned by Castro as the destination of the guerrillas' column that night, is located on this ridge line. [Note by Cuban editor.]

7. The battle in Uvero took place on 28 May 1957.

8. Castro and I [Ramonet] visited the Moncada barracks complex in Santiago de Cuba on 19 January 2003, where I saw that historic rifle.

9. General Abelardo 'Furri' Colomé Ibarra is currently a member of the Cuban Communist Party Politburo, vice president of the Council of State, and minister of the interior.

10. Juan Almeida Bosque (b. 1927) holds the rank of Comandante de la Revolución. He met Castro at university and joined the struggle against Batista after the coup on 10 March 1952. He took part in the assault on the Moncada barracks, was captured and sentenced to prison. He was one of the *Granma* expeditionary group and took part in many battles

and skirmishes in the Sierra Maestra. In 1958 he was promoted to *comandante* and given command of the Rebel Army's Third Front in the region around Santiago de Cuba. He has been a member of the Cuban Communist Party Politburo since its creation in 1965 and has held a number of government positions. He is currently president of the Association of Combatants of the Cuban Revolution.

11. Celia Sánchez Manduley (1920–80) was born in the small town of Media Luna in Oriente, now Granma province. Early in her life she joined the active opposition to the corrupt Authentic Party governments and after the coup on 10 March 1952, she joined the anti-Batista struggle. She entered the 26th of July organization when it was formally created in 1955, and she was charged with putting in place, throughout the south-west coastal region of the former Oriente province, the conditions for receiving the *Granma* expedition. Under the direction of Frank País, she was the main organizer of the first contingent of reinforcements sent from the plains area into the Sierra Maestra. In October 1957 she joined the guerrillas, and she soon became Fidel Castro's principal ally in organizing the rebel rear guard. After the triumph of the Revolution, she worked closely with Castro in many areas. In 1959 she was named secretary to the president, and in 1976, secretary to the Council of State, a position she held until her death in January 1980. See Pedro Álvarez Tabío, *Celia, ensayo para una biografía*, Havana: Oficina de Publicaciones del Consejo de Estado, 2003. [Note by Cuban editor.]

12. Rigoberto Sillero died as he was being transported by air to Santiago de Cuba; on that same flight was Lt Pedro Carreras, commander of the Uvero garrison, who'd also been wounded in the firefight. The other seriously wounded rebel, Mario Leal, survived and spent the rest of the war as a prisoner on Isla de Pinos. [Note by Cuban editor.]

13. [It has to be remembered that by this time, as Castro has pointed out several times along the way, the Rebel Army had been joined by a large number of *campesinos*, many if not most of whom were completely or functionally illiterate. – Trans.]

9: Lessons from a Guerrilla War

1. [Readers will note that this contradicts Castro's statement in Chapter 5, page 149, that the Rebel Army did not use this tactic. – Trans.]

2. Ernest Hemingway (1899–1961), winner of the Nobel Prize for Literature in 1954 was, as almost everyone knows, a correspondent in Spain during the Spanish Civil War (1936–9), and that experience led him in 1940 to write *For Whom the Bell Tolls*. (He wrote this novel in room 525 of the Hotel Ambos Mundos in Havana.) His is unquestionably the best known of the novels based on that conflict. In 1943 director Sam Wood made a film of the same name, starring Gary Cooper and Ingrid Bergman.

10: Revolution: First Steps, First Problems

1. At the time, this was the official name of the former Cuban Communist Party, whose secretary-general then was Blas Roca; Carlos Rafael Rodríguez was also a member.

2. In 1961, as part of the consolidation of the Revolution's forces, the 26th of July Movement merged with the 13th of March Revolutionary Directorate and the Popular Socialist Party to form the Integrated Revolutionary Organizations, the ORI. Later, the ORI became the Partido Unido de la Revolución Socialista de Cuba (the PURSC, or Cuban United Socialist Revolution Party), and in 1965, the Communist Party of Cuba.

3. Castro is referring here to Eutimio Guerra, a *campesino* who joined the guerrillas before the first battle at La Plata. Guerra was taken prisoner by Batista's army and, in exchange for a generous supply of material goods, was persuaded to assassinate Castro or provide aid to destroy the guerrilla forces, which he almost did on two occasions. His betrayal was discovered and Guerra was captured, tried and executed on 17 February 1957, the same day Castro was interviewed by Herbert Matthews. [Note by Cuban editor.]

4. Jesús Sosa Blanco, an army officer under Batista, was accused of 108 murders. One of his

most horrendous crimes was the mass murder, under his orders, of a dozen peaceful *campesino* inhabitants of the village of Oro de Guisa, in the Sierra Maestra, among them nine members of the Argote family. He was tried in the Sports City stadium in Havana on 22 January [dates attributed to this event vary; some sources say 18 January] 1959, sentenced to death, and summarily executed.

5. [The word used by Ramonet for his question is *testimonios*, which are, as the translation indicates, eyewitness reports of events. A *testimonio* is somewhat more than that, however, as it is a recognizable sub-literary genre in Latin America. What Ramonet is saying is that people produced documents attesting to their experiences in these camps. One such case was Reinaldo Arenas (1943–97), as part of his autobiography *Before Night Falls* (New York: Penguin, 1994). There are also works of fiction dealing with this subject, especially among the writings of Arenas. See, for example, 'The Brightest Star' ('Arturo, la estrella más brillante') in *Old Rosa* (New York: Grove Press, 1989). – Trans.]

6. Gustave Le Bon (1841–1931), French physician, archaeologist, anthropologist and psychologist, author of two very famous tracts: *Les Lois psychologiques de l'évolution des peuples* (1894) and *La Psychologie des foules*.

7. [Unfounded and often libellous rumours. – Trans.]

8. [The Cuban Missile Crisis, as it is known in the Anglophone world. – Trans.]

9. Here, Castro is referring to programmes under way at the time within the larger campaign of education, raising the level of general culture, and making the entire nation more aware of cultural and political affairs. This campaign is known generically as the 'Battle of Ideas'. The number of programmes within the campaign continues to grow, and by late 2005, there were more than 150, with encouraging results.

10. The 'Mariana Grajales' platoon, named in honour of Maceo's mother, a symbol of the female combatant in Cuba, was created by Castro in September 1958, after the last enemy offensive against the Rebel Army; the creation of this group necessitated overcoming the resistance of many rebel officers. The 'Marianas' played a distinguished role in many battles and actions. See Sara Mas, 'Mujeres en la línea de fuego: Las Marianas', *Granma*, Havana, 4 September 2003.

11. The active participation of the Catholic clergy in Miami and Cuba in this operation has been documented. See Ramón Torreira Crespo and José Buajasán Marawi, *La Operación Peter Pan*, Havana: Editora Política, 2000.

12. Mikhail Sholokhov (1905–84), Ukrainian author, winner of the Nobel Prize for Literature in 1965 and author of the famous tetralogy *And Quiet Flows the Don*.

13. In Mexico, from 1926 to 1929, the rebellion of the *cristeros* – indigenous converts to Catholicism and Catholic *campesinos* who marauded under the cry 'Long live Christ the King!' and attacked and killed the anti-clericals – translated into a virtual civil war and caused tens of thousands of deaths.

11: The Conspiracies Begin

1. Angel Sánchez Mosquera was a lieutenant [in Batista's army] at the beginning of the war who was promoted to colonel on the basis of his bloodthirsty actions in the Sierra Maestra. He was one of Batista's most capable and determined officers, and also one of the most murderous. It was his troops who came nearest the La Plata headquarters during the enemy offensive against the First Rebel Front in the summer of 1958, and in one of the final battles of that operation he was seriously wounded in the head. [Note by Cuban editor.]

2. Huber Matos (b. 1918) was a *comandante* in the rebel guerrillas who fought against Batista in the Sierra Maestra; he commanded the 'Antonio Guiteras' Column, Column 9, in the Third Front. In October 1959, while acting as governor of the military region of Camagüey, he became unhappy with the 'Communist direction' that, according to him, the Revolution was taking, and [according to Castro and the Revolution (see end of this note)] he began to organize a conspiracy. Camilo Cienfuegos went personally to Camagüey

to arrest Matos and thwart the conspiracy. Matos was tried and sentenced to twenty years in prison. He has lived in exile in Miami since he was released from prison in 1979, and he is the leader of the Cuba Independiente y Democrática movement (CID); he is the author of an autobiography titled *Cómo llegó la noche* (Madrid: Tusquets, 2003). [It should be noted that all Spanish editions insist on spelling Huber Matos's name 'Hubert'; this is an error; his name is spelled as given here. Likewise, it should be noted that Matos' and others' version of Matos's 'betrayal' of the Revolution and the alleged conspiracy he was organizing, an action he denies, is quite different from the version given here. Matos' letters to Castro, for example, seem never to have been published by him, and it seems to have been Castro who first made them public, probably in order to discredit Matos and bring him to trial. Obviously, both sides of this controversy have their own axe to grind; these clarifications are simply 'for the record'. – Trans.]

3. Antonio Núñez Jiménez (1923–98), geographer, speleologist and naturalist, was a captain in the Rebel Army. After the triumph of the Revolution he held high-ranking government posts, among them executive director of the National Institute of Agrarian Reform [an exceptionally important position in Cuba], which agency was created by the Agrarian Reform Act of May 1959. He was the author of numerous books on the geography of Cuba and other subjects, including a monumental encyclopaedia, *Cuba, la naturaleza y el hombre* ('Cuba, Nature and Man').

4. One *caballería* equals 13.4 hectares, or about 33 acres. See Chapter 1, note 6.

5. The collapse of the [Eastern] European Socialist bloc and the disintegration of the Soviet Union caused Cuba to abruptly lose its principal commercial markets and sources of credit, which in turn led, beginning in 1991, to a drastic contraction of the Cuban economy. Many people around the world predicted the imminent demise of the Cuban Revolution. The years during which the country lived under the effects of this difficult situation are called the 'special period', which lasted through to the end of the nineties, when the Cuban economy entered a sustained period of recovery. [Note by Cuban editor.]

6. In 1921, at the end of the civil war, Russia was in ruins and its population dying of starvation. At that point Lenin decided to abandon the Communism of the war years and launch the NEP (New Economic Policy), a partial return to capitalism – a mixed economy – and give priority to agriculture. The results were positive. Then Lenin died in 1924 and in 1928 Stalin abruptly abandoned the NEP and turned to a thoroughly Socialist economy, with top priority given to industrialization in order to 'build Socialism in a single country'.

7. In 1963–4, an important theoretical debate took place on the economic structure of the Cuban Revolution; in this debate, those in favour of economic calculus faced off with those in favour of the budget financing system. The first group, headed by Carlos Rafael Rodríguez, Alberto Mora, Marcelo Fernández Font and the French Marxist economist Charles Bettelheim, defended a political programme of mercantile Socialism, with businesses and industries largely decentralized and with limited financial autonomy, competing in the economy and exchanging their respective goods via money. Thus, in each business or industry, the stimulus of money, profit, held sway. Planning, argued these supporters of economic calculus, would operate through value and the market. This was the main path chosen and promoted by the Soviets during those years.

The second group, headed by Che Guevara and followed by Luis Alvarez Rom and the Belgian economist Ernest Mandel (director of the Fourth International), questioned the marriage of Socialism and a market economy. They defended a political programme in which 'planning' and 'market' were antagonistic terms. Che thought that planning was much more than a mere technical resource for helping the economy; it was, instead, the way to broaden the radius of human rationality, progressively reducing the amount of fetishism on which a belief in the 'autonomy of economic laws' was based.

The supporters, like Che, of the Budgetary System argued for the unification of all productive units under a single bank, with a single, centralized budget, so that all these elements were parts of a single huge Socialist enterprise (made up of the particular productive units). Between two factories of a single industry there would be no selling or buying mediated by money or the market, but rather exchange through a bank account register. Products would pass from one production unit to another without being 'merchandise'. Che and his supporters were in favour of volunteer work and moral incentives as the main, though not only, tools for raising the workers' Socialist awareness.

See Orlando Borrego (who worked with Che in the Ministry of Industry), *Che Guevara, el camino del fuego* (2001) and *Che, recuerdos en ráfaga* (2003), both Buenos Aires: Editorial Hombre Nuevo. See also Néstor Kohan, 'Che Guevara, lector de *El capital*, diálogo con Orlando Borrego', *Rebelión*, Buenos Aires, 13 August 2003.

8. On Che's ideas about the economy, see 'Socialism and Man in Cuba', in *Global Justice: Liberation and Socialism*, Melbourne: Ocean Press, 2002.

9. On 17 March 1960 the president of the United States approved a programme [signed an NSC directive approving a programme] undertaken by the CIA against Cuba, among whose actions were to be 'creation of a responsible, attractive and united Cuban opposition to the Castro regime', the 'development of a powerful propaganda offensive', 'the continuation of efforts to create a clandestine intelligence and action organization inside Cuba', and, finally, preparation outside Cuba of an 'appropriate paramilitary force'. This document was the direct antecedent of the campaign of subversion, destabilization and direct aggression that culminated in the Bay of Pigs invasion in April 1961. [Note by Cuban editor.]

10. See José Ramón Fernández and José Pérez Fernández, *La guerra de EE.UU. contra Cuba. La invasión de Playa Girón, 638 planes para asesinar a Fidel Castro, 40 años de agresiones*, Havana: Editorial Política, 2001, and Jacinto Valdés-Dapena, *La CIA contra Cuba: La actividad subversiva de la CIA y la contrarrevolución (1961–1968)*, Havana: Editorial Capitán San Luis, 2002. See also Luis Báez, *El mérito es vivir: Objetivo: asesinar a Fidel*, Barcelona: Editorial La Buganville, 2002.

11. Since publication of the first edition of this book, a media scandal has erupted in Miami due to revelations by a former member of the board of directors of the Cuban-American National Foundation in which he confirms the existence of this action group and gives details of plans to assassinate Fidel Castro during the Latin American Summit held on Isla Margarita in 1997. [Note by Cuban editor.]

12. See the Church Report of the United States Senate, *Alleged Assassination Plots Involving Foreign Leaders*, coordinated by Senator Frank Church, Washington, 1975. The Church Commission confirmed eight plans to assassinate Fidel Castro between 1960 and 1965, all with the direct participation and resources of the CIA.

13. Luis Posada Carriles (b. 1928) and three other Cubans linked to this plan to assassinate Castro – Pedro Remón Crispin, Guillermo Novo Sampoll and Gaspar Jiménez Escobedo – were arrested, tried and imprisoned in Panama. In August 2004, the outgoing president of Panama, Mireya Moscoso, commuted these four terrorists' sentences; three went immediately to the United States and were taken in by that country's authorities. In March 2005 Cuba denounced the fact that Posada Carriles had clandestinely entered the United States, and although this was initially denied by Washington, an intense international campaign spearheaded by Havana later forced the US to acknowledge Posada's presence in Miami. This created a difficult situation for the US government, which was championing a 'worldwide crusade against terrorism' yet giving refuge to a confessed terrorist. (See the interview with Posada Carriles in the *New York Times* of 12 July 1998: 'A Bomber's Tale: Taking Aim at Castro – Key Cuba Foe Claims Exiles' Backing', p. 1, column 1.) The US authorities had no choice but to arrest him and try him for 'illegally entering the country'. In September 2005 the courts decided that Posada should not be deported to Venezuela (where he had escaped from prison in 1985) or to Cuba, where he might, in their words 'be tortured'. The leaders of Latin American countries, meeting in Salamanca for the Latin American Summit in October 2005, expressed their solidarity with Venezuela and Cuba and backed those countries' attempts to extradite Posada Carriles or see him brought to justice. [For a recent detailed history of Posada's terrorist activities, see Ann Louise

Bardach, 'Twilight of the Assassins', *The Atlantic* (Washington, DC), Vol. 298, No. 4 (November 2006). – Trans.]

14. [While everyone agrees that this organization's acronym is CORU, there seems to be some doubt, in both Cuba and the US, as to whether the 'C' stands for '*coordinación*' or '*coordinadora.*' I have been unable to resolve the problem. – Trans.]

12: The Bay of Pigs/Playa Girón

1. In ancient Greece, a narrow pass between the mountains and the sea, measuring from twenty-five to about 150 feet wide, where a famous battle took place in 480 BC between the Spartans, under the command of Leonidas, and the Persian invaders led by emperor Xerxes. In this encounter, some 300 Spartans and 700 Thespians resisted the Persian army, said by some historians to number almost 5,000,000 men, for a period of three days. In the end, the Persians were able to get behind the Greeks and kill them.

2. In December 2001 a federal court in Miami gave long sentences to the five Cuban officers – Gerardo Hernández Nordelo, Ramón Labañino Salazar, Fernando González Llort, René González Sehwerert and Antonio Guerrero Rodríguez – who had infiltrated anti-Cuban terrorist organizations operating in that city; they had been arrested in Florida in 1998. Three of them were charged with conspiracy to commit espionage and all of them were charged with failure to register as agents of a foreign power. In December 2001 the People's Assembly in Cuba bestowed upon each of them the title 'Hero of the Republic of Cuba'. In August 2005 a panel of three judges from the Appeals Court in Atlanta overturned the Miami verdict and, therefore, the sentences, but one year later, in a most unusual action, that judgment was overturned by the court as a whole. At the time of this writing [July 2007], the five Cubans remain in US federal prisons, two of them forbidden to see their mothers, wives and children. These Five Heroes have inspired an international protest movement. (See also Chapter 21, note 9.)

3. Though it achieved its independence in 1975, Angola immediately fell into a long civil war in which the Luanda government, led by Agostinho Neto and the Marxist Popular Movement for the Liberation of Angola (the MPLA), was opposed by the National Union for the Total Independence of Angola (UNITA), backed by the United States and the Republic of South Africa and its apartheid regime. In the face of the direct intervention of South African and Zairean forces, which invaded Angola and threatened to occupy Luanda, Cuba launched 'Operation Carlota' and in November 1975 sent over a large expeditionary force. In the end, this force and the Angolan army halted the South Africans, turned them back, and inflicted on them a spectacular defeat in the battle of Cuito Cuanavale in 1987. (See also Chapter 15, 'Cuba and Africa'.)

4. [Mohamed Siad Barre (1919–95) was president of Somalia from 1969 to 1991. After training with Soviet army officers in the 1960s he became an advocate of Marxism. He was extremely nationalistic, making the Somali language the language of education, for example, and advocating the idea of a 'Greater Somalia', which would bring together all ethnic Somalis in one nation. To do this, it was necessary to annex Djibouti, the Somali region of Kenya, and the Ogaden region of Ethiopia. Thus, Siad Barre sent the Somali army in to invade the Ogaden. He was soon opposed by the Soviets, who came to the aid of Ethiopia, and by the Cubans, as Castro here points out. In the end, the Somali troops were expelled from the territory of Ethiopia. This conflict occurred in 1977–8. – Trans.]

5. In 1974 a rebellion of army officers backed by students, intellectuals and the people brought an end to the reign of Emperor Haile Selassie and with it, the Ethiopian empire. In 1977 Colonel Mengistu Haile Mariam assumed power at a time when the country had been invaded by Somalia, which occupied the region of Ogaden, over which it claimed sovereignty. The Soviet Union provided aid to Ethiopia, and Cuba sent in an expeditionary force. In 1978 the Cuban and Ethiopian forces, fighting together, won an important victory over the Somali army, which was forced to withdraw from Ogaden.

6. See Chapter 11, note 12.

7. Cardinal John O'Connor (1920–2000), archbishop of New York from 1984 until his death on 4 May 2000, visited Cuba with a delegation of his New York parishioners in January 1998, on the occasion of Pope John Paul II's visit to the island.

8. Alpha 66, a paramilitary organization founded in 1961, with a base in Miami containing training camps, carries out commando attacks and is responsible for assassination attempts and other actions in Cuba. Omega 7 is a Miami-based terrorist organization founded in 1974 and made up essentially of veterans of the Playa Girón invasion. It specializes in car bombs and shootings of Cuban government representatives in New York, New Jersey and Florida. These have been two of the most active organizations in the systematic terrorism practised against Cuba over the course of forty-six years.

9. [In the first edition, Castro makes an explicit comparison between these expectations and the expectations of the Bush–Cheney administration before the Iraq War. – Trans.]

13: The 'Cuban Missile Crisis' of October 1962

1. [For the text of the speech, see http://www.pbs.org/wgbh/amex/presidents/35_kennedy/psources/ps_armsbild.html. – Trans.]

2. These letters, translated, may now be found in various places on the internet. One site is the PBS (US public television) site for 'The Presidents'; links to the letters are at http://www.pbs.org/wgbh/amex/presidents/35_kennedy/psources/index.html. The texts included here follow, to a large degree, the translations there, though they have been edited for style for this book.

3. [Omitted parts of the letter:
   We have just drafted our response to the president's message. I will not include it here since it is being transmitted by radio.
   Because of this, we would now like to advise you, at this turning point of the crisis, not to be carried away by your feelings; be firm . . . We understand your profound indignation at the aggressive actions of the USA and its violation of the fundamental norms of international law . . .
   (Paragraph 2 of text quoted in main text goes here.)
   Because of this, we would like to advise you, in the spirit of friendship, to show patience, firmness, and more firmness. Naturally, if there is an invasion, it will be necessary to fight it with everything. But one must not allow oneself to be provoked. Now that a solution is being found, one that is in your favour and that guarantees against an invasion, the unbridled militarists in the Pentagon want to frustrate the agreement and provoke you into taking actions that could be used against you. We ask that you not give them a pretext for this.
   We on our side will do everything to stabilize the situation in Cuba, to defend Cuba from invasion, and to ensure the possibilities for the peaceful construction of the Socialist society in Cuba. – Trans.]

4. [Continuation of that paragraph, and the next two:
   It is possible that such feelings exist among the people. But we politicians and heads of state are the people's leaders, and the people do not know everything. That is why we must march at the head of the people. Then they will follow and respect us.
   If, by giving in to popular sentiment, we had allowed ourselves to be swept up by the more inflamed sectors of the populace, and if we had refused to reach a reasonable agreement with the government of the United States, war would likely have broken out, resulting in millions of deaths. Those who survived would have blamed the leaders for not having taken the measures that would have avoided this war of extermination.
   The prevention of war and of an attack on Cuba did not depend simply on the measures taken by our governments, but also on the analysis and examination of the enemy's actions near your territory. In short, the situation had to be considered as a whole. – Trans.]

5. [Continuation of letter in the next two paragraphs:
   In fact, we consider that consultations did take place, dear Comrade Fidel Castro, since

we received your cables, one more alarming than the other, and finally your cable of 17 October, in which you said that you were almost certain that an attack against Cuba was imminent. According to you it was only a matter of time: twenty-four to seventy-two hours.

Having received this very alarming cable from you, and knowing of your courage, we believed the alert to be totally justified. – Trans.]

6. [Continuation of that paragraph:

We struggle against imperialism not in order to die but in order to draw upon all of our potential, to lose as little as possible, and later to win more, so as to be a victor and ensure the triumph of Communism. – Trans.]

7. [Continuation in four brief paragraphs:

We believed that we had to take advantage of every possibility to defend Cuba, to strengthen its independence and sovereignty, to thwart military aggression, and to prevent a global thermonuclear war.

And we have succeeded.

Of course we have made concessions, we have made certain commitments. We have acted on the principle of reciprocal concessions. The United States has also made concessions; it has committed itself publicly, before the world, not to attack Cuba.

Therefore, if we compare a US attack and thermonuclear war on the one hand, and the commitments made on the other – the reciprocal concessions, the guarantee of the inviolability of the Republic of Cuba, and the prevention of a world war – then I think the conclusion is clear. – Trans.]

8. This important base, located within the city limits of Lourdes, forty kilometres, about twenty-five miles, south of Havana, covered an area of seventy-two square kilometres, some twenty-eight square miles or 18,000 acres. Some 1,500 engineers, technicians and Russian soldiers were stationed on it. It was opened during the period when the Soviet Union and Cuba had a close political, economic and military alliance and it was used to intercept all types of electronic communications. In 1994 Russia and Cuba agreed to retain the base, on which the USSR paid an annual rent of about $200 million. In October 2001 Moscow announced the closing of the electronic-surveillance bases at Lourdes and Cam Ranh, Vietnam. After closure of the base at Lourdes, the Cuban government modernized, remodelled and substantially expanded the facilities there and opened the Information Sciences University (UCI) on the site, one of the most ambitious and spectacular projects in the 'Battle of Ideas'. [Note by Cuban editor.]

9. Operation Mongoose was a covert programme of subversive warfare waged by the United States' National Security Council against Cuba. It included economic warfare, intelligence-gathering, psychological warfare, support of armed anti-Castro groups and support for counter-revolutionary political organizations. Launched in November 1961 on the suggestion of General Maxwell Taylor after the failure of the Playa Girón invasion, it did not officially conclude until 3 January 1963.

10. At the age of eighty-five, Arthur M. Schlesinger, Jr, former adviser to President John Kennedy, visited Cuba for the international conference titled 'The Cuban Missile Crisis, 1962: 40th Anniversary', as its name appears in English (the Spanish title is slightly different) on 11 and 12 October 2002. There, Schlesinger was asked whether, as rumour had it, President Kennedy had intentions of improving relations between the United States and Cuba after the missile crisis, to which Schlesinger answered: 'I was a direct witness of those intentions, since he mentioned them to me more than once, and I can tell you that despite the many issues that required his attention, the president was thinking about ways and means of implementing an approach to Havana.' Schlesinger mentioned, in this regard, 'a letter whose exact content I can't recall, addressed to the Cuban government and sent through the government of Brazil'. And he concluded: 'But his efforts were cut short with his assassination late that year.' Cable from the AIN news agency (the Cuban National Information Agency), 13 October 2002. [Schlesinger's comments are translated from the Spanish; I have not been able to find his exact words in English. – Trans.]

11. *A Thousand Days: John F. Kennedy in the White House*, Boston: Mariner Books, 1965.

14: The Death of Che Guevara

1. The Bandung Conference (Indonesia) was held on 18–24 April 1955, and was attended by twenty-nine countries of what had begun to be called the Third World. This conference gave rise to the Non-Aligned Movement. The most influential speakers at the conference were Nehru of India, Chou En-lai of China, Sukarno of Indonesia and Nasser of Egypt.

2. Rómulo Betancourt (1908–81) was a leader of the social-democratic Democratic Action Party in Venezuela and president of the country from 1945 to 1948. Then, in 1958, he was elected president again, this time democratically, and he waged a fierce fight against Venezuelan guerrillas. He was overthrown in 1964.

3. In July 1944 the Bretton Woods accords were signed by forty-four countries; the intention was to reform the monetary system and stimulate international exchange after the Second World War. These accords set the Gold Exchange Standard, made the dollar the international reserve currency, and created the International Monetary Fund (IMF) and the World Bank. (See also Chapter 20, note 10.)

4. In Guevara's 'Message to the Tricontinental', which he wrote in Cuba in 1966 before leaving for Bolivia. The message was addressed to the newly formed Organization of Solidarity with the Peoples of Asia, Africa and Latin America and published in April 1967 in the organization's magazine *Tricontinental*, under Guevara's title, 'Create two, three ... many Vietnams, that is the watchword'. The article is included in *Che Guevara and the Cuban Revolution: Writings and Speeches by Che Guevara*, Pathfinder, 1967, and also in *Global Justice: Liberation and Socialism*, Melbourne: Ocean Press, 2002.

5. Masetti interviewed Che Guevara in the Sierra Maestra in April 1958. See that interview in Ernesto 'Che' Guevara, *América Latina: Despertar de un continente*, Melbourne: Ocean Books, 2003, pp. 199–207.

6. The group of twenty-five men led by Masetti (Comandante Segundo), in the region of Salta, an area on the border between Argentina and Bolivia, 'disappeared' between 15 and 25 April 1964.

7. See Luis Báez, *Secretos de generales*, Buenos Aires: Losada, 1997. (See also Chapter 8, note 9.)

8. Patrice Lumumba (1925–61) was the Congolese (Kinshasa) leader of the war of independence against Belgium. He became prime minister in June 1960 and was assassinated in 1961.

9. Ahmed Ben Bella, 'Ainsi était le Che', *Le Monde Diplomatique*, October 1997. See Chapter 15.

10. Moises Tshombé (1919–69) was a political leader of the former Belgian Congo who founded the Conakat Party in the province of Katanga. In 1960, with the support of several Western powers, he led an opposition movement against Lumumba, had himself named president of Katanga, and declared the independence of that wealthy region of the country. Lumumba called on the United Nations for help but was assassinated by Katangan officers at the instigation of the CIA. Tshombé was forced out of power, so he went into exile in Europe, where he lived for a time in Spain. He died in Algeria.

11. Mobutu Sese Seko (1930–97), head of the Congolese armed forces after independence, overthrew President Kasavubu in 1965, combated guerrillas with the aid of a mercenary army, and was dictator of his country until his overthrow in 1997 by the forces of Laurent-Désiré Kabila. Mobutu was a tool of the CIA in the assassination of the great Congolese leader Patrice Lumumba; he enjoyed the full support of the US despite his notorious corruption and the brutality of his regime.

12. Ernesto 'Che' Guevara, *El año en que estuvimos en ninguna parte: Fragmentos del diario [de la guerrilla africana] de Ernesto Che Guevara*, ed. and notes by Paco Ignacio Taibo II, Froilán Escobar and Félix Guerra, Buenos Aires: Editorial Colihue (Ediciones del Pensamiento Nacional), 1995.

13. In Spanish, the exact quotation is: 'Mi única falta de alguna gravedad es no haber confiado más en ti desde los primeros momentos de la Sierra Maestra y no haber comprendido

con suficiente celeridad tus cualidades de conductor y de revolucionario.' Translated: 'My only error of any seriousness is not to have had more trust in you from the first moments in the Sierra Maestra and not to have quickly enough seen your qualities as leader and revolutionary.' See the complete text of this letter, which Castro made public on 3 October 1965, in *Che en la memoria de Fidel Castro, op.cit.*, pp. 34–6.

14. Che underwent plastic surgery and makeup, with a mouthpiece, by Cuban specialists.
15. The commando unit trained under Che's orders for the expedition in Bolivia was composed of the following men: Comandante Juan Vitalio Acuña ('Joaquín'), Comandante Antonio Sánchez Díaz ('Pinares', but 'Marcos' in Bolivia), Comandante Gustavo Machín ('Alejandro'), Comandante Alberto Fernández Montes de Oca ('Pacho'), Captain Jesús Suárez Gayol ('El Rubio'), Captain Eliseo Reyes ('Rolando', but 'Capitán San Luis' in Bolivia), Captain Orlando Pantoja ('Antonio'), Captain Manuel Hernández ('Miguel'), Octavio de la Concepción (Moro), Leonardo Tamayo ('Urbano'), Harry Villegas ('Pombo'), Dariel Alarcón Ramírez ('Benigno'), Carlos Coello ('Tuma'), José María Martínez Tamayo ('Ricardo'), Israel Reyes ('Braulio') and René Martínez Tamayo ('Arturo').
16. Their names were José María and René Martínez Tamayo.
17. Argentine Ciro Bustos, the only survivor of Jorge Masetti's group, and the liaison between Che's column and the Argentine militants who were supposed to join the guerrillas, had been captured and, under torture, apparently provided the information that Che was in Argentina and revealed his location.
18. Tamara Bunke Bider (1937–67), aka Laura González Bauer and generally known as 'Tania the guerrilla', an Argentine of German descent, took part in the guerrilla war in Bolivia in 'Joaquín's' group, whose members were ambushed and killed in El Yeso creek on 31 August 1967.
19. [Literally: Radio Big Lips; the usual English slang is 'the grapevine'. – Trans.]
20. Castro gave this speech at the solemn memorial for Che Guevara on 18 October 1967, in the Plaza de la Revolución in Havana before one million people.

15: Cuba and Africa

1. See Ahmed Ben Bella, 'Ainsi était le Che', *Le Monde Diplomatique*, Paris, October 1997.
2. The massacre at Kassinga took place on 4 May 1978, when South African forces bombed a Namibian refugee camp in the southern Angola province of Cunene, killing over 600 people, mostly women, children and old people.
3. The Henry Reeve Contingent (HRC), whose name honours a young American who fought in Cuba's first War of Independence and became a high-ranking officer in the Cuban Liberation Army (see Chapter 5, p. 146), was formed in 2005, just as the United States was rejecting a contingent of some 1,600 doctors and other health professionals, complete with medicines, equipment and field hospitals, to aid the victims of Hurricane Katrina, which had devastated the city of New Orleans and a wide area of Louisiana, Alabama and Georgia. The HRC's full name is the Henry Reeve International Contingent of Doctors Specializing in Disaster Situations and Serious Epidemics.
4. The first group of health workers sent to Algeria was composed of twenty-nine doctors, three orthodontists, fifteen nurses and eight medical technicians; there were forty-five men and ten women. [Note by Cuban editor.]
5. This Cuban detachment was under the command of *Comandante* Efigenio Ameijeiras, a veteran of the *Granma* crossing and the Sierra Maestra and former chief of Cuba's National Revolutionary Police.
6. For a detailed description of this operation, see Gabriel García Márquez, 'Operación Carlota', *Tricontinental*, No. 53, Havana, 1977.
7. [Actually, 'constructive engagement' rather than 'commitment' was Reagan's term for his relationship with South Africa. Cuba has always maintained that this 'commitment' (as the Cubans present the term in their official translations) or 'engagement' was a commitment to prolonging apartheid. – Trans.]

8. Currently lieutenant-general of the army, member of the Cuban Communist Party Polit-buro, and commander of the Army of the East.
9. Chester A. Crocker, *High Noon in Southern Africa: Making Peace in a Rough Neighbor-hood*, New York: Norton & Company, 1992.
10. A statue to Antonio Maceo, the 'Bronze Titan' (see Chapter 1, note 3), which stands in the Parque Antonio Maceo in Havana.
11. Operation Tribute took place on 7 December 1989, the anniversary of the death of General Antonio Maceo; this operation consisted of funeral ceremonies for the Cuban internationalist combatants who had fallen in battles fought in solidarity with Cuba's sister-states in Africa.

16: The Emigration Crises

1. [I.e., the triumph of the Revolution, after which tens of thousands of people emigrated, many thinking it was just 'until all this blows over'. – Trans.]
2. [Those immigrants who, according to law and US Immigration and Naturalization guide-lines, could be excluded from legal alien status because in their home countries they had been convicted of crimes, had been engaged in 'subversive activities', were unable to support themselves, had obtained their visa or other entry papers fraudulently, etc. – Trans.]
3. The Cuban Adjustment Act was passed by the US Congress on 2 November 1966, during the administration of Lyndon B. Johnson. It modified the immigration statute then in effect so as to categorize Cuban immigrants as 'political refugees' with the automatic right to political asylum and permission for permanent residency status. Cuba maintains that this law encourages illegal emigration from the island.
4. Up to 22 July 1994 the United States had granted only 544 visas, rather than the more than 10,000 that by that point in the year they should have issued, according to the 1984 agreement.
5. On 5 August 1994, in the middle of the special period, a group of people tried to take over a boat in Havana, and this action triggered demonstrations in the port area of the city. Soon after noon, a riot broke out there, in Old Havana, and in several neighbourhoods in the centre-city; the police were overrun and the situation was almost out of control when Castro himself stepped in.
6. Felipe Pérez Roque (b. 1965), current Cuban minister of foreign relations, was at the time Fidel Castro's personal assistant.
7. Carlos Lage (b. 1951), current vice president of the Cuban Council of State and secretary of the cabinet, the Council of Ministers.
8. [The period after the collapse of the Soviet Union when Cuba was left bereft of the material and economic support it had received from the Soviets; times were, indeed, very hard, as Castro mentions in Chapters 15, 16 and 17 especially. – Trans.]
9. It is estimated that over 100,000 Moroccans and sub-Saharans attempt to cross the Strait of Gibraltar every year. Few are successful: according to data from the Spanish authorities in Madrid, in the first nine months of 2003 some 15,985 foreigners were detained on the Spanish coastline; these people had crossed the Strait from Morocco in small boats. According to the Association of Friends and Families of Victims of Clandestine Immi-gration (AFVIC), between 1997 and 2001, some 10,000 illegal emigrants sailing from Morocco lost their lives in attempting to cross the Strait.
10. The North American Free Trade Agreement (usually referred to as NAFTA), between the US, Canada and Mexico, which went into effect on 1 January 1994.
11. [The Schengen Agreement takes its name from the place it was signed: the village of Schengen in Luxembourg; it was signed by its founding countries in 1985 and went into effect in 1990. The aim of the Schengen Agreement is to allow free circulation of people within the territory ('Schengen space') of the member countries. All persons who are legally resident in one of the Schengen member states can make short visits without a visa to any

other member state, provided they travel with their valid passport, which must be recognized by all the Schengen states, and a resident permit issued by the authorities of the country of residency. The following countries are today active members of the Schengen Agreement: Austria, Belgium, France, Germany, Greece, Italy, Luxembourg, The Netherlands, Spain and Portugal. Finland, Sweden, Norway and Iceland are associate members. – Trans.]

12. In April 2003 a Cuban citizen hijacked a passenger plane and forced it to fly to Miami. In September of that year, for the first time in forty years, the United States took action against a hijacker and this individual was sentenced to twenty years in jail by a court in Florida. In addition, in July 2003, also for the first time in forty years, US authorities returned a group of twelve Cubans who had hijacked a boat in Camagüey and sailed it to Florida.

13. Any illegal Cuban emigrant who sets foot on American soil ('dry foot') is automatically subject to the Cuban Adjustment Act and can enter the United States as a legal immigrant. Those who are intercepted at sea may be returned to Cuba, though the American authorities often ignore their own law and allow these 'wet feet' to remain in the US.

14. Robert 'Bob' Menendez, born in New York City to Cuban parents who had left Cuba under Batista in 1953, now junior senator from New Jersey, was the elected representative of New Jersey's District 13 from 1992 to 2006; in 2003 Menendez was elected chairman of the House Democratic Caucus, making him the third highest-ranking Democratic member of the House of Representatives. [On 17 January 2006, after the date of these interviews with Castro, Menendez was appointed to fill the Senate seat vacated by the resignation of New Jersey governor-elect John Corzine. In the November 2006 elections he won the Senate seat outright. – Trans.]

15. Eduard Shevardnadze (b. 1928), Soviet minister of foreign relations from 1985 to 1990. After the break-up of the Soviet Union, Shevardnadze served as president of Georgia (elected 1996 and 2000), one of the former Soviet republics. [He was overthrown by a popular insurrection in November 2003. – Trans.]

16. In 2003, despite the embargo that had been in place since 1962, the United States became the largest supplier of food to Cuba. In the first eight months of that year, according to Pedro Alvarez, president of Cuban import agency Alimport, the US had already sold food and agricultural products worth $238 million to Cuba. In September 2003 a delegation from the state of Montana, led by Democratic Senator Max Baucus and Republican Congressman Dennis Rehberg, went to Cuba with a group of businesspeople, including the president of the American Travel Agents Association, Robert Whitley. During this trip, agreements were signed to sell American foodstuffs to the amount of $10 million. Sales of US food and agricultural products to Cuba have continued throughout 2004 and 2005, despite the severe practical restrictions imposed on such transactions by US authorities.

17. [In the changes to the third Spanish-language edition, this statement, which is correct in the first edition, is 'amended' in such a way as to make it nonsensical in terms of US legislative proceedings. Thus, we have left it unchanged in the revisions to the English translation. – Trans.]

18. Despite the belligerence of the Bush administration, there are more and more people (in business, academia, tourism and Congress, both Democrats and Republicans) in favour of normalizing relations with Cuba. One example of this is the September 2003 visit to Cuba of Republican senator Norman Coleman, chair of the Senate Foreign Relations Western Hemisphere sub-committee, one of many Republican politicians in favour of making the economic embargo more flexible. Coleman met Castro on 21 September 2003.

19. Along those lines, in September 2003 the House of Representatives passed a bill (227 in favour, 188 opposed) to authorize American citizens to travel to Cuba. This law has been invalidated, however, by subsequent decisions of the Bush administration.

20. In May 2004 the Bush administration adopted a series of measures aimed at tightening the economic stranglehold on Cuba, among them extending the wait for Cubans to visit

the island to three years, restricting those trips as a general rule to immediate family members, and drastically limiting the amount of foreign currency a visitor to Cuba may take into the country.

17: The Collapse of the Soviet Union

1. On 25–26 April 1986, at the nuclear power plant in Chernobyl, in northern Ukraine, just twelve kilometres, or seven and a half miles, from the Belorussian border and some 125 kilometres, or eighty miles, north of Kiev, the greatest nuclear power accident in history took place. At first, local authorities concealed the true dimensions of the disaster from the public and the world, causing hundreds of deaths and leaving tens of thousands of people contaminated by radioactive materials.

2. [An inland sea, and the world's fourth largest lake, the Aral Sea is located east of the Caspian Sea in what was east-central Asian USSR. It spreads northwards up out of Uzbekistan across the border into Kazakhstan, and is 420 kilometres (260 miles) long and 280 kilometres (174 miles) wide, covering an area of 67,340 square kilometres (26,000 square miles). – Trans.]

3. André Voisin (1903–64), French agronomist and biochemist, author of *Soil, Grass and Cancer*, Austin, TX: Acres USA, 2000 (repr. of New York: Philosophical Library edition, 1959, trans. Catherine T. M. Herriot and Henry Kennedy). The edition that Castro knew was published by Tecnos, Madrid, in 1961.

4. [Used here in the general sense of 'organized crime or corruption', not to refer to the supposed Sicilian phenomenon. – Trans.]

5. Felipe González (b. 1942), leader of the Partido Socialista Obrero Español (PSOE; the Spanish Workers Socialist Party), was president of the Spanish government (in English generally referred to as 'prime minister') from 1982 to 1996. (See Chapter 23.)

6. [This is what is called the special period, when, indeed, calorie intake by Cuban citizens dropped precipitously, internal transport almost collapsed, and the basic commodities of life were lacking. Only the resourcefulness (and sense of humour) of the population prevented meltdown; conditions were truly deplorable. – Trans.]

7. The Torricelli Act, officially the Cuban Democracy Act of 1992, establishes two basic sanctions: (1) it prohibits US companies' subsidiaries based in third countries from selling to Cuba, and (2) it prohibits ships entering Cuban waters from entering the ports of the United States or its possessions for 180 days following their departure from the Cuban port.

8. Jesse Helms, Republican senator from North Carolina and then chairman of the Senate Foreign Relations Committee, and Dan Burton, Republican representative from Indiana, sponsored a bill, signed into law by President Bill Clinton on 12 March 1996, which gave American citizens the right to file in domestic courts for financial compensation for the property they lost to the Revolution and prohibited foreign companies from trading with Cuba by imposing sanctions on them and denying entrance to the US to their officers and major stockholders.

18: The Ochoa Case and the Death Penalty

1. In June 1989 Cuban authorities arrested three-star general Arnaldo Ochoa, forty-nine years of age, for drug trafficking and other offences. Ochoa was a 'Hero of the Revolution' who had fought with Castro and Camilo Cienfuegos in the Sierra Maestra; he had subsequently distinguished himself in the guerrilla forces in Venezuela and Nicaragua and in the wars fought by Cuban forces in Ethiopia and Angola. Along with Ochoa, high-ranking officials in the Ministry of the Interior were also arrested and charged with corruption and drug trafficking. These men were tried by a military tribunal in what became known as *Causa 1*, Trial Number 1, and found guilty; four of them were sentenced to execution by firing squad 'for high treason', and the others were sent to prison. On 9 July the Council

of State ratified the death sentences, and four days later, on 13 July, General Ochoa, Colonel Tony de la Guardia, Captain Jorge Martínez and Major Amado Padrón were executed. Under accusations of complicity in the drug trafficking, Minister of the Interior José Abrantes and several others were arrested, tried (Trial Number 2, 1989), and sentenced to prison. Abrantes, given a twenty-year sentence, died in prison on 21 January 1991.

2. Antonio Navarro Wolf, former leader of the M-19 guerrilla movement and currently independent senator in the Colombian Senate.

3. [The cult of personality as it relates to a *caudillo*, a Latin American political boss, or 'strongman'. – Trans.]

4. Norberto Fuentes (b. 1943), author of *Hemingway en Cuba* (with a foreword by Gabriel García Márquez; Havana: Editorial Letras Cubanas, 1985), now lives in Miami. Fuentes published his personal [3rd ed.: tendentious] version of the Ochoa case in *Dulces guerreros cubanos*, Madrid: Seix Barral, 1999, and in 2004, published [3rd ed.: the contemptible] *Autobiografía de Fidel Castro, 1: El paraíso de los otros*, Barcelona: Editorial Destino. [Bracketed notes added by Cuban editor.]

5. This part of the conversation took place in January 2003, before the hijacking of a boat on 1 April, the arrest of the hijackers, the trial and the sentencing of three of them to death on 11 April 2003. These executions put an end to the *de facto* suspension of the death penalty, a moratorium which had been in effect since April 2000. According to Amnesty International, in November 2003 some fifty-two people had been given the death sentence in Cuba and were awaiting execution; they have benefited from this moratorium.

6. See Seymour M. Hersh, *Chain of Command: From 9/11 to Abu Ghraib*, London: Allen Lane, 2004, especially Chapter VI, part 2, 'Manhunts', pp. 262–72.

7. The Red Brigades was an extreme left-wing Italian terrorist organization, supposedly Marxist, which was very active during the seventies and eighties. Its members carried out numerous firebombings and kidnappings, perhaps most notoriously that of former prime minister Aldo Moro, who was subsequently found murdered. Though the group began by fighting for labour unions against large capitalist enterprises, it later became more 'political', and its avowed purpose during this later time was to bring about a 'concentrated strike against the heart of the state, because the state is an imperialist collection of multinational corporations'.

8. GAL stands for Grupos Antiterroristas de Liberación (Antiterrorist Liberation Groups); these were illegal death squads (terrorism in the cause of anti-terrorism) set up by officials within the Spanish government to fight the ETA (Euskadi Ta Askatasuna; 'Basque Homeland and Freedom'), the Basque separatist [3rd ed.: pro-independence] group responsible for many bombings and other terrorist acts in Spain especially during the seventies and eighties, but dating from the late fifties into the new century. In pursuing their aims, from 1983 to 1987 the GALs committed kidnappings, torture and economic crimes; they had no clear ideology, but simply 'reacted' against the real or perceived members or supporters of the ETA. This period is called the 'dirty war' in Spain. At least twenty-six killings are attributed to these groups. The government of Felipe González was connected to the financing of the groups, and after an exposé by the newspaper *El Mundo*, lost the following elections to José María Aznar's People's Party.

19: Cuba and Neoliberal Globalization

1. Joseph E. Stiglitz (b. 1942), awarded the Nobel Prize in Economics in 2001, former vice president of the World Bank (1979–99), adviser to the Clinton administration, author of *Globalization and its Discontents* (London: Allen Lane, 2002) and *The Roaring Nineties: A New History of the World's Most Prosperous Decade* (London: Allen Lane, 2003).

2. George Soros (b. 1930), *The Crisis of Global Capitalism: Open Society Endangered* (NY: PublicAffairs [Perseus Group], 1998).

3. John Kenneth Galbraith (1908–2006), Harvard professor emeritus, generally regarded

as the United States' most distinguished economist and certainly the most read, author of, among over thirty works, *The Great Crash 1929* (NY: Mariner [Houghton Mifflin], 1997, repr. of 1954).

4. Ignacio Ramonet, *Un mundo sin rumbo*, Madrid: Debate, 1997.

5. Francis Fukuyama, *The End of History and the Last Man*, NY: Harper Perennial, 1993.

6. The 'Chicago Boys' were the free-market economists who worked in Chile during the regime of Augusto Pinochet, and they were given this somewhat sarcastic name because many of them had studied at the University of Chicago and were students or followers of Milton Friedman and the Chicago School of Economics. After the overthrow of Salvador Allende, they wrote a report calling for the immediate reprivatization of the industries and corporations nationalized by Allende. In the seventies and eighties their anti-Keynesian theories were applied not only by Pinochet's regime but also by Margaret Thatcher and Ronald Reagan.

7. Adam Smith (1723–90), Scottish economist, was the first great theorist of capitalism and the author of *The Wealth of Nations* (1776).

8. See Chapter 11, note 7, pp. 684–5.

9. Ernesto Che Guevara, 'Socialism and Man in Cuba', in *Global Justice: Liberation and Socialism*, Melbourne: Ocean Press, 2002.

10. Karl Marx, *Critique of the Gotha Programme*, with an introduction by Friedrich Engels, Moscow: Progress Publishers, 1971.

11. [The NEP, or New Economic Policy (*Novaya Ekonomicheskaya Politika*), was decreed in March 1921 and required farmers to send a certain quantity of agricultural goods (mainly foodstuffs) to central storehouses, as a sort of tax in kind. Basically, farmers were allowed some private ownership; crop yields increased because after remitting the required products, farmers were allowed to sell the remainder of their produce; thus, there were material incentives for agricultural work. When Stalin abandoned the plan in 1928 and instituted forced collectivization, Soviet agriculture virtually collapsed (in 1st ed.).]

12. *Le Monde Diplomatique*, an influential monthly published in Paris by Ignacio Ramonet; over ten editions are published around the world in other languages and in other countries. [Note by Cuban editor.]

13. The Club of Rome is a group of scientists and concerned laymen organized in 1968 by Italian industrialist/scholar Aurelio Peccei and Scottish scientist Alexander King; according to its website, it is composed of 'scientists, economists, businessmen, international high civil servants, heads of state and former heads of state from all five continents who are convinced that the future of humankind is not determined once and for all and that each human being can contribute to the improvement of our societies'. One of the Club of Rome's most important achievements has been to alert world societies to the dangers of overexploitation of the planet's natural resources, global warming and other effects of climate change, as set forth in several studies, but especially in the prescient book *Limits to Growth* (1972). [Note expanded by Trans.]

14. Ignacio Ramonet, *La tiranía de la comunicación*, Madrid: Debate, 2000.

15. Ibid., *Propagandas silenciosas*, Havana: Arte y Literatura, 2002.

20: President Jimmy Carter's Visit

1. Robert Scheer, *Playboy* interview with Jimmy Carter, *Playboy* magazine, November 1976.

2. [Carter's words were these: 'The Bible says, "Thou shalt not commit adultery." Christ said, I tell you that anyone who looks on a woman with lust has in his heart already committed adultery. I've looked on a lot of women with lust. *I've committed adultery in my heart many times* . . . This is something that God recognizes, that I will do and have done, and God forgives me for it. But that doesn't mean that I condemn someone who not only looks on a woman with lust but who leaves his wife and shacks up with somebody out of wedlock. Christ says, don't consider yourself better than someone else because one

guy screws a whole bunch of women while the other guy is loyal to his wife. The guy who's loyal to his wife ought not to be condescending or proud because of the relative degree of sinfulness.' (emphasis added) – Trans.]

3. Omar Torrijos (1929–81), Panamanian general, president of Panama from 1968 to 1978, brought important social and economic reforms to the country. In 1977 he negotiated an agreement with Carter to return the Canal to Panama; it had been under US jurisdiction since its completion in 1914. He died in a mysterious plane accident; his son Martín was elected president of Panama in 2005.

4. Gerald Ford (1913–2006), thirty-eighth president of the United States, served from August 1974, when Richard Nixon resigned due to the Watergate scandal, to January 1977. Ford is the only president never to have been elected either vice president or president, as he was called to fill the vice presidency after Nixon's vice president, Spiro Agnew, resigned in a tax scandal.

5. The true name of this diplomatic office is the American Interests Section in Havana; its counterpart is the Cuban Interests Section in Washington, DC. These names are diplomat-speak for 'embassies', in the absence of formal relations between the two countries, which were broken off by the US in January 1961, three months before the Playa Girón invasion. [Castro always refers to them as 'Interest Offices', and this text will reflect that usage. – Trans.]

6. In November 1979, during the height of the Islamic revolution in Iran, a group of followers of the Ayatollah Khomeini stormed the US embassy in Tehran and took fifty-two Americans hostage. All attempts to free the hostages failed. Carter authorized an attempt by Special Operations commandos to go in to rescue the people being held, but the expedition failed during execution due to technical problems and a series of accidents. It was not until 20 January 1981, the day Carter's successor Ronald Reagan was sworn in as president, that the hostages were finally freed.

7. At around midnight on 18–19 July 1969 Edward 'Ted' Kennedy had a strange car accident in Chappaquiddick (on Martha's Vineyard in Massachusetts) which cost the life of his secretary Mary Jo Kopechne and resulted in a huge scandal.

8. The Roman historian Gaius Suetonius (AD ?69–?140) lived during the reigns of emperors Trajan and Hadrian and is the author of *Lives of the Caesars*.

9. Winner of the Pulitzer Prize for history in 1957, the book details the moments of courage lived by important figures in US history as a way of describing the values and traits that in Kennedy's view allowed them to lead the nation: personal sacrifice, dedication, strength of character.

10. The Bretton Woods accords, signed by the great capitalist powers at the end of the Second World War, pegged currency parities against gold (at $35 an ounce) and created the new international economic system and its specialized institutions: the International Monetary Fund (IMF) and the World Bank.

11. Pierre Elliott Trudeau (1919–2000) was prime minister of Canada from 1968 to 1979 and then again from 1980 to 1984.

12. Michel Trudeau (1975–98) died in British Columbia on 15 November 1998. An avalanche in Kokanee Glacier Park swept him into Kokanee Lake, where he is presumed to have drowned; his body was never recovered.

13. The British ocean liner sunk by a German submarine on 7 May 1915, during the First World War; the [Cunard Line] ship was on its way from New York to Liverpool [Fastnet Rock, Ireland, was to be its berthing location], with over 1,200 passengers aboard and some 800 crew and service personnel.

14. [Carter is a devout Christian and has taught Sunday school throughout his life, but he is not ordained in the ministry. Carter's sister Ruth Carter Stapleton (1929–83) was, however, an evangelical minister. – Trans.]

15. Eunice Kennedy Shriver, sister of John, Robert and Edward Kennedy and mother of Maria Shriver, television personality and wife of actor-turned-California governor Arnold Schwarzenegger (elected in 2003 and re-elected in 2006).

16. [Here and in many other places in these interviews, Castro uses the first-person plural (*nosotros*: we) when talking about himself. This is not pompous, but actually somewhat self-effacing, in the Spanish-speaking cultures of the Caribbean. At any rate, what follows is slightly confusing, because after saying 'we're going out on the field', Castro invites Carter to go with him. Thus, in the first statement Castro is talking about himself as head of state. – Trans.]

17. [Named after Félix Varela, a nineteenth-century Cuban priest who called for Cuba's independence from Spain, the Varela Project began in March 2001. Based on a previously little-known provision in the Cuban Constitution, Article 88, which allows for citizens to introduce legislative initiatives to be decided by national referendum when accompanied by the signatures of at least 10,000 registered voters, the project sought to accumulate enough signatures to present the Cuban National Assembly with a list of reforms. The project was spearheaded by Osvaldo Payá (see note 20 below) of the Christian Liberation Movement. The Varela Project was supported by the US/Miami Cuban exile community and by the United States government, and the Cuban government has accused some of the dissidents within Cuba of receiving aid from James Cason, head of the American Interests Office in Havana. – Trans.]

18. [That is, while still linked to Spain commercially, financially and, to an extent, politically, Cuba would have a high degree of autonomy in matters of self-rule, much as the former members of the British Empire did, and the colonial aspects of life in Cuba would therefore not be so oppressive. These concessions were hard-won, but in the run-up to what would become the Spanish-American War, Spain allowed a certain amount of autonomy as a way of ensuring at least a degree of pro-Spanish sentiment to counter the growing consensus that Cuba might be better off either independent or under US rule, or tutelage. Obviously, there were also pressures from the second War of Independence, which began in 1895. – Trans.]

19. [Here, there is a bit of confusion: the petition associated with the Varela Project did not call for a constitutional amendment, but rather a change in law, or repeal of laws, whose effect would have been an expansion of certain freedoms, a reform of the electoral law, a general election, support for private business and an amnesty for political prisoners, while the 8-million-signature petition following George W. Bush's speech in Miami did call for a constitutional amendment limiting the right of the National Assembly to change the Socialist orientation of the Revolution. – Trans.]

20. Osvaldo Payá Sardiñas (b.1952) is the man behind the Varela Project and the coordinator of the Christian Liberation Movement (CLM), a counter-revolutionary political organization not recognized by the Cuban authorities but tolerated, which states that it 'fights for the freedom and human rights of all'. In April 2002 it supported the coup against Hugo Chávez, the constitutionally elected president of Venezuela. In 2002 Payá received the Sakharov Prize for 'his defence of human rights'.

21. Luis Jiménez de Asúa (1899–1970), Spanish jurist, chaired the parliamentary commission that drafted the Spanish Republican constitution in 1931. After the Spanish Civil War, he went into exile in Argentina, where he taught criminal law in Córdoba and Buenos Aires; he was the author of numerous books, most famously perhaps a treatise on criminal law.

22. In March 1999 four leaders of the Grupo de Trabajo de la Disidencia Interna (GTDI: the Taskforce on Internal Dissidence) [Martha Beatriz Roque, René Gómez Manzano, Félix Bonne Carcassés, Vladimiro Roca] were tried for 'acts against the security of the state' and sentenced to three to five years in prison.

21: The Arrests of Dissidents in March 2003

1. The foreign minister's press conference occurred on 9 April 2003.
2. John Bolton (b. 1948), the Bush administration's ambassador to the United Nations from August 2005 to December 2006 (he served in an interim capacity, his appointment never having been ratified by Congress), was at the time under secretary of state for arms control and international security. [In point of fact, Bolton went so far as to accuse Cuba not only of carrying out research, but of actually producing biological weapons and exporting them to other countries. The US intelligence community refused to support Bolton's claims. –Trans.]
3. Between 1985 and 1987, under President Ronald Reagan, the National Security Council (NSC) secretly sold arms to Iran (which was at war with Iraq, a country that at the time was a US ally) and with the profits from those arms sales aided the 'Contra' forces in Nicaragua. The revelation of this affair created a tremendous scandal, which the international news media dubbed 'Irangate' in allusion to that other earth-shaking scandal, under the Nixon administration, called 'Watergate'.
4. In July 2003 Reich was replaced as under secretary by Roger Noriega.
5. Oswaldo Guayasamín (1919–99) was an Ecuadorian painter and one of the most important figures in Latin American art in the twentieth century; he was also a defender of causes associated with the indigenous peoples of Latin America, an unconditional friend of the Cuban Revolution and a personal friend of Fidel Castro. The Chapel of Man, a monumental building inaugurated in Quito on 29 November 2002, is his crowning achievement.
6. The National Assembly of Popular Power is the supreme legislative body of the Cuban state. It is made up of over 600 deputies, or representatives, who are elected to five-year terms by a direct vote within their respective constituencies or precincts throughout the country. The legislature meets for two ordinary sessions each year, in addition to whatever extraordinary sessions may be necessary. At the beginning of each term, the National Assembly elects the Council of State and its president.
7. [See http://www.ruleoflawandcuba.fsu.edu/regime-21.cfm, where Cuban Foreign Minister Felipe Pérez Roque is interviewed about the dissident issue and shows a video of Cason. –Trans.]
8. In June 2003 the EU decided to impose a series of diplomatic sanctions on Cuba after the arrest and trial of some seventy-five dissidents and the execution of three hijackers of a boat.
9. During the nineties, Gerardo Hernández, René González, Fernando González, Antonio Guerrero and Ramón Labañino, agents of the Cuban intelligence services, infiltrated anti-Castro terrorist paramilitary groups in Miami that were organizing actions against economic objectives in Cuba in order to scare off tourism. One of the groups' actions took place on 4 September 1997, when a bomb went off in the Hotel Copacabana in Havana, causing the death of a young Italian tourist, Fabio DiCelmo. In June 1998 Havana sent the FBI the reports by its five agents, presuming that there was a shared interest in fighting terrorism. In September of that year, those same documents were used by US authorities to detain the five agents. Subjected to a murky trial in Miami, the agents were sentenced to long prison terms, which they began to serve under particularly harsh conditions. In August 2005, a panel of judges of the Atlanta Court of Appeals revoked the agents' sentences. One year later, in August 2006, the full Appeals Court overturned that decision, and all five Cubans are still, as of December 2006, in prison. (See Chapter 12, note 2.)
10. The 'hole' is an isolation cell measuring about six feet by six feet in which the prisoner is kept, clothed in only his underwear. The cell's light remains on twenty-four hours a day; all contact with other people, even the prison guards, is prohibited.
11. Rosa Miriam Elizalde and Luis Báez, 'Los disidentes': Agentes de la seguridad cubana revelan la historia real, Havana: Editora Política, 2003.
12. Raúl Rivero (b. 1945), Cuban journalist and poet, was a correspondent for Prensa

Latina in the Soviet Union. He has won the David Prize for Poetry (UNEAC, Havana, 1967) and the Julián del Casal National Poetry Prize (UNEAC, Havana, 1969). He was personal secretary to famed Cuban poet Nicolás Guillén. In 1991 he signed the 'Letter of Ten', which asked for political and economic openness. He founded the independent news agency CubaPress. He was arrested on 20 March and sentenced on 4 April 2003 to twenty years in prison for 'acts against the territorial integrity of the state'. He was released from prison on 30 November 2004, and went into exile in Spain.

13. Federico García Lorca (1899–1936), famed Spanish playwright and poet, was the author of *Romancero gitano* ('Gypsy Ballads', 1928) and *Bodas de Sangre* ('Blood Wedding', 1933), among other works, and was murdered by the Franco military authorities at the beginning of the Spanish Civil War. Lorca is universally recognized as one of Spain's greatest twentieth-century poets.

14. Antonio Machado (1875–1939), Spanish poet, was the author of *Soledades* ('Solitudes', 1902) and *Campos de Castilla* ('Fields of Castile', 1912); he died in exile in Collioure, France, at the end of the Spanish Civil War.

15. Miguel Hernández (1910–42), Spanish poet and playwright, was the author of *El rayo que no cesa* ('Unceasing Lightning', 1936) and *Vientos del pueblo* ('Winds of the People', 1937). He fought against Franco, and was captured as he tried to flee to Portugal. He died in prison of tuberculosis.

16. Armando Valladares (b. 1937) had been a police officer during the Batista dictatorship. He was arrested in 1960, condemned to thirty years in prison for 'acts of terrorism', and eventually served twenty-two years. An international campaign presented him as a poet who was the 'victim of the Cuban prison system', whose 'inhuman' rigours had produced neuropathological paralysis in his lower body. Freed in 1982, he was appointed by Ronald Reagan to be the US ambassador to the UN Human Rights Commission. [His memoirs, *Against All Hope* (trans. Andrew Hurley, orig. publ. NY: Knopf, 1986, repr. San Francisco: Encounter Books, 2001), came out in Spanish in 1985. – Trans.]

17. [On 26 June 2007 the CIA released some 700 pages of documents, dubbed the 'Family Jewels', detailing semi-legal and illegal CIA operations throughout the 1970s and 1980s. Pages 12 to 19 of this document discuss a government–Mafia plan to assassinate Fidel Castro. – Trans.]

18. There are, however, many exceptions. In France, for example, Lucien Léger, sentenced to life in prison in 1966, was freed on 3 October 2005, after forty-one years. On that date there were two other prisoners in France who had been in jail for more than forty years.

19. The Constitution of the Republic of Cuba, the draft of which was formulated by a commission of eminent jurists chaired by Blas Roca, was submitted to an open consultation [or referendum] with almost the entire population of Cuba, and whose text was approved in a national plebiscite by 97.7 per cent of the vote, was proclaimed on 24 February 1976. Since that time, amendments have been made to it, as approved by the National Assembly of People's Power in an amendment procedure set forth in the constitution itself.

20. ['Death . . . is not foretold' is an allusion to the title of a famous novel, *Chronicle of a Death Foretold* (*Crónica de una Muerte Anunciada*), by Gabriel García Márquez (trans. Gregory Rabassa, NY: Knopf, 1983). – Trans.]

21. Before France, other European countries that had abolished capital punishment were: Iceland in 1928, Austria in 1968, Finland and Sweden in 1972, Portugal in 1976, Luxembourg and Denmark in 1978 and Norway in 1979. The first countries to abolish the death penalty, however, were Latin American: Venezuela in 1863, Costa Rica in 1877, Ecuador in 1906, Uruguay in 1907 and Colombia in 1910.

22. The Czech Republic abolished the death penalty in 1990, Hungary in 1990 and Poland in 1997.

23. [The statement of the Council of Europe's origins and purpose can be found on its website (http://www. coe.int/T/e/Com/about_coe/) – Trans.]

24. [Abdullah Öcalan (Turkey, b. 1948) early on identified with the rights problems of the Kurdish people and in 1978 formed the Kurdistan Workers Party (PKK), of which he is

still the leader. In 1984 the PKK began a campaign of armed attacks against the government and civilians in Iraq, Iran and Turkey, seeking to create an independent Kurdish state. It is estimated that between 1984 and 2003 over 30,000 people were killed by the PKK, which has been labelled a terrorist organization by several states and international organizations (Turkey, the US, the EU, Syria, Canada, Iran). – Trans.]

25. [Turkey abolished the death penalty in 2002. – Trans.]

22: The Hijackings in April 2003

1. On 1 April 2003, in Havana harbour, a group of people hijacked a ferry with several dozen people aboard. The hijacking failed. The hijackers were arrested and tried, and three of them [Lorenzo Copello, Bárbaro Sevilla and Jorge Luis Martínez] were sentenced to death and executed by firing squad on 11 April 2003.

2. Several months later, on 19 September 2003, for the first time in forty years, a court in Florida sentenced the perpetrator of this hijacking to twenty years in prison. In addition, in July 2003, again for the first time, the US authorities deported a group of twelve Cubans who had hijacked a boat in Camagüey. For decades Cuba had been calling for this type of measure to combat piracy.

3. [The text in this section appears to be somewhat garbled; the translated text attempts to untangle the confusion, and it does reflect the facts of the case. – Trans.]

4. [Level 3 on the Beaufort scale indicates wind at seven to ten knots, with small waves and scattered whitecaps; the sea under those conditions is heavy enough to be a danger to a ferry-type vessel. – Trans.]

5. Oliver Stone (b. 1946), US film-maker and the director of some twenty-two films, among them *Platoon* (1986), *Born on the Fourth of July* (1989), *JFK* (1991), *Natural Born Killers* (1994), *Nixon* (1995), *Any Given Sunday* (1999) and *Alexander* (2004). In 2002 Stone had made a documentary in Cuba on Fidel Castro titled *Comandante* (released 2003). Although HBO had backed the film, the network later refused to broadcast it, alleging that it was not sufficiently critical of Castro and revolutionary Cuba. After the arrests of the dissidents in March 2003 and the execution of the three hijackers in April that year, Stone returned to Havana to film a second interview with Castro; it was to be a kind of extension of *Comandante*. It was released, under the title *Looking for Fidel*, in 2004.

6. José Saramago (b. 1922), Portuguese novelist, won the Nobel Prize for Fiction in 1998. On 14 April 2003, a few days after the execution of the three hijackers, Saramago published a brief text titled 'This is as far as I go' in the Spanish newspaper *El País*; in it, he announced that he was distancing himself from Cuba. On 12 October 2003, however, in an interview by Rosa Miriam Elizalde published in *La Jornada* in Mexico City and *Juventud Rebelde* in Havana, Saramago said, 'I have not broken with Cuba. I continue to be a friend of Cuba.'

23: Cuba and Spain

1. [The true title of the position held by González is 'president of the government', but in English the person holding this post is almost always referred to as the 'prime minister'. That usage will be followed here throughout. – Trans.]

2. Statements to Andrés Oppenheimer, *El Nuevo Herald*, Miami, 13 June 2003.

3. In a special programme on Cuban television on 25 April 2003 Castro made these statements. See Fidel Castro, *Jamás un pueblo tuvo cosas más sagradas que defender*, Havana: Oficina de Publicaciones del Consejo de Estado, 2003.

4. José Barrionuevo, minister of the interior in the González government, and Rafael Vera, secretary of state for security, were sentenced to eleven and seven years in prison, respectively.

5. Eloy Gutiérrez Menoyo was born in Madrid in 1935 to Republican parents who emigrated to Cuba when Gutiérrez was a child. Later, he took up arms against the Batista dictatorship

as a member of the Second National Escambray Front (SFNE), a group that was not associated with Fidel Castro's 26th of July Movement. In the SFNE, Gutiérrez attained the rank of *comandante*, but after the triumph of the Revolution he refused to accept the Revolution's precepts and in 1961 went to the United States. He returned secretly in 1965 and joined the dirty war against the Revolution. He was captured and spent twenty-two years in prison. When he was freed, he took up residence in Miami, where he founded an organization, Cambio Cubano (Cuban Change), which lobbies for dialogue between the Castro regime and its adversaries. In 1995 he returned to the island and met Castro. In the summer of 2003, now almost blind, Gutiérrez went to Cuba on holiday and announced that he was staying in Cuba in order to 'fight for a political space', a voice in Cuban politics.

6. The PSOE, under the leadership of Felipe González, held power in Spain for fourteen years, from 1982 to 1996. During this period there occurred a series of scandals involving corruption and abuse of power, and this caused a great deal of public alarm: the Filesa case, the Ibercorp case, the CESID wiretaps, the assassination of the GAL members, the diversion of assigned funds, the corruption of Luis Roldán and Juan Guerra . . . In those years Spain experienced what journalists began to call a *'cultura del pelotazo'* [that is, a sudden acquisition of great wealth, equivalent to 'hitting a homerun', scoring a perfect goal, etc.: making a killing in a very short time but, unlike the sports metaphor, by questionable methods] and what Carlos Solchaga, Socialist Party minister of economy, defined in this way: 'Spain is where a person can earn the most money in the least time.' See Mariano Sánchez Soler, *Negocios privados con dinero público: El vademecum de la corrupción de los políticos españoles*, Madrid: Foca, 2003.

7. Carlos Andrés Pérez (b. 1922), Social-Democratic president of Venezuela at two different times: from 1974 to 1979 and from 1989 to 1994. Pérez violently repressed several popular insurrections in February 1989 and the military insurrections in February and November 1992. On 30 May 1996 Pérez went down in history as the first Venezuelan president to be found guilty of misappropriation of public funds.

8. Numantia was a city in Hispania, bordering the Roman Empire, located about six kilometres, or four miles, from the current city of Soria, on the Duero River in north-central Spain about 230 kilometres, or 140 miles, north-east of modern-day Madrid. From its place on an isolated plateau above the Duero plain, Numantia played an important role in the Celtic-Iberian resistance to Rome, and for many years, from the time of Cato the Elder's campaign (195 BC) until Scipio Aemilianus finally took the city in 133 BC, after a brutal two-year siege, it held off the Roman forces. When Felipe González refers to Castro's 'Numantic attitude', he is saying Castro is stubbornly holding out against inexorable forces, and will eventually have to either surrender or die. Cervantes wrote about the Numantians' heroic but doomed defence of their city in a play, *La Numancia*.

9. [*Timbiriches* is a Cubanism; Ramonet seems not to have heard the word before and therefore to be puzzled by what Castro means. – Trans.]

10. On the programme *Mesa Redonda* (Round Table), 11 June 2003.

11. On 5 June 2003 the European Union imposed diplomatic sanctions on Cuba, including limits on official relations with the Cuban government and closer ties to internal opponents. On 30 April preceding that date, the European Commission, the Union's executive agency, had decided to table Cuba's demand to enter the Cotonou accords, which favour trade relations between the European Union and a number of developing countries. Cuba subsequently withdrew its request. On 3 January 2005 Havana normalized its contacts with the European Union nations, after the EU modified its stance.

12. On 12 June 2003, in protests against the EU's sanctions, approximately a million people marched in front of the Spanish and Italian embassies in Havana. Castro himself led the march in front of the Spanish embassy.

13. Jorge Mas Canosa was a millionaire Cuban exile who founded the Cuban-American National Foundation in Miami; he was considered the most extreme right-wing hawk opposed to the Castro government, and was linked by some with terrorist actions and attempts on Castro's life. He died in November, 1997.

14. [Aznar was the target of a car-bomb set by the Basque separatist group ETA; the attack occurred on 19 April 1995, before the general elections to be held in March of 1996. Aznar's popularity increased as a result of the bombing, and his conservative Popular Party won a victory over Felipe González' Socialist Workers Party. – Trans.]

15. [Santiago Carrillo (b. 1915) joined the Socialist Party (PSOE) as a teenager and by the age of nineteen was promoting the union of young Socialists and Communists in the Young Socialists Alliance. He joined the Spanish Communist Party in 1936 and has held many positions in that party. During the Spanish Civil War he was accused of ordering or countenancing mass executions, but was never tried; instead, he went into exile. When the Communist Party was recognized by the Spanish government in 1977, Carrillo was elected to the lower house of the Spanish parliament. Recently, he has moved to the right, towards Social-Democracy, and has said that Communism has lived out its life-cycle in Spain. – Trans.]

16. [Dolores Ibárruri Gómez, known as La Pasionaria (9 December 1895–12 November 1989), was a noted Spanish Communist and political figure. She was secretary-general of the Spanish Communist Party (the PCE) from 1944 to 1960, president of the Communist Party of Spain from 1960 to 1989, and a member of the Cortes, the Spanish parliament, twice: in 1936 and again from 1977 to 1979. She died of pneumonia in Madrid at the age of ninety-three. – Trans.]

17. [On 21 July 1921, against the Berbers under Abd el-Krim (1881–1963), the leader of the Rif Berber resistance against colonial Spain and France. – Trans.]

18. [Guernica, a city north-east of Bilbao in the Basque country, had long been a centre of Basque independence sentiment, and it was important that Franco and the Nationalists take it. Hitler, wishing to test some new methods of warfare, bombed it heavily in April 1937. Picasso's famous painting *Guernica* commemorates the devastation to the city and stands as an icon of anti-Fascism. – Trans.]

19. [In March 1937; Guadalajara is east of Madrid, and this battle was part of the 'battle for Madrid'. – Trans.]

20. ['Cortes' is the official name of the bicameral Spanish parliament. – Trans.]

21. See 'Eduardo Junco Bonet, el embajador de España en Cuba estuvo en la universidad cerca de la extrema derecha', *El País* (Madrid), 11 May 1998.

22. According to UNICEF and the Low Pay Unit association, in the United Kingdom there are approximately 2 million children working, mostly the children of immigrants, and almost always illegally.

23. Anthony Giddens, *The Third Way: The Renewal of Social Democracy*, Cambridge, England: Polity Press, 1998.

24. [On 23 February 1981 Lieutenant Colonel Antonio Tejero (b. 1932) led a group of about 200 Civil Guard troops into the Spanish parliament building during the voting for a new prime minister and held the congress at gunpoint while army tanks occupied streets around the Cortes building. Though the background to the coup is, predictably, complex, it can be said definitively and briefly that the coup took place in response to the fledgling republic's transition to democracy. King Juan Carlos went on television and called for calm and a respect for the democratic process, and within about eighteen hours the coup collapsed. – Trans.]

25. On 26 May 2003 a Yakovlev-42 aircraft belonging to the Ukrainian company Mediterranean Airlines and leased by the Spanish Ministry of Defence crashed near Trabzon, in Turkey, with sixty-two Spanish troops aboard; they were returning from a mission in Kabul, Afghanistan.

26. In a telephone conversation with [Ramonet] on 12 June 2006, Manuel Fraga denied having defended that thesis. According to Fraga, he had suggested to Castro the only way he knew of: the way the Spanish transition of 1975–8 had been accomplished. Fraga added: 'This conversation, which lasted several hours, took place during a meal in the private dining room of a restaurant in Santiago de Compostela. There were three of us at the table: Fidel Castro, Mario Vázquez Raña, a Mexican millionaire of Galician heritage

who is a media magnate in Mexico, and I. Vázquez Raña recorded the conversation on a miniature device hidden in his wristwatch. I made him promise that he would not make this conversation public until after my death, but given that Castro quotes it, although erroneously, I can free him [Vázquez Raña] from his promise. Therefore, I can bear witness to it.'

Informed of this clarification by Manuel Fraga, Fidel Castro maintains his version and reaffirms that the former president of the Galician Xunta proposed that he, Castro, do the same thing that had been done in Nicaragua after the electoral defeat of the Sandinistas in 1989.

27. Yuri Andropov (1914–84), Soviet leader who headed the powerful state security agency KGB and was a member of the Soviet Communist Party's Politburo. In November 1982, after the death of Leonid Brezhnev, Andropov was named secretary-general of the Communist Party and president of the Soviet Union, a position he held until his death less than two years later.

28. [The residence of the prime minister; like 'White House', this term refers to the seat of government. – Trans.]

29. [Sherry in Spanish is *jerez*, and is named after the city, Jerez de la Frontera, which makes the finest Spanish sherry; the fine cured ham known as *jabugo* is also named for the city where it is made, Jabugo; and manchego cheese is from the region of La Mancha. Except for La Mancha, which is part of the autonomous region known as Castilla-La Mancha (central Spain), these foods are Andalusian (southern Spain). Seville is the capital of the province of Andalusia. – Trans.]

24: Fidel and France

1. See Chapter 2, 'The Forging of a Rebel'.
2. Mario Mencía, *La prisión fecunda*, Havana: Editora Política, 1980.
3. [This description is not quite correct. The owner of the wild-ass skin is granted any wish, but with each wish the skin becomes smaller, and if it finally shrinks to nothing, the owner dies. Early on, the man makes wish after wish, paying no mind to the shrinkage of the skin, but as the skin dwindles, he becomes almost ascetic, trying not to wish for anything lest the skin disappear and he die. – Trans.]
4. Benito Pérez Galdós (1843–1920), Spanish novelist, author of *Fortunata and Jacinta* and others; in Spain, his best-known work is the historical saga *Episodios Nacionales* ('National Episodes'), in forty-six volumes. [Few of his works have been translated into English, although he is considered one of Spain's greatest novelists. – Trans.]
5. Romain Rolland (1866–1944), winner of the Nobel Prize for Literature in 1915.
6. [Jean Jaurès (1859–1914) was elected to the Chamber of Deputies in 1885 but lost the next election. After his defeat he returned to his teaching duties at the University of Toulouse, where he began reading Marx and becoming more and more radicalized. In 1893 he was re-elected to the Chamber of Deputies, but was again defeated in the following election, probably as a result of his support for Dreyfus. By 1900 he was the leader of the French Socialist Party, which began to make inroads in French politics. While he was out of power, Jaurès wrote his mammoth *Socialist History of the French Revolution*. In the run-up to the First World War, Jaurès was an outspoken advocate for a diplomatic solution to the growing German menace. He was assassinated on 31 July 1914 by a young pro-war nationalist. – Trans.]
7. [Adolphe Thiers (1797–1877) was a French statesman, journalist and politician; he was a founder and the first president (1871–3) of the Third Republic. The ten-volume work to which Castro refers is the *Histoire de la Révolution Française*. – Trans.]
8. [Alphonse de Lamartine (1790–1869), French writer, poet and politician, considered to be the first French Romantic poet; he influenced Verlaine and the Symbolistes. – Trans.]
9. [Claude-Joseph Rouget de Lisle (or l'Isle; 1760–1836) was an officer in the French Corps of Engineers. While on duty in Strasbourg in 1792, he composed 'Le Chant de guerre pour

l'armée du Rhin' (Battle Hymn for the Army of the Rhine), which was sung by the Marseilles troops on their march to Paris in that same year. Thus, the anthem soon became known as the 'Marseillaise', and in 1879 became France's official national anthem. – Trans.]

10. The lyrics are by French poet Eugène Pottier (a poem written in 1871 after the repression of the Paris Commune) and the music was composed by Pierre Degeyter, a Belgian musician, in 1888.

11. [*Histoire de la vie privée* (Paris: Seuil), series editors Philippe Ariès and Georges Duby, translated into English by Arthur Goldhammer as *A History of Private Life*, Cambridge, Mass: Belknap Press of Harvard University Press, 1987–91. The five volumes are as follows: Vol. 1. From Pagan Rome to Byzantium, Paul Veyne, editor; Vol. 2. Revelations of the Medieval World, Georges Duby, editor; Vol. 3. Passions of the Renaissance, Roger Chartier, editor; Vol. 4. From the Fires of Revolution to the Great War, Michelle Perrot, editor; Vol. 5. Riddles of Identity in Modern Times, Antoine Prost and Gérard Vincent, editors. – Trans.]

12. [?Lima: Editorial Prometeo, ?1962; in French, *Ouragan sur le sûcre*, 1961; in English, *Sartre on Cuba*, Westport, Conn: Greenwood Press, 1974, reprint of NY: Ballantine, 1961 original English translation (no translator given). According to Sartre biographer-critic Andrew Leak (London: Reaktion Books, 2006, pp. 113–14), a series of sixteen articles was produced by Sartre while he and de Beauvoir were in Cuba in February–March 1960; these articles were 'cleaned up' and to an extent extracted from the original 1,100 pages by *France-Dimanche* journalist Claude Lanzmann and they appeared in *France-Soir* in June and July 1960; they were then published in book form in 1961. – Trans.]

13. On 8 January 1959, the same day Fidel Castro entered Havana upon the triumph of the Revolution, de Gaulle was inaugurated as the first president of the Fifth Republic.

14. [In the original edition of this book in Spanish, the author cited Charles de Gaulle, *Vers l'armée de métier*, Paris: Berger-Levrault, 1934; English edition *The Army of the Future*, London/Melbourne: Hutchison, 1940/ New York: Lippincott, 1940. In the third edition, Ramonet or Castro cites, instead, *Le Fil de l'épée* (Paris, Berger-Levrault, 1932), translated as *The Edge of the Sword* by Frank L. Dash (London, New York: Hutchinson & Co., 1945). The translator believes that this second citation is erroneous, as the first book footnoted is, indeed, a study in the 'modern army' and its armoured divisions, its new technologies and strategies, etc., while the second does not fit the description in the text itself. – Trans.]

15. Régis Debray, *Révolution dans la révolution? Et autres essais*, Paris: François Maspéro, 1969, translated from the author's French and Spanish by Bobbye Ortiz as *Revolution in the Revolution? Armed Struggle and Political Struggle in Latin America*, New York: MR Press, 1967, repr. Westport, Conn: Greenwood Press, 1980.

16. [In 1986, Danielle Mitterrand (b. 1924) formed France-Libertés, a foundation dedicated to support of human rights. It backs initiatives promoting the right to justice, education and health care, assists in humanitarian aid campaigns, acts to eliminate all forms of torture, and fights poverty and social exclusion. It was formed by the merger of three earlier human-rights foundations. Its headquarters are located at 22 rue de Milan, Paris. – Trans.]

17. Jean-Edern Hallier (1936–97), *Fidel Castro: Conversation au clair de lune*, Paris: Messidor, 1990.

18. Jean-Edern Hallier, *L'Evangile du fou: Charles de Foucauld, le manuscrit de ma mère morte*, Paris: Albin Michel, 1986.

25: Latin America

1. [The alter-global movement arose after the fall of Socialism as an alternative anti-capitalist movement: '[There is] anti-globalism and alter- (or alternative) globalism ... For anti-globalism we either still live in the world structured according to the particularistic and pluralistic principles of sovereign statehood, or in the world where these principles are presently under attack from a "false universalism" of the discourse of globalisation, which can only result in the hegemony of particular states to the detriment of international pluralism. In contrast, alter-globalism may be said to accept the fundamental principles of globalisation and the overriding objective of "ever-greater" and "ever-deeper" international integration, but questions the specific modality of the contemporary processes of globalisation. In particular, alter-globalism opposes the equation of globalisation with the universalisation of neoliberal economic doctrines and the further unobstructed development of global capitalism. Thus, anti-globalism opposes globalisation as such, while alter-globalism accepts and welcomes the possibility of the establishment of a global order, but is critical of the present form of such an order.' (S. Prozorov, Petrozavodsk State University, Petrozavodsk, Russia, 'Critical Approaches to the Study of Globalisation and International Integration', at http://cua.karelia.ru/report11.doc, as of January 2007.) While this movement, or the theoretical aspects of it, seems to have begun in Russia, the spirit of the movement has now become 'global', and one of its avatars may be seen, for example, in the very widely read critique of worldwide capitalism represented by Naomi Klein's books, especially *No Logo: No Space, No Choice, No Jobs* (NY: Picador, 2002, first published UK: Flamingo, 2000). – Trans.]

2. Ignacio Ramonet, *Marcos, la dignidad rebelde. Conversaciones con el subcomandante Marcos*, Valencia, Spain: Cibermonde, 2001.

3. On 1 January 2006 Subcomandante Marcos began a new journey through Mexico lasting six months, this time by motorcycle (echoing the famous journey through South America made by Che Guevara and his friend Alberto Granado in 1951); its purpose was to visit the country's thirty-two states before the presidential election on 2 July 2006, and create an 'alternative national political front' opposed to the traditional parties. In June 2006 the Zapatista National Liberation Army (EZLN) renounced all 'military offensive operations'.

   During this journey, Marcos presented himself as 'Delegate [Congressman] Zero', and he said he rejected all Mexican parties, including the Party of Democratic Revolution (PRD), whose candidate, Andrés Manuel López Obrador, was considered by surveys at the time to be the favourite.

4. On 31 December 2005 Fidel Castro and Evo Morales (then president-elect of Bolivia) signed an agreement that promises strong medical and educational support to Bolivia. The document, which has eleven points, went into effect after Morales' inauguration on 22 January 2006. The two countries agreed to create a non-profit bi-national agency which guarantees eye operations for Bolivians of limited financial resources; for these operations, Cuba is to provide equipment and specialists (plus their salary), while the new government in La Paz will provide the physical facilities. The two countries also agreed that the National Ophthalmologic Institute in La Paz, newly equipped by Cuba, will open two new centres, one in Cochabamba and the other in Santa Cruz. Together, the two facilities will have the capacity to perform 50,000 operations per year. 'These capacities may increase if Bolivia offers its ophthalmological services to poor patients in neighbouring countries near the Bolivian clinics,' the agreement states.

5. The Palacio de Miraflores in Caracas is the official residence of that country's president.

6. ['*Lehendakari*' is the word Basques use for the president of their region. It is a neologism, as the words 'president' and 'gobernu' exist, but are used only for leaders of other nations or groups; it is used only for the head of the Basque Country. Before the establishment of standard Basque in the 1970s, it was spelled '*lendakari*', which is how Ramonet spells it in the Spanish edition. – Trans.]

7. General Efraín Vázquez Velasco, self-proclaimed 'commander-in-chief' of the Venezuelan

armed forces, served momentarily as leader and spokesman of the officers involved in the coup.

8. Pedro Carmona, president of the Fedecámaras consortium, was appointed 'provisional president' of Venezuela by the coup leaders. He served in this capacity for less than forty-eight hours; thus, his nickname.

9. Diosdado Cabello, constitutional vice president, became president of Venezuela briefly, between the disarticulation of the coup and the triumphant return of Hugo Chávez to Miraflores.

10. Juan Velasco Alvarado (1910–77) was an army general who led a military junta that took power in Peru and who then served as president from 1968 to 1975; he nationalized banks and strategic industries (oil, fishing, copper) and instituted a sweeping agricultural reform.

11. Jorge Amado (1912–2001), Brazilian novelist and author of a biography of Luiz Carlos Prestes titled in Spanish *Prestes, el caballero de la esperanza* (Buenos Aires: Editorial Futuro, 1958; in Portuguese, *Vida de Luiz Carlos Prestes, o cavaleiro da esperança* [1942]). [This book has not, so far as we can determine, been translated into English. – Trans.]

12. [Adolfo Pérez Esquivel was born in Buenos Aires, Argentina, in 1931 and trained as an architect. In 1974 he became an activist in the cause of non-violence as an instrument to combat human-rights abuses. He formed the organization Paz y Justicia (Peace and Justice), which is an umbrella organization for religious and civic groups opposing governmental abuses. While associated with the activist wing of the Catholic Church in Latin America, he is especially known for his defence of the *desaparecidos* in Argentina's dirty war of the seventies. He was awarded the Nobel Peace Prize in 1980. – Trans.]

13. In November 1999, Elián González (b. 1993) was taken illegally from Cuba by his mother. The raft on which they were making the crossing sank, and the mother drowned. Elián was rescued by fishermen and taken to the United States, where he was placed in the custody of an uncle in Miami, while his father demanded that he be returned to Cuba. This created a diplomatic crisis between Cuba and the US, and Elián became the focus of a heated custody battle. Though meeting fierce opposition from the Miami Cuban–American community, federal law enforcement officers under the orders of US Attorney General Janet Reno finally stormed the uncle's house and took custody of the child and, after a hearing by the US Supreme Court, returned the child to Cuba and his father.

14. During a state visit by Lula to Havana in September 2003, Brazil and Cuba signed twelve agreements of cooperation in the following areas: energy, fishing, tourism, medicine, industry, health, education and sport.

26: Cuba Today

1. Operation Miracle was created in 2004 in order to provide ophthalmological treatment to Venezuelans who come to Cuba to be operated on, essentially for cataracts; it has since been expanded to provide care to over twenty nationalities, thus, as of December 2005, enabling some 175,000 people to recover their sight. As of 2006, Operation Miracle has ophthalmological centres, run by Cuban medical personnel, in several Latin American countries.

2. In November 2006, for the fifteenth consecutive time, the United Nations General Assembly once again condemned the US blockade of Cuba; the vote was 184 in favour of the condemnation. The same four nations (the United States, Israel, the Marshall Islands and Palau) voted against the measure as they had the year before; one country (Micronesia) abstained, and three countries did not take part in the vote.

3. The Marshall Islands – 60,000 inhabitants in a total land area of 180 square kilometres, or about seventy square miles – were discovered in 1529 by Spanish sailors. A German protectorate from 1886 to 1914, the islands were then administered by Japan. In 1945 they became a territory entrusted to the United States under the mandate of the UN. From 1946 to 1958, sixty-seven atomic bombs were tested in the Bikini and Eniwetok atolls.

The islands have been independent since 1979 but linked to the United States by a Free Association Agreement; the nation has been a member of the UN since 1990.

4. The Rote Armee Fraktion (Red Army Faction or Fraction), more commonly known as the Baader-Meinhof group (or gang), described itself as a Communist 'urban guerrilla' group. It was an armed group that committed acts of what almost everyone considered terrorism in Germany between 1968 and 1972. Five of its principal members (and thirteen others) were arrested in June 1972 and sent to the Stammheim high-security prison in Stuttgart. In November 1974 Holger Meins died after several weeks on hunger strike. In May 1976 the authorities announced the death by suicide (hanging) of Ulrike Meinhof in her cell, and on 18 October 1977 Andreas Baader, Gudrun Ensslin and Jan-Carl Raspe were also found dead in mysterious circumstances: Baader had a gunshot wound to the back of his head; Ensslin was found hanged in her cell; and Raspe died in the hospital the next day from a gunshot wound to the head. [The authorities pronounced this a group suicide, but conspiracy theories abound, most blaming the authorities for the deaths. – Trans.]

5. In the United States, fifteen Puerto Ricans – five women and ten men – have been sentenced to the equivalent of life sentences for fighting for the independence of Puerto Rico; most of them have been in prison for over sixteen years.

6. [Mumia Abu-Jamal (born Wesley Cook on 24 April 1954) is a journalist and political activist from Philadelphia who was on death row after having been convicted of the murder of Philadelphia police officer Daniel Faulkner, but is now serving life in a Pennsylvania state prison after his death sentence was revoked by an appeals court. Many of his supporters claim that he is innocent, that his arrest and conviction were politically motivated, and that he qualifies as a political prisoner. – Trans.]

7. [Leonard Peltier (b. 12 September 1944) is a Native American activist and member of the American Indian Movement. In 1977 he was convicted and sentenced to two consecutive terms of life imprisonment for the murders of two FBI agents who died during a 1975 shoot-out on the Pine Ridge Indian Reservation. There has been considerable debate over Peltier's guilt and the fairness of his trial. Some supporters and organizations, including Amnesty International, consider him to be a political prisoner. He has been in prison since 1976. – Trans.]

8. In the face of Cuba's repeated denunciations of Luis Posada Carriles' presence in the United States and its demands for details as to how Posada Carriles entered the country and who allowed it, after ignoring these demands for weeks, the US government finally had no alternative but to detain Posada Carriles in Miami and charge him with 'illegal entry into the US'. In November 2005 Posada Carriles' accomplice Santiago Alvarez was also detained. Alvarez is the owner and skipper of the boat on which Posada entered the US; he was charged with illegal possession of firearms. At the time this note [in Spanish] was prepared, Posada's legal counsel was manoeuvring to have Posada's charges dropped.

9. [Not a medical *centre*, and not Havana, but in the sense of human capital, human resources. – Trans.]

10. As of mid-November 2006 a total of 485,476 patients from twenty-eight countries, of them over 290,000 Venezuelans, had been treated in Operation Miracle centres.

11. See the full text of Bush's speech at West Point at: http://www.whitehouse.gov/news/releases/2002/06/20020601–3.html (as of January 2007).

12. [The United Nations was officially founded on 26 June 1945, with the signing of the charter by fifty-one member-nations. – Trans.]

13. [One of these emissaries, the former Cuban UN ambassador Alcibíades Hidalgo, today in exile in the United States, has told in detail how a Cuban delegation headed by José Ramón Fernández, vice president of the Council of State, gave him a letter for Saddam Hussein from Fidel Castro: *Le Monde*, Paris, 11 March 2003 (in 1st ed.).]

14. [As of late July 2007 there had been over 3,600 US military deaths and almost 27,000 seriously wounded. – Trans.]

15. [See the full transcript of this address at: http://edition.cnn.com/2001/US/09/20/gen.bush.transcript. – Trans.]

16. [http://www.whitehouse.gov/news/releases/2002/06/20020601−3.html. – Trans.]
17. [Officially the Office of Cuban Affairs. – Trans.]
18. [The Office of Homeland Security (OHS) was established by executive order on 8 October 2001; after congressional approval on 19 November 2002 of a bill to create a new Department of Homeland Security, the former OHS became a cabinet-level department on 25 November 2002, with the president's signature of the bill into law, and it began operations on 1 March 2003. Thus, either Whitaker informed Castro of Homeland Security's opinion before late November 2002, and not in April 2003, or Castro has got the nomenclature wrong. – Trans.]
19. On 10 October 2003, the 135th anniversary of the beginning of the wars of independence against Spain, at a press conference in the White House, President George W. Bush announced the adoption of a series of measures against Cuba: a reduction in the possibilities of travel to Cuba; increase in aid to counter-revolutionary groups in Florida; and creation of a presidential commission – co-chaired by then secretary of state Colin Powell – to hasten the 'liberation' of Cuba.
20. Speech at Florida International University, Miami, 25 August 2000.

27: Summing Up a Life and a Revolution

1. [By 'authority' (here and throughout), Castro does not mean the power to command, or the responsibility attendant on leadership, but rather the power of persuasion – influence on the populace, respect from it. – Trans.]
2. This occurred in January–February 1957, in the Sierra Maestra, within a few weeks of the beginning of the war in the mountains; the guide was named Eutimio Guerra. The betrayal was discovered and the traitor confessed, was tried, and was shot by firing squad. (See also Chapter 10, note 3.) [Note by Cuban editor.]
3. Carlos Franqui (b. 1921), writer and journalist, founded the daily newspaper *Revolución* in 1956 while in the underground, and in 1958 joined the rebels in the Sierra Maestra, where he ran Radio Rebelde. In 1968 he went into exile in Italy. He is the author of several books, among them *Diary of the Cuban Revolution* (trans. Georgette Felix et al., New York: Viking Press, 1980; Spanish edition 1976), *Family Portrait with Fidel* (trans. Alfred MacAdam, NY: Random House, 1984, Spanish edition 1981) and *Camilo Cienfuegos* (Bogotá: Planeta, 2001).
4. See Chapter 11, note 2.
5. Rafael del Pino (b.1938), brigadier general and Cuban Air Force pilot. In April 1961, during the battle for Playa Girón, he piloted his T-33 when it downed two of the invaders' B-26s. In May 1987 he deserted and fled to the United States. He has published several autobiographical books, among them *Amanecer en Girón* ('Dawn at Playa Girón', 1982) and *Proa a la libertad* ('On Course for Freedom', 1990).
6. [Carlos Aldana (b. 1945), former head of the powerful Department of Revolutionary Orientation within the Communist Party Central Committee, in the eighties was considered the 'third man in power' in Cuba. Sanctioned in 1992, he was removed from his position after a scandal involving illegal appropriation of funds. He was also accused of wanting to become the 'Cuban Gorbachev'. For six years he directed an agricultural plan in the region of Escambray. He returned to the public spotlight in 2001 as an executive in Cimex, a corporation involved with foreign businesses. (in 1st ed.)]
7. [Roberto Robaina (b. 1956) is the former head of the Young Communists Union and former minister of foreign relations; he was removed from the latter post in 1999. Dishonourably thrown out of the Communist Party in May 2003 for disloyalty, corruption and having promoted himself as a candidate in the post-Castro transition, he now works in an urban environmental project in Havana. (in 1st ed.)]
8. [See English version of Fidel Castro's speech on 23 August 1968 in the *Granma Weekly Review* for 25 August 1968. – Trans.]

9. In 1970 Cuba set a goal of harvesting a record 10 million tons of sugar cane; the goal was not reached.

10. A submarine trench on the floor of the western Caribbean Sea between Jamaica and the Cayman Islands. It extends from the Windward Passage at the southeastern tip of Cuba towards Guatemala. The relatively narrow trough runs generally east–north-east to west–south-west and has a maximum depth of 25,216 feet (7,686 metres), the deepest point in the Caribbean Sea.

11. Stalin died on 5 March 1953, and was succeeded for a few months by a triumvirate made up of Nikolai Bulganin, Nikita Khrushchev and Gyorgy Malenkov. Nikita Khrushchev, first secretary of the Soviet Communist Party Central Committee, took power in 1956 and by 1958 had consolidated his hold on the Soviet leadership position. He was replaced in 1964 by Leonid Brezhnev.

12. On 8 January 1959 Fidel Castro gave his first public speech in Havana after the triumph of the Revolution; he spoke from a small stage set up on the parade field at the Columbia military facilities. In the middle of his speech, several white doves started fluttering around him. One perched on his shoulder and sat there for several minutes, in a scene that enthralled the people in the audience and the hundreds of thousands who were watching the spectacle on TV.

13. [While the answer that follows seems to be less 'oral' than many of Castro's answers, the speech Castro gave on the fiftieth anniversary of the attack on the Moncada barracks has many more specific statistics and figures than this answer, and it is much more highly focused on (and angry at) the Americans, rather than in favour of the Cubans. – Trans.]

14. In 2005 Cuba's infant mortality rate dropped below 6 per 1,000 live births, with no marked differences between regions.

15. Chinese leader Jiang Zemin (b. 1926) studied industrial engineering (electrical machinery); he entered the Communist Party in 1946. In 1978 he was promoted by Deng Xiaoping, the country's new leader after the death of Mao Zedong. In this promotion he was also supported by Hua Guofeng, Chinese Communist Party president and prime minister of the transition. As mayor of Shanghai, in 1985 Jiang accelerated the city's economic reforms. In 1989, after the Tiananmen Square killings, he was made secretary general of the Party; he was elected president of the People's Republic of China in March of 1993, where he was the creator of the 'market Socialist economy' formula. In March 2003 he stepped down and was succeeded by Hu Jintao, but became head of the powerful and influential Central Military Commission. In September 2004 Jiang retired from the Commission and was succeeded by Hu Jintao.

16. In 2003 a conversation between President Kennedy and his national security adviser, McGeorge Bundy, was made public; it showed that the president wanted to explore a *rapprochement* with Cuba, and had agreed to the possibility of a secret meeting with an emissary from Havana, on the suggestion of Fidel Castro.

17. Editor of *Le Nouvel Observateur*, an important French newspaper of the time.

18. [An author is given the Nobel Prize for a life's work, of course, not for an individual work. – Trans.]

19. [Hafizullah Amin (1929–79) was the second president of Afghanistan during the period of the Communist Democratic Republic of Afghanistan. His term was notorious for its brutality. After killing his predecessor Taraki in office, Amin began a purge during which, according to his own figures, some 18,000 'opponents' were killed; official Afghan figures put the number at up to 45,000. Finally, the Soviets intervened and the former 'advisers' and troops in Afghanistan overthrew the Amin regime and assassinated Amin himself. – Trans.]

20. [Ieng Sary (b. ?1922–5, current whereabouts unknown, possibly dead) was born in Vietnam but changed his name when he moved to Kampuchea as a young man. A high-ranking member of the Khmer Rouge, Sary was Pol Pot's second-in-command in the

Cambodian genocide. He was officially pardoned in 1996 by the king of Cambodia; he was at that time living in exile in poor health. – Trans.]

28: After Fidel, What?

1. [Castro means smoking, excessive alcohol use, drugs including 'soft drugs' such as marijuana, as well as the contextual 'vices' of petty theft, pilfering from the state, etc.; the cognate word is not as strong in Spanish as in English, but there is no easy or 'shorthand' way to convey its exact meaning. – Trans.]
2. [The word Castro uses is *sinvergüenza*, a very common term of opprobrium that can range from relatively mild to scathing, depending on circumstance and tone of voice: rascal, scoundrel, crook, cheeky, smart-mouthed, cynical, disrespectful, sneaky, opportunistic, etc., and even 'dirty' or 'swinish' when the circumstances are sexual, hygienic or scatological. Here, Castro is appealing to people's sense of what their mothers probably instilled in them: being 'ashamed of themselves' when they do something wrong. – Trans.]
3. [See Mauricio Vicent, 'El Gran Hermano Cubano' ('The Cuban Big Brother'), in the newspaper *El País* (Madrid), 26 December 2005, and 'Fidel Castro vigilará por satélite todos los autos estatales en Cuba' ('Fidel Castro Will Track All State Vehicles in Cuba by Satellite'), *El Clarín* (Buenos Aires), 28 December 2005: http://www.clarin.com/diario/2005/12/28/elmundo/i-02501.htm (not in 3rd Span. edition)]
4. [The English word is used to designate dollar shops, stores that sold articles not available in other stores in exchange for dollars, rather than Cuban pesos. – Trans.]
5. [This word, meaning 'palate', is used in Cuban now to designate 'privately owned restaurants', an innovation in post-Revolutionary Cuba. – Trans.]
6. Celia Sánchez (1920–80), Cuban heroine, first female guerrilla fighter in the Sierra Maestra and, from the triumph of the Revolution in 1959 until her death, one of Castro's closest collaborators. [See Pedro Alvarez Tabío, *Celia, ensayo para una biografía*. Havana: Oficina de Publicationes del Consejo de Estado, 2003 (not in 3rd Span. ed.).] See also Chapter 8, note 11.
7. [Against the World Trade Organization, in 1999. –Trans.]
8. [The explanation that follows in Castro's response appears, in Spanish, almost verbatim in the *Granma* newspaper edition of 22 October 2004, as a 'Letter from *Compañero* Castro to His Countrymen'. – Trans.]
9. [The fall occurred at the combined graduation ceremonies for all of Cuba's new schools for teachers of art, of which Castro was clearly very proud. The ceremonies were attended by some 30,000 people in the Plaza Ernesto Che Guevara in Santa Clara. The occasion explains this odd phrase that Castro uses here. – Trans.]
10. In late July 2006, Fidel Castro was forced to undergo delicate surgery as a result of intestinal bleeding. As a result, on 31 July he issued a statement announcing that because of the period of recovery necessary after such an operation and the extended rest he would be forced to take, he was temporarily turning over his responsibilities as head of the Cuban government to a constitutional replacement: the first vice president of the Council of State, Raúl Castro Ruz. At the time this note is being written, in early November 2006, to be included in the third Cuban edition of this book, Fidel Castro is recovering satisfactorily, and in fact has been working with dedicated intensity on the revision of the materials for the second edition and this third edition of the book. [Note by Cuban editor.]

A Note on the Text and the Translation

1. Barcelona: Random House Mondadori, 2006.

Some Key Dates in the Life of Fidel Castro and the Cuban Revolution
(1926–2007)

1. [The article detailing this interview was written by Ann Louise Bardach and Larry Rohter. An abstract may be found at http://select.nytimes.com/gst/abstract.html?res=F00B16F73 E550C718DDDAE0894D0494D81. It should be noted that this abstract includes an Editor's Note stating that Posada Carriles did *not* specifically say that Mas Canosa had financed the terrorist campaign, but rather that he had 'expressed his support for it'. There is no question, however, that Posada Carriles received money from the Cuban-American National Foundation for over a decade, and Posada Carriles himself says that Mas Canosa did not want to know how his money was being used. – Trans.]

2. See http://www.encyclopedia.com/doc/1G1-54176318.html

Index

NOVA SCOTIA COMMUNITY COLLEGE

3 1998 03271866 8

Res
ma